Monetary Theory and Policy

Monetary Theory and Policy

Third Edition

Carl E. Walsh

The MIT Press
Cambridge, Massachusetts
London, England

For information about special quantity discounts, please email ⟨special_sales@mitpress.mit.edu⟩.

This book was set in Times New Roman on 3B2 by Asco Typesetters, Hong Kong.
Printed and bound in the United States of America.

Library of Congress Cataloging-in-Publication Data

Walsh, Carl E.
Monetary theory and policy / Carl E. Walsh. — 3rd ed.
      p.   cm.
Includes bibliographical references and index.
ISBN 978-0-262-01377-2 (hardcover : alk. paper) 1. Monetary policy. 2. Money. I. Title.
HG230.3.W35   2010
332.4′6—dc22   2009028431

10   9   8   7   6   5   4   3   2

Contents

Preface

This book covers the most important topics in monetary economics and some of the models that economists have employed as they attempt to understand the interactions between real and monetary factors. It deals with topics in both monetary theory and monetary policy and is designed for second-year graduate students specializing in monetary economics, for researchers in monetary economics wishing to have a systematic summary of recent developments, and for economists working in policy institutions such as central banks. It can also be used as a supplement for first-year graduate courses in macroeconomics because it provides a more in-depth treatment of inflation and monetary policy topics than is customary in graduate macroeconomic textbooks. The chapters on monetary policy may be useful for advanced undergraduate courses.

In preparing the third edition of *Monetary Theory and Policy*, my objective has been to incorporate some of the new models, approaches, insights, and lessons that monetary economists have developed in recent years. As with the second edition, I have revised every chapter, with the goal of improving the exposition and incorporating new research contributions. At the time of the first edition, the use of models based on dynamic optimization and nominal rigidities in consistent general equilibrium frameworks was still relatively new. By the time of the second edition, these models had become the common workhorse for monetary policy analysis. And since the second edition appeared, these models have continued to provide the theoretical framework for most monetary analysis. They now also provide the foundation for empirical models that have been estimated for a number of countries, with many central banks now employing or developing dynamic stochastic general equilibrium (DSGE) models that build on the new Keynesian models covered in earlier editions.

This third edition incorporates new or expanded material on money in search equilibria, sticky information, adaptive learning, state-contingent pricing models, and channel systems of implementing monetary policy, among other topics. In addition, much of the material on models for policy analysis has been reorganized to reflect the dominance of the new Keynesian approach.

In the introduction to the first edition, I cited three innovations of the book: the use of calibration and simulation techniques to evaluate the quantitative significance of the channels through which monetary policy and inflation affect the economy; a stress on the need to understand the incentives facing central banks and to model the strategic interactions between the central bank and the private sector; and the focus on interest rates in the discussion of monetary policy. All three aspects remain in the current edition, but each is now commonplace in monetary research. For example, it is rare today to see research that treats monetary policy in terms of money supply control, yet this was common well into the 1990s.

When one is writing a book like this, several organizational approaches present themselves. Monetary economics is a large field, and one must decide whether to provide broad coverage, giving students a brief introduction to many topics, or to focus more narrowly and in more depth. I have chosen to focus on particular models, models that monetary economists have employed to address topics in theory and policy. I have tried to stress the major topics within monetary economics in order to provide sufficiently broad coverage of the field, but the focus within each topic is often on a small number of papers or models that I have found useful for gaining insight into a particular issue. As an aid to students, derivations of basic results are often quite detailed, but deeper technical issues of existence, multiple equilibria, and stability receive somewhat less attention. This choice was not made because the latter are unimportant. Instead, the relative emphasis reflects an assessment that to do these topics justice, while still providing enough emphasis on the core insights offered by monetary economics, would have required a much longer book. By reducing the dimensionality of problems and by not treating them in full generality, I hoped to achieve the right balance of insight, accessibility, and rigor. The many references will serve to guide students to the extensive treatments in the literature of all the topics touched upon in this book.

While new material has been added, and some material has been deleted, the organization of chapters 1–4 is similar to that of the second edition. Significant changes have been made to each of these chapters, however. Chapter 2 includes a discussion of steady states with a time-varying stock of money; and the empirical evidence on money demand and the connection between the interest elasticity of money demand and the costs of inflation are more fully discussed. The first-order conditions for the household's decision problem in the stochastic MIU model have been moved from an appendix into the text; the calibration for the simulation exercises has changed; and programs are provided (at ⟨http://people.ucsc.edu/~walshc/mtp3e⟩) for solving the stochastic MIU model using eigenvalue decomposition methods based on the programs of Harald Uhlig, Paul Söderlind, and Dynare as well as for employing an approach based on a linear regulator problem. Because Uhlig's tool kit is not the only approach used, the discussion of his methodology has been shortened.

Similar changes with regard to the simulation programs have been made for the CIA model of chapter 3. In addition, the timing of the asset and goods markets has been changed for the model used to study dynamics. Asset markets now open first, which ensures that the cash-in-advance constraint always holds as long as the nominal interest rate is positive. The major change to chapter 3 is the extended discussion of the literature on money in search equilibrium. Less detail is now provided on the Kiyotaki and Wright (1989) model; instead, the main focus is on the model of Lagos and Wright (2005).

Chapter 4 has been shortened by eliminating some of the discussion of time series methods for testing budget sustainability.

Chapters 5–11 have seen a major revision. Chapters 5 and 6 focus on the frictions that account for the short-run impact of monetary policy. In previous editions, this material was entirely contained in chapter 5. Given the enormous growth in the literature on topics like sticky information and state-dependent pricing models, the third edition devotes two chapters to the topic of frictions. Chapter 5 focuses on models with information rigidities, such as Lucas's island model and models of sticky information. It also discusses models based on portfolio frictions, such as limited-participation and asset-market-segmentation models. More formal development of a limited-participation model is provided, and a model of endogenous asset market segmentation is discussed. Chapter 6 focuses on nominal wage and price stickiness, and incorporates recent work on microeconomic evidence for price adjustment and research on state-contingent pricing models. The third edition focuses less on the issue of persistence in evaluating the new Keynesian Phillips curve but provides expanded coverage of empirical assessments of models of sticky prices, particularly related to the micro evidence now available.

Models of the average inflation bias of discretionary policy are discussed in chapter 7. Chapter 8 provides stand-alone coverage of new Keynesian models and their policy implications in the context of the closed economy. It incorporates material formerly split between chapters 5 and 11 of the second edition. The open economy is now the focus of chapter 9. Chapter 10 on credit frictions now includes a new section on macrofinance models as well as material on the term structure from the second edition. Finally, chapter 11, on operating procedures, has taken on a new relevance and provides a discussion of channel systems for implementing monetary policy.

It is not possible to discuss here all the areas of monetary economics in which economists are pursuing active research, or to give adequate credit to all the interesting work that has been done. The topics covered and the space devoted to them reflect my own biases toward research motivated by policy questions or influential in affecting the conduct of monetary policy. The field has simply exploded with new and interesting research, and at best this edition, like the earlier ones, can only scratch the surface of many topics. To those whose research has been slighted, I offer my apologies.

Previous editions were immensely improved by the thoughtful comments of many individuals who took the time to read parts of earlier drafts, and I have received many comments from users of the first two editions, which have guided me in revising the material. Luigi Buttiglione, Marco Hoeberichts, Michael Hutchison, Francesco Lippi, Jaewoo Lee, Doug Pearce, Gustavo Piga, Glenn Rudebusch, Willem Verhagen, and Chris Waller provided many insightful and useful comments on the first edition. Students at Stanford and the University of California, Santa Cruz (UCSC) gave important feedback on draft material; Peter Kriz, Jerry McIntyre, Fabiano Schivardi, Alina Carare, and especially Jules Leichter deserve special mention. A very special note of thanks is due Lars Svensson and Berthold Herrendorf. Each made extensive comments on complete drafts of the first edition. Attempting to address the issues they raised greatly improved the final product; it would have been even better if I had had the time and energy to follow all their suggestions. The comments and suggestions of Julia Chiriaeva, Nancy Jianakoplos, Stephen Miller, Jim Nason, Claudio Shikida, and participants in courses I taught based on the first edition at the IMF Institute, the Bank of Spain, the Bank of Portugal, the Bank of England, the University of Oslo, and the Swiss National Bank Studienzentrum Gerzensee all contributed to improving the second edition. Wei Chen, Ethel Wang, and Jamus Lim, graduate students at UCSC, also offered helpful comments and assistance in preparing the second edition.

I would like particularly to thank Henning Bohn, Betty Daniel, Jordi Galí, Eric Leeper, Tim Fuerst, Ed Nelson, Federico Ravenna, and Kevin Salyer for very helpful comments on early drafts of some chapters of the second edition. Many of the changes appearing in the third edition are the result of comments and suggestions from students and participants at intensive courses in monetary economics that I taught at the IMF Institute, the Swiss National Bank Studienzentrum Gerzensee, the Central Bank of Brazil, the University of Rome "Tor Vergata," the Norges Bank Training Program for Economists, the Finnish Post-Graduate Program in Economics, the ZEI Summer School, and the Hong Kong Institute for Monetary Research. Students at UCSC also contributed, and Conglin Xu provided excellent research assistance during the process of preparing this edition.

Henrik Jenson read penultimate versions of many of the current chapters and provided a host of useful suggestions that helped improve the book in terms of substance and clarity. Others I would like to thank, whose suggestions have improved this edition, include Ulf Söderström, Mario Nigrinis, Stephen Sauer, Sendor Lczel, Jizhong Zhou (who translated the second edition into Chinese), Oreste Tristani, Robert Tchaidze, Teresa Simões, David Coble Fernández, David Florian-Hoyle, Jonathan Benchimol, Carlo Migliardo, Oliver Fries, Yuichiro Waki, Cesar Carrera, Federico

Guerrero, Beka Lamazoshvili, Rasim Mutlu, Álvaro Pina, and Paul Söderlind (and my apologies to anyone I have failed to mention). As always, remaining errors are my own.

I would also like to thank Jane Macdonald, my editor at the MIT Press for the third edition, Nancy Lombardi, production editor for both the first and second editions, and Deborah Cantor-Adams, production editor, and Alice Cheyer, copy editor, for this edition, for their excellent assistance on the manuscript. Needless to say, all remaining weaknesses and errors are my own responsibility. Terry Vaughan, my original editor at the MIT Press, was instrumental in ensuring this project got off the ground initially, and Elizabeth Murry served ably as editor for the second edition.

Introduction

Monetary economics investigates the relationship between real economic variables at the aggregate level (such as real output, real rates of interest, employment, and real exchange rates) and nominal variables (such as the inflation rate, nominal interest rates, nominal exchange rates, and the supply of money). So defined, monetary economics has considerable overlap with macroeconomics more generally, and these two fields have to a large degree shared a common history over most of the past 50 years. This statement was particularly true during the 1970s after the monetarist/ Keynesian debates led to a reintegration of monetary economics with macroeconomics. The seminal work of Robert Lucas (1972) provided theoretical foundations for models of economic fluctuations in which money was the fundamental driving factor behind movements in real output. The rise of real-business-cycle models during the 1980s and early 1990s, building on the contribution of Kydland and Prescott (1982) and focusing explicitly on nonmonetary factors as the driving forces behind business cycles, tended to separate monetary economics from macroeconomics. More recently, the real-business-cycle approach to aggregate modeling has been used to incorporate monetary factors into dynamic general equilibrium models. Today, macroeconomics and monetary economics share the common tools associated with dynamic stochastic approaches to modeling the aggregate economy.

Despite these close connections, a book on monetary economics is not a book on macroeconomics. The focus in monetary economics is distinct, emphasizing price level determination, inflation, and the role of monetary policy. Today, monetary economics is dominated by three alternative modeling strategies. The first two, representative-agent models and overlapping-generations models, share a common methodological approach in building equilibrium relationships explicitly on the foundations of optimizing behavior by individual agents. The third approach is based on sets of equilibrium relationships that are often not derived directly from any decision problem. Instead, they are described as ad hoc by critics and as convenient approximations by proponents. The latter characterization is generally more appropriate, and these models have demonstrated great value in helping economists understand issues in monetary economics. This book deals with models in the representative-agent class and with ad hoc models of the type often used in policy analysis.

There are several reasons for ignoring the overlapping-generations (OLG) approach. First, systematic expositions of monetary economics from the perspective of overlapping generations are already available. For example, Sargent (1987) and Champ and Freeman (1994) covered many topics in monetary economics using OLG models. Second, many of the issues one studies in monetary economics require understanding the time series behavior of macroeconomic variables such as inflation or the relationship between money and business cycles. It is helpful if the theoretical framework can be mapped directly into implications for behavior that can be compared with actual data. This mapping is more easily done with infinite-horizon representative-agent models than with OLG models. This advantage, in fact, is one reason for the popularity of real-business-cycle models that employ the representative-agent approach, and so a third reason for limiting the coverage to representative-agent models is that they provide a close link between monetary economics and other popular frameworks for studying business cycle phenomena. Fourth, monetary policy issues are generally related to the dynamic behavior of the economy over time periods associated with business cycle frequencies, and here again the OLG framework seems less directly applicable. Finally, OLG models emphasize the store-of-value role of money at the expense of the medium-of-exchange role that money plays in facilitating transactions. McCallum (1983b) argued that some of the implications of OLG models that contrast most sharply with the implications of other approaches (the tenuousness of monetary equilibria, for example) are directly related to the lack of a medium-of-exchange role for money.

A book on monetary theory and policy would be seriously incomplete if it were limited to representative-agent models. A variety of ad hoc models have played, and continue to play, important roles in influencing the way economists and policy-makers think about the role of monetary policy. These models can be very helpful in highlighting key issues affecting the linkages between monetary and real economic phenomena. No monetary economist's tool kit is complete without them. But it is important to begin with more fully specified models so that one has some sense of what is missing in the simpler models. In this way, one is better able to judge whether the ad hoc models are likely to provide insight into particular questions.

This book is about monetary theory and the theory of monetary policy. Occasional references to empirical results are made, but no attempt has been made to provide a systematic survey of the vast body of empirical research in monetary economics. Most of the debates in monetary economics, however, have at their root issues of fact that can only be resolved by empirical evidence. Empirical evidence is needed to choose between theoretical approaches, but theory is also needed to interpret empirical evidence. How one links the quantities in the theoretical model to measurable data is critical, for example, in developing measures of monetary policy actions that can be used to estimate the impact of policy on the economy. Because empirical evidence aids in discriminating between alternative theories, it is helpful to begin with a brief overview of some basic facts. Chapter 1 does so, providing a discussion that focuses primarily on the estimated impact of monetary policy actions on real output. Here, as in the chapters that deal with some of the institutional details of monetary policy, the evidence comes primarily from research on the United States. However, an attempt has been made to cite cross-country studies and to focus on empirical regularities that seem to characterize most industrialized economies.

Chapters 2–4 emphasize the role of inflation as a tax, using models that provide the basic microeconomic foundations of monetary economics. These chapters cover topics of fundamental importance for understanding how monetary phenomena affect the general equilibrium behavior of the economy and how nominal prices, inflation, money, and interest rates are linked. Because the models studied in these chapters assume that prices are perfectly flexible, they are most useful for understanding longer-run correlations between inflation, money, and output and cross-country differences in average inflation. However, they do have implications for short-run dynamics as real and nominal variables adjust in response to aggregate productivity disturbances and random shocks to money growth. These dynamics are examined by employing simulations based on linear approximations around the steady-state equilibrium.

Chapters 2 and 3 employ a neoclassical growth framework to study monetary phenomena. The neoclassical model is one in which growth is exogenous and money has no effect on the real economy's long-run steady state or has effects that are likely to be small empirically. However, because these models allow one to calculate the welfare implications of exogenous changes in the economic environment, they provide a natural framework for examining the welfare costs of alternative steady-state rates of inflation. Stochastic versions of the basic models are calibrated, and simulations are used to illustrate how monetary factors affect the behavior of the economy. Such simulations aid in assessing the ability of the models to capture correlations observed in actual data. Since policy can be expressed in terms of both exogenous shocks and endogenous feedbacks from real shocks, the models can be used to study how economic fluctuations depend on monetary policy.

In chapter 4, the focus turns to public finance issues associated with money, inflation, and monetary policy. The ability to create money provides governments with a means of generating revenue. As a source of revenue, money creation, along with the inflation that results, can be analyzed from the perspective of public finance as one among many tax tools available to governments.

The link between the dynamic general equilibrium models of chapters 2–4 and the models employed for short-run and policy analysis is developed in chapters 5 and 6.

Chapter 5 discusses information and portfolio rigidities, and chapter 6 focuses on nominal rigidities that can generate important short-run real effects of monetary policy. Chapter 5 begins by reviewing some attempts to replicate the empirical evidence on the short-run effects of monetary policy shocks while still maintaining the assumption of flexible prices. Lucas's misperceptions model provides an important example of one such attempt. Models of sticky information with flexible prices, due to the work of Mankiw and Reis, provide a modern approach that can be thought of as building on Lucas's original insight that imperfect information is important for understanding the short-run effects of monetary shocks. Despite the growing research on sticky information and on models with portfolio rigidities (also discussed in chapter 5), it remains the case that most research in monetary economics in recent years has adopted the assumption that prices and/or wages adjust sluggishly in response to economic disturbances. Chapter 6 discusses some important models of price and inflation adjustment, and reviews some of the new microeconomic evidence on price adjustment by firms. This evidence is helping to guide research on nominal rigidities and has renewed interest in models of state-contingent pricing.

Chapter 7 turns to the analysis of monetary policy, focusing on monetary policy objectives and the ability of policy authorities to achieve these objectives. Understanding monetary policy requires an understanding of how policy actions affect macroeconomic variables (the topic of chapters 2–6), but it also requires models of policy behavior to understand why particular policies are undertaken. A large body of research over the past three decades has used game-theoretic concepts to model the monetary policymaker as a strategic agent. These models have provided new insights into the rules-versus-discretion debate, provided positive theories of inflation, and provided justification for many of the actual reforms of central banking legislation that have been implemented in recent years.

Models of sticky prices in dynamic stochastic general equilibrium form the foundation of the new Keynesian models that have become the standard models for monetary policy analysis over the past decade. These models build on the joint foundations of optimizing behavior by economic agents and nominal rigidities, and they form the core material of chapter 8. The basic new Keynesian model and some of its policy implications are explored.

Chapter 9 extends the analysis to the open economy by focusing on two questions. First, what additional channels from monetary policy actions to the real economy are present in the open economy that were absent in the closed-economy analysis? Second, how does monetary policy affect the behavior of nominal and real exchange rates? New channels through which monetary policy actions are transmitted to the real economy are present in open economies and involve exchange rate movements and interest rate linkages.

Traditionally, economists have employed simple models in which the money stock or even inflation is assumed to be the direct instrument of policy. In fact, most central banks have employed interest rates as their operational policy instrument, so chapter 10 emphasizes the role of the interest rate as the instrument of monetary policy and the term structure that links policy rates to long-term interest rates. While the channels of monetary policy emphasized in traditional models operate primarily through interest rates and exchange rates, an alternative view is that credit markets play an independent role in affecting the transmission of monetary policy actions to the real economy. The nature of credit markets and their role in the transmission process are affected by market imperfections arising from imperfect information, so chapter 10 also examines theories that stress the role of credit and credit market imperfections in the presence of moral hazard, adverse selection, and costly monitoring.

Finally, in chapter 11 the focus turns to monetary policy implementation. Here, the discussion deals with the problem of monetary instrument choice and monetary policy operating procedures. A long tradition in monetary economics has debated the usefulness of monetary aggregates versus interest rates in the design and implementation of monetary policy, and chapter 11 reviews the approach economists have used to address this issue. A simple model of the market for bank reserves is used to stress how the observed responses of short-term interest rates and reserve aggregates will depend on the operating procedures used in the conduct of policy. New material on channel systems for interest rate control has been added in this edition. A basic understanding of policy implementation is important for empirical studies that attempt to measure changes in monetary policy.[1]

---

1. Central bank operating procedures have changed significantly in recent years. For example, the Federal Reserve now employs a penalty rate on discount window borrowing and pays interest on reserves. Several other central banks employ channel systems (see section 11.4.3). For these reasons, the reserve market model discussed in the first two editions, based as it was on a zero interest rate on reserves and a nonpenalty discount rate, is less relevant. However, because the previous model may still be of interest to some readers, section 9.4 of the second edition is available online at ⟨http://people.ucsc.edu/~walshc/mtp3e⟩.

Monetary Theory and Policy

1 Empirical Evidence on Money, Prices, and Output

1.1 Introduction

This chapter reviews some of the basic empirical evidence on money, inflation, and output. This review serves two purposes. First, these basic facts about long-run and short-run relationships serve as benchmarks for judging theoretical models. Second, reviewing the empirical evidence provides an opportunity to discuss the approaches monetary economists have taken to estimate the effects of money and monetary policy on real economic activity. The discussion focuses heavily on evidence from vector autoregressions (VARs) because these have served as a primary tool for uncovering the impact of monetary phenomena on the real economy. The findings obtained from VARs have been criticized, and these criticisms as well as other methods that have been used to investigate the money-output relationship are also discussed.

1.2 Some Basic Correlations

What are the basic empirical regularities that monetary economics must explain? Monetary economics focuses on the behavior of prices, monetary aggregates, nominal and real interest rates, and output, so a useful starting point is to summarize briefly what macroeconomic data tell us about the relationships among these variables.

1.2.1 Long-Run Relationships

A nice summary of long-run monetary relationships is provided by McCandless and Weber (1995). They examined data covering a 30-year period from 110 countries using several definitions of money. By examining average rates of inflation, output growth, and the growth rates of various measures of money over a long period of time and for many different countries, McCandless and Weber provided evidence on relationships that are unlikely to depend on unique country-specific events (such as the particular means employed to implement monetary policy) that might influence the actual evolution of money, prices, and output in a particular country. Based on their analysis, two primary conclusions emerge.

The first is that the correlation between inflation and the growth rate of the money supply is almost 1, varying between 0.92 and 0.96, depending on the definition of the money supply used. This strong positive relationship between inflation and money growth is consistent with many other studies based on smaller samples of countries and different time periods.[1] This correlation is normally taken to support one of the basic tenets of the quantity theory of money: a change in the growth rate of money induces "an equal change in the rate of price inflation" (Lucas 1980b, 1005). Using U.S. data from 1955 to 1975, Lucas plotted annual inflation against the annual growth rate of money. While the scatter plot suggests only a loose but positive relationship between inflation and money growth, a much stronger relationship emerged when Lucas filtered the data to remove short-run volatility. Berentsen, Menzio, and Wright (2008) repeated Lucas's exercise using data from 1955 to 2005, and like Lucas, they found a strong correlation between inflation and money growth as they removed more and more of the short-run fluctuations in the two variables.[2]

This high correlation between inflation and money growth does not, however, have any implication for causality. If countries followed policies under which money supply growth rates were exogenously determined, then the correlation could be taken as evidence that money growth causes inflation, with an almost one-to-one relationship between them. An alternative possibility, equally consistent with the high correlation, is that other factors generate inflation, and central banks allow the growth rate of money to adjust. Any theoretical model not consistent with a roughly one-for-one long-run relationship between money growth and inflation, though, would need to be questioned.[3]

The appropriate interpretation of money-inflation correlations, both in terms of causality and in terms of tests of long-run relationships, also depends on the statistical properties of the underlying series. As Fischer and Seater (1993) noted, one cannot ask how a permanent change in the growth rate of money affects inflation unless

1. Examples include Lucas (1980b); Geweke (1986); and Rolnick and Weber (1994), among others. A nice graph of the close relationship between money growth and inflation for high-inflation countries is provided by Abel and Bernanke (1995, 242). Hall and Taylor (1997, 115) provided a similar graph for the G-7 countries. As will be noted, however, the interpretation of correlations between inflation and money growth can be problematic.

2. Berentsen, Menzio, and Wright (2008) employed an HP filter and progressively increased the smoothing parameter from 0 to 160,000.

3. Haldane (1997) found, however, that the money growth rate–inflation correlation is much less than 1 among low-inflation countries.

actual money growth has exhibited permanent shifts. They showed how the order of integration of money and prices influences the testing of hypotheses about the long-run relationship between money growth and inflation. In a similar vein, McCallum (1984b) demonstrated that regression-based tests of long-run relationships in monetary economics may be misleading when expectational relationships are involved.

McCandless and Weber's second general conclusion is that there is no correlation between either inflation or money growth and the growth rate of real output. Thus, there are countries with low output growth and low money growth and inflation, and countries with low output growth and high money growth and inflation—and countries with every other combination as well. This conclusion is not as robust as the money growth–inflation one; McCandless and Weber reported a positive correlation between real growth and money growth, but not inflation, for a subsample of OECD countries. Kormendi and Meguire (1984) for a sample of almost 50 countries and Geweke (1986) for the United States argued that the data reveal no long-run effect of money growth on real output growth. Barro (1995; 1996) reported a negative correlation between inflation and growth in a cross-country sample. Bullard and Keating (1995) examined post–World War II data from 58 countries, concluding for the sample as a whole that the evidence that permanent shifts in inflation produce permanent effects on the level of output is weak, with some evidence of positive effects of inflation on output among low-inflation countries and zero or negative effects for higher-inflation countries.[4] Similarly, Boschen and Mills (1995b) concluded that permanent monetary shocks in the United States made no contribution to permanent shifts in GDP, a result consistent with the findings of R. King and Watson (1997).

Bullard (1999) surveyed much of the existing empirical work on the long-run relationship between money growth and real output, discussing both methodological issues associated with testing for such a relationship and the results of a large literature. Specifically, while shocks to the level of the money supply do not appear to have long-run effects on real output, this is not the case with respect to shocks to money growth. For example, the evidence based on postwar U.S. data reported in King and Watson (1997) is consistent with an effect of money growth on real output. Bullard and Keating (1995) did not find any real effects of permanent inflation shocks with a cross-country analysis, but Berentsen, Menzio, and Wright (2008), using the same filtering approach described earlier, argued that inflation and unemployment are positively related in the long run.

---

4. Kormendi and Meguire (1985) reported a statistically significant positive coefficient on average money growth in a cross-country regression for average real growth. This effect, however, was due to a single observation (Brazil), and the authors reported that money growth became insignificant in their growth equation when Brazil was dropped from the sample. They did find a significant negative effect of monetary volatility on growth.

However, despite this diversity of empirical findings concerning the long-run relationship between inflation and real growth, and other measures of real economic activity such as unemployment, the general consensus is well summarized by the proposition, "about which there is now little disagreement, . . . that there is no long-run trade-off between the rate of inflation and the rate of unemployment" (Taylor 1996, 186).

Monetary economics is also concerned with the relationship between interest rates, inflation, and money. According to the Fisher equation, the nominal interest rate equals the real return plus the expected rate of inflation. If real returns are independent of inflation, then nominal interest rates should be positively related to expected inflation. This relationship is an implication of the theoretical models discussed throughout this book. In terms of long-run correlations, it suggests that the level of nominal interest rates should be positively correlated with average rates of inflation. Because average rates of inflation are positively correlated with average money growth rates, nominal interest rates and money growth rates should also be positively correlated. Monnet and Weber (2001) examined annual average interest rates and money growth rates over the period 1961–1998 for a sample of 31 countries. They found a correlation of 0.87 between money growth and long-term interest rates. For developed countries, the correlation is somewhat smaller (0.70); for developing countries, it is 0.84, although this falls to 0.66 when Venezuela is excluded.[5] This evidence is consistent with the Fisher equation.[6]

1.2.2 Short-Run Relationships

The long-run empirical regularities of monetary economics are important for gauging how well the steady-state properties of a theoretical model match the data. Much of our interest in monetary economics, however, arises because of a need to understand how monetary phenomena in general and monetary policy in particular affect the behavior of the macroeconomy over time periods of months or quarters. Short-run dynamic relationships between money, inflation, and output reflect both the way in which private agents respond to economic disturbances and the way in which the monetary policy authority responds to those same disturbances. For this reason, short-run correlations are likely to vary across countries, as different central banks implement policy in different ways, and across time in a single country, as the sources of economic disturbances vary.

Some evidence on short-run correlations for the United States are provided in figures 1.1 and 1.2. The figures show correlations between the detrended log of real

---

5. Venezuela's money growth rate averaged over 28 percent, the highest among the countries in Monnet and Weber's sample.

6. Consistent evidence on the strong positive long-run relationship between inflation and interest rates was reported by Berentsen, Menzio, and Wright (2008).

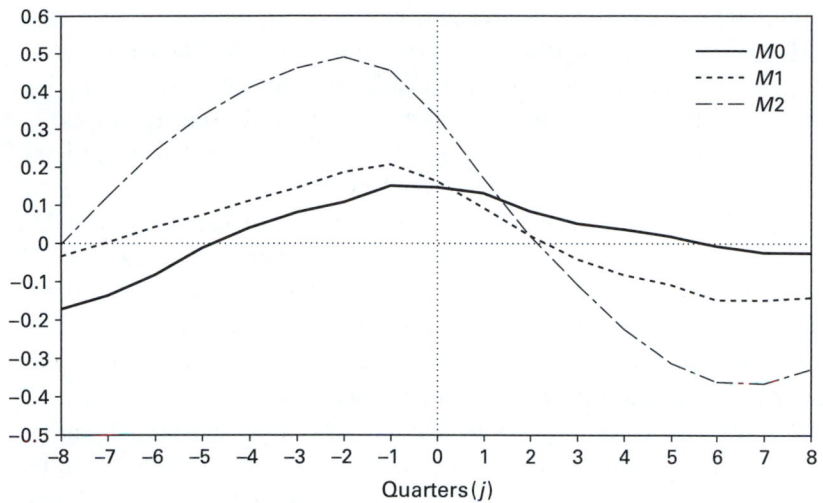

Figure 1.1
Dynamic correlations, GDP_t and M_{t+j}, 1967:1–2008:2.

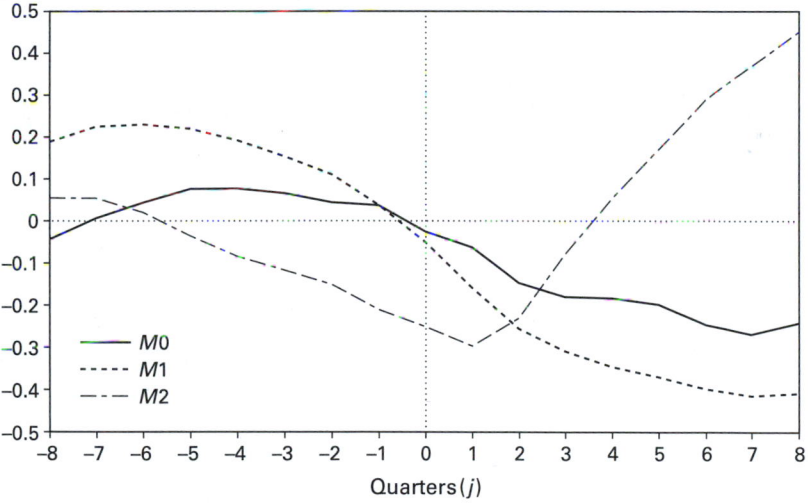

Figure 1.2
Dynamic correlations, GDP_t and M_{t+j}, 1984:1–2008:2.

GDP and three different monetary aggregates, each also in detrended log form.[7]
Data are quarterly from 1967:1 to 2008:2, and the figures plot, for the entire sample
and for the subperiod 1984:1–2008:2, the correlation between real GDP_t and M_{t+j}
against j, where M represents a monetary aggregate. The three aggregates are the
monetary base (sometimes denoted $M0$), $M1$, and $M2$. $M0$ is a narrow definition of
the money supply, consisting of total reserves held by the banking system plus currency in the hands of the public. $M1$ consists of currency held by the nonbank public,
travelers checks, demand deposits, and other checkable deposits. $M2$ consists of $M1$
plus savings accounts and small-denomination time deposits plus balances in retail
money market mutual funds. The post-1984 period is shown separately because
1984 often is identified as the beginning of a period characterized by greater macroeconomic stability, at least until the onset of the financial crisis in 2007.[8]

As figure 1.1 shows, the correlations with real output change substantially as one
moves from $M0$ to $M2$. The narrow measure $M0$ is positively correlated with real
GDP at both leads and lags over the entire period, but future $M0$ is negatively correlated with real GDP in the period since 1984. $M1$ and $M2$ are positively correlated
at lags but negatively correlated at leads over the full sample. In other words, high
GDP (relative to trend) tends to be preceded by high values of $M1$ and $M2$ but followed by low values. The positive correlation between GDP_t and M_{t+j} for $j < 0$
indicates that movements in money lead movements in output. This timing pattern
played an important role in M. Friedman and Schwartz's classic and highly influential *A Monetary History of the United States* (1963a). The larger correlations between
GDP and $M2$ arise in part from the endogenous nature of an aggregate such as $M2$,
depending as it does on banking sector behavior as well as on that of the nonbank
private sector (see King and Plosser 1984; Coleman 1996). However, these patterns
for $M2$ are reversed in the later period, though $M1$ still leads GDP. Correlations
among endogenous variables reflect the structure of the economy, the nature of
shocks experienced during each period, and the behavior of monetary policy. One
objective of a structural model of the economy and a theory of monetary policy is
to provide a framework for understanding why these dynamic correlations differ
over different periods.

Figures 1.3 and 1.4 show the cross-correlations between detrended real GDP and
several interest rates and between detrended real GDP and the detrended GDP deflator. The interest rates range from the federal funds rate, an overnight interbank rate
used by the Federal Reserve to implement monetary policy, to the 1-year and 10-year
rates on government bonds. The three interest rate series display similar correlations

---

7. Trends are estimated using a Hodrick-Prescott filter.

8. Perhaps reflecting the greater volatility during 1967–1983, cross-correlations during this period are similar to those obtained using the entire 1967–2008 period.

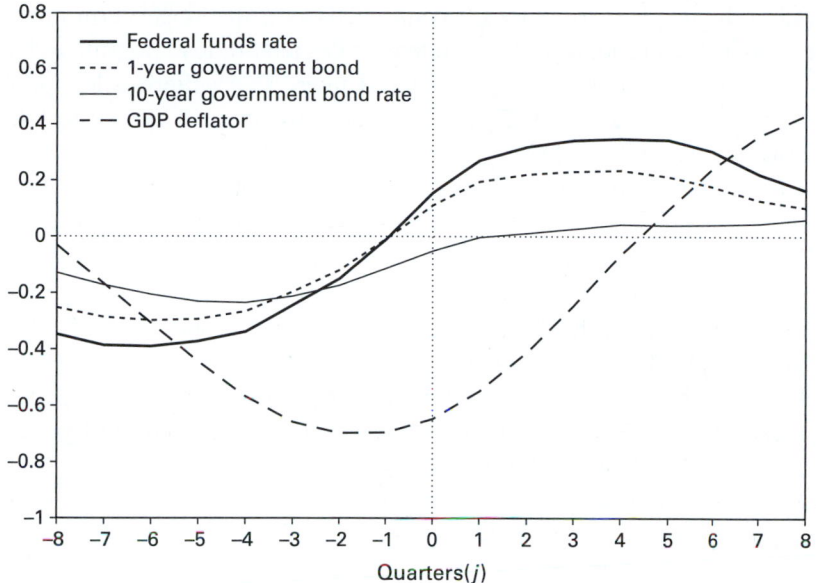

Figure 1.3
Dynamic correlations, output, prices, and interest rates, 1967:1–2008:2.

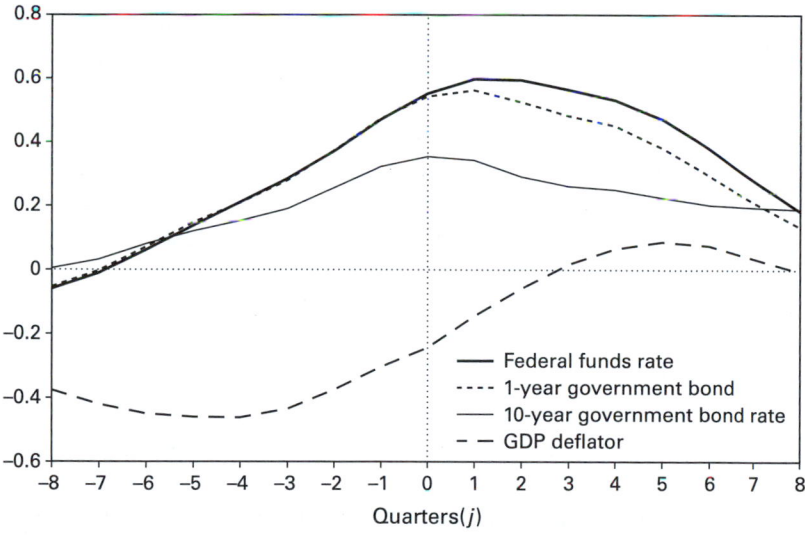

Figure 1.4
Dynamic correlations, output, prices, and interest rates, 1984:1–2008:2.

with real output, although the correlations become smaller for the longer-term rates. For the entire sample period (figure 1.3), low interest rates tend to lead output, and a rise in output tends to be followed by higher interest rates. This pattern is less pronounced in the 1984:1–2008:2 period (figure 1.4), and interest rates appear to rise prior to an increase in detrended GDP.

In contrast, the GDP deflator tends to be below trend when output is above trend, but increases in real output tend to be followed by increases in prices, though this effect is absent in the more recent period. Kydland and Prescott (1990) argued that the negative contemporaneous correlation between the output and price series suggests that supply shocks, not demand shocks, must be responsible for business cycle fluctuations. Aggregate supply shocks would cause prices to be countercyclical, whereas demand shocks would be expected to make prices procyclical. However, if prices were sticky, a demand shock would initially raise output above trend, and prices would respond very little. If prices did eventually rise while output eventually returned to trend, prices could be rising as output was falling, producing a negative unconditional correlation between the two even though it was demand shocks generating the fluctuations (Ball and Mankiw 1994; Judd and Trehan 1995). Den Haan (2000) examined forecast errors from a vector autoregression (see section 1.3.4) and found that price and output correlations are positive for short forecast horizons and negative for long forecast horizons. This pattern seems consistent with demand shocks playing an important role in accounting for short-run fluctuations and supply shocks playing a more important role in the long-run behavior of output and prices.

Most models used to address issues in monetary theory and policy contain only a single interest rate. Generally, this is interpreted as a short-term rate of interest and is often viewed as an overnight market interest rate that the central bank can, to a large degree, control. The assumption of a single interest rate is a useful simplification if all interest rates tend to move together. Figure 1.5 shows several longer-term market rates of interest for the United States. As the figure suggests, interest rates do tend to display similar behavior, although the 3-month Treasury bill rate, the shortest maturity shown, is more volatile than the other rates. There are periods, however, when rates at different maturities and riskiness move in opposite directions. For example, during 2008, a period of financial crisis, the rate on corporate bonds rose while the rates on government debt, both at 3-month and 10-year maturities, were falling.

Although figures 1.1–1.5 produce evidence for the behavior of money, prices, interest rates, and output, at least for the United States, one of the challenges of monetary economics is to determine the degree to which these data reveal causal relationships, relationships that should be expected to appear in data from other countries and during other time periods, or relationships that depend on the particular characteristics of the policy regime under which monetary policy is conducted.

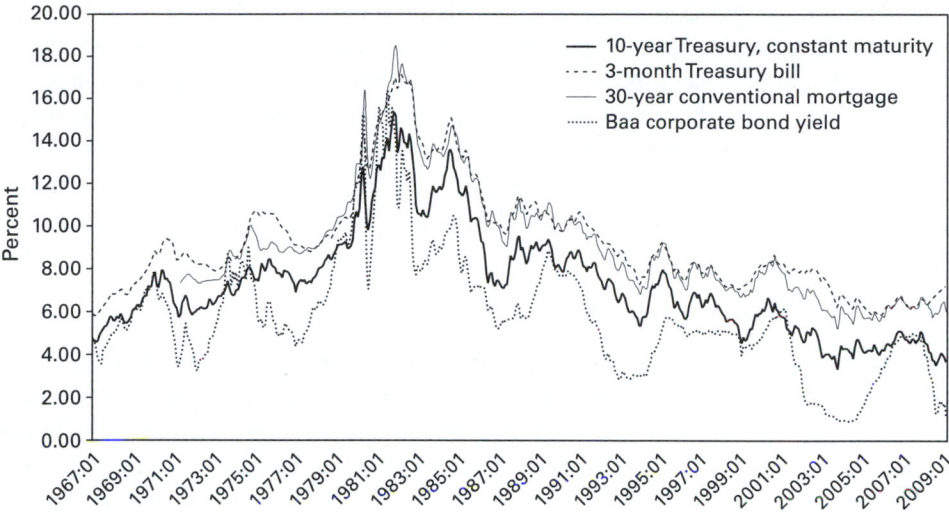

Figure 1.5
Interest rates, 1967:01–2008:09.

1.3 Estimating the Effect of Money on Output

Almost all economists accept that the long-run effects of money fall entirely, or almost entirely, on prices, with little impact on real variables, but most economists also believe that monetary disturbances can have important effects on real variables such as output in the short run.[9] As Lucas (1996) put it in his Nobel lecture, "This tension between two incompatible ideas—that changes in money are neutral unit changes and that they induce movements in employment and production in the same direction—has been at the center of monetary theory at least since Hume wrote" (664).[10] The time series correlations presented in the previous section suggest the short-run relationships between money and income, but the evidence for the effects of money on real output is based on more than these simple correlations.

The tools that have been employed to estimate the impact of monetary policy have evolved over time as the result of developments in time series econometrics and changes in the specific questions posed by theoretical models. This section reviews some of the empirical evidence on the relationship between monetary policy and U.S. macroeconomic behavior. One objective of this literature has been to determine

9. For an exposition of the view that monetary factors have not played an important role in U.S. business cycles, see Kydland and Prescott (1990).

10. The reference is to David Hume's 1752 essays *Of Money* and *Of Interest*.

whether monetary policy disturbances actually have played an important role in U.S. economic fluctuations. Equally important, the empirical evidence is useful in judging whether the predictions of different theories about the effects of monetary policy are consistent with the evidence. Among the excellent recent discussions of these issues are Leeper, Sims, and Zha (1996) and Christiano, Eichenbaum, and Evans (1999), where the focus is on the role of identified VARs in estimating the effects of monetary policy, and R. King and Watson (1996), where the focus is on using empirical evidence to distinguish among competing business-cycle models.

1.3.1 The Evidence of Friedman and Schwartz

M. Friedman and Schwartz's (1963a) study of the relationship between money and business cycles still represents probably the most influential empirical evidence that money does matter for business cycle fluctuations. Their evidence, based on almost 100 years of data from the United States, relies heavily on patterns of timing; systematic evidence that money growth rate changes lead changes in real economic activity is taken to support a causal interpretation in which money causes output fluctuations. This timing pattern shows up most clearly in figure 1.1 with $M2$.

Friedman and Schwartz concluded that the data "decisively support treating the rate of change series [of the money supply] as conforming to the reference cycle positively with a long lead" (36). That is, faster money growth tends to be followed by increases in output above trend, and slowdowns in money growth tend to be followed by declines in output. The inference Friedman and Schwartz drew was that variations in money growth rates cause, with a long (and variable) lag, variations in real economic activity.

The nature of this evidence for the United States is apparent in figure 1.6, which shows two detrended money supply measures and real GDP. The monetary aggregates in the figure, $M1$ and $M2$, are quarterly observations on the deviations of the actual series from trend. The sample period is 1967:1–2008:2, so that is after the period of the Friedman and Schwartz study. The figure reveals slowdowns in money leading most business cycle downturns through the early 1980s. However, the pattern is not so apparent after 1982. B. Friedman and Kuttner (1992) documented the seeming breakdown in the relationship between monetary aggregates and real output; this changing relationship between money and output has affected the manner in which monetary policy has been conducted, at least in the United States (see chapter 11).

While it is suggestive, evidence based on timing patterns and simple correlations may not indicate the true causal role of money. Since the Federal Reserve and the banking sector respond to economic developments, movements in the monetary aggregates are not exogenous, and the correlation patterns need not reflect any causal effect of monetary policy on economic activity. If, for example, the central

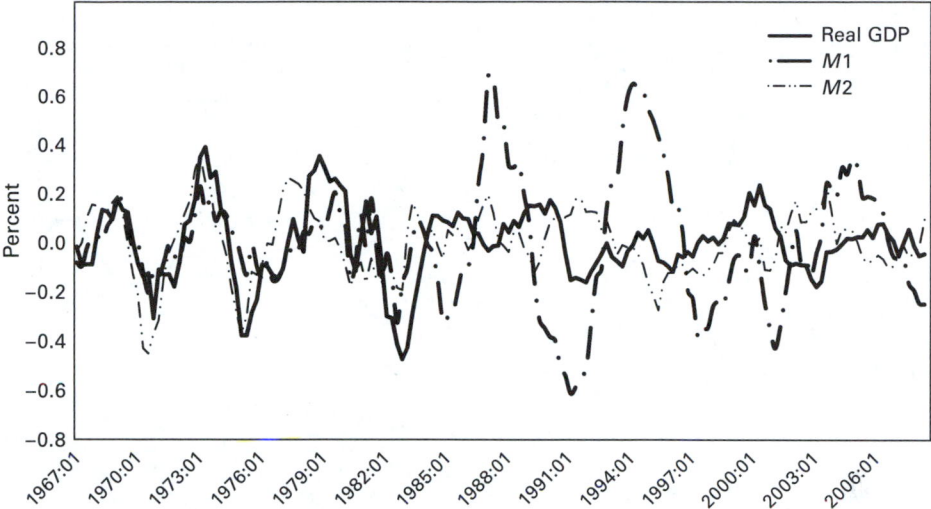

Figure 1.6
Detrended money and real GDP, 1967:1–2008:2.

bank is implementing monetary policy by controlling the value of some short-term market interest rate, the nominal stock of money will be affected both by policy actions that change interest rates and by developments in the economy that are not related to policy actions. An economic expansion may lead banks to expand lending in ways that produce an increase in the stock of money, even if the central bank has not changed its policy. If the money stock is used to measure monetary policy, the relationship observed in the data between money and output may reflect the impact of output on money, not the impact of money and monetary policy on output.

Tobin (1970) was the first to model formally the idea that the positive correlation between money and output—the correlation that Friedman and Schwartz interpreted as providing evidence that money caused output movements—could in fact reflect just the opposite—output might be causing money. A more modern treatment of what is known as the *reverse causation argument* was provided by R. King and Plosser (1984). They show that inside money, the component of a monetary aggregate such as $M1$ that represents the liabilities of the banking sector, is more highly correlated with output movements in the United States than is outside money, the liabilities of the Federal Reserve. King and Plosser interpreted this finding as evidence that much of the correlation between broad aggregates such as $M1$ or $M2$ and output arises from the endogenous response of the banking sector to economic disturbances that are not the result of monetary policy actions. More recently, Coleman (1996), in an estimated equilibrium model with endogenous money, found that

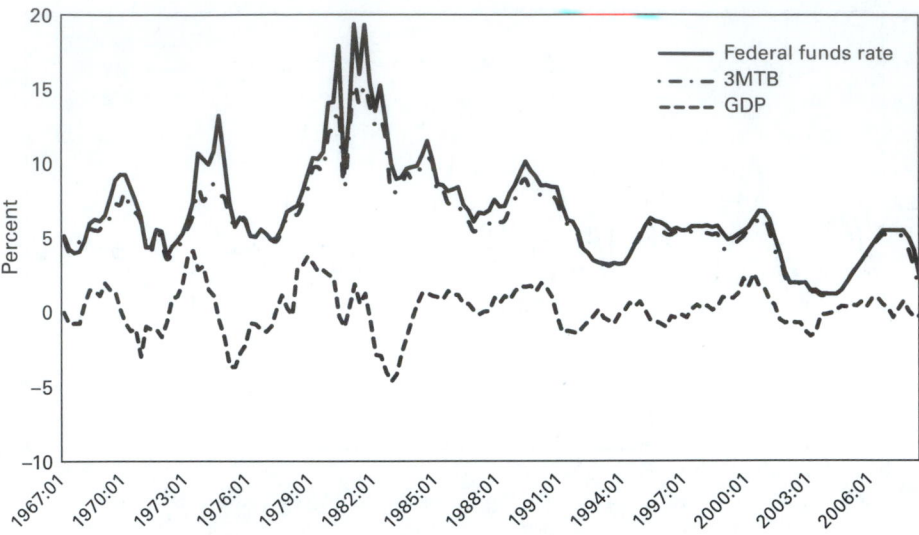

Figure 1.7
Interest rates and detrended real GDP, 1967:1–2008:2.

the implied behavior of money in the model cannot match the lead-lag relationship in the data. Specifically, a money supply measure such as $M2$ leads output, whereas Coleman found that his model implies that money should be more highly correlated with lagged output than with future output.[11]

The endogeneity problem is likely to be particularly severe if the monetary authority has employed a short-term interest rate as its main policy instrument, and this has generally been the case in the United States. Changes in the money stock will then be endogenous and cannot be interpreted as representing policy actions. Figure 1.7 shows the behavior of two short-term nominal interest rates, the 3-month Treasury bill rate (3MTB) and the federal funds rate, together with detrended real GDP. Like figure 1.6, figure 1.7 provides some support for the notion that monetary policy actions have contributed to U.S. business cycles. Interest rates have typically increased prior to economic downturns. But whether this is evidence that monetary policy has caused or contributed to cyclical fluctuations cannot be inferred from the figure; the movements in interest rates may simply reflect the Fed's response to the state of the economy.

Simple plots and correlations are suggestive, but they cannot be decisive. Other factors may be the cause of the joint movements of output, monetary aggregates,

---

11. Lacker (1988) showed how the correlations between inside money and future output could also arise if movements in inside money reflect new information about future monetary policy.

and interest rates. The comparison with business cycle reference points also ignores much of the information about the time series behavior of money, output, and interest rates that could be used to determine what impact, if any, monetary policy has on output. And the appropriate variable to use as a measure of monetary policy will depend on how policy has been implemented.

One of the earliest time series econometric attempts to estimate the impact of money was due to M. Friedman and Meiselman (1963). Their objective was to test whether monetary or fiscal policy was more important for the determination of *nominal* income. To address this issue, they estimated the following equation:[12]

$$y_t^n \equiv y_t + p_t = y_0^n + \sum_{i=0} a_i A_{t-i} + \sum_{i=0} b_i m_{t-i} + \sum_{i=0} h_i z_{t-i} + u_t, \tag{1.1}$$

where y^n denotes the log of nominal income, equal to the sum of the logs of output and the price level, A is a measure of autonomous expenditures, and m is a monetary aggregate; z can be thought of as a vector of other variables relevant for explaining nominal income fluctuations. Friedman and Meiselman reported finding a much more stable and statistically significant relationship between output and money than between output and their measure of autonomous expenditures. In general, they could not reject the hypothesis that the a_i coefficients were zero, while the b_i coefficients were always statistically significant.

The use of equations such as (1.1) for policy analysis was promoted by a number of economists at the Federal Reserve Bank of St. Louis, so regressions of nominal income on money are often called *St. Louis equations* (see L. Andersen and Jordon 1968; B. Friedman 1977a; Carlson 1978). Because the dependent variable is nominal income, the St. Louis approach does not address directly the question of how a money-induced change in nominal spending is split between a change in real output and a change in the price level. The impact of money on nominal income was estimated to be quite strong, and Andersen and Jordon (1968, 22) concluded, "Finding of a strong empirical relationship between economic activity and ... monetary actions points to the conclusion that monetary actions can and should play a more prominent role in economic stabilization than they have up to now."[13]

---

12. This is not exactly correct; because Friedman and Meiselman included "autonomous" expenditures as an explanatory variable, they also used consumption as the dependent variable (basically, output minus autonomous expenditures). They also reported results for real variables as well as nominal ones. Following modern practice, (1.1) is expressed in terms of logs; Friedman and Meiselman estimated their equation in levels.

13. B. Friedman (1977a) argued that updated estimates of the St. Louis equation did yield a role for fiscal policy, although the statistical reliability of this finding was questioned by Carlson (1978). Carlson also provided a bibliography listing many of the papers on the St. Louis equation (see his footnote 2, p. 13).

The original Friedman-Meiselman result generated responses by Modigliani and Ando (1976) and De Prano and Mayer (1965), among others. This debate emphasized that an equation such as (1.1) is misspecified if m is endogenous. To illustrate the point with an extreme example, suppose that the central bank is able to manipulate the money supply to offset almost perfectly shocks that would otherwise generate fluctuations in nominal income. In this case, y^n would simply reflect the random control errors the central bank had failed to offset. As a result, m and y^n might be completely uncorrelated, and a regression of y^n on m would not reveal that money actually played an important role in affecting nominal income. If policy is able to respond to the factors generating the error term u_t, then m_t and u_t will be correlated, ordinary least-squares estimates of (1.1) will be inconsistent, and the resulting estimates will depend on the manner in which policy has induced a correlation between u and m. Changes in policy that altered this correlation would also alter the least-squares regression estimates one would obtain in estimating (1.1).

1.3.2 Granger Causality

The St. Louis equation related nominal output to the past behavior of money. Similar regressions employing *real* output have also been used to investigate the connection between real economic activity and money. In an important contribution, Sims (1972) introduced the notion of *Granger causality* into the debate over the real effects of money. A variable X is said to Granger-cause Y if and only if lagged values of X have marginal predictive content in a forecasting equation for Y. In practice, testing whether money Granger-causes output involves testing whether the a_i coefficients equal zero in a regression of the form

$$y_t = y_0 + \sum_{i=1} a_i m_{t-i} + \sum_{i=1} b_i y_{t-i} + \sum_{i=1} c_i z_{t-i} + e_t, \tag{1.2}$$

where key issues involve the treatment of trends in output and money, the choice of lag lengths, and the set of other variables (represented by z) that are included in the equation.

Sims's original work used log levels of U.S. nominal GNP and money (both $M1$ and the monetary base). He found evidence that money Granger-caused GNP. That is, the past behavior of money helped to predict future GNP. However, using the index of industrial production to measure real output, Sims (1980) found that the fraction of output variation explained by money was greatly reduced when a nominal interest rate was added to the equation (so that z consists of the log price level and an interest rate). Thus, the conclusion seemed sensitive to the specification of z. Eichenbaum and Singleton (1987) found that money appeared to be less important if the regressions were specified in log first difference form rather than in log levels with a time trend. Stock and Watson (1989) provided a systematic treatment of the trend specification in testing whether money Granger-causes real output. They concluded that money does help to predict future output (they actually used industrial production) even when prices and an interest rate are included.

A large literature has examined the value of monetary indicators in forecasting output. One interpretation of Sims's finding was that including an interest rate reduces the apparent role of money because, at least in the United States, a short-term interest rate rather than the money supply provides a better measure of monetary policy actions (see chapter 11). B. Friedman and Kuttner (1992) and Bernanke and Blinder (1992), among others, looked at the role of alternative interest rate measures in forecasting real output. Friedman and Kuttner examined the effects of alternative definitions of money and different sample periods and concluded that the relationship in the United States is unstable and deteriorated in the 1990s. Bernanke and Blinder found that the federal funds rate "dominates both money and the bill and bond rates in forecasting real variables."

Regressions of real output on money were also popularized by Barro (1977; 1978; 1979b) as a way of testing whether only unanticipated money matters for real output. By dividing money into anticipated and unanticipated components, Barro obtained results suggesting that only the unanticipated part affects real variables (see also Barro and Rush 1980 and the critical comment by Small 1979). Subsequent work by Mishkin (1982) found a role for anticipated money as well. Cover (1992) employed a similar approach and found differences in the impacts of positive and negative monetary shocks. Negative shocks were estimated to have significant effects on output, whereas the effect of positive shocks was usually small and statistically insignificant.

1.3.3   Policy Uses

Before reviewing other evidence on the effects of money on output, it is useful to ask whether equations such as (1.2) can be used for policy purposes. That is, can a regression of this form be used to design a policy rule for setting the central bank's policy instrument? If it can, then the discussions of theoretical models that form the bulk of this book would be unnecessary, at least from the perspective of conducting monetary policy.

Suppose that the estimated relationship between output and money takes the form

$$y_t = y_0 + a_0 m_t + a_1 m_{t-1} + c_1 z_t + c_2 z_{t-1} + u_t. \tag{1.3}$$

According to (1.3), systematic variations in the money supply affect output. Consider the problem of adjusting the money supply to reduce fluctuations in real output. If this objective is interpreted to mean that the money supply should be manipulated to minimize the variance of y_t around y_0, then m_t should be set equal to

$$m_t = -\frac{a_1}{a_0}m_{t-1} - \frac{c_2}{a_0}z_{t-1} + v_t$$

$$= \pi_1 m_{t-1} + \pi_2 z_{t-1} + v_t, \tag{1.4}$$

where for simplicity it is assumed that the monetary authority's forecast of z_t is equal to zero. The term v_t represents the control error experienced by the monetary authority in setting the money supply. Equation (1.4) represents a feedback rule for the money supply whose parameters are themselves determined by the estimated coefficients in the equation for y. A key assumption is that the coefficients in (1.3) are independent of the choice of the policy rule for m. Substituting (1.4) into (1.3), output under the policy rule given in (1.4) would be equal to $y_t = y_0 + c_1 z_t + u_t + a_0 v_t$.

Notice that a policy rule has been derived using only knowledge of the policy objective (minimizing the expected variance of output) and knowledge of the estimated coefficients in (1.3). No theory of how monetary policy actually affects the economy was required. Sargent (1976) showed, however, that the use of (1.3) to derive a policy feedback rule may be inappropriate. To see why, suppose that real output actually depends only on unpredicted movements in the money supply; only surprises matter, with predicted changes in money simply being reflected in price level movements with no impact on output.[14] From (1.4), the unpredicted movement in m_t is just v_t, so let the true model for output be

$$y_t = y_0 + d_0 v_t + d_1 z_t + d_2 z_{t-1} + u_t. \tag{1.5}$$

Now from (1.4), $v_t = m_t - (\pi_1 m_{t-1} + \pi_2 z_{t-1})$, so output can be expressed equivalently as

$$y_t = y_0 + d_0[m_t - (\pi_1 m_{t-1} + \pi_2 z_{t-1})] + d_1 z_t + d_2 z_{t-1} + u_t$$

$$= y_0 + d_0 m_t - d_0 \pi_1 m_{t-1} + d_1 z_t + (d_2 - d_0 \pi_2)z_{t-1} + u_t, \tag{1.6}$$

which has exactly the same form as (1.3). Equation (1.3), which was initially interpreted as consistent with a situation in which systematic feedback rules for monetary policy could affect output, is *observationally equivalent* to (1.6), which was derived under the assumption that systematic policy had no effect and only money surprises mattered. The two are observationally equivalent because the error term in both (1.3) and (1.6) is just u_t; both equations fit the data equally well.

A comparison of (1.3) and (1.6) reveals another important conclusion. The coefficients of (1.6) are functions of the parameters in the policy rule (1.4). Thus, changes in the conduct of policy, interpreted to mean changes in the feedback rule parame-

---

14. The influential model of Lucas (1972) has this implication. See chapter 5.

ters, will change the parameters estimated in an equation such as (1.6) (or in a St. Louis–type regression). This is an example of the Lucas (1976) critique: empirical relationships are unlikely to be invariant to changes in policy regimes.

Of course, as Sargent stressed, it may be that (1.3) is the true structure that remains invariant as policy changes. In this case, (1.5) will not be invariant to changes in policy. To demonstrate this point, note that (1.4) implies

$$m_t = (1 - \pi_1 L)^{-1}(\pi_2 z_{t-1} + v_t),$$

where L is the lag operator.[15] Hence, we can write (1.3) as

$$y_t = y_0 + a_0 m_t + a_1 m_{t-1} + c_1 z_t + c_2 z_{t-1} + u_t$$

$$= y_0 + a_0(1 - \pi_1 L)^{-1}(\pi_2 z_{t-1} + v_t)$$

$$+ a_1(1 - \pi_1 L)^{-1}(\pi_2 z_{t-2} + v_{t-1}) + c_1 z_t + c_2 z_{t-1} + u_t$$

$$= (1 - \pi_1)y_0 + \pi_1 y_{t-1} + a_0 v_t + a_1 v_{t-1} + c_1 z_t$$

$$+ (c_2 + a_0 \pi_2 - c_1 \pi_1)z_{t-1} + (a_1 \pi_2 - c_2 \pi_1)z_{t-2} + u_t - \pi_1 u_{t-1}, \tag{1.7}$$

where output is now expressed as a function of lagged output, the z variable, and money surprises (the v realizations). If this were interpreted as a policy-invariant expression, one would conclude that output is independent of any predictable or systematic feedback rule for monetary policy; only unpredicted money appears to matter. Yet, under the hypothesis that (1.3) is the true invariant structure, changes in the policy rule (the π_1 coefficients) will cause the coefficients in (1.7) to change.

Note that starting with (1.5) and (1.4), one derives an expression for output that is observationally equivalent to (1.3). But starting with (1.3) and (1.4), one ends up with an expression for output that is not equivalent to (1.5); (1.7) contains lagged values of output, v, and u, and two lags of z, whereas (1.5) contains only the contemporaneous values of v and u and one lag of z. These differences would allow one to distinguish between the two, but they arise only because this example placed a priori restrictions on the lag lengths in (1.3) and (1.5). In general, one would not have the type of a priori information that would allow this.

The lesson from this simple example is that policy cannot be designed without a theory of how money affects the economy. A theory should identify whether the coefficients in a specification of the form (1.3) or in a specification such as (1.5) will remain invariant as policy changes. While output equations estimated over a single

---

15. That is, $L^i x_t = x_{t-i}$.

policy regime may not allow the true structure to be identified, information from several policy regimes might succeed in doing so. If a policy regime change means that the coefficients in the policy rule (1.4) have changed, this would serve to identify whether an expression of the form (1.3) or one of the form (1.5) was policy-invariant.

1.3.4 The VAR Approach

Much of the understanding of the empirical effects of monetary policy on real economic activity has come from the use of vector autoregression (VAR) frameworks. The use of VARs to estimate the impact of money on the economy was pioneered by Sims (1972; 1980). The development of the approach as it moved from bivariate (Sims 1972) to trivariate (Sims 1980) to larger and larger systems as well as the empirical findings the literature has produced were summarized by Leeper, Sims, and Zha (1996). Christiano, Eichenbaum, and Evans (1999) provided a thorough discussion of the use of VARs to estimate the impact of money, and they provided an extensive list of references to work in this area.[16]

Suppose there is a bivariate system in which y_t is the natural log of real output at time t, and x_t is a candidate measure of monetary policy such as a measure of the money stock or a short-term market rate of interest.[17] The VAR system can be written as

$$\begin{bmatrix} y_t \\ x_t \end{bmatrix} = A(\text{L}) \begin{bmatrix} y_{t-1} \\ x_{t-1} \end{bmatrix} + \begin{bmatrix} u_{yt} \\ u_{xt} \end{bmatrix}, \tag{1.8}$$

where $A(\text{L})$ is a 2×2 matrix polynomial in the lag operator L, and u_{it} is a time t serially independent innovation to the ith variable. These innovations can be thought of as linear combinations of independently distributed shocks to output (e_{yt}) and to policy (e_{xt}):

$$\begin{bmatrix} u_{yt} \\ u_{xt} \end{bmatrix} = \begin{bmatrix} e_{yt} + \theta e_{xt} \\ \phi e_{yt} + e_{xt} \end{bmatrix} = \begin{bmatrix} 1 & \theta \\ \phi & 1 \end{bmatrix} \begin{bmatrix} e_{yt} \\ e_{xt} \end{bmatrix} = B \begin{bmatrix} e_{yt} \\ e_{xt} \end{bmatrix}. \tag{1.9}$$

The one-period-ahead error made in forecasting the policy variable x_t is equal to u_{xt}, and since, from (1.9), $u_{xt} = \phi e_{yt} + e_{xt}$, these errors are caused by the exogenous output and policy disturbances e_{yt} and e_{xt}. Letting Σ_u denote the 2×2 variance-covariance matrix of the u_{it}, $\Sigma_u = B\Sigma_e B'$, where Σ_e is the (diagonal) variance matrix of the e_{it}.

---

16. Two references on the econometrics of VARs are Hamilton (1994) and Maddala (1992).

17. How one measures monetary policy is a critical issue in the empirical literature (see, e.g., C. Romer and Romer 1990a; Bernanke and Blinder 1992; D. Gordon and Leeper 1994; Christiano, Eichenbaum, and Evans 1996a; 1999; Bernanke and Mihov 1998; Rudebusch 1997; Leeper, Sims, and Zha 1996; and Leeper 1997). Zha (1997) provided a useful discussion of the general identification issues that arise in attempting to measure the impact of monetary policy; see chapter 11.

The random variable e_{xt} represents the exogenous shock to policy. To determine the role of policy in *causing* movements in output or other macroeconomic variables, one needs to estimate the effect of e_x on these variables. As long as $\phi \neq 0$, the innovation to the observed policy variable x_t will depend both on the shock to policy e_{xt} and on the nonpolicy shock e_{yt}; obtaining an estimate of u_{xt} does not provide a measure of the policy shock unless $\phi = 0$.

To make the example even more explicit, suppose the VAR system is

$$\begin{bmatrix} y_t \\ x_t \end{bmatrix} = \begin{bmatrix} a_1 & a_2 \\ 0 & 0 \end{bmatrix} \begin{bmatrix} y_{t-1} \\ x_{t-1} \end{bmatrix} + \begin{bmatrix} u_{yt} \\ u_{xt} \end{bmatrix}, \tag{1.10}$$

with $0 < a_1 < 1$. Then $x_t = u_{xt}$, and $y_t = a_1 y_{t-1} + u_{yt} + a_2 u_{xt-1}$, and one can write y_t in moving average form as

$$y_t = \sum_{i=0}^{\infty} a_1^i u_{yt-i} + \sum_{i=0}^{\infty} a_1^i a_2 u_{xt-i-1}.$$

Estimating (1.10) yields estimates of $A(L)$ and Σ_u, and from these the effects of u_{xt} on $\{y_t, y_{t+1}, \ldots\}$ can be calculated. If one interpreted u_x as an exogenous policy disturbance, then the implied response of $y_t, y_{t+1}, \ldots$ to a policy shock would be[18]

$$0, a_2, a_1 a_2, a_1^2 a_2, \ldots .$$

To estimate the impact of a policy shock on output, however, one needs to calculate the effect on $\{y_t, y_{t+1}, \ldots\}$ of a realization of the policy shock e_{xt}. In terms of the true underlying structural disturbances e_y and e_x, (1.9) implies

$$y_t = \sum_{i=0}^{\infty} a_1^i (e_{yt-i} + \theta e_{xt-i}) + \sum_{i=0}^{\infty} a_1^i a_2 (e_{xt-i-1} + \phi e_{yt-i-1})$$

$$= e_{yt} + \sum_{i=0}^{\infty} a_1^i (a_1 + a_2 \phi) e_{yt-i-1} + \theta e_{xt} + \sum_{i=0}^{\infty} a_1^i (a_1 \theta + a_2) e_{xt-i-1}, \tag{1.11}$$

so the impulse response function giving the true response of y to the exogenous policy shock e_x is

$$\theta, a_1 \theta + a_2, a_1 (a_1 \theta + a_2), a_1^2 (a_1 \theta + a_2), \ldots .$$

---

18. This represents the response to an nonorthogonalized innovation. The basic point, however, is that if θ and ϕ are nonzero, the underlying shocks are not identified, so the estimated response to u_x or to the component of u_x that is orthogonal to u_y will not identify the response to the policy shock e_x.

This response involves the elements of $A(L)$ *and* the elements of B. And while $A(L)$ can be estimated from (1.8), B and Σ_e are not identified without further restrictions.[19]

Two basic approaches to solving this identification problem have been followed. The first imposes additional restrictions on the matrix B that links the observable VAR residuals to the underlying structural disturbances (see (1.9)). This approach was used by Sims (1972; 1988); Bernanke (1986); Walsh (1987); Bernanke and Blinder (1992); D. Gordon and Leeper (1994); and Bernanke and Mihov (1998), among others. If policy shocks affect output with a lag, for example, the restriction that $\theta = 0$ would allow the other parameters of the model to be identified. The second approach achieves identification by imposing restrictions on the long-run effects of the disturbances on observed variables. For example, the assumption of long-run neutrality of money would imply that a monetary policy shock (e_x) has no long-run permanent effect on output. In terms of the example that led to (1.11), long-run neutrality of the policy shock would imply that $\theta + (a_1\theta + a_2) \sum a_1^i = 0$ or $\theta = -a_2$. Examples of this approach include Blanchard and Watson (1986); Blanchard (1989); Blanchard and Quah (1989); Judd and Trehan (1989); Hutchison and Walsh (1992); and Galí (1992). The use of long-run restrictions is criticized by Faust and Leeper (1997).

In Sims (1972), the nominal money supply ($M1$) was treated as the measure of monetary policy (the x variable), and policy shocks were identified by assuming that $\phi = 0$. This approach corresponds to the assumption that the money supply is predetermined and that policy innovations are exogenous with respect to the nonpolicy innovations (see (1.9)). In this case, $u_{xt} = e_{xt}$, so from the fact that $u_{yt} = \theta e_{xt} + e_{yt} = \theta u_{xt} + e_{yt}$, θ can be estimated from the regression of the VAR residuals u_{yt} on the VAR residuals u_{xt}.[20] This corresponds to a situation in which the policy variable x does not respond contemporaneously to output shocks, perhaps because of information lags in formulating policy. However, if x depends contemporaneously on nonpolicy disturbances as well as policy shocks ($\phi \neq 0$), using u_{xt} as an estimate of e_{xt} will compound the effects of e_{yt} on u_{xt} with the effects of policy actions.

An alternative approach seeks a policy measure for which $\theta = 0$ is a plausible assumption; this corresponds to the assumption that policy shocks have no contemporaneous impact on output.[21] This type of restriction was imposed by Bernanke and Blinder (1992) and Bernanke and Mihov (1998). How reasonable such an assumption might be clearly depends on the unit of observation. In annual data, the assump-

---

19. In this example, the three elements of Σ_u, the two variances and the covariance term, are functions of the four unknown parameters, ϕ, θ, and the variances of e_y and e_x.

20. This represents a Choleski decomposition of the VAR residuals with the policy variable ordered first.

21. This represents a Choleski decomposition with output ordered before the policy variable.

tion of no contemporaneous effect would be implausible; with monthly data, it might be much more plausible.

This discussion has, for simplicity, treated both y and x as scalars. In fact, neither assumption is appropriate. One is usually interested in the effects of policy on several dimensions of an economy's macroeconomic performance, and policy is likely to respond to unemployment and inflation as well as to other variables, so y would normally be a vector of nonpolicy variables. Then the restrictions that correspond to either $\phi = 0$ or $\theta = 0$ may be less easily justified. While one might argue that policy does not respond contemporaneously to unemployment when the analysis involves monthly data, this is not likely to be the case with respect to market interest rates. And, using the same example, one might be comfortable assuming that the current month's unemployment rate is unaffected by current policy actions, but this would not be true of interest rates, since financial markets will respond immediately to policy actions.

In addition, there generally is no clear scalar choice for the policy variable x. If policy were framed in terms of strict targets for the money supply, for a specific measure of banking sector reserves, or for a particular short-term interest rate, then the definition of x might be straightforward. In general, however, several candidate measures of monetary policy will be available, all depending in various degrees on both policy actions and nonpolicy disturbances. What constitutes an appropriate candidate for x, and how x depends on nonpolicy disturbances, will depend on the operating procedures the monetary authority is following as it implements policy.

Money and Output

Sims (1992) provided a useful summary of the VAR evidence on money and output from France, Germany, Japan, the United Kingdom, and the United States. He estimated separate VARs for each country, using a common specification that includes industrial production, consumer prices, a short-term interest rate as the measure of monetary policy, a measure of the money supply, an exchange rate index, and an index of commodity prices. Sims ordered the interest rate variable first. This corresponds to the assumption that $\phi = 0$; innovations to the interest rate variable potentially affect the other variables contemporaneously (Sims used monthly data), whereas the interest rate is not affected contemporaneously by innovations in any of the other variables.[22]

The response of real output to an interest rate innovation was similar for all five of the countries Sims examined. In all cases, monetary shocks led to an output response that is usually described as following a hump-shaped pattern. The negative output

---

22. Sims noted that the correlations among the VAR residuals, the u'_{it}, are small so that the ordering has little impact on his results (i.e., sample estimates of ϕ and θ are small).

effects of a contractionary shock, for example, build to a peak after several months and then gradually die out.

Eichenbaum (1992) compared the estimated effects of monetary policy in the United States using alternative measures of policy shocks and discussed how different choices can produce puzzling results, at least puzzling relative to certain theoretical expectations. He based his discussion on the results obtained from a VAR containing four variables: the price level and output (these correspond to the elements of y in (1.8)), $M1$ as a measure of the money supply, and the federal funds rate as a measure of short-term interest rates (these correspond to the elements of x). He considered interpreting shocks to $M1$ as policy shocks versus the alternative of interpreting funds rate shocks as policy shocks. He found that a positive innovation to $M1$ is followed by an increase in the federal funds rate and a decline in output. This result is puzzling if $M1$ shocks are interpreted as measuring the impact of monetary policy. An expansionary monetary policy shock would be expected to lead to increases in both $M1$ and output. The interest rate was also found to rise after a positive $M1$ shock, also a potentially puzzling result; a standard model in which money demand varies inversely with the nominal interest rate would suggest that an increase in the money supply would require a decline in the nominal rate to restore money market equilibrium. D. Gordon and Leeper (1994) showed that a similar puzzle emerges when total reserves are used to measure monetary policy shocks. Positive reserve innovations are found to be associated with increases in short-term interest rates and unemployment increases. The suggestion that a rise in reserves or the money supply might raise, not lower, market interest rates generated a large literature that attempted to search for a liquidity effect of changes in the money supply (e.g., Reichenstein 1987; Christiano and Eichenbaum 1992a; Leeper and Gordon 1992; Strongin 1995; Hamilton 1996).

When Eichenbaum used innovations in the short-term interest rate as a measure of monetary policy actions, a positive shock to the funds rate represented a contractionary policy shock. No output puzzle was found in this case; a positive interest rate shock was followed by a decline in the output measure. Instead, what has been called the *price puzzle* emerges: a contractionary policy shock is followed by a rise in the price level. The effect is small and temporary (and barely statistically significant) but still puzzling. The most commonly accepted explanation for the price puzzle is that it reflects the fact that the variables included in the VAR do not span the full information set available to the Fed. Suppose the Fed tends to raise the funds rate whenever it forecasts that inflation might rise in the future. To the extent that the Fed is unable to offset the factors that led it to forecast higher inflation, or to the extent that the Fed acts too late to prevent inflation from rising, the increase in the funds rate will be followed by a rise in prices. This interpretation would be consistent

with the price puzzle. One solution is to include commodity prices or other asset prices in the VAR. Since these prices tend to be sensitive to changing forecasts of future
inflation, they serve as a proxy for some of the Fed's additional information (Sims
1992; Chari, Christiano, and Eichenbaum 1995; Bernanke and Mihov 1998). Sims
(1992) showed that the price puzzle is not confined to U.S. studies. He reported
VAR estimates of monetary policy effects for France, Germany, Japan, and the
United Kingdom as well as for the United States, and in all cases a positive shock
to the interest rate led to a positive price response. These price responses tended to
become smaller, but did not in all cases disappear, when a commodity price index
and a nominal exchange rate were included in the VAR.

An alternative interpretation of the price puzzle is provided by Barth and Ramey
(2002). They argued that contractionary monetary policy operates on aggregate supply as well as aggregate demand. For example, an increase in interest rates raises the
cost of holding inventories and thus acts as a positive cost shock. This negative supply effect raises prices and lowers output. Such an effect is called the *cost channel*
of monetary policy. In this interpretation, the price puzzle is simply evidence of the
cost channel rather than evidence that the VAR is misspecified. Barth and Ramey
combined industry-level data with aggregate data in a VAR and reported evidence
supporting the cost channel interpretation of the price puzzle (see also Ravenna and
Walsh 2006).

One difficulty in measuring the impact of monetary policy shocks arises when
operating procedures change over time. The best measure of policy during one period
may no longer accurately reflect policy in another period if the implementation of
policy has changed. Many authors have argued that over most of the past 35 years,
the federal funds rate has been the key policy instrument in the United States, suggesting that unforecasted changes in this interest rate may provide good estimates of
policy shocks. This view has been argued, for example, by Bernanke and Blinder
(1992) and Bernanke and Mihov (1998). While the Fed's operating procedures have
varied over time, the funds rate is likely to be the best indicator of policy in the
United States during the pre-1979 and post-1982 periods.[23] Policy during the period
1979–1982 is less adequately characterized by the funds rate.[24]

While researchers have disagreed on the best means of identifying policy shocks,
there has been a surprising consensus on the general nature of the economic responses to monetary policy shocks. A variety of VARs estimated for a number of

23. Chapter 11 provides a brief history of Fed operating procedures.

24. During this period, nonborrowed reserves were set to achieve a level of interest rates consistent with
the desired monetary growth targets. In this case, the funds rate may still provide a satisfactory policy indicator. Cook (1989) found that most changes in the funds rate during the 1979–1982 period reflected policy actions. See chapter 11 for a discussion of operating procedures and the reserve market.

countries all indicate that in response to a policy shock, output follows a hump-shaped pattern in which the peak impact occurs several quarters after the initial shock. Monetary policy actions appear to be taken in anticipation of inflation, so that a price puzzle emerges if forward-looking variables such as commodity prices are not included in the VAR.

If monetary policy shocks cause output movements, how important have these shocks been in accounting for actual business cycle fluctuations? Leeper, Sims, and Zha (1996) concluded that monetary policy shocks have been relatively unimportant. However, their assessment is based on monthly data for the period from the beginning of 1960 until early 1996. This sample contains several distinct periods characterized by differences in the procedures used by the Fed to implement monetary policy, and the contribution of monetary shocks may have differed over various subperiods. Christiano, Eichenbaum, and Evans (1999) concluded that estimates of the importance of monetary policy shocks for output fluctuations are sensitive to the way monetary policy is measured. When they used a funds-rate measure of monetary policy, policy shocks accounted for 21 percent of the four-quarter-ahead forecast error variance for quarterly real GDP. This figure rose to 38 percent of the 12-quarter-ahead forecast error variance. Smaller effects were found using policy measures based on monetary aggregates. Christiano, Eichenbaum, and Evans found that very little of the forecast error variance for the price level could be attributed to monetary policy shocks.

Criticisms of the VAR Approach

Measures of monetary policy based on the estimation of VARs have been criticized on several grounds.[25] First, some of the impulse responses do not accord with most economists' priors. In particular, the price puzzle—the finding that a contractionary policy shock, as measured by a funds rate shock, tends to be followed by a rise in the price level—is troublesome. As noted earlier, the price puzzle can be solved by including oil prices or commodity prices in the VAR system, and the generally accepted interpretation is that lacking these inflation-sensitive prices, a standard VAR misses important information that is available to policymakers. A related but more general point is that many of the VAR models used to assess monetary policy fail to incorporate forward-looking variables. Central banks look at a lot of information in setting policy. Because policy is likely to respond to forecasts of future economic conditions, VARs may attribute the subsequent movements in output and inflation to the policy action. However, the argument that puzzling results indicate a misspecification implicitly imposes a prior belief about what the correct effects of

---

25. These criticisms are detailed in Rudebusch (1998).

monetary shocks should look like. Eichenbaum (1992), in fact, argued that short-term interest rate innovations have been used to represent policy shocks in VARs because they produce the types of impulse response functions for output that economists expect.

In addition, the residuals from the VAR regressions that are used to represent exogenous policy shocks often bear little resemblance to standard interpretations of the historical record of past policy actions and periods of contractionary and expansionary policy (Sheffrin 1995; Rudebusch 1998). They also differ considerably depending on the particular specification of the VAR. Rudebusch (1998) reported low correlations between the residual policy shocks he obtained based on funds rate futures and those obtained from a VAR by Bernanke and Mihov. How important this finding is depends on the question of interest. If the objective is to determine whether a particular recession was caused by a policy shock, then it is important to know if and when the policy shock occurred. If alternative specifications provide differing and possibly inconsistent estimates of when policy shocks occurred, then their usefulness as a tool of economic history would be limited. If, however, the question of interest is how the economy responds when a policy shock occurs, then the discrepancies among the VAR residual estimates may be of less importance. Sims (1998a) argued that in a simple supply-demand model different authors using different supply curve shifters may obtain quite similar estimates of the demand curve slope (since they all obtain consistent estimators of the true slope). At the same time, they may obtain quite different residuals for the estimated supply curve. If the true interest is in the parameters of the demand curve, the variations in the estimates of the supply shocks may not be of importance. Thus, the type of historical analysis based on a VAR, as in Walsh (1993), is likely to be more problematic than the use of a VAR to determine the way the economy responds to exogenous policy shocks.

While VARs focus on residuals that are interpreted as policy shocks, the systematic part of the estimated VAR equation for a variable such as the funds rate can be interpreted as a policy reaction function; it provides a description of how the policy instrument has been adjusted in response to lagged values of the other variables included in the VAR system. Rudebusch (1998) argued that the implied policy reaction functions look quite different than results obtained from more direct attempts to estimate reaction functions or to model actual policy behavior.[26] A related point is that VARs are typically estimated using final, revised data and will therefore not capture accurately the historical behavior of the monetary policymaker who is reacting

26. For example, Taylor (1993a) employed a simple interest rate rule that closely matches the actual behavior of the federal funds rate in recent years. As Khoury (1990) noted in a survey of many earlier studies of the Fed's reaction function, few systematic conclusions have emerged from this empirical literature.

to preliminary and incomplete data. Woolley (1995) showed how the perception of the stance of monetary policy in the United States in 1972 and President Richard Nixon's attempts to pressure Fed Chairman Arthur F. Burns into adopting a more expansionary policy were based on initial data on the money supply that were subsequently very significantly revised.

At best the VAR approach identifies only the effects of monetary policy shocks, shifts in policy unrelated to the endogenous response of policy to developments in the economy. Yet most, if not all, of what one thinks of in terms of policy and policy design represents the endogenous response of policy to the economy, and "most variation in monetary policy instruments is accounted for by responses of policy to the state of the economy, not by random disturbances to policy" (Sims 1998a, 933). So it is unfortunate that a primary empirical tool—VAR analysis—used to assess the impact of monetary policy is uninformative about the role played by policy rules. If policy is completely characterized as a feedback rule on the economy, so that there are no exogenous policy shocks, then the VAR methodology would conclude that monetary policy doesn't matter. Yet while monetary policy is not causing output movements in this example, it does not follow that policy is unimportant; the response of the economy to nonpolicy shocks may depend importantly on the way monetary policy endogenously adjusts.

Cochrane (1998) made a similar point related to the issues discussed in section 1.3.3. In that section, it was noted that one must know whether it is anticipated money that has real effects (as in (1.3)) or unanticipated money that matters (as in (1.5)). Cochrane argued that while most of the VAR literature has focused on issues of lag length, detrending, ordering, and variable selection, there is another fundamental identification issue that has been largely ignored—is it anticipated or unanticipated monetary policy that matters? If only unanticipated policy matters, then the subsequent systematic behavior of money after a policy shock is irrelevant. This means that the long hump-shaped response of real variables to a policy shock must be due to inherent lags of adjustment and the propagation mechanisms that characterize the structure of the economy. If anticipated policy matters, then subsequent systematic behavior of money after a policy shock is relevant. This means that the long hump-shaped response of real variables to a policy shock may only be present because policy shocks are followed by persistent, systematic policy actions. If this is the case, the direct impact of a policy shock, if it were not followed by persistent policy moves, would be small.

Attempts have been made to use VAR frameworks to assess the systematic effects of monetary policy. Sims (1998b), for example, estimated a VAR for the interwar years and used it to simulate the behavior of the economy if policy had been determined according to the feedback rule obtained from a VAR estimated using postwar data.

1.3.5   Structural Econometric Models

The empirical assessment of the effects of alternative feedback rules for monetary policy has traditionally been carried out using structural macroeconometric models. During the 1960s and early 1970s, the specification, estimation, use, and evaluation of large-scale econometric models for forecasting and policy analysis represented a major research agenda in macroeconomics. Important contributions to the understanding of investment, consumption, the term structure, and other aspects of the macroeconomy grew out of the need to develop structural equations for various sectors of the economy. An equation describing the behavior of a policy instrument such as the federal funds rate was incorporated into these structural models, allowing model simulations of alternative policy rules to be conducted. These simulations would provide an estimate of the impact on the economy's dynamic behavior of changes in the way policy was conducted. For example, a policy under which the funds rate was adjusted rapidly in response to unemployment movements could be contrasted with one in which the response was more muted.

A key maintained hypothesis, one necessary to justify this type of analysis, was that the estimated parameters of the model would be invariant to the specification of the policy rule. If this were not the case, then one could no longer treat the model's parameters as unchanged when altering the monetary policy rule (as the example in section 1.3.3 shows). In a devastating critique of this assumption, Lucas (1976) argued that economic theory predicts that the decision rules for investment, consumption, and expectations formation will not be invariant to shifts in the systematic behavior of policy. The Lucas critique emphasized the problems inherent in the assumption, common in the structural econometric models of the time, that expectations adjust adaptively to past outcomes.

While large-scale econometric models of aggregate economies continued to play an important role in discussions of monetary policy, they fell out of favor among academic economists during the 1970s, in large part as a result of Lucas's critique, the increasing emphasis on the role of expectations in theoretical models, and the dissatisfaction with the empirical treatment of expectations in existing large-scale models.[27] The academic literature witnessed a continued interest in small-scale rational-expectations models, both single and multicountry versions (for example, the work of Taylor 1993b), as well as the development of larger-scale models (Fair 1984), all of which incorporated rational expectations into some or all aspects of the model's behavioral relationships. Other examples of small models based on rational expectations and forward-looking behavior include Fuhrer (1994b; 1997c), and Fuhrer and Moore (1995a; 1995b).

---

27. For an example of a small-scale model in which expectations play no explicit role, see Rudebusch and Svensson (1997).

More recently, empirical work investigating the impact of monetary policy has relied on estimated dynamic stochastic general equilibrium (DSGE) models. These models combine rational expectations with a microeconomic foundation in which households and firms are assumed to behave optimally, given their objectives (utility maximization, profit maximization) and the constraints they face. Many central banks have built and estimated DSGE models to use for policy analysis, and many more central banks are in the process of doing so. Examples of such models include Adolfson et al. (2007b) for Sweden and Gouvea et al. (2008) for Brazil. In general, these models are built on the theoretical foundations of the new Keynesian model. As discussed in chapter 8, this model is based on the assumption that prices and wages display rigidities and that this nominal stickiness accounts for the real effects of monetary policy. Early examples include Yun (1996); Ireland (1997a); and Rotemberg and Woodford (1998). Among the recent examples of DSGE models are Christiano, Eichenbaum, and Evans (2005), who estimated the model by matching VAR impulse responses, and Smets and Wouter (2003), who estimated their model using Bayesian techniques. The use of Bayesian estimation is now common; recent examples include Levin et al. (2006); Smets and Wouter (2003; 2007); and Lubik and Schorfheide (2007).

1.3.6   Alternative Approaches

Although the VAR approach has been the most commonly used empirical methodology, and although the results have provided a fairly consistent view of the impact of monetary policy shocks, other approaches have also influenced views on the role policy has played. Two such approaches, one based on deriving policy directly from a reading of policy statements, the other based on case studies of disinflations, have influenced academic discussions of monetary policy.

Narrative Measures of Monetary Policy
An alternative to the VAR statistical approach is to develop a measure of the stance of monetary policy from a direct examination of the policy record. In recent years, this approach has been taken by C. Romer and Romer (1990a) and Boschen and Mills (1991), among others.[28]

Boschen and Mills developed an index of policy stance that takes on integer values from -2 (strong emphasis on inflation reduction) to $+2$ (strong emphasis on "promoting real growth"). Their monthly index is based on a reading of the Fed's Federal Open Market Committee (FOMC) policy directives and the records of the FOMC meetings. Boschen and Mills showed that innovations in their index corre-

---

28. Boschen and Mills (1991) provided a discussion and comparison of some other indices of policy. For a critical view of Romer and Romer's approach, see Leeper (1993).

sponding to expansionary policy shifts are followed by subsequent increases in monetary aggregates and declines in the federal funds rate. They also concluded that all the narrative indices they examined yield relatively similar conclusions about the impact of policy on monetary aggregates and the funds rates. And in support of the approach used in section 1.3.4, Boschen and Mills concluded that the funds rate is a good indicator of monetary policy. These findings are extended in Boschen and Mills (1995a), which compared several narrative-based measures of monetary policy, finding them to be associated with permanent changes in the level of $M2$ and the monetary base and temporary changes in the funds rate.

Romer and Romer (1990a) used the Fed's "Record of Policy Actions" and, prior to 1976 when they were discontinued, minutes of FOMC meetings to identify episodes in which policy shifts occurred that were designed to reduce inflation.[29] They found six different months during the postwar period that saw such contractionary shifts in Fed policy: October 1947, September 1955, December 1968, April 1974, August 1978, and October 1979. Leeper (1993) argued that the Romer-Romer index is equivalent to a dummy variable that picks up large interest rate innovations. Hoover and Perez (1994) provided a critical assessment of the Romers' narrative approach, noting that the Romer dates are associated with oil price shocks, and Leeper (1997) found that the exogenous component of the Romers' policy variable does not produce dynamic effects on output and prices that accord with general beliefs about the effects of monetary policy.

The narrative indices of Boschen and Mills and the dating system employed by Romer and Romer to isolate episodes of contractionary policy provide a useful and informative alternative to the VAR approach that associates policy shocks with serially uncorrelated innovations. The VAR approach attempts to identify exogenous shifts in policy; the estimated effects of these exogenous shifts are the conceptual parallels to the comparative static exercises for which theoretical models make predictions. To determine whether the data are consistent with a model's predictions about the effects of an exogenous policy action, one needs to isolate empirically such exogenous shifts. Doing so, however, does not yield a measure of whether policy is, on net, expansionary or contractionary.[30] The narrative indices can provide a better measure of the net stance of policy, but they capture both exogenous shifts in policy and the endogenous response of monetary policy to economic developments. It is presumably the latter that accounts for most of the observed changes in policy variables such as the funds rate as policy responds to current and future expected economic conditions. In fact, a major conclusion of Leeper, Sims, and Zha (1996), and one they viewed as not surprising, was that most movements in monetary policy

---

29. The FMOC resumed publishing its minutes in 2005.

30. Bernanke and Mihov (1998) used their VAR estimates in an attempt to develop such a measure.

instruments represent responses to the state of the economy, not exogenous policy shifts.

Case Studies of Disinflation

Case studies of specific episodes of disinflation provide, in principle, an alternative means of assessing the real impact of monetary policy. Romer and Romer's approach to dating periods of contractionary monetary policy is one form of case study. However, the most influential example of this approach is that of Sargent (1986), who examined the ends of several hyperinflations. As discussed more fully in chapter 5, the distinction between anticipated and unanticipated changes in monetary policy has played an important role during the past 30 years in academic discussions of monetary policy, and a key hypothesis is that anticipated changes should affect prices and inflation with little or no effect on real economic activity. This implies that a credible policy to reduce inflation should succeed in actually reducing inflation without causing a recession. This implication contrasts sharply with the view that any policy designed to reduce inflation would succeed only by inducing an economic slowdown and temporarily higher unemployment.

Sargent tested these competing hypotheses by examining the ends of the post–World War I hyperinflations in Austria, German, Hungary, and Poland. In each case, Sargent found that the hyperinflations ended abruptly. In Austria, for example, prices rose by over a factor of 20 from December 1921 to August 1922, an annual inflation rate of over 8800 percent. Prices then stopped rising in September 1922, actually declining by more than 10 percent during the remainder of 1922. While unemployment did rise during the price stabilizations, Sargent concluded that the output cost "was minor compared with the \$220 billion GNP that some current analysts estimate would be lost in the United States per one percentage point inflation reduction" (Sargent 1986, 55). Sargent's interpretation of the experiences in Germany, Poland, and Hungary is similar. In each case, the hyperinflation was ended by a regime shift that involved a credible change in monetary and fiscal policy designed to reduce government reliance on inflationary finance. Because the end of inflation reduced the opportunity cost of holding money, money demand grew and the actual stock of money continued to grow rapidly after prices had stabilized.

Sargent's conclusion that the output costs of these disinflations were small has been questioned, as have the lessons he drew for the moderate inflations experienced by the industrialized economies in the 1970s and early 1980s. As Sargent noted, the ends of the hyperinflations "were not isolated restrictive actions within a given set of rules of the game" but represented changes in the rules of the game, most importantly in the ability of the fiscal authority to finance expenditures by creating money. In contrast, the empirical evidence from VARs of the type discussed earlier in this chapter reflects the impact of policy changes within a given set of rules.

Schelde-Andersen (1992) and Ball (1993) provided more recent examples of the case study approach. In both cases, the authors examined disinflationary episodes in order to estimate the real output costs associated with reducing inflation.[31] Their cases, all involving OECD countries, represent evidence on the costs of ending moderate inflations. Ball calculated the deviation of output from trend during a period of disinflation and expressed this as a ratio to the change in trend inflation over the same period. The 65 disinflation periods he identified in annual data yield an average sacrifice ratio of 0.77 percent; each percentage point reduction in inflation was associated with a 0.77 percent loss of output relative to trend. The estimate for the United States was among the largest, averaging 2.3 percent based on annual data. The sacrifice ratios are negatively related to nominal wage flexibility; countries with greater wage flexibility tend to have smaller sacrifice ratios. The costs of a disinflation also appear to be larger when inflation is brought down more gradually over a longer period of time.[32]

The case study approach can provide interesting evidence on the real effects of monetary policy. Unfortunately, as with the VAR and other approaches, the issue of identification needs to be addressed. To what extent have disinflations been exogenous, so that any resulting output or unemployment movements can be attributed to the decision to reduce inflation? If policy actions depend on whether they are anticipated or not, then estimates of the cost of disinflating obtained by averaging over episodes, episodes that are likely to have differed considerably in terms of whether the policy actions were expected or, if announced, credible, may yield little information about the costs of ending any specific inflation.

1.4   Summary

The consensus from the empirical literature on the long-run relationship between money, prices, and output is clear. Money growth and inflation essentially display a correlation of 1; the correlation between money growth or inflation and real output growth is probably close to zero, although it may be slightly positive at low inflation rates and negative at high rates.

The consensus from the empirical literature on the short-run effects of money is that exogenous monetary policy shocks produce hump-shaped movements in real

---

31. See also R. Gordon (1982) and R. Gordon and King (1982).

32. Brayton and Tinsley (1996) showed how the costs of disinflation can be estimated under alternative assumptions about expectations and credibility using the FRB/U.S. structural model. Their estimates of the sacrifice ratio, expressed in terms of the cumulative annual unemployment rate increase per percentage point decrease in the inflation rate, range from 2.6 under imperfect credibility and VAR expectations to 1.3 under perfect credibility and VAR expectations. Under full-model expectations, the sacrifice ratio is 2.3 with imperfect credibility and 1.7 with full credibility.

economic activity. The peak effects occur after a lag of several quarters (as much as two or three years in some of the estimates) and then die out. The exact manner in which policy is measured makes a difference, and using an incorrect measure of monetary policy can significantly affect the empirical estimates one obtains.

There is less consensus, however, on the effects, not of policy shocks but of the role played by the systematic feedback responses of monetary policy. Structural econometric models have the potential to fill this gap, and they are widely used in policy-making settings. Disagreements over the true structure and the potential dependence of estimated relationships on the policy regime have, however, posed problems for the structural modeling approach. A major theme of subsequent chapters is that the endogenous response of monetary policy to economic developments can have important implications for the empirical relationships observed among macroeconomic variables.

2 Money-in-the-Utility Function

2.1 Introduction

The neoclassical growth model due to Ramsey (1928) and Solow (1956) provides the basic framework for much of modern macroeconomics. Solow's growth model has just three key ingredients: a production function allowing for smooth substitutability between labor and capital in the production of output, a capital accumulation process in which a fixed fraction of output is devoted to investment each period, and a labor supply process in which the quantity of labor input grows at an exogenously given rate. Solow showed that such an economy would converge to a steady-state growth path along which output, the capital stock, and the effective supply of labor all grew at the same rate.

When the assumption of a fixed savings rate is replaced by a model of forward-looking households choosing savings and labor supply to maximize lifetime utility, the Solow model becomes the foundation for dynamic stochastic general equilibrium (DSGE) models of the business cycle. Productivity shocks or other real disturbances affect output and savings behavior, with the resultant effect on capital accumulation propagating the effects of the original shock over time in ways that can mimic some features of actual business cycles (see Cooley 1995).

The neoclassical growth model is a model of a nonmonetary economy, and although goods are exchanged and transactions must be taking place, there is no medium of exchange—that is, no "money"—that is used to facilitate these transactions. Nor is there an asset like money that has a zero nominal rate of return and is therefore dominated in rate of return by other interest-bearing assets. To employ the neoclassical framework to analyze monetary issues, a role for money must be specified so that the agents will wish to hold positive quantities of money. A positive demand for money is necessary if, in equilibrium, money is to have positive value.[1]

---

1. This is just another way of saying that the money price of goods should be bounded. If the price of goods in terms of money is denoted by P, then one unit of money will purchase $1/P$ units of goods. If money has positive value, $1/P > 0$ and P is bounded ($0 < P < \infty$). Bewley (1983) refers to the issue of why money has positive value as the *Hahn problem* (Hahn 1965).

Fundamental questions in monetary economics are the following: How should we model the demand for money? How do real economies differ from Arrow-Debreu economies in ways that give rise to a positive value for money? Three general approaches to incorporating money into general equilibrium models have been followed: (1) assume that money yields direct utility by incorporating money balances into the utility functions of the agents of the model (Sidrauski 1967); (2) impose transaction costs of some form that give rise to a demand for money, by making asset exchanges costly (Baumol 1952; Tobin 1956), requiring that money be used for certain types of transactions (Clower 1967), assuming that time and money can be combined to produce transaction services that are necessary for obtaining consumption goods (Brock 1974; McCallum and Goodfriend 1987; Croushore 1993), or assuming that direct barter of commodities is costly (Kiyotaki and Wright 1989); or (3) treat money like any other asset used to transfer resources intertemporally (Samuelson 1958).

All three approaches involve shortcuts in one form or another; some aspects of the economic environment are simply specified exogenously to introduce a role for money. This can be a useful device, allowing one to focus attention on questions of primary interest without being unduly distracted by secondary issues. But confidence in the ability of a model to answer questions brought to it is reduced if exogenously specified aspects appear to be critical to the issue of focus. An important consideration in evaluating different approaches is to determine whether conclusions generalize beyond the specific model or depend on the exact manner in which a role for money has been introduced. Subsequent examples include results that are robust, such as the connection between money growth and inflation, and others that are sensitive to the specification of money's role, such as the impact of inflation on the steady-state capital stock.

This chapter develops the first of the three approaches by incorporating into the basic neoclassical model agents whose utility depends directly on their consumption of goods *and* their holdings of money.[2] Given suitable restrictions on the utility function, such an approach can guarantee that in equilibrium agents choose to hold positive amounts of money, and money will be positively valued. The money-in-the-utility function (MIU) model is originally due to Sidrauski (1967) and has been used widely.[3] It can be employed to examine some of the critical issues in monetary economics—the relationship between money and prices, the effects of inflation on

2. The second approach, focusing on the transactions role of money, is discussed in chapter 3. The third approach was developed primarily within the context of overlapping-generation models; see Sargent (1987) or Champ and Freeman (1994).

3. Patinkin (1965, ch. 4) provided an earlier discussion of an MIU model, although he did not integrate capital accumulation into his model. However, the first-order condition for optimal money holdings that he presented (see his equation 1, p. 89) is equivalent to the one derived in the next section.

equilibrium, and the optimal rate of inflation. To better understand the role of money in such a framework, a linear approximation is presented. This approximation can be used to derive some analytical implications and to study numerically the MIU model's implications for macrodynamics.

2.2   The Basic MIU Model

To develop the basic MIU approach, we will initially ignore uncertainty and any labor-leisure choice, focusing instead on the implications of the model for money demand, the value of money, and the costs of inflation.

Suppose that the utility function of the representative household takes the form

$$U_t = u(c_t, z_t),$$

where z_t is the flow of services yielded by money holdings and c_t is time t per capita consumption. Utility is assumed to be increasing in both arguments, strictly concave and continuously differentiable. The demand for monetary services will always be positive if one assumes that $\lim_{z \to 0} u_z(c, z) = \infty$ for all c, where $u_z = \partial u(c, z) / \partial z$.

What constitutes z_t? To maintain the assumption of rational economic agents, what enters the utility function cannot just be the number of dollars (or euros or yen) that the individual holds. What should matter is the command over goods represented by those dollar holdings, or some measure of the transaction services, expressed in terms of goods, that money yields. In other words, z should be related to something like the number of dollars, M, times their price, $1/P$, in terms of goods: $M(1/P) = M/P$. If the service flow is proportional to the real value of the stock of money, and N_t is the population, then z can be set equal to real per capita money holdings:

$$z_t = \frac{M_t}{P_t N_t} \equiv m_t.$$

To ensure that a monetary equilibrium exists, it is often assumed that for all c, there exists a finite $\bar{m} > 0$ such that $u_m(c, m) \leq 0$ for all $m > \bar{m}$. This means that the marginal utility of money eventually becomes negative for sufficiently high money balances. The role of this assumption will be made clear later when the existence of a steady state is discussed. It is, however, not necessary for the existence of equilibrium, and some common functional forms employed for the utility function (used later in this chapter) do not satisfy this condition.[4]

---

4. For example, $u(c, m) = \log c + b \log m$ does not exhibit this property because $u_m = b/m > 0$ for all finite m.

Assuming that money enters the utility function is often criticized on the grounds that money itself is intrinsically useless (as with a paper currency) and that it is only through its use in facilitating transactions that it yields valued services. Approaches that emphasize the transaction role of money are discussed in chapter 3, but models in which money helps to reduce the time needed to purchase consumption goods can be represented by the money-in-the-utility function approach adopted in this chapter.[5]

The representative household is viewed as choosing time paths for consumption and real money balances subject to budget constraints to be specified, with total utility given by

$$W = \sum_{t=0}^{\infty} \beta^t u(c_t, m_t), \tag{2.1}$$

where $0 < \beta < 1$ is a subjective rate of discount.

Equation (2.1) implies a much stronger notion of the utility provided by holding money than simply that the household would prefer having more money to less money. If the marginal utility of money is positive, then (2.1) implies that *holding constant the path of real consumption for all t*, the individual's utility is increased by an increase in money holdings. That is, even though the money holdings are never used to purchase consumption, they yield utility. This should seem strange; one usually thinks the demand for money is instrumental in that we hold money to engage in transactions leading to the purchase of the goods and services that actually yield utility. All this is just a reminder that the money-in-the-utility function may be a useful shortcut for ensuring that there is a demand for money, but it is just a shortcut.

To complete the specification of the model, assume that households can hold money, bonds that pay a nominal interest rate i_t, and physical capital. Physical capital produces output according to a standard neoclassical production function. Given its current income, its assets, and any net transfers received from the government (τ_t), the household allocates its resources between consumption, gross investment in physical capital, and gross accumulation of real money balances and bonds.

If the rate of depreciation of physical capital is δ, the aggregate economywide budget constraint of the household sector takes the form

$$Y_t + \tau_t N_t + (1-\delta)K_{t-1} + \frac{(1+i_{t-1})B_{t-1}}{P_t} + \frac{M_{t-1}}{P_t} = C_t + K_t + \frac{M_t}{P_t} + \frac{B_t}{P_t}, \tag{2.2}$$

where Y_t is aggregate output, K_{t-1} is the aggregate stock of capital at the start of period t, and $\tau_t N_t$ is the aggregate real value of any lump-sum transfers or taxes.

---

5. Brock (1974), for example, developed two simple transactions stories that can be represented by putting money directly in the utility function. See also Feenstra (1986).

The timing implicit in this specification of the MIU model assumes that it is the household's real money holdings at the end of the period, M_t/P_t, *after* having purchased consumption goods, that yield utility. Carlstrom and Fuerst (2001) criticized this timing assumption, arguing that the appropriate way to model the utility from money is to assume that money balances available *before* going to purchase consumption goods yield utility. As they demonstrate, alternative timing assumptions can affect the correct definition of the opportunity cost of holding money and whether multiple real equilibria can be ruled out. Because it is standard in the MIU approach to assume that it is the end-of-period money holdings that yield utility, we will continue to maintain that assumption in the development of the model.[6]

The aggregate production function relates output Y_t to the available capital stock K_{t-1} and employment N_t: $Y_t = F(K_{t-1}, N_t)$.[7] Assuming that this production function is linear homogeneous with constant returns to scale, output per capita y_t will be a function of the per capita capital stock k_{t-1}:[8]

$$y_t = f\left(\frac{k_{t-1}}{1+n}\right), \tag{2.3}$$

where n is the population growth rate (assumed to be constant). Note that output is produced in period t using capital carried over from period $t-1$. The production function is assumed to be continuously differentiable and to satisfy the usual Inada conditions ($f_k \geq 0$, $f_{kk} \leq 0$, $\lim_{k\to 0} f_k(k) = \infty$, $\lim_{k\to\infty} f_k(k) = 0$).

Dividing both sides of the budget constraint (2.2) by population N_t, the per capita version becomes

$$\omega_t \equiv f\left(\frac{k_{t-1}}{1+n}\right) + \tau_t + \left(\frac{1-\delta}{1+n}\right)k_{t-1} + \frac{(1+i_{t-1})b_{t-1} + m_{t-1}}{(1+\pi_t)(1+n)} = c_t + k_t + m_t + b_t, \tag{2.4}$$

where π_t is the rate of inflation, $b_t = B_t/P_tN_t$, and $m_t = M_t/P_tN_t$.

The household's problem is to choose paths for c_t, k_t, b_t, and m_t to maximize (2.1) subject to (2.4). This is a problem in dynamic optimization, and it is convenient to formulate the problem in terms of a value function. The value function gives the maximized present discounted value of utility that the household can achieve by

---

6. Problems 1 and 2 at the end of this chapter ask you to derive the first-order conditions for money holdings under an alternative timing assumption.

7. Since any labor-leisure choice is ignored in this section, N_t is used interchangably for population and employment.

8. That is, if $Y_t = F(K_{t-1}, N_t)$, where Y is output, K is the capital stock, and N is labor input, and $F(\lambda K, \lambda N) = \lambda F(K, N) = \lambda Y$, one can write $Y_t/N_t \equiv y_t = F(K_{t-1}, N_t)/N_t = F(K_{t-1}/N_t, 1) \equiv f(k_{t-1}/(1+n))$, where $n = (N_t - N_{t-1})/N_{t-1}$ is the constant labor force growth rate. In general, a lowercase letter denotes the per capita value of the corresponding uppercase variable.

optimally choosing consumption, capital holdings, bond holdings, and money balances, given its current state.[9] The state variable for the problem is the household's initial level of resources ω_t, and the value function is defined by

$$V(\omega_t) = \max_{c_t, k_t, b_t, m_t} \{u(c_t, m_t) + \beta V(\omega_{t+1})\},$$ (2.5)

where the maximization is subject to the budget constraint (2.4) and

$$\omega_{t+1} = f\left(\frac{k_t}{1+n}\right) + \tau_{t+1} + \left(\frac{1-\delta}{1+n}\right)k_t + \frac{(1+i_t)b_t + m_t}{(1+\pi_{t+1})(1+n)}.$$

Using (2.4) to express k_t as $\omega_t - c_t - m_t - b_t$ and making use of the definition of ω_{t+1}, (2.5) can be written as

$$V(\omega_t) = \max_{c_t, b_t, m_t} \left\{ u(c_t, m_t) + \beta V \left(f\left(\frac{\omega_t - c_t - m_t - b_t}{1+n}\right) + \tau_{t+1} \right. \right.$$

$$\left. \left. + \left(\frac{1-\delta}{1+n}\right)(\omega_t - c_t - m_t - b_t) + \frac{(1+i_t)b_t + m_t}{(1+\pi_{t+1})(1+n)} \right) \right\},$$

with the maximization problem now an unconstrained one over c_t, b_t, and m_t. The first-order necessary conditions for this problem are

$$u_c(c_t, m_t) - \frac{\beta}{1+n}[f_k(k_t') + 1 - \delta]V_\omega(\omega_{t+1}) = 0$$ (2.6)

$$\frac{1+i_t}{(1+\pi_{t+1})} - [f_k(k_t') + 1 - \delta] = 0$$ (2.7)

$$u_m(c_t, m_t) - \frac{\beta}{1+n}\left[f_k(k_t') + 1 - \delta - \left(\frac{1}{1+\pi_{t+1}}\right)\right]V_\omega(\omega_{t+1}) = 0,$$ (2.8)

where $k_t' \equiv k_t/(1+n)$, together with the transversality conditions

$$\lim_{t \to \infty} \beta^t \lambda_t x_t = 0 \qquad \text{for } x = k, b, m,$$ (2.9)

where λ_t is the marginal utility of period t consumption. The envelope theorem implies

$$V_\omega(\omega_t) = \frac{\beta}{1+n}[f(k_t') + 1 - \delta]V_\omega(\omega_{t+1}),$$

---

9. Introductions to dynamic optimization designed for economists can be found in Sargent (1987); Lucas and Stokey (1989); Dixit (1990); Chiang (1992); Obstfeld and Rogoff (1996); or Ljungquist and Sargent (2000).

which together with (2.6) yields

$$\lambda_t = u_c(c_t, m_t) = V_\omega(\omega_t). \tag{2.10}$$

The first-order conditions have straightforward interpretations. Since initial resources ω_t must be divided between consumption, capital, bonds, and money balances, each use must yield the same marginal benefit at an optimum allocation.[10] Using (2.6) and (2.10), (2.8) can be written as

$$u_m(c_t, m_t) + \frac{\beta u_c(c_{t+1}, m_{t+1})}{(1 + \pi_{t+1})(1 + n)} = u_c(c_t, m_t), \tag{2.11}$$

which states that the marginal benefit of adding to money holdings at time t must equal the marginal utility of consumption at time t. The marginal benefit of additional money holdings has two components. First, money directly yields utility u_m. Second, real money balances at time t add $1/(1 + \pi_{t+1})(1 + n)$ to real per capita resources at time $t + 1$; this addition to ω_{t+1} is worth $V_\omega(\omega_{t+1})$ at $t + 1$, or $\beta V_\omega(\omega_{t+1})$ at time t. Thus, the total marginal benefit of money at time t is $u_m(c_t, m_t) + \beta V_\omega(\omega_{t+1})/(1 + \pi_{t+1})(1 + n)$. Equation (2.11) is then obtained by noting that $V_\omega(\omega_{t+1}) = u_c(c_{t+1}, m_{t+1})$.

From (2.6), (2.7), and (2.11),

$$\frac{u_m(c_t, m_t)}{u_c(c_t, m_t)} = 1 - \left[\frac{1}{(1 + \pi_{t+1})(1 + n)} \right] \frac{\beta u_c(c_{t+1}, m_{t+1})}{u_c(c_t, m_t)}$$

$$= 1 - \frac{1}{(1 + r_t)(1 + \pi_{t+1})}$$

$$= \frac{i_t}{1 + i_t} \equiv \Upsilon_t, \tag{2.12}$$

where $1 + r_t \equiv f(k'_t) + 1 - \delta$ is the real return on capital, and (2.6) implies $\beta u_c(c_{t+1}, m_{t+1})/u_c(c_t, m_t) = (1 + n)/(1 + r_t)$. Equation (2.12) also makes use of (2.7), which links the nominal return on bonds, inflation, and the real return on capital. This latter equation can be written as

$$1 + i_t = [f(k'_t) + 1 - \delta](1 + \pi_{t+1}) = (1 + r_t)(1 + \pi_{t+1}). \tag{2.13}$$

This relationship between real and nominal rates of interest is called the *Fisher relationship* after Irving Fisher (1896). It expresses the gross nominal rate of interest as equal to the gross real return on capital times 1 plus the expected rate of inflation.

---

10. For a general equilibrium analysis of asset prices in an MIU framework, see LeRoy (1984a; 1984b).

If one notes that $(1 + x)(1 + y) \approx 1 + x + y$ when x and y are small, (2.13) is often written as

$$i_t = r_t + \pi_{t+1}.$$

To interpret (2.12), consider a very simple choice problem in which the agent must pick x and z to maximize $u(x, z)$ subject to a budget constraint of the form $x + pz = y$, where p is the relative price of z. The first-order conditions imply $u_z/u_x = p$; in words, the marginal rate of substitution between z and x equals the relative price of z in terms of x. Comparing this to (2.12) shows that Υ can be interpreted as the relative price of real money balances in terms of the consumption good. The marginal rate of substitution between money and consumption is set equal to the price, or opportunity cost, of holding money. The opportunity cost of holding money is directly related to the nominal rate of interest. The household could hold one unit less of money, purchasing instead a bond yielding a nominal return of i; the real value of this payment is $i/(1 + \pi)$, and since it is received in period $t + 1$, its present value is $i/[(1 + r)(1 + \pi)] = i/(1 + i)$.[11] Since money is assumed to pay no rate of interest, the opportunity cost of holding money is affected both by the real return on capital and the rate of inflation. If the price level is constant (so $\pi = 0$), then the forgone earnings from holding money rather than capital are determined by the real return to capital. If the price level is rising ($\pi > 0$), the real value of money in terms of consumption declines, and this adds to the opportunity cost of holding money.

In deriving the first-order conditions for the household's problem, it could have been equivalently assumed that the household rented its capital to firms, receiving a rental rate of r_k, and sold its labor services at a wage rate of w. Household income would then be $r_k k + w$ (expressed on a per capita basis and ignoring population growth). With competitive firms hiring capital and labor in perfectly competitive factor markets under constant returns to scale, $r_k = f'(k)$ and $w = f(k) - kf'(k)$, so household income would be $r_k k + w = f_k(k)k + [f(k) - kf_k(k)] = f(k)$, as in (2.4).[12]

While this system could be used to study analytically the dynamic behavior of the economy (e.g., Sidrauski 1967; S. Fischer 1979b; Blanchard and Fischer 1989), we will focus first on the properties of the steady-state equilibrium. And, since the main focus here is not on the exogenous growth generated by population growth, it will provide some slight simplification to set $n = 0$ in the following. After examining the

---

11. Suppose households gain utility from the real money balances they have at the start of period t rather than the balances they hold at the end of the period, as has been assumed. Then the marginal rate of substitution between money and consumption will be set equal to i_t (see Lucas 1982; Carlstrom and Fuerst 2001). See also problem 1 at the end of this chapter.

12. This follows from Euler's theorem: If the aggregate constant-returns-to-scale production function is $F(N, K)$, then $F(N, K) = F_N N + F_K K$. In per capita terms, this becomes $f(k) = F_N + F_K k = w + rk$ if labor and capital are paid their marginal products.

steady state, we will study the dynamic properties implied by a stochastic version of the model, a version that also includes uncertainty, a labor-leisure choice, and variable employment.

2.2.1 Steady-State Equilibrium

Consider the properties of this economy when it is in a steady-state equilibrium with $n = 0$ and the nominal supply of money growing at the rate θ. Let the superscript ss denote values evaluated at the steady state. The steady-state, constant values of consumption, the capital stock, real money balances, inflation, and the nominal interest rate must satisfy the first-order necessary conditions for the household's decision problem given by (2.6)–(2.8), the economywide budget constraint, and the specification of the exogenous growth rate of M. Note that with real money balances constant in the steady state, it must be that the prices are growing at the same rate as the nominal stock of money, or $\pi^{ss} = \theta$.[13] Using (2.10) to eliminate $V_\omega(\omega^{ss})$, the equilibrium conditions can be written as

$$u_c(c^{ss}, m^{ss}) - \beta[f_k(k^{ss}) + 1 - \delta]u_c(c^{ss}, m^{ss}) = 0 \tag{2.14}$$

$$\frac{1 + i^{ss}}{1 + \theta} - [f_k(k^{ss}) + 1 - \delta] = 0 \tag{2.15}$$

$$u_m(c^{ss}, m^{ss}) - \beta[f_k(k^{ss}) + 1 - \delta]u_c(c^{ss}, m^{ss}) + \frac{\beta u_c(c^{ss}, m^{ss})}{1 + \theta} = 0 \tag{2.16}$$

$$f(k^{ss}) + \tau^{ss} + (1 - \delta)k^{ss} + \frac{m^{ss}}{1 + \theta} = c^{ss} + k^{ss} + m^{ss}, \tag{2.17}$$

where $\omega^{ss} = f(k^{ss}) + \tau^{ss} + (1 - \delta)k^{ss} + m^{ss}/(1 + \pi)$. In (2.14)–(2.17), use has been made of the fact that in the equilibrium of this representative agent model, $b = 0$. Equation (2.15) is the steady-state form of the Fisher relationship linking real and nominal interest rates. This can be seen by noting that the real return on capital (net of depreciation) is $r^{ss} \equiv f_k(k^{ss}) - \delta$, so (2.15) can be written as

$$1 + i^{ss} = (1 + r^{ss})(1 + \theta) = (1 + r^{ss})(1 + \pi^{ss}). \tag{2.18}$$

Notice that in (2.14)–(2.17) money appears only in the form of real money balances. Thus, any change in the nominal quantity of money that is matched by a proportional change in the price level, leaving m^{ss} unchanged, has no effect on the economy's real equilibrium. This is described by saying that the model exhibits

---

13. If the population is growing at the rate n, then $1 + \pi^{ss} = (1 + \theta)/(1 + n)$.

neutrality of money. If prices do not adjust immediately in response to a change in M, then a model might display non-neutrality with respect to changes in M in the short run but still exhibit monetary neutrality in the long run, once all prices have adjusted. In fact, this is the case with the models used in chapters 5–11 to examine issues related to short-run monetary policy. One-time changes in the level of the nominal quantity of money ultimately affect only the level of prices.

Dividing (2.14) by $u_c(c^{ss}, m^{ss})$ yields $1 - \beta[f_k(k^{ss}) + 1 - \delta] = 0$, or

$$f_k(k^{ss}) = \frac{1}{\beta} - 1 + \delta. \tag{2.19}$$

This equation defines the steady-state capital-labor ratio k^{ss} as a function of β and δ. If the production function is Cobb-Douglas, say $f(k) = k^{\alpha}$ for $0 < \alpha \leq 1$, then $f_k(k) = \alpha k^{\alpha-1}$ and

$$k^{ss} = \left[\frac{\alpha\beta}{1 + \beta(\delta - 1)}\right]^{1/(1-\alpha)}. \tag{2.20}$$

What is particularly relevant here is the implication from (2.19) that the steady-state capital-labor ratio is independent of (1) all parameters of the utility function other than the subjective discount rate β, and (2) the steady-state rate of inflation π^{ss}. In fact, k^{ss} depends only on the production function, the depreciation rate, and the discount rate. It is independent of the rate of inflation and the growth rate of money.

Because changes in the nominal quantity of money are engineered in this model by making lump-sum transfers to the public, the real value of these transfers must equal $(M_t - M_{t-1})/P_t = \theta M_{t-1}/P_t = \theta m_{t-1}/(1 + \pi_t)$. Hence, steady-state transfers are given by $\tau^{ss} = \theta m^{ss}/(1 + \pi^{ss}) = \theta m^{ss}/(1 + \theta)$, and the budget constraint (2.17) reduces to the economy's resource constraint

$$c^{ss} = f(k^{ss}) - \delta k^{ss}. \tag{2.21}$$

The steady-state level of consumption per capita is equal to output minus replacement investment and is completely determined once the level of steady-state capital is known. Assuming that $f(k) = k^{\alpha}$, then k^{ss} is given by (2.20) and

$$c^{ss} = \left[\frac{\alpha\beta}{1 + \beta(\delta - 1)}\right]^{\alpha/(1-\alpha)} - \delta\left[\frac{\alpha\beta}{1 + \beta(\delta - 1)}\right]^{1/(1-\alpha)}.$$

Steady-state consumption per capita depends on the parameters of the production function (α), the rate of depreciation (δ), and the subjective rate of time discount (β).

The Sidrauski MIU model exhibits a property called the *superneutrality of money*; the steady-state values of the capital stock, consumption, and output are all independent of the *rate of growth* of the nominal money stock. That is, not only is money neutral, so that proportional changes in the *level* of nominal money balances and prices have no real effects, but changes in the *rate of growth* of nominal money also have no effect on the steady-state capital stock or, therefore, on output or per capita consumption. Since the real rate of interest is equal to the marginal product of capital, it also is invariant across steady states that differ only in their rates of money growth. Thus, the Sidrauski MIU model possesses the properties of both neutrality and superneutrality.

To understand why superneutrality holds, note that from (2.10), $u_c = V_\omega(\omega_t)$, so using (2.6),

$$u_c(c_t, m_t) = \beta[f_k(k_t) + 1 - \delta]u_c(c_{t+1}, m_{t+1}),$$

or

$$\frac{u_c(c_{t+1}, m_{t+1})}{u_c(c_t, m_t)} = \frac{1/\beta}{f_k(k_t) + 1 - \delta}. \tag{2.22}$$

Recall from (2.19) that the right side of this expression is equal to 1 in the steady state. If $k < k^{ss}$ so that $f_k(k) > f_k(k^{ss})$, then the right side is smaller than 1, and the marginal utility of consumption will be declining over time. It will be optimal to postpone consumption to accumulate capital and have consumption grow over time (so u_c declines over time). As long as $f_k + 1 - \delta > 1/\beta$, this process continues, but as the capital stock grows, the marginal product of capital declines until eventually $f_k(k) + 1 - \delta = 1/\beta$. The converse holds if $k > k^{ss}$. Consumption remains constant only when $f_k + 1 - \delta = 1/\beta$. If an increase in the rate of money growth (and therefore an increase in the rate of inflation) were to induce households to accumulate more capital, this would lower the marginal product of capital, leading to a situation in which $f_k + 1 - \delta < 1/\beta$. Households would then want their consumption path to decline over time, so they would immediately attempt to increase current consumption and reduce their holdings of capital. The value of k^{ss} consistent with a steady state is independent of the rate of inflation.

What is affected by the rate of inflation? One thing to expect is that the interest rate on any asset that pays off in units of money at some future date will be affected; the real value of those future units of money will be affected by inflation, and this will be reflected in the interest rate required to induce individuals to hold the asset, as shown by (2.13). To understand this equation, consider the nominal interest rate that an asset must yield if it is to give a real return of r_t in terms of the consumption good. That is, consider an asset that costs 1 unit of consumption in period t and yields $(1 + r_t)$ units of consumption at $t + 1$. In units of money, this asset costs P_t units of money at time t. Since the cost of each unit of consumption at $t + 1$ is P_{t+1} in terms of money, the asset must pay an amount equal to $(1 + r)P_{t+1}$. Thus, the nominal return is $[(1 + r_t)P_{t+1} - P_t]/P_t = (1 + r_t)(1 + \pi_{t+1}) - 1 \equiv i_t$. In the steady state, $1 + r^{ss} = 1/\beta$, and $\pi^{ss} = \theta$, so the steady-state nominal rate of interest is given by $[(1 + \theta)/\beta] - 1$ and varies (approximately) one for one with inflation.[14]

Existence of the Steady State

To ensure that a steady-state monetary equilibrium exists, there must exist a positive but finite level of real money balances m^{ss} that satisfies (2.12), evaluated at the steady-state level of consumption. If utility is separable in consumption and money balances, say $u(c, m) = v(c) + \phi(m)$, this condition can be written as $\phi_m(m^{ss}) = \Upsilon^{ss} v_c(c^{ss})$. The right side of this expression is a non-negative constant; the left side approaches ∞ as $m \to 0$. If $\phi_m(m) \leq 0$ for all m greater than some finite level, a steady-state equilibrium with positive real money balances is guaranteed to exist. This was the role of the earlier assumption that the marginal utility of money eventually becomes negative. Note that this assumption is not necessary; $\phi(m) = \log m$ yields a positive solution to (2.12) as long as $\Upsilon^{ss} v_c(c^{ss}) > 0$. When utility is not separable, one can still write (2.12) as $u_m(c^{ss}, m^{ss}) = \Upsilon^{ss} u_c(c^{ss}, m^{ss})$. If $u_{cm} < 0$ so that the marginal utility of consumption decreases with increased holdings of money, both u_m and u_c decrease with m and the solution to (2.12) may not be unique; multiple steady-state equilibria may exist.[15] Note, however, that it may be more plausible to assume money and consumption are complements in utility, an assumption that would imply $u_{cm} \geq 0$.

When $u(c, m) = v(c) + \phi(m)$, the dynamics of real balances around the steady state can be described easily by multiplying both sides of (2.12) by M_t and noting that $M_{t+1} = (1 + \theta)M_t$:

$$B(m_{t+1}) \equiv \frac{\beta}{1 + \theta} v_c(c_{ss})m_{t+1} = [v_c(c^{ss}) - \phi_m(m_t)]m_t \equiv A(m_t), \tag{2.23}$$

which gives a difference equation in m. The properties of this equation have been examined by Brock (1974) and Obstfeld and Rogoff (1983; 1986). A steady-state value for m satisfies $B(m^{ss}) = A(m^{ss})$. The functions $B(m)$ and $A(m)$ are illustrated in figure 2.1. $B(m)$ is a straight line with slope $\beta v_c(c^{ss})/(1 + \theta)$. $A(m)$ has slope $(v_c - \phi_m - \phi_{mm}m)$. For the case drawn, $\lim_{m \to 0} \phi_m m = 0$, so there are two steady-state solutions to (2.23), one at m' and one at zero. Only one of these involves positive real money balances (and a positive value for money). If $\lim_{m \to 0} \phi_m m = \tilde{m} > 0$, then $\lim_{m \to 0} A(m) < 0$ and there is only one solution. Paths for m_t originating to the

14. Outside of the steady state, the nominal rate can still be written as the sum of the expected real rate plus the expected rate of inflation, but there is no longer any presumption that short-run variations in inflation will leave the real rate unaffected.

15. For more on the conditions necessary for the existence of monetary equilibria, see Brock (1974; 1975) and Bewley (1983).

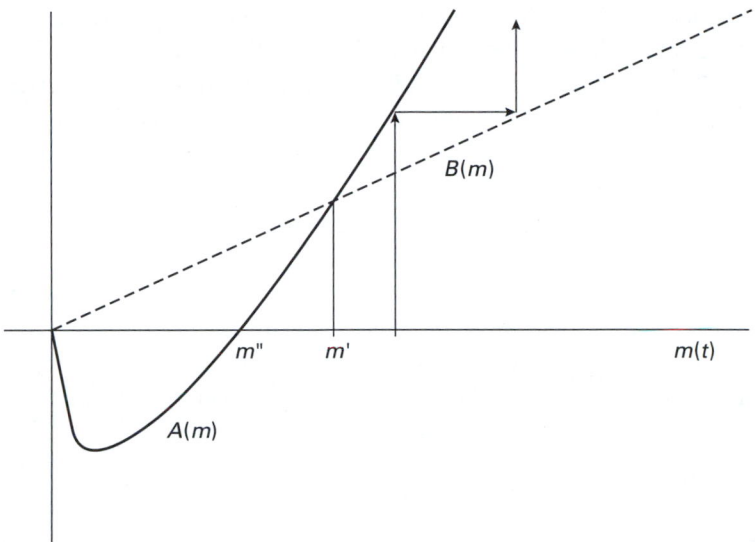

Figure 2.1
Steady-state real balances (separate utility).

right of m' involve $m_{t+s} \to \infty$ as $s \to \infty$. When $\theta \geq 0$ (non-negative money growth), such explosive paths for m, involving a price level going to zero, violate the transversality condition that the discounted value of asset holdings must go to zero (see Obstfeld and Rogoff 1983; 1986).[16] More recently, Benhabib, Schmitt-Grohé, and Uribe (2001a; 2001b; 2002) noted that the zero lower bound on the nominal interest rate may not allow one to rule out paths that begin to the right of m'. As the rate of deflation rises along these paths, the nominal interest rate must fall. Once it reaches zero, the process cannot continue, so the economy may find itself in a zero interest rate equilibrium that does not violate any transversality condition.[17]

When $\lim_{m \to 0} A(m) < 0$, paths originating to the left of m' converge to $m < 0$; but this is clearly not possible, since real balances cannot be negative. For the case drawn in figure 2.1, however, some paths originating to the left of m' converge to zero without ever involving negative real balances. For example, a path that reaches m'' at which $A(m'') = 0$ then jumps to $m = 0$. Along such an equilibrium path, the price level is growing faster than the nominal money supply (so that m declines). Even if $\theta = 0$, so that the nominal money supply is constant, the equilibrium path

16. Obstfeld and Rogoff (1986) show that any such equilibrium path with an implosive price level violates the transversality condition unless $\lim_{m \to \infty} \phi(m) = \infty$. This condition is implausible because it would require that the utility yielded by money be unbounded.

17. See the discussion of liquidity traps in chapter 10.

would involve a speculative hyperinflation with the price level going to infinity.[18] Unfortunately, Obstfeld and Rogoff showed that the conditions needed to ensure $\lim_{m \to 0} \phi_m m = \tilde{m} > 0$ so that speculative hyperinflations can be ruled out are restrictive. They showed that $\lim_{m \to 0} \phi_m m > 0$ implies $\lim_{m \to 0} \phi(m) = -\infty$; essentially, money must be so necessary that the utility of the representative agent goes to minus infinity if real balances fall to zero.[19]

When paths originating to the left of m' cannot be ruled out, the model exhibits multiple equilibria. For example, suppose that the nominal stock of money is held constant, with $M_t = M_0$ for all $t > 0$. Then there is a rational expectations equilibrium path for the price level and real money balances starting at any price level P_0 as long as $M_0/P_0 < m'$. Chapter 4 examines an approach called the *fiscal theory of the price level*, which argues that the initial price level may be determined by fiscal policy.

2.2.2   Steady States with a Time-Varying Money Stock

The previous section considered the steady state associated with a constant growth rate of the nominal supply of money. Often, particularly when the focus is on the relationship between money and prices, one might be more interested in a steady state in which real quantities such as consumption and the capital stock are constant but the growth rate of money varies over time. Assume, then, that $c_t = c^*$ and $k_t = k^*$ for all t. Setting population growth n to zero and using (2.10), the equilibrium conditions (2.6) and (2.7) can be written as

$$u_c(c^*, m_t) = \beta[f_k(k^*) + 1 - \delta]u_c(c^*, m_{t+1}) \tag{2.24}$$

$$\frac{1 + i_t}{(1 + \pi_{t+1})} = [f_k(k^*) + 1 - \delta], \tag{2.25}$$

and (2.12) implies

$$\frac{u_m(c^*, m_t)}{u_c(c^*, m_t)} = \frac{i_t}{1 + i_t}. \tag{2.26}$$

The budget constraint becomes

$$c^* = f(k^*) - \delta k^*,$$

---

18. The hyperinflation is labeled speculative because it is not driven by fundamentals such as the growth rate of the nominal supply of money.

19. Speculative hyperinflations are shown by Obstfeld and Rogoff to be ruled out if the government holds real resources to back a fraction of the outstanding currency. This ensures a positive value below which the real value of money cannot fall.

and the evolution of the real stock of money is given by

$$m_t = \left(\frac{1+\theta_t}{1+\pi_t}\right) m_{t-1}. \tag{2.27}$$

If θ is constant, one has the situation previously studied. There is a steady state with inflation equal to the rate of growth of money ($\pi = \theta$), and real money balances are constant. With m constant, (2.24) uniquely determines the capital stock such that $\beta[f_k(k^{ss}) + 1 - \delta] = 1$. The economy's resource constraint then determines c^*.

There may also be steady-state equilibria in which m is changing over time. Reis (2007) investigated how monetary policies that allow the monetary stock to be time-varying can alter the steady-state values of consumption and capital. To understand intuitively how c^* and k^* could be affected by monetary policy, consider (2.24) for $k^* > k^{ss}$.[20] Because of diminishing marginal productivity, $\beta[f_k(k^*) + 1 - \delta] < 1$, so for (2.24) to hold requires the marginal utility of consumption to rise over time such that

$$\frac{u_c(c^*, m_{t+1})}{u_c(c^*, m_t)} = \frac{1}{\beta[f_k(k^*) + 1 - \delta]} > 1. \tag{2.28}$$

For example, suppose $u_{cm} > 0$ so that higher levels of real money balances increase the marginal utility of consumption. Then (2.28) can be satisfied if real money balances grow over time. For real money balances to grow over time, (2.12) implies that the nominal interest rate must be decreasing, reducing the opportunity cost of holding money. Of course, a steady state that satisfies (2.28) may not be feasible. If the marginal utility of money goes to zero for some $\bar{m} > 0$, then such a steady state does not exist. Note also that if utility is separable in consumption and real money balances, (2.24) becomes $u_c(c^*) = \beta[f_k(k^*) + 1 - \delta]u_c(c^*)$, which implies $k^* = k^{ss}$, and the steady state is independent of real money balances.

If, following Fischer (1979b), the utility function takes the form

$$u(c,m) = \frac{(c^{1-\gamma}m^\gamma)^{1-\eta}}{1-\eta},$$

with $\eta < 1$ and $\gamma \in (0,1)$, then (2.28) requires that real money balances evolve according to

$$\left(\frac{m_{t+1}}{m_t}\right) = \left\{\frac{1}{\beta[f_k(k^*) + 1 - \delta]}\right\}^{1/(1-\gamma(1-\eta))}. \tag{2.29}$$

20. Recall k^{ss} is such that $\beta[f_k(k^{ss}) + 1 - \delta] = 1$.

Rather than characterize the steady state in terms of the growth rate of the nominal stock of money, Reis (2007) examined the behavior of the nominal interest rate directly, since central banks today generally employ a nominal interest rate and not a nominal quantity as their policy instrument. The equilibrium condition (2.26) implicitly defines a money demand function of the form

$$m_t = \phi(i_t, c^*),$$

so (2.29) implies the path of the nominal rate must satisfy

$$\frac{\phi(i_{t+1}, c^*)}{\phi(i_t, c^*)} = \left\{ \frac{1}{\beta[f_k(k^*) + 1 - \delta]} \right\}^{1/(1 - \gamma(1 - \eta))}.$$

With k constant, (2.25) implies the real interest rate, given by $(1 + i_t)/(1 + \pi_{t+1})$, is constant, so the required path for the nominal rate also pins down the path followed by the inflation rate. Advancing (2.27) one period then determines the growth rate of the nominal money stock consistent with the specified equilibrium path. Reis (2007) discussed how the monetary authority could, through a policy of declining nominal interest rates, sustain a steady state in which consumption and output remain above the levels that would be reached under a constant growth rate of money policy.

2.2.3   The Interest Elasticity of Money Demand

Returning to (2.12), this equation characterizes the demand for real money balances as a function of the nominal rate of interest and real consumption. For example, suppose that the utility function in consumption and real balances is of the constant elasticity of substitution (CES) form:

$$u(c_t, m_t) = [ac_t^{1-b} + (1 - a)m_t^{1-b}]^{1/(1-b)}, \tag{2.30}$$

with $0 < a < 1$ and $b > 0$, $b \neq 1$. Then

$$\frac{u_m}{u_c} = \left(\frac{1-a}{a}\right)\left(\frac{c_t}{m_t}\right)^b,$$

and (2.12) can be written as[21]

$$m_t = \left(\frac{1-a}{a}\right)^{1/b} \left(\frac{i}{1+i}\right)^{-1/b} c_t. \tag{2.31}$$

---

21. In the limit, as $b \to \infty$, (2.31) implies that $m = c$. This is then equivalent to the cash-in-advance models examined in chapter 3.

In terms of the more common log specification used to model empirical money demand equations,

$$\log \frac{M_t}{P_t N_t} = \frac{1}{b} \log\left(\frac{1-a}{a}\right) + \log c - \frac{1}{b} \log \frac{i}{1+i},$$ (2.32)

which gives the real demand for money as a negative function of the nominal rate of interest and a positive function of consumption.[22] The consumption (income) elasticity of money demand is equal to 1 in this specification. The elasticity of money demand with respect to the opportunity cost variable $\Upsilon_t = i_t/(1+i_t)$ is $1/b$. For simplicity, this will often be referred to as the *interest elasticity of money demand*.[23]

For $b = 1$, the CES specification becomes $u(c_t, m_t) = c_t^a m_t^{1-a}$. Note from (2.32) that in this case, the consumption (income) elasticity of money demand and the elasticity with respect to the opportunity cost measure Υ_t are both equal to 1.

While the parameter b governs the interest elasticity of demand, the steady-state level of money holdings depends on the value of a. From (2.31), the ratio of real money balances to consumption in the steady state will be[24]

$$\frac{m^{ss}}{c^{ss}} = \left(\frac{1-a}{a}\right)^{1/b} \left(\frac{1+\pi^{ss}-\beta}{1+\pi^{ss}}\right)^{-1/b}.$$

The ratio of m^{ss} to c^{ss} is decreasing in a; an increase in a reduces the weight given to real money balances in the utility function and results in smaller holdings of money (relative to consumption) in the steady state. Increases in inflation also reduce the ratio of money holdings to consumption by increasing the opportunity cost of holding money.

Empirical Evidence on the Interest Elasticity of Money Demand

The empirical literature on money demand is vast. See, for example, the references in Judd and Scadding (1982); Laidler (1985); or Goldfeld and Sichel (1990) for earlier surveys. Recent contributions include Lucas (1988); Hoffman and Rasche (1991);

---

22. The standard specification of money demand would use income in place of consumption, although see Mankiw and Summers (1986).

23. The elasticity of money demand with respect to the nominal interest rate is

$$-\frac{\partial m_t}{\partial i_t} \frac{i_t}{m_t} = \frac{1}{b} \frac{1}{1+i_t}.$$

Empirical work often estimates money demand equations in which the log of real money balances is a function of log income and the *level* of the nominal interest rate. The coefficient on the nominal interest rate is then equal to the semielasticity of money demand with respect to the nominal interest rate ($m^{-1} \partial m/\partial i$), which for (2.32) is $1/bi(1+i)$.

24. This makes use of the fact that $1 + i^{ss} = (1+r^{ss})(1+\pi^{ss}) = (1+\pi^{ss})/\beta$ in the steady state.

Stock and Watson (1993); Ball (2001); Knell and Stix (2005); Teles and Zhou (2005); and Ireland (2008). Ball argued that in postwar samples ending prior to the late 1980s, the high degree of collinearity between output and interest rates made it difficult to obtain precise estimates of the income and interest elasticities of money demand. Based on data from 1946 to 1996, he found the income elasticity of the demand for the $M1$ monetary aggregate to be around 0.5 and the interest semielasticity to be around -0.5. An income elasticity less than 1 is consistent with the findings of Knell and Stix (2005). Teles and Zhou argued that $M1$ is not the relevant measure of money after 1980 because of the widespread changes in financial regulations. They focused on a monetary aggregate constructed by the Federal Reserve Bank of St. Louis, called money zero maturity (MZM), which measures balances available immediately for transactions at zero cost. Teles and Zhou also assumed an income elasticity of 1 and estimated the interest elasticity of money demand to be -0.24.

Holman (1998) directly estimated the parameters of the utility function under various alternative specifications of its functional form, including (2.30), using annual U.S. data from 1889 to 1991.[25] She obtained estimates of b of around 0.1 and a of around 0.95. This value of b implies an elasticity of money demand equal to 10. However, in shorter samples, the data failed to reject $b = 1$, the case of Cobb-Douglas preferences, indicating that the interest elasticity of money demand is estimated very imprecisely.

Using annual data, Lucas (2000) obtained an estimate of 0.5 for the interest elasticity of $M1$ demand. Chari, Kehoe, and McGrattan (2000) estimated (2.32) using quarterly U.S. data and the $M1$ definition of money. They obtained an estimate for a of around 0.94 and an estimate of the interest elasticity of money demand of 0.39, implying a value of b on the order of $1/0.39 \approx 2.6$. Christiano, Eichenbaum, and Evans (2005) reported an interest semielasticity of 0.86 (the partial of log real money holdings with respect to the gross nominal interest rate), obtained as part of the estimation of a DSGE model of the United States.

Hoffman, Rasche, and Tieslau (1995) conducted a cross-country study of money demand and found a value of around 0.5 for the U.S. and Canadian money demand interest elasticity, with somewhat higher values for the United Kingdom and lower values for Japan and Germany. An elasticity of 0.5 implies a value of 2 for b. Ireland (2001a) estimated the interest elasticity as part of a general equilibrium model and obtained a value of 0.19 for the pre-1979 period and 0.12 for the post-1979 period. These translate into values for b of 5.26 and 8.33, respectively.

Ireland (2009) focused on what recent data on interest rates and $M1$ reveal about the appropriate functional form for the money demand equation. He contrasted two

25. Holman (1998) considered a variety of specifications for the utility function, including Cobb-Douglas ($b = 1$) and nested CES functions of the form used in section 2.5.

Table 2.1
Estimated Money Demand (MZM), U.S., 1984:1–2007:2

m	Const	$\ln C$	$\ln Y$	$\ln\left(\frac{i}{1+i}\right)$	m_{t-1}
1.	−8.482	1.357		−0.090	
	(0.192)	(0.024)		(0.010)	
2.	−10.380		1.500	−0.107	
	(0.241)		(0.028)	(0.010)	
3.	−0.965	0.153		−0.016	0.886
	(0.251)	(0.040)		(0.004)	(0.029)
4.	−1.036		0.149	−0.016	0.898
	(0.275)		(0.030)	(0.004)	(0.020)

Note: Standard errors in parentheses.

alternative functions. The first is a standard log-log specification, in which the log of real money balances relative to income is related to the log of the nominal interest rate. The second is a semi-log specification linking the log real money balances relative to income to the *level* of the nominal interest rate. Estimated elasticities for the log-log form were in the range of −0.05 to −0.09, and the semi-log form yielded a coefficient in the range of −1.5 to −1.9 on the level of the interest rate. Ireland found that the semi-log specification fits the post-1980 data for the United States much better than the log-log specification. The form of the money demand equation and the sensitivity of money demand to the opportunity cost of holding money are important for assessing the welfare cost of inflation (see section 2.3).

Reynard (2004) found that the increase in financial market participation has increased the interest elasticity of money demand in the United States. He reported that interest rate elasticity rose from −0.065 for the 1949–1969 period to −0.134 for 1977–1999.

Table 2.1 reports estimates of money demand for the United States based on quarterly data from the period 1984:1 to 2007:2. One advantage of this period is that the Federal Reserve employed an interest rate instrument to implement monetary policy. Because the Federal Reserve was not attempting to control monetary aggregates, simultaneity should not be a significant problem, allowing money demand to be estimated using ordinary least-squares.[26] Results are reported for MZM.[27] The theory leading to (2.32) implies that consumption should appear in the money demand

---

26. Under a monetary aggregates policy, a shock to money demand would affect the nominal interest rate, inducing correlation between one of the explanatory variables (the nominal rate) and the error term. Under an interest rate policy procedure, shocks to money demand are allowed to affect the quantity of money but not the nominal interest rate.

27. MZM is zero-maturity money calculated by the Federal Reserve Bank of St Louis as $M2$ less small-denomination time deposits plus institutional money funds.

equation, but it is more common to use a measure of income such as GDP. Thus, results are reported for both real personal consumption expenditures (in which case the corresponding personal consumption expenditures chain-type price index is employed) and real GDP (and the chain-type price index for GDP). To obtain a measure of the opportunity cost of holding MZM, the own return on MZM is subtracted from the 3-month secondary market Treasury bill rate. Using either consumption or income, the income elasticity of money demand is greater than 1. Using real consumption, the interest elasticity is estimated to be -0.09 according to row 1, and row 3 implies a long-run elasticity of -0.144. According to (2.32), these values would imply values for b of from just under 7 to over 11.

Most empirical estimates of the interest elasticity of money demand employ aggregate time series data. At the household level, many U.S. households hold no interest-earning assets, so the normal substitution between money and interest-earning assets as the nominal interest rate changes is absent. As nominal interest rates rise, more households find it worthwhile to hold interest-earning assets. Changes in the nominal interest rate then affect both the extensive margin (the decision whether to hold interest-earning assets) and the intensive margin (the decision of how much to hold in interest-earning assets, given that the household already holds some wealth in this form). Mulligan and Sala-i-Martin (2000) focused on these two margins and used cross-sectional evidence on household holdings of financial assets to estimate the interest elasticity of money demand. They found that the elasticity increases with the level of nominal interest rates and is low at low nominal rates of interest.

2.2.4   Limitations

Before moving on to use the MIU framework to analyze the welfare cost of inflation, we need to consider the limitations of the money-in-the-utility function approach. In the MIU model, there is a clearly defined reason for individuals to hold money—it provides utility. However, this essentially solves the problem of generating a positive demand for money by assumption; it doesn't address the reasons that money, particularly money in the form of unbacked pieces of paper, might yield utility. The money-in-the-utility function approach has to be thought of as a shortcut for a fully specified model of the transaction technology faced by households that gives rise to a positive demand for a medium of exchange.

Shortcuts are often extremely useful. But one problem with such a shortcut is that it does not provide any real understanding of, or possible restrictions on, partial derivatives such as u_m or u_{cm} that play a role in determining equilibrium and the outcome of comparative static exercises. One possible story that can generate a money-in-the-utility function is based on the idea that money can reduce the time needed to purchase consumption goods. This shopping-time story will be discussed in chapter 3.

2.3   The Welfare Cost of Inflation

Because money holdings yield direct utility and higher inflation reduces real money balances, inflation generates a welfare loss. This raises two questions: How large is the welfare cost of inflation? Is there an optimal rate of inflation that maximizes the steady-state welfare of the representative household? Some important results on both of these questions are illustrated here, and chapters 4 and 8 provide more discussion of the optimal rate of inflation.

The second question—the optimal rate of inflation—was originally addressed by Bailey (1956) and M. Friedman (1969). Their basic intuition was the following. The private opportunity cost of holding money depends on the nominal rate of interest (see (2.12)). The social marginal cost of producing money, that is, running the printing presses, is essentially zero. The wedge that arises between the private marginal cost and the social marginal cost when the nominal rate of interest is positive generates an inefficiency. This inefficiency would be eliminated if the private opportunity cost were also equal to zero, and this will be the case if the nominal rate of interest equals zero. But $i = 0$ requires that $\pi = -r/(1+r) \approx -r$. So the optimal rate of inflation is a rate of *deflation* approximately equal to the real return on capital.[28]

In the steady state, real money balances are directly related to the inflation rate, so the optimal rate of inflation is also frequently discussed under the heading of the *optimal quantity of money* (M. Friedman 1969). With utility depending directly on m, one can think of the government choosing its policy instrument θ (and therefore π) to achieve the steady-state optimal value of m. Steady-state utility will be maximized when $u(c^{ss}, m^{ss})$ is maximized subject to the constraint that $c^{ss} = f(k^{ss}) - \delta k^{ss}$. But since c^{ss} is independent of θ, the first-order condition for the optimal θ is just $u_m(\partial m/\partial \theta) = 0$, or $u_m = 0$, and from (2.12), this occurs when $i = 0$.[29]

The major criticism of this result is due to Phelps (1973), who pointed out that money growth generates revenue for the government—the inflation tax. The implicit assumption so far has been that variations in money growth are engineered via lump-sum transfers. Any effects on government revenue can be offset by a suitable adjustment in these lump-sum transfers (taxes). But if governments only have distortionary taxes available for financing expenditures, then reducing inflation tax revenues to achieve the Friedman rule of a zero nominal interest rate requires that the lost revenue be replaced through increases in other distortionary taxes. Reducing the nominal

---

28. Since $(1+i) = (1+r)(1+\pi)$, $i = 0$ implies $\pi = -r/(1+r) \approx -r$.

29. Note that the earlier assumption that the marginal utility of money goes to zero at some finite level of real balances ensures that $u_m = 0$ has a solution with $m < \infty$. The focus here is on the steady state, but a more appropriate perspective for addressing the optimal inflation question would not restrict attention solely to the steady state. The more general case is considered in chapter 4.

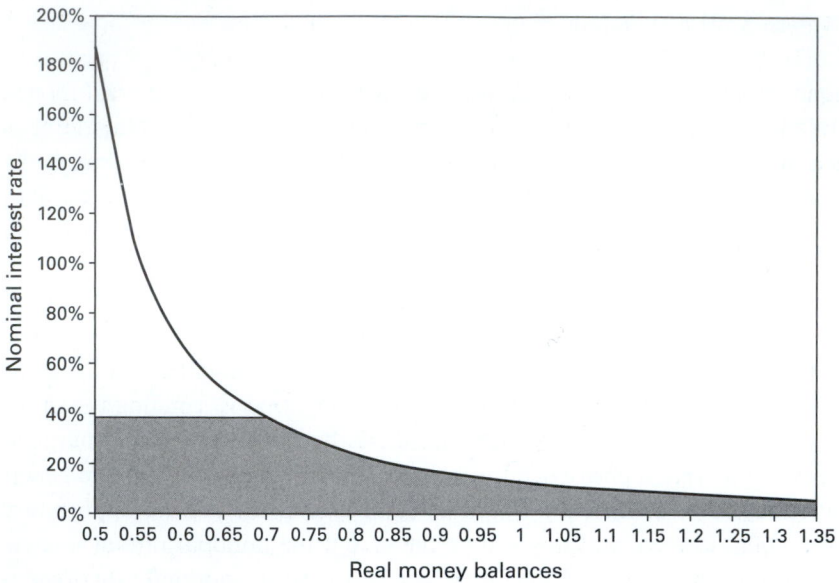

Figure 2.2
Welfare costs of inflation as measured by the area under the demanded curve.

rate of interest to zero would increase the inefficiencies generated by the higher level of other taxes that would be needed to replace the lost inflation tax revenues. To minimize the total distortions associated with raising a given amount of revenue, it may be optimal to rely on the inflation tax to some degree. Recent work has re-examined these results (see Chari, Christiano, and Kehoe 1991; 1996; Correia and Teles 1996; 1999; Mulligan and Sala-i-Martin 1997). The revenue implications of inflation and optimal inflation are major themes of chapter 4.

Now let's return to the first question—what is the welfare cost of inflation? Beginning with Bailey (1956), this welfare cost has been calculated from the area under the money demand curve (showing money demand as a function of the nominal rate of interest) because this provides a measure of the consumer surplus lost as a result of having a positive nominal rate of interest. Figure 2.2 is based on the money demand function given by (2.31) with $a = 0.9$ and Chari, Kehoe, and McGrattan (2000)'s implied value for b of 2.56. At a nominal interest rate of i^*, the deadweight loss is measured by the shaded area under the money demand curve.

Nominal interest rates reflect *expected* inflation, so calculating the area under the money demand curve provides a measure of the costs of *anticipated* inflation and is therefore appropriate for evaluating the costs of alternative constant rates of inflation. There are other costs of inflation associated with tax distortions and with variability in the rate of inflation; these are discussed in the survey on the costs of inflation by Driffill, Mizon, and Ulph (1990); relative price distortions generated by inflation when prices are sticky are discussed in chapter 8.

Lucas (1994) provided estimates of the welfare costs of inflation by starting with the following specification of the instantaneous utility function:

$$u(c,m) = \frac{1}{1-\sigma}\left\{\left[c\varphi\left(\frac{m}{c}\right)\right]^{1-\sigma} - 1\right\}. \tag{2.33}$$

With this utility function, (2.12) becomes

$$\frac{u_m}{u_c} = \frac{\varphi'(x)}{\varphi(x) - x\varphi'(x)} = \frac{i}{1+i} = \Upsilon, \tag{2.34}$$

where $x \equiv m/c$.[30] Normalizing so that steady-state consumption equals 1, $u(1,m)$ will be maximized when $\Upsilon = 0$, implying that the optimal x is defined by $\varphi'(m^*) = 0$. Lucas proposed to measure the costs of inflation by the percentage increase in steady-state consumption necessary to make the household indifferent between a nominal interest rate of i and a nominal rate of 0. If this cost is denoted $w(\Upsilon)$, it is defined by

$$u(1 + w(\Upsilon), m(\Upsilon)) \equiv u(1, m^*), \tag{2.35}$$

where $m(\Upsilon)$ denotes the solution of (2.34) for real money balances evaluated at steady-state consumption $c = 1$.

Suppose, following Lucas, that $\varphi(m) = (1 + Bm^{-1})^{-1}$, where B is a positive constant. Solving (2.34), one obtains $m(i) = B^{0.5}\Upsilon^{-0.5}$.[31] Note that $\varphi' = 0$ requires that $m^* = \infty$. But $\varphi(\infty) = 1$ and $u(1, \infty) = 0$, so $w(\Upsilon)$ is the solution to $u(1 + w(\Upsilon), B^{0.5}\Upsilon^{-0.5}) = u(1, \infty) = 0$. Using the definition of the utility function, one obtains $1 + w(\Upsilon) = 1 + \sqrt{B\Upsilon}$, or

$$w(\Upsilon) = \sqrt{B\Upsilon}. \tag{2.36}$$

Based on U.S. annual data from 1900 to 1985, Lucas reported an estimate of 0.0018 for B. Hence, the welfare loss arising from a nominal interest rate of 10 percent would be $\sqrt{(0.0018)(0.1/1.1)} = 0.013$, or just over 1 percent of aggregate consumption.

---

30. In the framework Lucas employed, the relevant expression is $u_m/u_c = i$; problem 1 at the end of this chapter provides an example of the timing assumptions Lucas employed.

31. Lucas actually started with the assumption that money demand is equal to $m = Ai^{-0.5}$ for A equal to a constant. He then derived $\varphi(m)$ as the utility function necessary to generate such a demand function, where $B = A^2$.

Since U.S. government bond yields were around 10 percent in 1979 and 1980, one can use 1980 aggregate personal consumption expenditures of $2447.1 billion to get a rough estimate of the dollar welfare loss (although consumption expenditures includes purchases of durables). In this example, 1.3 percent of $2447.1 billion is about $32 billion. Since this is the annual cost in terms of steady-state consumption, one needs the present discounted value of $32 billion. With a real rate of return of 2 percent, this amounts to $32(1.02)/0.02 = $1632 billion; at 4 percent the cost would be $832 billion.

An annual welfare cost of $32 billion seems a small number, especially when compared to the estimated costs of reducing inflation. For example, Ball (1993) reported a "sacrifice ratio" of 2.4 percent of output per 1 percent inflation reduction for the United States. Since inflation was reduced from about 10 to about 3 percent in the early 1980s, Ball's estimate would put the cost of this disinflation at approximately 17 percent of GDP (2.4 percent times an inflation reduction of 7 percent). Based on 1980 GDP of $3776.3 billion (1987 prices), this would be $642 billion. This looks large when compared to the $32 billion annual welfare cost, but the trade-off starts looking more worthwhile if the costs of reducing inflation are compared to the present discounted value of the annual welfare cost. (See also Feldstein 1979.)

Gillman (1995) provides a useful survey of different estimates of the welfare cost of inflation. The estimates differ widely. One important reason for these differences arises from the choice of the base inflation rate. Some estimates compare the area under the money demand curve between an inflation rate of zero and, say, 10 percent. This is incorrect in that a zero rate of inflation still results in a positive nominal rate (equal to the real rate of return) and therefore a positive opportunity cost associated with holding money. Gillman concluded, based on the empirical estimates he surveyed, that a reasonable value of the welfare cost of inflation for the United States is in the range of 0.85 percent to 3 percent of real GNP per percentage rise in the nominal interest rate above zero, a loss in 2008 dollars of $120 billion to $426 billion per year.[32]

It should be clear from figure 2.2 that the size of the area under the demand curve will depend importantly on both the shape and the position of the demand curve. For example, if money demand exhibits a constant elasticity with respect to the nominal interest rates, than at low levels of interest rates, further declines in the interest rate generate larger and larger increases in the absolute level of money demand, as illustrated in the figure. The area under the demand curve, and thus the welfare costs of inflation, will correspondingly be large.

---

32. These estimates apply to the United States, which has experienced relatively low rates of inflation. They may not be relevant for high-inflation countries.

Lucas (2000) calculated the welfare costs of inflation for two alternative specifications of money demand. The first takes the form

$$\ln(m) = \ln(A) - \eta \ln(i); \tag{2.37}$$

the second takes the form

$$\ln(m) = \ln(B) - \xi i. \tag{2.38}$$

Based on annual U.S. data from the period 1900–1994, Lucas obtained estimates of 0.5 for η and 7 for ξ. Ireland (2009) illustrated how these two functional forms have very different curvatures at low nominal interest rates. Real money demand becomes very large as i approaches zero under the log-log specification but approaches the finite limit $\ln(B)$ with the semi-log version. Equation (2.38) implies that a fall of interest rates from 3 to 2 percent produces the same increase in money demand as a fall from 10 to 9 percent, unlike the functional form in figure 2.2. If the welfare costs of positive nominal interest rates is measured from the area under the money demand function, these costs will appear much larger when using (2.37) rather than (2.38). For example, at a real interest rate of 3 percent, an average inflation rate of 2 percent carries a welfare cost of just over 1 percent of income if (2.37) is the correct specification of money demand, but only 0.25 percent if (2.38) is correct.

Ireland (2009) argued that the support for the log-log specification comes primarily from two historical periods. The first is the late 1940s, when interest rates were very low and money demand very high (relative to income). The second is the period of disinflation beginning in 1979 through the early 1980s, when interest rates were very high and money demand was unexpectedly low (often referred to as the period of missing money; see Goldfeld 1976). Ireland found, using a measure of the money stock that accounts for some of the changes due to financial market deregulation, that the data since 1980 provide much more support for the semi-log specification with a small value of ξ. Rather than the value of 7 estimated by Lucas, Ireland found values below 2. His estimates translate into a welfare cost of 2 percent inflation of less than 0.04 percent of income.

The Sidrauski model provides a convenient framework for calculating the steady-state welfare costs of inflation, both because the lower level of real money holdings that result at higher rates of inflation has a direct effect on welfare when money enters the utility function and because the superneutrality property of the model means that the other argument in the utility function, real consumption, is invariant across different rates of inflation. This latter property simplifies the calculation because it is not necessary to account for both variations in money holdings and variations in consumption when making the welfare cost calculation. However, the area under the demand curve is a partial equilibrium measure of the welfare costs of inflation if superneutrality does not hold, since steady-state consumption will no longer be independent of the inflation rate. Gomme (1993) and Dotsey and Ireland (1996) examined the effects of inflation in general equilibrium frameworks that allow for the supply of labor and the average rate of economic growth to be affected (in models that do not display superneutrality; see section 2.4.2). Gomme found that even though inflation reduces the supply of labor and economic growth, the welfare costs are small due to the increased consumption of leisure that households enjoy.[33] Dotsey and Ireland found much larger welfare costs of inflation in a model that generates an interest elasticity of money demand that matches estimates for the United States. (See also De Gregorio 1993 and Imrohoroğlu and Prescott 1991.)

2.4 Extensions

2.4.1 Interest on Money

If the welfare costs of inflation are related to the positive private opportunity costs of holding money, paying explicit interest on money would be an alternative to deflation as a means of eliminating these costs. There are obvious technical difficulties in paying interest on cash, but ignoring these, assume that the government pays a nominal interest rate of i^m on money balances. Assume further that these interest payments are financed by lump-sum taxes s. The household's budget constraint, (2.4), now becomes (setting $n = 0$)

$$f(k_{t-1}) - s_t + \tau_t + (1 - \delta)k_{t-1} + (1 + r_{t-1})b_{t-1} + \frac{1 + i_t^m}{1 + \pi_t} m_{t-1} = c_t + k_t + m_t + b_t$$

(2.39)

and the first-order condition (2.8) becomes

$$-u_c(c_t, m_t) + u_m(c_t, m_t) + \frac{\beta(1 + i_t^m) V_\omega(\omega_{t+1})}{(1 + \pi_{t+1})} = 0,$$

(2.40)

whereas (2.12) is now

$$\frac{u_m(c_t, m_t)}{u_c(c_t, m_t)} = \frac{i_t - i_t^m}{1 + i_t}.$$

The opportunity cost of money is related to the interest rate gap $i - i^m$, which represents the difference between the nominal return on bonds and the nominal return on

---

33. The effect of money (and inflation) on labor supply is discussed in section 2.4.2.

money. Thus, the optimal quantity of money can be achieved as long as $i - i^m = 0$, regardless of the rate of inflation. If $\theta = 0$, so that the rate of inflation in the steady state is also zero, the optimal quantity of money is obtained with a positive nominal interest rate as long as $i^{ss} = i^m = r^{ss} > 0$.

The assumption that the interest payments are financed by the revenue from lump-sum taxes is critical for this result. Problem 6 at the end of this chapter considers what happens if the government simply finances the interest payments on money by printing more money.

2.4.2 Nonsuperneutrality

Calculations of the steady-state welfare costs of inflation in the Sidrauski model are greatly simplified by the fact that the model exhibits superneutrality. But how robust is the result that money is superneutral? The empirical evidence of Barro (1995) suggests that inflation has a negative effect on growth, a finding inconsistent with super-neutrality.[34] One channel through which inflation can have real effects in the steady state is introduced if households have a labor supply choice. That is, suppose utility depends on consumption, real money holdings, and leisure:

$$u = u(c, m, l). \tag{2.41}$$

The economy's production function becomes

$$y = f(k, n), \tag{2.42}$$

where n is employment. If the total supply of time is normalized to equal 1, then $n = 1 - l$. The additional first-order condition implied by the optimal choice of leisure is

$$\frac{u_l(c, m, l)}{u_c(c, m, l)} = f_n(k, 1 - l). \tag{2.43}$$

Now, both steady-state labor supply and consumption may be affected by variations in the rate of inflation. Specifically, an increase in the rate of inflation reduces holdings of real money balances. If this affects the marginal utility of leisure, then (2.43) implies the supply of labor will be affected, leading to a change in the steady-state per capita stock of capital, output, and consumption. But why would changes in money holdings affect the marginal utility of leisure? Because money has simply been assumed to yield utility, with no explanation for the reason, it is difficult to answer this question. Chapter 3 examines a model in which money helps to reduce the time spent in carrying out the transactions necessary to purchase consumption goods; in

---

34. Of course, the empirical relationship may not be causal; both growth and inflation may be reacting to common factors. As noted in chapter 1, McCandless and Weber (1995) found no relationship between inflation and average real growth.

this case, a rise in inflation would lead to more time spent engaged in transactions, and this would raise the marginal utility of leisure. But one might expect that this channel is unlikely to be important empirically, so superneutrality may remain a reasonable first approximation to the effects of inflation on steady-state real magnitudes.

Equation (2.43) suggests that if u_l/u_c were independent of m, then superneutrality would hold. This is the case because the steady-state values of k, c, and l could then be found from

$$\frac{u_l}{u_c} = f_n(k^{ss}, 1 - l^{ss}),$$

$$f_k(k^{ss}, 1 - l^{ss}) = \frac{1}{\beta} - 1 + \delta,$$

and

$$c^{ss} = f(k^{ss}, 1 - l^{ss}) + \delta k^{ss}.$$

If u_l/u_c does not depend on m, these three equations determine the steady-state values of consumption, capital, and labor independently of inflation. So superneutrality reemerges when the utility function takes the general form $u(c, m, l) = v(c, l)g(m)$. Variations in inflation will affect the agent's holdings of money, but the consumption-leisure choice will not be directly affected. As McCallum (1990a) noted, Cobb-Douglas specifications, which are quite common in the literature, satisfy this condition. So with a Cobb-Douglas utility function, the ratio of the marginal utility of leisure to the marginal utility of consumption will be independent of the level of real money balances, and superneutrality will hold.

Another channel through which inflation can affect the steady-state stock of capital occurs if money enters directly into the production function (Fischer 1974). Since steady states with different rates of inflation will have different equilibrium levels of real money balances, they will also lead to different marginal products of capital for given levels of the capital-labor ratio. With the steady-state marginal product of capital determined by $1/\beta - 1 + \delta$ (see (2.19)), the two steady states can have the same marginal product of capital only if their capital-labor ratios differ. If $\partial \text{MPK}/\partial m > 0$ (so that money and capital are complements), higher inflation, by leading to lower real money balances, also leads to a lower steady-state capital stock.[35] This is the opposite of the *Tobin effect*; Tobin (1965) argued that higher inflation would induce a portfolio substitution toward capital that would increase the steady-state capital-

---

35. That is, in the steady state, $f_k(k^{ss}, m^{ss}) = \beta^{-1} - 1 + \delta$, where $f(k, m)$ is the production function and f_i denotes the partial derivative with respect to argument i. It follows that $dk^{ss}/dm^{ss} = -f_{km}/f_{kk}$, so with $f_{kk} \leq 0$, $\text{sign}(dk^{ss}/dm^{ss}) = \text{sign}(f_{km})$.

labor ratio (see also Stein 1969; S. Fischer 1972). For higher inflation to be associated with a higher steady-state capital-labor ratio requires that $\partial \text{MPK}/\partial m < 0$ (that is, higher money balances reduce the marginal product of capital; money and capital are substitutes in production).

This discussion actually has, by ignoring taxes, excluded what is probably the most important reason that superneutrality may fail in actual economies. Taxes generally are not indexed to inflation and are levied on nominal capital gains instead of real capital gains. Effective tax rates will depend on the inflation rate, generating real effects on capital accumulation and consumption as inflation varies. (See, for example, Feldstein 1978; 1998; Summers 1981.)

2.5 Dynamics in an MIU Model

The analysis of the MIU approach has, up to this point, focused on steady-state properties. It is also important to understand the model's implications for the dynamic behavior of the economy as it adjusts to exogenous disturbances. Even the basic Sidrauski model can exhibit nonsuperneutralities during the transition to the steady state. For example, S. Fischer (1979a) showed that for the constant relative risk aversion class of utility functions, the rate of capital accumulation is positively related to the rate of money growth except for the case of log separable utility; earlier it was noted how the steady state can be affected when money growth varies over time (Reis 2007).[36]

In addition, theoretical and empirical work in macroeconomics and monetary economics are closely tied, and it is important to reflect on how the theoretical models can illuminate actual observations on inflationary experiences.

One way to study the model's dynamics is to employ numerical methods to carry out simulations using the model. The results can then be compared to actual data generated by real economies. This approach was popularized by the real-business-cycle literature (see Cooley 1995). Since the parameters of theoretical models can be varied in ways that the characteristics of real economies cannot, simulation methods permit answering a variety of "what if" questions. For example, how does the dynamic response to a temporary change in the growth rate of the money supply depend on the degree of intertemporal substitution characterizing individual preferences or the persistence of money growth rate disturbances?

---

36. Superneutrality holds during the transition if $u(c, m) = \ln(c) + b \ln(m)$. The general class of utility functions Fischer considered is of the form $u(c, m) = \frac{1}{1-\Phi}(c^a m^b)^{1-\Phi}$; log utility obtains when $\Phi = 1$. See also Asako (1983), who showed that faster money growth can lead to slower capital accumulation under certain conditions if c and m are perfect complements. These effects of inflation on capital accumulation apply during the transition from one steady-state equilibrium to another; they differ therefore from the Tobin (1965) effect of inflation on the steady-state capital-labor ratio.

It can also be helpful to have an analytic solution to a model; often explicit solutions help to indicate whether simulation results are likely to be sensitive to parameter values and to highlight directly the mechanisms through which changes in the processes followed by the exogenous variables lead to effects on the endogenous variables and to alterations in the equilibrium decision rules of the agents in the model. In addition, easily adaptable programs for solving linear dynamic stochastic rational-expectations models are now freely available.[37]

This section develops a linearized version of an MIU model that also incorporates a labor-leisure choice. This introduces a labor supply decision into the analysis, an important and necessary extension for studying business cycle fluctuations, since employment variation is an important characteristic of cycles. It is also important to allow for uncertainty by adding exogenous shocks that disturb the system from its steady-state equilibrium. The two types of shocks considered are productivity shocks, the driving force in real-business-cycle models, and shocks to the growth rate of the nominal stock of money.

2.5.1 The Decision Problem

The household's problem is conveniently expressed using the value function. In studying a similar problem without a labor-leisure choice (see section 2.2), the state could be summarized by the resource variable ω_t that included current income. When the household chooses how much labor to supply, current income is no longer predetermined from the perspective of the household's choices of money, bonds, and capital investment. Consequently, income (output) y_t cannot be part of the state vector for period t. Instead, let

$$a_t = \tau_t + [(1 + i_{t-1})/(1 + \pi_t)]b_{t-1} + [1/(1 + \pi_t)]m_{t-1}$$

be the household's real financial wealth plus transfer at the start of period t where b_{t-1} and m_{t-1} are real bond and money balances at the end of the previous period, and τ_t is the real transfer payment received at the start of period t; π_t is the inflation rate. Define the value function $V(a_t, k_{t-1})$ as the maximum present value of utility the household can achieve if the current state is (a_t, k_{t-1}), where k_{t-1} is the per capita (or household) stock of capital at the start of the period. If n_t denotes the fraction of time the household devotes to market employment (so that $n_t = 1 - l_t$, where l_t is the fraction of time spent in leisure activities), output per household y_t is given by

$$y_t = f(k_{t-1}, n_t, z_t).$$

---

37. For example, Matlab programs provided by Harald Uhlig can be obtained from ⟨http://www.wiwi .hu-berlin.de/wpol/html/toolkit.htm⟩ and Paul Söderlind's Gauss and Matlab programs are available at ⟨http://home.datacomm.ch/paulsoderlind/⟩. Dynare for Matlab is available at ⟨http://www.cepremap .cnrs.fr/dynare/⟩.

The household's decision problem is defined by

$$V(a_t, k_{t-1}) = \max\{u(c_t, m_t, 1 - n_t) + \beta \mathrm{E}_t V(a_{t+1}, k_t)\}, \tag{2.44}$$

where the maximization is over $(c_t, m_t, b_t, k_t, n_t)$ and is subject to

$$f(k_{t-1}, n_t, z_t) + (1 - \delta)k_{t-1} + a_t \geq c_t + k_t + b_t + m_t \tag{2.45}$$

$$a_{t+1} = \tau_{t+1} + \left(\frac{1 + i_t}{1 + \pi_{t+1}}\right)b_t + \frac{m_t}{1 + \pi_{t+1}}. \tag{2.46}$$

Note that the presence of uncertainty arising from the stochastic productivity and money growth rate shocks means that it is the expected value of $V(a_{t+1}, k_t)$ that appears in the value function (2.44). The treatment of a_t as a state variable assumes that the money growth rate is known at the time the household decides on c_t, k_t, b_t, and m_t because it determines the current value of the transfer τ_t. It is also assumed that the productivity disturbance z_t is known at the start of period t.

Equation (2.45) will always hold with equality (as long as $u_c > 0$); it can be used to eliminate k_t, and (2.46) can be used to substitute for a_{t+1}, allowing the value function to be rewritten as

$$V(a_t, k_{t-1}) = \max_{c_t, n_t, b_t, m_t} \left\{ u(c_t, m_t, 1 - n_t) + \beta \mathrm{E}_t V\left(\tau_{t+1} + \left(\frac{1 + i_t}{1 + \pi_{t+1}}\right)b_t + \frac{m_t}{1 + \pi_{t+1}}, \right. \right.$$

$$\left. \left. f(k_{t-1}, n_t, z_t) + (1 - \delta)k_{t-1} + a_t - c_t - b_t - m_t \right) \right\},$$

where this is now an unconstrained maximization problem. The first-order necessary conditions with respect to c_t, n_t, b_t, and m_t are

$$u_c(c_t, m_t, 1 - n_t) - \beta \mathrm{E}_t V_k(a_{t+1}, k_t) = 0 \tag{2.47}$$

$$-u_l(c_t, m_t, 1 - n_t) + \beta \mathrm{E}_t V_k(a_{t+1}, k_t) f_n(k_{t-1}, n_t, z_t) = 0 \tag{2.48}$$

$$\beta \mathrm{E}_t \left(\frac{1 + i_t}{1 + \pi_{t+1}}\right) V_a(a_{t+1}, k_t) - \beta \mathrm{E}_t V_k(a_{t+1}, k_t) = 0 \tag{2.49}$$

$$u_m(c_t, m_t, 1 - n_t) + \beta \mathrm{E}_t \left[\frac{V_a(a_{t+1}, k_t)}{1 + \pi_{t+1}}\right] - \beta \mathrm{E}_t V_k(a_{t+1}, k_t) = 0 \tag{2.50}$$

and the envelope theorem yields

$$V_a(a_t, k_{t-1}) = \beta \mathrm{E}_t V_k(a_{t+1}, k_t) \tag{2.51}$$

$$V_k(a_t, k_{t-1}) = \beta \mathrm{E}_t V_k(a_{t+1}, k_t)[1 - \delta + f_k(k_{t-1}, n_t, z_t)]. \tag{2.52}$$

Updating (2.52) one period and using (2.51), one obtains

$$V_k(a_{t+1}, k_t) = E_t\{[1 - \delta + f_k(k_t, n_{t+1}, z_{t+1})] V_a(a_{t+1}, k_t)\}.$$

Now substituting this for $V_k(a_{t+1}, k_t)$ in (2.47) yields

$$u_c(c_t, m_t, 1 - n_t) - \beta E_t\{[1 - \delta + f_k(k_t, n_{t+1}, z_{t+1})] V_a(a_{t+1}, k_t)\} = 0. \tag{2.53}$$

When it is recognized that $u_c(c_t, m_t, 1 - n_t) = \beta E_t V_k(a_{t+1}, k_t)$, (2.50), (2.53), and (2.51) take the same form as (2.8), (2.6), and (2.10), the first-order conditions for the basic Sidrauski model, which did not include a labor-leisure choice. The only new condition is (2.48), which can be written, using (2.47), as

$$\frac{u_l(c_t, m_t, 1 - n_t)}{u_c(c_t, m_t, 1 - n_t)} = f_n(k_{t-1}, n_t, z_t).$$

This states that at an optimum, the marginal rate of substitution between consumption and leisure must equal the marginal product of labor.

The equilibrium values of consumption, capital, money holdings, and labor supply must satisfy the conditions given in (2.47)–(2.51). These conditions can be simplified, however. Note that (2.47), (2.49), and (2.51) imply that

$$u_c(c_t, m_t, 1 - n_t) = \beta(1 + i_t) E_t \left[\frac{u_c(c_{t+1}, m_{t+1}, 1 - n_{t+1})}{1 + \pi_{t+1}} \right].$$

Using this relationship and (2.47), one can now write (2.50), (2.48), and (2.53) as

$$u_m(c_t, m_t, 1 - n_t) = u_c(c_t, m_t, 1 - n_t) \left(\frac{i_t}{1 + i_t} \right) \tag{2.54}$$

$$u_l(c_t, m_t, 1 - n_t) = u_c(c_t, m_t, 1 - n_t) f_n(k_{t-1}, n_t, z_t) \tag{2.55}$$

$$u_c(c_t, m_t, 1 - n_t) = \beta E_t(1 + r_t) u_c(c_{t+1}, m_{t+1}, 1 - n_{t+1}), \tag{2.56}$$

where, in (2.56),

$$r_t = f_k(k_t, n_{t+1}, z_{t+1}) - \delta \tag{2.57}$$

is the marginal product of capital net of depreciation. In addition, the economy's aggregate resource constraint, expressed in per capita terms, requires that

$$k_t = (1 - \delta)k_{t-1} + y_t - c_t, \tag{2.58}$$

and the production function is

$$y_t = f(k_{t-1}, n_t, z_t). \tag{2.59}$$

Finally, real money balances evolve according to

$$m_t = \left(\frac{1+\theta_t}{1+\pi_t}\right)m_{t-1}, \tag{2.60}$$

where θ_t is the stochastic growth rate of the nominal stock of money.

Once processes for the exogenous disturbances z_t and θ_t have been specified, equations (2.54)–(2.60) constitute a nonlinear system of equations to determine the equilibrium values of the model's seven endogenous variables: y_t, c_t, k_t, m_t, n_t, r_t, π_t.

2.5.2 The Steady State

Consider a steady-state equilibrium of this model in which all real variables (including m) are constant and shocks are set to zero. It follows immediately from (2.56) that $1 + r^{ss} = \beta^{-1}$ and from (2.57) that

$$f_k(k^{ss}, n^{ss}, 0) = \beta^{-1} - 1 + \delta. \tag{2.61}$$

Thus, the marginal product of capital is a function only of β and δ. If the production function exhibits constant returns to scale, f_k will depend only on the capital-labor ratio k^{ss}/n^{ss}. In this case, (2.61) uniquely determines k/n. That is, the capital-labor ratio is independent of inflation or the real quantity of money.

With constant returns to scale, $\phi(k/n) = f/n$ can be defined as the intensive production function. Then, from the economy's resource constraint,

$$c^{ss} = f(k^{ss}, n^{ss}, 0) - \delta k^{ss} = \left[\phi\left(\frac{k^{ss}}{n^{ss}}\right) - \delta\left(\frac{k^{ss}}{n^{ss}}\right)\right]n^{ss} = \bar{\phi}n^{ss},$$

where $\bar{\phi} \equiv \phi(k^{ss}/n^{ss}) - \delta(k^{ss}/n^{ss})$ does not depend on anything related to money. Now, (2.55) implies that

$$\frac{u_l(c^{ss}, m^{ss}, 1 - n^{ss})}{u_c(c^{ss}, m^{ss}, 1 - n^{ss})} = f_n(k^{ss}, n^{ss}, 0).$$

In the case of constant returns to scale, f_n depends only on k^{ss}/n^{ss}, which is a function of β and δ, so using the definition of $\bar{\phi}$, one can rewrite this last equation as

$$\frac{u_l(\bar{\phi}n^{ss}, m^{ss}, 1 - n^{ss})}{u_c(\bar{\phi}n^{ss}, m^{ss}, 1 - n^{ss})} = \phi\left(\frac{k^{ss}}{n^{ss}}\right) - \left(\frac{k^{ss}}{n^{ss}}\right)\phi'\left(\frac{k^{ss}}{n^{ss}}\right). \tag{2.62}$$

This relationship provides the basic insight into how money can affect the real equilibrium. Suppose the utility function is separable in money so that neither the marginal utility of leisure nor the marginal utility of consumption depend on the household's holdings of real money balances. Then (2.62) becomes

$$\frac{u_l(\bar{\phi} n^{ss}, 1 - n^{ss})}{u_c(\bar{\phi} n^{ss}, 1 - n^{ss})} = \phi\left(\frac{k^{ss}}{n^{ss}}\right) - \left(\frac{k^{ss}}{n^{ss}}\right)\phi'\left(\frac{k^{ss}}{n^{ss}}\right),$$

which determines the steady-state supply of labor. Steady-state consumption is then given by $\bar{\phi} n^{ss}$. Thus, separable preferences imply superneutrality. Changes in the steady-state rate of inflation will alter nominal interest rates and the demand for real money balances (see (2.54)), but different inflation rates have no effect on the steady-state values of the capital stock, labor supply, or consumption.

If utility is nonseparable, so that either u_l or u_c (or both) depend on m^{ss}, then money is not superneutral. Variations in average inflation that affect the opportunity cost of holding money will affect m^{ss}. Different levels of m^{ss} will change the value of n^{ss} that satisfies (2.62). Since $1 + i^{ss} = (1 + r^{ss})(1 + \pi^{ss}) = \beta^{-1}(1 + \theta^{ss})$, equation (2.54) can be rewritten as

$$\frac{u_m(\bar{\phi} n^{ss}, m^{ss}, 1 - n^{ss})}{u_c(\bar{\phi} n^{ss}, m^{ss}, 1 - n^{ss})} = \left(\frac{i^{ss}}{1 + i^{ss}}\right) = \frac{1 + \theta^{ss} - \beta}{1 + \theta^{ss}}.$$

This equation, together with (2.62) must be jointly solved for m^{ss} and n^{ss}. Even in this case, however, the ratios of output, consumption, and capital to labor are independent of the rate of money growth. The steady-state *levels* of the capital stock, output, and consumption will depend on the money growth rate through the effects of inflation on labor supply, with inflation-induced changes in n^{ss} affecting y^{ss}, c^{ss}, and k^{ss} equiproportionally.

The effect of faster money growth will depend on how u_c, and u_l are affected by m. For example, suppose money holdings do not affect the marginal utility of leisure ($u_{lm} = 0$) but money and consumption are Edgeworth complements; higher inflation that reduces real money balances decreases the marginal utility of consumption ($u_{cm} > 0$). In this case, faster money growth reduces m^{ss} and decreases the marginal utility of consumption. Households substitute away from labor and toward leisure. Steady-state employment, output, and consumption fall. These effects go in the opposite direction if consumption and money are Edgeworth substitutes ($u_{cm} < 0$).

2.5.3 The Linear Approximation

To further explore the effects of money outside the steady state, it is useful to approximate the model's equilibrium conditions around the steady state. The steps involved in obtaining the linear approximation around the steady state follow the approach of Campbell (1994) and Uhlig (1999). Details on the approach used to linearize (2.54)–(2.60) are discussed in the appendix to this chapter (section 2.7). With the exception of interest rates and inflation, variables will be expressed as percentage deviations around the steady state. Percentage deviations of a variable q_t around its steady-state value will be denoted by $\hat{q}_t$, where $q_t \equiv q^{ss}(1 + \hat{q}_t)$. For interest rates and inflation, $\hat{r}_t$, $\hat{i}_t$, and $\hat{\pi}_t$ will denote $r_t - r^{ss}$, $i_t - i^{ss}$, and $\pi_t - \pi^{ss}$, respectively.[38] In what follows, uppercase letters denote economywide variables, lowercase letters denote random disturbances and variables expressed in per capita terms, and the superscript ss indicates the steady-state value of a variable. However, m, m^{ss}, and $\hat{m}$ refer to *real* money balances per capita, whereas M represents the aggregate *nominal* stock of money.

As is standard, the production function is taken to be Cobb-Douglas with constant returns to scale, so

$$y_t = e^{z_t} k_{t-1}^{\alpha} n_t^{1-\alpha} \tag{2.63}$$

with $0 < \alpha < 1$. For the utility function, it is assumed that

$$u(c_t, m_t, 1 - n_t) = \frac{[ac_t^{1-b} + (1-a)m_t^{1-b}]^{(1-\Phi)/(1-b)}}{1 - \Phi} + \Psi \frac{(1 - n_t)^{1-\eta}}{1 - \eta}. \tag{2.64}$$

R. King, Plosser, and Rebelo (1988) demonstrated that with the exception of the log case, utility must be multiplicatively separable in labor to be consistent with steady-state growth, in which the share of time devoted to work remains constant as real wages rise. Equation (2.64) does not have this property. However, we will abstract from growth factors, and the assumption of linear separability in leisure is common in the recent literature on business cycles. The end-of-chapter problems present an example using a utility function that is consistent with growth.

The resulting linearized system consists of the exogenous processes for the productivity shock and the money growth rate plus the eight additional equilibrium conditions: the production function, the goods market clearing condition, the definition of the real return on capital, the Euler equation for optimal intertemporal consumption allocation, the first-order conditions for labor supply and money holdings, the Fisher equation linking nominal and real interest rates, and the money market equilibrium condition. These can be solved for the capital stock, money holdings, output, consumption, employment, the real rate of interest, the nominal interest rate, and the inflation rate.

To this system of eight endogenous variables, it will be convenient to add investment, x_t, given by $x_t = k_t - (1 - \delta)k_{t-1}$, and to define λ_t as the marginal utility of consumption. The linearized expression for $\hat{\lambda}_t$ is

---

38. That is, if the interest rate is 0.0125 at a quarterly rate (i.e., 5 percent at an annual rate) and the steady-state value of the interest rate is 0.01, then $\hat{r}_t = 0.0125 - 0.01 = 0.0025$, not $(0.0125 - 0.01)/0.01 = 0.25$, a 25 percent deviation.

$$\hat{\lambda}_t = \Omega_1 \hat{c}_t + \Omega_2 \hat{m}_t, \tag{2.65}$$

where $\Omega_1 = [(b - \Phi)\gamma - b]$, $\Omega_2 = (b - \Phi)(1 - \gamma)$, and the parameter γ is equal to $a(c^{ss})^{1-b}/[a(c^{ss})^{1-b} + (1-a)(m^{ss})^{1-b}]$.

Then, in linearized form, the equilibrium conditions include (2.65) and (see the chapter appendix):

$$\left(\frac{x^{ss}}{k^{ss}}\right)\hat{x}_t = \hat{k}_t - (1-\delta)\hat{k}_{t-1}, \tag{2.66}$$

$$\hat{y}_t = \alpha\hat{k}_{t-1} + (1-\alpha)\hat{n}_t + z_t \tag{2.67}$$

$$\left(\frac{y^{ss}}{k^{ss}}\right)\hat{y}_t = \left(\frac{c^{ss}}{k^{ss}}\right)\hat{c}_t + \delta\hat{x}_t \tag{2.68}$$

$$\hat{r}_t = \alpha\left(\frac{y^{ss}}{k^{ss}}\right)(E_t\hat{y}_{t+1} - \hat{k}_t) \tag{2.69}$$

$$\hat{\lambda}_t = E_t\hat{\lambda}_{t+1} + \hat{r}_t \tag{2.70}$$

$$-\hat{\lambda}_t + \eta\left(\frac{n^{ss}}{1 - n^{ss}}\right)\hat{n}_t = \hat{y}_t - \hat{n}_t \tag{2.71}$$

$$\hat{\imath}_t = \hat{r}_t + E_t\hat{\pi}_{t+1} \tag{2.72}$$

$$\hat{m}_t - \hat{c}_t = -\left(\frac{1}{b}\right)\left(\frac{1}{\imath^{ss}}\right)\hat{\imath}_t \tag{2.73}$$

$$\hat{m}_t = \hat{m}_{t-1} - \hat{\pi}_t + u_t. \tag{2.74}$$

Consistent with the real-business-cycle literature, a stochastic disturbance to total factor productivity is incorporated that follows an AR(1) process:

$$z_t = \rho_z z_{t-1} + e_t. \tag{2.75}$$

Assume that e_t is a serially uncorrelated mean zero process and $|\rho_z| < 1$. Note the timing convention in (2.67): the capital carried over from period $t - 1$, K_{t-1}, is available for use in producing output during period t.

It is also necessary to specify the process followed by the nominal stock of money. In previous sections, θ denoted the growth rate of the nominal money supply. Assume then that the average growth rate is θ^{ss}, and let $u_t \equiv \theta_t - \theta^{ss}$ be the deviation in period t of the growth rate from its unconditional average value. This deviation will be treated as a stochastic process given by

$$u_t = \rho_u u_{t-1} + \phi z_{t-1} + \varphi_t, \qquad 0 \le \gamma < 1, \tag{2.76}$$

where φ_t is a white noise process and $|\rho_u| < 1$. This formulation allows the growth rate of the money stock to display persistence (if $\rho_u > 0$), respond to the real productivity shock z, and be subject to random disturbances through the realizations of φ_t.

Equation (2.67) is the economy's production function in which output deviations from the steady state are a linear function of the percentage deviations of the capital stock and labor supply from the steady state plus the productivity shock. Equation (2.68) is the resource constraint derived from the condition that output equals consumption plus investment. Deviations of the marginal product of capital are tied to deviations of the real return by (2.69). Equations (2.70)–(2.73) are derived from the representative household's first-order conditions for consumption, leisure, and money holdings. Finally, (2.74) relates the change in the deviation from steady state of real money balances to the inflation rate and the growth of the nominal money stock. To complete the specification, the exogenous disturbances for productivity and nominal money growth were given earlier by (2.75) and (2.76).

One conclusion follows immediately from inspecting this system. If $\Phi = b$, (2.65) shows that money no longer affects the marginal utility of consumption. Thus, money drops out of both (2.70) and (2.71) so that (2.67)–(2.71) can be solved for $\hat{y}$, $\hat{c}$, $\hat{r}$, $\hat{k}$, and $\hat{n}$ independently of the money supply process and inflation. This implies that superneutrality will characterize dynamics around the steady state as well as the steady state itself. Thus, the system will exhibit superneutrality along its dynamic adjustment path.[39]

Separability allows the real equilibrium to be solved independent of money and inflation, but it has more commonly been used in monetary economics to allow the study of inflation and money growth to be conducted independent of the real equilibrium. When $\Phi = b$, (2.73) and (2.74) constitute a two-equations system in inflation and real money balances, with u representing an exogenous random disturbance and $\hat{c}$ and $\hat{r}$ determined by (2.67)–(2.71) and exogenous to the determination of inflation and real money balances. Equation (2.73) can then be written as

$$E_t \pi_{t+1} \equiv E_t \hat{p}_{t+1} - \hat{p}_t = -(bi^{ss})\hat{m}_t + \chi_t = -(bi^{ss})(\hat{M}_t - \hat{p}_t) + \chi_t.$$

This is an expectational difference equation that can be solved for the equilibrium path of $\hat{p}$ for a given process for the nominal money supply and the exogenous variable $\chi_t \equiv [(bi^{ss})\hat{c}_t - \hat{r}_t]$. Models of this type have been widely employed in monetary economics, and they are studied further in chapter 4.

---

39. This result, for the preferences given by (2.64), generalizes the findings of Brock (1974) and Fischer (1979a).

A second conclusion revealed by the dynamic system is that when money does matter (i.e., when $b \neq \Phi$), it is only *anticipated* changes in money growth that matter. To see this, suppose $\rho_u = \phi = 0$, so that $u_t = \varphi_t$ is a purely unanticipated change in the growth rate of money that has no effect on anticipated future values of money growth. Now consider a positive realization of φ_t (nominal money growth is faster than average). This increases the nominal stock of money. If $\rho_u = \phi = 0$, future money growth rates are unaffected by the value of φ_t. This means that future expected inflation, $E_t \pi_{t+1}$, is also unaffected. Therefore, a permanent jump in the price level that is proportional to the unexpected rise in the nominal money stock leaving m_t unaffected also leaves (2.67)–(2.73) unaffected. From (2.74), for φ_t to have no effect on $\hat{m}_t$ requires that $\pi_t = \varphi_t$. So an unanticipated money growth rate disturbance has no real effects and simply leads to a one-period change in the inflation rate (and a permanent change in the price level). Unanticipated money doesn't matter.[40]

Now consider what happens when one continues to assume that $\phi = 0$ but allows ρ_u to differ from zero. In the United States, money growth displays positive serial correlation, so assume that $\rho_u > 0$. A positive shock to money growth ($\varphi_t > 0$) now has implications for the future growth rate of money. With $\rho_u > 0$, future money growth will be above average, so expectations of future inflation will rise. From (2.73), however, for real consumption and the expected real interest rate to remain unchanged in response to a rise in expected future inflation, current real money balances must fall. This means that $\hat{p}_t$ would need to rise more than in proportion to the rise in the nominal money stock. But when $\Omega_2 \neq 0$, the decline in $\hat{m}_t$ affects the first-order conditions given by (2.71) and (2.73), so the real equilibrium will not remain unchanged. Monetary disturbances have real effects by affecting the expected rate of inflation.

A positive monetary shock *increases* the nominal rate of interest. Monetary policy actions that increase the growth rate of money are usually thought to reduce nominal interest rates, at least initially. The negative effect of money on nominal interest rates is usually called the *liquidity effect*, and it arises if an increase in the nominal quantity of money also increases the real quantity of money because nominal interest rates would need to fall to ensure that real money demand also increased. However, in the MIU model, prices have been assumed to be perfectly flexible; the main effect of money growth rate shocks when $\rho_u > 0$ is to increase expected inflation and raise the nominal interest rate. Because prices are perfectly flexible, the monetary shock generates a jump in the price level immediately. The real quantity of money actually falls,

---

40. During the 1970s, macroeconomics was heavily influenced by a model developed by Lucas (1972), in which only unanticipated changes in the money supply had real effects. See chapter 5.

consistent with the decline in real money demand that occurs as a result of the increase in the nominal interest rate.

To actually determine how the equilibrium responds to money growth rate shocks and how the response depends quantitatively on ρ_u and ϕ, one must calibrate the parameters of the model and numerically solve for the rational-expectations equilibrium.

2.5.4   Calibration

Thirteen parameters appear in the equations that characterize behavior around the steady state: α, δ, ρ_z, σ_e^2, β, a, b, η, Φ, θ^{ss}, ρ_u, ϕ, σ_φ^2. Some of these parameters are common to standard real-business-cycle models; for example, Cooley and Prescott (1995, 22) reported values of, in the present notation, α (the share of capital income in total income), δ (the rate of depreciation of physical capital), ρ_z (the autoregressive coefficient in the productivity process), σ_e (the standard deviation of productivity innovations), and β (the subjective rate of time discount in the utility function). These values are based on a time period equal to three months (one quarter). Cooley and Prescott's values are adopted except for the depreciation rate δ; Cooley and Prescott calibrated $\delta = 0.012$ based on a model that explicitly incorporates growth. Here the somewhat higher value of 0.019 given in Cooley and Hansen (1995, 201) is used. The value of σ_e is set to match the standard deviation of quarterly HP-filtered log U.S. real GDP for the 1959–2008 period of 1.5 percent. For the period from 1984 to 2007, the average annual growth rate of $M1$ in the United States was 4.1 percent, and the growth rate of MZM was 7.2 percent. An annual rate of 4 percent (7 percent) would imply a quarterly value of 1.01 (1.017) for $1 + \theta^{ss}$, so set $1 + \theta^{ss} = 1.01$ to match $M1$. Estimating an AR(1) process for $M1$ growth yields $\rho_u = 0.75$ with a value of 0.9 for σ_φ, the standard deviation of innovations to the nominal money growth rate.[41] Various alternative values are considered for the autoregression coefficient for money growth, ρ_u, and the coefficient on the productivity shock, ϕ, to see how the implications of the model are affected by the manner in which money growth evolves.

The remaining parameters are those in the utility function. The value of Ψ can be chosen so that the steady-state value of n^{ss} is equal to one-third, as in Cooley and Prescott. The results of table 2.1 suggest a value of at least 7 for b for MZM, but estimates for $M1$ (not reported) suggest a lower value, closer to 3. The chapter appendix shows that the steady-state value of real money balances relative to consumption is equal to $(a\Upsilon^{ss}/(1-a))^{-1/b}$, $\Upsilon^{ss} = (1 + \theta^{ss} - \beta)/(1 + \theta^{ss})$. For real $M1$, this ratio in the data is about 0.8 when consumption is expressed at a quarterly rate. If

---

41. For the growth rate of MZM, one obtains $\rho_u = 0.68$ with a value of 4.1 for σ_φ.

$b = 3$, this would imply $a = 0.99$, and the ratio of real MZM to consumption is 2.64, which, for $b = 7$ implies $a = 0.04$. Thus, for the purposes of the simulation exercise, values of $a = 0.99$ and $b = 3$ are used.

The inverse of the intertemporal elasticity of substitution, Φ, is set equal to 2 in the benchmark simulations. With $b = 3$, this means $b - \Phi > 0$, and faster expected money growth will decrease employment and output. Finally, η is set equal to 1. With $n^{ss} = 1/3$, a value of $\eta = 1$ yields a labor supply elasticity of $[\eta n^{ss}/(1 - n^{ss})]^{-1} = 2$.

These parameter values are as follows:

Baseline Parameter Values

α	δ	β	Φ	η	a	b	$1 + \theta^{ss}$	ρ_z	σ_e	ρ_u	σ_φ
0.36	0.019	0.989	2	1	0.99	3	1.01	0.95	0.34	0.75	0.9

Using the information in this table, the steady-state values for the variables can be evaluated:

Steady-State Values at Baseline Parameter Values

$1 + r^{ss}$	$\frac{y^{ss}}{k^{ss}}$	$\frac{c^{ss}}{k^{ss}}$	$\frac{m^{ss}}{k^{ss}}$	$\frac{n^{ss}}{k^{ss}}$
1.011	0.084	0.065	0.051	0.021

The effect of money growth on the steady-state level of employment can be derived using (2.77) in the appendix. The elasticity of the steady-state labor supply with respect to the growth rate of the nominal money supply depends on the sign of u_{cm}; this in turn depends on the sign of $b - \Phi$. For the benchmark parameter values, this is positive. With Φ less than b, the marginal utility of consumption is increasing in real money balances. Hence, higher inflation decreases the marginal utility of consumption, increases the demand for leisure, and decreases the supply of labor (see (2.43)). If $b - \Phi$ is negative, higher inflation leads to a rise in labor supply and output. The dependence of the elasticity of labor with respect to inflation on the partial derivatives of the utility function in a general MIU model is discussed more fully by Wang and Yip (1992).

2.5.5 Simulation Results

Several Matlab programs for solving linear rational-expectations models numerically are publicly available (see the appendix and the programs available at ⟨http://people.ucsc.edu/~walshc/mtp3e⟩). Figure 2.3 shows that the magnitude of the effect of a one standard deviation monetary shock on output and labor is small, but the

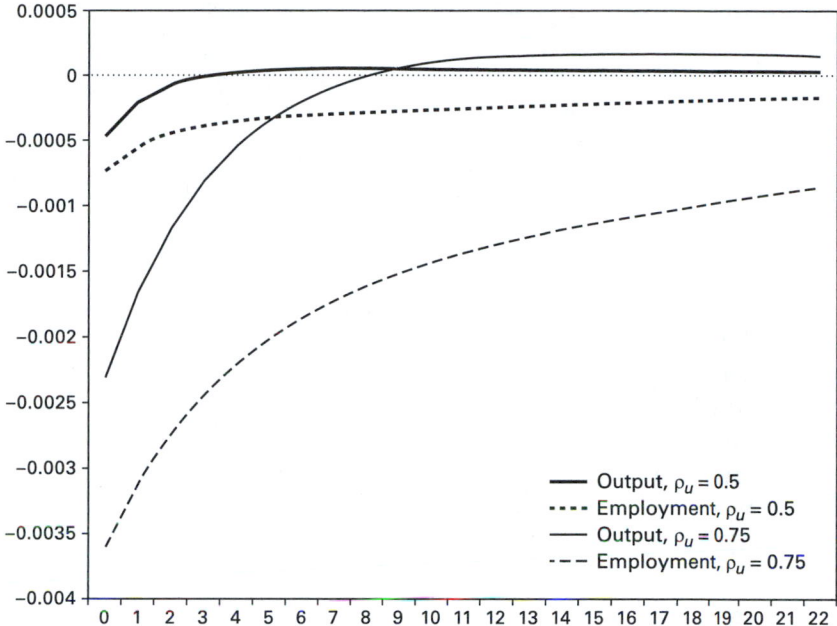

Figure 2.3
Response of output and employment to a positive money growth shock.

effects clearly depend on the degree of persistence in the money growth process.[42] Higher values of ρ_u generate larger effects on labor input and output.[43]

Figure 2.4 shows how the nominal interest rate response depends on ρ_u. A positive monetary shock *increases* the nominal rate of interest; when $\rho_u > 0$, money growth rate shocks increase expected inflation and raise the nominal interest rate, while the real quantity of money actually falls.

How do the properties of the model vary if money growth responds to productivity shocks? Table 2.2 illustrates the effects of varying ϕ, the response of money growth to the productivity shock.[44] The major effect of ϕ is on the behavior of inflation and the nominal rate of interest. When money growth does not respond to a productivity shock or when it decreases in response (i.e., when $\phi \leq 0$), output and inflation are negatively correlated, as the positive shock to productivity increases output

---

42. Recall that the transitional dynamics exhibit superneutrality when $\Phi = b$. In this case, neither output nor employment would be affected by the monetary shock.

43. Effects would also be larger if the model were calibrated to match a broader monetary aggregate by reducing a, increasing b, and increasing σ_φ.

44. When $\phi \neq 0$, the variance of the innovation to u is adjusted to keep the standard deviation of nominal money growth equal to 0.9, as in the benchmark case.

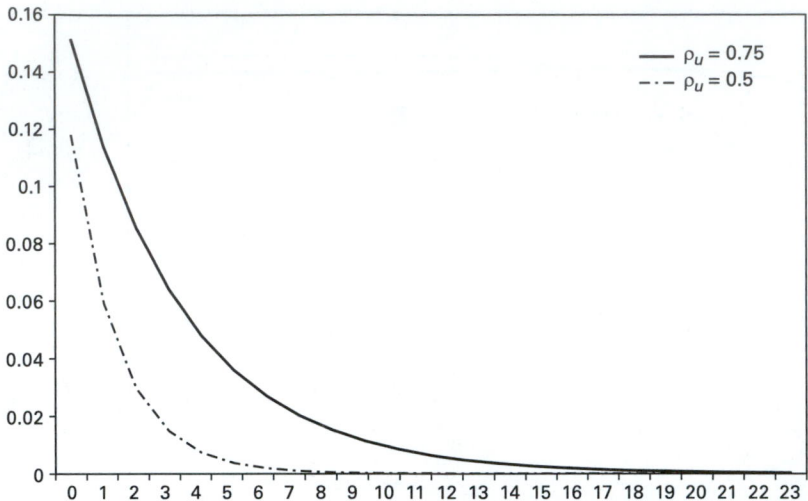

Figure 2.4
Response of the nominal interest rate to a positive money growth shock.

Table 2.2
Effects of the Money Process

	$\phi = -0.15$			$\phi = 0$			$\phi = 0.15$		
	s.d.	s.d. rel. to y	Corr. with y	s.d.	s.d. rel. to y	Corr. with y	s.d.	s.d. rel. to y	Corr. with y
y	1.51	1.00	1.00	1.49	1.00	1.00	1.48	1.00	1.00
n	0.58	0.38	0.02	0.58	0.39	−0.04	0.59	0.40	−0.10
c	0.91	0.60	0.88	0.88	0.59	0.87	0.86	0.58	0.86
x	4.22	2.79	0.94	4.25	2.84	0.94	4.28	2.90	0.94
r	0.04	0.02	0.19	0.04	0.02	0.17	0.04	0.02	0.14
m	7.86	5.20	0.90	3.59	2.40	0.24	6.35	4.30	−0.84
i	0.45	0.30	−0.88	0.22	0.15	−0.03	0.44	0.30	0.87
π	3.59	2.37	−0.11	3.23	2.16	−0.00	3.51	2.38	0.11

and reduces prices. When $\phi > 0$, however, the output-inflation correlation becomes positive.

When $\phi < 0$, a positive technology shock leads to lower expected money growth and inflation. Lower expected inflation raises real money balances, increases the marginal utility of consumption, and increases the labor supply when, as in the case here, $b > \Phi$. Hence, employment and output are slightly higher after a technology shock when $\phi < 0$ than when $\phi = 0$. When $\phi > 0$, a positive technology shock leads to higher expected inflation, and employment and output respond less than in the base case. Simulations reveal these differences to be small. Changes in the money growth process have their main effect on the behavior of the nominal interest rate and inflation. Both the sign and the magnitude of the correlation between these variables and output depends on the money growth process.

Consistent with the earlier discussion, the monetary shock φ_t affects the labor-leisure choice only when the nominal money growth rate process exhibits serial correlation ($\rho_u \neq 0$) or responds to the technology shock ($\phi \neq 0$). But for the base value of 0.5 for ρ_u, the effect of a money growth shock on n_t is very small. As (2.43) showed, variations in money holdings can affect the agent's labor-leisure choice by affecting the ratio of the marginal utility of leisure to the marginal utility of consumption. A positive realization of φ_t implies a rise in expected inflation when money growth is positively serially correlated ($\rho_u > 0$); this reduces holdings of real money balances (m), and with $\Phi = 2 < b$, lowers the marginal utility of consumption, and causes the agent to substitute toward leisure. As a consequence, labor supply and output fall. If $\Phi > b$, higher expected inflation (and therefore lower real money balances) would raise the marginal utility of consumption and lead to a decrease in leisure demand; labor supply and output would rise in this case.

2.6 Summary

Assuming that holdings of real money balances yield direct utility is a means of ensuring a positive demand for money so that, in equilibrium, money is held and has value. This assumption is clearly a shortcut; it does not address the issue of why money yields utility or why certain pieces of paper that we call money yield utility but other pieces of paper presumably do not.

The Sidrauski model, because it assumes that agents act systematically to maximize utility, allows welfare comparisons to be made. The model can be used to assess the welfare costs of inflation and to determine the optimal rate of inflation. Friedman's conclusion that the optimal inflation rate is the rate that produces a zero nominal rate of interest is quite robust (see chapter 4).

Finally, by developing a linear approximation to the basic money-in-the-utility function model (augmented to include a labor supply choice), it was shown how the effects of variations in the growth rate of the money supply on the short-run dynamic adjustment of the economy depended on the effect of money holdings on the marginal utility of consumption and leisure.

2.7   Appendix: Solving the MIU Model

The basic MIU model will be linearized around the nonstochastic steady state, so the first task is to derive the steady-state equilibrium. Setting all shocks to zero and all endogenous variables equal to constants, and using the functional forms assumed for production and utility, the Euler condition, the definition of the real return, the production function, the capital accumulation equation, and the goods market clearing condition imply

$$\lambda^{ss} = \beta(1 + r^{ss})\lambda^{ss} \Rightarrow 1 + r^{ss} = \frac{1}{\beta},$$

$$r^{ss} = \alpha\left(\frac{y^{ss}}{k^{ss}}\right) - \delta \Rightarrow \left(\frac{y^{ss}}{k^{ss}}\right) = \left(\frac{1}{\alpha}\right)\left(\frac{1}{\beta} - 1 + \delta\right)$$

$$y^{ss} = (k^{ss})^{\alpha}(n^{ss})^{1-\alpha} \Rightarrow \frac{n^{ss}}{k^{ss}} = \left(\frac{y^{ss}}{k^{ss}}\right)^{1/(1-\alpha)} = \left(\frac{\frac{1}{\beta} - 1 + \delta}{\alpha}\right)^{1/(1-\alpha)}$$

$$x^{ss} = k^{ss} - (1-\delta)k^{ss} = \delta k^{ss} \Rightarrow \frac{x^{ss}}{k^{ss}} = \delta$$

$$c^{ss} = y^{ss} - x^{ss} \Rightarrow \frac{c^{ss}}{k^{ss}} = \left(\frac{y^{ss}}{k^{ss}}\right) - \delta = \left(\frac{1}{\alpha}\right)\left[\frac{1}{\beta} - 1 + (1-\alpha)\delta\right].$$

These five equations pin down the steady-state values of the real return as well as the steady-state ratios of output, employment, investment, and consumption to the capital stock.

In the text, the intensive production function was defined as

$$\phi\left(\frac{k^{ss}}{n^{ss}}\right) = \left(\frac{k^{ss}}{n^{ss}}\right)^{\alpha}.$$

Then $y^{ss}/n^{ss} = \phi(k^{ss}/n^{ss})$, $c^{ss} = y^{ss} - \delta k^{ss} = [\phi - \delta(k^{ss}/n^{ss})]n^{ss} = \bar{\phi}n^{ss}$. Section 2.5.2 also made use of the fact that since $y = f = \phi n$, $f_n = \phi - (k^{ss}/n^{ss})\phi'$.

From

$$m^{ss} = \left(\frac{1 + \theta^{ss}}{1 + \pi^{ss}}\right) m^{ss},$$

one obtains $\pi^{ss} = \theta^{ss}$, and this then means

$$1 + r^{ss} = \frac{1 + i^{ss}}{1 + \pi^{ss}} \Rightarrow 1 + i^{ss} = (1 + r^{ss})(1 + \pi^{ss}) = \frac{1 + \theta^{ss}}{\beta},$$

or $i^{ss} = (1 + \theta^{ss} - \beta)/\beta$. The first-order condition for money holdings then becomes

$$\frac{u_m(c^{ss}, m^{ss}, 1 - n^{ss})}{\lambda^{ss}} = \left(\frac{m^{ss}}{c^{ss}}\right)^{-b} = \left(\frac{i^{ss}}{1 + i^{ss}}\right) = \left(\frac{a}{1 - a}\right)\left(\frac{1 + \theta^{ss} - \beta}{1 + \theta^{ss}}\right),$$

or

$$\left(\frac{m^{ss}}{c^{ss}}\right) = \left[\left(\frac{a}{1 - a}\right)\left(\frac{1 + \theta^{ss} - \beta}{1 + \theta^{ss}}\right)\right]^{-1/b}.$$

From the first-order condition for the household's choice of hours and the definition of the marginal utility of consumption,

$$\frac{u_l(c^{ss}, m^{ss}, 1 - n^{ss})}{\lambda^{ss}} = \frac{\Psi(1 - n^{ss})^{-\eta}}{a[a(c^{ss})^{1-b} + (1 - a)(m^{ss})^{1-b}]^{(b-\Phi)/(1-b)}(c^{ss})^{-b}} = (1 - \alpha)\left(\frac{y^{ss}}{n^{ss}}\right).$$

This can be rewritten as

$$\frac{\Psi(1 - n^{ss})^{-\eta}}{a\left[a + (1 - a)\left(\frac{m^{ss}}{c^{ss}}\right)^{1-b}\right]^{(b-\Phi)/(1-b)}(c^{ss})^{-\Phi}} = (1 - \alpha)\left(\frac{y^{ss}}{k^{ss}}\right)\left(\frac{k^{ss}}{n^{ss}}\right).$$

Rearranging, and using the earlier results, n^{ss} satisfies

$$(1 - n^{ss})^{-\eta}(n^{ss})^{\Phi} = \frac{H}{\Psi}, \qquad (2.77)$$

where

$$H = (1 - \alpha)\left(\frac{y^{ss}}{k^{ss}}\right)a\left[a + (1 - a)\left(\frac{m^{ss}}{c^{ss}}\right)^{1-b}\right]^{(b-\Phi)/(1-b)}\left(\frac{c^{ss}}{k^{ss}}\right)^{-\Phi}\left(\frac{k^{ss}}{n^{ss}}\right)^{1-\Phi}$$

$$= (1 - \alpha)a\left[a + (1 - a)\left(\frac{m^{ss}}{c^{ss}}\right)^{1-b}\right]^{(b-\Phi)/(1-b)}\left(\frac{c^{ss}}{k^{ss}}\right)^{-\Phi}\left(\frac{y^{ss}}{k^{ss}}\right)^{(\Phi-\alpha)/(1-\alpha)}$$

$$= a(1-\alpha)\left(\frac{\frac{1}{\beta}-1+\delta}{\alpha}\right)^{(\Phi-\alpha)/(1-\alpha)}\left[a+(1-a)\left(\frac{1+\theta^{ss}-\beta}{1+\theta^{ss}}\right)^{-(1-b)/b}\right]^{(b-\Phi)/(1-b)}$$

$$\times\left[\frac{\frac{1}{\beta}-1+(1-\alpha)\delta}{\alpha}\right]^{-\Phi}.$$

Only H depends on the rate of money growth (and so on the steady-state rate of inflation), and if $b = \Phi$, then H too is independent of $1 + \theta^{ss}$. In this case, n^{ss} and all other real variables (except m^{ss}) are independent of the rate of money growth.

The next step is to obtain the linear approximation for each equilibrium condition of the model so that the dynamic behavior as the economy fluctuates around the steady state can be studied.

2.7.1   The Linear Approximation

Three basic rules are employed in deriving the linear approximations (see Uhlig 1999). First, for two variables u and w,

$$uw = u^{ss}(1+\hat{u})w^{ss}(1+\hat{w}) \approx u^{ss}w^{ss}(1+\hat{u}+\hat{w}). \tag{2.78}$$

That is, assume that product terms like $\hat{u}\hat{w}$ are approximately equal to zero. Second,

$$u^a = (u^{ss})^a(1+\hat{u})^a \approx (u^{ss})^a(1+a\hat{u}), \tag{2.79}$$

which can be obtained as a repeated application of the first rule. Furthermore,

$$\ln u = \ln u^{ss}(1+\hat{u}) = \ln u^{ss} + \ln(1+\hat{u}) \approx \ln u^{ss} + \hat{u}. \tag{2.80}$$

Finally, since variables such as interest rates and inflation rates are already expressed in percentages, it seems natural to write them as absolute deviations from steady state. So, for example, $\hat{r}_t \equiv r_t - r^{ss}$. Assuming interest rates and inflation rates are small, (2.80) permits approximating the log deviation of $(1 + r_t)$ around the steady state by $\ln(1 + r_t) - \ln(1 + r^{ss}) \approx r_t - r^{ss} = \hat{r}_t$, and similarly for i_t and π_t. This also means $(1 + r_t)/(1 + r^{ss})$ is approximated by $1 + r_t - r^{ss} = 1 + \hat{r}_t$.[45] By applying these rules, one obtains a system of linear equations that characterizes the dynamic behavior of the MIU model for small deviations around its steady state.

---

45. This requires that terms such as r_t be small. Otherwise, one should use the exact Taylor series expansion. For example, in the case of $(1 + r_t)/(1 + r^{ss})$, this would be

$$\frac{1+r_t}{1+r^{ss}} \approx 1+\left(\frac{1}{1+r^{ss}}\right)(r_t - r^{ss}) = 1+\left(\frac{1}{1+r^{ss}}\right)\hat{r}_t.$$

With the calibration employed, $r^{ss} = 0.011$, so $1/(1 + r^{ss}) = \beta = 0.989$.

The Production Function

First, rewrite the production relationship (2.63) by replacing each variable with its steady-state value times 1 plus the percent deviation of its time t value from the steady state, noting that e^{z_t} can be approximated by $1 + z_t$ for small z_t:

$$y^{ss}(1 + \hat{y}_t) = (1 + z_t)(k^{ss})^a(1 + \hat{k}_{t-1})^{\alpha}(n^{ss})^{1-\alpha}(1 + \hat{n}_t)^{1-\alpha}.$$

Since

$$y^{ss} = (k^{ss})^a(n^{ss})^{1-\alpha},$$

divide both sides by y^{ss} to obtain

$$(1 + \hat{y}_t) = (1 + z_t)(1 + \hat{k}_{t-1})^{\alpha}(1 + \hat{n}_t)^{1-\alpha}$$

$$\approx 1 + \alpha \hat{k}_{t-1} + (1 - \alpha)\hat{n}_t + z_t,$$

or

$$\hat{y}_t = \alpha \hat{k}_{t-1} + (1 - \alpha)\hat{n}_t + z_t. \tag{2.81}$$

Goods Market Clearing

Goods market clearing requires that $y_t = c_t + x_t$, where x_t is investment. One can write this as

$$y^{ss}(1 + \hat{y}_t) = c^{ss}(1 + \hat{c}_t) + x^{ss}(1 + \hat{x}_t).$$

Since $y^{ss} = c^{ss} + x^{ss}$, it follows that

$$y^{ss}\hat{y}_t = c^{ss}\hat{c}_t + x^{ss}\hat{x}_t.$$

Dividing both sides by k^{ss} and noting that $x^{ss}/k^{ss} = \delta$ gives

$$\left(\frac{y^{ss}}{k^{ss}}\right)\hat{y}_t = \left(\frac{c^{ss}}{k^{ss}}\right)\hat{c}_t + \delta \hat{x}_t. \tag{2.82}$$

Capital Accumulation

The capital stock evolves according to $k_t = (1 - \delta)k_{t-1} + x_t$, or

$$k^{ss}(1 + \hat{k}_t) = (1 - \delta)k^{ss}(1 + \hat{k}_{t-1}) + x^{ss}(1 + \hat{x}_t),$$

which implies

$$\hat{k}_t = (1 - \delta)\hat{k}_{t-1} + \left(\frac{x^{ss}}{k^{ss}}\right)\hat{x}_t,$$

but $x^{ss}/k^{ss} = \delta$, so

$$\hat{k}_t = (1 - \delta)\hat{k}_{t-1} + \delta\hat{x}_t. \tag{2.83}$$

Labor Hours

The first-order condition for the choice of labor hours is

$$u_l(c_t, m_t, 1 - n_t) = \lambda_t f_n(k_{t-1}, n_t, z_t),$$

where λ_t is the marginal utility of consumption. Using the production and utility functions, this becomes

$$\frac{u_l}{\lambda_t} = \frac{\Psi(1 - n_t)^{-\eta}}{\lambda_t} = \frac{\Psi l_t^{-\eta}}{\lambda_t} = (1 - \alpha)\left(\frac{y_t}{n_t}\right).$$

Written in terms of deviations, this is

$$\frac{\Psi(l^{ss})^{-\eta}(1 + \hat{l}_t)^{-\eta}}{\lambda^{ss}(1 + \hat{\lambda}_t)} = (1 - \alpha)\left(\frac{y^{ss}}{n^{ss}}\right)\left(\frac{1 + \hat{y}_t}{1 + \hat{n}_t}\right).$$

But in the steady state,

$$\frac{\Psi(l^{ss})^{-\eta}}{\lambda^{ss}} = (1 - \alpha)\left(\frac{y^{ss}}{n^{ss}}\right),$$

so

$$\frac{(1 + \hat{l}_t)^{-\eta}}{(1 + \hat{\lambda}_t)} = \left(\frac{1 + \hat{y}_t}{1 + \hat{n}_t}\right),$$

or

$$(1 - \eta\hat{l}_t)(1 - \hat{\lambda}_t) \approx 1 - \eta\hat{l}_t - \hat{\lambda}_t \approx 1 + \hat{y}_t - \hat{n}_t.$$

From $l_t = 1 - n_t$,

$$l^{ss}(1 + \hat{l}_t) = 1 - n^{ss}(1 + \hat{n}_t) \Rightarrow \hat{l}_t = -\left(\frac{n^{ss}}{l^{ss}}\right)\hat{n}_t.$$

Hence,

$$-\eta\hat{l}_t - \hat{\lambda}_t = \eta\left(\frac{n^{ss}}{l^{ss}}\right)\hat{n}_t - \hat{\lambda}_t \approx \hat{y}_t - \hat{n}_t,$$

which can be written as

$$\left[1 + \eta\left(\frac{n^{ss}}{l^{ss}}\right)\right]\hat{n}_t = \hat{y}_t + \hat{\lambda}_t. \tag{2.84}$$

Marginal Utility of Consumption

The marginal utility of consumption is

$$\lambda_t = a[ac_t^{1-b} + (1-a)m_t^{1-b}]^{(b-\Phi)/(1-b)}c_t^{-b}.$$

Define

$$Q_t = ac_t^{1-b} + (1-a)m_t^{1-b}.$$

Then

$$\lambda_t = aQ_t^{(b-\Phi)/(1-b)}c_t^{-b},$$

or

$$\lambda^{ss}(1 + \hat{\lambda}_t) = a(Q^{ss})^{(b-\Phi)/(1-b)}(c^{ss})^{-b}\left[1 + \left(\frac{b-\Phi}{1-b}\right)\hat{q}_t\right](1 - b\hat{c}_t).$$

Since

$$\lambda^{ss} = a(Q^{ss})^{(b-\Phi)/(1-b)}(c^{ss})^{-b},$$

the right side of the previous equation can be approximated by

$$\lambda^{ss}\left[1 + \left(\frac{b-\Phi}{1-b}\right)\hat{q}_t - b\hat{c}_t\right],$$

so

$$\hat{\lambda}_t = \left(\frac{b-\Phi}{1-b}\right)\hat{q}_t - b\hat{c}_t.$$

To obtain an expression for $\hat{q}_t$, note that from the definition of Q_t,

$$(1 + \hat{q}_t) = \frac{a(c^{ss})^{1-b}}{Q^{ss}}(1 + \hat{c}_t)^{1-b} + \frac{(1-a)(m^{ss})^{1-b}}{Q^{ss}}(1 + \hat{m}_t)^{1-b}$$

$$= \gamma[1 + (1-b)\hat{c}_t] + (1-\gamma)[1 + (1-b)\hat{m}_t],$$

where

$$\gamma \equiv \frac{a(c^{ss})^{1-b}}{Q^{ss}}.$$

Hence,

$$\hat{q}_t = \gamma(1 - b)\hat{c}_t + (1 - \gamma)(1 - b)\hat{m}_t.$$

Combining these results,

$$\hat{\lambda}_t = \Omega_1 \hat{c}_t + \Omega_2 \hat{m}_t, \tag{2.85}$$

where $\Omega_1 = b(\gamma - 1) - \gamma\Phi$ and $\Omega_2 = (b - \Phi)(1 - \gamma)$. Note that if $b = \Phi$, $\hat{\lambda}_t = -b\hat{c}_t$.

Euler Condition

The Euler condition is

$$\lambda_t = \beta E_t(1 + r_t)\lambda_{t+1},$$

which, because $\beta = (1 + r^{ss})^{-1}$, can be written as

$$\lambda^{ss}(1 + \hat{\lambda}_t) = \beta\lambda^{ss}(1 + r_t)E_t(1 + \hat{\lambda}_{t+1}) = \lambda^{ss}\left(\frac{1 + r_t}{1 + r^{ss}}\right)E_t(1 + \hat{\lambda}_{t+1}).$$

Dividing both sides by λ^{ss}, recalling that $\hat{r}_t \equiv r_t - r^{ss}$, and using (2.78),

$$(1 + \hat{\lambda}_t) \approx (1 + \hat{r}_t + E_t\hat{\lambda}_{t+1}).$$

Then

$$\hat{\lambda}_t = \hat{r}_t + E_t\hat{\lambda}_{t+1}.$$

Marginal Product, Real Return Condition

Start with

$$1 + r_t = 1 - \delta + \alpha E_t\left(\frac{y_{t+1}}{k_t}\right).$$

Using the same general approach as applied to the other equations,

$$1 + r_t \approx 1 - \delta + \alpha\left(\frac{y^{ss}}{k^{ss}}\right)E_t(1 + \hat{y}_{t+1} - \hat{k}_t).$$

Since $r^{ss} = \alpha(y^{ss}/k^{ss}) - \delta$,

$$\hat{r}_t = r_t - r^{ss} = \alpha\left(\frac{y^{ss}}{k^{ss}}\right)E_t(\hat{y}_{t+1} - \hat{k}_t). \tag{2.86}$$

It is convenient to eliminate $E_t\hat{y}_{t+1}$ from this equation. This can be done by noting that the linearized production function implies that

$$E_t\hat{y}_{t+1} = \alpha\hat{k}_t + (1 - \alpha)E_t\hat{n}_{t+1} + \rho_z z_t,$$

after using the fact that $E_t z_{t+1} = \rho_z z_t$. The linearized labor supply condition and the Euler condition (derived above) imply

$$\left[1 + \eta\left(\frac{n^{ss}}{l^{ss}}\right)\right] E_t \hat{n}_{t+1} = E_t \hat{y}_{t+1} + E_t \hat{\lambda}_{t+1} = E_t \hat{y}_{t+1} + \hat{\lambda}_t - \hat{r}_t.$$

Hence, $E_t \hat{y}_{t+1}$ can be expressed as

$$E_t \hat{y}_{t+1} = \alpha \hat{k}_t + (1-\alpha) E_t \hat{n}_{t+1} + \rho_z z_t = \alpha \hat{k}_t + \left[\frac{1-\alpha}{1 + \eta\left(\frac{n^{ss}}{l^{ss}}\right)}\right] (E_t \hat{y}_{t+1} + \hat{\lambda}_t - \hat{r}_t) + \rho_z z_t.$$

Solving for expected future output,

$$E_t \hat{y}_{t+1} = \alpha \left[\frac{1 + \eta\left(\frac{n^{ss}}{l^{ss}}\right)}{\alpha + \eta\left(\frac{n^{ss}}{l^{ss}}\right)}\right] \hat{k}_t + \left(\frac{1-\alpha}{\alpha + \eta\left(\frac{n^{ss}}{l^{ss}}\right)}\right) (\hat{\lambda}_t - \hat{r}_t) + \left[\frac{1 + \eta\left(\frac{n^{ss}}{l^{ss}}\right)}{\alpha + \eta\left(\frac{n^{ss}}{l^{ss}}\right)}\right] \rho_z z_t.$$

Substituting this into the expression for the real rate of interest gives

$$(1 + \kappa)\hat{r}_t = -\kappa \eta \left(\frac{n^{ss}}{l^{ss}}\right) \hat{k}_t + \kappa \hat{\lambda}_t + \kappa \left(\frac{1 + \eta\left(\frac{n^{ss}}{l^{ss}}\right)}{1 - \alpha}\right) \rho_z z_t,$$

where

$$\kappa \equiv \alpha \left(\frac{y^{ss}}{k^{ss}}\right) \left(\frac{1-\alpha}{\alpha + \eta\left(\frac{n^{ss}}{l^{ss}}\right)}\right).$$

Money Holdings

The first-order condition for money holdings is

$$\frac{u_m(c_t, m_t, 1 - n_t)}{u_c(c_t, m_t, 1 - n_t)} = \left(\frac{i_t}{1 + i_t}\right).$$

From the specification of the utility function, the left side can be approximated as

$$\frac{u_m(c_t, m_t, 1 - n_t)}{u_c(c_t, m_t, 1 - n_t)} = \frac{(1-a)m_t^{-b}}{ac_t^{-b}} \approx \left(\frac{1-a}{a}\right) \left(\frac{m^{ss}}{c^{ss}}\right)^{-b} (1 - b\hat{m}_t + b\hat{c}_t)$$

$$= \left(\frac{i^{ss}}{1 + i^{ss}}\right)(1 - b\hat{m}_t + b\hat{c}_t).$$

Therefore,

$$\left(\frac{i^{ss}}{1 + i^{ss}}\right)(1 - b\hat{m}_t + b\hat{c}_t) \approx \left(\frac{i_t}{1 + i_t}\right),$$

or

$$-b\hat{m}_t + b\hat{c}_t \approx \left(\frac{1 + i^{ss}}{i^{ss}}\right)\left(\frac{i_t}{1 + i_t}\right) - 1.$$

But

$$\left(\frac{1 + i^{ss}}{i^{ss}}\right)\left(\frac{i_t}{1 + i_t}\right) - 1 = \frac{i_t(1 + i^{ss})}{i^{ss}(1 + i_t)} - 1,$$

so, ignoring second-order terms such as $i_t i^{ss}$,

$$\frac{i_t(1 + i^{ss})}{i^{ss}(1 + i_t)} - 1 \approx \left(\frac{i_t - i^{ss}}{i^{ss}}\right) = \left(\frac{1}{i^{ss}}\right)\hat{i}_t.$$

Therefore, the money demand equation is given by

$$\hat{m}_t = \hat{c}_t - \left(\frac{1}{b}\right)\left(\frac{1}{i^{ss}}\right)\hat{i}_t. \tag{2.87}$$

Real Money Growth

Since $\theta^{ss} = \pi^{ss}$, one can approximate

$$m_t = \left(\frac{1 + \theta_t}{1 + \pi_t}\right)m_{t-1}$$

by

$$m_t = \left(\frac{1 + \theta_t}{1 + \pi_t}\right)m_{t-1} = \left(\frac{1 + \theta_t}{1 + \pi_t}\right)\left(\frac{1 + \pi^{ss}}{1 + \theta^{ss}}\right)m_{t-1} \approx \left(\frac{1 + \hat{\theta}_t}{1 + \hat{\pi}_t}\right)m_{t-1},$$

or

$$m^{ss}(1 + \hat{m}_t) \approx (1 + \hat{\theta}_t - \hat{\pi}_t)m^{ss}(1 + \hat{m}_{t-1}),$$

where $\hat{\theta}_t \equiv \theta_t - \theta^{ss}$. Dividing both sides by m^{ss} and using (2.78) yields

$$\hat{m}_t \approx \hat{\theta}_t - \hat{\pi}_t + \hat{m}_{t-1} = u_t - \hat{\pi}_t + \hat{m}_{t-1}.$$

Fisher Equation

The relationship between the nominal interest rate, the real interest rate, and expected inflation is

$$1 + r_t = E_t\left(\frac{1 + i_t}{1 + \pi_{t+1}}\right),$$

or

$$r_t \approx i_t - E_t \pi_{t+1}.$$

Subtracting steady-state values from both sides,

$$\hat{r}_t = \hat{i}_t - E_t \hat{\pi}_{t+1}.$$

2.7.2   Collecting All Equations

The linearized model consists of twelve equations to determine the exogenous disturbances $\hat{z}_t$ and $\hat{u}_t$ and the ten endogenous variables $\hat{y}_t$, $\hat{k}_t$, $\hat{n}_t$, $\hat{x}_t$, $\hat{c}_t$, $\hat{\lambda}_t$, $\hat{r}_t$, $\hat{i}_t$, $\hat{\pi}_t$, $\hat{m}_t$. These twelve equations are:

$$z_t = \rho_z z_{t-1} + e_t$$

$$u_t = \rho_u u_{t-1} + \phi z_{t-1} + \varphi_t$$

$$\hat{y}_t = z_t + \alpha \hat{k}_{t-1} + (1-\alpha)\hat{n}_t$$

$$\left(\frac{y^{ss}}{k^{ss}}\right)\hat{y}_t = \left(\frac{c^{ss}}{k^{ss}}\right)\hat{c}_t + \delta\hat{x}_t$$

$$\hat{k}_t = (1-\delta)\hat{k}_{t-1} + \delta\hat{x}_t$$

$$\left[1 + \eta\left(\frac{n^{ss}}{l^{ss}}\right)\right]\hat{n}_t = \hat{y}_t + \hat{\lambda}_t$$

$$(1+\kappa)\hat{r}_t = -\kappa\eta\left(\frac{n^{ss}}{l^{ss}}\right)\hat{k}_t + \kappa\hat{\lambda}_t + \kappa\left(\frac{1 + \eta\left(\frac{n^{ss}}{l^{ss}}\right)}{1-\alpha}\right)\rho_z z_t$$

$$\hat{\lambda}_t = \Omega_1 \hat{c}_t + \Omega_2 \hat{m}_t$$

$$\hat{m}_t = \hat{c}_t - \left(\frac{1}{b}\right)\left(\frac{1}{i^{ss}}\right)\hat{i}_t$$

$$\hat{m}_t = u_t - \hat{\pi}_t + \hat{m}_{t-1}$$

$$\hat{\lambda}_t = \hat{r}_t + E_t\hat{\lambda}_{t+1}$$

$$\hat{i}_t = \hat{r}_t + E_t\hat{\pi}_{t+1},$$

where $\kappa = (1-\alpha)\alpha(y^{ss}/k^{ss})/(\alpha + \eta n^{ss}/l^{ss})$, $\Omega_1 = b(\gamma-1) - \gamma\Phi$,   and $\Omega_2 = (b-\Phi)(1-\gamma)$. Note that if $b = \Phi$ so that $\Omega_2 = 0$, the first eight equations can be solved for the behavior of the real variables z_t, $\hat{y}_t$, $\hat{k}_t$, $\hat{n}_t$, $\hat{x}_t$, $\hat{c}_t$, $\hat{\lambda}_t$, and $\hat{r}_t$, and the last four then determine u_t, $\hat{i}_t$, $\hat{\pi}_t$, and $\hat{m}_t$.

2.7.3 Solving Linear Rational-Expectations Models with Forward-Looking Variables

This sections provides a brief overview of the approach used to solve linear rational-expectations models numerically. The basic reference is Blanchard and Kahn (1980). General discussions can be found in Farmer (1993, ch. 3) or the user's guide in Hoover, Hartley, and Salyer (1998). See also Turnovsky (1995); Wickens (2008, app. 15.8); and Cochrane (2007).

Following the solutions methods of Blanchard and Kahn (1980), the basic specification of a linear rational-expectations model can be written in the form

$$A_1 \begin{bmatrix} X_{t+1} \\ E_t x_{t+1} \end{bmatrix} = A_2 \begin{bmatrix} X_t \\ x_t \end{bmatrix} + \begin{bmatrix} \psi_{t+1} \\ 0 \end{bmatrix},$$

where X are predetermined variables (n_1 in number) and x are nonpredetermined (forward-looking) variables (n_2 in number). Predetermined means that X_t is known at time t and not jointly determined with x_t, whereas x_t are endogenously determined at time t. Premultiplying both sides by A_1 inverse, one obtains

$$\begin{bmatrix} X_{t+1} \\ E_t x_{t+1} \end{bmatrix} = A \begin{bmatrix} X_t \\ x_t \end{bmatrix} + A_1^{-1} \begin{bmatrix} \psi_{t+1} \\ 0 \end{bmatrix},$$

where $A = A_1^{-1} A_2$. R. King and Watson (1998) consider the case in which A_1 is singular.

Blanchard and Kahn showed that the number of eigenvalues of A that are outside the unit circle must equal the number of forward-looking variables. Decompose A as $Q^{-1} \Lambda Q$, where Λ is a diagonal matrix of the eigenvalues of A, and Q is the corresponding matrix of eigenvectors, and order Λ so that λ_1 is the smallest and $\lambda_{n_1+n_2}$ is the largest eigenvalue. Then, the Blanchard and Kahn conditions require that the first n_1 eigenvalues must be inside the unit circle and the last n_2 must be outside the unit circle if the system is to have a unique stationary rational-expectations equilibrium. If there are fewer than n_2 eigenvalues outside the unit circle, multiple equilibria exist, and the system is said to be characterized by indeterminacy. If there are too many eigenvalues outside the unit circle, then no solution exists.

If a unique equilibrium exists, then the solution takes the form

$$X_{t+1} = MX_t + N\psi_{t+1}$$

and

$$x_t = CX_t.$$

Further details on solving the linearized forward-looking rational-expectations model of this chapter can be found at ⟨http://people.ucsc.edu/~walshc/mtp3e⟩.

Matlab Programs

Matlab code is available at ⟨http://people.ucsc.edu/~walshc/mtp3e⟩ to solve the MIU model. Programs are provided to use with (1) Harald Uhlig's tool kit (Uhlig 1999), (2) a modification of Paul Söderlind's programs for optimal policy based on the Blanchard-Kahn approach (Söderlind 1999), (3) Dynare (⟨http://www.cepremap.cnrs.fr/dynare/⟩), a suite of programs set up to solve linear models but also to derive second-order approximations to nonlinear models, and (4) an approach based on a linear regulator problem (Gerali and Lippi 2003).

2.8 Problems

1. The MIU model of section 2.2 implied that the marginal rate of substitution between money and consumption was set equal to $i_t/(1 + i_t)$ (see (2.12)). That model assumed that agents entered period t with resources ω_t and used those to purchase capital, consumption, nominal bonds, and money. The real value of these money holdings yielded utility in period t. Assume instead that money holdings chosen in period t do not yield utility until period $t + 1$. Utility is $\sum \beta^i U(c_{t+i}, M_{t+i}/P_{t+i})$ as before, but the budget constraint takes the form

$$\omega_t = c_t + \frac{M_{t+1}}{P_t} + b_t + k_t,$$

and the household chooses c_t, k_t, b_t, and M_{t+1} in period t. The household's real wealth ω_t is given by

$$\omega_t = f(k_{t-1}) + (1 - \delta)k_{t-1} + (1 + r_{t-1})b_{t-1} + m_t.$$

Derive the first-order condition for the household's choice of M_{t+1} and show that

$$\frac{U_m(c_{t+1}, m_{t+1})}{U_c(c_{t+1}, m_{t+1})} = i_t.$$

(Suggested by Kevin Salyer.)

2. (Carlstrom and Fuerst 2001) Assume that the representative household's utility depends on consumption and the level of real money balances available for spending on consumption. Let A_t/P_t be the real stock of money that enters the utility function. If capital is ignored, the household's objective is to maximize $\sum \beta^i U(c_{t+i}, A_{t+i}/P_{t+i})$ subject to the budget constraint

$$Y_t + \frac{M_{t-1}}{P_t} + \tau_t + \frac{(1 + i_{t-1})B_{t-1}}{P_t} = C_t + \frac{M_t}{P_t} + \frac{B_t}{P_t},$$

where income Y_t is treated as an exogenous process. Assume that the stock of money that yields utility is the real value of money holdings after bonds have been purchased but before income has been received or consumption goods have been purchased:

$$\frac{A_t}{P_t} = \frac{M_{t-1}}{P_t} + \tau_t + \frac{(1 + i_{t-1})B_{t-1}}{P_t} - \frac{B_t}{P_t}.$$

a. Derive the first-order conditions for B_t and for A_t.

b. How do these conditions differ from those obtained in the text?

3. Suppose $W = \sum \beta^t (\ln c_t + m_t e^{-\gamma m_t})$, $\gamma > 0$, and $\beta = 0.95$. Assume that the production function is $f(k_t) = k_t^{0.5}$ and $\delta = 0.02$. What rate of inflation maximizes steady-state welfare? How do real money balances at the welfare-maximizing rate of inflation depend on γ?

4. Suppose that the utility function (2.64) is replaced by

$$u(c_t, m_t, l_t) = \left(\frac{1}{1 - \Phi}\right) \{[ac_t^{1-b} + (1 - a)m_t^{1-b}]^{1/(1-b)} l_t^{1-\eta}\}^{1-\Phi}.$$

a. Derive the first-order conditions for the household's optimal money holdings.

b. Show how (2.70) and (2.71) are altered with this specification of the utility function.

5. Suppose the utility function (2.64) is replaced by

$$u(c_t, m_t, 1 - n_t) = \frac{[aC_t^{1-b} + (1 - a)m_t^{1-b}]^{(1-\Phi)/(1-b)}}{1 - \Phi} \left[\frac{(1 - n_t)^{1-\eta}}{1 - \eta}\right].$$

a. Derive the first-order conditions for the household's optimal money holdings.

b. Show how (2.70) and (2.71) are altered with this specification of the utility function.

6. Suppose a nominal interest rate of i_m is paid on money balances. These payments are financed by a combination of lump-sum taxes and printing money. Let a be the fraction financed by lump-sum taxes. The government's budget identity is $\tau_t + v_t = i_m m_t$, with $\tau_t = a i_m m_t$ and $v = \theta m_t$. Using Sidrauski's model, do the following:

a. Show that the ratio of the marginal utility of money to the marginal utility of consumption depends on $r + \pi - i_m = i - i_m$. Explain why.

b. Show how $i - i_m$ is affected by the method used to finance the interest payments on money. Explain the economics behind your result.

7. Suppose the representative agent does not treat τ_t as a lump-sum transfer but instead assumes the transfer will be proportional to her own holdings of money (since in equilibrium, $\tau = \theta m$). Solve for the agent's demand for money. What is the welfare cost of inflation?

8. Suppose money is a productive input into production so that the aggregate production function becomes $y = f(k, m)$. Incorporate this modification into the model of section 2.2. Is money still superneutral? Explain.

9. Consider the following two alternative specifications for the demand for money given by (2.37) and (2.38).

a. Using (2.37), calculate the welfare cost as a function of η.

b. Using (2.38), calculate the welfare cost as a function of ξ.

10. In Sidrauski's MIU model augmented to include a variable labor supply, money is superneutral if the representative agent's preferences are given by

$$\sum \beta^i u(c_{t+i}, m_{t+i}, l_{t+i}) = \sum \beta^i (c_{t+i} m_{t+i})^b l_{t+i}^d$$

but not if they are given by

$$\sum \beta^i u(c_{t+i}, m_{t+i}, l_{t+i}) = \sum \beta^i (c_{t+i} + k m_{t+i})^b l_{t+i}^d.$$

Discuss. (Assume output depends on capital and labor and the aggregate production function is Cobb-Douglas.)

11. In the limiting case with $\Phi = b = 1$, preferences over consumption and money holdings are log linear $(u = a \ln c_t + (1 - a) \ln m_t + \Psi l_t^{1-\eta}/(1 - \eta))$. S. Fischer (1979b) showed that the transition paths are independent of the money supply in this case since the marginal rate of substitution between leisure and consumption is independent of real money balances. Write down the equilibrium conditions for this case, and show that the model dichotomizes into a real sector that determines output, consumption, and investment, and a monetary sector that determines the price level and the nominal interest rate.

12. For the model of section 2.5, is the response of output and employment to u_t increasing or decreasing in b? Explain. (Use the programs available at ⟨http://people.ucsc.edu/~walshc/mtp3e⟩ to answer this question.)

13. For the model of section 2.5, is the response of output and employment to u_t increasing or decreasing in a? Explain. (Use the programs available at ⟨http://people.ucsc.edu/~walshc/mtp3e⟩ to answer this question.)

3 Money and Transactions

3.1 Introduction

The previous chapter introduced a role for money by assuming that individuals derived utility directly from holding real money balances. Therefore, real money balances appeared in the utility function alongside consumption and leisure. Yet money is usually thought of as yielding utility indirectly through use; it is valued because it is useful in facilitating transactions to obtain the consumption goods that do directly provide utility. As described by Clower (1967), goods buy money, and money buys goods, but goods don't buy goods. And because goods don't buy goods, a monetary medium of exchange that serves to aid the process of transacting will have value.

A medium of exchange that facilitates transactions yields utility indirectly by allowing certain transactions to be made that would not otherwise occur or by reducing the costs associated with transactions. The demand for money is then determined by the nature of the economy's transactions technology. The first formal models of money demand that emphasized the role of transaction costs were due to Baumol (1952) and Tobin (1956).[1] Niehans (1978) developed a systematic treatment of the theory of money in which transaction costs play a critical role. These models were partial equilibrium models, focusing on the demand for money as a function of the nominal interest rate and income. In keeping with the approach used in examining money-in-the-utility (MIU) models, the focus in this chapter is on *general* equilibrium models in which the demand for money arises from its use in carrying out transactions.

The first models examined in this chapter are ones in which real resources and money are used to produce transaction services, with these services being required to purchase consumption goods. These real resources can take the form of either time or goods. Most of this chapter, however, is devoted to the study of models that

---

1. Jovanovic (1982) and D. Romer (1986) embedded the Baumol-Tobin model in general equilibrium frameworks.

impose a rigid restriction on the nature of transactions. Rather than allowing substitutability between time and money in carrying out transactions, *cash-in-advance* (CIA) models simply require that money balances be held to finance certain types of purchases; without money, these purchases cannot be made. CIA models, like MIU models, assume that money is special; unlike other financial assets, it either yields direct utility and therefore belongs in the utility function, or it has unique properties that allow it to be used to facilitate transactions. This chapter concludes with a look at some recent work based on search theory to explain how the nature of transactions gives rise to money.

3.2 Resource Costs of Transacting

A direct approach to modeling the role of money in facilitating transactions is to assume that the purchase of goods requires the input of transaction services. First a model is considered in which theses services are produced using inputs of money and time. Then an alternative approach is studied in which there are real resource costs in terms of goods that are incurred in purchasing consumption goods. Larger holdings of money allow the household to reduce the resource costs of producing transaction services.

3.2.1 Shopping-Time Models

When transaction services are produced by time and money, the consumer must balance the opportunity cost of holding money against the value of leisure in deciding how to combine time and money to purchase consumption goods. The production technology used to produce transaction services determines how much time must be spent "shopping" for given levels of consumption and money holdings. Higher levels of money holdings reduce the time needed for shopping, thereby increasing the individual agent's leisure. When leisure enters the utility function of the representative agent, shopping-time models provide a link between the MIU approach and models of money that focus more explicitly on transaction services and money as a medium of exchange.[2]

Suppose that purchasing consumption requires transaction services ψ, with units chosen so that consumption of c requires transaction services $\psi = c$. These transaction services are produced with inputs of real cash balances $m \equiv M/P$ and shopping time n^s:

---

2. See Brock (1974) for an earlier use of a shopping-time model to motivate an MIU approach. The use of a shopping-time approach to the study of the demand for money is presented in McCallum and Goodfriend (1987) and Croushore (1993).

$$\psi = \psi(m, n^s) = c, \tag{3.1}$$

where $\psi_m \geq 0$, $\psi_{n^s} \geq 0$ and $\psi_{mm} \leq 0$, $\psi_{n^s n^s} \leq 0$. This specification assumes that it is the agent's holdings of *real* money balances that produce transaction services; a change in the price level requires a proportional change in nominal money holdings to generate the same level of real consumption purchases, holding shopping time n^s constant. Rewriting (3.1) in terms of the shopping time required for given levels of consumption and money holdings,

$$n^s = g(c, m), \qquad g_c > 0, g_m \leq 0.$$

Household utility is assumed to depend on consumption and leisure: $v(c, l)$. Leisure is equal to $l = 1 - n - n^s$, where n is time spent in market employment and n^s is time spent shopping. Total time available is normalized to equal 1. With shopping time n^s an increasing function of consumption and a decreasing function of real money holdings, time available for leisure is $1 - n - g(c, m)$. Now define a function

$$u(c, m, n) \equiv v[c, 1 - n - g(c, m)]$$

that gives utility as a function of consumption, labor supply, and money holdings. Thus, a simple shopping-time model can motivate the appearance of an MIU function and, more important, can help determine the properties of the partial derivatives of the function u with respect to m. By placing restrictions on the partial derivatives of the shopping time production function $g(c, m)$, one potentially can determine what restrictions might be placed on the utility function $u(c, m, n)$. For example, if the marginal productivity of money goes to zero for some finite level of real money balances $\bar{m}$, that is, $\lim_{m \to \bar{m}} g_m = 0$, then this property will carry over to u_m.

In the MIU model, higher expected inflation lowered money holdings, but the effect on leisure and consumption depended on the signs of u_{lm} and u_{cm}.[3] The shopping-time model implies that $u_m = -v_l g_m \geq 0$, so

$$u_{cm} = (v_{ll} g_c - v_{cl}) g_m - v_l g_{cm}. \tag{3.2}$$

The sign of u_{cm} will depend on such factors as the effect of variations in leisure time on the marginal utility of consumption (v_{cl}) and the effect of variations in consumption on the marginal productivity of money in reducing shopping time (g_{cm}). In the benchmark MIU model, u_{cm} was taken to be positive.[4] Relating u_{cm} to the partials of the underlying utility function v and the transaction production function g can

---

3. This is a statement about the partial equilibrium effect of inflation on the representative agent's decision. In general equilibrium, consumption and leisure are independent of inflation in models that display superneutrality.

4. This corresponded to $b > \Phi$ in the benchmark utility function used in chapter 2.

suggest whether this assumption was reasonable. From (3.2), the assumption of diminishing marginal utility of leisure ($v_{ll} \leq 0$) and $g_m \leq 0$ implies that $v_{ll}g_cg_m \geq 0$. If greater consumption raises the marginal productivity of money in reducing shopping time ($g_{cm} \leq 0$), then $-v_lg_{cm} \geq 0$ as well. Wang and Yip (1992) characterized the situation in which these two dominate, so that $u_{cm} \geq 0$ as the transaction services version of the MIU model. In this case, the MIU model implies that a rise in expected inflation would lower m and u_c, and this would lower consumption, labor supply, and output (see section 2.3.2). The reduction in labor supply is reinforced by the fact that $u_{lm} = -v_{ll}g_m < 0$, so that the reduction in m raises the marginal utility of leisure.[5] If consumption and leisure are strong substitutes so that $v_{cl} \leq 0$, then u_{cm} could be negative, a situation Wang and Yip described as corresponding to an asset substitution model. With $u_{cm} < 0$, a monetary injection that raises expected inflation will increase consumption, labor supply, and output.

The household's intertemporal problem analyzed in chapter 2 for the MIU model can be easily modified to incorporate a shopping time role for money. The household's objective is to maximize

$$\sum_{i=0}^{\infty} \beta^i v[c_{t+i}, 1 - n_{t+i} - g(c_{t+i}, m_{t+i})], \qquad 0 < \beta < 1$$

subject to

$$f(k_{t-1}, n_t) + \tau_t + (1 - \delta)k_{t-1} + \frac{(1 + i_{t-1})b_{t-1} + m_{t-1}}{1 + \pi_t} = c_t + k_t + b_t + m_t, \qquad (3.3)$$

where f is a standard neoclassical production function, k is the capital stock, δ is the depreciation rate, b and m are real bond and money holdings, and τ is a real lump-sum transfer from the government.[6] Defining $a_t = \tau_t + [(1 + i_{t-1})b_{t-1} + m_{t-1}]/(1 + \pi_t)$, the household's decision problem can be written in terms of the value function $V(a_t, k_{t-1})$:

$$V(a_t, k_{t-1}) = \max\{v[c_t, 1 - n_t - g(c_t, m_t)] + \beta V(a_{t+1}, k_t)\},$$

where the maximization is subject to the constraints $f(k_{t-1}, n_t) + (1 - \delta)k_{t-1} + a_t = c_t + k_t + b_t + m_t$ and $a_{t+1} = \tau_{t+1} + [(1 + i_t)b_t + m_t]/(1 + \pi_{t+1})$. Proceeding as in chapter 2 by using these two constraints to eliminate k_t and a_{t+1} from the expression

5. I thank Henrik Jensen for pointing this out.

6. Note that it is assumed that transaction services are needed only for the purchase of consumption goods and not for the purchase of capital goods. In the next section, alternative treatments of investment and the transaction technology are shown to have implications for the steady state.

for the value function, the necessary first-order conditions for consumption, real money holdings, real bond holdings, and labor supply are

$$v_c - v_l g_c - \beta V_k(a_{t+1}, k_t) = 0 \tag{3.4}$$

$$-v_l g_m + \beta \frac{V_a(a_{t+1}, k_t)}{1 + \pi_{t+1}} - \beta V_k(a_{t+1}, k_t) = 0 \tag{3.5}$$

$$-v_l + \beta V_k(a_{t+1}, k_t) f_n(k_{t-1}, n_t) = 0 \tag{3.6}$$

$$\beta \left(\frac{1 + i_t}{1 + \pi_{t+1}} \right) V_a(a_{t+1}, k_t) - \beta V_k(a_{t+1}, k_t) = 0, \tag{3.7}$$

and the envelope theorem yields

$$V_a(a_t, k_{t-1}) = \beta V_k(a_{t+1}, k_t) \tag{3.8}$$

$$V_k(a_t, k_{t-1}) = \beta V_k(a_{t+1}, k_t)[f_k(k_{t-1}, n_t) + 1 - \delta]. \tag{3.9}$$

Letting w_t denote the marginal product of labor (i.e., $w_t = f_n(k_{t-1}, n_t)$), (3.6) and (3.8) yield $v_l = w_t V_a(a_t, k_{t-1})$. This implies that (3.4) can be written as

$$v_c(c_t, l_t) = V_a(a_t, k_{t-1})[1 + w_t g_c(c_t, m_t)]. \tag{3.10}$$

The marginal utility of consumption is set equal to the marginal utility of wealth, $V_a(a_t, k_{t-1})$, plus the cost, in utility units, of the marginal time needed to purchase consumption. Thus, the total cost of consumption includes the value of the shopping time involved. A marginal increase in consumption requires an additional g_c in shopping time. The value of this time in terms of goods is obtained by multiplying g_c by the real wage w, and its value in terms of utility is $V_a(a, k) w g_c$.

With $g_m \leq 0$, $v_l g_m = V_a w g_m$ is the value in utility terms of the shopping time savings that results from additional holdings of real money balances. Equations (3.5) and (3.8) imply that money will be held to the point where the marginal net benefit, equal to the value of shopping time savings plus the discounted value of money's wealth value in the next period, or $-v_l g_m + \beta V_a(a_{t+1}, k_t)/(1 + \pi_{t+1})$, just equals the net marginal utility of wealth. The first-order condition for optimal money holdings, together with (3.7) and (3.8), implies

$$-v_l g_m = \beta V_k(a_{t+1}, k_t) - \beta \frac{V_a(a_{t+1}, k_t)}{1 + \pi_{t+1}}$$

$$= V_a(a_t, k_{t-1}) \left[1 - \beta \frac{V_a(a_{t+1}, k_t)/V_a(a_t, k_{t-1})}{1 + \pi_{t+1}} \right]$$

$$= V_a(a_t, k_{t-1}) \left[1 - \left(\frac{1}{1 + i_t} \right) \right]$$

$$= V_a(a_t, k_{t-1}) \left(\frac{i_t}{1 + i_t} \right), \tag{3.11}$$

where i_t is the nominal rate of interest and, using (3.7) and (3.8),[7]

$$\frac{V_a(a_{t+1}, k_t)}{V_a(a_t, k_{t-1})} = \frac{1 + \pi_{t+1}}{1 + i_t}.$$

Further insight can be gained by using (3.6) and (3.8) to note that (3.11) can also be written as

$$-w_t g_m = \frac{i_t}{1 + i_t}. \tag{3.12}$$

The left side of this equation is the value of the transaction time saved by holding additional real money balances. At the optimal level of money holdings, this is just equal to the opportunity cost of holding money, $i/(1 + i)$.

Since no social cost of producing money has been introduced, optimality would require that the private marginal product of money, g_m, be driven to zero. Equation (3.12) implies that $g_m = 0$ if and only if $i = 0$; one thus obtains the standard result for the optimal rate of inflation, as seen earlier in the MIU model.

The chief advantage of the shopping-time approach as a means of motivating the presence of money in the utility function is its use in tying the partials of the utility function with respect to money to the specification of the production function relating money, shopping time, and consumption. But this representation of the medium-of-exchange role of money is also clearly a shortcut. The transaction services production function $\psi(m, n^s)$ is simply postulated; this approach does not help to determine what constitutes money. Why, for example, do certain types of green paper facilitate transactions (at least in the United States), whereas yellow pieces of paper don't? Section 3.4 reviews models based on search theory that attempt to derive money demand from a more primitive specification of the transaction process.

---

7. Note that (3.11) implies $-v_l g_m / V_a = i/(1 + i)$. The left side is the value of the shopping-time savings from holding additonal real money balances relative to the marginal utility of income. The right side is the opportunity cost of holding money. This expression can be compared to the result from the MIU model, which showed that the marginal utility of real balances relative to the marginal utility of income would equal $i/(1 + i)$. In the MIU model, however, the marginal utility of income and the marginal utility of consumption were equal.

3.2.2 Real Resource Costs

An alternative approach to the CIA or shopping-time models is to assume that transaction costs take the form of real resources that are used up in the process of exchange (Brock 1974; 1990). An increase in the volume of goods exchanged leads to a rise in transaction costs, whereas higher average real money balances for a given volume of transactions lower costs. In a shopping-time model, these costs are time costs and so enter the utility function indirectly by affecting the time available for leisure.

If goods must be used up in transacting, the household's budget constraint must be modified, for example, by adding a transaction cost term $\Upsilon(c, m)$ that depends on the volume of transactions (represented by c) and the level of money holdings. The budget constraint (3.18) then becomes

$$f(k_{t-1}) + (1 - \delta)k_{t-1} + \tau_t + (1 + r_{t-1})b_{t-1} + \frac{m_{t-1}}{1 + \pi_t} \geq c_t + m_t + b_t + k_t + \Upsilon(c_t, m_t).$$

Feenstra (1986) considered a variety of transaction costs formulations and showed that they all lead to the presence of a function involving c and m appearing on the right side of the budget constraint. He also showed that transaction costs satisfy the following condition for all $c, m \geq 0$: Υ is twice continuously differentiable and $\Upsilon \geq 0$; $\Upsilon(0, m) = 0$; $\Upsilon_c \geq 0$; $\Upsilon_m \leq 0$; $\Upsilon_{cc}, \Upsilon_{mm} \geq 0$; $\Upsilon_{cm} \leq 0$; and $c + \Upsilon(c, m)$ is quasi-convex, with expansion paths having a non-negative slope. These conditions all have intuitive meaning: $\Upsilon(0, m) = 0$ means that the consumer bears no transaction costs if consumption is zero. The sign restrictions on the partial derivatives reflect the assumptions that transaction costs rise at an increasing rate as consumption increases and that money has positive but diminishing marginal productivity in reducing transaction costs. The assumption that $\Upsilon_{cm} \leq 0$ means that the marginal transaction costs of additional consumption do not increase with money holdings. Expansion paths with non-negative slopes imply that $c + \Upsilon$ increases with income. Positive money holdings can be ensured by the additional assumption that $\lim_{m \to 0} \Upsilon_m(c, m) = -\infty$; that is, money is essential.

Now consider how the MIU approach compares to a transaction cost approach. Suppose a function $W(x, m)$ has the following properties: for all $x, m \geq 0$; W is twice continuously differentiable and satisfies $W \geq 0$; $W(0, m) = 0$; $W(x, m) \to \infty$ as $x \to \infty$ for fixed m; $W_m \geq 0$; $0 \leq W_x \leq 1$; $W_{xx} \leq 0$; $W_{mm} \leq 0$; $W_{xm} \geq 0$; W is quasi-concave with Engel curves with a non-negative slope.

Now simplify by dropping capital and consider the following two static problems representing simple transaction cost and MIU approaches:

$$\max \ U(c) \text{ subject to } c + \Upsilon(c, m) + b + m = y \tag{3.13}$$

and

$$\max\ V(x,m)\ \text{subject to}\ x + b + m = y, \tag{3.14}$$

where $V(x,m) = U[W(x,m)]$. These two problems are equivalent if (c^*,b^*,m^*) solves (3.13) if and only if (x^*,b^*,m^*) solves (3.14) with $x^* = c^* + \Upsilon(c^*,m^*)$. Feenstra (1986) showed that equivalence holds if the functions $\Upsilon(c,m)$ and $W(x,m)$ satisfy the stated conditions.

This "functional equivalence" (Wang and Yip 1992) between the transaction cost and MIU approaches suggests that conclusions derived within one framework will also hold under the alternative approach. However, this equivalence is obtained by redefining variables. So, for example, the "consumption" variable x in the utility function is equal to consumption *inclusive* of transaction costs (i.e., $x = c + \Upsilon(c,m)$) and is therefore not independent of money holdings. At the very least, the appropriate definition of the consumption variable needs to be considered if one attempts to use either framework to draw implications for actual macroeconomic time series.[8]

3.3 CIA Models

A direct approach to generating a role for money, proposed by Clower (1967) and developed formally by Grandmont and Younes (1972) and Lucas (1980a), captures the role of money as a medium of exchange by requiring explicitly that money be used to purchase goods. Such a requirement can also be viewed as replacing the substitution possibilities between time and money highlighted in the shopping-time model with a transaction technology in which shopping time is zero if $M/P \geq c$ and infinite otherwise (McCallum 1990a). This specification can be represented by assuming that the individual faces, in addition to a standard budget constraint, a cash-in-advance (CIA) constraint.[9]

The exact form of the CIA constraint depends on which transactions or purchases are subject to the CIA requirements. For example, both consumption goods and investment goods might be subject to the requirement. Or only consumption might be subject to the constraint. Or only a subset of all consumption goods may require cash for their purchase. The constraint will also depend on what constitutes cash. Can bank deposits that earn interest, for example, also be used to carry out transactions? The exact specification of the transactions subject to the CIA constraint can be important.

---

8. When distortionary taxes are introduced, Mulligan and Sala-i-Martin (1997) showed the functional equivalence between the two approaches can depend on whether money is required to pay taxes.

9. Boianovsky (2002) discussed the early use in the 1960s of a CIA constraint by the Brazilian economist Mario Simonsen.

Timing assumptions also are important in CIA models. In Lucas (1982), agents are able to allocate their portfolios between cash and other assets at the start of each period, after observing any current shocks but prior to purchasing goods. This timing is often described by saying that the asset market opens first and then the goods market opens. If there is a positive opportunity cost of holding money and the asset market opens first, agents will only hold an amount of money that is just sufficient to finance their desired level of consumption. In Svensson (1985), the goods market opens first. This implies that agents have available for spending only the cash carried over from the previous period, and so cash balances must be chosen before agents know how much spending they will wish to undertake. For example, if uncertainty is resolved *after* money balances are chosen, an agent may find that he is holding cash balances that are too low to finance his desired spending level. Or he may be left with more cash than he needs, thereby forgoing interest income.

To understand the structure of CIA models, the next section reviews a simplified version of a model due to Svensson (1985). The simplification involves eliminating uncertainty. Once the basic framework has been reviewed, however, a stochastic CIA model is considered as a means of studying the role of money in a dynamic stochastic general equilibrium (DSGE) model in which business cycles are generated by both real productivity shocks and shocks to the growth rate of money. Developing a linearized version of the model will serve to illustrate how the CIA approach differs from the MIU approach discussed in chapter 2.

3.3.1 The Certainty Case

This section develops a simple cash-in-advance model. Issues arising in the presence of uncertainty are postponed until section 3.3.2. The timing of transactions and markets follows Svensson (1985), although the alternative timing used by Lucas (1982) is also discussed. After the model and its equilibrium conditions are set out, the steady state is examined and the welfare costs of inflation in a CIA model are discussed.

The Model

Consider the following representative agent model. The agent's objective is to chose a path for consumption and asset holdings to maximize

$$\sum_{t=0}^{\infty} \beta^t u(c_t) \tag{3.15}$$

for $0 < \beta < 1$, where $u(.)$ is bounded, continuously differentiable, strictly increasing, and strictly concave, and the maximization is subject to a sequence of CIA and budget constraints. The agent enters the period with money holdings M_{t-1} and receives a lump-sum transfer T_t (in nominal terms). If goods markets open first, the CIA constraint takes the form

$P_t c_t \leq M_{t-1} + T_t,$

where c is real consumption, P is the aggregate price level, and T is the nominal lump-sum transfer. In real terms,

$$c_t \leq \frac{M_{t-1}}{P_t} + \frac{T_t}{P_t} = \frac{m_{t-1}}{1 + \pi_t} + \tau_t, \tag{3.16}$$

where $m_{t-1} = M_{t-1}/P_{t-1}$, $\pi_t = (P_t/P_{t-1}) - 1$ is the inflation rate, and $\tau_t = T_t/P_t$. Note the timing: M_{t-1} refers to nominal money balances chosen by the agent in period $t-1$ and carried into period t. The real value of these balances is determined by the period t price level P_t. Since we have assumed away any uncertainty, the agent knows P_t at the time M_{t-1} is chosen. This specification of the CIA constraint assumes that income from production during period t will not be available for consumption purchases until period $t+1$.

The budget constraint, in nominal terms, is

$$P_t \omega_t \equiv P_t f(k_{t-1}) + (1-\delta) P_t k_{t-1} + M_{t-1} + T_t + (1 + i_{t-1}) B_{t-1}$$

$$\geq P_t c_t + P_t k_t + M_t + B_t, \tag{3.17}$$

where ω_t is the agent's time t real resources, consisting of income generated during period t $f(k_{t-1})$, the undepreciated capital stock $(1-\delta)k_{t-1}$, money holdings, the transfer from the government, and gross nominal interest earnings on the agent's $t-1$ holdings of nominal one-period bonds, B_{t-1}. Physical capital depreciates at the rate δ. These resources are used to purchase consumption, capital, bonds, and nominal money holdings that are then carried into period $t+1$. Dividing through by the time t price level, the budget constraint can be rewritten in real terms as

$$\omega_t \equiv f(k_{t-1}) + (1-\delta)k_{t-1} + \tau_t + \frac{m_{t-1} + (1 + i_{t-1})b_{t-1}}{1 + \pi_t} \geq c_t + m_t + b_t + k_t, \tag{3.18}$$

where m and b are real cash and bond holdings. Note that real resources available to the representative agent in period $t+1$ are given by

$$\omega_{t+1} = f(k_t) + (1-\delta)k_t + \tau_{t+1} + \frac{m_t + (1 + i_t)b_t}{1 + \pi_{t+1}}. \tag{3.19}$$

The period t gross nominal interest rate $1 + i_t$ divided by $1 + \pi_{t+1}$ is the gross real rate of return from period t to $t+1$ and can be denoted by $1 + r_t = (1 + i_t)/(1 + \pi_{t+1})$. With this notation, (3.19) can be written as

$$\omega_{t+1} = f(k_t) + (1-\delta)k_t + \tau_{t+1} + (1 + r_t)a_t - \left(\frac{i_t}{1 + \pi_{t+1}}\right)m_t,$$

where $a_t \equiv m_t + b_t$ is the agent's holding of nominal financial assets (money and bonds). This form highlights that there is a cost to holding money when the nominal interest rate is positive. This cost is $i_t/(1 + \pi_{t+1})$; since this is the cost in terms of period $t + 1$ real resources, the discounted cost at time t of holding an additional unit of money is $i_t/(1 + r_t)(1 + \pi_{t+1}) = i_t/(1 + i_t)$. This is the same expression for the opportunity cost of money obtained in chapter 2 in an MIU model.

Equation (3.16) is based on the timing convention that goods markets open before asset markets. The model of Lucas (1982) assumed the reverse, and individuals can engage in asset transactions at the start of each period before the goods market has opened. In the present model, this would mean that the agent enters period t with financial wealth that can be used to purchase nominal bonds B_t or carried as cash into the goods market to purchase consumption goods. The CIA constraint would then take the form

$$c_t \leq \frac{m_{t-1}}{1 + \pi_t} + \tau_t - b_t. \tag{3.20}$$

In this case, the household is able to adjust its portfolio between money and bonds before entering the goods market to purchase consumption goods.

To understand the implications of this alternative timing, suppose there is a positive opportunity cost of holding money. Then, if the asset market opens first, the agent will only hold an amount of money that is just sufficient to finance the desired level of consumption. Since the opportunity cost of holding m is positive whenever the nominal interest rate is greater than zero, (3.20) will always hold with equality as long as the nominal rate of interest is positive. When uncertainty is introduced, the CIA constraint may not bind when (3.16) is used and the goods market opens before the asset market. For example, if period $t's$ income is uncertain and is realized after M_{t-1} has been chosen, a bad income realization may cause the agent to reduce consumption to a point where the CIA constraint is no longer binding. Or a disturbance that causes an unexpected price decline might, by increasing the real value of the agent's money holdings, result in a nonbinding constraint.[10] Since a nonstochastic environment holds in this section, the CIA constraint will bind under either timing assumption if the opportunity cost of holding money is positive. For a complete discussion and comparison of alternative assumptions about the timing of the asset and goods markets, see Salyer (1991). In the remainder of this chapter, we shall follow Svensson (1985) in using (3.16) and assume that consumption in period t is limited by the cash carried over from period $t - 1$ plus any net transfer.

---

10. Uncertainty may cause the CIA constraint to not bind, but it does not follow that the nominal interest rate will be zero. If money is held, the constraint must be binding in some states of nature. The nominal interest rate will equal the discounted expected value of money; see problem 4.

The choice variables at time t are c_t, m_t, b_t, and k_t. An individual agent's state at time t can be characterized by her resources ω_t and her real cash holdings m_{t-1}; both are relevant because consumption choice is constrained by the agent's resources and by cash holdings. To analyze the agent's decision problem, one can define the value function

$$V(\omega_t, m_{t-1}) = \max_{c_t, k_t, b_t, m_t} \{u(c_t) + \beta V(\omega_{t+1}, m_t)\}, \tag{3.21}$$

where the maximization is subject to the budget constraint (from 3.18)

$$\omega_t \geq c_t + m_t + b_t + k_t, \tag{3.22}$$

the CIA constraint (3.16), and the definition of ω_{t+1} given by (3.19). Using this expression for ω_{t+1} in (3.21) and letting λ_t (μ_t) denote the Lagrangian multiplier associated with the budget constraint (the CIA constraint), the first-order necessary conditions for the agent's choice of consumption, capital, bond, and money holdings take the form[11]

$$u_c(c_t) - \lambda_t - \mu_t = 0 \tag{3.23}$$

$$\beta[f_k(k_t) + 1 - \delta]V_\omega(\omega_{t+1}, m_t) - \lambda_t = 0 \tag{3.24}$$

$$\beta(1 + r_t)V_\omega(\omega_{t+1}, m_t) - \lambda_t = 0 \tag{3.25}$$

$$\beta\left[1 + r_t - \frac{i_t}{1 + \pi_{t+1}}\right]V_\omega(\omega_{t+1}, m_t) + \beta V_m(\omega_{t+1}, m_t) - \lambda_t = 0. \tag{3.26}$$

From the envelope theorem,

$$V_\omega(\omega_t, m_{t-1}) = \lambda_t \tag{3.27}$$

$$V_m(\omega_t, m_{t-1}) = \left(\frac{1}{1 + \pi_t}\right)\mu_t. \tag{3.28}$$

From (3.27), λ_t is equal to the marginal utility of wealth. According to (3.23), the marginal utility of consumption exceeds the marginal utility of wealth by the value of liquidity services, μ_t. The individual must hold money in order to purchase consumption, so the "cost," to which the marginal utility of consumption is set equal, is the marginal utility of wealth plus the cost of the liquidity services needed to finance the transaction.[12]

---

11. The first-order necessary conditions also include the transversality conditions.

12. Equation (3.23) can be compared to (3.10) from the shopping-time model.

In terms of λ, (3.25) becomes

$$\lambda_t = \beta(1 + r_t)\lambda_{t+1}, \qquad (3.29)$$

which is a standard asset pricing equation and is a familiar condition from problems involving intertemporal optimization. Along the optimal path, the marginal cost (in terms of today's utility) from reducing wealth slightly, λ_t, must equal the utility value of carrying that wealth forward one period, earning a gross real return $1 + r_t$, where tomorrow's utility is discounted back to today at the rate β; that is, $\lambda_t = \beta(1 + r_t)\lambda_{t+1}$ along the optimal path.

Using (3.27) and (3.28), the first-order condition (3.26) can be expressed as

$$\lambda_t = \beta\left(\frac{\lambda_{t+1} + \mu_{t+1}}{1 + \pi_{t+1}}\right). \qquad (3.30)$$

Equation (3.30) can also be interpreted as an asset pricing equation for money. The price of a unit of money in terms of goods is just $1/P_t$ at time t; its value in utility terms is λ_t/P_t. Now, by dividing (3.30) through by P_t, it can be rewritten as $\lambda_t/P_t = \beta(\lambda_{t+1}/P_{t+1} + \mu_{t+1}/P_{t+1})$. Solving this equation forward[13] implies that

$$\frac{\lambda_t}{P_t} = \sum_{i=1}^{\infty} \beta^i \left(\frac{\mu_{t+i}}{P_{t+i}}\right). \qquad (3.31)$$

From (3.28), μ_{t+i}/P_{t+i} is equal to $V_m(\omega_{t+i}, m_{t+i-1})/P_{t+i-1}$. This last expression, though, is just the partial of the value function with respect to time $t + i - 1$ *nominal* money balances:

$$\frac{\partial V(\omega_{t+i}, m_{t+i-1})}{\partial M_{t+i-1}} = V_m(\omega_{t+i}, m_{t+i-1})\left(\frac{\partial m_{t+i-1}}{\partial M_{t+i-1}}\right)$$

$$= \frac{V_m(\omega_{t+i}, m_{t+i-1})}{P_{t+i-1}}$$

$$= \left(\frac{\mu_{t+i}}{P_{t+i}}\right).$$

This means (3.31) can be rewritten as

$$\frac{\lambda_t}{P_t} = \sum_{i=1}^{\infty} \beta^i \frac{\partial V(\omega_{t+i}, m_{t+i-1})}{\partial M_{t+i-1}}.$$

13. For references on solving difference equations forward in the context of rational-expectations models, see Blanchard and Kahn (1980) or McCallum (1989).

In other words, the current value of money in terms of utility is equal to the present value of the marginal utility of money in all future periods. Equation (3.31) is an interesting result; it says that money is just like any other asset in the sense that its value (i.e., its price today) can be thought of as equal to the present discounted value of the stream of returns generated by the asset. In the case of money, these returns take the form of liquidity services.[14] If the CIA constraint were not binding, these liquidity services would not have value ($\mu = V_m = 0$) and neither would money. But if the constraint is binding, then money has value because it yields valued liquidity services.[15]

The result that the value of money, λ/P, satisfies an asset pricing relationship is not unique to the CIA approach. For example, a similar relationship is implied by the MIU approach. The model employed in the analysis of the MIU approach (see chapter 2) implied that

$$\frac{\lambda_t}{P_t} = \beta\left(\frac{\lambda_{t+1}}{P_{t+1}}\right) + \frac{u_m(c_t, m_t)}{P_t},$$

which can be solved forward to yield

$$\frac{\lambda_t}{P_t} = \sum_{i=0}^{\infty} \beta^i \left[\frac{u_m(c_{t+i}, m_{t+i})}{P_{t+i}}\right].$$

Here, the marginal utility of money u_m plays a role exactly analogous to that played by the Lagrangian on the CIA constraint μ. The one difference is that in the MIU approach, m_t yields utility at time t, whereas in the CIA approach, the value of money accumulated at time t is measured by μ_{t+1} because the cash cannot be used to purchase consumption goods until period $t+1$.[16]

An expression for the nominal rate of interest can be obtained by using (3.29) and (3.30) to obtain $\lambda_t = \beta(1 + r_t)\lambda_{t+1} = \beta(\lambda_{t+1} + \mu_{t+1})/(1 + \pi_{t+1})$, or $(1 + r_t)(1 + \pi_{t+1})\lambda_{t+1} = (\lambda_{t+1} + \mu_{t+1})$. Since $1 + i_t = (1 + r_t)(1 + \pi_{t+1})$, the nominal interest rate is given by

$$i_t = \left(\frac{\lambda_{t+1} + \mu_{t+1}}{\lambda_{t+1}}\right) - 1 = \frac{\mu_{t+1}}{\lambda_{t+1}}. \tag{3.32}$$

14. The parallel expression for the shopping-time model can be obtained from (3.5) and (3.8). See problem 2.

15. Bohn (1991b) analyzed the asset pricing implications of a CIA model. See also Salyer (1991).

16. Carlstrom and Fuerst (2001) argued that utility at time t should depend on money balances available for spending during period t, or M_{t-1}/P_t. This would make the timing more consistent with CIA models. With this timing, m_t is chosen at time t but yields utility at $t+1$. In this case, $\lambda_t/P_t = \sum_{i=1}^{\infty} \beta^i[u_m(c_{t+i}, m_{t+i})/P_{t+i}]$, and the timing is the same as in the CIA model.

Thus, the nominal rate of interest is positive if and only if money yields liquidity services ($\mu_{t+1} > 0$). In particular, if the nominal interest rate is positive, the CIA constraint is binding ($\mu > 0$).

One can use the relationship between the nominal rate of interest and the Lagrangian multipliers to rewrite the expression for the marginal utility of consumption, given in (3.23), as

$$u_c = \lambda(1 + \mu/\lambda) = \lambda(1 + i) \geq \lambda. \tag{3.33}$$

Since λ represents the marginal value of income, the marginal utility of consumption exceeds that of income whenever the nominal interest rate is positive. Even though the economy's technology allows output to be directly transformed into consumption, the "price" of consumption is not equal to 1; it is $1 + i$ because the household must hold money to finance consumption. Thus, in this CIA model, a positive nominal interest rate acts as a tax on consumption; it raises the price of consumption above its production cost.[17]

The CIA constraint holds with equality when the nominal rate of interest is positive, so $c_t = M_{t-1}/P_t + \tau_t$. Since the lump-sum monetary transfer τ_t is equal to $(M_t - M_{t-1})/P_t$, this implies that $c_t = M_t/P_t = m_t$. Consequently, the consumption velocity of money is identically equal to 1 (velocity $= P_t c_t/M_t = 1$). Since actual velocity varies over time, CIA models have been modified in ways that break this tight link between c and m. One way to avoid this is to introduce uncertainty (see Svensson 1985). If money balances have to be chosen prior to the resolution of uncertainty, it may turn out after the realizations of shocks that the desired level of consumption is less than the amount of real money balances being held. In this case, some money balances will be unspent, and velocity can be less than 1. Velocity may also vary if the CIA constraint only applies to a subset of consumption goods. Then variations in the rate of inflation can lead to substitution between goods whose purchase requires cash and those whose purchase does not (see problem 6 at the end of this chapter).

The Steady State
In the steady state, (3.29) implies that $(1 + r^{ss}) = 1/\beta$, and $i = (1 + \pi^{ss})/\beta - 1 \approx 1/\beta - 1 + \pi^{ss}$. In addition, (3.24) gives the steady-state capital stock as the solution to

$$f_k(k^{ss}) = r^{ss} + \delta = \frac{1}{\beta} - 1 + \delta.$$

So this CIA model, like the Sidrauski MIU model, exhibits superneutrality. The steady-state capital stock depends only on the time preference parameter β, the rate

---

17. In the shopping-time model, consumption is also taxed. See problem 3.

of depreciation δ, and the production function. It is independent of the rate of inflation. Since steady-state consumption is equal to $f(k^{ss}) - \delta k^{ss}$, it too is independent
of the rate of inflation.[18]

It has been shown that the marginal utility of consumption could be written as the
marginal utility of wealth (λ) times 1 plus the nominal rate of interest, reflecting the
opportunity cost of holding the money required to purchase goods for consumption.
Using (3.32), the ratio of the liquidity value of money, measured by the Lagrangian
multiplier μ, to the marginal utility of consumption is

$$\frac{\mu}{u_c} = \frac{\mu}{\lambda(1+i)} = \frac{i}{1+i}.$$

This expression is exactly parallel to the result in the MIU framework, where the
ratio of the marginal utility of money to the marginal utility of consumption was
equal to the nominal interest rate divided by 1 plus the nominal rate, that is, the relative price of money in terms of consumption.

With the CIA constraint binding, real consumption is equal to real money balances. In the steady state, constant consumption implies that the stock of nominal
money balances and the price level must be changing at the same rate. Define θ as
the growth rate of the nominal quantity of money (so that $T_t = \theta M_{t-1}$); then

$$\pi^{ss} = \theta^{ss}.$$

The steady-state inflation rate is, as usual, determined by the rate of growth of the
nominal money stock.

One difference between the CIA model and the MIU model is that with c^{ss} independent of inflation and the cash-in-advance constraint binding, the fact that
$c^{ss} = m^{ss}$ in the CIA model implies that steady-state money holdings are also independent of inflation.

The Welfare Costs of Inflation
The CIA model, because it is based explicitly on behavioral relationships consistent
with utility maximization, can be used to assess the welfare costs of inflation and to
determine the optimal rate of inflation. The MIU approach had very strong implications for the optimal inflation rate. Steady-state utility of the representative household was maximized when the nominal rate of interest equaled zero. It has already

---

18. The expression for steady-state consumption can be obtained from (3.18) by noting that $m_t = \tau_t + m_{t-1}/\Pi_t$ and, with all households identical, $b = 0$ in equilibrium. Then (3.18) reduces to

$$c^{ss} + k^{ss} = f(k^{ss}) + (1-\delta)k^{ss},$$

or $c^{ss} = f(k^{ss}) - \delta k^{ss}$.

been suggested that this conclusion continues to hold when money produces transaction services.

In the basic CIA model, however, there is no optimal rate of inflation that maximizes the steady-state welfare of the representative household. The reason follows directly from the specification of utility as a function only of consumption and the result that consumption is independent of the rate of inflation (superneutrality). Steady-state welfare is equal to

$$\sum_{t=0}^{\infty} \beta^t u(c^{ss}) = \frac{u(c^{ss})}{1-\beta}$$

and is invariant to the inflation rate. Comparing across steady states, any inflation rate is as good as any other.[19]

This finding is not robust to modifications in the basic CIA model. In particular, once the model is extended to incorporate a labor-leisure choice, consumption will no longer be independent of the inflation rate, and there will be a well-defined optimal rate of inflation. Because leisure can be "purchased" without the use of money (i.e., leisure is not subject to the CIA constraint), variations in the rate of inflation will affect the marginal rate of substitution between consumption and leisure (see section 3.3.2). With different inflation rates leading to different levels of steady-state consumption and leisure, steady-state utility will be a function of inflation. This type of substitution plays an important role in the model of Cooley and Hansen (1989), discussed in the next section; in their model, inflation leads to an increased demand for leisure and a reduction in labor supply. But before including a labor-leisure choice, it will be useful to briefly review some other modifications of the basic CIA model, modifications that will, in general, generate a unique optimal rate of inflation.

Cash and Credit Goods   Lucas and Stokey (1983; 1987) introduced the idea that the CIA constraint may only apply to a subset of consumption goods. They modeled this by assuming that the representative agent's utility function is defined over consumption of two types of goods: "cash" goods and "credit" goods. In this case, paralleling (3.23), the marginal utility of cash goods is equated to $\lambda + \mu \geq \lambda$, and the marginal utility of credit goods is equated to λ. Hence, the CIA requirement for cash goods drives a wedge between the marginal utilities of the two types of goods. It is exactly as if the consumer faced a tax of $\mu/\lambda = i$ on purchases of the cash good. Higher inflation, by raising the opportunity cost of holding cash, serves to raise the tax on cash

---

19. By contrast, the optimal rate of inflation was well defined even in the basic Sidrauski model that exhibited superneutrality, since real money balances vary with inflation and directly affect utility in an MIU model.

goods and generates a substitution away from the cash good and toward the credit good. (See also Hartley 1988.)

The obvious difficulty with this approach is that the classifications of goods into cash and credit goods is exogenous. And it is common to assume a one-good technology so that the goods are not differentiated by any technological considerations. The advantage of these models is that they can produce time variation in velocity. Recall that in the basic CIA model, any equilibrium with a positive nominal rate of interest is characterized by a binding CIA constraint, and this means that $c = m$. With both cash and credit goods, m will equal the consumption of cash goods, allowing the ratio of total consumption to money holdings to vary with expected inflation.[20]

CIA and Investment Goods A second modification to the basic model involves extending the CIA constraint to cover investment goods. In this case, the inflation tax applies to both consumption and investment goods. Higher rates of inflation will tend to discourage capital accumulation, and Stockman (1981) showed that higher inflation would lower the steady-state capital-labor ratio (see also Abel 1985 and problem 9 at the end of this chapter).[21]

Implications for Optimal Inflation In CIA models, inflation acts as a tax on goods or activities whose purchase requires cash. This tax then introduces a distortion by creating a wedge between the marginal rates of transformation implied by the economy's technology and the marginal rates of substitution faced by consumers. Since the CIA model, like the MIU model, offers no reason for such a distortion to be introduced (there is no inefficiency that calls for Pigovian taxes or subsidies on particular activities, and the government's revenue needs can be met through lump-sum taxation), optimality calls for setting the inflation tax equal to zero. The inflation tax is directly related to the nominal rate of interest; a zero inflation tax is achieved when the nominal rate of interest is equal to zero.

3.3.2 A Stochastic CIA Model

While the models of Lucas (1982), Svensson (1985), and Lucas and Stokey (1987) provide theoretical frameworks for assessing the role of inflation on asset prices and interest rates, they do not provide any guide to the empirical magnitude of inflation effects or to the welfare costs of inflation. What one would like is a dynamic equilibrium model that could be simulated under alternative monetary policies—for example, for alternative steady-state rates of inflation—in order to assess quantitatively

20. Woodford (1998) studied a model with a continuum of goods indexed by $i \in [0, 1]$. A fraction s, $0 \le s \le 1$, are cash goods. He then approximated a cashless economy by letting $s \to 0$.

21. Abel (1985) studied the dynamics of adjustment in a model in which the CIA constraint applies to both consumption and investment.

the effects of inflation. Such an exercise was first conducted by Cooley and Hansen (1989; 1991). Cooley and Hansen followed the basic framework of Lucas and Stokey (1987). However, important aspects of their specification include (1) the introduction of capital and, consequently, an investment decision; (2) the introduction of a labor-leisure choice; and (3) the identification of consumption as the cash good and investment and leisure as credit goods.

Inflation represents a tax on the purchases of the cash good, and therefore higher rates of inflation shift household demand away from the cash good and toward the credit good. In Cooley and Hansen's formulation, this implies that higher inflation increases the demand for leisure. One effect of higher inflation, then, is to reduce the supply of labor. This then reduces output, consumption, investment, and the steady-state capital stock.

Cooley and Hansen expressed welfare losses across steady states in terms of the consumption increase (as a percentage of output) required to yield the same utility as would arise if the CIA constraint were nonbinding.[22] For a 10 percent inflation rate, they reported a welfare cost of inflation of 0.387 percent of output if the CIA constraint is assumed to apply at a quarterly time interval. Not surprisingly, if the constraint binds only at a monthly time interval, the cost falls to 0.112 percent of output. These costs are small. For much higher rates of inflation, they start to look significant. For example, with a monthly time period for the CIA constraint, a 400 percent annual rate of inflation generates a welfare loss equal to 2.137 percent of output. The welfare costs of inflation are discussed further in chapter 4.

The Basic Model

To model the behavior of the representative agent faced with uncertainty and a CIA constraint, assume the agent's objective is to maximize

$$
E_t \sum_{i=0}^{\infty} \beta^i u(c_{t+i}, 1 - n_{t+i}) = E_0 \sum_{i=0}^{\infty} \beta^i \left[\frac{c_{t+i}^{1-\Phi}}{1-\Phi} + \Psi \frac{(1 - n_{t+i})^{1-\eta}}{1-\eta} \right],
\tag{3.34}
$$

with $0 < \beta < 1$. Here c_t is real consumption, and n_t is labor supplied to market activities, expressed as a fraction of the total time available, so that $1 - n_t$ is equal to leisure time.[23] The parameters Φ, Ψ, and η are restricted to be positive.

---

22. Refer to Cooley and Hansen (1989, sec. II) or Hansen and Prescott (Cooley 1995, ch. 2) for discussions of the computational aspects of this exercise.

23. In order to allow for comparison between the MIU model developed earlier and a CIA model, the preference function used earlier, (2.38) of chapter 2, is modified by setting $a = 1$ and $b = 0$ so that real balances do not yield direct utility. The resulting utility function given in (3.34) differs from Cooley and Hansen's specification; they assume that the preferences of the identical (ex ante) households are log-separable in consumption and leisure, a case obtained when $\Phi = \eta = 1$.

Households supply labor and rent capital to firms that produce goods. The household enters each period with nominal money balances M_{t-1} and receives a nominal lump-sum transfer equal to T_t. In the aggregate, this transfer is related to the growth rate of the nominal supply of money. Letting the stochastic variable θ_t denote the rate of money growth ($M_t = (1 + \theta_t)M_{t-1}$), the per capita transfer will equal $\theta_t M_{t-1}$. At the start of period t, θ_t is known to all households. Households purchase bonds B_t, and their remaining cash is available for purchasing consumption goods. Thus, the timing has asset markets opening first, and the CIA constraint, which is taken to apply only to the purchase of consumption goods, takes the form

$$P_t c_t \leq M_{t-1} + T_t - B_t,$$

where P_t is the time t price level. Note that time t transfers are available to be spent in period t. In real terms, the CIA constraint becomes

$$c_t \leq \frac{m_{t-1}}{1 + \pi_t} + \tau_t - b_t. \tag{3.35}$$

Here $1 + \pi_t$ is equal to 1 plus the rate of inflation. The CIA constraint will always be binding if the nominal interest rate is positive.[24]

In addition to the CIA constraint, the household faces a flow budget constraint in nominal terms of the form

$$M_t = P_t[Y_t + (1 - \delta)K_{t-1} - K_t] + (1 + i_t)B_t + (M_{t-1} + T_t - P_t c_t - B_t).$$

In real terms, this becomes

$$m_t = y_t + (1 - \delta)k_{t-1} + i_t b_t - k_t + \frac{m_{t-1}}{1 + \pi_t} + \tau_t - c_t, \tag{3.36}$$

where $0 \leq \delta \leq 1$ is the depreciation rate.

The individual's decision problem is characterized by the value function

$$V(k_{t-1}, b_{t-1}, m_{t-1}) = \max_{c_t, n_t, k_t, b_t, m_t} \left[\frac{c_t^{1-\Phi}}{1 - \Phi} + \Psi \frac{(1 - n_t)^{1-\eta}}{1 - \eta} + \beta E_t V(k_t, b_t, m_t) \right],$$

where the maximization is subject to the constraints (3.36) and (3.35).

The first-order conditions for the representative agent's decision problem must be satisfied in equilibrium. If λ_t is the Lagrangian multiplier on the budget constraint and μ_t is the multiplier on the cash-in-advance constraint, then these first-order conditions take the form

---

24. Previous editions followed Cooley and Hansen in assuming the goods market opened first. In this case, the cash-in-advance constraint took the form $P_t c_t \leq M_{t-1} + T_t$.

$$c_t^{-\Phi} = \lambda_t + \mu_t \tag{3.37}$$

$$\Psi(1-n)^{-\eta} = (1-\alpha)\left(\frac{y_t}{n_t}\right)\lambda_t \tag{3.38}$$

$$\lambda_t = \beta E_t(1+r_t)\lambda_{t+1} \tag{3.39}$$

$$i_t\lambda_t - \mu_t = 0 \tag{3.40}$$

$$\lambda_t = \beta E_t\left[\frac{\lambda_{t+1} + \mu_{t+1}}{1 + \pi_{t+1}}\right], \tag{3.41}$$

where $r_t = \alpha(y_{t+1}/k_t) - \delta$.

To complete the specification of the model, assume the economy's technology is given by a Cobb-Douglas constant-returns-to-scale production function, expressed in per capita terms as

$$y_t = e^{z_t}k_{t-1}^{\alpha}n_t^{1-\alpha}, \tag{3.42}$$

where $0 \leq \alpha \leq 1$. The exogenous productivity shock z_t is assumed to follow an AR(1) process:

$$z_t = \rho_z z_{t-1} + e_t,$$

with $0 \leq \rho \leq 1$. The innovation e_t has mean zero and variance σ_e^2.

Finally, let $u_t = \theta_t - \theta^{ss}$ be the deviation of money growth from its steady-state average rate and assume

$$u_t = \rho_u u_{t-1} + \phi z_{t-1} + \varphi_t,$$

where φ_t is a white noise innovation with variance σ_φ^2. This is the same process for the nominal growth rate of money that was used in chapter 2.

The Steady State

Adopting the same parameter calibrations as those reported in section 2.5.4 for the MIU model, the steady-state values of the ratios that were reported for the MIU model are also the steady-state values for the CIA model (see the chapter appendix). The Euler condition ensures $1 + r^{ss} = 1/\beta$, which then implies $y^{ss}/k^{ss} = (r^{ss} + \delta)/\alpha$ and, with investment in the steady state equal to δk^{ss}, $c^{ss}/k^{ss} = (y^{ss}/k^{ss}) - \delta$. Even though the method used to generate a demand for money has changed with the move from the MIU model to the CIA model, the steady-state values of the output-capital and consumption-capital ratios are unchanged. Note that none of these steady-state ratios depends on the growth rate of the nominal money supply. The level of real money balances in the steady state is then determined by the cash-in-advance constraint, which is binding as long as the nominal rate of interest is positive. Hence, $c^{ss} = m^{ss}/(1 + \pi^{ss}) + \tau^{ss} = m^{ss}$, so $m^{ss}/k^{ss} = c^{ss}/k^{ss}$.

The steady-state labor supply will depend on the money growth rate and therefore on the rate of inflation. The appendix shows that n^{ss} satisfies

$$(1 - n^{ss})^{-\eta}(n^{ss})^{\Phi} = \left(\frac{1 - \alpha}{\Psi}\right)\left(\frac{\beta}{1 + \theta^{ss}}\right)\left(\frac{y^{ss}}{k^{ss}}\right)^{(\Phi - \alpha)/(1 - \alpha)}\left(\frac{c^{ss}}{k^{ss}}\right)^{-\Phi}, \tag{3.43}$$

where θ is the steady-state rate of money growth. Since the left side of this expression is increasing in n^{ss}, a rise in θ^{ss}, which implies a rise in the inflation rate, lowers the steady-state labor supply. Higher inflation taxes consumption and causes households to substitute toward more leisure. This is the source of the welfare cost of inflation in this CIA model. The elasticity of labor supply with respect to the growth rate of money is negative.

It is useful to note the similarity between the expression for steady-state labor supply in the CIA model and the corresponding expression (given in (2.77) in chapter 2) that was obtained in the MIU model. With the MIU specification, faster money growth had an ambiguous effect on the supply of labor. With the calibrated values of the parameters of the utility function used in chapter 2, money and consumption were complements, so higher inflation, by reducing real money holdings, lowered the marginal utility of consumption and also reduced the supply of labor.

Dynamics

The dynamic implications of the CIA model can be explored by obtaining a first-order linear approximation around the steady state. The derivation of the approximation is contained in the chapter appendix. As in chapter 2, a variable $\hat{x}$ denotes the percentage deviation of x around the steady state.[25] The CIA model can be approximated around the steady state by the following nine linear equations:

$$\hat{y}_t = \alpha \hat{k}_{t-1} + (1 - \alpha)\hat{n}_t + z_t \tag{3.44}$$

$$\left(\frac{y^{ss}}{k^{ss}}\right)\hat{y}_t = \left(\frac{c^{ss}}{k^{ss}}\right)\hat{c}_t + \hat{k}_t - (1 - \delta)\hat{k}_{t-1} \tag{3.45}$$

$$\hat{y}_t + \hat{\lambda}_t = \left(1 + \eta\frac{n^{ss}}{1 - n^{ss}}\right)\hat{n}_t \tag{3.46}$$

$$\hat{r}_t = \alpha\left(\frac{y^{ss}}{k^{ss}}\right)(E_t\hat{y}_{t+1} - \hat{k}_t) \tag{3.47}$$

---

25. The exceptions again being that $\hat{r}$ and $\hat{i}$ are expressed in percentage terms (e.g., $\hat{r}_t = r_t - r_t^{ss}$).

$$\hat{\lambda}_t = \hat{r}_t + E_t\hat{\lambda}_{t+1} \tag{3.48}$$

$$-\Phi\hat{c}_t = \hat{\lambda}_t + \hat{\imath}_t \tag{3.49}$$

$$\hat{\lambda}_t = -\Phi E_t\hat{c}_{t+1} - E_t\hat{\pi}_{t+1} \tag{3.50}$$

$$\hat{c}_t = \hat{m}_t \tag{3.51}$$

$$\hat{m}_t = \hat{m}_{t-1} - \hat{\pi}_t + u_t. \tag{3.52}$$

Note that the first five equations (the production function, the resource constraint, the labor-leisure condition, the marginal product of capital equation, and the Euler condition) are identical to those found with the MIU approach. The critical differences between the two approaches appear in a comparison of (3.49), (3.50), and (3.51) with (2.65) and (2.73) of chapter 2. In the MIU model, utility depended directly on money holdings, so (2.65) expressed the marginal utility of consumption in terms of $\hat{c}_t$ and $\hat{m}_t$. In the CIA model, the marginal utility of income can differ from the marginal utility of consumption; (3.50) reflects the fact that an extra dollar of income received in period t cannot be spent on consumption until $t+1$. Equation (3.41) gives $\lambda_t = \beta E_t(\lambda_{t+1} + \mu_{t+1})/(1 + \pi_{t+1})$.[26] Since the marginal utility of consumption $c_t^{-\Phi}$ is equated to $\lambda_t + \mu_t$, this becomes $\lambda_t = \beta E_t c_{t+1}^{-\Phi}/(1 + \pi_{t+1}) = \beta E_t m_{t+1}^{-\Phi}/(1 + \pi_{t+1})$. Linearizing this result produces (3.50). Equation (2.73) was the MIU money demand condition derived from the first-order condition for the household's holdings of real money balances. In the CIA model, (3.49) and (3.51) reflect the presence of the nominal interest rate as a tax on consumption and the binding cash-in-advance constraint in the CIA model. Finally, note that (3.48)–(3.50) can be combined to yield the Fisher equation: $\hat{\imath}_t = \hat{r}_t + E_t\hat{\pi}_{t+1}$.

Calibration and Simulations

In order to assess the effects of money in this CIA model, values must be assigned to the specific parameters; that is, the model must be calibrated. The steady state depends on the values of α, β, δ, η, Ψ, and Φ. The baseline values reported in section 2.5.4 for the MIU model can be employed for the CIA model as well. This implies that $\alpha = 0.36$, $\beta = 0.989$, and $\delta = 0.019$. Assuming $\eta = 1$ implies that the utility is log-linear in leisure. The value of Ψ is then determined so that the steady-state value of n is 0.31. For the baseline parameters, this yields $\Psi = 1.34$. To maintain comparability with the MIU model, the utility function parameter Φ will be set equal to 2 for the baseline solutions. The remaining parameters are set to the same values reported in section 2.5.4.

---

26. Equation (3.30) is the corresponding equation for the nonstochastic CIA model of section 3.3.1.

Recall that the MIU model displayed short-run dynamics in which the real variables such as output, consumption, capital stock, and employment were independent of the nominal money supply process when utility was log-linear in consumption and money balances.[27] While $\hat{m}$ does not directly enter the utility function in the CIA model, note that in the case of log utility in consumption (that is, when $\Phi = 1$), the short-run real dynamics in the CIA model are not independent of the process followed by $\hat{m}$, as they were in the MIU model. Note that (3.46), (3.50), and (3.52) imply, when $\Phi = 1$, that

$$\hat{\lambda}_t = -E_t(\hat{m}_{t+1} + \hat{\pi}_{t+1}) = -(\hat{m}_t + E_t u_{t+1}) = \left(1 + \eta \frac{n^{ss}}{l^{ss}}\right)\hat{n}_t - \hat{y}_t.$$

Thus, variations in the expected future growth rate of money, $E_t u_{t+1}$, force adjustment to either $\hat{y}$, $\hat{c}$ $(\hat{m})$, or $\hat{n}$ (or all three). In particular, for given output and consumption, higher expected money growth (and therefore higher expected inflation) produces a fall in $\hat{n}_t$. This is the effect by which higher inflation reduces labor supply and output.

The current growth rate of the nominal money stock, u_t, and the current rate of inflation, π_t, only appear in the form $u_t - \pi_t$ (see (3.52)). Hence, as in the MIU model, *unanticipated* monetary shocks affect only current inflation and have no real effects unless they alter expectations of future money growth (i.e., unless $E_t u_{t+1}$ is affected).

The response of money growth to productivity shocks has real effects, and the economy's response to a productivity shock is decreasing in ϕ. For example, when ϕ is negative, a positive productivity shock implies that money growth will decline in the future. Consequently, expected inflation also declines. The resulting reduction in the nominal interest rate lowers the effective inflation tax on consumption and increases labor supply. In contrast, when ϕ is positive, a positive productivity shock increases expected inflation and reduces labor supply. This tends to partially offset the effect of the productivity shock on output. Thus, output variability is less when ϕ is positive than when it is zero or negative. However, the effects are small; as ϕ goes from -0.15 to 0 to 0.15, the standard deviation of output falls from 1.57 to 1.50 to 1.43.

The response of the nominal interest rate is shown in figure 3.1. As with the MIU model, a positive money growth shock, by raising expected inflation when $\rho_u > 0$, raises the nominal rate of interest. Greater persistence of the money growth rate process leads to larger movements in expected inflation in response to a monetary shock. This, in turn, produces larger adjustments of labor supply and output. As illustrated

---

27. This was the case in which $\Phi = b = 1$.

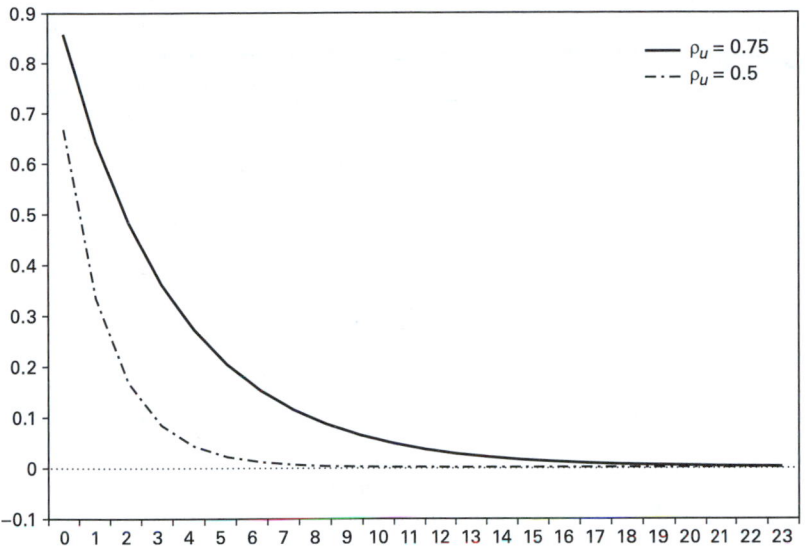

Figure 3.1
Response of the nominal interest rate to a positive money growth shock.

in figure 3.2, a one-unit positive shock, by raising the expected rate of inflation and thereby increasing the inflation tax on consumption, induces a substitution toward leisure that lowers labor supply. When $\rho_u = 0.75$, employment falls by 7 percent. Comparing this figure with figure 2.3 reveals that a money growth shock has a much larger real impact in the CIA model than in the MIU model.

3.4   Search

Both the MIU and the CIA approaches are useful alternatives for introducing money into a general equilibrium framework. However, neither approach is very specific about the exact role played by money. MIU models assume that the direct utility yielded by money proxies for the services money produces in facilitating transactions. However, the nature of these transactions and, more important, the resource costs they might involve, and how these costs might be reduced by holding money, are not specified. Use of the CIA model is motivated by appealing to the idea that some form of nominal asset is required to facilitate transactions. Yet the constraint used is extreme, implying that there are no alternative means of carrying out certain transactions. The CIA constraint is meant to capture the essential role of money as a medium of exchange, but in this case one might wish to start from a specification of

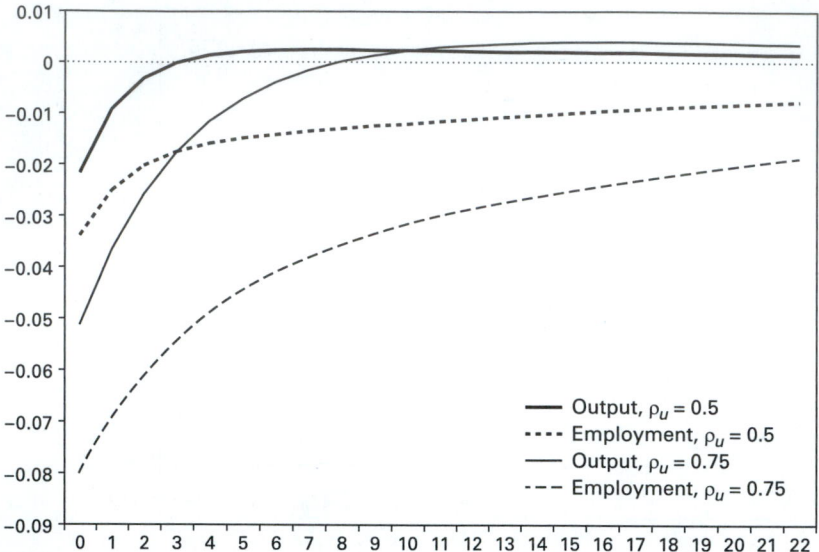

Figure 3.2
Response of output and employment to a positive money growth shock.

the transactions technology to understand why some commodities and assets serve as money and others do not.

A number of papers have employed search theory to motivate the development of media of exchange; this has been one of the most active areas of monetary theory (examples include Jones 1976; Diamond 1983; Kiyotaki and Wright 1989; 1993; Oh 1989; Trejos and Wright 1993; 1995; Ritter 1995; Shi 1995; Rupert, Schindler, and Wright 2001; Lagos and Wright 2005; Rocheteau and Wright (2005); and the papers in the May 2005 issue of the *International Economic Review*). In these models, individual agents must exchange the goods they produce (or with which they are endowed) for the goods they consume. During each period, individuals randomly meet other agents; exchange takes place if it is mutually beneficial. In a barter economy, exchange is possible only if an agent holding good i and wishing to consume good j (call this an ij agent) meets an individual holding good j who wishes to consume good i (a ji agent). This requirement is known as the *double coincident of wants* and limits the feasibility of direct barter exchange when production is highly specialized. Trade could occur if agent ij meets a ki agent for $k \neq j$ as long as exchange of goods is costless and the probability of meeting a jk agent is the same as meeting a ji agent. In this case, agent ij would be willing to exchange i for k (thereby becoming an kj agent).

In the basic Kiyotaki-Wright model, direct exchange of commodities is assumed to be costly, but there exists a fiat money that can be traded costlessly for commodities. The assumption that there exists money with certain exchange properties (costless trade with commodities) serves a role similar to that of putting money directly into the utility function in the MIU approach or specifying that money must be used in certain types of transactions in the CIA approach.[28] More recent work on search and exchange assumes trading is anonymous so that credit is precluded—you will not accept an IOU from a trading partner if you would be unable to identify or locate that person when you wish to collect.[29] However, whether an agent will accept money in exchange for goods will depend on the probability the agent places on being able later to exchange money for a consumption good.

Suppose agents are endowed with a new good according to a Poisson process with arrival rate a.[30] Trading opportunities arrive at rate b. A successful trade can occur if there is a double coincidence of wants. If x is the probability that another agent chosen at random is willing to accept the trader's commodity, the probability of a double coincidence of wants is x^2. A successful trade can also take place if there is a single coincidence of wants (i.e., one of the agents has a good the other wants), if one agent has money and the other agent is willing to accept it. That is, a trade can take place when an ij agent meets a jk agent if the ij agent has money and the jk agent is willing to accept it.

In this simple framework, agents can be in one of three states; an agent can be waiting for a new endowment to arrive (state 0), have a good to trade and be waiting to find a trading partner (state 1), or have money and be waiting for a trading opportunity (state m).

Three equilibria are possible. Suppose the probability of making a trade holding money is less than the probability of making a trade holding a commodity. In this case, individuals will prefer to hold on to their good when they meet another trader (absent a double coincidence) rather than trade for money. With no one willing to trade for money, money will be valueless in equilibrium. A second equilibrium arises when holding money makes a successful trade more likely than continuing to hold a commodity. So every agent will be willing to hold money, and in equilibrium all agents will be willing to accept money in exchange for goods. A mixed monetary

---

28. In an early analysis, Alchian (1977) attempted to explain why there might exist a commodity with the types of exchange properties assumed in the new search literature. He stressed the role of information and the costs of assessing quality. Any commodity whose quality can be assessed at low cost can facilitate the acquisition of information about other goods by serving as a medium of exchange.

29. Anonymity is treated as given, and the role of third parties, such as credit card companies and banks, that solve this problem in monetary economies are precluded by assumption.

30. In Kiyotaki and Wright (1993), this is interpreted as a production technology.

equilibrium can also exist; agents accept money with some probability as long as they believe other agents will accept it with the same probability.

The Kiyotaki-Wright model emphasized the exchange process and the possibility for an intrinsically valueless money to be accepted in trade. It did so, however, by assuming a fixed rate of exchange—one unit of money is exchanged for one unit of goods whenever a trade takes place. The value of money in terms of goods is either 0 (in a nonmonetary equilibrium) or 1. In the subsequent literature, however, the goods price of money is determined endogenously as part of the equilibrium. For example, in Trejos and Wright (1995), this price is the outcome of a bargaining process between buyers and sellers who meet through a process similar to that in Kiyotaki and Wright. However, Trejos and Wright assumed money is indivisible, whereas goods are infinitely divisible (i.e., all trades involve one dollar, but the quantity of goods exchanged for that dollar may vary). Shi (1997) extended the Kiyotaki-Wright search model to include divisible goods *and* divisible money, and Shi (1999) also analyzed inflation and its effects on growth in a search model.

Lagos and Wright (2005) and Rocheteau and Wright (2005) are good examples of search models and the insights about the costs of inflation that this literature has provided. Money is perfectly divisible and is the only storable good available to agents. Assume each period is divided into subperiods, called day and night. Agents consume and supply labor (produce) in both subperiods. The subperiods differ in terms of their market structure. Night markets are centralized and competitive; day markets are decentralized and prices (and quantities) are set via bargaining between individual agents in bilateral meetings.

The preferences of agents are identical and given by

$$U = U(x, h, X, H) = u(x) - c(h) + U(X) - H,$$

where x (X) is consumption during the day (night), and h (H) is labor supply during the day (night). The utility functions u, c, and U have standard properties, and it is assumed that there exist q^* and X^* such that $u'(q^*) = c'(q^*)$ and $U'(X^*) = 1$. Utility is linear in night labor supply H. The technology allows one unit of H to be transformed into one unit of X. Hence X^* is the quantity of the night good such that marginal utility equals marginal cost.

During the night, trading takes place in a centralized Walrasian market. Consider the decision problem of an agent who enters the night market with nominal money balances m. Let ϕ_t denote the price of money in terms of goods (i.e., the price level, the price of goods in terms of money, is $1/\phi_t$). Let $W_t(m)$ be the value function for an agent at the start of the night market with money holds m. Let $V_{t+1}(m')$ be the value function for the agent entering the day market (described later). Then the agent will choose X, H, and m' to maximize

$$U(X) - H + \beta V_{t+1}(m')$$

subject to a budget constraint of the form

$$\phi_t m + H = X + \phi_t m'.$$

The left side of this equation represents the agent's real money holdings on entering the night market plus income generated from production. The right side is consumption plus real balances carried into the next day market. Using the budget constraint, the problem can be rewritten as

$$W_t(m) = \max_{X,m'}[U(X) + \phi_t m - X + \phi_t m' + \beta V_{t+1}(m')]. \tag{3.53}$$

The first-order conditions for an interior solution take the form[31]

$$U'(X) = 1 \Rightarrow X = X^* \tag{3.54}$$

and

$$\phi_t + \beta V'_{t+1}(m') = 0. \tag{3.55}$$

Equations (3.54) and (3.55) imply that X and m' are independent of m. This is a consequence of the assumption that utility is linear in H. Intuitively, the marginal value of accumulating an extra dollar in the centralized market is $\beta V'_{t+1}(m'_{t+1})$. The marginal cost of acquiring an extra dollar is ϕ_t times the utility cost of the extra labor needed to produce and sell more output. But the marginal disutility of work is a constant (equal to 1). So the marginal costs of acquiring an extra dollar is just ϕ_t, which is the same for all agents. But if all agents exit the night market holding the same level of money balances, i.e, the same m', the distribution of money holdings across agents at the start of each day will be degenerate. This is extremely useful in dealing with a model in which agents may have different market experiences, as they will in Lagos and Wright's day market, while still preserving the idea of a representative agent. Shi (1999) adopted the notion of a large family whose individual members may have different experiences during each period but who reunite into a representative family at the end of each period. This approach, originally introduced by Lucas (1990), is used in chapter 5 when discussing models that impose restrictions on access by some agents to credit markets.

---

31. Because of the linearity of utility in H, Lagos and Wright (2005) needed to verify that $H < \bar{H}$ in equililibrium, where $\bar{H}$ is the maximum labor time an agent has available.

A final result from (3.53) that will be useful is that W can be written as

$$W_t(m) = \phi_t m + \max_{X,m'}[U(X) - X + \phi_t m' + \beta V_{t+1}(m')],$$

showing that W is linear in m.

The subperiods differ in the nature of the trading process that occurs in each. The day good x comes in different varieties, and each agent consumes a different variety than the one he produces. Hence, there is a motive for trade. As in the night market, one unit of labor can be converted into one unit of the good. In the day market, agents search for trading partners. With probability α, they meet another agent. One of three possible outcomes can occur as a result of this meeting. First, each consumes what the other produces. This corresponds to a double coincidence of wants; no money or credit is necessary for a trade to occur. Assume the probability of a double coincidence of wants is δ. Second, there could be a single coincidence of wants; one agent consumes what the other produces, but not vice versa. Assume the probability of this occurring is 2σ.[32] Finally, neither agent consumes what the other produces, an event that occurs with probability $1 - \delta - 2\sigma$.

Recall that $V_t(m)$ is the value function for an agent with money holdings m who is entering the decentralized day market, and $W_t(m)$ is the value function when entering the centralized night market. Let $F_t(\tilde{m})$ be the fraction of agents at the beginning of day t with $m \leq \tilde{m}$. Then

$$V_t(m) = \alpha\delta \int B_t(m, \tilde{m}) \, dF_t(\tilde{m})$$

$$+ \alpha\sigma \int \{u[q_t(m, \tilde{m})] + W_t[m - d_t(m, \tilde{m})]\} \, dF_t(\tilde{m})$$

$$+ \alpha\sigma \int \{-c[q_t(\tilde{m}, m)] + W_t[m + d_t(\tilde{m}, m)]\} \, dF_t(\tilde{m})$$

$$+ (1 - \alpha\delta - 2\alpha\sigma) W_t(m), \tag{3.56}$$

where $B_t(m, \tilde{m})$ is the payoff to an agent holding m who meets an agent holding $\tilde{m}$ when there is a double coincidence of wants. The four terms in $V_t(m)$ are (1) the probability of a double coincidence times the expected payoff; (2) the probability the agent meets another agent with $\tilde{m}$, there is a single coincidence of want, and $d_t(m, \tilde{m})$ is exchanged for $q_t(m, \tilde{m})$ of the consumption good; (3) the probability of a single co-

---

32. For agents i and j, the probability that i consumes what j produces but not vice versa is σ; the probability that j consumes what i produces but not vice versa is also σ. Thus, the probability that a meeting satisfies a single coincidence of wants is 2σ.

incidence meeting in which the agent produces $q_t(\tilde{m}, m)$ and receives $d_t(\tilde{m}, m)$; and (4) the probability that no meeting (or trade) occurs and the agent enters the night market with m.

Because the day meetings each involve just two agents, the search literature has generally assumed the price and quantity exchanged, q_t and d_t, are determined by Nash bargaining between the agents. When a double coincidence of wants occurs, the joint surplus is maximized when q^* is exchanged, where

$$u'(q^*) = c'(q^*).$$

Hence, $B_t(m, \tilde{m}) = u(q^*) - c(q^*) + W_t(m)$.

When a single coincidence occurs, bargaining is more complicated. Let the buyer's share of the joint surplus from a bargain be $\theta \in [0 \quad 1]$. The threat point of a buyer is $W_t(m)$; that of the seller is $W_t(\tilde{m})$, where m and $\tilde{m}$ are the buyer's and the seller's initial money holdings. The exchange of q for d units of money maximizes

$$[u(q) + W_t(m - d) - W_t(m)]^\theta [-c(q) + W_t(m + d) - W_t(m)]^{1-\theta}, \qquad (3.57)$$

subject to $d \geq 0$, $q \geq 0$. Recall that $W_t(m)$ is linear in m. Hence, (3.57) can be rewritten as

$$[u(q) - \phi_t d]^\theta [-c(q) + \phi_t d]^{1-\theta}. \qquad (3.58)$$

If $d \leq m$, money holdings are not a binding constraint, and the first-order conditions with respect to d and q yield

$$-\theta \phi_t [u(q) - \phi_t d]^{-1} + (1 - \theta)\phi_t [-c(q) + \phi_t d]^{-1} = 0$$

$$\theta u'(q)[u(q) - \phi_t d]^{-1} - (1 - \theta)c'(q)[-c(q) + \phi_t d]^{-1} = 0,$$

or

$$u'(q) = c'(q) \Rightarrow q_t = q^*$$

$$\phi_t d^* = \theta c(q^*) + (1 - \theta)u(q^*).$$

The monetary cost of q, d^*, is a weighted average of the cost of producing it and the value of consuming it, with weights reflecting the bargaining power of the buyer and seller.

If $d^* > m$, then the buyer does not have the cash necessary to purchase q^*; in effect, the cash-in-advance constraint is binding. In this case, Lagos and Wright (2005) showed, the seller receives all the buyer's money, so

$$\phi_t d_t = \phi_t m = z(q_t),\tag{3.59}$$

where q_t is the solution to the constrained Nash bargaining problem.[33] The quantity transacted and the price depend on the buyer's money holdings but do not depend on the seller's; this quantity can be expressed as a function of m: $q_t = q_t(m)$.

Lagos and Wright showed that m', the amount of money agents carry out of the night market is less than d^* whenever the inflation rate, $(\phi_t/\phi_{t+1}) - 1$, exceeds $\beta - 1$. Recall that an inflation rate of $\beta - 1$ corresponds to the Friedman rule of a zero nominal interest rate. So, just as in the earlier CIA models, the cash-in-advance constraint is binding when the nominal rate of interest is positive. Of course, the constraint only binds for agents who find buyers in single coincidence of wants meetings. Sellers, or those in a double coincidence of wants meeting or in no meeting, exit the period with unchanged money holdings.

Now consider the value to an agent of entering the day market with money holdings m. This value arises from the effects of m on price and quantity when the agent is the buyer in a single coincidence of wants meeting. Since the probability that this occurs is $\alpha\sigma$, it can be expressed, using (3.56), as

$$v_t(m) = \alpha\sigma \int \{u[q_t(m)] - \phi_t d_t(m)\} \, dF_t(\tilde{m}).$$

The value of money is then given by the pricing equation

$$\phi_t = \beta[v'_{t+1}(M) + \phi_{t+1}],\tag{3.60}$$

where M is the aggregate nominal quantity of money. Because $d'_{t+1}(M) = 1$ (an increase in the quantity of money increases the number of dollars needed to purchase goods by the same amount),

$$v'_{t+1}(M) = \alpha\sigma[u'[q_{t+1}(M)]q'_{t+1}(M) - \phi_{t+1}].$$

Using this in (3.60),

$$\phi_t = \beta\alpha\sigma u'[q_{t+1}]q'_{t+1}(M) + \beta(1 - \alpha\sigma)\phi_{t+1}.\tag{3.61}$$

---

33. $\hat{q}(m)$ solves

$$\frac{\theta c(q)u'(q) + (1-\theta)u(q)c'(q)}{\theta u'(q) + (1-\theta)c'(q)} = \phi_t m.$$

See Lagos and Wright (2005) for details.

The value of money is determined by the marginal utility of the goods the agent is able to consume when faced with a single coincidence of wants trading opportunity. If such meetings are uncommon ($\alpha\sigma$ is small), money will be less useful and therefore less valuable. This implication of search models of money emphasizes the importance of the trading environment for determining the value of money.

Equation (3.61) can be rewritten, using (3.59), as[34]

$$\phi_t = \beta \left[\alpha\sigma \frac{u'(q_{t+1})}{z'(q_{t+1})} + (1 - \alpha\sigma) \right] \phi_{t+1}.$$

Now consider a steady state in which the money stock grows at the rate τ. The inflation rate will also equal τ: $(\phi_t/\phi_{t+1}) - 1 = \tau$. Thus,

$$\phi_t = \beta \left[\alpha\sigma \frac{u'(q_{t+1})}{z'(q_{t+1})} + (1 - \alpha\sigma) \right] \phi_{t+1} \Rightarrow 1 = \beta \left[\alpha\sigma \frac{u'(q)}{z'(q)} + (1 - \alpha\sigma) \right] \left(\frac{1}{1+\tau} \right),$$

using (3.59). Solving for u'/z',

$$\frac{u'(q)}{z'(q)} = \frac{1 + \tau - \beta(1 - \alpha\sigma)}{\beta\alpha\sigma} = 1 + \frac{1 + \tau - \beta}{\beta\alpha\sigma}.$$

The left side of this equation, u'/z', is the marginal utility of consumption divided by the marginal cost of the good. The right side is 1 plus a term that can be written as $\beta^{-1}(1 + \tau) - 1$ divided by $\alpha\sigma$. But since β^{-1} is the gross real interest rate, and τ is the inflation rate, $\beta^{-1}(1 + \tau) - 1$ is the nominal rate of interest, so

$$\frac{u'(q)}{z'(q)} = 1 + \frac{i}{\alpha\sigma}. \tag{3.62}$$

This looks very similar to earlier results from a CIA model (see (3.33)). A positive nominal interest rate acts as a tax on consumption. But this tax now also depends on the nature of trading. An increase in the frequency of single coincidence of wants meetings, by raising the usefulness of money, reduces the net cost of holding money.

While it is clear that the tax is zero if the Friedman rule of a zero nominal interest rate is followed, Lagos and Wright showed that the equilibrium with $i = 0$ is still not fully efficient because of the trading frictions associated with bargaining in the decentralized market. Efficiency requires that all the surplus go to the buyer ($\theta = 1$).[35] In standard models such as the MIU model in chapter 2, or the CIA model developed in

---

34. Equation (3.59) implies $q' = \phi/z'$.

35. This is essentially the Hosios (1990) condition for this model; since the quantity transacted is independent of the seller's money holdings, all the surplus is due to the buyer, so efficiency would require $\theta = 1$.

section 3.3, full efficiency is attained with $i = 0$. Then, since $i = 0$ maximizes welfare, small deviations have small effects on welfare (basically an application of the envelope theorem). But if $\theta < 1$, the equilibrium with $i = 0$ in the search model does not fully maximize utility. Hence, small deviations from the Friedman rule can have first-order effects on welfare. By calibrating their model, Lagos and Wright found much larger welfare costs of positive nominal interest rates than other authors had found.

The importance of the trading environment in determining the costs of inflation was further explored by Rocheteau and Wright (2005). They compared welfare costs in three settings: a search model similar to Lagos and Wright (2005), a competitive market model, and a search model with posted prices (rather than the bilateral bargaining of the basic search model). By allowing for endogenous determination of the number of market participants, Rocheteau and Wright introduced an extensive margin (the effects on the value of money as the number of traders varies) as well as an intensive margin (the effects for a given number of traders as individual agent's money holdings vary). The Friedman rule always ensures efficiency along the intensive margin, but the extensive margin may still generate a source of inefficiency. Interestingly, if the market makers in the competitive search version of the model internalize the effects of the prices they post on the number of traders they attract, the model endogenously ensures that the Hosios condition is satisfied and the equilibrium is fully efficient when the nominal rate of interest is zero. Lagos and Rocheteau (2005) explored the interactions of the pricing mechanism (bilateral bargaining versus posted pricing) and found that with directed search, inflation can increase search intensities when inflation is low but reduce them when inflation is high. Thus, at low inflation rates, an increase in inflation can raise output, but they showed that this actually reduces welfare and that the Friedman rule supports the efficient equilibrium.

The Lagos and Wright model has only one nominal asset—money. If an interest-bearing nominal asset such as a bond were introduced into the analysis, it would dominate money whenever the nominal interest rate is positive. To explain the simultaneous existence of interest-bearing nominal bonds and non-interest-bearing money, Shi (2005) employed a model with a decentralized goods market and a centralized bond market but in which there are assumed to be barriers to trading across markets. Households can use either bonds or money in the goods market, but only money can be used to purchase bonds. At the start of each period, the household must allocate its money holdings between the two markets. Assume a fraction a is sent to the goods market and $1 - a$ to the bond market. Let ω_t^m denote the value of money at the end of period t. Then Shi showed that

$$\omega_t^m = \beta a \alpha \sigma \lambda_{t+1}^m + \beta \omega_{t+1}^m,$$

where β is the discount factor, α and σ are the probability of meeting a potential trading partner and the probability that there is single coincidence of wants, and λ^m is the Lagrangian multiplier on the constraint that the money payment from buyer to seller in the goods market must be less than the buyer's money holdings. Thus, $a\alpha\sigma\lambda^m_{t+1}$ is the service value of money in facilitating a goods purchase. The current value of money is equal to this service value plus the discounted future value of money.

Money that the household sends to the bond market cannot be used to purchase current goods, nor can the newly purchased bonds be used to exchange for goods. While bonds can, in future periods, be used to purchase goods, purchasing bonds initially entails a one-period loss of liquidity. Therefore, bonds must sell at a discount relative to money; if S is the money price of a bond, $S < 1$. Shi demonstrated that the nominal interest rate, $(1 - S)/S$, is given by

$$\frac{1 - S}{S} = \frac{a\alpha\sigma\lambda^m}{\omega^m},$$ (3.63)

which is positive if λ^m is positive. This expression for the nominal interest rate can be compared to (3.32) obtained in a basic cash-in-advance model. Similar to the result in other models in the search literature, (3.63) reveals how the nature of transactions in the decentralized market as reflected in the parameters α and σ affect the value of money and the nominal interest rate.

In Shi's basic model, old bonds and money can both circulate in the goods market and be used in purchasing goods. Suppose, however, that the government also engages as a seller in the goods market, and assume the government only accepts money in payment for goods. Since there is a chance a household will encounter a government seller in the decentralized market, and frictions are assumed to prevent the household from locating another seller, there is a smaller probability of a successful trade if the household carries only bonds into the goods market than if it carries money. This difference drives bonds out of the goods market, and Shi showed that only money circulates as a means of payment.

The search-theoretic approach to monetary economics provides a natural framework for addressing a number of issues. Ritter (1995) used it to examine the conditions necessary for fiat money to arise, linking it to the credibility of the issuer. Governments lacking credibility would be expected to overissue the currency to gain seigniorage. In this case, agents would be unwilling to hold the fiat money. Soller and Waller (2000) used a search-theoretic approach to study the coexistence of legal and illegal currencies. By stressing the role of money in facilitating exchange, the search-theoretic approach emphasizes the role of money as a medium of exchange. The approach also emphasizes the social aspect of valued money; agents are willing to accept fiat money only in environments in which they expect others to accept such money.[36]

3.5 Summary

The models studied in this chapter are among the basic frameworks monetary economists have found useful for understanding the steady-state implications of inflation and the steady-state welfare implications of alternative rates of inflation. These models and those of chapter 2 assume prices are perfectly flexible, adjusting to ensure that market equilibrium is continuously maintained. The MIU, CIA, shopping-time, and search models all represent means of introducing valued money into a general equilibrium framework. Each approach captures some aspects of the role that money plays in facilitating transactions.

Despite the different approaches, several conclusions are common to all. First, because the price level is completely flexible, the value of money, equal to 1 over the price of goods, behaves like an asset price.[37] The return money yields, however, differs in the various approaches. In the MIU model, the marginal utility of money is the direct return, whereas in the CIA model, this return is measured by the Lagrangian multiplier on the CIA constraint. In the shopping-time model, the return arises from the time savings provided by money in carrying out transactions, and the value of this time savings depends on the real wage. In search models it depends on the probability of trading opportunities.

All these models have similar implications for the optimal rate of inflation. An efficient equilibrium will be characterized by equality between social and private costs. Because the social cost of producing money is taken to be zero, the private opportunity cost of holding money must be zero in order to achieve optimality. The private opportunity cost is measured by the nominal interest rate, so the optimal rate of inflation in the steady state is the rate that achieves a zero nominal rate of interest. While this result is quite general, two important considerations—the effects of inflation on government revenues and the interaction of inflation with other taxes in a nonindexed tax system—have been ignored. These are among the topics of chapter 4.

3.6 Appendix: The CIA Approximation

The method used to obtain a linear approximation around the steady state for the CIA model is discussed here. Since the approach is similar to the one followed for

---

36. Samuelson (1958) was one of the earliest modern treatments of money as a social construct.
37. Of course, this is clearly not the case in the search models that assume fixed prices.

the MIU model, some details are skipped. The basic equations of the model are given by (3.37)–(3.42).

3.6.1 The Steady State

The steady-state values of the ratios that were reported in section 2.5.4 for the MIU model also characterize the steady state for the CIA model. See the appendix to chapter 2 for details.

With a binding CIA constraint, $c^{ss} = \tau^{ss} + m^{ss}/(1 + \pi^{ss})$, but in a steady state with m constant, $\tau^{ss} + m^{ss}/(1 + \pi^{ss}) = m^{ss}$. Thus, $c^{ss} = m^{ss}$, and $m^{ss}/c^{ss} = 1$.

From the first-order condition for the household's choice of n,

$$\Psi(1 - n^{ss})^{-\eta} = (1 - \alpha)\left(\frac{y^{ss}}{n^{ss}}\right)\lambda^{ss}, \tag{3.64}$$

and since y^{ss}/k^{ss} takes on the same values as in the MIU model (because the production technology and the discount factor are identical), it only remains to determine the marginal utility of income λ^{ss}. From (3.37) and (3.40), $(c^{ss})^{-\Phi} = \lambda^{ss} + \mu^{ss} = \lambda^{ss}(1 + i^{ss})$. Using this relationship in (3.41) yields

$$\lambda^{ss} = \beta\left[\frac{\lambda^{ss}(1 + i^{ss})}{1 + \theta^{ss}}\right] \Rightarrow 1 + i^{ss} = \frac{1 + \theta^{ss}}{\beta},$$

where $\theta^{ss} = \pi^{ss}$. This is the steady-state version of the Fisher equation, and it means one can write

$$\lambda^{ss} = \frac{(c^{ss})^{-\Phi}}{1 + i^{ss}} = \frac{\beta(c^{ss})^{-\Phi}}{1 + \theta^{ss}}.$$

Combining this with (3.64) and multiplying and dividing appropriately by k^{ss} and n^{ss},

$$\Psi(1 - n^{ss})^{-\eta} = (1 - \alpha)\left(\frac{\beta}{1 + \theta^{ss}}\right)\left(\frac{y^{ss}}{k^{ss}}\right)\left(\frac{c^{ss}}{k^{ss}}\right)^{-\Phi}\left(\frac{k^{ss}}{n^{ss}}\right)^{1-\Phi}(n^{ss})^{-\Phi}.$$

The production function implies that $n^{ss}/k^{ss} = (y^{ss}/k^{ss})^{1/(1-\alpha)}$, so one obtains

$$(1 - n^{ss})^{-\eta}(n^{ss})^{\Phi} = \left(\frac{1 - \alpha}{\Psi}\right)\left(\frac{\beta}{1 + \theta^{ss}}\right)\left(\frac{y^{ss}}{k^{ss}}\right)^{(\Phi-\alpha)/(1-\alpha)}\left(\frac{c^{ss}}{k^{ss}}\right)^{-\Phi}.$$

It is useful to note that the expressions for y^{ss}/k^{ss}, c^{ss}/k^{ss}, r^{ss}, and n^{ss}/k^{ss} are identical to those obtained in the MIU model. Only the equation determining n^{ss} differs from the one found in chapter 2.

3.6.2 The Linear Approximation

Expressions linear in the percentage deviations around the steady state can be obtained for the economy's production function, resource constraint, the definition of the marginal product of capital, and the first-order conditions for consumption, money holdings, and labor supply, as was done for the MIU model. The economy's production function, resource constraint, the definition of the marginal product of capital, and the labor-leisure first-order condition are identical to those of the MIU model,[38] so they are simply stated here:

$$\hat{y}_t = \alpha \hat{k}_{t-1} + (1 - \alpha)\hat{n}_t + z_t \tag{3.65}$$

$$\hat{k}_t = (1 - \delta)\hat{k}_{t-1} + \left(\frac{y^{ss}}{k^{ss}}\right)\hat{y}_t - \left(\frac{c^{ss}}{k^{ss}}\right)\hat{c}_t \tag{3.66}$$

$$\hat{r}_t = \alpha \left(\frac{y^{ss}}{k^{ss}}\right)(E_t\hat{y}_{t+1} - \hat{k}_t) \tag{3.67}$$

$$\left(1 + \eta\frac{n^{ss}}{l^{ss}}\right)\hat{n}_t = \hat{y}_t + \hat{\lambda}_t. \tag{3.68}$$

Proceeding in exactly the same manner as was done for the MIU model, $E_t\hat{y}_{t+1}$ is eliminated from (3.67) to obtain

$$(1 + \kappa)\hat{r}_t = -\kappa\eta\left(\frac{n^{ss}}{l^{ss}}\right)\hat{k}_t + \kappa\hat{\lambda}_t + \kappa\left(\frac{1 + \eta\left(\frac{n^{ss}}{l^{ss}}\right)}{1 - \alpha}\right)\rho_z z_t, \tag{3.69}$$

where

$$\kappa \equiv \alpha\left(\frac{y^{ss}}{k^{ss}}\right)\left(\frac{1 - \alpha}{\alpha + \eta\left(\frac{n^{ss}}{l^{ss}}\right)}\right).$$

From the CIA constraint, $c_t = m_t$, so

$$\hat{c}_t = \hat{m}_t \tag{3.70}$$

in an equilibrium with a positive nominal rate of interest. Eliminating consumption and noting that $\lambda_{t+1} + \mu_{t+1} = c_{t+1}^{-\Phi} = m_{t+1}^{-\Phi}$, (3.41) implies

$$\lambda_t = \beta E_t\left[\frac{m_{t+1}^{-\Phi}}{1 + \pi_{t+1}}\right],$$

---

38. See the chapter 2 appendix.

and (3.37) and (3.40), together with the cash-in-advance constraint, imply

$$m_t^{-\Phi} = \lambda_t(1 + i_t).$$

Linearizing these last two equations, together with (3.38)–(3.40) around the steady state, one obtains

$$\hat{\lambda}_t = -E_t[\Phi \hat{m}_{t+1} + \hat{\pi}_{t+1}]$$

$$= -\Phi(\hat{m}_t + \rho_u u_t + \phi z_t) - (1 - \Phi)E_t\hat{\pi}_{t+1} \tag{3.71}$$

$$\hat{\lambda}_t = E_t\hat{\lambda}_{t+1} + \hat{r}_t \tag{3.72}$$

$$\hat{i}_t = -\left(\frac{1}{1 + i^{ss}}\right)(\Phi \hat{m}_t + \hat{\lambda}_t). \tag{3.73}$$

Notice that in (3.71), (3.52) has been used to replace $E_t\hat{m}_{t+1}$ by $\hat{m}_t - E_t\hat{\pi}_{t+1} + E_t u_{t+1}$ $= \hat{m}_t - E_t\hat{\pi}_{t+1} + \rho_u u_t + \phi z_t$.

Finally, introduce $\hat{x}_t$ as the percentage deviation of investment around the steady state:

$$\hat{k}_t = (1 - \delta)\hat{k}_{t-1} + \delta\hat{x}_t. \tag{3.74}$$

Collecting All Equations

To summarize, the linearized model consists of equations (3.65), (3.66), (3.68), (3.69), (3.70), (3.71), (3.72), (3.73) and (3.74), together with the processes for the two exogenous shocks and the equation governing the evolution of real money balances. The resulting twelve equations solve for z_t, u_t, $\hat{y}_t$, $\hat{k}_t$, $\hat{n}_t$, $\hat{\lambda}_t$, $\hat{c}_t$, $\hat{x}_t$, $\hat{m}_t$, $\hat{r}_t$, $\hat{i}_t$, and $\hat{\pi}_t$. Collecting all the equilibrium conditions together, they are

$$z_t = \rho_z z_{t-1} + e_t$$

$$u_t = \rho_u u_{t-1} + \phi z_{t-1} + \varphi_t$$

$$\hat{y}_t = \alpha\hat{k}_{t-1} + (1 - \alpha)\hat{n}_t + z_t$$

$$\left(\frac{y^{ss}}{k^{ss}}\right)\hat{y}_t = \left(\frac{c^{ss}}{k^{ss}}\right)\hat{c}_t + \delta\hat{x}_t$$

$$\hat{k}_t = (1 - \delta)\hat{k}_{t-1} + \delta\hat{x}_t$$

$$\left[1 + \eta\left(\frac{n^{ss}}{l^{ss}}\right)\right]\hat{n}_t = \hat{y}_t + \lambda_t$$

$$(1+\kappa)\hat{r}_t = -\kappa\eta\left(\frac{n^{ss}}{l^{ss}}\right)\hat{k}_t + \kappa\hat{\lambda}_t + \kappa\left(\frac{1+\eta\left(\frac{n^{ss}}{l^{ss}}\right)}{1-\alpha}\right)\rho_z z_t$$

$$\hat{c}_t = \hat{m}_t$$

$$\hat{\lambda}_t = -\Phi(\hat{m}_t + \rho_u u_t + \phi z_t) - (1-\Phi)E_t\hat{\pi}_{t+1}$$

$$\hat{\imath}_t = -\left(\frac{1}{1+i^{ss}}\right)(\Phi\hat{m}_t + \hat{\lambda}_t)$$

$$\hat{m}_t = u_t - \hat{\pi}_t + \hat{m}_{t-1}$$

$$\hat{\lambda}_t = \hat{r}_t + E_t\hat{\lambda}_{t+1}.$$

The Matlab program used to simulate this CIA model and additional details on the derivation of the linearized model are available at ⟨http://people.ucsc.edu/~walshc/mtp3e/⟩.

3.7   Problems

1. Suppose the production function for shopping takes the form $\psi = c = e^x(n^s)^a m^b$, where a and b are both positive but less than 1, and x is a productivity factor. The agent's utility is given by $v(c,l) = c^{1-\Phi}/(1-\Phi) + l^{1-\eta}/(1-\eta)$, where $l = 1 - n - n^s$ and n is time spent in market employment.

a. Derive the transaction time function $g(c,m) = n^s$.

b. Derive the money-in-the-utility function specification implied by the shopping production function. How does the marginal utility of money depend on the parameters a and b? How does it depend on x?

c. Is the marginal utility of consumption increasing or decreasing in m?

2. Using (3.5) and (3.8), show that

$$\frac{V_a(a_t, k_{t-1})}{P_t} = -\sum_{i-0}^{\infty}\beta^i\left(\frac{v_l(a_{t+i}, k_{t+i-1})g_m(c_{t+i}, m_{t+i})}{P_{t+i}}\right).$$

Interpret this equation. How does it compare to (3.31)?

3. Show that for the shopping-time model of section 3.2.1, the tax on consumption is given by

$$-\left(\frac{i_t}{1+i_t}\right)\left(\frac{g_c}{g_m}\right).$$

(Recall that money reduced shopping time, so $g_m \leq 0$.) Provide an intuitive interpretation for this expression.

4. Use (3.40) and (3.41) to demonstrate that the Lagrangian multipliers λ_t and λ_{t+1} are linked by $(1 + i_{t+1})/(1 + \pi_{t+1})$.

5. MIU and CIA models are alternative approaches to constructing models in which money has positive value in equilibrium.

a. What strengths and weaknesses do you see in each of these approaches?

b. Suppose you wanted to study the effects of the growth of credit cards on money demand. Which approach would you adopt? Why?

6. Modify the basic model of section 3.3.1 by assuming utility depends on the consumption of two goods, denoted C_t^m and C_t^c. Purchases of C_t^m are subject to a cash-in-advance constraint; purchases of C_t^c are not. The two goods are produced by the same technology: $C_t^m + C_t^c = Y_t = f(k_t)$.

a. Write down the household's decision problem.

b. Write down the first-order conditions for the household's optimal choices for C_t^m and C_t^c. How are these affected by the cash-in-advance constraint?

c. Show that the nominal rate of interest acts as a tax on the consumption of C_t^m.

7. Assume the model of section 3.3.1 is modified so that only a fraction ψ of consumption must be purchased using cash. In this case, the cash-in-advance constraint takes the form

$$\psi c_t \leq \frac{m_{t-1}}{1 + \pi_t} + \tau_t, \qquad 0 < \psi \leq 1.$$

a. Write down the household's decision problem.

b. Write down the household's first-order conditions. How are these affected by ψ?

c. If ψ were a choice variable of the household, would it ever choose $\psi > 0$?

8. Modify the model of section 3.3.1 so that only a fraction ψ of consumption is subject to the cash-in-advance constraint. How is the impact of a serially correlated shock to the money growth rate on real output affected by ψ? (Use the programs available at ⟨http://people.ucsc.edu/~walshc/mtp3e⟩ to answer this question, and compare the impulse response of output for $\psi = 0.25, 0.5, 0.75$, and 1.)

9. Consider the model of section 3.3.1. Suppose that money is required to purchase both consumption and investment goods. The CIA constraint then becomes $c_t + x_t \leq m_{t-1}/(1 + \pi_t) + \tau_t$, where x is investment. Assume that the aggregate production function takes the form $y_t = e^{z_t} k_{t-1}^{\alpha} n_t^{1-\alpha}$. Show that the steady-state capital-labor ratio is affected by the rate of inflation. Does a rise in inflation raise or lower the steady-state capital-labor ratio? Explain.

10. Consider the following model. Preferences are given by

$$E_t \sum_{i=0}^{\infty} \beta^i [\ln c_{t+i} + \theta \ln d_{t+i}],$$

and the budget and CIA constraints take the form

$$c_t + d_t + m_t + k_t = Ak_{t-1}^a + (1 - \delta)k_{t-1} + \tau_t + \frac{m_{t-1}}{1 + \pi_t}$$

$$c_t \le \tau_t + \frac{m_{t-1}}{1 + \pi_t},$$

where m denotes real money balances, and π_t is the inflation rate from period $t - 1$ to period t. The two consumption goods, c and d, represent cash (c) and credit (d) goods. The net transfer τ is viewed as a lump-sum payment (or tax) by the household.

a. Does this model exhibit superneutrality? Explain.

b. What is the rate of inflation that maximizes steady-state utility?

11. Consider the following model. Preferences are given by

$$E_t \sum_{i=0}^{\infty} \beta^i [\ln c_{t+i} + \ln d_{t+i}],$$

and the budget constraint is

$$c_t + d_t + m_t + k_t = Ak_{t-1}^a + \tau_t + \frac{m_{t-1}}{1 + \pi_t} + (1 - \delta)k_{t-1},$$

where m denotes real money balances, and π_t is the inflation rate from period $t - 1$ to period t. Utility depends on the consumption of two types of good; c must be purchased with cash, whereas d can be purchased using either cash or credit. The net transfer τ is viewed as a lump-sum payment (or tax) by the household. If a fraction θ of d is purchased using cash, then the household also faces a CIA constraint of the form

$$c_t + \theta d_t \le \frac{m_{t-1}}{1 + \pi_t} + \tau_t.$$

What is the relationship between the nominal rate of interest and whether the CIA constraint is binding? Explain. Will the household ever use cash to purchase d (i.e., will the optimal θ ever be greater than zero)?

12. Suppose the representative household enters period t with nominal money balances M_{t-1} and receives a lump-sum transfer T_t. During period t, the bond market opens first, and the household receives interest payments and purchases nominal bonds in the amount B_t. With its remaining money $(M_{t-1} + T_t + (1 + i_{t-1})B_{t-1} - B_t)$, the household enters the goods market and purchases consumption goods subject to

$$P_t c_t \leq M_{t-1} + T_t + (1 + i_{t-1})B_{t-1} - B_t.$$

The household receives income at the end of the period and ends period t with nominal money holdings M_t, given by

$$M_t = P_t e^{z_t} K_{t-1}^{\alpha} N_t^{1-\alpha} + (1 - \delta)P_t K_{t-1} - P_t K_t + M_{t-1}$$

$$+ T_t + (1 + i_{t-1})B_{t-1} - B_t - P_t c_t.$$

If the household's objective is to maximize

$$E_0 \sum_{i=0}^{\infty} \beta^i u(c_{t+i}, 1 - N_{t+i}) = E_0 \sum_{i=0}^{\infty} \beta^i \left[\frac{c_{t+i}^{1-\Phi}}{1 - \Phi} + \Psi \frac{(1 - N_{t+i})^{1-\eta}}{1 - \eta} \right],$$

do the equilibrium conditions differ from (3.37)–(3.41)?

13. Trejos and Wright (1993) found that if no search is allowed while bargaining takes place, output tends to be too low (the marginal utility of output exceeds the marginal production costs). Show that output is also too low in a basic CIA model. (For simplicity, assume that only labor is needed to produce output according to the production function $y = n$.) Does the same hold true in an MIU model?

14. For the bargaining problem of section 3.4, the buyer and seller exchange q for d, where these two values maximize (3.57). Verify that when money holdings are not a constraint

$$\phi_t d^* = \theta c(q^*) + (1 - \theta)u(q^*).$$

15. Equation (3.62) shows how the nominal interest rate acts as a positive tax on consumption. Discuss how this condition compares to (3.33) from the basic CIA model. If the CIA model is interpreted as one in which trading takes place with certainty and always involves a single coincidence of wants, can the CIA model be viewed as a special case of the search model?

4 Money and Public Finance

4.1 Introduction

Inflation is a tax. And as a tax, it both generates revenue for the government and distorts private sector behavior. Chapters 2 and 3 focused on these distortions. In the Sidrauski model, inflation distorts the demand for money, thereby generating welfare effects because real money holdings directly yield utility. In the cash-in-advance model, inflation serves as an implicit tax on consumption, so a higher inflation rate generates a substitution toward leisure, leading to lower labor supply, output, and consumption.

In the analysis of these distortions, the revenue side of the inflation tax was ignored except to note that the Friedman rule for the optimal rate of inflation may need to be modified if the government does not have lump-sum sources of revenue available. Any change in inflation that affects the revenue from the inflation tax will have budgetary implications for the government. If higher inflation allows other forms of distortionary taxation to be reduced, this fact must be incorporated into any assessment of the costs of the inflation tax. This chapter introduces the government sector's budget constraint and examines the revenue implications of inflation. This allows a more explicit focus on the role of inflation in a theory of public finance and draws on the literature on optimal taxation to analyze the effects of inflation.

A public finance approach yields several insights. Among the most important is the recognition that fiscal and monetary policies are linked through the government sector's budget constraint. Variations in the inflation rate can have implications for the fiscal authority's decisions about expenditures and taxes, and, conversely, decisions by the fiscal authority can have implications for money growth and inflation. When inflation is viewed as a distortionary revenue-generating tax, the degree to which it should be relied upon depends on the set of alternative taxes available to the government and on the reasons individuals hold money. Whether the most appropriate strategy is to think of money as entering the utility function as a final good or as an intermediate input into the production of transaction services can have implications for whether money should be taxed. The optimal tax perspective also has empirical implications for inflation.

In the next section, the consolidated government's budget identity is set out, and some of the revenue implications of inflation are examined. Section 4.3 introduces various assumptions that can be made about the relationship between monetary and fiscal policies. Section 4.4 discusses situations of fiscal dominance in which a fixed amount of revenue must be raised from the inflation tax. It then discusses the equilibrium relationship between money and the price level. Section 4.5 turns to recent theories that emphasize what has come to be called the *fiscal theory of the price level*. In section 4.6, inflation revenue (seigniorage) and other taxes are brought together to analyze the joint determination of the government's tax instruments. This theme is developed first in a partial equilibrium model, and then Friedman's rule for the optimal inflation rate is revisited. The implications of optimal Ramsey taxation for inflation are discussed. Finally, section 4.6.4 contains a brief discussion of some additional effects that arise when the tax system is not fully indexed.

4.2   Budget Accounting

To obtain goods and services, governments in market economies need to generate revenue. And one way that they can obtain goods and services is to print money that is then used to purchase resources from the private sector. However, to understand the revenue implications of inflation (and the inflation implications of the government's revenue needs), one must start with the government's budget constraint.[1]

Consider the following identity for the fiscal branch of a government:

$$G_t + i_{t-1}B_{t-1}^T = T_t + (B_t^T - B_{t-1}^T) + \text{RCB}_t, \tag{4.1}$$

where all variables are in nominal terms. The left side consists of government expenditures on goods, services, and transfers G_t, plus interest payments on the outstanding debt $i_{t-1}B_{t-1}^T$ (the superscript T denoting total debt, assumed to be one period in maturity, where debt issued in period $t - 1$ earns the nominal interest rate i_{t-1}), and the right side consists of tax revenue T_t, plus new issues of interest-bearing debt $B_t^T - B_{t-1}^T$, plus any direct receipts from the central bank RCB_t. As an example of RCB, the U.S. Federal Reserve turns over to the Treasury almost all the interest

---

1. Bohn (1992) provided a general discussion of government deficits and accounting.

earnings on its portfolio of government debt.[2] Equation (4.1) is referred to as the *Treasury's budget constraint.*

The monetary authority, or central bank, also has a budget identity that links changes in its assets and liabilities. This takes the form

$$(B_t^M - B_{t-1}^M) + \text{RCB}_t = i_{t-1}B_{t-1}^M + (H_t - H_{t-1}), \tag{4.2}$$

where $B_t^M - B_{t-1}^M$ is equal to the central bank's purchases of government debt, $i_{t-1}B_{t-1}^M$ is the central bank's receipt of interest payments from the Treasury, and $H_t - H_{t-1}$ is the change in the central bank's own liabilities. These liabilities are called *high-powered money*, or sometimes the *monetary base*, because they form the stock of currency held by the nonbank public plus bank reserves, and they represent the reserves private banks can use to back deposits. Changes in the stock of high-powered money lead to changes in broader measures of the money supply, measures that normally include various types of bank deposits as well as currency held by the public (see chapter 11).

By letting $B = B^T - B^M$ be the stock of government interest-bearing debt held by the public, the budget identities of the Treasury and the central bank can be combined to produce the consolidated government sector budget identity:

$$G_t + i_{t-1}B_{t-1} = T_t + (B_t - B_{t-1}) + (H_t - H_{t-1}). \tag{4.3}$$

From the perspective of the consolidated government sector, only debt held by the public (i.e., outside the government sector) represents an interest-bearing liability.

According to (4.3), the dollar value of government purchases G_t, plus its payment of interest on outstanding privately held debt $i_{t-1}B_{t-1}$, must be funded by revenue that can be obtained from one of three alternative sources. First, T_t represents revenues generated by taxes (other than inflation). Second, the government can obtain funds by borrowing from the private sector. This borrowing is equal to the change in the debt held by the private sector, $B_t - B_{t-1}$. Finally, the government can print currency to pay for its expenditures, and this is represented by the change in the outstanding stock of non-interest-bearing debt, $H_t - H_{t-1}$.

Equation (4.3) can be divided by the price level P_t to obtain

$$\frac{G_t}{P_t} + i_{t-1}\left(\frac{B_{t-1}}{P_t}\right) = \frac{T_t}{P_t} + \frac{B_t - B_{t-1}}{P_t} + \frac{H_t - H_{t-1}}{P_t}.$$

Note that terms like B_{t-1}/P_t can be multiplied and divided by P_{t-1}, yielding

---

2. In 2007 the Federal Reserve banks turned over $34.6 billion to the Treasury (*93d Annual Report of the Federal Reserve System* 2007, 161). Klein and Neumann (1990) showed how the revenue generated by seigniorage and the revenue received by the fiscal branch may differ.

$$\frac{B_{t-1}}{P_t} = \left(\frac{B_{t-1}}{P_{t-1}}\right)\left(\frac{P_{t-1}}{P_t}\right) = b_{t-1}\left(\frac{1}{1+\pi_t}\right),$$

where $b_{t-1} = B_{t-1}/P_{t-1}$ represents real debt and π_t is the inflation rate.[3] With the convention that lowercase letters denote variables deflated by the price level, the government's budget identity is

$$g_t + \bar{r}_{t-1}b_{t-1} = t_t + (b_t - b_{t-1}) + h_t - \frac{h_{t-1}}{(1+\pi_t)}, \tag{4.4}$$

where $\bar{r}_{t-1} = [(1+i_{t-1})/(1+\pi_t)] - 1$ is the ex post real return from $t-1$ to t.

To highlight the respective roles of anticipated and unanticipated inflation, let r_t be the ex ante real rate of return and let π_t^e be the expected rate of inflation; then $1 + i_{t-1} = (1 + r_{t-1})(1 + \pi_t^e)$. Adding $(r_{t-1} - \bar{r}_{t-1})b_{t-1} = (\pi_t - \pi_t^e)(1 + r_{t-1})b_{t-1}/(1+\pi_t)$ to both sides of (4.4), and rearranging, the budget constraint becomes

$$g_t + r_{t-1}b_{t-1} = t_t + (b_t - b_{t-1}) + \left(\frac{\pi_t - \pi_t^e}{1+\pi_t}\right)(1 + r_{t-1})b_{t-1} + \left[h_t - \left(\frac{1}{1+\pi_t}\right)h_{t-1}\right]. \tag{4.5}$$

The third term on the right side of this expression, involving $(\pi_t - \pi_t^e)b_{t-1}$, represents the revenue generated when unanticipated inflation reduces the real value of the government's outstanding interest-bearing nominal debt. To the extent that inflation is anticipated, this term will be zero; π_t^e will be reflected in the nominal interest rate that the government must pay. Inflation by itself does not reduce the burden of the government's interest-bearing debt; only unexpected inflation has such an effect.

The last bracketed term in (4.5) represents seigniorage, the revenue from money creation. Seigniorage can be written as

$$s_t \equiv \frac{H_t - H_{t-1}}{P_t} = (h_t - h_{t-1}) + \left(\frac{\pi_t}{1+\pi_t}\right)h_{t-1}. \tag{4.6}$$

Seigniorage arises from two sources. First, $h_t - h_{t-1}$ is equal to the change in real high-powered money holdings. Since the government is the monopoly issuer of high-powered money, an increase in the amount of high-powered money that the private sector is willing to hold allows the government to obtain real resources in return. In a steady-state equilibrium, h is constant, so this source of seigniorage then equals zero.

---

3. If one is dealing with a growing economy, it is appropriate to deflate nominal variables by the price level and the level of output, i.e., by $P_t Y_t$. If the growth rate of output is μ_t, then $B_{t-1}/P_t Y_t = b_{t-1}[1/(1+\pi_t)(1+\mu_t)]$.

The second term in (4.6) is normally the focus of analyses of seigniorage because it can be nonzero even in the steady state. To maintain a constant level of real money holdings, the private sector needs to increase its nominal holdings of money at the rate π (approximately) to offset the effects of inflation on real holdings. By supplying money to meet this demand, the government is able to obtain goods and services or reduce other taxes.

Denote the growth rate of the nominal monetary base H by θ; the growth rate of h will equal $(\theta - \pi)/(1 + \pi) \approx \theta - \pi$.[4] In a steady state, h will be constant, implying that $\pi = \theta$. In this case, (4.6) shows that seigniorage will equal

$$\left(\frac{\pi}{1+\pi}\right)h = \left(\frac{\theta}{1+\theta}\right)h. \tag{4.7}$$

For small values of the rate of inflation, $\pi/(1+\pi)$ is approximately equal to π, so s can be thought of as the product of a tax rate of π, the rate of inflation, and a tax base of h, the real stock of base money. Since base money does not pay interest, its real value is depreciated by inflation whether or not inflation is anticipated.

The definition of s would appear to imply that the government receives no revenue if inflation is zero. But this inference neglects the real interest savings to the government of issuing h, which is non-interest-bearing debt, as opposed to b, which is interest-bearing debt. That is, for a given level of the government's total real liabilities $d = b + h$, interest costs will be a decreasing function of the fraction of this total that consists of h. A shift from interest-bearing to non-interest-bearing debt would allow the government to reduce total tax revenues or increase transfers or purchases.

This observation suggests that one should consider the government's budget constraint expressed in terms of the total liabilities of the government. Using (4.5) and (4.6), the budget constraint can be rewritten as[5]

$$g_t + r_{t-1}d_{t-1} = t_t + (d_t - d_{t-1}) + \left(\frac{\pi_t - \pi_t^e}{1 + \pi_t}\right)(1 + r_{t-1})d_{t-1} + \left(\frac{i_{t-1}}{1 + \pi_t}\right)h_{t-1}. \tag{4.8}$$

Seigniorage, defined as the last term in (4.8), becomes

$$\bar{s} = \left(\frac{i}{1+\pi}\right)h. \tag{4.9}$$

This shows that the relevant tax rate on high-powered money depends directly on the nominal rate of interest. Thus, under the Friedman rule for the optimal rate of

---

4. Problem 1 at the end of this chapter deals with the case in which there is population and real per capita income growth.

5. To obtain this, add $r_{t-1}h_{t-1}$ to both sides of (4.5).

inflation, which calls for setting the nominal rate of interest equal to zero (see chapters 2 and 3), the government collects no revenue from seigniorage. The budget constraint also illustrates that any change in seigniorage requires an offsetting adjustment in the other components of (4.8). Reducing the nominal interest rate to zero implies that the lost revenue must be replaced by an increase in other taxes, real borrowing that increases the government's net indebtedness, or reductions in expenditures.

The various forms of the government's budget identity suggest at least three alternative measures of the revenue from money creation. First, the measure that might be viewed as appropriate from the perspective of the Treasury is simply RCB, total transfers from the central bank to the Treasury (see 4.1). For the United States, R. King and Plosser (1985) reported that the real value of these transfers amounted to 0.02% of real GNP during the 1929–1952 period and 0.15% of real GNP in the 1952–1982 period. Under this definition, shifts in the ownership of government debt between the private sector and the central bank affect the measure of seigniorage even if high-powered money remains constant. That is, from (4.2), if the central bank used interest receipts to purchase debt, B^M would rise, RCB would fall, and the Treasury would, from (4.1), need to raise other taxes, reduce expenditures, or issue more debt. But this last option means that the Treasury could simply issue debt equal to the increase in the central bank's debt holdings, leaving private debt holdings, government expenditures, and other taxes unaffected. Thus, changes in RCB do not represent real changes in the Treasury's finances and are therefore not the appropriate measure of seigniorage.

A second possible measure of seigniorage is given by (4.6), the real value of the change in high-powered money. King and Plosser reported that s equaled 1.37 percent of real GNP during 1929–1952 but only 0.3 percent during 1952–1982. This measure of seigniorage equals the revenue from money creation for a given path of interest-bearing government debt. That is, s equals the total expenditures that could be funded, holding constant other tax revenues and the total private sector holdings of interest-bearing government debt. While s, expressed as a fraction of GNP, was quite small during the postwar period in the United States, King and Plosser reported much higher values for other countries. For example, it was more than 6 percent of GNP in Argentina and over 2 percent in Italy.

Finally, (4.9) provides a third definition of seigniorage as the nominal interest savings from issuing non-interest-bearing as opposed to interest-bearing debt.[6] Using the four- to six-month commercial paper rate as a measure of the nominal interest rate, King and Plosser reported that this measure of seigniorage equaled 0.2 percent of U.S. GNP during 1929–1952 and 0.47 percent during 1952–1982. This third defi-

6. These are not the only three possible definitions. See King and Plosser (1985) for an additional three.

nition equals the revenue from money creation for a given path of total (interest- and non-interest-bearing) government debt; it equals the total expenditures that could be funded, holding constant other tax revenues and the total private sector holdings of real government liabilities.

The difference between s and $\bar{s}$ arises from alternative definitions of fiscal policy. To understand the effects of monetary policy, one normally wants to consider changes in monetary policy while holding fiscal policy constant. Suppose tax revenues t are simply treated as lump-sum taxes. Then one definition of fiscal policy would be in terms of a time series for government purchases and interest-bearing debt: $\{g_{t+i}, b_{t+i}\}_{i=0}^{\infty}$. Changes in s, together with the changes in t necessary to maintain $\{g_{t+i}, b_{t+i}\}_{i=0}^{\infty}$ unchanged, would constitute monetary policy. Under this definition, monetary policy would change the total liabilities of the government (i.e., $b + h$). An open market purchase by the central bank would, ceteris paribus, lower the stock of interest-bearing debt held by the public. The Treasury would then need to issue additional interest-bearing debt to keep the b_{t+i} sequence unchanged. Total government liabilities would rise. Alternatively, under the definition $\bar{s}$, fiscal policy sets the path $\{g_{t+i}, d_{t+i}\}_{i=0}^{\infty}$ and monetary policy determines the division of d between interest- and non-interest-bearing debt but not its total.

4.2.1 Intertemporal Budget Balance

The budget relationships derived in the previous section link the government's choices concerning expenditures, taxes, debt, and seigniorage at each point in time. However, unless there are restrictions on the government's ability to borrow or to raise revenue from seigniorage, (4.8) places no direct constraint on expenditure or tax choices. If governments, like individuals, are constrained in their ability to borrow, then this constraint limits the government's choices. To see exactly how it does so requires focusing on the intertemporal budget constraint of the government.

Ignoring the effect of surprise inflation, the single-period budget identity of the government given by (4.5) can be written as

$$g_t + r_{t-1}b_{t-1} = t_t + (b_t - b_{t-1}) + s_t.$$

Assuming the interest factor r is a constant (and is positive), this equation can be solved forward to obtain

$$(1+r)b_{t-1} + \sum_{i=0}^{\infty} \frac{g_{t+i}}{(1+r)^i} = \sum_{i=0}^{\infty} \frac{t_{t+i}}{(1+r)^i} + \sum_{i=0}^{\infty} \frac{s_{t+i}}{(1+r)^i} + \lim_{i \to \infty} \frac{b_{t+i}}{(1+r)^i}. \qquad (4.10)$$

The government's expenditure and tax plans are said to satisfy the requirement of intertemporal budget balance (the *no Ponzi condition*) if the last term in (4.10) equals zero:

$$\lim_{i \to \infty} \frac{b_{t+i}}{(1+r)^i} = 0. \tag{4.11}$$

In this case, the right side of (4.10) becomes the present discounted value of all current and future tax and seigniorage revenues, and this is equal to the left side, which is the present discounted value of all current and future expenditures plus current outstanding debt (principal plus interest). In other words, the government must plan to raise sufficient revenue, in present value terms, to repay its existing debt and finance its planned expenditures. Defining the primary deficit as $\Delta = g - t - s$, intertemporal budget balance implies, from (4.10), that

$$(1+r)b_{t-1} = -\sum_{i=0}^{\infty} \frac{\Delta_{t+i}}{(1+r)^i}. \tag{4.12}$$

Thus, if the government has outstanding debt ($b_{t-1} > 0$), the present value of future primary deficits must be negative (i.e., the government must run a primary surplus in present value). This surplus can be generated through adjustments in expenditures, taxes, or seigniorage.

Is (4.12) a constraint on the government? Must the government (the combined monetary and fiscal authorities) pick expenditures, taxes, and seigniorage to ensure that (4.12) holds for all possible values of the initial price level and interest rates? Or is it an equilibrium condition that need only hold at the equilibrium price level and interest rate? Buiter (2002) argued strongly that the intertemporal budget balance condition represents a constraint on government behavior, and this is the perspective generally adopted here. However, Sims (1994), Woodford (1995; 2001a), and Cochrane (1999) argued that (4.12) is an equilibrium condition; this alternative perspective is taken up in section 4.5.

4.3   Money and Fiscal Policy Frameworks

Most analyses of monetary phenomena and monetary policy assume, usually without statement, that variations in the stock of money matter but that how a variation occurs does not. The nominal money supply could change because of a shift from tax-financed government expenditures to seigniorage-financed expenditures. Or it could change as the result of an open market operation in which the central bank purchases interest-bearing debt, financing the purchase by an increase in non-interest-bearing debt, holding other taxes constant (see (4.2)). Because these two means of increasing the money stock have differing implications for taxes and the stock of interest-bearing government debt, they may lead to different effects on prices and/or interest rates.

The government sector's budget constraint links monetary and fiscal policies in ways that can matter for determining how a change in the money stock affects the equilibrium price level.[7] The budget link also means that one needs to be precise about defining monetary policy as distinct from fiscal policy. An open market purchase increases the stock of money, but by reducing the interest-bearing government debt held by the public, it has implications for the future stream of taxes needed to finance the interest cost of the government's debt. So an open market operation potentially has a fiscal side to it, and this fact can lead to ambiguity in defining what one means by a change in monetary policy, *holding fiscal policy constant.*

The literature in monetary economics has analyzed several alternative assumptions about the relationship between monetary and fiscal policies. In most traditional analyses, fiscal policy is assumed to adjust to ensure that the government's intertemporal budget is always in balance while monetary policy is free to set the nominal money stock or the nominal rate of interest. This situation is described as one of *monetary dominance*, or one in which fiscal policy is passive and monetary policy is active (Leeper 1991). The models of chapters 2 and 3 implicitly fall into this category in that fiscal policy was ignored and monetary policy determined the price level.

If fiscal policy affects the real rate of interest, then the price level is not independent of fiscal policy, even under regimes of monetary dominance. A balanced budget increase in expenditures that raises the real interest rate raises the nominal interest rate and lowers the real demand for money. Given an exogenous path for the nominal money supply, the price level must jump to reduce the real supply of money.

A second policy regime is one in which the fiscal authority sets its expenditure and taxes without regard to any requirement of intertemporal budget balance. If the present discounted value of these taxes is not sufficient to finance expenditures (in present value terms), seigniorage must adjust to ensure that the government's intertemporal budget constraint is satisfied. This regime is one of *fiscal dominance* (or active fiscal policy) and passive monetary policy, as monetary policy must adjust to deliver the level of seigniorage required to balance the government's budget. Prices and inflation are affected by changes in fiscal policy because these fiscal changes, if they require a change in seigniorage, alter the current and/or future money supply. Any regime in which either taxes and/or seigniorage always adjust to ensure that the government's intertemporal budget constraint is satisfied is called a *Ricardian* regime (Sargent 1982). Regimes of fiscal dominance are analyzed in section 4.4.

A final regime leads to what has become known as the fiscal theory of the price level (Sims 1994; Woodford 1995; 2001a; Cochrane 1999). In this regime, the government's intertemporal budget constraint may not be satisfied for arbitrary price levels.

---

7. See, for example, Sargent and Wallace (1981) and Wallace (1981). The importance of the budget constraint for the analysis of monetary topics is clearly illustrated in Sargent (1987).

Following Woodford (1995), these regimes are described as *non-Ricardian*. The discussion of non-Ricardian regimes is postponed until section 4.5.

4.4 Deficits and Inflation

The intertemporal budget constraint implies that any government with a current outstanding debt must run, in present value terms, future surpluses. One way to generate a surplus is to increase revenues from seigniorage, and for that reason, economists have been interested in the implications of budget deficits for future money growth. Two questions have formed the focus of studies of deficits and inflation: First, do fiscal deficits necessarily imply that inflation will eventually occur? Second, if inflation is not a necessary consequence of deficits, is it in fact a historical consequence?

The literature on the first question has focused on the implications for inflation if the monetary authority must act to ensure that the government's intertemporal budget is balanced. This interpretation views fiscal policy as set independently, so that the monetary authority is forced to generate enough seigniorage to satisfy the intertemporal budget balance condition.

From (4.12), the government's intertemporal budget constraint takes the form

$$b_{t-1} = -R^{-1} \sum_{i=0}^{\infty} R^{-i}(g_{t+i} - t_{t+i} - s_{t+i}),$$

where $R = 1 + r$ is the gross real interest rate, $g_t - t_t - s_t$ is the primary deficit, and s_t is real seigniorage revenue. Let $s_t^f \equiv t_t - g_t$ be the primary *fiscal* surplus (i.e., tax revenues minus expenditures but excluding interest payments and seigniorage revenue). Then the government's budget constraint can be written as

$$b_{t-1} = R^{-1} \sum_{i=0}^{\infty} R^{-i} s_{t+i}^f + R^{-1} \sum_{i=0}^{\infty} R^{-i} s_{t+i}. \tag{4.13}$$

The current real liabilities of the government must be financed, in present value terms, by either a fiscal primary surplus or seigniorage.

Given the real value of the government's liabilities b_{t-1}, (4.13) illustrates what Sargent and Wallace (1981) described as "unpleasant monetarist arithmetic" in a regime of fiscal dominance. If the present value of the fiscal primary surplus is reduced, the present value of seigniorage must rise to maintain (4.13). Or, for a given present value of s^f, an attempt by the monetary authority to reduce inflation and seigniorage today must lead to higher inflation and seigniorage in the future because the present discounted value of seigniorage cannot be altered. The mechanism is straightforward;

if current inflation tax revenues are lowered, the deficit grows and the stock of debt rises. This implies an increase in the present discounted value of future tax revenues, including revenues from seigniorage. If the fiscal authority does not adjust, the monetary authority will be forced eventually to produce higher inflation.[8]

The literature on the second question—has inflation been a consequence of deficits historically?—has focused on estimating empirically the effects of deficits on money growth. Joines (1985) found money growth in the United States to be positively related to major war spending but not to nonwar deficits. Grier and Neiman (1987) summarized a number of earlier studies of the relationship between deficits and money growth (and other measures of monetary policy) in the United States. That the results are generally inconclusive is perhaps not surprising because the studies they review were all based on postwar but pre-1980 data. Thus, the samples covered periods in which there was relatively little deficit variation and in which much of the existing variation arose from the endogenous response of deficits to the business cycle as tax revenues varied procyclically.[9] Grier and Neiman did find that the structural (high-employment) deficit is a determinant of money growth. This finding is consistent with that of R. King and Plosser (1985), who reported that the fiscal deficit does help to predict future seigniorage for the United States. They interpreted this as mixed evidence for fiscal dominance.

Demopoulos, Katsimbris, and Miller (1987) provided evidence on debt accommodation for eight OECD countries. These authors estimated a variety of central bank reaction functions (regression equations with alternative policy instruments on the left-hand side) in which the government deficit is included as an explanatory variable. For the post–Bretton Woods period, they found a range of outcomes, from no accommodation by the Federal Reserve and the Bundesbank to significant accommodation by the Bank of Italy and the Nederlandse Bank.

One objection to this empirical literature is that simple regressions of money growth on deficits, or unrestricted VAR used to assess Granger causality (i.e., whether deficits contain any predictive information about future money growth), ignore information about the long-run behavior of taxes, debt, and seigniorage that is implied by intertemporal budget balance. Intertemporal budget balance implies a cointegrating relationship between the primary deficit and the stock of debt. This link between the components of the deficit and the stock of debt restricts the time series

8. In a regime of monetary dominance, the monetary authority can determine inflation and seigniorage; the fiscal authority must then adjust either taxes or spending to ensure that (4.13) is satisfied.

9. For that reason, some of the studies cited by Grier and Neiman employed a measure of the high employment surplus (i.e., the surplus estimated to occur if the economy had been at full employment). Grier and Neiman concluded, "The high employment deficit (surplus) seems to have a better 'batting average'" (204).

behavior of expenditures, taxes, and seigniorage, and this fact in turn implies that empirical modeling of their behavior should be carried out within the framework of a vector error correction model (VECM).[10]

Suppose $X_t = (g_t \quad T_t \quad b_{t-1})$, where $T = t + s$ is defined as total government receipts from taxes and seigniorage. If the elements of X are nonstationary, intertemporal budget balance implies that the deficit inclusive of interest, or $(1 \quad -1 \quad r)X_t = \beta' X_t = g_t - T_t + rb_{t-1}$, is stationary. Hence, $\beta' = (1 \quad -1 \quad r)$ is a cointegrating vector for X. The appropriate specification of the time series process is then a VECM of the form

$$C(L)\Delta X_t = -\alpha\beta' X_t + e_t. \tag{4.14}$$

The presence of the deficit inclusive of interest, $\beta' X_t$, ensures that the elements of X cannot drift too far apart; doing so would violate intertemporal budget balance. A number of authors have tested for cointegration to examine the sustainability of budget policies (e.g., Trehan and Walsh 1988; 1991). However, Bohn (2007) argued that time series tests based on cointegration relationships are not capable of rejecting intertemporal budget balance.

Bohn (1991a) estimated a model of the form (4.14) using U.S. data from 1800 to 1988. Unfortunately for the purposes here, Bohn did not treat seigniorage separately, and thus his results are not directly relevant for determining the effects of spending or tax shocks on the adjustment of seigniorage. He did find, however, that one-half to two-thirds of deficits initiated by a tax revenue shock were eventually eliminated by spending adjustments, and about one-third of spending shocks were essentially permanent and resulted in tax changes.

4.4.1 Ricardian and (Traditional) Non-Ricardian Fiscal Policies

Changes in the nominal quantity of money engineered through lump-sum taxes and transfers (as in chapters 2 and 3) may have different effects than changes introduced through open market operations in which non-interest-bearing government debt is exchanged for interest-bearing debt. In an early contribution, Metzler (1951) argued that an open market purchase, that is, an increase in the nominal quantity of money held by the public and an offsetting reduction in the nominal stock of interest-bearing debt held by the public, would raise the price level less than proportionally to the increase in M. An open market operation would therefore affect the real stock of money and lead to a change in the equilibrium rate of interest. Metzler assumed that households' desired portfolio holdings of bonds and money depended on the expected return on bonds. An open market operation, by altering the ratio of bonds

---

10. See Engle and Granger (1987).

to money, requires a change in the rate of interest to induce private agents to hold the new portfolio composition of bonds and money. A price level change proportional to the change in the nominal money supply would not restore equilibrium, because it would not restore the original ratio of nominal bonds to nominal money.

An important limitation of Metzler's analysis was its dependence on portfolio behavior that was not derived directly from the decision problem facing the agents of the model. The analysis was also limited in that it ignored the consequence for future taxes of shifts in the composition of the government's debt, a point made by Patinkin (1965). It has been noted that the government's intertemporal budget constraint requires the government to run surpluses in present value terms equal to its current outstanding interest-bearing debt. An open market purchase by the monetary authority reduces the stock of interest-bearing debt held by the public, and this reduction will have consequences for future expected taxes.

Sargent and Wallace (1981) showed that the backing for government debt, whether it is ultimately paid for by taxes or by printing money, is important in determining the effects of debt issuance and open market operations. This finding can be illustrated following the analysis of Aiyagari and Gertler (1985). They used a two-period overlapping-generations model that allows debt policy to affect the real intergenerational distribution of wealth. This effect is absent from the representative-agent models used here, but the representative-agent framework can still be used to show how the specification of fiscal policy will have important implications for conclusions about the link between the money supply and the price level.[11]

In order to focus on debt, taxes, and seigniorage, set government purchases equal to zero and ignore population and real income growth, in which case the government's budget constraint takes the simplified form

$$(1 + r_{t-1})b_{t-1} = t_t + b_t + s_t, \tag{4.15}$$

with s_t denoting seigniorage.

In addition to the government's budget constraint, the budget constraint of the representative agent must be specified. Assume that this agent receives an exogenous endowment y in each period and pays (lump-sum) taxes t_t in period t. She also receives interest payments on any government debt held at the start of the period; these payments, in real terms, are given by $(1 + i_{t-1})B_{t-1}/P_t$, where i_{t-1} is the nominal interest rate in period $t - 1$, B_{t-1} is the number of bonds held at the start of period t, and P_t is the period t price level. This can be written equivalently as $(1 + r_{t-1})b_{t-1}$, where $r_{t-1} = (1 + i_{t-1})/(1 + \pi_t) - 1$ is the ex post real rate of interest. Finally, the agent has real money balances equal to $M_{t-1}/P_t = (1 + \pi_t)^{-1}m_{t-1}$ that

---

11. See also Woodford (1995; 2001a) and section 4.5.2.

are carried into period t from period $t - 1$. The agent allocates these resources to consumption, real money holdings, and real bond purchases, subject to

$$c_t + m_t + b_t = y + (1 + r_{t-1})b_{t-1} + \frac{m_{t-1}}{1 + \pi_t} - t_t. \tag{4.16}$$

Aiyagari and Gertler (1985) asked whether the price level will depend only on the stock of money or whether debt policy and the behavior of the stock of debt might also be relevant for price level determination. They assumed that the government sets taxes to back a fraction ψ of its interest-bearing debt liabilities, with $0 \leq \psi \leq 1$. If $\psi = 1$, government interest-bearing debt is completely backed by taxes in the sense that the government commits to maintaining the present discounted value of current and future tax receipts equal to its outstanding debt liabilities. Such a fiscal policy was called Ricardian by Sargent (1982).[12] If $\psi < 1$, Aiyagari and Gertler characterized fiscal policy as non-Ricardian. To avoid confusion with the more recent interpretations of non-Ricardian regimes (see section 4.5.2), let regimes where $\psi < 1$ be referred to as *traditional non-Ricardian* regimes. In such regimes, seigniorage must adjust to maintain the present value of taxes plus seigniorage equal to the government's outstanding debt.

Let T_t now denote the present discounted value of taxes. Under the assumed debt policy, the government ensures that $T_t = \psi(1 + r_{t-1})b_{t-1}$ because $(1 + r_{t-1})b_{t-1}$ is the net liability of the government (including its current interest payment). Because T_t is a present value, one can also write

$$T_t = t_t + \mathrm{E}_t\left(\frac{T_{t+1}}{1 + r_t}\right) = t_t + \mathrm{E}_t\left[\frac{\psi(1 + r_t)b_t}{(1 + r_t)}\right],$$

or $T_t = t_t + \psi b_t$. Now because $T_t = \psi(1 + r_{t-1})b_{t-1}$, it follows that

$$t_t = \psi(R_{t-1}b_{t-1} - b_t), \tag{4.17}$$

where $R = 1 + r$. Similarly, $s_t = (1 - \psi)(R_{t-1}b_{t-1} - b_t)$. With taxes adjusting to ensure that the fraction ψ of the government's debt liabilities is backed by taxes, the remaining fraction, $1 - \psi$, represents the portion backed by seigniorage.

Using (4.17), the household's budget constraint (4.16) becomes

$$c_t + m_t + (1 - \psi)b_t = y + (1 - \psi)R_{t-1}b_{t-1} + \frac{m_{t-1}}{1 + \pi_t}.$$

12. It is more common for Ricardo's name to be linked with debt in the form of the Ricardian equivalence theorem, under which shifts between debt and tax financing of a given expenditure stream have no real effects. See Barro (1974) or D. Romer (2006). Ricardian equivalence holds in the representative agent framework; the issue is whether debt policy, as characterized by ψ, matters for price level determination.

In the Ricardian case ($\psi = 1$), all terms involving the government's debt drop out; only the stock of money matters. If $\psi < 1$, however, debt does not drop out. The budget constraint can then be written as $y + R_{t-1}w_{t-1} = c_t + w_t + i_{t-1}m_{t-1}/(1 + \pi_t)$, where $w = m + (1 - \psi)b$, showing that the relevant measure of household income is $y + R_{t-1}w_{t-1}$ and this is then used to purchase consumption, financial assets, or money balances (where the opportunity cost of money is $i/(1 + \pi)$). With asset demand depending on ψ through w_{t-1}, the equilibrium price level and nominal rate of interest will generally depend on ψ.[13]

Having derived the representative agent's budget constraint and shown how it is affected by the means the government uses to back its debt, in order to actually determine the effects on the equilibrium price level and nominal interest rate, one must determine the agent's demand for money and bonds and then equate these demands to the (exogenous) supplies. To illustrate the role of debt policy, assume log-separable utility, $\ln c_t + \delta \ln m_t$, and consider a perfect foresight equilibrium. From chapter 2, the marginal rate of substitution between money and consumption will be set equal to $i_t/(1 + i_t)$. With log utility, this implies $m_t = \delta c_t(1 + i_t)/i_t$. The Euler condition for the optimal consumption path yields $c_{t+1} = \beta(1 + r_t)c_t$. Using these in the agent's budget constraint,

$$y + R_{t-1}w_{t-1} = c_t + w_t + \left(\frac{i_{t-1}}{1 + \pi_t}\right)\delta\left(\frac{1 + i_{t-1}}{i_{t-1}}\right)\frac{c_t}{\beta(1 + r_{t-1})}$$

$$= \left(1 + \frac{\delta}{\beta}\right)c_t + w_t.$$

In equilibrium, $c_t = y$, so this becomes $R_{t-1}w_{t-1} = (\delta/\beta)y + w_t$. In the steady state, $w_t = w_{t-1} = w^{ss} = \delta y/\beta(R - 1)$. But $w = [M + (1 - \psi)B]/P$, so the equilibrium steady-state price level is equal to

$$P^{ss} = \left(\frac{\beta r^{ss}}{\delta y}\right)[M + (1 - \psi)B]. \tag{4.18}$$

If government debt is entirely backed by taxes ($\psi = 1$), one gets the standard result; the price level is proportional to the nominal stock of money. The stock of debt has no effect on the price level. With $0 < \psi < 1$, however, both the nominal money supply and the nominal stock of debt play a role in price level determination. Proportional changes in M and B produce proportional changes in the price level.

In a steady state, all nominal quantities and the price level must change at the same rate because real values are constant. Thus, if M grows, then B must also

---

13. In this example, $c = y$ in equilibrium because there is no capital good that would allow the endowment to be transferred over time.

grow at the same rate. The real issue is whether the composition of the government's liabilities matters for the price level. To focus more clearly on that issue, let $\lambda = M/(M + B)$ be the fraction of government liabilities that consists of non-interest-bearing debt. Since open market operations affect the relative proportions of money and bonds in government liabilities, open market operations determine λ. Equation (4.18) can then be written as

$$P^{ss} = \left(\frac{\beta r^{ss}}{\delta y}\right)[1 - \psi(1 - \lambda)](M + B).$$

Open market purchases (an increase in λ) that substitute money for bonds but leave $M + B$ unchanged raise P^{ss} when $\psi > 0$. The rise in P^{ss} is not proportional to the increase in M. Shifting the composition of its liabilities away from interest-bearing debt reduces the present discounted value of the private sector's tax liabilities by less than the fall in debt holdings; a rise in the price level proportional to the rise in M would leave households' real wealth lower (their bond holdings are reduced in real value, but the decline in the real value of their tax liabilities is only $\psi < 1$ times as large).

Leeper (1991) argued that even if $\psi = 1$ on average (that is, all debt is backed by taxes), the means used to finance shocks to the government's budget have important implications. He distinguished between active and passive policies; with an active monetary policy and a passive fiscal policy, monetary policy acts to target nominal interest rates and does not respond to the government's debt, while fiscal policy must then adjust taxes to ensure intertemporal budget balance. Conversely, with an active fiscal policy and a passive monetary policy, the monetary authority must adjust seigniorage revenues to ensure intertemporal budget balance, while fiscal policy does not respond to shocks to debt. Leeper showed that the inflation and debt processes are unstable if both policy authorities follow active policies, and there is price level indeterminacy if both follow passive policies.

4.4.2   The Government Budget Constraint and the Nominal Rate of Interest

Earlier, we examined Sargent and Wallace's "unpleasant monetarist arithmetic" using (4.13). Given the government's real liabilities, the monetary authority would be forced to finance any difference between these real liabilities and the present discounted value of the government's fiscal surpluses. Fiscal considerations determine the money supply, but the traditional quantity theory holds and the price level is proportional to the nominal quantity of money. Suppose, however, that the initial nominal stock of money is set exogenously by the monetary authority. Does this mean that the price level is determined solely by monetary policy, with no effect of fiscal policy? The following example shows that the answer is no; fiscal policy can affect the initial equilibrium price level, even when the initial nominal quantity of money is given and the government's intertemporal budget constraint must be satisfied at all price levels.

Consider a perfect-foresight equilibrium. In such an equilibrium, the government's budget constraint must be satisfied and the real demand for money must equal the real supply of money. The money-in-the-utility function (MIU) model of chapter 2 can be used, for example, to derive the real demand for money. That model implied that agents would equate the marginal rate of substitution between money and consumption to the cost of holding money, where this cost depended on the nominal rate of interest:

$$\frac{u_m(c_t, m_t)}{u_c(c_t, m_t)} = \frac{i_t}{1 + i_t}.$$

Using the utility function employed in chapter 2,[14] this condition implies that

$$m_t = \frac{M_t}{P_t} = \left[\left(\frac{i_t}{1 + i_t}\right)\left(\frac{a}{1 - a}\right)\right]^{-1/b} c_t.$$

Evaluated at the economy's steady state, this can be written as

$$\frac{M_t}{P_t} = f(R_{m,t}),\tag{4.19}$$

where $R_m = 1 + i$ is the gross nominal rate of interest and

$$f(R_m) = \left[\left(\frac{R_m - 1}{R_m}\right)\left(\frac{a}{1 - a}\right)\right]^{-1/b} c_t.$$

Given the nominal interest rate, (4.19) implies a proportional relationship between the nominal quantity of money and the equilibrium price level. If the initial money stock is M_0, then the initial price level is $P_0 = M_0/f(R_m)$.

The government's budget constraint must also be satisfied. In a perfect-foresight equilibrium, there are no inflation surprises, so the government's budget constraint given by (4.5) can be written as

$$g_t + rb_{t-1} = t_t + (b_t - b_{t-1}) + m_t - \left(\frac{1}{1 + \pi_t}\right)m_{t-1}.\tag{4.20}$$

14. In chapter 2 it was assumed that

$$u(c_t, m_t) = \frac{[ac_t^{1-b} + (1 - a)m_t^{1-b}]^{(1-\Phi)/(1-b)}}{1 - \Phi}.$$

Now consider a stationary equilibrium in which government expenditures and taxes are constant, as are the real stocks of government interest-bearing debt and money. In such a stationary equilibrium, the budget constraint becomes

$$g + \left(\frac{1}{\beta} - 1\right)b = t + \left(\frac{\pi_t}{1 + \pi_t}\right)m = t + \left(\frac{\beta R_m - 1}{\beta R_m}\right)f(R_m), \tag{4.21}$$

which uses the steady-state results that the gross real interest rate is $1/\beta$, $R_m \equiv (1 + \pi_t)/\beta$, and real money balances must be consistent with the demand given by (4.19).

Suppose the fiscal authority sets g, t, and b. Then (4.21) determines the nominal interest rate R_m. With g, t, and b given, the government needs to raise $g + (1/\beta - 1)b - t$ in seigniorage. The nominal interest rate is determined by the requirement that this level of seigniorage be raised.[15] Because the nominal interest rate is equal to $(1 + \pi)/\beta$, one can alternatively say that fiscal policy determines the inflation rate. Once the nominal interest rate is determined, the initial price level is given by (4.19) as $P_0 = M_0/f(R_m)$, where M_0 is the initial stock of money. In subsequent periods, the price level is equal to $P_t = P_0(\beta R_m)^t$, where $\beta R_m = (1 + \pi)$ is the gross inflation rate. The nominal stock of money in each future period is endogenously determined by $M_t = P_t f(R_m)$. In this case, even though the monetary authority has set M_0 exogenously, the initial price level is determined by the need for fiscal solvency because the fiscal authority's budget requirement (4.21) determines R_m and therefore the real demand for money. The initial price level is proportional to the initial money stock, but the factor of proportionality, $1/f(R_m)$, is determined by fiscal policy, and both the rate of inflation and the path of the future nominal money supply are determined by the fiscal requirement that seigniorage equal $g + (1/\beta - 1)b - t$.

If the fiscal authority raises expenditures, holding b and t constant, then seigniorage must rise. The equilibrium nominal interest rate rises to generate this additional seigniorage.[16] With a higher R_m, the real demand for money falls, and this increases the equilibrium value of the initial price level P_0, even though the initial nominal quantity of money is unchanged.

4.4.3 Equilibrium Seigniorage

Suppose that, given its expenditures and other tax sources, the government has a fiscal deficit of Δ^f that must be financed by money creation. When will it be feasible

---

15. The nominal interest rate that raises seigniorage equal to $g + (1/\beta - 1)b - t$ may not be unique. A rise in R_m increases the tax rate on money, but it also erodes the tax base by reducing the real demand for money. A given amount of seigniorage may be raised with a low tax rate and a high base or a high tax rate and a low base.

16. This assumes that the economy is on the positively sloped portion of the Laffer curve so that raising the tax rate increases revenue; see sections 4.4.3.

to raise Δ^f in a steady-state equilibrium? And what will be the equilibrium rate of inflation?

The answers to these questions would be straightforward if there were a one-to-one relationship between the revenue generated by the inflation tax and the inflation rate. If this were the case, the inflation rate would be uniquely determined by the amount of revenue that must be raised. But the inflation rate affects the base against which the tax is levied. For a given base, a higher inflation rate raises seigniorage, but a higher inflation rate raises the opportunity cost of holding money and reduces the demand for money, thereby lowering the base against which the tax is levied. This raises the possibility that a given amount of revenue can be raised by more than one rate of inflation. For example, the nominal rate of interest R_m that satisfies (4.21) may not be unique.

It will be helpful to impose additional structure so that one can say more about the demand for money. The standard approach used in most analyses of seigniorage is to specify directly a functional form for the demand for money as a function of the nominal rate of interest. An early example of this approach, and one of the most influential, is that of Cagan (1956). This approach is discussed later, but first Calvo and Leiderman (1992) are followed in using a variant of the Sidrauski model of chapter 2 to motivate a demand for money. That is, suppose the economy consists of identical individuals, and the utility of the representative agent is given by

$$\sum_{t=0}^{\infty} \beta^t u(c_t, m_t), \tag{4.22}$$

where $0 < \beta < 1$, c is per capita consumption, m is per capita real money holdings, and the function $u(.)$ is strictly concave and twice continuously differentiable. The representative agent chooses consumption, money balances, and holdings of interest-earning bonds to maximize the expected value of (4.22), subject to the following budget constraint:

$$c_t + b_t + m_t = y_t - \tau_t + (1 + r)b_{t-1} + \frac{m_{t-1}}{\Pi_t},$$

where b is the agent's holdings of bonds, y is real income, τ is equal to the net taxes of the agent, r is the real rate of interest, assumed constant for simplicity, and $\Pi_t \equiv P_t/P_{t-1} = 1 + \pi_t$, where π_t is the inflation rate. Thus, the last term in the budget constraint, m_{t-1}/Π_t, is equal to the period t real value of money balances carried into period t, that is, M_{t-1}/P_t, where M represents nominal money holdings. Attention is restricted to perfect-foresight equilibria.

If w_t is the agent's real wealth in period t, $w_t = b_t + m_t$, and $R_t = 1 + r_t$, then the budget constraint can be rewritten as

$$c_t + w_t = y_t - \tau_t + R_{t-1}w_{t-1} - \left(\frac{R_{t-1}\Pi_t - 1}{\Pi_t}\right)m_{t-1}$$

$$= y_t - \tau_t + R_{t-1}w_{t-1} - \left(\frac{i_{t-1}}{\Pi_t}\right)m_{t-1}$$

by using the fact that $R\Pi = 1 + i$, where i is the nominal rate of interest. When the budget constraint is written in this way, it is clear that the cost of holding wealth in the form of money as opposed to interest-earning bonds is i/Π.[17] The first-order condition for optimal money holdings sets the marginal utility of money equal to the cost of holding money times the marginal utility of wealth. Since the interest forgone by holding money in period t is a cost that is incurred in period $t + 1$, this cost must be discounted back to period t using the discount factor β to compare with the marginal utility of money in period t. Thus, $u_m(c_t, m_t) = \beta(i_t/\Pi_{t+1})u_c(c_{t+1}, m_{t+1})$. But the standard Euler condition for optimal consumption implies that $u_c(c_t, m_t) = \beta R_t u_c(c_{t+1}, m_{t+1})$. Combining these first-order conditions yields

$$u_m(c_t, m_t) = \left(\frac{i_t}{R_t\Pi_{t+1}}\right)u_c(c_t, m_t) = \left(\frac{i_t}{1 + i_t}\right)u_c(c_t, m_t). \tag{4.23}$$

Now suppose the utility function takes the form $u(c_t, m_t) = \ln c_t + m_t(B - D \ln m_t)$. Using this functional form in (4.23), one obtains

$$m_t = Ae^{-\omega_t/Dc_t}, \tag{4.24}$$

where $A = e^{(B/D - 1)}$ and $\omega = i/(1 + i)$. Equation (4.24) provides a convenient functional representation for the demand for money.

Since the time of Cagan's seminal contribution to the study of seigniorage and hyperinflations (Cagan 1956, 158–161), many economists have followed him in specifying a money demand function of the form $m = Ke^{-\alpha\pi^e}$; (4.24) shows how something similar can be derived from an underlying utility function. As Calvo and Leiderman (1992) pointed out, the advantage is that one sees how the parameters K and α depend on more primitive parameters of the representative agent's preferences and how they may actually be time-dependent. For example, α depends on c_t and therefore will be time-dependent unless K varies appropriately or c itself is constant.

The reason for deriving the demand for money as a function of the rate of inflation is that, having done so, one can express seigniorage as a function of the rate of inflation. Recall from (4.9) that seigniorage was equal to $im/(1 + \pi) = (1 + r)im/(1 + i)$. Using the expression for the demand for money, steady-state seigniorage is equal to

---

17. Recall from the derivation of (4.8) that the term for the government's revenue from seigniorage was $(i_{t-1}/\Pi_t)h_{t-1}$. Comparing this to the household's budget constraint (with $h_{t-1} = m_{t-1}$) shows that the cost of holding money is exactly equal to the revenue obtained by the government.

Seigniorage

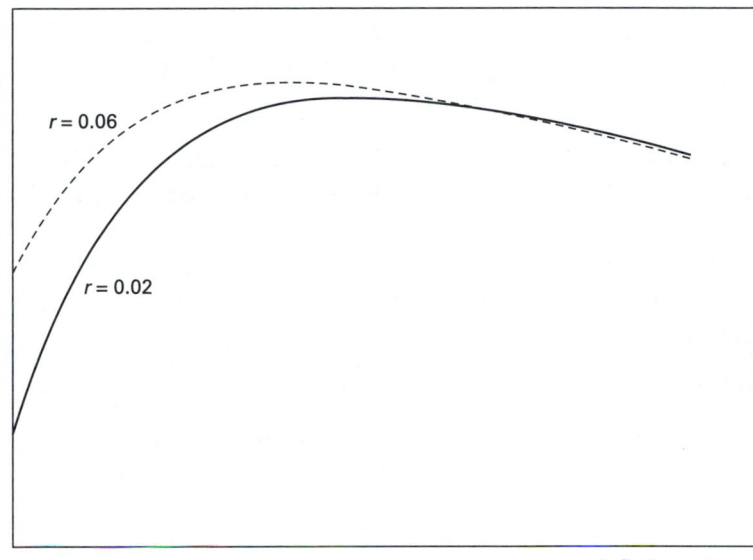

Inflation rate

Figure 4.1
Seigniorage as a function of inflation.

$$\bar{s} = (1+r)\left(\frac{i}{1+i}\right) A \, \exp\left[-\frac{i}{Dc(1+i)}\right].$$

If superneutrality is assumed to characterize the model, then c will be constant in the steady state and independent of the rate of inflation. The same will be true of the real rate of interest.

To determine how seigniorage varies with the rate of inflation, think of choosing $\omega = i/(1+i)$ through the choice of π. Then $\bar{s} = (1+r)\omega Ae^{-\omega/Dc}$ and $\partial\bar{s}/\partial\pi = (\partial\bar{s}/\partial\omega)(\partial\omega/\partial i)(\partial i/\partial\pi) = (\partial\bar{s}/\partial\omega)(1+r)/(1+i)^2$, so the sign of $\partial\bar{s}/\partial\pi$ will be determined by the sign of $(\partial\bar{s}/\partial\omega)$. Since

$$\frac{\partial\bar{s}}{\partial\omega} = (1+r)Ae^{-\omega/Dc}\left[1 - \frac{\omega}{Dc}\right] = \frac{\bar{s}}{\omega}\left[1 - \frac{\omega}{Dc}\right],$$

the sign of $\partial\bar{s}/\partial\omega$ depends on the sign of $1 - (\omega/Dc)$. As illustrated in figure 4.1, seigniorage increases with inflation initially but eventually begins to decline with further increases in π as the demand for real balances shrinks.[18]

---

18. Whether a Laffer curve exists for seigniorage depends on the specification of utility. For example, in chapter 2 it was noted that with a CES utility function, the demand for money was given by $m_t = A[i/(1+i)]^{-1/b}c_t$, where A is a constant. Hence, seigniorage is $A[i/(1+i)]^{1-1/b}c_t$, which is monotonic in i.

To determine the inflation rate that maximizes seigniorage, note that $\partial \bar{s} / \partial \pi = 0$ if and only if

$$\omega = \frac{i}{1+i} = Dc, \quad \text{or} \quad \pi^{\max} = \left(\frac{1}{1+r}\right)\left(\frac{1}{1-Dc}\right) - 1.$$

For inflation rates less than $\pi^{\max}$, the government's revenue is increasing in the inflation rate. The effect of an increase in the tax rate dominates the effect of higher inflation in reducing the real demand for money. As inflation increases above $\pi^{\max}$, the tax base shrinks sufficiently that revenues from seigniorage decline. Consequently, governments face a seigniorage Laffer curve; raising inflation beyond a certain point results in lower real tax revenue.

4.4.4 Cagan's Model

Since 1970 the consumer price index for the United States has risen just over 5.5-fold; that is inflation.[19] In Hungary, the index of wholesale prices was 38,500 in January 1923 and 1,026,000 in January 1924, one year later, a 27-fold increase; that is hyperinflation (Sargent 1986, 64).

One of the earliest studies of the dynamics of money and prices during hyperinflation was done by Cagan (1956). The discussion here follows Cagan in using continuous time. Suppose the real per capita fiscal deficit that needs to be financed is exogenously given and is equal to Δ^f. This means that

$$\Delta^f = \frac{\dot{H}}{H}\frac{H}{PY} = \theta h,$$

where h is expressed as real balances relative to income to allow for real economic growth. The demand for real balances will depend on the nominal interest rate and therefore the expected rate of inflation. Treating real variables such as the real rate of interest and the growth rate of real output as constant (which is appropriate in a steady state characterized by superneutrality and is usually taken as reasonable during hyperinflations because all the action involves money and prices), write the demand for the real monetary base as $h = \exp(-\alpha \pi^e)$. Then the government's revenue requirement implies that

$$\Delta^f = \theta e^{-\alpha \pi^e}. \tag{4.25}$$

For h to be constant in equilibrium requires that $\pi = \theta - \mu$, where μ is the growth rate of real income. And in a steady-state equilibrium, $\pi^e = \pi$, so (4.25) becomes

---

19. The CPI was equal to 38.8 in 1970 and reached 216.6 in May 2008.

Inflation

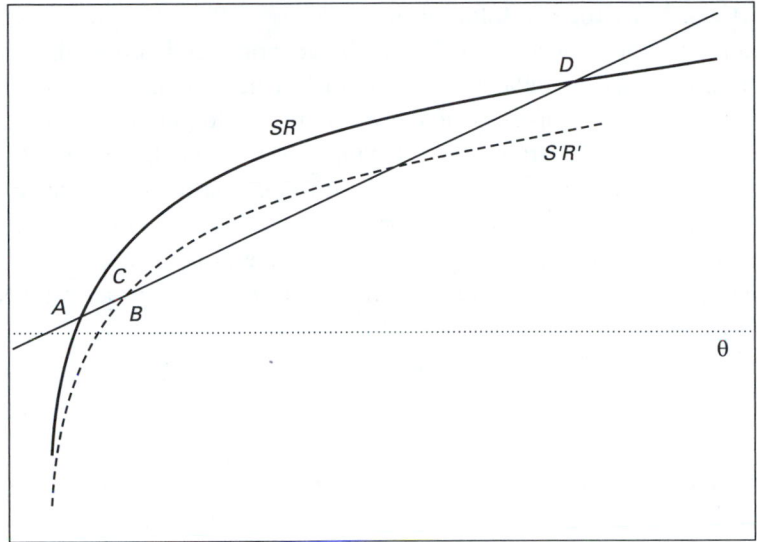

Figure 4.2
Money growth and seigniorage revenue.

$$\Delta^f = \theta e^{-\alpha(\theta - \mu)}, \tag{4.26}$$

the solution(s) of which give the rates of money growth that are consistent with raising the amount Δ^f through seigniorage. The right side of (4.26) equals zero when money growth is equal to zero, rises to a maximum at $\theta = (1/\alpha)$, and then declines.[20] That is, for rates of money growth above $(1/\alpha)$, and therefore inflation rates above $(1/\alpha) - \mu$, higher inflation actually leads to lower revenues because the tax base falls sufficiently to offset the rise in inflation. Thus, any deficit less than $\Delta^* = (1/\alpha)\exp(\alpha\mu - 1)$ can be financed by either a low rate of inflation or a high rate of inflation.

Figure 4.2, based on Bruno and Fischer (1990), illustrates the two inflation rates consistent with seigniorage revenues of Δ^f. The curve SR is derived from (4.25) and shows, for each rate of money growth, the expected rate of inflation needed to generate the required seigniorage revenues.[21] The 45° line gives the steady-state inflation

---

20. More generally, with h a function of the nominal interest rate and r a constant, seigniorage can be written as $s = \theta h(\theta)$. This is maximized at the point where the elasticity of real money demand with respect to θ is equal to -1: $\theta h'(\theta)/h = -1$.

21. That is, SR plots $\pi^e = (\ln \theta - \ln \Delta^f)/\alpha$. A reduction in θ continues to yield Δ^f only if money holdings rise, and this would require a fall in expected inflation.

rate as a function of the money growth rate: $\pi^e = \pi = \theta - \mu$. The two points of intersection labeled A and D are the two solutions to (4.26).

What determines whether, for a given deficit, the economy ends up at the high-inflation equilibrium or the low-inflation equilibrium? Which equilibrium is picked out depends on the stability properties of the economy. Determining this in turn requires a more complete specification of the dynamics of the model. Recall that the demand for money depends on expected inflation through the nominal rate of interest, whereas the inflation tax rate depends on actual inflation. In considering the effects of variations in the inflation rate, one needs to determine how expectations will adjust. Cagan (1956) addressed this by assuming that expectations adjust adaptively to actual inflation:

$$\frac{\partial \pi^e}{\partial t} = \dot{\pi}^e = \eta(\pi - \pi^e), \tag{4.27}$$

where η captures the "speed of adjustment" of expectations. A low η implies that expectations respond slowly to inflation forecast errors. Since $h = \exp(-\alpha\pi^e)$, differentiate this expression with respect to time, obtaining

$$\frac{\dot{h}}{h} = \theta - \mu - \pi = -\alpha\dot{\pi}^e.$$

Solving for π using (4.27) yields $\pi = \theta - \mu + \alpha\dot{\pi}^e = \theta - \mu + \alpha\eta(\pi - \pi^e)$, or $\pi = (\theta - \mu - \alpha\eta\pi^e)/(1 - \alpha\eta)$. Substituting this back into the expectations adjustment equation gives

$$\dot{\pi}^e = \frac{\eta(\theta - \mu - \pi^e)}{1 - \alpha\eta}, \tag{4.28}$$

which implies that the low-inflation equilibrium will be stable as long as $\alpha\eta < 1$. This requires that expectations adjust sufficiently slowly ($\eta < 1/\alpha$).

If expectations adjust adaptively and sufficiently slowly, what happens when the deficit is increased? Since the demand for real money balances depends on expected inflation, and because the adjustment process does not allow the expected inflation rate to jump immediately, the higher deficit can be financed by an increase in the rate of inflation (assuming the new deficit is still below the maximum that can be financed, Δ^*). Since actual inflation now exceeds expected inflation, $\dot{\pi}^e > 0$ and π^e begins to rise. The economy converges into a new equilibrium at a higher rate of inflation.

In terms of figure 4.2, an increase in the deficit shifts the SR line to the right to $S'R'$ (for a given expected rate of inflation, money growth must rise in order to generate more revenue). Assume that initially the economy is at point A, the low-inflation equilibrium. Budget balance requires that the economy be on the $S'R'$ line, so θ jumps to the rate associated with point B. But now, at point B, inflation has risen and $\pi^e < \pi = \theta - \mu$. Expected inflation rises (as long as $\alpha\eta < 1$; see (4.28)), and the economy converges to C. The high-inflation equilibrium, in contrast, is unstable.

Adaptive expectations of the sort Cagan assumed disappeared from the literature under the onslaught of the rational-expectations revolution begun by Lucas and Sargent in the early 1970s. If agents are systematically attempting to forecast inflation, then their forecast will depend on the actual process governing the evolution of inflation; rarely will this imply an adjustment process such as (4.27). Stability in the Cagan model also requires that expectations not adjust too quickly ($\eta < 1/\alpha$), and this requirement conflicts with the rational-expectations notion that expectations adjust quickly in response to new information. Bruno and Fischer (1990) showed that, to some degree, assuming that agents adjust their holdings of real money balances slowly plays a role under rational expectations similar to the role played by the slow adjustment of expectations in Cagan's model in ensuring stability under adaptive expectations.

4.4.5   Rational Hyperinflation

Why do countries find themselves in situations of hyperinflation? Most explanations of hyperinflation point to fiscal policy as the chief culprit. Governments that are forced to print money to finance real government expenditures often end up generating hyperinflations. In that sense, rapid money growth does lead to hyperinflation, consistent with the relationship between money growth and inflation implied by the models examined so far, but money growth is no longer exogenous. Instead, it is endogenously determined by the need to finance a fiscal deficit.[22]

Two explanations for the development of hyperinflation suggest themselves. In the Cagan model with adaptive expectations, suppose that $\alpha\eta < 1$ so that the low-inflation equilibrium is stable. Now suppose that a shock pushes the inflation rate above the high-inflation equilibrium (above point D in figure 4.2). If that equilibrium is unstable, the economy continues to diverge, moving to higher and higher rates of inflation. So one explanation for hyperinflations is that they represent situations in which exogenous shocks push the economy into an unstable region.

Alternatively, suppose the deficit that needs to be financed with seigniorage grows. If it rises above Δ^*, the maximum that can be financed by money creation, the government finds itself unable to obtain enough revenue, so it runs the printing presses faster, further reducing the real revenue it obtains and forcing it to print money even

---

22. The current modern example of such a fiscally driven hyperinflation is provided by Zimbabwe.

faster. Most hyperinflations have occurred after wars (and on the losing side). Such countries face an economy devastated by war and a tax system that no longer functions effectively. At the same time, there are enormous demands on the government for expenditures to provide the basics of food and shelter and to rebuild the economy. Revenue needs outpace the government's ability to raise tax revenues. The ends of such hyperinflations usually involve a fiscal reform that allows the government to reduce its reliance on seigniorage (see Sargent 1986).

When expected inflation falls in response to the reforms, the opportunity cost of holding money is reduced and the demand for real money balances rises. Thus, the growth rate of the nominal money supply normally continues temporarily at a very high rate after a hyperinflation has ended. A similar, if smaller-scale, phenomenon occurred in the United States in the mid-1980s. The money supply, as measured by $M1$, grew very rapidly. At the time, there were concerns that this growth would lead to a return of higher rates of inflation. Instead, it seemed to reflect the increased demand for money resulting from the decline in inflation from its peak levels in 1979–1980. The need for real money balances to grow as inflation is reduced often causes problems for establishing and maintaining the credibility of policies designed to reduce inflation. If a disinflation is credible, so that expected inflation falls, it may be necessary to increase the growth rate of the nominal money supply temporarily. But when inflation and rapid money growth are so closely related, letting money growth rise may be misinterpreted as a signal that the central bank has given up on its disinflation policy.

Fiscal theories of seigniorage, inflation, and hyperinflations are based on fundamentals—there really is a deficit that needs to be financed, and that is what leads to money creation. An alternative view of hyperinflations is that they are simply *bubbles*, similar to bubbles in financial markets. Such phenomena are based on the possibility of multiple equilibria in which expectations can be self-fulfilling.

To illustrate this possibility, suppose the real demand for money is given, in log terms, by

$$m_t - p_t = -\alpha(\mathrm{E}_t p_{t+1} - p_t),$$

where $\mathrm{E}_t p_{t+1}$ denotes the expectation formed at time t of time $t+1$ prices and $\alpha > 0$. This money demand function is the log version of Cagan's demand function. This equation can be rearranged to express the current price level as

$$p_t = \left(\frac{1}{1+\alpha}\right)m_t + \left(\frac{\alpha}{1+\alpha}\right)\mathrm{E}_t p_{t+1}. \qquad (4.29)$$

Suppose that the growth rate of the nominal money supply process is given by $m_t = \theta_0 + (1-\gamma)\theta_1 t + \gamma m_{t-1}$. Since m is the log money supply, the growth rate of the money supply is $m_t - m_{t-1} = (1 - \gamma)\theta_1 + \gamma(m_{t-1} - m_{t-2})$, and the trend (average) growth rate is θ_1. Given this process, and the assumption that agents make use of it and the equilibrium condition (4.29) in forming their expectations, one solution for the price level is given by

$$p_t = \frac{\alpha[\theta_0 + (1 - \gamma)\theta_1(1 + \alpha)]}{1 + \alpha(1 - \gamma)} + \left[\frac{\alpha(1 - \gamma)\theta_1}{1 + \alpha(1 - \gamma)}\right]t + \left[\frac{1}{1 + \alpha(1 - \gamma)}\right]m_t$$

$$= A_0 + A_1 t + A_2 m_t.$$

That this is a solution can be verified by noting that it implies $E_t p_{t+1} = A_0 + A_1(t + 1) + A_2 E_t m_{t+1} = A_0 + A_1(t + 1) + A_2[\theta_0 + (1 - \gamma)\theta_1(t + 1) + \gamma m_t]$; substituting this into (4.29) yields the proposed solution. Under this solution, the inflation rate $p_t - p_{t-1}$ converges to θ_1, the average growth rate of the nominal supply of money.[23]

Consider an alternative solution:

$$p_t = A_0 + A_1 t + A_2 m_t + B_t, \tag{4.30}$$

where B_t is time-varying. Does there exist a B_t process consistent with (4.29)? Substituting the new proposed solution into the equilibrium condition for the price level yields

$$A_0 + A_1 t + A_2 m_t + B_t = \frac{m_t}{1 + \alpha} + \frac{\alpha[A_0 + A_1(t + 1) + A_2 E_t m_{t+1} + E_t B_{t+1}]}{1 + \alpha},$$

which, to hold for all realizations of the nominal money supply, requires that, as before, $A_0 = \alpha[\theta_0 + (1 - \gamma)\theta_1(1 + \alpha)]/[1 + \alpha(1 - \gamma)]$, $A_1 = \alpha(1 - \gamma)\theta_1/[1 + \alpha(1 - \gamma)]$, and $A_2 = 1/[1 + \alpha(1 - \gamma)]$. This then implies that the B_t process must satisfy

$$B_t = \left(\frac{\alpha}{1 + \alpha}\right) E_t B_{t+1},$$

which holds if B follows the explosive process

$$B_{t+1} = k B_t \tag{4.31}$$

for $k = (1 + \alpha)/\alpha > 1$. In other words, (4.30) is an equilibrium solution for *any* process B_t satisfying (4.31). Since B grows at the rate $k - 1 = 1/\alpha$, and since α, the elasticity of money demand with respect to expected inflation, is normally thought to be small, its inverse would be large. The actual inflation rate along a bubble solution path could greatly exceed the rate of money growth.

23. This follows because $p_t - p_{t-1} = A_1 + A_2(m_t - m_{t-1})$ converges to $A_1 + A_2\theta_1 = \theta_1$.

Obstfeld and Rogoff (1983; 1986) considered whether speculative hyperinflations are consistent with equilibrium when agents are utility-maximizing. As discussed in section 2.2.1, they showed that speculative hyperinflation in unbacked fiat money systems cannot generally be ruled out. Equilibrium paths may exist along which real money balances eventually converge to zero as the price level goes to $+\infty$ (see also section 4.5.1).

The methods developed to test for bubbles are similar to those that have been employed to test for intertemporal budget balance. For example, if the nominal money stock is nonstationary, then the absence of bubbles implies that the price level will be nonstationary *but cointegrated with the money supply*. This is a testable implication of the no-bubble assumption. Equation (4.31) gives the simplest example of a bubble process. Evans (1991) showed how the cointegration tests can fail to detect bubbles that follow periodically collapsing processes. For more on asset prices and bubbles, see Shiller (1981); Mattey and Meese (1986); West (1987; 1988); Diba and Grossman (1988a; 1988b); and Evans (1991).

4.5   The Fiscal Theory of the Price Level

A number of researchers have examined models in which fiscal factors replace the money supply as the key determinant of the price level (see Leeper 1991; Sims 1994; Woodford 1995; 1999a; 2001a; Bohn 1999; Cochrane 1999; Kocherlakota and Phelen 1999; Daniel 2001; the excellent discussions by Carlstrom and Fuerst 1999b and by Christiano and Fitzgerald 2000 and references they list; and the criticisms of the approach by McCallum 2001; Buiter 2002; and McCallum and Nelson 2005). The *fiscal theory of the price level* raises some important issues for both monetary theory and monetary policy.

There are two ways fiscal policy might matter for the price level. First, equilibrium requires that the real quantity of money equal the real demand for money. If fiscal variables affect the real demand for money, the equilibrium price level will also depend on fiscal factors (see section 4.4.2). This, however, is not the channel emphasized in fiscal theories of the price level. Instead, these theories focus on a second aspect of monetary models—there may be multiple price levels consistent with a given nominal quantity of money and equality between money supply and money demand. Fiscal policy may then determine which of these is the equilibrium price level. And in some cases, the equilibrium price level picked out by fiscal factors may be independent of the nominal supply of money.

In contrast to the standard monetary theories of the price level, the fiscal theory assumes that the government's intertemporal budget equation represents an equilibrium condition rather than a constraint that must hold for all price levels. At some price levels, the intertemporal budget constraint would be violated. Such price levels are not consistent with equilibrium. Given the stock of nominal debt, the equilibrium price level must ensure that the government's intertemporal budget is balanced.

The next section illustrates why the requirement that the real demand for money equal the real supply of money may not be sufficient to uniquely determine the equilibrium price level, even for a fixed nominal money supply. The subsequent section shows how fiscal considerations may serve to pin down the equilibrium price level.

4.5.1   Multiple Equilibria

The traditional quantity theory of money highlights the role the nominal stock of money plays in determining the equilibrium price level. Using the demand for money given by (4.19), a proportional relationship is obtained between the nominal quantity of money and the equilibrium price level that depends on the nominal rate of interest. However, the nominal interest rate is also an endogenous variable, so (4.19) by itself may not be sufficient to determine the equilibrium price level. Because the nominal interest rate depends on the rate of inflation, (4.19) can be written as

$$\frac{M_t}{P_t} = f\left(R_t \frac{P_{t+1}}{P_t}\right),$$

where R is the gross real rate of interest. This forward difference equation in the price level may be insufficient to determine a unique equilibrium path for the price level.

Consider a perfect-foresight equilibrium with a constant nominal supply of money, M_0. Suppose the real rate of return is equal to its steady-state value of $1/\beta$, and the demand for real money balances is given by (4.19). One can then write the equilibrium between the real supply of money and the real demand for money as

$$\frac{M_0}{P_t} = g\left(\frac{P_{t+1}}{P_t}\right), \qquad g' < 0.$$

Under suitable regularity conditions on $g(\ )$, this condition can be rewritten as

$$P_{t+1} = P_t g^{-1}\left(\frac{M_0}{P_t}\right) \equiv \phi(P_t). \tag{4.32}$$

Equation (4.32) defines a difference equation in the price level. One solution is $P_{t+i} = P^*$ for all $i \geq 0$, where $P^* = M_0/g(1)$. In this equilibrium, the quantity theory holds, and the price level is proportional to the money supply.

This constant price level equilibrium is not, however, the only possible equilibrium. As noted in section 4.4.5 and chapter 2, there may be equilibrium price paths starting from $P_0 \neq P^*$ that are fully consistent with the equilibrium condition (4.32). For example, in figure 4.3, the convex curve shows $\phi(P_t)$ as an increasing function of

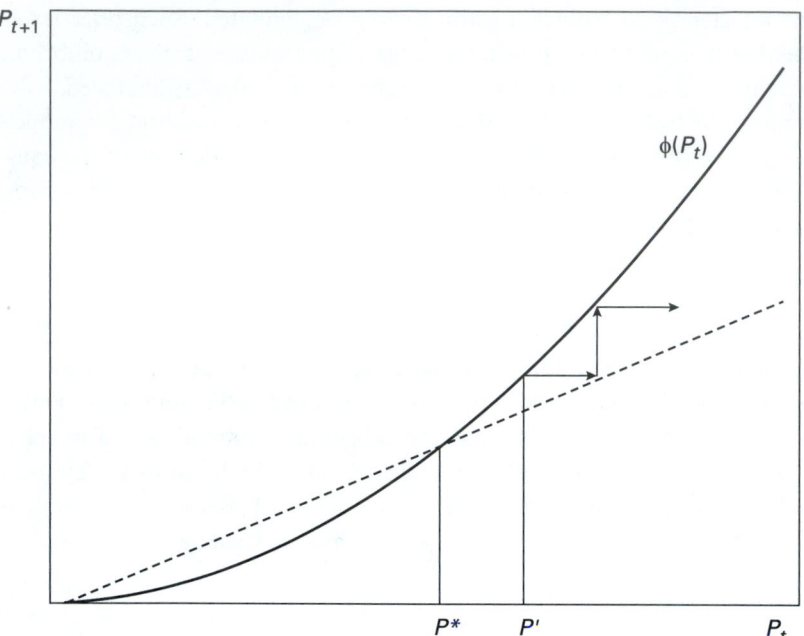

Figure 4.3
Equilibrium with a fixed nominal money supply.

P_t. Also shown in the figure is the 45° line. Using the fact that $g^{-1}(M_0/P^*) = 1$, the slope of $\phi(P_t)$, evaluated at P^*, is

$$\phi'(P^*) = g^{-1}(M_0/P^*) - [\partial g^{-1}(M_0/P^*)/\partial(M_0/P^*)](M_0/P^*)$$

$$= 1 - [\partial g^{-1}(M_0/P^*)/\partial(M_0/P^*)](M_0/P^*) > 1.$$

Thus, ϕ cuts the 45° line from below at P^*. Any price path starting at $P_0 = P' > P^*$ is consistent with (4.32) and involves a positive rate of inflation. As the figure illustrates, $P \to \infty$, but the equilibrium condition (4.32) is satisfied along this path. As the price level explodes, real money balances go to zero. But this is consistent with private agents' demand for money because inflation and therefore nominal interest rates are rising, lowering the real demand for money. Any price level to the right of P^* is a valid equilibrium. These equilibria all involve speculative hyperinflations. (Equilibria originating to the left of P^* eventually violate a transversality condition because M/P is exploding as $P \to 0$.) By itself, (4.32) is not sufficient to uniquely determine the equilibrium value of P_0, even though the nominal quantity of money is fixed.

4.5.2 The Fiscal Theory

Standard models in which equilibrium depends on forward-looking expectations of the price level, a property of the models discussed in chapters 2 and 3, generally have multiple equilibria. Thus, an additional equilibrium condition may be needed to uniquely determine the price level. The fiscal theory of the price level focuses on situations in which the government's intertemporal budget constraint may supply that additional condition.

The Basic Idea

The fiscal theory can be illustrated in the context of a model with a representative household and a government but no capital. The implications of the fiscal theory will be easiest to see if attention is restricted to perfect-foresight equilibria.

The representative household chooses its consumption and asset holdings optimally, subject to an intertemporal budget constraint. Suppose the period t budget constraint of the representative household takes the form

$$D_t + P_t y_t - T_t \geq P_t c_t + M_t^d + B_t^d = P_t c_t + \left(\frac{i_t}{1+i_t}\right) M_t^d + \left(\frac{1}{1+i_t}\right) D_{t+1}^d,$$

where D_t is the household's beginning-of-period financial wealth and $D_{t+1}^d = (1+i_t) B_t^d + M_t^d$. The superscripts denote that M^d and B^d are the household's demand for money and interest-bearing debt. In real terms, this budget constraint becomes

$$d_t + y_t - \tau_t \geq c_t + m_t^d + b_t^d = c_t + \left(\frac{i_t}{1+i_t}\right) m_t^d + \left(\frac{1}{1+r_t}\right) d_{t+1}^d,$$

where $\tau_t = T_t/P_t$, $m_t^d = M_t^d/P_t$, $1 + r_t = (1+i_t)(1+\pi_{t+1})$, and $d_t = D_t/P_t$. Let

$$\lambda_{t,t+i} = \prod_{j=1}^{i} \left(\frac{1}{1+r_{t+j}}\right)$$

be the discount factor, with $\lambda_{t,t} = 1$. Under standard assumptions, the household intertemporal budget constraint takes the form

$$d_t + \sum_{i=0}^{\infty} \lambda_{t,t+i}(y_{t+i} - \tau_{t+i}) = \sum_{i=0}^{\infty} \lambda_{t,t+i}\left[c_{t+i} + \left(\frac{i_{t+i}}{1+i_{t+i}}\right) m_{t+i}^d\right]. \tag{4.33}$$

Household choices must satisfy this intertemporal budget constraint. The left side is the present discounted value of the household's initial real financial wealth and after-tax income. The right side is the present discounted value of consumption spending plus the real cost of holding money. This condition holds with equality because any path of consumption and money holdings for which the left side exceeded the right side would not be optimal; the household could increase its consumption at time t without reducing consumption or money holdings at any other date. As long as the household is unable to accumulate debts that exceed the present value of its resources, the right side cannot exceed the left side.

The budget constraint for the government sector, in nominal terms, takes the form

$$P_t g_t + (1 + i_{t-1})B_{t-1} = T_t + M_t - M_{t-1} + B_t. \tag{4.34}$$

Dividing by P_t, this can be written as

$$g_t + d_t = \tau_t + \left(\frac{i_t}{1+i_t}\right)m_t + \left(\frac{1}{1+r_t}\right)d_{t+1}.$$

Recursively substituting for future values of d_{t+i}, this budget constraint implies that

$$d_t + \sum_{i=0}^{\infty} \lambda_{t,t+i}[g_{t+i} - \tau_{t+i} - \bar{s}_{t+i}] = \lim_{T \to \infty} \lambda_{t,t+T} d_T, \tag{4.35}$$

where $\bar{s}_t = i_t m_t / (1 + i_t)$ is the government's real seigniorage revenue. In previous sections, it was assumed that the expenditures, taxes, and seigniorage choices of the consolidated government (the combined monetary and fiscal authorities) were constrained by the requirement that $\lim_{T \to \infty} \lambda_{t,t+T} d_T = 0$ for *all* price levels P_t. Policy paths for $(g_{t+i}, \tau_{t+i}, s_{t+i}, d_{t+i})_{i \geq 0}$ such that

$$d_t + \sum_{i=0}^{\infty} \lambda_{t,t+i}[g_{t+i} - \tau_{t+i} - \bar{s}_{t+i}] = \lim_{T \to \infty} \lambda_{t,t+T} d_T = 0$$

for all price paths p_{t+i}, $i \geq 0$ are called *Ricardian* policies. Policy paths for $(g_{t+i}, \tau_{t+i}, \bar{s}_{t+i}, d_{t+i})_{i \geq 0}$ for which $\lim_{T \to \infty} \lambda_{t,t+T} d_T$ may not equal zero for all price paths are called *non-Ricardian*.[24]

Now consider a perfect-foresight equilibrium. Regardless of whether the government follows a Ricardian or a non-Ricardian policy, equilibrium in the goods market in this simple economy with no capital requires that $y_t = c_t + g_t$. The demand for money must also equal the supply of money: $m_t^d = m_t$. Substituting $y_t - g_t$ for c_t and m_t for m_t^d in (4.33) and rearranging yields

---

24. Notice that this usage differs somewhat from the way Sargent (1982) and Aiyagari and Gertler (1985) employed the terms. In those papers, a Ricardian policy was one in which the fiscal authority fully adjusted taxes to ensure intertemporal budget balance for all price paths. A non-Ricardian policy was a policy in which the monetary authority was required to adjust seigniorage to ensure intertemporal budget balance for all price paths. Both of these policies would be labeled Ricardian under the current section's use of the term.

$$d_t + \sum_{i=0}^{\infty} \lambda_{t,t+i} \left[g_{t+i} - \tau_{t+i} - \left(\frac{i_{t+i}}{1 + i_{t+i}} \right) m_{t+i} \right] = 0. \tag{4.36}$$

Thus, an implication of the representative household's optimization problem and market equilibrium is that (4.36) must hold in equilibrium. Under Ricardian policies, (4.36) does not impose any additional restrictions on equilibrium because the policy variables are always adjusted to ensure that this condition holds. Under a non-Ricardian policy, however, it does impose an additional condition that must be satisfied in equilibrium. To see what this condition involves, use the definition of d_t and seigniorage to write (4.36) as

$$\frac{D_t}{P_t} = \sum_{i=0}^{\infty} \lambda_{t,t+i} [\tau_{t+i} + \bar{s}_{t+i} - g_{t+i}]. \tag{4.37}$$

At time t, the government's outstanding nominal liabilities D_t are predetermined by past policies. Given the present discounted value of the government's future surpluses (the right side of (4.37)), the only endogenous variable is the current price level P_t. The price level must adjust to ensure that (4.37) is satisfied.

Equation (4.37) is an equilibrium condition under non-Ricardian policies, but it is not the only equilibrium condition. It is still the case that real money demand and real money supply must be equal. Suppose the real demand for money is given by (4.19), rewritten here as

$$\frac{M_t}{P_t} = f(1 + i_t). \tag{4.38}$$

Equations (4.37) and (4.38) must both be satisfied in equilibrium. However, which two variables are determined jointly by these two equations depends on the assumptions that are made about fiscal and monetary policies. For example, suppose the fiscal authority determines g_{t+i} and τ_{t+i} for all $i \geq 0$, and the monetary authority pegs the nominal rate of interest $i_{t+i} = \bar{i}$ for all $i \geq 0$. Seigniorage is equal to $\bar{i}f(1 + \bar{i})/(1 + \bar{i})$ and so is fixed by monetary policy. With this specification of monetary and fiscal policies, the right side of (4.37) is given. Since D_t is predetermined at date t, (4.37) can be solved for the equilibrium price level P_t^* given by

$$P_t^* = \frac{D_t}{\sum_{i=0}^{\infty} \lambda_{t,t+i} [\tau_{t+i} + \bar{s}_{t+i} - g_{t+i}]}. \tag{4.39}$$

The current nominal money supply is then determined by (4.38):

$$M_t = P_t^* f(1 + \bar{i}).$$

One property of this equilibrium is that changes in fiscal policy (g or τ) directly alter the equilibrium price level, even though seigniorage as measured by $\sum_{i=0}^{\infty} \lambda_{t,t+i} \bar{s}_{t+i}$ is unaffected.[25] The finding that the price level is uniquely determined by (4.39) contrasts with a standard conclusion that the price level is indeterminate under a nominal interest rate peg. This conclusion is obtained from (4.38): with i pegged, the right side of (4.38) is fixed, but this only determines the real supply of money. Any price level is consistent with equilibrium, as M then adjusts to ensure that (4.38) holds.

Critical to the fiscal theory is the assumption that (4.37), the government's intertemporal budget constraint, is an *equilibrium* condition that holds at the equilibrium price level and not a condition that must hold at all price levels. This means that at price levels not equal to P_t^*, the government is planning to run surpluses (including seigniorage) whose real value, in present discounted terms, is not equal to the government's outstanding real liabilities. Similarly, it means that the government could cut current taxes, leaving current and future government expenditures and seigniorage unchanged, and not simultaneously plan to raise future taxes.[26] When (4.37) is interpreted as a budget *constraint* that must be satisfied for all price levels, that is, under Ricardian policies, any decision to cut taxes today (and so lower the right side of (4.37)) must be accompanied by planned future tax increases to leave the right side unchanged.

In standard infinite-horizon, representative-agent models, a tax cut (current and future government expenditures unchanged) has no effect on equilibrium (i.e., Ricardian equivalence holds) because the tax reduction does not have a real wealth effect on private agents. Agents recognize that in a Ricardian regime, future taxes have risen in present value terms by an amount exactly equal to the reduction in current taxes. Alternatively expressed, the government cannot engineer a permanent tax cut unless government expenditures are also cut (in present value terms). Because the fiscal theory of the price level assumes that (4.37) holds only when evaluated at the equilibrium price level, the government can plan a permanent tax cut. If it does, the price level must rise to ensure that the new, lower value of discounted surpluses is again equal to the real value of government debt.

For (4.39) to define an equilibrium price level, it must hold that $D_t \neq 0$. Niepelt (2004) argued that the fiscal theory cannot hold if there is no initial outstanding stock of nominal government debt. However, Daniel (2007) showed that one can define non-Ricardian policies in a consistent manner when the initial stock of debt is zero. Her argument is most clearly seen in a two-period example. If the monetary author-

---

25. A change in g or τ causes the price level to jump, and this transfers resources between the private sector and the government. This transfer can also be viewed as a form of seigniorage.

26. However, as Bassetto (2002) emphasized, the ability of the government to run a deficit in any period under a non-Ricardian policy regime is contrained by the willingness of the public to lend to the government.

ity pegs the nominal rate of interest, then any initial value of the price level is consistent with equilibrium, a standard result under interest rate pegs (see chapter 11). The nominal interest rate peg does pin down the expected inflation rate, or equivalently, the expected price level in the second period. However, this policy does not pin down the actual price level in period 2. Under a Ricardian fiscal policy, *any* realization of the price level in period 2, consistent with the value expected, is an equilibrium. If the realized price level were to result in the government's budget constraint not balancing, then the Ricardian nature of policy means that taxes and/or spending must adjust to ensure intertemporal budget balance at the realized price level. Under a non-Ricardian fiscal policy, only realizations of the price level that satisfy intertemporal budget balance can be consistent with an equilibrium. Thus, whatever quantity of nominal debt the government issued in the first period, the realized price level must ensure the real value of this debt in period 2 balances with the real value the government chooses for its primary surplus (including seigniorage). Under rational expectations, however, a non-Ricardian government cannot systematically employ price surprises in period 2 to finance spending because the monetary authority's interest peg has determined the expected value of the period 2 price level. Equilibrium must be consistent with those expectations.

An interest rate peg is just one possible specification for monetary policy. As an alternative, suppose as before that the fiscal authority sets the paths for g_{t+i} and τ_{t+i}, but now suppose that the government adjusts tax revenues to offset any variations in seigniorage. In this case, $\tau_{t+i} + \bar{s}_{t+i}$ becomes an exogenous process. Then (4.37) can be solved for the equilibrium price level independent of the nominal money stock. Equation (4.38) must still hold in equilibrium. If the monetary authority sets M_t, this equation determines the nominal interest rate that ensures that the real demand for money is equal to the real supply. If the monetary authority sets the nominal rate of interest, (4.38) determines the nominal money supply. The extreme implication of the fiscal theory (relative to traditional quantity theory results) is perhaps most stark when the monetary authority fixes the nominal supply of money: $M_{t+i} = \bar{M}$ for all $i \geq 0$. Then, under a fiscal policy that makes $\tau_{t+i} + \bar{s}_{t+i}$ an exogenous process, the price level is proportional to D_t and, for a given level of D_t, is independent of the value chosen for $\bar{M}$.

Empirical Evidence on the Fiscal Theory

Under the fiscal theory of the price level, (4.37) holds at the equilibrium value of the price level. Under traditional theories of the price level, (4.37) holds for all values of the price level. If only equilibrium outcomes are observed, it will be impossible empirically to distinguish between the two theories. As Sims (1994, 381) puts it, "Determinacy of the price level under any policy depends on the public's beliefs about what the policy authority would do under conditions that are never observed in equilibrium."

Canzoneri, Cumby, and Diba (2001) examined VAR evidence on the response of U.S. liabilities to a positive innovation to the primary surplus. Under a non-Ricardian policy, a positive innovation to $\tau_t + \bar{s}_t - g_t$ should increase D_t/P_t (see (4.37)) unless it also signals future reductions in the surplus, that is, unless $\tau_t + \bar{s}_t - g_t$ is negatively serially correlated. The authors argued that in a Ricardian regime, a positive innovation to the current primary surplus will reduce real liabilities. This can be seen by writing the budget constraint (4.34) in real terms as

$$d_{t+1} = R[d_t - (\tau_t + s_t - g_t)]. \tag{4.40}$$

Examining U.S. data, the authors found that the responses are inconsistent with a non-Ricardian regime. Increases in the surplus are associated with declines in current and future real liabilities, and the surplus does not display negative serial correlation.

Cochrane pointed out the fundamental problem with this test: both (4.40) and (4.37) must hold in equilibrium, so it can be difficult to develop testable restrictions that can distinguish between the two regimes. The two regimes have different implications only if nonequilibrium values of the price level can be observed.

Bohn (1999) examined the U.S. deficit and debt processes and concluded that the primary surplus responds positively to the debt to GDP ratio. In other words, a rise in the debt to GDP ratio leads to an increase in the primary surplus. Thus, the surplus does adjust, and Bohn found that it responds enough to ensure that the intertemporal budget constraint is satisfied. This is evidence that the fiscal authority seems to act in a Ricardian fashion.

Finally, there is an older literature that attempted to estimate whether fiscal deficits tend to lead to faster money growth. Such evidence might be interpreted to imply a Ricardian regime of fiscal dominance. Some of this literature was reviewed in section 4.4.

4.6 Optimal Taxation and Seigniorage

If the government can raise revenue by printing money, how much should it raise from this source? Suppose only distortionary revenue sources are available. To raise a given amount of revenue while causing the minimum deadweight loss from tax-induced distortions, the government should generally set its tax instruments so that the marginal distortionary cost per dollar of revenue raised is equalized across all taxes. As first noted by Phelps (1973), this suggests that an optimal tax package should include some seigniorage. This prescription links the optimal inflation tax to a more general problem of determining the optimal levels of all tax instruments. If governments are actually attempting to minimize the distortionary costs of raising revenue, then the optimal tax literature provides a positive theory of inflation.

This basic idea is developed in the next section and was originally used by Mankiw (1987) to explain nominal interest rate setting by the Federal Reserve. However, the implications of this approach are rejected for industrialized economies (Poterba and Rotemberg 1990; Trehan and Walsh 1990), although this may not be too surprising because seigniorage plays a fairly small role as a revenue source for these countries. Calvo and Leiderman (1992) used the optimal tax approach to examine the experiences of some Latin American economies, with more promising results. A survey of optimal seigniorage that links the topic with the issues of time inconsistency treated in chapter 7 can be found in Herrendorf (1997). Section 4.6.2 considers the role inflation might play as an optimal response to the need to finance temporary expenditure shocks. Section 4.6.3 revisits Friedman's rule for the optimal rate of inflation in an explicit general equilibrium framework.

4.6.1   A Partial Equilibrium Model

This section assumes a Ricardian regime in which the government has available to it two revenue sources. The government can also borrow. It needs to finance a constant exogenous level of real expenditures g, plus interest on any borrowing. To simplify the analysis, the real rate of interest is assumed to be constant, and ad hoc descriptions are specified for both money demand and the distortions associated with the two tax instruments.

With these assumptions, the basic real budget identity of the government can be obtained by dividing (4.3) by the time t price level to obtain

$$b_t = Rb_{t-1} + g - \tau_t - s_t, \tag{4.41}$$

where R is the gross interest factor (i.e., 1 plus the rate of interest), τ is nonseigniorage tax revenue, and s is seigniorage revenue. Seigniorage is given by

$$s_t = \frac{M_t - M_{t-1}}{P_t} = m_t - \frac{m_{t-1}}{1 + \pi_t}. \tag{4.42}$$

Taking expectations of (4.41) conditional on time t information and recursively solving forward yields the intertemporal budget constraint of the government:

$$E_t \sum_{i=0}^{\infty} R^{-i}(\tau_{t+i} + s_{t+i}) = Rb_{t-1} + \left(\frac{R}{R-1}\right)g. \tag{4.43}$$

Note that, given b_{t-1}, (4.43) imposes a constraint on the government because $E_t \lim_{i \to \infty} R^{-i}b_{t+i}$ has been set equal to zero. Absent this constraint, the problem of choosing the optimal time path for taxes and seigniorage becomes trivial. Just set both equal to zero and borrow continually to finance expenditures plus interest, because debt never needs to be repaid.

The government is assumed to set τ_t and the inflation rate π_t, as well as planned paths for their future values to minimize the present discounted value of the distortions generated by these taxes, taking as given the inherited real debt b_{t-1}, the path of expenditures, and the financing constraint given by (4.43). The assumption that the government can commit to a planned path for future taxes and inflation is an important one. Much of chapter 7 deals with outcomes when governments cannot precommit to future policies.

In order to illustrate the key implications of the joint determination of inflation and taxes, assume that the distortions arising from income taxes are quadratic in the tax rate: $(\tau_t + \phi_t)^2/2$, where ϕ is a stochastic term that allows the marginal costs of taxes to vary randomly.[27] Similarly, costs associated with seigniorage are taken to equal $(s_t + \varepsilon_t)^2/2$, where ε is a stochastic shift in the cost function. Thus, the present discounted value of tax distortions is given by

$$\frac{1}{2}E_t \sum_{i=0}^{\infty} R^{-i}[(\tau_{t+i} + \phi_{t+i})^2 + (s_{t+i} + \varepsilon_{t+i})^2]. \tag{4.44}$$

The government's objective is to choose paths for the tax rate and inflation to minimize (4.44) subject to (4.43).

Letting λ represent the Lagrangian multiplier associated with the intertemporal budget constraint, the necessary first-order conditions for the government's setting of τ and s take the form

$$E_t(\tau_{t+i} + \phi_{t+i}) = \lambda, \qquad i \geq 0$$

$$E_t(s_{t+i} + \varepsilon_{t+i}) = \lambda, \qquad i \geq 0.$$

These conditions simply state that the government will arrange its tax collections to equalize the marginal distortionary costs across tax instruments, that is, $E_t(\tau_{t+i} + \phi_{t+i}) = E_t(s_{t+i} + \varepsilon_{t+i})$ for each $i \geq 0$, and across time, that is, $E_t(\tau_{t+i} + \phi_{t+i}) = E_t(\tau_{t+j} + \phi_{t+j})$ and $E_t(s_{t+i} + \varepsilon_{t+i}) = E_t(s_{t+j} + \varepsilon_{t+j})$ for all i and j.

For $i = 0$, the first-order condition implies that $\tau_t + \phi_t = s_t + \varepsilon_t = \lambda$; this represents an *intratemporal* optimality condition. Since the value of λ will depend on the total revenue needs of the government, increases in $Rg/(R-1) + Rb_{t-1}$ will cause the government to increase the revenue raised from both tax sources. Thus, one would expect to observe τ_t and s_t moving in similar directions (given ϕ_t and ε_t).

Intertemporal optimality requires that marginal costs be equated across time periods for each tax instrument:

---

27. This approach follows that of Poterba and Rotemberg (1990), who specified tax costs directly, as is done here, although they assumed a more general functional form for which the quadratic specification is a special case. See also Trehan and Walsh (1988).

$$E_t \tau_{t+1} = \tau_t - E_t \phi_{t+1} + \phi_t \tag{4.45}$$

$$E_t s_{t+1} = s_t - E_t \varepsilon_{t+1} + \varepsilon_t. \tag{4.46}$$

These intertemporal conditions lead to standard *tax-smoothing* conclusions; for each tax instrument, the government will equate the expected marginal distortionary costs in different time periods. If the random shocks to tax distortions follow $I(1)$ processes such that $E_t \phi_{t+1} - \phi_t = E_t \varepsilon_{t+1} - \varepsilon_t = 0$, these intertemporal optimality conditions imply that both τ and s follow Martingale processes, an implication of the tax-smoothing model originally developed by Barro (1979). If $E_t \varepsilon_{t+1} - \varepsilon_t = 0$, (4.46) implies that changes in seigniorage revenues should be unpredictable based on information available at time t.

Changes in revenue sources might be predictable and still be consistent with this model of optimal taxation if the expected $t+1$ values of ϕ and/or ε, conditional on period t information, are nonzero. For example, if $E_t \varepsilon_{t+1} - \varepsilon_t > 0$, that is, if the distortionary cost of seigniorage revenue were expected to rise, it would be optimal to plan to reduce future seigniorage.

Using a form of (4.46), Mankiw (1987) argued that the near random walk behavior of inflation (actually nominal interest rates) is consistent with U.S. monetary policy having been conducted in a manner consistent with optimal finance considerations. Poterba and Rotemberg (1990) provided some cross-country evidence on the joint movements of inflation and other tax revenues. In general, this evidence is not favorable to the hypothesis that inflation (or seigniorage) has been set on the basis of optimal finance considerations. Although Poterba and Rotemberg found the predicted positive relationship between tax rates and inflation for the United States and Japan, there was a negative relationship for France, Germany, and the United Kingdom.

The implications of the optimal finance view of seigniorage are, however, much stronger than simply that seigniorage and other tax revenues should be positively correlated. Since the unit root behavior of both s and τ arises from the same source (their dependence on $Rg/(R-1) + Rb_{t-1}$ through λ), the optimizing model of tax setting has the joint implication that both tax rates and inflation should contain unit roots (they respond to permanent shifts in government revenue needs) and that they should be cointegrated.[28] Trehan and Walsh (1990) showed that this implication is rejected for U.S. data.

The optimal finance view of seigniorage fails for the United States because seigniorage appears to behave more like the stock of debt than like general tax revenues. Under a tax-smoothing model, temporary variations in government expenditures

---

28. That is, if ϕ and ε are $I(0)$ processes, then τ and s are $I(1)$ but $\tau - s = \varepsilon - \phi$ is $I(0)$.

should be met through debt financing. Variations in seigniorage should reflect changes in expected permanent government expenditures or, from (4.46), stochastic shifts in the distortions associated with raising seigniorage (due to the ε realizations). In contrast, debt should rise in response to a temporary revenue need (such as a war) and then gradually decline over time. However, the behavior of seigniorage in the United States, particularly during the World War II period, mimics that of the deficit much more than it does that of other tax revenues (Trehan and Walsh 1988).

One drawback of this analysis is that the specification of the government's objective function is ad hoc; the tax distortions were not related in any way to the underlying sources of the distortions in terms of the allocative effects of taxes or the welfare costs of inflation. These costs depend on the demand for money; therefore, the specification of the distortions should be consistent with the particular approach used to motivate the demand for money.

Calvo and Leiderman (1992) provided an analysis of optimal intertemporal inflation taxation using a money demand specification consistent with utility maximization. They showed that the government's optimality condition requires that the nominal rate of interest vary with the expected growth of the marginal utility of consumption. Optimal tax considerations call for high taxes when the marginal utility of consumption is low and low taxes when the marginal utility of consumption is high. Thus, models of inflation in an optimal finance setting will generally imply restrictions on the joint behavior of inflation and the marginal utility of consumption, not just on inflation alone. Calvo and Leiderman estimated their model using data from three countries that have experienced periods of high inflation: Argentina, Brazil, and Israel. While the overidentifying restrictions implied by their model are not rejected for the first two countries, they are for Israel.

4.6.2   Optimal Seigniorage and Temporary Shocks

The prescription to smooth marginal distortionary costs over time implies that tax levels are set on the basis of some estimate of permanent expenditure needs. Allowing tax rates to fluctuate in response to temporary and unanticipated fluctuations in expenditures would result in a higher total efficiency loss in present value terms because of the distortions induced by non-lump-sum taxes. As extended to seigniorage by Mankiw (1987), the same argument implies that seigniorage should be set on the basis of permanent expenditure needs and not adjusted in response to unanticipated temporary events.

The allocative distortions induced by the inflation tax, however, were shown in chapters 2 and 3 to be based on anticipated inflation. Consumption, labor supply, and money holding decisions are made by households on the basis of expected inflation, and for this reason variations in expected inflation generate distortions. In contrast, unanticipated inflation has wealth effects but no substitution effects. It therefore serves as a form of lump-sum tax. Given real money holdings, which are based on the public's expectations about inflation, a government interested in minimizing distortionary tax costs should engineer a surprise inflation. If sufficient revenue could be generated in this way, socially costly distortionary taxes could be avoided.[29]

Unfortunately, private agents are likely to anticipate that the government will have an incentive to attempt a surprise inflation; the outcome in such a situation is the major focus of chapter 7. But suppose the government can commit itself to, on average, only inflating at a rate consistent with its revenue needs based on average expenditures. That is, average inflation is set according to permanent expenditures, as implied by the tax-smoothing model. But if there are unanticipated fluctuations in expenditures, these should be met through socially costless unanticipated inflation.

Calvo and Guidotti (1993) made this argument rigorous. They showed that when the government can commit to a path for anticipated inflation, it is optimal for unanticipated inflation to respond flexibly to unexpected disturbances. This implication is consistent with the behavior of seigniorage in the United States, which for most of the twentieth century followed a pattern that appeared to be more similar to that of the federal government deficit than to a measure of the average tax rate. During war periods, when most of the rise in expenditures could be viewed as temporary, taxes were not raised sufficiently to fund the war effort. Instead, the U.S. government borrowed heavily, just as the Barro tax-smoothing model implies. But the United States did raise the inflation tax; seigniorage revenues rose during the war, falling back to lower levels at the war's conclusion. This behavior is much closer to that implied by Calvo and Guidotti's theory than to the basic implications of Mankiw's.[30]

4.6.3   Friedman's Rule Revisited

The preceding analysis has gone partway toward integrating the choice of inflation with the general public finance choice of tax rates, and the discussion was motivated by Phelps's conclusion that if only distortionary tax sources are available, some revenue should be raised from the inflation tax. However, this conclusion has been questioned by Kimbrough (1986a; 1986b); Faig (1988); Chari, Christiano, and Kehoe (1991; 1996); and Correia and Teles (1996; 1999).[31] They showed that there are conditions under which Friedman's rule for the optimal inflation rate—a zero nominal

---

29. Auernheimer (1974) provided a guide to seigniorage for an "honest" government, one that does not generate revenue by allowing the price level to jump unexpectedly, even though this would represent an efficient lump-sum tax.

30. Chapter 8 revisits the optimal choice of taxes and inflation in a new Keynesian model.

31. An early example of the use of optimal tax models to study the optimal inflation rate issue is Drazen (1979). See also Walsh (1984). Chari and Kehoe (1999) provided a survey.

rate of interest—continues to be optimal even in the absence of lump-sum taxes. Mulligan and Sala-i-Martin (1997) provided a general discussion of the conditions necessary for taxing (or not taxing) money.

This literature integrates the question of the optimal inflation tax into the general problem of optimal taxation. By doing so, the analysis can build on findings in the optimal tax literature that identify situations in which the structure of optimal indirect taxes calls for different final goods to be taxed at the same rate or for the tax rate on goods that serve as intermediate inputs to be zero (see Diamond and Mirrlees 1971; Atkinson and Stiglitz 1972). Using an MIU approach, for example, treats money as a final good; in contrast, a shopping-time model, or a more general model in which money serves to produce transaction services, treats money as an intermediate input. Thus, it is important to examine the implications these alternative assumptions about the role of money have for the optimal tax approach to inflation determination, and how optimal inflation tax results might depend on particular restrictions on preferences or on the technology for producing transaction services.

The Basic Ramsey Problem

The problem of determining the optimal structure of taxes to finance a given level of expenditures is called the *Ramsey problem*, after the classic treatment of Frank Ramsey (1928). In the representative-agent models studied here, the Ramsey problem involves setting taxes to maximize the utility of the representative agent, subject to the government's revenue requirement.

The following static Ramsey problem, based on Mulligan and Sala-i-Martin (1997), can be used to highlight the key issues. The utility of the representative agent depends on consumption, real money balances, and leisure:

$$u = u(c, m, l).$$

Agents maximize utility subject to the following budget constraint:

$$f(n) \geq (1 + \tau)c + \tau_m m, \tag{4.47}$$

where $f(n)$ is a standard production function, $n = 1 - l$ is the supply of labor, c is consumption, τ is the consumption tax, $\tau_m = i/(1 + i)$ is the tax on money, and m is the household's holdings of real money balances. The representative agent picks consumption, money holdings, and leisure to maximize utility, taking the tax rates as given. Letting λ be the Lagrangian multiplier on the budget constraint, the first-order conditions from the agent's maximization problem are

$$u_c = \lambda(1 + \tau) \tag{4.48}$$

$$u_m = \lambda \tau_m \tag{4.49}$$

$$u_l = \lambda f'. \tag{4.50}$$

From these first-order conditions and the budget constraint, the choices of c, m, and l can be expressed as functions of the two tax rates: $c(\tau, \tau_m)$, $m(\tau, \tau_m)$, and $l(\tau, \tau_m)$.

The government's problem is to set τ and τ_m to maximize the representative agent's utility, subject to three types of constraints. First, the government must satisfy its budget constraint; tax revenues must be sufficient to finance expenditures. This constraint takes the form

$$\tau c + \tau_m m \geq g, \tag{4.51}$$

where g is real government expenditures. These expenditures are taken to be exogenous. Second, the government is constrained by the fact that consumption, labor supply, and real money must be consistent with the choices of private agents. That means that (4.48)–(4.50) represent constraints on the government's choices. Finally, the government is constrained by the economy's resource constraint:

$$f(1 - l) \geq c + g. \tag{4.52}$$

The government's problem is to pick τ and τ_m to maximize $u(c, m, l)$ subject to (4.48)–(4.52).

There are two approaches to solving this problem. The first approach, often called the *dual approach*, employs the indirect utility function to express utility as a function of taxes. These tax rates are treated as the government's control variables, and the optimal values of the tax rates are found by solving the first-order conditions from the government's optimization problem. The second approach, called the *primal approach*, treats quantities as the government's controls. The tax rates are found from the representative agent's first-order conditions to ensure that private agents choose the quantities that solve the government's maximization problem. The dual approach is considered first, and the primal approach is discussed later in this section.

The government's problem can be written as

$$\max_{\tau, \tau_m} \{ v(\tau, \tau_m) + \mu[\tau_m m(\tau, \tau_m) + \tau c(\tau, \tau_m) - g] + \theta[f(1 - l(\tau, \tau_m)) - c(\tau, \tau_m) - g] \},$$

where $v(\tau, \tau_m) = u[c(\tau, \tau_m), m(\tau, \tau_m), l(\tau, \tau_m)]$ is the indirect utility function, and μ and θ are Lagrangian multipliers on the budget and resource constraints. Notice that the constraints represented by (4.48)–(4.50) have been incorporated by writing consumption, money balances, and leisure as functions of the tax rates. The first-order conditions for the two taxes are

$$v_\tau + \mu(\tau_m m_\tau + c + \tau c_\tau) - \theta(f'l_\tau + c_\tau) \le 0$$

$$v_{\tau_m} + \mu(m + \tau_m m_{\tau_m} + \tau c_{\tau_m}) - \theta(f'l_{\tau_m} + c_{\tau_m}) \le 0,$$

where $v_\tau = u_c c_\tau + u_m m_\tau + u_l l_\tau$ and $v_{\tau_m} = u_c c_{\tau_m} + u_m m_{\tau_m} + u_l l_{\tau_m}$. These conditions will hold with equality if the solution is an interior one with positive taxes on both consumption and money. If the left side of the second first-order condition is negative when evaluated at a zero tax on money, then a zero tax on money ($\tau_m = 0$) will be optimal. From the resource constraint (4.52), $-f'l_x - c_x = 0$ for $x = \tau$, τ_m since g is fixed, so the two first-order conditions can be simplified to yield

$$u_c c_\tau + u_m m_\tau + u_l l_\tau + \mu(\tau_m m_\tau + c + \tau c_\tau) \le 0 \tag{4.53}$$

$$u_c c_{\tau_m} + u_m m_{\tau_m} + u_l l_{\tau_m} + \mu(m + \tau_m m_{\tau_m} + \tau c_{\tau_m}) \le 0. \tag{4.54}$$

The first three terms in (4.53) can be written using the agent's first-order conditions and the budget constraint (4.47) as

$$u_c c_\tau + u_m m_\tau + u_l l_\tau = u_l \left(\frac{u_c}{u_l} c_\tau + \frac{u_m}{u_l} m_\tau + l_\tau \right)$$

$$= \left(\frac{u_l}{f'} \right) [(1 + \tau)c_\tau + \tau_m m_\tau + f'l_\tau].$$

However, differentiating the budget constraint (4.47) by τ yields

$$c + (1 + \tau)c_\tau + \tau_m m_\tau + f'l_\tau = 0,$$

so $u_c c_\tau + u_m m_\tau + u_l l_\tau = -(u_l/f')c$. Thus, (4.53) becomes

$$\left(\frac{u_l}{f'} \right) c \ge \mu(\tau_m m_\tau + c + \tau c_\tau),$$

while following similar steps implies that (4.54) becomes

$$\left(\frac{u_l}{f'} \right) m \ge \mu(m + \tau_m m_{\tau_m} + \tau c_{\tau_m}).$$

Hence, if the solution is an interior one with positive taxes on consumption and money holdings,

$$\frac{m}{c} = \frac{m + \tau_m m_{\tau_m} + \tau c_{\tau_m}}{\tau_m m_\tau + c + \tau c_\tau}. \tag{4.55}$$

To interpret this condition, note that $v_{\tau_m} = u_c c_{\tau_m} + u_m m_{\tau_m} + u_l l_{\tau_m} = -u_l m/f'$ is the effect of the tax on money on utility, and $v_\tau = u_c c_\tau + u_m m_\tau + u_l l_\tau = -u_l c/f'$ is the effect of the consumption tax on utility. Thus, their ratio, m/c, is the marginal rate of substitution between the two tax rates, holding constant the utility of the representative agent.[32] The right side of (4.55) is the marginal rate of transformation, holding the government's revenue constant.[33] At an optimum, the government equates the marginal rates of substitution and transformation.

Our interest is in determining when the Friedman rule, $\tau_m = 0$, is optimal. Assume, following Friedman, that at a zero nominal interest rate, the demand for money is finite. Since the tax on consumption must be positive if the tax on money is zero (since the government does need to raise revenue), (4.53) will hold with equality. Then

$$\frac{m}{c} \geq \frac{m + \tau_m m_{\tau_m} + \tau c_{\tau_m}}{\tau_m m_\tau + c + \tau c_\tau}, \tag{4.56}$$

or

$$\frac{m}{m + \tau_m m_{\tau_m} + \tau c_{\tau_m}} \geq \frac{c}{\tau_m m_\tau + c + \tau c_\tau}.$$

The left side is proportional to the marginal impact of the inflation tax on utility per dollar of revenue raised. The right side is proportional to the marginal impact of the consumption tax on utility per dollar of revenue raised. If the inequality is strict at $\tau_m = 0$, then the distortion caused by using the inflation tax (per dollar of revenue raised) exceeds the cost of raising that same revenue with the consumption tax. Thus, it is optimal to set the tax on money equal to zero if

$$\frac{m}{c} \geq \frac{m + \tau c_{\tau_m}}{c + \tau c_\tau}, \tag{4.57}$$

or (since $c_\tau \leq 0$)

---

32. That is, if $v(\tau, \tau_m)$ is the utility of the representative agent as a function of the two tax rates, then $v_\tau \, d\tau + v_{\tau_m} \, d\tau_m = 0$ yields

$$\frac{d\tau}{d\tau_m} = -\frac{v_{\tau_m}}{v_\tau} = -\frac{m}{c}.$$

33. That is, from the government's budget constraint,

$$(m + \tau_m m_{\tau_m} + \tau c_{\tau_m}) \, d\tau_m + (\tau_m m_\tau + c + \tau c_\tau) \, d\tau = 0,$$

yielding

$$\frac{d\tau_m}{d\tau} = -\frac{\tau_m m_\tau + c + \tau c_\tau}{m + \tau_m m_{\tau_m} + \tau c_{\tau_m}}.$$

$$\frac{m}{c} \leq \frac{c_{\tau_m}}{c_\tau},$$
(4.58)

where these expressions are evaluated at $\tau_m = 0$.[34]

Mulligan and Sala-i-Martin (1997) considered (4.56) for a variety of special cases that have appeared in the literature. For example, if utility is separable in consumption and money holdings, then $c_{\tau_m} = 0$; in this case, the right side of (4.58) is equal to zero, and the left side is positive. Hence, (4.58) cannot hold, and it is optimal to tax money.

A second case that leads to clear results occurs if $c_{\tau_m} > 0$. In this case, the right side of (4.58) is negative (since $c_\tau < 0$, an increase in the consumption tax reduces consumption). Since the left side is non-negative, $m/c > c_{\tau_m}/c_\tau$, and money should always be taxed. This corresponds to a case in which money and consumption are substitutes so that an increase in the tax on money (which reduces money holdings) leads to an increase in consumption. Finally, if money and consumption are complements, $c_{\tau_m} < 0$. The ratio c_{τ_m}/c_τ is then positive, and whether money is taxed will depend on a comparison of m/c and c_{τ_m}/c_τ. Recall that the calibration exercises in chapter 2 used parameter values that implied that m and c were complements.

Chari, Christiano, and Kehoe (1996) examined the optimality of the Friedman rule in an MIU model with taxes on consumption, labor supply, and money. They showed that if preferences are homothetic in consumption and money balances and separable in leisure, the optimal tax on money is zero. When preferences satisfy these assumptions, one can write

$$u(c, m, l) = \bar{u}[s(c, m), l],$$

where $s(c, m)$ is homothetic.[35] Mulligan and Sala-i-Martin (1997) showed that in this case,

$$\frac{m}{c} = \frac{c_{\tau_m}}{c_\tau},$$

so (4.58) implies that the optimal tax structure yields $\tau_m = 0$.

Chari, Christiano, and Kehoe related their results to the optimal taxation literature in public finance. Atkinson and Stiglitz (1972) showed that if two goods are produced under conditions of constant returns to scale, a sufficient condition for uniform tax rates is that the utility function is homothetic. With equal tax rates, the ratio of marginal utilities equals the ratio of producer prices. To see how this applies

---

34. This is Proposition 2 in Mulligan and Sala-i-Martin (1997, 692).

35. Homothetic preferences imply that $s(c, m)$ is homogeneous of degree 1 and that s_i is homogeneous of degree 0. With homothetic preferences, indifference curves are parallel to each other, with constant slope along any ray; $s_2(c, m)/s_1(c, m) = f(m/c)$.

in the present case, suppose the budget constraint for the representative household takes the form

$$(1 + \tau_t^c)Q_t c_t + M_t + B_t = (1 - \tau_t^h)Q_t(1 - l_t) + (1 + i_{t-1})B_{t-1} + M_{t-1},$$

where M and B are the nominal money and bond holdings, i is the nominal rate of interest, Q is the producer price of output, and τ^c and τ^h are the tax rates on consumption (c) and hours of work ($1 - l$). In addition, it is assumed that the production function exhibits constant returns to scale and that labor hours, $1 - l$, are transformed into output according to $y = 1 - l$. Define $P \equiv (1 + \tau^c)Q$. Household real wealth is $w_t = (M_t + B_t)/P_t = m_t + b_t$, and the budget constraint can be written as

$$c_t + w_t = \left(\frac{1 - \tau_t^h}{1 + \tau_t^c}\right)(1 - l_t) + (1 + r_{t-1})b_{t-1} + \frac{m_{t-1}}{1 + \pi_t}$$

$$= (1 - \tau_t)(1 - l_t) + (1 + r_{t-1})w_{t-1} - \left(\frac{i_{t-1}}{1 + \pi_t}\right)m_{t-1}, \tag{4.59}$$

where $1 - \tau_t \equiv (1 - \tau_t^h)/(1 + \tau_t^c)$ and $(1 + r_{t-1}) = (1 + i_{t-1})/(1 + \pi_t)$, and $\pi_t = P_t/P_{t-1} - 1$. Thus, the consumption and labor taxes only matter through the composite tax τ, so without loss of generality, set the consumption tax equal to zero. If the representative household's utility during period t is given by $\bar{u}[s(c, m), l]$ and the household maximizes $E_t \sum_{i=0}^{\infty} \beta^i \bar{u}[s(c_{t+i}, m_{t+i}), l_{t+i}]$ subject to the budget constraint given by (4.59), then the first-order conditions for the household's decision problem imply that consumption, money balances, and leisure will be chosen such that

$$\frac{\bar{u}_m(c_t, m_t, l_t)}{\bar{u}_c(c_t, m_t, l_t)} = \frac{s_m(c_t, m_t)}{s_c(c_t, m_t)} = \frac{i_t}{1 + i_t} \equiv \tau_{m,t}.$$

With the production costs of money assumed to be zero, the ratio of marginal utilities differs from the ratio of production costs unless $\tau_{m,t} = 0$. Hence, with preferences that are homothetic in c and m, the Atkinson-Stiglitz result implies that it will be optimal to set the nominal rate of interest equal to zero.

Correia and Teles (1999) considered other cases in which (4.57) holds so that the optimal tax on money equals zero. They followed M. Friedman (1969) in assuming a satiation level of money holdings m^* such that the marginal utility of money is positive for $m < m^*$ and nonpositive for $m \geq m^*$. This satiation level can depend on c and l. Correia and Teles showed that the optimal tax on money is zero if $m^* = \bar{k}c$ for a positive constant $\bar{k}$. They also showed that the optimal tax on money is zero if $m^* = \infty$. Intuitively, at an optimum, the marginal benefit of additional money holdings must balance the cost of the marginal effect on government revenues. This contrasts with the case of normal goods, where the marginal benefit must balance the costs of the marginal impact on the government's revenue *and* the marginal resource cost of producing the goods. Money, in contrast, is assumed to be costless to produce. At the satiation point, the marginal benefit of money is zero. The conditions studied by Correia and Teles ensure that the marginal revenue effect is also zero.

Friedman's rule for the optimal rate of inflation can be recovered even in the absence of lump-sum taxes. But it is important to recognize that the restrictions on preferences necessary to restore Friedman's rule are very strong and, as discussed by Braun (1991), different assumptions about preferences will lead to different conclusions. The assumption that the ratio of the marginal utilities of consumption and money is independent of leisure can certainly be questioned. However, it is very common in the literature to assume separability between leisure, consumption, and money holdings. The standard log utility specification, for example, displays this property and so would imply that a zero nominal interest rate is optimal.

A CIA Model

The examples so far have involved MIU specifications. Suppose instead that the consumer faces a CIA constraint on a subset of its purchases. Specifically, assume that c_1 represents cash goods, and c_2 represents credit goods. Let l denote leisure. The household's objective is to maximize

$$E_t \sum_{i=0}^{\infty} \beta^i U(c_{1,t+i}, c_{2,t+i}, l_{t+i})$$

subject to the budget constraint

$$(1 + \tau_t^c) Q_t(c_{1,t} + c_{2,t}) + M_t + B_t = (1 - \tau_t^h) Q_t(1 - l_t) + (1 + i_{t-1}) B_{t-1} + M_{t-1},$$

where variables are as defined previously. In addition, the CIA constraint requires that

$$c_{1,t} \leq \frac{m_{t-1}}{1 + \pi_t}.$$

Before considering when the optimal inflation tax might be positive, ignore the credit good c_2 for the moment so that the model is similar to the basic CIA model studied in chapter 3. Recall that inflation served as a tax on labor supply in that model. But according to the budget constraint, the government already has, in τ^h, a tax on labor supply. Thus, the inflation tax is redundant.[36] Because it is redundant, the government can achieve an optimal allocation without using the inflation tax.

---

36. See Chari, Christiano, and Kehoe (1996).

In a cash-and-credit-goods economy, the inflation tax is no longer redundant if the government cannot set different commodity taxes on the two types of goods. So returning to the model with both cash and credit goods, the first-order conditions for the household's decision problem imply that consumption and leisure will be chosen such that

$$\frac{U_1(c_{1,t}, c_{2,t}, l_t)}{U_2(c_{1,t}, c_{2,t}, l_t)} = 1 + i_t.$$

The analysis of Atkinson and Stiglitz (1972) implies that if preferences are homothetic in $c_{1,t}$ and $c_{2,t}$, the ratio of the marginal utility of cash and credit goods should equal 1, the ratio of their production prices. This occurs only if $i = 0$; hence, homothetic preferences imply that the nominal rate of interest should be set equal to zero. But this is just the Friedman rule for the optimal rate of inflation.

Thus, the optimal inflation tax should be zero if for all $\lambda > 0$,

$$\frac{U_1(\lambda c_{1,t}, \lambda c_{2,t}, l_t)}{U_2(\lambda c_{1,t}, \lambda c_{2,t}, l_t)} = \frac{U_1(c_{1,t}, c_{2,t}, l_t)}{U_2(c_{1,t}, c_{2,t}, l_t)}, \tag{4.60}$$

in which case the utility function has the form

$$U(c_1, c_2, l) = V(\phi(c_1, c_2), l),$$

where ϕ is homogeneous of degree 1. If this holds, the government should avoid using the inflation tax even though it must rely on other distortionary taxes. Positive nominal rates of interest impose an efficiency cost by distorting the consumer's choice between cash and credit goods.[37]

How reasonable is this condition? Recall that no explanation has been offered for why one good is a cash good and the other is a credit good. This distinction has simply been assumed, and therefore it is difficult to argue intuitively why the preferences for cash and credit goods should (or should not) satisfy condition (4.60). In aggregate analysis, it is common to combine all goods into one composite good; this is standard in writing utility as $u(c, l)$, with c representing an aggregation over all consumption goods. Interpreting c as $\phi(c_1, c_2)$, where ϕ is a homogeneous of degree 1 aggregator function, implies that preferences would satisfy the properties necessary for the optimal inflation tax to be zero. However, this is not an innocuous restriction. It requires, for example, that the ratio of the marginal utility of coffee at the local coffee cart (a

---

37. As Chari, Christiano, and Kehoe (1996) noted, the preference restrictions are sufficient for the Friedman rule to be optimal but not necessary. For example, in the cash/credit model, suppose preferences are not homothetic and the optimal tax structure calls for taxing credit goods more heavily. A positive nominal interest rate taxes cash goods, and negative nominal rates are not feasible. Thus, a corner solution can arise in which the optimal nominal interest rate is zero. This assumes that the government cannot impose separate goods taxes on cash and credit goods.

cash good) to that of books at the bookstore (a credit good) remain constant if coffee and book consumption double.

Money as an Intermediate Input

The approach in the previous sections motivated a demand for money by including real money balances as an element of the representative agent's utility function or by imposing a CIA constraint that applied to a subset of goods. If the role of money arises because of the services it provides in facilitating transactions, then it might be more naturally viewed as an intermediate good, a good used as an input in the production of the final goods that directly enter the utility function. The distinction between final goods and intermediate goods is important for determining the optimal structure of taxation; Diamond and Mirrlees (1971), for example, showed that under certain conditions it may be optimal to tax only final goods. In particular, when the government can levy taxes on each final good, intermediate goods should not be taxed.

The importance of money's role as an intermediate input was first stressed by Kimbrough (1986a; 1986b) and Faig (1988).[38] Their work suggested that the Friedman rule might apply even in the absence of lump-sum taxes, and conclusions to the contrary arose from the treatment of money as a final good that enters the utility function directly. Under conditions of constant returns to scale, the Diamond-Mirrlees result called for efficiency in production, implying that money and labor inputs into producing transactions should not be taxed. Since the MIU approach is usually used as a shortcut for modeling situations in which money serves as a medium of exchange by facilitating transactions, the work of Kimbrough and Faig indicates that such shortcuts can have important implications. However, the requirement that taxes be available for every final good is not satisfied in practice, and the properties of the transactions technology of the economy are such that until these are better understood, there is no clear case for assuming constant returns to scale.

Correia and Teles (1996) provided further results on the applicability of the Friedman rule. They showed that Friedman's result holds for any shopping-time model in which shopping time is a homogeneous function of consumption and real money balances. To investigate this result, and to illustrate the primal approach to the Ramsey problem, consider a generalized shopping-time model in which money and time are inputs into producing transaction services. Specifically, assume that the representative agent has a total time allocation normalized to 1, which can be allocated to leisure (l), market activity (n), or shopping (n^s):

$$l_t + n_t + n_t^s = 1. \tag{4.61}$$

38. See also Guidotti and Végh (1993).

Shopping time depends on the agent's choice of consumption and money holdings, with n_t^s increasing in c_t and decreasing in m_t according to the shopping production function

$$n_t^s = G(c_t, m_t).$$

Assume that G is homogeneous of degree η, so that $G(\lambda_t c_t, \lambda_t m_t) = \lambda_t^\eta G(c_t, m_t)$. Letting $\lambda_t = 1/c_t$,

$$n_t^s = c_t^\eta G\left(1, \frac{m_t}{c_t}\right) \equiv c_t^\eta g\left(\frac{m_t}{c_t}\right).$$

In addition, assume that g is a convex function, $g' \leq 0$, $g'' \geq 0$, which implies that shopping time is nonincreasing in m_t/c_t but real money balances exhibit diminishing marginal productivity. Constant returns to scale correspond to $\eta = 1$. Assume that there exists a level of real balances relative to consumption $\bar{\mu}$ such that $g'(x) = 0$ for $x \geq \bar{\mu}$, corresponding to a satiation level of real balances.

The representative agent chooses paths for consumption, labor supply, money holdings, and capital holdings to maximize

$$\sum_{i=0}^{\infty} \beta^i u\left[c_{t+i}, 1 - n_{t+i} - c_{t+i}^\eta g\left(\frac{m_{t+i}}{c_{t+i}}\right)\right] \tag{4.62}$$

subject to the following budget constraint:

$$w_t \equiv \left(\frac{1 + i_{t-1}}{1 + \pi_t}\right) d_{t-1} - \left(\frac{i_{t-1}}{1 + \pi_t}\right) m_{t-1} \geq c_t + d_t - (1 - \tau_t) f(n_t), \tag{4.63}$$

where $f(n_t)$ is a standard, neoclassical production function, τ_t is the tax rate on income, $d_t = m_t + b_t$ is total real assets holdings, equal to government interest-bearing debt holdings (b_t) plus real money holdings, i_{t-1} is the nominal interest rate from $t-1$ to t, and π_t is the inflation rate from $t-1$ to t. Notice that capital accumulation is ignored in this analysis. Further assume that initial conditions include $M_{t-1} = B_{t-1} = 0$, where these are the nominal levels of money and bond stocks. A final important assumption in Correia and Teles's analysis is that production exhibits constant returns to scale, with $f(n) = 1 - l - n^s$.[39]

---

39. Notice that the utility function in (4.62) can be written as $v(c_{t+i}, m_{t+i}, n_{t+i})$ and so can be used to justify an MIU function (see section 3.3.1). When the shopping-time function takes the form assumed here, Correia and Teles (1999) show that $m^* = \bar{k}c$ for a positive constant $\bar{k}$, where m^* is the satiation level of money balances such that $g'(m^*/c) = 0$. As noted earlier, the optimal tax on money is zero when $m^* = \bar{k}c$.

The government's optimal tax problem is to pick time paths for τ_{t+i} and i_{t+i} to maximize (4.62) subject to the economy resource constraint $c_t + g_t \le 1 - l_t - n_t^s$ and to the requirement that consumption and labor supply be consistent with the choices of private agents. Following Lucas and Stokey (1983), this problem can be recast by using the first-order conditions from the individual agent's decision problem to express, in terms of the government's tax instruments, the equilibrium prices that will support the paths of consumption and labor supply that solve the government's problem. This leads to an additional constraint on the government's choices and can be summarized in terms of an *implementability condition*.

To derive this implementability condition, start with the first-order conditions for the representative agent's problem. Define the value function

$$v(w_t) = \max_{c_t, n_t, m_t, d_t} \left\{ u\left[c_t, 1 - n_t - c_t^{\eta} g\left(\frac{m_t}{c_t}\right)\right] + \beta v(w_{t+1}) \right\},$$

where the maximization is subject to the budget constraint (4.63). Letting λ_t denote the Lagrangian multiplier associated with the time t budget constraint, the first-order conditions imply

$$u_c - u_l\left(\eta g - \frac{m}{c} g'\right) c_t^{\eta-1} = \lambda_t \tag{4.64}$$

$$u_l = \lambda_t(1 - \tau_t) \tag{4.65}$$

$$-u_l g' c_t^{\eta-1} = \lambda_t I_t \tag{4.66}$$

$$\lambda_t = \beta R_t \lambda_{t+1}, \tag{4.67}$$

where $I_t = i_t/(1 + i_t)$ and the real interest rate is $R_t = (1 + i_t)/(1 + \pi_{t+1})$.

The next step is to recast the budget constraint (4.63). This constraint can be written as

$$R_{t-1}d_{t-1} = \sum_{i=0}^{\infty} D_i[c_{t+i} - (1 - \tau_{t+i})(1 - l_{t+i} - n_{t+i}^s) + R_{t-1+i}I_{t-1+i}m_{t-1+i}], \tag{4.68}$$

where a no Ponzi condition is imposed and the discount factor D_i is defined as $D_i = 1$ for $i = 0$ and $D_i = \prod_{j=1}^{i} R_{t+j-1}^{-1}$ for $i \ge 1$. Since it is assumed that the initial stocks of money and bonds equal zero, $d_{t-1} = 0$, so the right side of (4.68) must also equal zero.[40] The implementability condition is obtained by replacing the prices in

---

40. If the government's initial nominal liabilities were positive, it would be optimal to immediately inflate away their value because this would represent a nondistortionary source of revenue. It is to avoid this outcome that the initial stocks are assumed to be zero.

this budget constraint using the first-order conditions of the agent's problem to express the prices in terms of quantities.[41]

Recalling that $c^\eta g = n^s$, first multiply and divide the intertemporal budget constraint by λ_{t+i}; then use the result from the first-order conditions (4.67) that $D_i = \beta^i D_0 \lambda_{t+i}/\lambda_t$ to write (4.68) as[42]

$$\sum_{i=0}^{\infty} \beta^i [\lambda_{t+i} c_{t+i} - \lambda_{t+i}(1-\tau_{t+i})(1-l_{t+i}-n^s_{t+i}) + \lambda_{t+i} I_{t+i} m_{t+i}] = 0.$$

Now use the first-order conditions (4.64)–(4.66) to obtain

$$\sum_{i=0}^{\infty} \beta^i \left\{ \left[u_c - u_l \left(\eta g - u_l \frac{m}{c} g' \right) c_{t+i}^{\eta-1} \right] c_{t+i} - u_l(1-l_{t+i}-n^s_{t+i}) - u_l \frac{m_{t+i}}{c_{t+i}} g' c_{t+i}^{\eta} \right\} = 0.$$

Since the term $u_l \frac{m}{c} g' c_{t+i}^\eta$ appears twice, with opposite signs, these cancel, and this condition becomes

$$\sum_{i=0}^{\infty} \beta^i [u_c c_{t+i} - u_l(1-l_{t+i}) + u_l(1-\eta)n^s_{t+i})] = 0. \tag{4.69}$$

Equation (4.69) is the implementability condition. The government's problem now is to choose c_{t+i}, m_{t+i}, and l_{t+i} to maximize the utility of the representative agent, subject to the economy's resource constraint, the production function for shopping time, and (4.69). That is, $\max \sum \beta^i u(c_{t+i}, l_{t+i})$ subject to (4.69) and $c_t + g_t \leq (1 - l_t - n^s_t)$, where $n^s_t = g(m_t/c_t)c_t^\eta$. This formulation of the Ramsey problem illustrates the primal approach; the first-order conditions for the representative agent are used to eliminate prices from the agent's intertemporal budget constraint.

Since m appears in this problem only in the production function for shopping time, the first-order condition for the optimal choice of m_{t+1} is

$$[\beta^i \psi u_l(1-\eta) - \mu_{t+i}]g' = 0, \tag{4.70}$$

---

41. The price of consumption is 1, the price of leisure is $1 - \tau$, and the price of real balances is I.

42. This uses the fact that $m_{t-1} = 0$, so

$$\sum_{i=0}^{\infty} D_i R_{t-1+i} I_{t-1+i} m_{t-1+i} = \sum_{i=1}^{\infty} D_i R_{t-1+i} I_{t-1+i} m_{t-1+i} = \sum_{i=1}^{\infty} D_{i-1} I_{t-1+i} m_{t-1+i}$$

$$= \sum_{i=1}^{\infty} \frac{D_{i-1}}{\lambda_{t-1+i}} \lambda_{t-1+i} I_{t-1+i} m_{t-1+i} = \sum_{i=0}^{\infty} \frac{D_i}{\lambda_{t+i}} \lambda_{t+i} I_{t+i} m_{t+i}$$

$$= \frac{1}{\lambda_t} \sum_{i=0}^{\infty} \beta^i \lambda_{t+i} I_{t+i} m_{t+i}.$$

where $\psi \geq 0$ is the Lagrangian multiplier on the implementability constraint (4.69) and $\mu \geq 0$ is the Lagrangian multiplier on the resource constraint. Correia and Teles showed that $\beta^i \psi u_l(1 - \eta) - \mu_{t+i} = 0$ cannot characterize the optimum, so for (4.70) to be satisfied requires that $g' = 0$. From the first-order conditions in the representative agent's problem, $-u_l g' c_t^{\eta-1} = \lambda_t I_t$; this implies that $g' = 0$ requires $I = 0$. That is, the nominal rate of interest should equal zero and the optimal tax on money should be zero.

The critical property of money, according to Correia and Teles, is its status as a free primary good. *Free* in this context means that it can be produced at zero variable cost. The costless production assumption is standard in monetary economics, and it provided the intuition for Friedman's original result. With a zero social cost of production, optimality requires that the private cost also be zero. This occurs only if the nominal rate of interest is zero.

It is evident that there are general cases in which Phelps's conclusion does not hold. Even in the absence of lump-sum taxation, optimal tax policy should not distort the relative price of cash and credit goods or distort money holdings. But, as discussed by Braun (1991) and Mulligan and Sala-i-Martin (1997), different assumptions about preferences or technology can lead to different conclusions. Correia and Teles (1999) attempted to quantify the deviations from the Friedman rule when the preference and technology restrictions required for a zero nominal interest rate to be optimal do not hold. They found that the optimal nominal rate of interest is still close to zero.

4.6.4   Nonindexed Tax Systems

Up to this point, the discussion has assumed that the tax system is indexed so that taxes are levied on real income; a one-time change in all nominal quantities and the price level would leave the real equilibrium unchanged. This assumption requires that a pure price change have no effect on the government's real tax revenues or the tax rates faced by individuals and firms in the private sector. Most actual tax systems, however, are not completely indexed to ensure that pure price level changes leave real tax rates and real tax revenue unchanged. Inflation-induced distortions generated by the interaction of inflation and the tax system have the potential to be much larger than the revenue-related effects on which most of the seigniorage and optimal inflation literature has focused. Feldstein (1998) analyzed the net benefits of reducing inflation from 2 percent to zero,[43] and he concluded that for his preferred parameter values, the effects due to reducing distortions related to the tax system are roughly twice those associated with the change in government revenue.

---

43. Feldstein allowed for an upward bias in the inflation rate, as measured by the consumer price index, so that his estimates apply to reducing consumer price inflation from 4 percent to 2 percent.

One important distortion arises when nominal interest income, and not real interest income, is taxed. After-tax real rates of return will be relevant for individual agents in making savings and portfolio decisions, and if nominal income is subject to a tax rate of τ, the real after-tax return will be

$$r_a = (1 - \tau)i - \pi$$

$$= (1 - \tau)r - \tau\pi,$$

where $i = r + \pi$ is the nominal return and r is the before-tax real return. Thus, for a given pretax real return r, the after-tax real return is decreasing in the rate of inflation.

To see how this distortion affects the steady-state capital-labor ratio, consider the basic MIU model of chapter 2 with an income tax of τ on total nominal income. Nominal income is assumed to include any nominal capital gain on capital holdings:

$$Y_t \equiv P_t f(k_{t-1}) + i_{t-1} B_{t-1} + P_t T_t + (P_t - P_{t-1})(1 - \delta)k_{t-1}.$$

The representative agent's budget constraint becomes

$$(1 - \tau)Y_t = P_t c_t + P_t k_t - P_t(1 - \delta)k_{t-1} + (B_t - B_{t-1}) + (M_t - M_{t-1}),$$

where M is the agent's nominal money holdings, B is his bond holdings, and $P_t T_t$ is a nominal transfer payment.[44] In real terms, the budget constraint becomes[45]

$$(1 - \tau)\left[f(k_{t-1}) + \frac{i_{t-1} b_{t-1}}{1 + \pi_t} + T_t \right] - \tau\left(\frac{\pi_t}{1 + \pi_t} \right)(1 - \delta)k_{t-1}$$

$$= c_t + k_t - (1 - \delta)k_{t-1} + \left(b_t - \frac{b_{t-1}}{1 + \pi_t} \right) + \left(m_t - \frac{m_{t-1}}{1 + \pi_t} \right).$$

Assuming the agent's objective is to maximize the present discounted value of expected utility, which depends on consumption and money holdings, the first-order conditions for capital and bonds imply, in the steady state,

$$(1 - \tau)f_k(k) + \left[\frac{1 + (1 - \tau)\pi}{1 + \pi} \right](1 - \delta) = \frac{1}{\beta} \tag{4.71}$$

---

44. For simplicity, assume that T is adjusted in a lump-sum fashion to ensure that variations in inflation and the tax rate on income leave the government's budget balanced. Obviously, if lump-sum taxes actually were available, the optimal policy would involve setting $\tau = 0$ and following Friedman's rule for the optimal rate of inflation. The purpose here is to examine the effects of a nonindexed tax system on the steady-state capital stock in the easiest possible manner.

45. This formulation assumes that real economic depreciation is tax-deductible. If depreciation allowances are based on historical nominal cost, a further inflation-induced distortion would be introduced.

and

$$(1 - \tau)\left(\frac{1 + i}{1 + \pi}\right) + \frac{\tau}{1 + \pi} = \frac{1}{\beta}. \tag{4.72}$$

The steady-state capital-labor ratio is determined by

$$f_k(k^{ss}) = \left(\frac{1}{1 - \tau}\right)\left\{\frac{1}{\beta} - \left[\frac{1 + (1 - \tau)\pi}{1 + \pi}\right](1 - \delta)\right\}.$$

Since $[1 + (1 - \tau)\pi]/(1 + \pi)$ is decreasing in π, k^{ss} is decreasing in the inflation rate. Higher inflation leads to larger nominal capital gains on existing holdings of capital, and since these are taxed, inflation increases the effective tax rate on capital.

Equation (4.72) can be solved for the steady-state nominal rate of interest to yield

$$1 + i^{ss} = \frac{1}{\beta}\left(\frac{1 + \pi}{1 - \tau}\right) - \frac{\tau}{1 - \tau}.$$

Thus, the pretax real return on bonds, $(1 + i)/(1 + \pi)$, increases with the rate of inflation, implying that nominal rates rise more than proportionately with an increase in inflation.

It is important to recognize that only one aspect of the effects of inflation and the tax system has been examined.[46] Because of the taxation of nominal returns, higher inflation distorts the individual's decisions, but it also generates revenue for the government that, with a constant level of expenditures (in present value terms), would allow other taxes to be reduced. Thus, the distortions associated with higher inflation are potentially offset by the reduction in the distortions caused by other tax sources. As noted earlier, however, Feldstein (1998) argued that the offset is only partial, leaving a large net annual cost of positive rates of inflation. Feldstein identified the increased effective tax rate on capital that occurs because of the treatment of depreciation and the increased subsidy on housing associated with the deductibility of nominal mortgage interest in the United States as important distortions generated by higher inflation interacting with a nonindexed tax system. Including these effects with an analysis of the implications for government revenues and consequently possible adjustments in other distortionary taxes, Feldstein estimated that a 2 percent reduction in inflation (from 2 percent to zero) increases net welfare by 0.63 percent to 1.01 percent of GDP annually.[47] Since these are annual gains, the

---

46. Feldstein, Green, and Sheshinski (1978) employed a version of Tobin's money and growth model (Tobin 1965) to explore the implications of a nonindexed tax system when firms use both debt and equity to finance capital.

47. These figures assume an elasticity of savings with respect to the after-tax real return of 0.4 and a deadweight loss of taxes of between 40 cents for every dollar of revenue (leading to the 0.63 percent figure) and $1.50 per dollar of revenue (leading to the 1.01 percent figure).

present discounted value of permanently reducing inflation to zero would be quite large.

4.7   Summary

Monetary and fiscal actions are linked through the government's budget constraint. Under Ricardian regimes, changes in the money stock or its growth rate will require some other variable in the budget constraint—taxes, expenditures, or borrowing—to adjust. With fiscal dominance, changes in government taxes or expenditures can require changes in inflation. Under non-Ricardian regimes, changes in government debt can affect prices even if monetary policy is exogenous. A complete analysis of price level determinacy requires a specification of the relationship between fiscal and monetary policies.

   Despite this, and despite the emphasis budget relationships have received in the work of Sargent and Wallace and the work on the fiscal theory of the price level initiated by Sims and Woodford, much of monetary economics ignores the implications of the budget constraint. This is valid in the presence of lump-sum taxes; any effects on the government's budget can simply be offset by an appropriate variation in lump-sum taxes. Traditional analyses that focus only on the stock of high-powered money are also valid when governments follow a Ricardian policy of fully backing interest-bearing debt with tax revenues, either now or in the future. In general, though, one should be concerned with the fiscal implications of any analysis of monetary policy because changes in the quantity of money that alter the interest payments of the government have implications for future tax liabilities.

4.8   Problems

1. Suppose the rate of population growth is n and the rate of growth of real per capita income is λ. Show that (4.6) becomes

$$s_t = (h_t - h_{t-1}) + \left[\frac{(1+\pi_t)(1+\mu) - 1}{(1+\pi_t)(1+\mu)}\right]h_{t-1},$$

where $1 + \mu = (1+n)(1+\lambda)$. Now consider the steady state in which $h_t = h_{t-1}$ and inflation is constant. Does seigniorage depend on μ? Explain.

2. Suppose utility is given by $u(c_t, m_t) = w(c_t) + v(m_t)$, with $w(c_t) = \ln c_t$ and $v(m_t) = m_t(B - D \ln m_t)$, where B and D are positive parameters. Approximate steady-state revenues from seigniorage by θm, where θ is the growth rate of the money supply.

a. Is there a Laffer curve for seigniorage (i.e., are revenues increasing in θ for all $\theta \le \theta^*$ and decreasing in θ for all $\theta > \theta^*$ for some θ^*)?

b. What rate of money growth maximizes steady-state revenues from seigniorage?

c. Assume that the economy's rate of population growth is λ, and reinterpret m as real money balances per capita. What *rate of inflation* maximizes seigniorage? How does it depend on λ?

3. Suppose the demand for real money balances is $m = f(R_m)$, where R_m is the gross nominal rate of interest. Assume the gross real interest rate is fixed at its steady-state value of $1/\beta$ so that $R_m = (1 + \pi)/\beta$, where π is the rate of inflation. Using the definition of seigniorage revenues employed in (4.21), what rate of inflation maximizes steady-state seigniorage?

4. Suppose the government faces the following budget identity:

$$b_t = Rb_{t-1} + g_t - \tau_t y_t - s_t,$$

where the terms are one-period debt, gross interest payments, government purchases, income tax receipts, and seigniorage. Assume seigniorage is given by $f(\pi_t)$, where π is the rate of inflation. The interest factor R is constant, and the expenditure process $\{g_{t+i}\}_{i=0}^{\infty}$ is exogenous. The government sets time paths for the income tax rate and for inflation to minimize

$$E_t \sum_{i=0}^{\infty} \beta^i [h(\tau_{t+i}) + k(\pi_{t+i})],$$

where the functions h and k represent the distortionary costs of the two tax sources. Assume that the functions h and k imply positive and increasing marginal costs of both revenue sources.

a. What is the *intratemporal* optimality condition linking the choices of τ and π at each point in time?

b. What is the *intertemporal* optimality condition linking the choice of π at different points in time?

c. Suppose $y = 1$, $f(\pi) = a\pi$, $h(\tau) = b\tau^2$, and $k(\pi) = c\pi^2$. Evaluate the inter- and intratemporal conditions. Find the optimal settings for τ_t and π_t in terms of b_{t-1} and $\sum R^{-i} g_{t+i}$.

d. Using your results from part (c), when will optimal financing imply constant planned tax rates and inflation over time?

5. The model of section 4.6.1 assumed that the distortions of taxes and seigniorage were quadratic functions of the level of taxes and that the government desired to minimize

$$\frac{1}{2} \mathrm{E}_t \sum_{i=0}^{\infty} R^{-i}[(\tau_{t+i} + \phi_{t+i})^2 + (s_{t+i} + \varepsilon_{t+i})^2],$$

subject to

$$\mathrm{E}_t \sum_{i=0}^{\infty} R^{-i}(\tau_{t+i} + s_{t+i}) = Rb_{t-1} + \left(\frac{R}{R-1}\right)g,$$

where s is seigniorage revenue, τ represents other tax revenues, b_{t-1} is the initial stock of outstanding govenerment debt, g is the fixed level of expenditures the government needs to finance each period, and ϕ and ε are stochastic shocks to the distortionary costs of each tax source. Suppose $\phi_t = \rho_\phi \phi_{t-1} + z_t$ and $\varepsilon_t = \rho_{ge} + e_t$, where z and e are mutually and serially uncorrelated white noise innovations to ϕ and ε. Derive the intratemporal and intertemporal optimality conditions for the two taxes. How does the behavior of each tax depend on ρ_ϕ and ρ_ε?

6. Mankiw (1987) suggested that the nominal interest rate should evolve as a random walk under an optimal tax policy. Suppose that the real rate of interest is constant and that the equilibrium price level is given by (4.29). Suppose that the nominal money supply is given by $m_t = m_t^p + v_t$, where m_t^p is the central bank's planned money supply and v_t is a white noise control error. Let θ be the optimal rate of inflation. There are different processes for m^p that lead to the same average inflation rate but different time series behavior of the nominal interest rate. For each of the processes for m_t^p given below, demonstrate that average inflation is θ. In each case, is the nominal interest rate a random walk?

a. $m_t^p = \theta(1-\gamma)t + \gamma m_{t-1}$.

b. $m_t^p = m_{t-1} + \theta$.

7. Suppose utility is given by $U = c^{1-\sigma}/(1-\sigma) + m^{1-\theta}/(1-\theta)$. Find the function $\phi(P)$ defined in (4.32) and verify that it has the shape shown in figure 4.3. Solve for the stationary equilibrium price level P^* such that $P^* = \phi(P^*)$.

8. Consider (4.37) implied by the fiscal theory of the price level. Seigniorage $\bar{s}_t$ was defined as $i_t m_t/(1+i_t)$. Assume that the utility function of the representative agent takes the form $u(c, m) = \ln c + b \ln m$. Show that $\bar{s}_t = bc_t$ and that the price level is independent of the nominal supply of money as long as $\tau_t - g_t + bc_t$ is independent of M_t.

9. Consider the optimal tax problem of section 4.6.3. The government wishes to maximize $u(c, m, l) = v(c, m) + \phi(l)$ subject to the economy's resource constraint: $f(1-l) \geq c + g$.

a. Derive the implementability constraint by using the first-order conditions (4.48)–(4.50) to eliminate the tax rates from the representative agent's budget constraint (4.47).

b. Set up the government's optimization problem and derive the first-order conditions.

c. Show that the first-order condition for m is satisfied if $v_m = v_{mc} = v_{mm} = 0$. Argue that these conditions are met if the satiation level m^* is equal to ∞.

10. Suppose the Correia-Teles model of section 4.6.3 is modified so that output is equal to $f(n)$, where f is a standard neoclassical production function exhibiting positive but diminishing marginal productivity of n. Show that if $f(n) = n^a$ for $a > 0$, the optimality condition given by (4.70) continues to hold.

5 Money in the Short Run: Informational and Portfolio Rigidities

5.1 Introduction

The empirical evidence from the United States is consistent with the notion that positive monetary shocks lead to a hump-shaped positive response of output that persists for appreciable periods of time, and Sims (1992) found similar patterns for other OECD economies. The models of chapters 2–4 did not seem capable of producing such an effect. So why does money matter?[1] Is it only through the tax effects that arise from inflation? Or are there other channels through which monetary actions have real effects? This question is critical for any normative analysis of monetary policy because designing good policy requires understanding how monetary policy affects the real economy and how changes in the way policy is conducted might affect economic behavior.

In the models examined in earlier chapters, monetary disturbances did cause output movements, but these movements arose from substitution effects induced by expected inflation. Most analysis suggests that these effects are too small to account for the empirical evidence on the output responses to monetary shocks. In addition, the evidence in many countries is that inflation responds only slowly to monetary shocks.[2] If actual inflation responds gradually, so should expectations. Thus, the evidence does not appear to support theories that require monetary shocks to affect labor supply decisions and output by causing shifts in expected inflation.

In this chapter, the focus shifts away from the role of inflation as a tax and toward the effects of policy-induced changes in real interest rates that affect aggregate spending decisions. Monetary models designed to capture the real effects of money in the short run incorporate frictions that fall into one of three classes: informational

---

1. For a survey on this topic, see Blanchard (1990). See also D. Romer (2006, ch. 6).

2. For example, see Nelson (1998) or Christiano, Eichenbaum, and Evans (2005) for evidence on the United States. Sims (1992) and Taylor (1993b) provided evidence for other countries.

frictions, portfolio frictions, and nominal price rigidities. This chapter discusses the first two of these classes; nominal price rigidities are the focus of chapter 6.

5.2 Informational Frictions

To account for the empirical evidence on the short-run impact of money, models that maintain the assumption of price flexibility need to introduce new channels through which money can affect the real equilibrium. This section reviews two attempts to resolve the tension between the long-run neutrality of money and the short-run real effects of money while maintaining the assumption that wages and prices are flexible. The first approach focuses on misperceptions about aggregate economic conditions; the second focuses on delays in information acquisition.

5.2.1 Imperfect Information

During the 1960s the need to reconcile the long-run neutrality of money with the apparent short-run non-neutrality of money was not considered a major research issue in macroeconomics. Models used for policy analysis incorporated a Phillips curve relationship between wage (or price) inflation and unemployment that allowed for a long-run trade-off between the two. In 1968, Milton Friedman and Edmund Phelps independently argued on theoretical grounds that the inflation-unemployment trade-off was only a short-run trade-off at best; attempts to exploit the trade-off by engineering higher inflation to generate lower unemployment would ultimately result only in higher inflation.

Milton Friedman (1968; 1977) reconciled the apparent short-run trade-off with the neutrality of money by distinguishing between actual real wages and perceived real wages.[3] The former were relevant for firms making hiring decisions; the latter were relevant for workers making labor supply choices. In a long-run equilibrium, the two would coincide; the real wage would adjust to clear the labor market. Since economic decisions depend on real wages, the same labor market equilibrium would be consistent with any level of nominal wages and prices or any rate of change of wages and prices that left the real wage equal to its equilibrium level.

An unexpected increase in inflation would disturb this real equilibrium. As nominal wages and prices rose more rapidly than previously expected, workers would see their nominal wages rising but would initially not realize that the prices of all the goods and services they consumed were also rising more rapidly. They would misinterpret the nominal wage increase as a rise in their real wage. Labor supply would increase, shifting the labor market equilibrium to a point of higher employment and

---

3. A nice exposition of Friedman's model was provided by Rasche (1973).

lower actual real wages. As workers then engaged in shopping activities, they would discover not only that the nominal price of their labor services had risen unexpectedly but that all prices had risen. Real wages had actually fallen, not risen. The labor supply curve would shift back, and equilibrium would eventually be restored at the initial levels of employment and real wages.

The critical insight is that changes in wages and prices that are unanticipated generate misperceptions about relative prices (the real wage, in Friedman's version). Economic agents, faced with what they perceive to be changes in relative prices, alter their real economic decisions, and the economy's real equilibrium is affected. Once expectations adjust, however, the economy's natural equilibrium is reestablished. Expectations, and the information on which they are based, become central to understanding the short-run effects of money.

5.2.2   The Lucas Model

Friedman's insight was given an explicit theoretical foundation by Lucas (1972). Lucas showed how unanticipated changes in the money supply could generate short-run transitory movements in real economic activity. He did so by analyzing the impact of monetary fluctuations in an overlapping-generations environment with physically separate markets. The demand for money in each location was made random by assuming that the allocation of the population to each location was stochastic.[4] The key features of this environment can be illustrated by employing the analogy of an economy consisting of a large number of individual islands. Agents are randomly reallocated among islands after each period, so individuals care about prices on the island they currently are on and prices on other islands to which they may be reassigned. Individuals on each island are assumed to have imperfect information about aggregate economic variables such as the nominal money supply and price level. Thus, when individuals observe changes in the prices on their island, they must decide whether they reflect purely nominal changes in aggregate variables or island-specific relative price changes.

To illustrate how variations in the nominal quantity of money can have real effects when information is imperfect, assume a basic money-in-the-utility function (MIU) model such as the one developed in chapter 2, but simplify it in three ways. First, ignore capital. This choice implies that only labor is used to produce output and, with no investment, equilibrium requires that output equal consumption. Second, assume that money is the only available asset. Third, assume that monetary transfers associated with changes in the nominal quantity of money are viewed by agents as being proportional to their own holdings of cash. This change has substantive

---

4. In Lucas's formulation, agents had two-period lives; young agents were distributed randomly to each location.

implications and is not done just to simplify the model. It implies that the transfers will appear to money holders as interest payments on their cash holdings. This approach eliminates inflation tax effects so that one can concentrate on the role of imperfect information.[5]

Suppose the aggregate economy consists of several islands, indexed by i; thus, x^i denotes the value of variable x on island i, and x denotes its economywide average value. Since information will differ across islands, let $E^i x_t$ denote the expectations of a variable x_t based on the information available on island i. Using the model from the chapter 2 appendix, express equilibrium deviations from the steady state on each island by the following conditions:[6]

$$y_t^i = (1 - \alpha)n_t^i \tag{5.1}$$

$$\left[1 + \eta\left(\frac{n^{ss}}{1 - n^{ss}}\right)\right]n_t^i = y_t^i + \lambda_t^i \tag{5.2}$$

$$m_t^i - p_t^i = y_t^i + \left(\frac{1}{b}\right)\left(\frac{\beta}{1 - \beta}\right)[E^i \tau_{t+1} - (E^i p_{t+1} - p_t^i) + E^i(\lambda_{t+1} - \lambda_t^i)] \tag{5.3}$$

$$\lambda_t^i = \Omega_1 y_t^i + \Omega_2(m_t^i - p_t^i), \tag{5.4}$$

where λ_t^i is the marginal utility of consumption on island i, and Ω_1 and Ω_2 depend on parameters from the utility function.[7] Note that the goods market equilibrium condition, $y_t = c_t$, has been used and, in contrast to chapters 2–4, m^i now denotes the *nominal* supply of money on island i. Equation (5.1) is the production function linking labor input (n_t^i) to output.[8] Equation (5.2) comes from the first-order condition linking the marginal utility of leisure, the marginal utility of consumption, and the real wage.[9] Equation (5.3) is derived from the first-order condition for the individ-

---

5. Recall that in chapter 2 transfers were viewed as lump-sum. With higher inflation, the transfers rose (as the seigniorage revenues were returned to private agents), but each individual viewed these transfers as unrelated to his or her own money holdings. If the transfers are viewed as interest payments, higher inflation does not raise the opportunity cost of holding money because the interest payment on cash also rises. In this case, money is superneutral.

6. All variables are expressed as natural log deviations around steady-state values. Since all values will be in terms of deviations, the "hat" notation of chapters 2–4 is dropped for convenience. For an early exposition of a linearized version of Lucas's model, see McCallum (1984a).

7. The underlying utility function that leads to (5.1)–(5.4) is the same as employed in chapter 2. Details can be found in the appendix (section 5.5).

8. Note that any productivity disturbance has been eliminated; the focus is on monetary disturbances.

9. Equation (5.2) arises from the requirement that the marginal utility of leisure ($[\eta n^{ss}/(1 + n^{ss})]n_t$ in percentage deviation around the steady state) equal the real wage times the marginal utility of consumption. The marginal product of labor (the real wage) is equal to $(1 - \alpha)Y/N$, or $y - n$ in terms of percentage deviations.

ual agent's holdings of real money balances. This first-order condition requires that reducing consumption at time t slightly, thereby carrying higher money balances into period $t + 1$ and then consuming them, must, at the margin, have no effect on total utility over the two periods. In the present context, the cost of reducing consumption in period t is the marginal utility of consumption; the additional money balances yield the marginal utility of money in period t and a gross return of T_{t+1}/Π_{t+1} in period $t + 1$, where T_{t+1} is the gross nominal transfer per dollar on money holdings and Π_{t+1} is 1 plus the inflation rate from t to $t + 1$. This return can be consumed at $t + 1$, yielding, in terms of period t utility, $\beta(T_{t+1}/\Pi_{t+1})$ times the marginal utility of consumption, where β is the representative household's discount factor. Linearizing the result around the steady state leads to (5.3). Finally, (5.4) defines the marginal utility of consumption as a function of output (consumption) and real money balances; see the chapter appendix (section 5.5).

If agents are reallocated randomly across islands in each period, then the relevant period $t + 1$ variables in (5.3) are the aggregate price level p_{t+1}, marginal utility of consumption λ_{t+1}, and nominal transfer τ_{t+1}.

The final component of the model is the specification of the nominal money supply process. Assume the aggregate average nominal money supply evolves as[10]

$$m_t = \rho_m m_{t-1} + v_t + u_t. \tag{5.5}$$

The aggregate supply is assumed to depend on two serially uncorrelated shocks, v and u, assumed to have zero means and variances σ_v^2 and σ_u^2. The difference between the two is that v is public information whereas u is not. Including both will help to illustrate how imperfect information (in this case about u) will influence the real effects of money shocks. The nominal money stock on island i is given by

$$m_t^i = \rho_m m_{t-1} + v_t + u_t + u_t^i,$$

where u^i is a serially uncorrelated island-specific money shock that averages to zero across all islands and has variance σ_i^2. If the aggregate money stock at time $t - 1$, as well as v, is public information, then observing the island-specific nominal money stock m_t^i allows individuals on island i to infer $u_t + u_t^i$ but not u and u^i separately. This is important because only u affects the aggregate money stock (see (5.5)), and as long as $\rho_m \neq 0$, knowledge about u would be useful in forecasting m_{t+1}.

Since $m_{t+1} = \rho_m m_t + v_{t+1} + u_{t+1}$, the expectation of the time $t + 1$ money supply, conditional on the information available on island i, will be $\mathrm{E}^i m_{t+1} = \rho_m \mathrm{E}^i m_t$

10. With money supply changes engineered via transfers,

$$\tau_t = m_t - m_{t-1} = (\gamma - 1)m_{t-1} + v_t + u_t.$$

$= \rho_m^2 m_{t-1} + \rho_m v_t + \rho_m E^i u_t$. If expectations are equated with linear least-squares projections,

$$E^i u_t = \kappa(u_t + u_t^i),$$

where $\kappa = \sigma_u^2/(\sigma_u^2 + \sigma_i^2)$, $0 \leq \kappa \leq 1$. If aggregate money shocks are large relative to island-specific shocks (i.e., σ_u is large relative to σ_i), κ will be close to 1; movements in $u + u^i$ are interpreted as predominantly reflecting movements in the aggregate shock u. In contrast, if the variance of the island-specific shocks is large, κ will be close to zero; movements in $u + u^i$ are interpreted as predominantly reflecting island-specific shocks.

Using (5.1)–(5.4), the chapter appendix shows that the equilibrium solutions for the price level and employment are given by

$$p_t = \rho_m m_{t-1} + v_t + \left(\frac{\kappa + K}{1 + K}\right) u_t \tag{5.6}$$

and

$$n_t = A(m_t - p_t) = A\left(\frac{1 - \kappa}{1 + K}\right) u_t, \tag{5.7}$$

where A and K depend on the underlying parameters of the model.

Equation (5.7) reveals Lucas's basic result; aggregate monetary shocks, represented by u, have real effects on employment (and therefore output) if and only if there is imperfect information ($\kappa < 1$), and their effect depends on the aggregate errors agents make in inferring u: $u - \int E^i u_t \, di = (1 - \kappa)u$, where $\int E^i u_t \, di$ is the aggregate average (over all islands) of the expected value of u. Publicly announced changes in the money supply, represented by the v shocks, have no real effects on output (v does not appear in (5.7)) but simply move the price level one-for-one (v has a coefficient equal to 1 in (5.6)). But the u shocks will affect employment and output if private agents are unable to determine whether the money stock movements they observe on island i reflect aggregate or island-specific movements. Predictable movements in money (captured here by $\rho_m m_{t-1}$) or announced changes (captured by v) have no real effects. Only unanticipated changes in the money supply have real effects.

Equation (5.7) can be rewritten in a form that emphasizes the role of money surprises in producing employment and output effects. From (5.5), $u_t = m_t - E(m_t \mid \Gamma_{t-1}, v_t)$, where $E(m_t \mid \Gamma_{t-1}, v_t)$ denotes the expectation of m_t conditional on aggregate information on variables dated $t - 1$ or earlier, summarized by the information set Γ_{t-1} and the announced money injection v_t. Thus,

$$n_t = A\left(\frac{1 - \kappa}{1 + K}\right)[m_t - E(m_t \mid \Gamma_{t-1}, v_t)].$$

Equations of this form provided the basis for the empirical work of Barro (1977; 1978) and others in testing whether unanticipated or anticipated changes in money matter for real output.

In writing employment as a function of money surprises, it is critically important to specify correctly the information set on which agents base their expectations. In empirical work, this information set was often assumed to consist simply of lagged values of the relevant variables. But in the example here, $E(m_t \mid \Gamma_{t-1}) = \rho_m m_{t-1}$, and $m_t - E(m_t \mid \Gamma_{t-1}) = u_t + v_t \neq u_t$. Misspecifying the information set can create difficulties in testing models that imply that only surprises matter.

Because (5.7) is derived directly from a model consistent with optimizing behavior, the effects of an unanticipated money supply shock on employment can be related to the basic parameters of the production and utility functions.[11] Using the basic parameter values given in section 2.5.4, $A/[1 + K] = 0.007$. This implies that even if κ is close to zero, the elasticity of employment with respect to a money surprise is tiny; a 10 percent surprise increase in the money supply would raise employment by 0.07 percent and output by less than $(1 - \alpha) \times 0.07 = 0.64 \times 0.07 \approx 0.05$ percent.[12]

The impact of money surprises in this example works through labor supply decisions. An increase in real money balances raises the marginal utility of consumption and induces agents to increase consumption and labor supply (since $\Omega_2 > 0$). This effect is larger, the more willing agents are to substitute consumption over time. Thus, the impact of a money surprise is larger when the degree of intertemporal substitution is larger.[13] The effect of a money surprise on output is increasing in the wage elasticity of labor supply.

The basic idea behind Lucas's island model is that unpredicted variations in money generate price movements that agents may misinterpret as relative price movements. If a general price rise is falsely interpreted to be a rise in the relative price of what the individual or firm sells, the price rise will induce an increase in employment and output. Once individuals and firms correctly perceive that the price rise was part of an increase in all prices, output returns to its former equilibrium level.

Implications

Lucas's model makes clear the important distinction between expected and unexpected variations in money. Economic agents face a signal extraction problem because they have imperfect information about the current money supply. If changes in the nominal supply of money were perfectly predictable, money would have no real

---

11. McCallum (1984a) presented a linearized approximation to Lucas's model within an overlapping-generations framework. See also D. Romer (2006). However, both simply postulated some of the basic behavioral relationships of the model.

12. Because the calibration employed in chapter 2 of this edition differs from that used in previous editions, the value reported for $A/(1 + K)$ is larger than in earlier editions (see section 2.5.4).

13. See Barro and King (1984).

effects. Short-run fluctuations in the money supply are likely to be at least partially unpredictable, so they will cause output and employment movements. In this way, Lucas was able to reconcile the neutrality of money in the long run with its important real effects in the short run. Sargent and Wallace (1975) and Barro (1976) provided important early contributions that employed the general approach pioneered by Lucas to examine its implications for monetary policy issues.

Lucas's model has several important testable implications, and these were the focus of a great deal of empirical work in the late 1970s and early 1980s. A first implication is that the distinction between anticipated and unanticipated money matters. Barro (1977; 1978; 1979b) was the first to directly examine whether output was related to anticipated or unanticipated money. He concluded that the evidence supported Lucas's model, but subsequent empirical work by Mishkin (1982) and others showed that both anticipated and unanticipated money appear to influence real economic activity. A survey of the general approach motivated by Lucas's work and of the empirical literature can be found in Barro (1981, ch. 2).

A second implication is that the short-run relationship between output and inflation will depend on the relative variance of real and nominal disturbances. The parameter κ in (5.7) depends on the predictability of aggregate changes in the money supply, and this can vary across time and across countries. Lucas (1973) examined the slopes of short-run Phillips curves in a cross-country study and showed that, as predicted by his model, there was a positive correlation between the slope of the Phillips curve and the relative variance of nominal aggregate volatility. A rise in aggregate volatility (an increase in σ_u^2 in the version of Lucas's model developed in the previous section) implies that an observed increase in prices is more likely to be interpreted as resulting from an aggregate price increase. A smaller real response occurs as a result, and aggregate money surprises have smaller real effects.

A third influential implication of Lucas's model was demonstrated by Sargent and Wallace (1975) and became known as the *policy irrelevance hypothesis*. If changes in money have real effects only when they are unanticipated, then any policy that generates systematic, predictable variations in the money supply will have no real effect. For example, (5.7) shows that employment and therefore output are independent of the degree of serial correlation in m as measured by ρ_m. Because the effects of lagged money on the current aggregate money stock are completely predictable, no informational confusion is created and the aggregate price level simply adjusts, leaving real money balances unaffected (see (5.6)). A similar conclusion would hold if policy responded to lagged values of u (or to lagged values of anything else), as long as private agents knew the rule being followed by the policymaker.[14]

---

14. Chapter 9 considers a variant of Lucas's model in which nominal wages are set in advance. In the resulting model, systematic policy can have real effects.

The empirical evidence that both anticipated and unanticipated money affect output implies, however, that the policy irrelevance hypothesis does not hold. Systematic responses to lagged variables seem to matter, and therefore the choice of policy rule is not irrelevant for the behavior of real economic activity.

Lucas's misperceptions model was popularized by Sargent and Wallace (1975) and Barro (1976), who employed tractable log-linear versions of the basic model. Although these models are no longer viewed as providing an adequate explanation for the short-run real effects of monetary policy, they have had, and continue to have, an enormous influence on modern monetary economics. For example, these models play an important role in the analysis of time inconsistency of optimal policy (see chapter 7). And the finding that announced changes in money (the v term) have no real effect implies that inflation could be reduced at no output cost simply by announcing a reduction in money growth. But such announcements must be credible so that expectations are actually reduced as money growth falls; disinflations will be costly if announcements are not credible. This point has produced a large literature on the role of credibility (see chapter 7).

5.2.3   Sticky Information

As an alternative to the misperceptions view of imperfect information (and in contrast to the models of sticky prices discussed in chapter 6), Mankiw and Reis (2002) argued that *sticky information*—the slow dispersal of information about macroeconomic conditions—can help account for the sluggish adjustment of prices and for the real effects that occur in response to monetary shocks. The implications of sticky information have been developed in a number of papers, including Mankiw and Reis (2003; 2006b); Ball, Mankiw, and Reis (2005); and Reis (2006a; 2006b).[15]

Mankiw and Reis developed a simple model in which each firm adjusts its price in every period but its decision may be based on outdated information. In every period, a fraction of firms update their information so that, over time, new information reaches all firms in a delayed manner. To illustrate the implications of sticky information, assume that in period t, firm $j's$ optimal price is, in log terms,

$$p_t^*(j) = p_t + \alpha x_t, \tag{5.8}$$

where p_t is the log aggregate price level and x_t is an output gap measure of output relative to the natural rate of output. Equation (5.8) reflects the fact that individual firms care about their price relative to other firms, $p_t^*(j) - p_t$, and variation in the output gap leads to variation in the firm's marginal costs, which affect its optimal price. Notice that if all firms are identical, as is assumed here, $p_t^*(j) = p_t^*$ for all j,

---

15. See also Sims (2003).

and (5.8) can be written as $p_t^* = p_t + \alpha x_t$. Further, if all firms set their price equal to p_t^*, then the aggregate average price level is $p_t = p_t^*$, from which it follows that $x_t = 0$; output is equal to its natural rate. The effect of sticky information will be to cause firms to set different prices, even if, under full information, they all have the same desired price.

Specifically, assume a firm that updated its information i periods in the past sets the price

$$p_t^i = \mathrm{E}_{t-i} p_t^*.$$

All firms with information sets that are i period old will set the same price, so it is not necessary to index p_t^i by j. Now assume that each period a fraction λ of all firms are randomly selected to update their information.[16] This assumption implies that, at time t, λ of all firms will set their price equal to p_t^* because they have fully updated information. Of the remaining $1 - \lambda$ fraction of all firms that do not update their information at time t, λ of them will have updated their information in $t - 1$. These firms, of whom there are $(1 - \lambda)\lambda$, set their price at time t equal to $\mathrm{E}_{t-1} p_t^*$. Following a similar logic, there remain $1 - \lambda - (1 - \lambda)\lambda = (1 - \lambda)^2$ of the firms that do not update at either t or $t - 1$. However, λ of these firms updated at $t - 2$ and, at time t, set their price equal to $\mathrm{E}_{t-2} p_t^*$; there are $(1 - \lambda)^2 \lambda$ such firms. For any period i in the past, there will be $(1 - \lambda)^i \lambda$ firms that have not updated their information since period $t - i$. It follows that the average aggregate log price level will be

$$p_t = \lambda \sum_{i=0}^{\infty} (1 - \lambda)^i \mathrm{E}_{t-i} p_t^* = \lambda \sum_{i=0}^{\infty} (1 - \lambda)^i \mathrm{E}_{t-i} (p_t + \alpha x_t). \tag{5.9}$$

The parameter λ provides a measure of the degree of information stickiness. If λ is large, most firms update frequently; if λ is small, many firms will be basing time t decisions on old information.

To derive an expression for the inflation rate from (5.9), let $z_t = p_t + \alpha x_t$, and then one can write

$$p_t = \lambda z_t + \lambda \sum_{i=1}^{\infty} (1 - \lambda)^i \mathrm{E}_{t-i} z_t$$

$$= \lambda z_t + \lambda(1 - \lambda) \mathrm{E}_{t-1} z_t + \lambda(1 - \lambda)^2 \mathrm{E}_{t-2} z_t + \cdots,$$

and

---

16. This structure borrows from a common modeling strategy employed to deal with sticky prices, originally due to Calvo (1983) (see section 6.2.4).

$$p_{t-1} = \lambda \sum_{i=0}^{\infty} (1-\lambda)^i E_{t-1-i} z_{t-1}$$

$$= \lambda E_{t-1} z_{t-1} + \lambda (1-\lambda) E_{t-2} z_{t-1} + \lambda (1-\lambda)^2 E_{t-3} z_{t-1} + \cdots.$$

Subtracting the second equation from the first yields

$$\pi_t = p_t - p_{t-1} = \lambda z_t + \lambda \sum_{i=1}^{\infty} (1-\lambda)^i E_{t-i} \Delta z_t - \lambda^2 \sum_{i=0}^{\infty} (1-\lambda)^i E_{t-1-i} z_t, \tag{5.10}$$

where $\Delta z_t \equiv z_t - z_{t-1}$. Recalling that $z_t = p_t + \alpha x_t$, (5.9) also implies

$$p_t = \left(\frac{\lambda}{1-\lambda}\right) \alpha x_t + \left(\frac{\lambda}{1-\lambda}\right) \sum_{i=1}^{\infty} (1-\lambda)^i E_{t-i} z_t$$

$$= \left(\frac{\lambda}{1-\lambda}\right) \alpha x_t + \lambda \sum_{i=0}^{\infty} (1-\lambda)^i E_{t-1-i} z_t.$$

This means that the last term in (5.10) is equal to $\lambda p_t - \left(\frac{\lambda^2}{1-\lambda}\right) \alpha x_t$. Making this substitution, (5.10) becomes

$$\pi_t = \lambda z_t + \lambda \sum_{i=1}^{\infty} (1-\lambda)^i E_{t-i} \Delta z_t - \lambda p_t + \left(\frac{\lambda^2}{1-\lambda}\right) \alpha x_t$$

$$= \left(\frac{\lambda}{1-\lambda}\right) \alpha x_t + \lambda \sum_{i=1}^{\infty} (1-\lambda)^i E_{t-i} (\pi_t + \alpha \Delta x_t). \tag{5.11}$$

Equation (5.11) is the sticky information Phillips curve (SIPC). The coefficient on the current output gap is increasing in λ; the more frequently firms update their information, the more sensitive current pricing decisions are to current economic conditions. The key aspect of the SIPC is the presence of expectations of current variables based on lagged information sets. The presence of these terms means that a shock that occurs at time t will only gradually affect inflation as the information on which expectations are based is only gradually updated. The faster information is updated (the larger is λ), the more rapidly will inflation respond to current movements in real output.

To complete the determination of inflation and the output gap, Mankiw and Reis (2002) assumed a simple quantity theory equation and an exogenous AR(1) process for the growth rate of the money supply. In log terms, the quantity theory relation is $m_t + v_t = p_t + x_t$. Taking first differences, this becomes

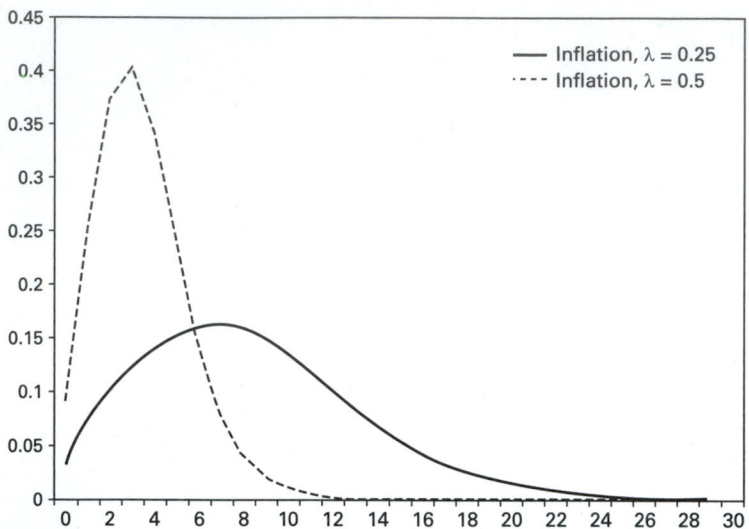

Figure 5.1
Response of inflation to a unit innovation in money growth in the sticky information model.

$$m_t - m_{t-1} + \Delta v_t = \pi_t + \Delta x_t.$$

Assume further that the money process is given by

$$m_t - m_{t-1} = \rho(m_{t-1} - m_{t-2}) + u_t,$$

and velocity v_t follows a random walk, with Δv_t a mean zero serially uncorrelated process.

Figure 5.1 illustrates the response of inflation to a unit realization of u_t for two different values of λ when $\rho = 0.5$. Mankiw and Reis set $\lambda = 0.25$ in their baseline calibration. Figure 5.2 shows the corresponding behavior of output.

These impulse responses display the hump-shaped pattern observed in estimated VARs, and Mankiw and Reis argued that sticky information can provide an explanation for the real effects of monetary policy shocks and for the persistence seen in the inflation process. In contrast to the Lucas model of imperfect information, a key aspect of the sticky information model is the presence of heterogeneity in information sets across firms, heterogeneity that persists over time due to the staggered updating of information.

In their original development of sticky information, Mankiw and Reis (2002) used a calibrated version of their model to argue that sticky information was better able to capture inflation and output dynamics than were the models based on sticky prices discussed in chapter 6. H. Khan and Zhu (2006) estimated a sticky informa-

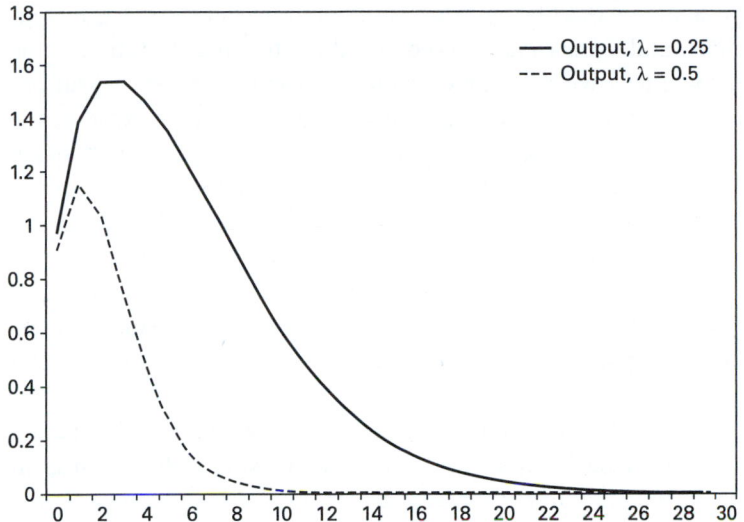

Figure 5.2
Response of output to a unit innovation in money growth in the sticky information model.

tion Phillips curve using quarterly U.S. data from the period 1980–2000. To generate expectations of current inflation and output on old information, they employed VAR forecasts. They found the average duration of information stickiness ranges from three to seven quarters, consistent with the findings of Mankiw and Reis (2002).

A number of authors have estimated sticky information Phillips curves and compared them to the inflation equations based on sticky prices. This empirical work is discussed in chapter 6.

5.2.4 Learning

Standard rational-expectations models assume that agents know the true model of the economy. Typically, only information on the current innovations to exogenous shocks may be incomplete. Once these innovations become known to all agents, after one period in the Lucas islands model or only as part of a staggered multiperiod process in the Mankiw-Reis model of sticky information, the model is characterized by complete information. A growing literature has investigated situations in which the underlying state of the economy may never be known or in which the structure of the economy is unknown and agents must engage in a process of learning.

Brunner, Meltzer, and Cukierman (1980) provided an early example of a model in which observed disturbances are composed of permanent and transitory components. These individual components are not directly observed, so agents must estimate them based on the past history of the observed disturbance. This signal extraction problem leads to richer dynamics than would be generated in the basic islands model. For instance, Brunner, Meltzer, and Cukierman showed that the rational expectation of the permanent component will be a weighted average of all current and past realizations of the observed disturbance, with weights depending on the relative variance of the permanent and transitory innovations. When a realization of the permanent shock occurs, agents initially interpret part of the change in the observed disturbance as due to the transitory component. They underestimate the change in the permanent component and, as a consequence, underestimate future realizations of the disturbance. Since the true values of the two components are never observed, forecast errors can be serially correlated. In the case of a money supply disturbance, money surprises will be serially correlated, leading to real effects that persist for several periods.

In the Brunner, Meltzer, and Cukierman model, agents know the model structure but each period update their beliefs about the value of the persistent disturbance. In contrast, the adaptive learning literature pioneered by Evans and Honkapohja (2001) assumed agents do not know the true model structure. However, agents have beliefs about the true model, and they update their beliefs using recursive least-squares as new data become available. A key question is whether the adaptive learning process will converge to the rational-expectations equilibrium. If it does, the model is said to be e-stable under learning.

To illustrate the adaptive learning approach, consider a general model of the form

$$y_t = \alpha + M E_t y_{t+1} + \delta y_{t-1} + \phi e_t, \tag{5.12}$$

and $e_t = \rho e_{t-1} + \varepsilon_t$. The minimum state-variable rational-expectations solution (McCallum 1983a) takes the form

$$y_t = a + b y_{t-1} + c e_t. \tag{5.13}$$

Assume agents know the solution takes this general form, and given values for the parameters a, b, and c, they treat (5.13) as their perceived law of motion (PLM) of y_t. Then agents use the PLM to form expectations:

$$E_t y_{t+1} = a + b y_t + c \rho e_t. \tag{5.14}$$

Given these expectations, the actual law of motion (ALM) for y_t is obtained by substituting (5.14) into (5.12). Solving for y_t yields

$$y_t = \alpha + M[a + b y_t + c \rho e_t] + \delta y_{t-1} + \phi e_t$$

$$= \frac{\alpha + Ma}{1 - Mb} + \left(\frac{\delta}{1 - Mb}\right) y_{t-1} + \left(\frac{\phi + Mc\rho}{1 - Mb}\right) e_t.$$

The mapping from the PLM to the ALM is defined by

$$T(a,b,c) = \left[\frac{\alpha + Ma}{1 - Mb}, \left(\frac{\delta}{1 - Mb} \right), \left(\frac{\phi + Mc\rho}{1 - Mb} \right) \right].$$

Evans and Honkapohja (2001) showed that if the mapping $T(a,b,c) \to (a,b,c)$ is locally asymptotically stable at the fixed point $T(a,b,c) = (a,b,c)$ that corresponds to the minimum state-variable solution, the system is e-stable. Evans and Honkapohja then showed that this ensures stability under real-time learning in which the PLM is

$$y_t = a_{t-1} + b_{t-1} y_{t-1} + c_{t-1} e_t$$

and the coefficients are updated by running recursive least-squares.

Because agents are using macroeconomic outcomes to update their beliefs about the structure of the economy, and these beliefs then influence both expectations and macroeconomic outcomes, learning can have important implications for economic dynamics. For example, Erceg and Levin (2003) showed that accounting for learning about the central bank's inflation goals can be important for understanding the real effects on the economy during periods of disinflation such as the early 1980s in the United States.

Much of the recent literature on learning in the context of monetary policy has employed the new Keynesian model (see chapter 8). Evans and Honkapohja (2009) provided a survey of some of the important implications of learning for monetary policy and references to the relevant literature.

5.3 Limited Participation and Liquidity Effects

The impact of a monetary disturbance on market interest rates can be decomposed into its effect on the expected real rate of return and its effect on the expected inflation rate. If money growth is positively serially correlated, an increase in money growth will be associated with higher future inflation and therefore higher *expected* inflation. As noted in chapters 2 and 3, the flexible-price MIU and CIA models implied that faster money growth would immediately increase nominal interest rates.

Most economists, and certainly monetary policymakers, believe that central banks can reduce short-term nominal interest rates by employing policies that lead to faster growth in the money supply. This belief is often interpreted to mean that faster money growth will initially cause nominal interest rates to fall, an impact called the *liquidity effect*. This effect is usually viewed as an important channel through which a monetary expansion affects real consumption, investment, and output.[17]

---

17. A thorough discussion of possible explanations of liquidity effects was provided by Ohanian and Stockman (1995) and Hoover (1995).

A number of authors have explored flexible-price models in which monetary injections reduce nominal interest rates (Lucas 1990; Christiano 1991; Christiano and Eichenbaum 1992a; 1995; Fuerst 1992; Dotsey and Ireland 1995; R. King and Watson 1996; Cooley and Quadrini 1999; Alvarez, Lucas, and Weber 2001, Alvarez, Atkeson, and Kehoe 2002; Williamson 2004; 2005). These models generate effects of monetary shocks on real interest rates by imposing restrictions on the ability of agents to engage in certain types of financial transactions.[18] For example, Lucas modified a basic CIA framework to study effects that arise when monetary injections are not distributed equally across a population of otherwise representative agents. If a monetary injection affects agents differentially, a price level increase proportional to the aggregate change in the money stock will not restore the initial real equilibrium. Some agents will be left with higher real money holdings, others with lower real balances.

Fuerst (1992) and Christiano and Eichenbaum (1995) introduced a liquidity effect by modifying a basic CIA model to distinguish between households, firms, and financial intermediaries. Households can allocate resources between bank deposits and money balances that are then used to finance consumption. Intermediaries lend out their deposits to firms that borrow to finance purchases of labor services from households. After households have made their choice between money and bank deposits, financial intermediaries receive lump-sum monetary injections. Only firms and intermediaries interact in financial markets after the monetary injection.[19]

In a standard representative-agent CIA model, monetary injections are distributed proportionately to all agents. Thus, a proportional rise in the price level leaves all agents with the same level of real money balances as previously. In contrast, if the injections initially affect only the balance sheets of the financial intermediaries, a new channel is introduced by which employment and output will be affected. As long as the nominal interest rate is positive, intermediaries will wish to increase their lending in response to a positive monetary injection. To induce firms to borrow the additional funds, the interest rate on loans must fall. Hence, a liquidity effect is generated; interest rates decline in response to a positive monetary injection.[20] The

18. The first limited-participation models were due to Grossman and Weiss (1983) and Rotemberg (1984). Models that restrict financial transactions can be viewed as variants of the original Baumol-Tobin models with infinite costs for certain types of transactions, rather than the finite costs of exchanging money and interest-earning assets assumed by Baumol (1952) and Tobin (1956).

19. Allowing for heterogeneity greatly complicates the analysis, but these limited-participation models overcome this problem by following the modeling strategy introduced by Lucas (1980) in which each representative family consists of a household supplying labor and purchasing goods, a firm hiring labor, producing goods, and borrowing from the intermediary, and an intermediary. At the end of each period, the various units of the family are reunited and pool resources. As a result, there can be heterogeneity within periods because the new injections of money affect only firms and intermediaries, but between periods all families are identical, so the advantages of the representative agent formulation are preserved.

20. Expected inflation effects will also be at work, so the net impact on nominal interest rates will depend on, among other things, the degree of positive serial correlation in the growth rate of the money supply.

restrictions on trading mean that cash injections create a wedge between the value of cash in the hands of household members shopping in the goods market and the value of cash in the financial market.[21] Because Fuerst and Christiano and Eichenbaum assume that firms must borrow to fund their wage bill, the appropriate marginal cost of labor to firms is the real wage times the gross rate of interest on loans. The interest rate decline generated by the liquidity effect lowers the marginal cost of labor; at each real wage, labor demand increases. As a result, equilibrium employment and output rise.

5.3.1   A Basic Limited-Participation Model

The real effects of money in a limited-participation model can be illustrated in a version of Fuerst's (1992) model. The basic model follows Lucas (1990) in assuming that each representative household consists of several members. The household members play different roles within each period, thus allowing for heterogeneity, but because all members reunite at the end of each period, all households remain identical in equilibrium. Specifically, the household consists of a shopper, a firm manager, a worker, and a financial intermediary (a bank). The household enters the period with money holdings M_t. An amount equal to D_t in nominal terms is deposited in the bank, and the shopper takes $M_t - D_t$ to be used in the goods market to purchase consumption goods. The purchase of such goods is subject to a cash-in-advance constraint:

$$P_t C_t \leq M_t - D_t.$$

The worker sells labor services N_t^s to firms, but firms must pay wages prior to receiving the receipts from production. To accomplish this, firms must take out bank loans to pay workers. If N_t^d is the firm's demand for labor hours and L_t equals nominal bank loans, than the wages-in-advance constraint in nominal terms is

$$P_t \omega_t N_t^d \leq L_t,$$

where ω_t is the real wage. Firm profits, expressed in nominal terms, are

$$\Pi_t^f = P_t Y(N_t^d) - P_t \omega_t N_t^d - R_t^L L_t,$$

where $Y(N^d)$ is the firm's production technology and R^L is the interest rate charged on bank loans.

---

21. In Fuerst (1992), this wedge is measured by the difference between the Lagrangian multiplier on the household's CIA constraint and that on the firm's CIA constraint. A cash injection lowers the value of cash in the financial market and lowers the nominal rate of interest. Similarly, positive nominal interest rates arise in the search model of Shi (2005) because money balances taken to the bond market cannot be used in the goods market within the same period (see section 3.4).

Banks accept deposits from households and pay interest R^D on them. Banks make loans to firms, charging R^L. Finally, the central bank makes transfers to banks. The balance sheet of the representative bank is

$$L_t = D_t + H_t,$$

where H represents transfers from the central bank. Profits for the representative bank are

$$\Pi_t^b = R_t^L L_t + H_t - R_t^D D_t = (R_t^L - R_t^D)D_t + (1 + R_t^L)H_t.$$

Competition and profit maximization in the banking sector ensures

$$R_t^L = R_t^D \equiv R,$$

so bank profits are $(1 + R_t)H_t$.

Key to the structure of this model is the assumption that households must make their financial portfolio decision in choosing D_t prior to learning the current realization of the central bank transfer H_t. Hence, households will be unable to adjust their portfolio in response to the monetary injection. Banks and firms are able to respond after H_t is realized. Thus, the effects of H_t on the supply of bank loans will affect the equilibrium interest rate on loans needed to balance loan supply and loan demand.

Before writing the decision problem of the representative household and deriving the equilibrium conditions, it will be useful to divide all nominal variables by the aggregate price level and let lowercase letters denote the resulting real quantities. Hence, m_t will equal real money holdings of the representative household. Thus, the cash-in-advance constraint becomes $C_t \leq m_t - d_t$, and the wage-in-advance constraint becomes $\omega_t N_t^d \leq l_t$. The household's budget constraint is, in nominal terms,

$$P_t \omega_t N_t^s + M_t - D_t + (1 + R_t)D_t + \Pi_t^b + \Pi_t^f - P_t C_t = M_{t+1},$$

so that after using the expressions for Π_t^b and Π_t^f and dividing by P_t, this becomes

$$\omega_t N_t^s + m_t + R_t d_t + (1 + R_t)h_t + [Y(N_t^d) - w_t N_t^d - R_t l_t] - C_t = \left(\frac{P_{t+1}}{P_t}\right)m_{t+1}.$$

In equilibrium, $m_t = M_t^s/P_t$, where M_t^s is the nominal supply of money, $N_t^s = N_t^d = N_t$, and $l_t = d_t + h_t$.

Let the household's preferences over consumption and hours of work be given by

$$u(C_t) - v(N_t^s),$$

where $u_c, v_N \geq 0$, $u_{cc} \leq 0$, $v_{NN} \geq 0$. The value function for the household can be written as

$$V(m_t) = \max_{d} \; E \left\{ \max_{C_t, N_t^s, N_t^d, l_t, m_{t+1}} [u(C_t) - v(N_t^s) + \beta V(m_{t+1})] \right\},$$

where the maximization is subject to

$$m_t - d_t \geq C_t$$

$$\omega_t N_t^s + m_t + R_t^D d_t + \pi_t^b + [Y(N_t^d) - \omega_t N_t^d - R_t^L l_t] - C_t - \left(\frac{P_{t+1}}{P_t}\right) m_{t+1} = 0$$

and

$$l_t \geq \omega_t N_t^d.$$

Let λ_1, λ_2, and λ_3 be the Lagrangian multipliers associated with these three constraints. Note that d_t is chosen before the household knows the current level of transfers and so must be picked based on expectations but knowing the other variables will subsequently be chosen optimally. The first-order necessary conditions for the optimal choice of d_t, C_t, N_t^s, N_t^d, l_t, and m_{t+1} include

$$d: E_h[-\lambda_{1t} + R_t^D \lambda_{2t}] = 0 \tag{5.15}$$

$$C: u'(C_t) = \lambda_{1t} + \lambda_{2t} \tag{5.16}$$

$$N^s: -v'(N_t^s) + \omega_t \lambda_{2t} = 0 \tag{5.17}$$

$$N^d: \lambda_{2t} Y'(N_t^d) - \omega_t(\lambda_{2t} + \lambda_{3t}) = 0 \tag{5.18}$$

$$l: \lambda_{3t} - R_t^L \lambda_{2t} = 0 \tag{5.19}$$

$$m: -\lambda_{2t}\left(\frac{P_{t+1}}{P_t}\right) + \beta V_m(m_{t+1}) = 0 \tag{5.20}$$

$$V_m(m_t) = E_h(\lambda_{1t} + \lambda_{2t}). \tag{5.21}$$

The operator E_h denotes expectations with respect to the distribution of h_t and is applied to (5.15) and the envelope condition (5.21) because d is chosen before observing h_t. Conditions such as (5.16) are familiar from cash-in-advance models (see chapter 3). The marginal utility of consumption can differ from the marginal utility of income (λ_{2t}) if the cash-in-advance constraint binds (i.e., when $\lambda_{1t} > 0$).

The multipliers λ_{1t} and λ_{3t} measure the value of liquidity in the goods market and the loan market, respectively. Subtracting (5.16) from (5.19) yields

$$\lambda_{3t} - \lambda_{1t} = (1 + R_t)\lambda_{2t} - u'(C_t),$$

and (5.16), (5.20), and (5.21) imply

$$\lambda_{2t} = \beta\left(\frac{P_t}{P_{t+1}}\right) V_m(m_{t+1}) = \beta\left(\frac{P_t}{P_{t+1}}\right) E_h u'(C_{t+1}). \qquad (5.22)$$

Using (5.22), these last two equations can be rearranged as

$$u'(C_t) = \beta\left(\frac{1 + R_t}{1 + \pi_{t+1}}\right) E_h u'(C_{t+1}) - (\lambda_{3t} - \lambda_{1t}), \qquad (5.23)$$

where $1 + \pi_{t+1} = P_{t+1}/P_t$. This expression would, in the absence of the last term, simply be a standard Euler condition linking the marginal utility of consumption at t and $t+1$ with the real return on the bond. When the value of cash in the goods market differs from its value in the loan market, $\lambda_{3t} - \lambda_{1t} \neq 0$, and a wedge is created between the current marginal utility of consumption and its future value adjusted for the expected real return.

From (5.19) and the earlier result that $R_t^D = R_t^L$, equation (5.15) can be rewritten as

$$E_h \lambda_{1t} = E_h \lambda_{3t}.$$

When the household makes its portfolio choice, the value of sending money to the goods market (as measured by λ_{1t}) and of sending it to the loan market by depositing it in a bank (as measured by λ_{3t}) must be equal. Ex post, the two multipliers can differ, because households cannot reallocate funds between the two markets during the period.

Turning to the labor market, (5.18) and (5.19) imply

$$Y'(N_t^d) = (1 + R_t^L)\omega_t; \qquad (5.24)$$

the firm equates the marginal product of labor to the marginal cost of labor, but this is greater than the real wage because of the cost of borrowing funds to finance the firm's wage bill. Thus, the nominal interest rate drives a wedge between the real wage and the marginal product of labor.[22]

From the perspective of labor suppliers, wages earned in period t cannot be used to purchase consumption goods until period $t+1$. Thus, from (5.17), the marginal rate of substitution between leisure and income is set equal to the real wage:

---

22. A rise in the interest rate increases labor costs for each value of the wage and has a negative effect on aggregate employment and output. This effect of interest rates is usually called the cost channel of monetary policy (see Ravenna and Walsh 2006 and chapter 10).

$$\frac{v'(N_t^s)}{\lambda_{2t}} = \omega_t.$$

Combining this expression with the labor demand condition and noting that $N_t^d = N_t^s = N_t$ in equilibrium,

$$\frac{v'(N_t)}{\lambda_{2t}} = \frac{Y'(N_t)}{1 + R_t}, \tag{5.25}$$

revealing how the nominal interest rate drives a wedge between the marginal rate of substitution and the marginal product of labor.

Now consider what happens when there is an unexpected monetary injection H_t. Since the injection is received initially by banks, it increases the supply of loans $D_t + H_t$ because D_t is predetermined by the household's portfolio choice. Equilibrium requires a rise in loan demand, and this is induced by a fall in the interest rate on loans. From (5.24), the fall in R_t^L increases the demand for labor at each real wage. This increase in labor demand leads to a rise in the real wage, which in turn induces households to supply more labor. In equilibrium, both employment and the real wage rise until the demand for loans, $\omega_t N_t$, has increased to absorb the rise in the supply of loans. Hence, both employment and the real wage rise in response to the monetary injection.

Monetary injections have real effects in this model because households must make their portfolio choices before observing the current monetary shock. Any change in the money supply that is anticipated would not have real effects since it would be factored into the household's portfolio choice. Once households are able to reallocate their money and bond holdings, changes in the level of the money supply are neutral, affecting only the level of prices.[23]

5.3.2   Endogenous Market Segmentation

The standard limited-participation model assumes all agents participate in all markets, just not all the time. Some agents make portfolio choices before all information is revealed and are then restricted until the next period from reallocating their portfolio once the information is available. An alternative approach is to assume that some agents access some markets infrequently. For example, Alvarez, Atkeson, and Kehoe (2002) developed a model of endogenous market segmentation. Fixed costs of

---

23. To produce more persistent real effects of monetary shocks, Chari, Christiano, and Eichenbaum (1995) introduced quadratic costs of portfolio adjustment. A similar mechanism was employed by Cooley and Quadrini (1999).

exchanging bonds for money leads agents to trade infrequently.[24] Monetary injections into the bond market cause distributional effects because the new money must be held by the subset of agents active in the bond market. These effects will depend on the level of inflation, however. When inflation is low, the opportunity cost of holding money is low, and few agents will find it worthwhile to pay the fixed cost of exchanging money for bonds; market segmentation will be high and monetary shocks will have large distributional effects. When inflation is high, the opportunity cost of holding money is also high, and most agents will find it worthwhile to pay the fixed cost of exchanging money for bonds; market segmentation will be low and monetary shocks will have small distributional effects.

The basic structure of the Alvarez, Atkeson, and Kehoe (2002) model consists of a goods market and an asset market. Changes in the supply of money are engineered via open market operations in the asset market. Purchases in the goods market are subject to a cash-in-advance constraint. Suppose a household's desired consumption is greater than the real value of its initial cash holdings. The household can sell bonds to obtain additional cash, but each transfer of cash between the asset market and the goods market incurs a fixed cost of γ. Let m be the household's real money balances, and let c denote the consumption level it would choose if it incurs the fixed cost of obtaining additional money. Then it will pay the fixed cost and make an asset exchange if

$$h(c,m) \equiv U(c) - U(m) - U_c(c)(c + \gamma - m) > 0, \tag{5.26}$$

where $U(c)$ is utility of consumption and U_c is marginal utility. To understand this condition, note that if the household does not make an asset transfer, the cash-in-advance constraint implies it can consume m, yielding utility $U(m)$. If it does make a transfer, it can consume c, yielding utility $U(c)$, but it must also pay the fee γ, and the last term in (5.26) is the cost of the fee in terms of utility.[25]

Importantly, the function h defined in (5.26) is minimized when $m = c$, in which case $h(c,c) = -U_c(c)\gamma < 0$. Because h is continuous, for m near c, h will be negative, the condition in (5.26) will not be satisfied, and the household will be in what Alvarez, Atkeson, and Kehoe described as a zone of inactivity. The gain from an asset exchange is not sufficient to justify the fixed cost, so the household does not participate in the asset market. If m is further away from c, the gains are larger. Alvarez, Atkeson, and Kehoe showed that m_L and m_H can be defined such that if $m < m_L$ or

---

24. Alvarez, Lucas, and Weber (2001) provided a simplified model with segmented markets in which an exogenous fraction of agents do not participate in the bond market.

25. The cost of consuming c is $c + \gamma$, since the fee must be paid. The cost of consuming m is just m, so the extra cost of consuming c is $c + \gamma - m$, which carries a utility cost of $U_c(c)(c + \gamma - m)$.

$m > m_H$, the household will find it worthwhile to be active in the asset market. In the former case (i.e., when $m < m_L$), the household will sell bonds for money; in the latter case (i.e., when $m > m_H$), the household will use money to buy bonds. Thus, markets are segmented in that some households are actively participating in the asset markets while others are inactive, but this segmentation is endogenously determined.

Given market segmentation, a monetary injection has real effects just as in the earlier limited-participation models that treated segmentation or lack of market access as an exogenous characteristic of the environment. An increase in the growth rate of money increases expected inflation, and this acts to raise the nominal interest rate. However, the increase in real balances raises the consumption of the households who are active in the asset market. As in all the models that have been examined, the real return links the marginal utility of consumption today with the expected future marginal utility of consumption, but it is only the marginal utility of the active households that is relevant in the asset market.[26] Since their current consumption has risen relative to their expected future consumption, the real interest rate falls. Alvarez, Atkeson, and Kehoe called this the segmentation effect. Thus, nominal interest rates may fall with an increase in the growth rate of money if the segmentation effect is larger than the expected inflation effect.

To illustrate the competing effects on the nominal interest rate, Alvarez, Atkeson, and Kehoe assumed money growth rates, expressed as deviations around the steady state, following an AR(1) process:

$$\hat{\mu}_t = \rho \hat{\mu}_{t-1} + e_t,$$

where $\hat{\mu}$ denotes the log deviation of μ. They then showed that expected inflation is equal to $E_t\hat{\mu}_{t+1}$, and the marginal utility of active households is $-\phi\hat{\mu}_t$, with $\phi > 0$. Let $\hat{u}_c(t)$ denote the log deviation of the marginal utility of active households at date t. Then, the log-linear approximation to the Euler condition implies that the real interest rate is

$$\hat{r}_t = -[E_t\hat{u}_c(t+1) - \hat{u}_c(t)] = \phi(E_t\hat{\mu}_{t+1} - \hat{\mu}_t) = \phi(\rho - 1)\hat{\mu}_t.$$

The effect of money growth on the nominal interest rate is then equal to

$$\hat{i}_t = \hat{r}_t + E_t\hat{\pi}_{t+1} = \phi(\rho - 1)\hat{\mu}_t + \rho\hat{\mu}_t = [\phi(\rho - 1) + \rho]\hat{\mu}_t,$$

which is negative (faster money growth lowers the nominal interest rate) if $\phi > \rho/(1-\rho)$. The authors then discussed possible calibrations of ϕ consistent with their model. For example, if half of all households are inactive and the coefficient of

---

26. The standard Euler condition, $U_c(t) = \beta(1 + r_t)E_tU_c(t+1)$, still holds for active households, but it no longer holds for the representative household.

relative risk aversion is 2, then $\phi = 1$. In this case, nominal interest rates fall in response to a rise in money growth as long as $\rho < 1/2$.

5.3.3   Assessment

Models that generate real effects of money by restricting financial transactions can account for nominal (and real) interest rate declines in response to monetary policy shocks. But as Dotsey and Ireland (1995) showed, this class of models does not account for interest rate effects of the magnitude actually observed in the data. Similarly, R. King and Watson (1996) found that monetary shocks do not produce significant business cycle fluctuations in their version of a limited-participation model (which they call a *liquidity-effect model*). Christiano, Eichenbaum, and Evans (1997) showed that their limited-participation model is able to match evidence on the effects of monetary shocks on prices, output, real wages, and profits only if the labor supply wage elasticity is assumed to be very high. They argued that this outcome is due, in part, to the absence of labor market frictions in the current generation of limited-participation models.

Because limited-participation models were developed to account for the observation that monetary injections lower market interest rates, the real test of whether they have isolated an important channel through which monetary policy operates must come from evaluating their other implications. Christiano, Eichenbaum, and Evans (1997) examined real wage and profit movements to test their models. They argued that limited-participation models are able to account for the increase in profits that follows a monetary expansion. A further implication of such models relates to the manner in which the impact of monetary injections will change over time as financial sectors evolve and the cost of transactions falls. Financial markets today are very different than they were 25 years ago, and these differences should show up in the way money affects interest rates now as compared to 25 years ago.[27] While financial market frictions are likely to be important in understanding the effects of monetary policy actions on short-term market interest rates, the relevance of the channels emphasized in limited-participation models for understanding the broader effects of monetary policy on the aggregate economy remains an open debate.

5.4   Summary

Monetary economists generally agree that the models discussed in chapters 2–4, while useful for examining issues such as the welfare cost of inflation and the optimal

---

27. Cole and Ohanian (2002) argued that the impact of money shocks in the United States has declined with the ratio of $M1$ to nominal GDP, a finding consistent with the implications of limited-participation models.

inflation tax, need to be modified to account for the short-run effects of monetary factors on the economy. In this chapter, two such modifications were explored: informational frictions, and frictions that limit the ability of some agents to adjust their portfolios. Aggregate informational or portfolio frictions can allow money to have real effects in the short run even when prices are completely flexible, but most monetary models designed to address short-run monetary issues assume that prices and/or wages do not adjust instantaneously in response to changes in economic conditions. The next chapter discusses models of nominal price and wage rigidities.

5.5 Appendix: An Imperfect-Information Model

This appendix provides details on the derivation of equilibrium in the Lucas imperfect-information model of section 5.2.2. Additional details on the derivations employed in this appendix can be found at ⟨http://people.ucsc.edu/~walshc/mtp3e⟩.

Using (5.4) to eliminate the marginal utility of consumption from (5.1)–(5.3), the equilibrium in local market i, or island i, can be represented by the following three equations, where the goods equilibrium condition $y^i = c^i$ has been used:

$$y_t^i = (1 - \alpha)n_t^i \tag{5.27}$$

$$\left[1 + \eta\left(\frac{n^{ss}}{1 - n^{ss}}\right)\right]n_t^i = (1 + \Omega_1)y_t^i + \Omega_2(m_t^i - p_t^i) \tag{5.28}$$

$$m_t^i - p_t^i = y_t^i + \left(\frac{1}{b}\right)\left(\frac{\beta}{1 - \beta}\right)[\mathrm{E}^i\tau_{t+1} - (\mathrm{E}^i p_{t+1} - p_t^i)$$

$$+ \Omega_1\mathrm{E}^i(y_{t+1} - y_t^i) + \Omega_2\mathrm{E}^i(m_{t+1} - p_{t+1} - m_t^i + p_t^i)], \tag{5.29}$$

where $\Omega_1 = [\varphi(b - \Phi) - b]$, $\Omega_2 = (b - \Phi)(1 - \varphi)$, and[28]

$$\varphi \equiv \frac{a(C^{ss})^{1-b}}{a(C^{ss})^{1-b} + (1 - a)[(M/P)^{ss}]^{1-b}}.$$

The chapter 2 appendix contains a more complete derivation of the basic MIU model. Equation (5.28) is derived from the condition that the marginal utility of

---

28. The parameters β, Φ, b, and η are from the utility function of the representative agent:

$$u\left(C_t, \frac{M_t}{P_t}, 1 - N_t\right) = \frac{\left[aC_t^{1-b} + (1 - a)\left(\frac{M_t}{P_t}\right)^{1-b}\right]^{(1-\Phi)/(1-b)}}{1 - \Phi} + \Psi\frac{[(1 - N_t)^{1-\eta}]}{1 - \eta}.$$

leisure divided by the marginal utility of consumption must equal the marginal product of labor. Equation (5.29) is derived from the first-order condition that for an agent on island i,

$$u_c^i(t) = u_m^i(t) + \beta E^i \left(\frac{T_{t+1}}{\Pi_{t+1}} \right) u_c(t+1), \tag{5.30}$$

where the left side is the utility cost of reducing consumption marginally in order to hold more money, and the right side is the return from higher money holdings. This return consists of the direct utility yield $u_m^i(t)$, plus the utility from using the real balances to increase consumption in period $t+1$. With transfers viewed as proportional to money holdings, the individual treats money as if it yielded a real return of T_{t+1}/Π_{t+1}. Given the assumed utility function, both sides of (5.30) can be divided by $u_c^i(t)$ and written as

$$1 = \left(\frac{1-a}{a} \right) \left(\frac{M_t^i/P_t^i}{C_t^i} \right)^{-b} + \beta E^i \left(\frac{T_{t+1}}{\Pi_{t+1}} \right) \left(\frac{X_{t+1}^{(b-\Phi)/(1-b)} C_{t+1}^{-b}}{X_t^{(b-\Phi)/(1-b)} C_t^{-b}} \right),$$

where

$$X_t = aC_t^{1-b} + (1-a) \left(\frac{M_t}{P_t} \right)^{1-b}.$$

Expressed in terms of percentage deviations around the steady state (denoted by lowercase letters), the two terms on the right side become

$$\left(\frac{1-a}{a} \right) \left(\frac{M_t^i/P_t^i}{C_t^i} \right)^{-b} \approx \left(\frac{1-a}{a} \right) \left[\left(\frac{M/P}{C} \right)^{ss} \right]^{-b} [1 + bc_t^i - b(m_t^i - p_t^i)]$$

and

$$\beta E^i \left(\frac{T_{t+1}}{\Pi_{t+1}} \right) \left(\frac{X_{t+1}^{(b-\Phi)/(1-b)} C_{t+1}^{-b}}{X_t^{(b-\Phi)/(1-b)} C_t^{-b}} \right)$$

$$\approx \beta E^i [1 + \tau_{t+1} - p_{t+1} + p_t^i + \Omega_1 \Delta c_{t+1} + \Omega_2(\Delta m_{t+1} - \Delta p_{t+1})],$$

where Δ is the first difference operator ($\Delta c_{t+1} = c_{t+1} - c_t^i$) and the fact that in the steady state, $T^{ss} = \Pi^{ss}$ has been used. This condition also implies

$$1 = \left(\frac{1-a}{a} \right) \left[\left(\frac{M/P}{C} \right)^{ss} \right]^{-b} + \beta \left(\frac{T^{ss}}{\Pi^{ss}} \right) = \left(\frac{1-a}{a} \right) \left[\left(\frac{M/P}{C} \right)^{ss} \right]^{-b} + \beta, \tag{5.31}$$

so the first-order condition becomes

$$0 = (1 - \beta)[bc_t^i - b(m_t^i - p_t^i)]$$

$$+ \beta E^i[\tau_{t+1} - p_{t+1} + p_t^i + \Omega_1 \Delta c_{t+1} + \Omega_2 (\Delta m_{t+1} - \Delta p_{t+1})],$$

which can be rearranged to yield (5.29), since $c^i = y^i$.

The nominal money supply on island i is assumed to evolve according to

$$m_t^i = \rho_m m_{t-1} + v_t + u_t + u_t^i.$$

The value of v is announced (or observed) at the start of period t. Individuals on island i observe the island-specific nominal money stock m_t^i. This allows them to infer $u_t + u_t^i$ but not u and u^i separately. The expectation of the time $t + 1$ money supply, conditional on the information available on island i, will be $E^i m_{t+1} = \rho_m^2 m_{t-1} + \rho_m v_t + \rho_m E^i u_t$. Equating expectations with linear least-squares projections, $E^i u_t = \kappa(u_t + u_t^i)$, where $\kappa = \sigma_u^2 / (\sigma_u^2 + \sigma_i^2)$.

The time t transfer τ_t is $\tau_t = m_t - m_{t-1} = (\rho_m - 1)m_{t-1} + v_t + u_t$, so

$$E_t \tau_{t+1} = (\rho_m - 1)E^i m_t + E^i[v_{t+1} + u_{t+1}]$$

$$= (\rho_m - 1)[\rho_m m_{t-1} + v_t + \kappa(u_t + u_t^i)].$$

Eliminating output and the expected transfer from (5.27)–(5.29), these equations yield the following two equations for employment and prices:

$$n_t^i = \left[\frac{\Omega_2}{1 + \eta\left(\frac{n^{ss}}{l^{ss}}\right) - (1 + \Omega_1)(1 - \alpha)} \right] (m_t^i - p_t^i) = A(m_t^i - p_t^i) \tag{5.32}$$

$$m_t^i - p_t^i = (1 - \alpha)n_t^i + \left(\frac{1}{b}\right)\left(\frac{\beta}{1 - \beta}\right)\Omega_2 E^i[m_{t+1} - p_{t+1} - m_t^i + p_t^i]$$

$$+ \left(\frac{1}{b}\right)\left(\frac{\beta}{1 - \beta}\right)(1 - \alpha)\Omega_1 E^i \Delta n_{t+1}$$

$$+ \left(\frac{1}{b}\right)\left(\frac{\beta}{1 - \beta}\right)[(\rho_m - 1)E^i m_t - E^i p_{t+1} + p_t^i]. \tag{5.33}$$

By substituting (5.32) into (5.33), one obtains a single equation that involves the price process and the exogenous nominal money supply process:

$(m_t^i - p_t^i) = (1 - \alpha)A(m_t^i - p_t^i)$

$$+ \left(\frac{1}{b}\right)\left(\frac{\beta}{1-\beta}\right)[\Omega_2 + (1 - \alpha)\Omega_1 A]E^i[m_{t+1} - p_{t+1} - m_t^i + p_t^i]$$

$$+ \left(\frac{1}{b}\right)\left(\frac{\beta}{1-\beta}\right)[(\rho_m - 1)E^i m_t - E^i p_{t+1} + p_t^i]. \tag{5.34}$$

Equation (5.34) can be solved using the method of undetermined coefficients (see McCallum 1989; Attfield, Demery, and Duck 1991). This method involves guessing a solution for p_t^i and then verifying that the solution is consistent with (5.34). Since m_t depends on m_{t-1}, v_t, u_t, and u_t^i, a guess for the minimum state-variable solution (McCallum 1983a) for the equilibrium price level takes the following form:

$$p_t^i = a_1 m_{t-1} + a_2 v_t + a_3 u_t + a_4 u_t^i, \tag{5.35}$$

where the a_j coefficients are yet to be determined parameters. Equation (5.35) implies that the aggregate price level is $p_t = a_1 m_{t-1} + a_2 v_t + a_3 u_t$, so

$$E^i p_{t+1} = a_1 E^i m_t = a_1(\rho_m m_{t-1} + v_t + E^i u_t)$$

$$= a_1[\rho_m m_{t-1} + v_t + \kappa(u_t + u_t^i)]$$

$$E^i m_{t+1} = \rho_m^2 m_{t-1} + \rho_m v_t + \rho_m E^i u_t.$$

Now all the terms in (5.34) can be evaluated. The left side of (5.34) is equal to

$$(m_t^i - p_t^i) = (\rho_m - a_1)m_{t-1} + (1 - a_2)v_t + (1 - a_3)u_t + (1 - a_4)u_t^i,$$

and the terms on the right side equal

$$(1 - \alpha)A[(\rho_m - a_1)m_{t-1} + (1 - a_2)v_t + (1 - a_3)u_t + (1 - a_4)u_t^i],$$

$$B[\rho_m^2 m_{t-1} + \rho_m v_t + \rho_m \kappa(u_t + u_t^i)] - Ba_1[\rho_m m_{t-1} + v_t + \kappa(u_t + u_t^i)]$$

$$- B[\rho_m m_{t-1} + v_t + u_t + u_t^i] + B(a_1 m_{t-1} + a_2 v_t + a_3 u_t + a_4 u_t^i),$$

where $B = (\beta/b(1-\beta))[\Omega_2 - (1-\alpha)\Omega_1 A]$, and

$$\left(\frac{1}{b}\right)\left(\frac{\beta}{1-\beta}\right)(\rho_m - 1)[\rho_m m_{t-1} + v_t + \kappa(u_t + u_t^i)]$$

$$- \left(\frac{1}{b}\right)\left(\frac{\beta}{1-\beta}\right)[a_1(\rho_m m_{t-1} + v_t + \kappa(u_t + u_t^i)) - (a_1 m_{t-1} + a_2 v_t + a_3 u_t + a_4 u_t^i)].$$

For the two sides of (5.34) to be equal for all possible realizations of m_{t-1}, v_t, u_t, and u_t^i requires that the following hold. First, the coefficient on m_{t-1} on the right side must be equal to the coefficient on the left side, which holds if $a_1 = \rho_m$. Second, the coefficient of v_t on the right side must be equal to the coefficient of v_t on the left side, or $a_2 = 1$ (since $a_1 = \rho_m$). Third, the coefficient of u_t on the right side must be equal to the coefficient of u_t on the left side, or

$$a_3 = \frac{\kappa + K}{1 + K} < 1,$$

where

$$K = b\left(\frac{1 - \beta}{\beta}\right)[1 - (1 - \alpha)A + B].$$

Finally, the coefficient on u_t^i on the right side must be equal to its coefficient on the left side, or $a_4 = a_3$.

Combining these results, one obtains the expressions for the equilibrium economy-wide price level and employment given by (5.6) and (5.7).

5.6 Problems

1. Using (5.1)–(5.4), show that if $\Omega_2 = 0$, then $y_t = y_t^i = n_t^i = n_t = 0$.

2. Suppose the central bank becomes more transparent in that σ_u^2 falls, so that the aggregate money stock becomes more predictable. Using the Lucas model of section 5.2.2, explain how the variance of the price level and the variance of employment would be affected by this change.

3. According to the sticky information model of section 5.2.3, the impact of the output gap on inflation (holding constant expectations) is equal to $\alpha\lambda/(1 - \lambda)$, where λ is the fraction of firms that update their information. Explain why the impact of the output gap on inflation is increasing in λ.

4. Using the model of section 5.2.3 and the calibrated values used to obtain figures 5.1 and 5.2, construct impulse responses for inflation and output to innovations to the money growth rate for $\rho = 0, 0.25, 0.5$, and 0.75. How are the responses affected by the degree of serial correlation in the growth rate of money?

5. Using the limited-participation model of section 5.3.1, and ignoring uncertainty, show that when the household makes its portfolio decision, it anticipates that the marginal rate of substitution between leisure and consumption will equal the marginal product of labor divided by $(1 + R_t)^2$. Explain the intuition for this result.

6 Money in the Short Run: Nominal Price and Wage Rigidities

6.1 Introduction

In this chapter, the focus shifts away from models with flexible wages and prices to models of sticky wages and prices. It starts with a simple example of a model with nominal wage rigidities that last for one period. Then it reviews models that account for the observation that prices and wages may take several periods to adjust to changes in macroeconomic conditions. Time-dependent and state-dependent models of price adjustment are discussed. Time-dependent pricing models assume the probability that a firm changes its price is a function only of time, and state-dependent models make this probability a function of the current state of the economy.

The focus in this chapter is on various models of nominal rigidities. In chapter 8, the new Keynesian Phillips curve developed in section 6.3.2 is incorporated into a general equilibrium framework so that the implications of price and wage rigidities for monetary policy can be studied.

6.2 Sticky Prices and Wages

Most macroeconomic models attribute the short-run real effects of monetary disturbances not to imperfect information or limited participation in financial markets but to the presence of nominal wage and/or price rigidities. These rigidities mean that nominal wages and prices fail to adjust immediately and completely to changes in the nominal quantity of money. In the 1980s it was common to model nominal rigidities by imposing the assumption that prices (or wages) were fixed for one period. This approach is illustrated in section 6.2.1 and employed extensively in chapter 7. This modification increases the impact that monetary disturbances have on real output but cannot account for persistent real effects of monetary policy. The model of staggered multiperiod nominal wage contracts due to Taylor (1979; 1980) can generate the persistent output responses observed in the data, but Taylor's model was not based on an explicit model of optimizing behavior by workers or firms. The literature in recent years has turned to models of monopolistic competition and price stickiness in which the decision problem faced by firms in setting prices can be made explicit. The objective in this section is to review some of the standard models of nominal rigidities and their implications. The new generation of dynamic stochastic general equilibrium (DSGE) models based on nominal rigidites and their implications for monetary policy analysis is the chief focus of chapter 8.

6.2.1   An Example of Nominal Rigidities in General Equilibrium

The first model considered adds a one-period nominal wage rigidity to the MIU model of chapter 2. This approach is not based on optimizing behavior by wage setters, but it leads to a reduced-form model that has been widely used in monetary economics. This model plays an important role in the analysis of time inconsistency in chapter 7.

Wage Rigidity in an MIU Model
One way to introduce nominal price stickiness is to modify a flexible-price model, such as an MIU model, by simply assuming that prices and/or wages are set at the start of each period and are unresponsive to developments within the period. In chapter 2 a linear approximation was used to examine the time series implications of an MIU model. Wages and prices were assumed to adjust to ensure market equilibrium, and consequently the behavior of the money supply mattered only to the extent that anticipated inflation was affected. A positive disturbance to the growth rate of money would, assuming that the growth rate of money was positively serially correlated, raise the expected rate of inflation, leading to a rise in the nominal rate of interest that affects labor supply and output. These last effects depended on the form of the utility function; if utility was separable in money, changes in expected inflation had no effect on labor supply or real output. Introducing wage stickiness into an MIU model serves to illustrate the effect such a modification has on the impact of monetary disturbances.

Consider the linear approximation to the Sidrauski MIU model developed in chapter 2. To simplify the model, assume utility is separable in consumption and money holdings ($b = \Phi$, or $\Omega_2 = 0$ in terms of the parameters of the model used in chapter 2). This implies that money and monetary shocks have no effect on output when prices are perfectly flexible.[1] In addition, the capital stock is treated as fixed, and investment is zero. This follows McCallum and Nelson (1999), who argued that for most monetary policy and business cycle analyses, fluctuations in the stock of

---

1. From (5.32), money surprises also have no effect on employment and output when $\Omega_2 = 0$ in Lucas's imperfect-information model.

capital do not play a major role. The equations characterizing equilibrium in the resulting MIU model are

$$y_t = (1 - \alpha)n_t + e_t \tag{6.1}$$

$$y_t = c_t \tag{6.2}$$

$$y_t - n_t = w_t - p_t \tag{6.3}$$

$$\Phi E_t(c_{t+1} - c_t) - r_t = 0 \tag{6.4}$$

$$\eta \left(\frac{n^{ss}}{1 - n^{ss}} \right) n_t + \Phi c_t = w_t - p_t \tag{6.5}$$

$$m_t - p_t = c_t - \left(\frac{1}{bi^{ss}} \right) i_t \tag{6.6}$$

$$i_t = r_t + E_t p_{t+1} - p_t \tag{6.7}$$

$$m_t = \rho_m m_{t-1} + s_t. \tag{6.8}$$

All variables are expressed as log derivations from steady state. The system is written in terms of the log price level p rather than the inflation rate, and in contrast to the notation of chapter 2, m represents the nominal stock of money. Equation (6.1) is the economy's production function in which output deviations from the steady state are a linear function of the deviations of labor supply from steady state and a productivity shock. Equation (6.2) is the resource constraint derived from the condition that in the absence of investment or government purchases, output equals consumption. Labor demand is derived from the condition that labor is employed up to the point where the marginal product of labor equals the real wage. With the Cobb-Douglas production function underlying (6.1), this condition, expressed in terms of percentage deviations from the steady state, can be written as (6.3).[2] Equations (6.4)–(6.6) are derived from the representative household's first-order conditions for consumption, leisure, and money holdings. Equation (6.7) is the Fisher equation linking the nominal and real rates of interest. Finally, (6.8) gives the exogenous process for the nominal money supply.[3]

When prices are flexible, (6.1)–(6.5) form a system of equations that can be solved for the equilibrium time paths of output, labor, consumption, the real wage, and the

2. If $Y = \bar{K}^{\alpha} N^{1-\alpha}$, then the marginal product of labor is $(1 - \alpha) Y/N$, where $\bar{K}$ is the fixed stock of capital. In log terms, the real wage is then equal to $\ln W - \ln P = \ln(1 - \alpha) + \ln Y - \ln N$, or, in terms of deviations from steady state, $w - p = y - n$.

3. Alternatively, the nominal interest rate i_t could be taken as the instrument of monetary policy, with (6.6) then determining m_t.

real rate of interest. Equations (6.6)–(6.8) then determine the evolution of real money balances, the nominal interest rate, and the price level. Thus, realizations of the monetary disturbance s_t have no effect on output when prices are flexible. This version of the MIU model displays the *classical dichotomy* (Modigliani 1963; Patinkin 1965); real variables such as output, consumption, investment, and the real interest rate are determined independently of both the money supply process and money demand factors.[4]

Now suppose the nominal wage rate is set prior to the start of the period, and that it is set equal to the level *expected* to produce the *real* wage that equates labor supply and labor demand. Since workers and firms are assumed to have a real wage target in mind, the nominal wage will adjust fully to reflect expectations of price level changes held at the time the nominal wage is set. This means that the information available at the time the wage is set, and on which expectations will be based, will be important. If unanticipated changes in prices occur, the actual real wage will differ from its expected value. In the standard formulation, firms are assumed to determine employment on the basis of the actual, realized real wage. If prices are unexpectedly low, the actual real wage will exceed the level expected to clear the labor market, and firms will reduce employment.[5]

The equilibrium level of employment and the real wage with flexible prices can be obtained by equating labor supply and labor demand (from (6.5) and (6.3)) and then using the production function (6.1) and the resource constraint (6.2) to obtain

$$n_t^* = \left[\frac{1 - \Phi}{1 + \bar{\eta} + (1 - \alpha)(\Phi - 1)} \right] e_t = b_0 e_t$$

and

$$\omega_t^* = \left[\frac{\bar{\eta} + \Phi}{1 + \bar{\eta} + (1 - \alpha)(\Phi - 1)} \right] e_t = b_1 e_t,$$

where n^* is the flexible-wage equilibrium employment, ω^* is the flexible-wage equilibrium real wage, and $\bar{\eta} \equiv \eta n^{ss}/(1 - n^{ss})$.

The contract nominal wage w^c will satisfy

$$w_t^c = E_{t-1}\omega_t^* + E_{t-1}p_t. \tag{6.9}$$

---

4. This is stronger than the property of monetary superneutrality, in which the real variables are independent of the money supply process. For example, Lucas's model does not display the classical dichotomy as long as $\Omega_2 \neq 0$ because the production function, the resource constraint, and the labor supply condition cannot be solved for output, consumption, and employment without knowing the real demand for money, since real balances enter (5.4).

5. This implies that the real wage falls in response to a positive money shock. Using a VAR approach based on U.S. data, Christiano, Eichenbaum, and Evans (1997) found that an expansionary monetary policy shock actually leads to a slight increase in real wages.

With firms equating the marginal product of labor to the actual real wage, actual employment will equal $n_t = y_t - (w_t^c - p_t) = y_t - E_{t-1}\omega_t^* + (p_t - E_{t-1}p_t)$, or using the production function and noting that $E_{t-1}\omega_t^* = -\alpha E_{t-1}n_t^* + E_{t-1}e_t$,

$$n_t = E_{t-1}n_t^* + \left(\frac{1}{\alpha}\right)(p_t - E_{t-1}p_t) + \left(\frac{1}{\alpha}\right)\varepsilon_t, \tag{6.10}$$

where $\varepsilon_t = (e_t - E_{t-1}e_t)$. Equation (6.10) shows that employment deviates from the expected flexible-wage equilibrium level in the face of unexpected movements in prices. An unanticipated increase in prices reduces the real value of the contract wage and leads firms to expand employment. An unexpected productivity shock ε_t raises the marginal product of labor and leads to an employment increase.

By substituting (6.10) into the production function, one obtains

$$y_t = (1 - \alpha)\left[E_{t-1}n_t^* + \left(\frac{1}{\alpha}\right)(p_t - E_{t-1}p_t) + \left(\frac{1}{\alpha}\right)\varepsilon_t\right] + e_t,$$

which implies that

$$y_t - E_{t-1}y_t^* = a(p_t - E_{t-1}p_t) + (1 + a)\varepsilon_t, \tag{6.11}$$

where $E_{t-1}y^* = (1 - \alpha)E_{t-1}n_t^* + E_{t-1}e_t$ is expected equilibrium output under flexible wages and $a = (1 - \alpha)/\alpha$. Innovations to output are positively related to price innovations. Thus, monetary shocks which produce unanticipated price movements directly affect real output.

The linear approximation to the MIU model, augmented with one-period nominal wage contracts, produces one of the basic frameworks often used to address policy issues. This framework generally assumes serially uncorrelated disturbances, so $E_{t-1}y^* = 0$ and the aggregate supply equation (6.11), often called a *Lucas supply function* (see chapter 5) becomes

$$y_t = a(p_t - E_{t-1}p_t) + (1 + a)\varepsilon_t. \tag{6.12}$$

The demand side often consists of a simple quantity equation of the form

$$m_t - p_t = y_t. \tag{6.13}$$

This model can be obtained from the model of the chapter appendix (section 6.5) by letting $b \to \infty$; this implies that the interest elasticity of money demand goes to zero. According to (6.12), a 1 percent deviation of p from its expected value will cause a $(1 - \alpha)/\alpha \approx 1.8$ percent deviation of output if the benchmark value of 0.36 is used for α. To solve the model for equilibrium output and the price level, given the nominal quantity of money, note that (6.13) and (6.8) imply

$$p_t - E_{t-1}p_t = m_t - E_{t-1}m_t - (y_t - E_{t-1}y_t) = s_t - y_t.$$

Substituting this result into (6.12), one obtains

$$y_t = \left(\frac{a}{1+a}\right)s_t + \left(\frac{1+a}{1+a}\right)\varepsilon_t = (1-\alpha)s_t + \varepsilon_t. \qquad (6.14)$$

A 1 percent money surprise increases output by $1 - \alpha \approx 0.64$ percent. Notice that in (6.12) the coefficient a on price surprises depends on parameters of the production function. This is in contrast to Lucas's misperceptions model, in which the impact on output of a price surprise depends on the variances of shocks (see section 5.2.2). The model consisting of (6.12) and (6.13) will play an important role in the analysis of monetary policy in chapter 7.

When (6.13) is replaced with an interest-sensitive demand for money, the systematic behavior of the money supply can matter for the real effects of money surprises. For example, if money is positively serially correlated ($\rho_m > 0$), a positive realization of s_t implies that the money supply will be higher in the future as well. This leads to increases in $E_t p_{t+1}$, expected inflation, and the nominal rate of interest. The rise in the nominal rate of interest reduces the real demand for money today, causing, for a given shock s_t, a larger increase in the price level today than occurs when $\rho_m = 0$. This means the price surprise today is larger and implies that the real output effect of s_t will be increasing in ρ_m.[6]

Bénassy (1995) shows how one-period wage contracts affect the time series behavior of output in a model similar to the one used here but in which capital is not ignored. However, the dynamics associated with consumption smoothing and capital accumulation are inadequate on their own to produce anything like the output persistence that is revealed by the data.[7] That is why real business cycle models assume that the productivity disturbance itself is highly serially correlated. Because it is assumed here that nominal wages are fixed for only one period, the estimated effects of a monetary shock on output die out almost completely after one period.[8] This would continue to be the case even if the money shock were serially correlated. While serial correlation in the s_t shock would affect the behavior of the price level, this will be incorporated into expectations, and the nominal wage set at the start of $t + 1$ will adjust fully to make the expected real wage (and therefore employment and output) independent of the predictable movement in the price level. Just adding one-period

---

6. See problem 1 at the end of this chapter. I thank Henrik Jensen for pointing out this effect of systematic policy.

7. Cogley and Nason (1995) demonstrated this for standard real business cycle models.

8. With Bénassy's model and parameters ($\alpha = 0.40$ and $\delta = 0.019$), equilibrium output (expressed as a deviation from trend) is given by $y_t \approx 0.6 \times (1 + 0.006L - 0.002L^2 \ldots)(m_t - m_t^e)$, so that the effects of a money surprise die out almost immediately (Bénassy 1995, 313, eq. 51).

sticky nominal wages will not capture the persistent effects of monetary shocks, but it will significantly influence the effect of a money shock on the economy.

6.2.2   Early Models of Intertemporal Nominal Adjustment

The model just discussed assumes that wages remain fixed for one period. More interesting from the perspective of understanding the implications for macroeconomic dynamics of nominal rigidities are models that allow prices and/or wages to adjust gradually over several periods. Two such models are discussed here.

Taylor's Model of Staggered Nominal Adjustment
One of the first models of nominal rigidities that also assumed rational expectations is due to Taylor (1979; 1980). Because his model was originally developed in terms of nominal wage-setting behavior, that approach is followed here. Prices are assumed to be a constant markup over wage costs, so the adjustment of wages translates directly into a model of the adjustment of prices.

Assume that wages are set for two periods, with one-half of all contracts negotiated each period. Let x_t equal the log contract wage set at time t. The average wage faced by the firm is equal to $w_t = (x_t + x_{t-1})/2$ because in period t, contracts set in the previous period (x_{t-1}) are still in effect. Assuming a constant markup, the log price level is given by $p_t = w_t + \mu$, where μ is the log markup. For convenience, normalize so that $\mu = 0$.

For workers covered by the contract set in period t, the average expected real wage over the life of the contract is $\frac{1}{2}[(x_t - p_t) + (x_t - E_t p_{t+1})] = x_t - \frac{1}{2}(p_t + E_t p_{t+1}).$[9] In Taylor (1980), the expected average real contract wage is assumed to be increasing in the level of economic activity, represented by log output:

$$x_t = \frac{1}{2}(p_t + E_t p_{t+1}) + k y_t. \tag{6.15}$$

With $p_t = 0.5(x_t + x_{t-1})$,

$$p_t = \frac{1}{2}\left[\frac{1}{2}(p_t + E_t p_{t+1}) + k y_t + \frac{1}{2}(p_{t-1} + E_{t-1} p_t) + k y_{t-1}\right]$$

$$= \frac{1}{4}[2p_t + E_t p_{t+1} + p_{t-1} + \eta_t] + \frac{k}{2}(y_t + y_{t-1}),$$

where $\eta_t \equiv E_{t-1} p_t - p_t$ is an expectational error term. Rearranging,

---

9. It would be more appropriate to assume that workers care about the present discounted value of the real wage over the life of the contract. This would lead to a specification of the form $0.5(1 + \beta)x_t - 0.5(p_t + \beta E_t p_{t+1})$ for $0 < \beta < 1$, where β is a discount factor.

$$p_t = \frac{1}{2}p_{t-1} + \frac{1}{2}E_t p_{t+1} + k(y_t + y_{t-1}) + \frac{1}{2}\eta_t. \tag{6.16}$$

The basic Taylor specification leads to inertia in the aggregate price level. The value of p_t is influenced both by expectations of future prices and by the price level in the previous period.

Expressed in terms of the rate of inflation $\pi_t = p_t - p_{t-1}$, (6.16) implies

$$\pi_t = E_t \pi_{t+1} + 2k(y_t + y_{t-1}) + \eta_t. \tag{6.17}$$

The key implication of (6.17) is that while prices display inertia, the inflation rate need not exhibit inertia, that is, it depends on expected future inflation but not on past inflation. This is important, as can be seen by considering the implications of Taylor's model for a policy of disinflation. Suppose that the economy is in an initial, perfect-foresight equilibrium with a constant inflation rate π_1. Now suppose that in period $t - 1$ the policymaker announces a policy that will lower the inflation rate to π_2 in period t and then maintain inflation at this new lower rate. Using (6.17) and the definition of η_t, it can be shown that this disinflation has no impact on total output. As a consequence, inflation can be costlessly reduced. The price level is sticky in Taylor's specification, but the rate at which it changes, the rate of inflation, is not. The backward-looking aspect of price behavior causes unanticipated reductions in the *level* of the money supply to cause real output declines. Prices set previously are too high relative to the new path for the money supply; only as contracts expire can their real value be reduced to levels consistent with the new lower money supply. However, as Ball (1994a) has shown, price rigidities based on such backward-looking behavior need not imply that policies to reduce inflation by reducing the *growth rate* of money will cause a recession. Since m continues to grow, just at a slower rate, the real value of preset prices continues to be eroded, unlike the case of a level reduction in m.[10]

Quadratic Costs of Price Changes

Rotemberg (1982) modeled the sluggish adjustment of prices by assuming that firms faced quadratic costs of making price changes. Unlike the Taylor model, the Rotemberg model assumed all firms could adjust their price each period, but because of the adjustment costs, they would only close partially any gap between their current price and the optimal price.[11]

---

10. For example, when the policy to reduce inflation from π_1 to π_2 is announced in period $t - 1$, $E_{t-1}\pi_t$ falls. For a given level of output, this decline would reduce π_{t-1}. If the policymaker acts to keep inflation at the time of the announcement (i.e., π_{t-1}) unchanged, output must rise.

11. Ireland (2004) provided a recent example of a model employing quadratic costs of adjusting prices.

Suppose, for example, that the desired price of firm j depends on the aggregate average price level and a measure of real economic activity. As with the sticky information model of chapter 5, assume the firm's desired price in log terms is given by

$$p_t^*(j) = p_t + \alpha x_t. \tag{6.18}$$

Furthermore, assume profits are a decreasing quadratic function of the deviation of the firm's actual log price from $p_t^*(j)$:

$$\Pi_t(j) = -\delta[p_t(j) - p_t^*(j)]^2 = -\delta[p_t(j) - p_t - \alpha x_t]^2.$$

The costs of adjusting price are also quadratic and equal to

$$c_t(j) = \phi[p_t(j) - p_{t-1}(j)]^2.$$

Each period, firm j chooses $p_t(j)$ to maximize

$$\sum_{i=0}^{\infty} \beta^i E_t[\Pi_{t+i}(j) - c_{t+i}(j)].$$

The first-order condition for the firm's problem is

$$-\delta[p_t(j) - p_t^*(j)] - \phi[p_t(j) - p_{t-1}(j)] + \beta\phi[E_t p_{t+1}(j) - p_t(j)] = 0.$$

Since all firms are identical, $p_t(j) = p_t(s) = p_t$, and one can rewrite this first-order condition in terms of inflation as

$$\pi_t = \beta E_t \pi_{t+1} + \left(\frac{\alpha\delta}{\phi}\right) x_t. \tag{6.19}$$

Actual inflation depends on the real activity variable x_t and expected future inflation. Because firms are concerned with their price relative to other firms' prices, and they recognize that future price changes are costly, the price they set at time t is higher if they anticipate higher inflation in the future. The expression for inflation given by (6.19) is very similar to those obtained from other models of price stickiness (see following sections), particularly in the role given to expected future inflation.[12] Ireland (1997a; 2001a) estimated a general equilibrium model of inflation and output that is based on quadratic costs of adjusting prices.[13]

---

12. This is a point made by Roberts (1995).

13. Ireland (2001a) also introduced quadratic costs of changing the inflation rate to capture the idea that inflation might be sticky. His empirical results support the hypothsis that prices are sticky but inflation is not. However, in his model, the persistence of inflation that is observed in the data is attributed to persistence in the exogenous shocks rather than to large costs of adjustment.

However, while the assumption that firms face quadratic costs of adjusting prices provides a very tractable specification that leads to a simple expression for inflation, the quadratic cost formulation has not been as widely used as the models discussed in section 6.2.4. The more common approach has been to imbed sticky prices into an explicit model of monopolistic competition, to assume not all firms adjust prices each period, and consequently to allow prices to differ across firms. In contrast, the quadratic cost model, in its basic form, assumes all firms adjust prices every period and so set the same price. The microeconomic evidence (see section 6.3.1) is not consistent with models in which all firms adjust prices every period.

6.2.3 Imperfect Competition

A common argument is that nominal rigidities arise because of small *menu costs*, essentially fixed costs, associated with changing wages or prices. As economic conditions change, a firm's *optimal* price will also change, but if there are fixed costs of changing prices, it may not be optimal for the firm to adjust its price continually to economic changes. Only if the firm's actual price diverges sufficiently from the equilibrium price will it be worthwhile to bear the fixed cost and adjust prices. The macroeconomic implications of menu cost models were first explored by Akerlof and Yellen (1985) and Mankiw (1985) and were surveyed by D. Romer (2006, ch. 7). Ball and Romer (1991) showed how small menu costs can interact with imperfect competition in either goods or labor markets to amplify the impact of monetary disturbances, create strategic complementaries, and lead potentially to multiple equilibria. While menu costs rationalize sluggish price-setting behavior, such costs may seem implausible as the reason that monetary disturbances have significant real effects. After all, adjusting production is also costly, and it is difficult to see why shutting down an assembly line is less costly than reprinting price catalogs. And computers have lowered the cost of changing prices for most retail establishments, although it seems unlikely that this has had an important effect on the ability of monetary authorities to have short-run real effects on the economy. Money seems to matter in important ways because of nominal rigidities, but there is no satisfactory integration of microeconomic models of nominal adjustment with monetary models of macroeconomic equilibrium.

A problem with simply introducing price or wage stickiness into an otherwise competitive model is that any sort of nominal rigidity naturally raises the question of who is setting wages and prices, a question the perfectly competitive model begs. To address the issue of price setting, one must examine models that incorporate some aspect of imperfect competition, such as monopolistic competition.

A Basic Model of Monopolistic Competition
To explore the implications of nominal rigidities, a basic model that incorporates monopolistic competition among intermediate goods producers is developed. Exam-

ples of similar models include Blanchard and Kiyotaki (1987); Ball and Romer (1991); Beaudry and Devereux (1995); and R. King and Watson (1996). Imperfect competition can lead to aggregate demand externalities (Blanchard and Kiyotaki 1987), equilibria in which output is inefficiently low, and multiple equilibria (Ball and Romer 1991; Rotemberg and Woodford 1995), but imperfect competition alone does not lead to monetary non-neutrality. If prices are free to adjust, one-time permanent changes in the level of the money supply induce proportional changes in all prices, leaving the real equilibrium unaffected. Price stickiness remains critical to generating significant real effects of money. The present example follows Chari, Kehoe, and McGrattan (2000), and in the following section, price stickiness is added by assuming that intermediate goods producers engage in multiperiod staggered price setting.

Let Y_t be the output of the final good; it is produced using inputs of the intermediate goods according to

$$Y_t = \left[\int Y_t(i)^q \, di \right]^{1/q}, \qquad 0 < q \leq 1, \tag{6.20}$$

where $Y_t(i)$ is the input of intermediate good i. Firms producing final goods operate in competitive output markets and maximize profits given by $P_t Y_t - \int P_t(i) Y_t(i) \, di$, where P_t is the price of final output and $P_t(i)$ is the price of input i. The first-order conditions for profit maximization by final goods producers yield the following demand function for intermediate good i:

$$Y_t^d(i) = \left[\frac{P_t}{P_t(i)} \right]^{1/(1-q)} Y_t. \tag{6.21}$$

Final goods firms earn zero profit as long as

$$P_t = \left[\int P_t(i)^{q/(q-1)} \, di \right]^{(q-1)/q}.$$

Each intermediate good is produced according to a constant-returns-to-scale Cobb-Douglas production function:

$$Y_t(i) = K_t(i)^a L_t(i)^{1-a}, \tag{6.22}$$

where K and L denote capital and labor inputs purchased in competitive factor markets at prices r and W. The producer of good $Y(i)$ chooses $P(i)$, $K(i)$, and $L(i)$ to maximize profits subject to the demand function (6.21) and the production function (6.22). Intermediate profits are equal to

$$\Pi_t(i) = P_t(i)\, Y_t(i) - r_t K_t(i) - W_t L_t(i)$$

$$= [P_t(i) - P_t V_t]\left[\frac{P_t}{P_t(i)}\right]^{1/(1-q)} Y_t, \tag{6.23}$$

where V_t is equal to minimized unit costs of production (so $P_t V_t$ is nominal unit cost). The first-order condition for the value of $P_t(i)$ that maximizes profits for the intermediate goods producing firm is

$$\left[\frac{P_t}{P_t(i)}\right]^{1/(1-q)} Y_t - \frac{1}{1-q}[P_t(i) - P_t V_t]\left[\frac{P_t}{P_t(i)}\right]^{(2-q)/(1-q)}\left(\frac{1}{P_t}\right) Y_t = 0.$$

After some rearranging, this yields

$$P_t(i) = \frac{P_t V_t}{q}. \tag{6.24}$$

Thus, the price of intermediate good i is set as a constant markup $1/q$ over unit nominal costs PV.

For the intermediate goods producers, labor demand involves setting

$$\frac{W_t}{P_t(i)} = q\left[\frac{(1-\alpha)\, Y_t(i)}{L_t(i)}\right], \tag{6.25}$$

where W_t is the nominal wage rate and $(1-\alpha)\, Y_t(i)/L_t(i)$ is the marginal product of labor. In a symmetric equilibrium, all intermediate firms charge the same relative price, employ the same labor and capital inputs, and produce at the same level, so $P_t(i) = P_t(j) = P_t$, and (6.25) implies

$$L_t = \frac{q(1-\alpha)\, Y_t}{W_t/P_t}. \tag{6.26}$$

Firms will be concerned with their relative price, not the absolute price level, so money remains neutral. As (6.25) and (6.26) show, proportional changes in all nominal prices (i.e., $P(i)$, P, and W) leave firm $i's$ optimal relative price and aggregate labor demand unaffected. If the household's decision problem is not altered from the earlier analysis, consumption, labor supply, and investment decisions would not be altered by proportional changes in all nominal prices and the nominal stock of money.[14]

---

14. The household's budget constraint is altered because real profits of the intermediate goods producers must be paid out to households. However, as (6.23) shows, nominal profits are homogeneous of degree 1 in prices, so their real value will be homogeneous of degree 0. Thus, proportional changes in the nominal money stock and all prices leave the household's budget constraint unaffected.

To complete the specification of the model, the aggregate demand for labor given by (6.26) must be equated to the aggregate labor supply derived from the outcome of household choices. In the flexible-price models examined so far, labor market equilibrium with competitive factor markets required that the marginal rate of substitution between leisure and consumption be equal to the real wage, which, in turn, was equal to the marginal product of labor. With imperfect competition, (6.26) shows that q drives a wedge between the real wage and the marginal product of labor.[15] Thus, labor market equilibrium requires that

$$\frac{U_l}{U_c} = \frac{W}{P} = q\text{MPL} \leq \text{MPL}. \tag{6.27}$$

If the model is linearized around the steady state, q drops out of the labor market equilibrium condition because of the way in which it enters multiplicatively.

This example of a model of monopolistic competition assumed flexible prices (and wages). The basic structure of this example is used to explore alternative models of nominal rigidities.

6.2.4   Time-Dependent Pricing (TDP) Models

An important class of models treats the adjustment of prices (and wages) as depending on time but not on the state of the economy. That is, they assume the probability that a firm adjusts its price does not depend on whether there have been big shocks since the price was last changed or whether inflation has been high or low since the last adjustment. Instead, this probability may depend simply on how many periods since the firm last adjusted its price, or the probability of adjustment might be the same, regardless of how long it has been since the last price change or how economic conditions may have changed. The Taylor model discussed earlier is an example of a time-dependent pricing (TDP) model. Time-dependent models of price adjustment are more tractable than models in which the decision to change price depends on the state of the economy. As a consequence, time-dependent models are very popular and are the basis of most models employed for policy analysis. State-dependent models are discussed in section 6.2.5.[16]

The Taylor Model Revisited

Taylor (1979; 1980) argued that the presence of multiperiod nominal contracts, with only a fraction of wages or prices negotiated each period, could generate the type of real output persistence in response to monetary shocks observed in the data. When

---

15. In their calibrations, Chari, Kehoe, and McGrattan used a value of 0.9 for q.

16. The focus of this section is on models of price adjustment; similar models have been applied to explain the adjustment of nominal wages. Chapter 8 examines the implications of incorporating both sticky prices and sticky wages into a general equilibrium model.

setting a price during period t that will remain in effect for several periods, a firm will base its decisions on its expectations of conditions in future periods. But the aggregate price level will also depend on those prices set in earlier periods that are still in effect. This imparts both forward-looking and backward-looking aspects to the aggregate price level and, as Taylor showed, provides a framework capable of replicating aggregate dynamics.

To develop a simple example based on Chari, Kehoe, and McGrattan (2000) and their model of monopolistic competition (see section 6.2.3), suppose that each intermediate goods producing firm sets its price $P(i)$ for two periods, with half of all firms adjusting in each period.[17] Thus, if $i \in [0, 0.5)$, assume that $P(i)$ is set in period t, $t + 2$, $t + 4$, and so on. If $i \in [0.5, 1]$, the firm sets prices in periods $t + 1$, $t + 3$, and so on. Since only symmetric equilibria are considered in which all firms setting prices at time t pick the same price, one can drop the index i and let $\bar{P}_{t+j}$ denote the intermediate goods price set in period $t + j$ for periods $t + j$ and $t + j + 1$.

Consider a firm i setting its price in period t. This price will be in effect for periods t and $t + 1$. Thus, if R_t is the gross interest rate, $\bar{P}_t$ will be chosen to maximize

$$
E_t\left[(\bar{P}_t - P_t V_t)\left(\frac{P_t}{\bar{P}_t}\right)^{1/(1-q)} Y_t + R_t^{-1}(\bar{P}_t - P_{t+1}V_{t+1})\left(\frac{P_{t+1}}{\bar{P}_t}\right)^{1/(1-q)} Y_{t+1}\right],
$$

which represents the expected discounted profits over periods t and $t + 1$.[18] After some manipulation of the first-order condition, one obtains

$$
\bar{P}_t = \frac{E_t(P_t^{\theta} V_t Y_t + R_t^{-1} P_{t+1}^{\theta} V_{t+1} Y_{t+1})}{q E_t(P_t^{1/(1-q)} Y_t + R_t^{-1} P_{t+1}^{1/(1-q)} Y_{t+1})}, \tag{6.28}
$$

where $\theta = (2 - q)/(1 - q)$. If prices are set for only one period, the terms involving $t + 1$ drop out, and one obtains the earlier pricing equation (6.24).

What does (6.28) imply about aggregate price adjustment? Let $\bar{p}$, p, and v denote percentage deviations of $\bar{P}$, P, and V around a zero inflation steady state. If discounting is ignored, for simplicity, (6.28) can be approximated in terms of percentage deviations around the steady state as

$$
\bar{p}_t = \frac{1}{2}(p_t + E_t p_{t+1}) + \frac{1}{2}(v_t + E_t v_{t+1}). \tag{6.29}
$$

17. This is a form of time-dependent pricing; prices are set for a fixed length of time, regardless of economic conditions.

18. Chari, Kehoe, and McGrattan (2000) considered situations in which a fraction $1/N$ of all firms set prices each period for N periods. They then varied N to examine its role in affecting aggregate dynamics. They altered the interpretation of the time period so that N always corresponds to one year; thus, varying N alters the degree of staggering. They concluded that N has little effect.

The average price of the final good, expressed in terms of deviations from the steady state, is $p_t = \frac{1}{2}(\bar{p}_{t-1} + \bar{p}_t)$, where $\bar{p}_{t-1}$ is the price of intermediate goods set at time $t-1$ and $\bar{p}_t$ is the price set in period t. Similarly, $E_t p_{t+1} = \frac{1}{2}(\bar{p}_t + \bar{p}_{t+1})$. Substituting these expressions into the equation for $\bar{p}_t$ yields

$$\bar{p}_t = \frac{1}{2}\bar{p}_{t-1} + \frac{1}{2}E_t\bar{p}_{t+1} + (v_t + E_t v_{t+1}).$$

This reveals the backward-looking (via the presence of $\bar{p}_{t-1}$) and forward-looking (via the presence of $E_t\bar{p}_{t+1}$ and $E_t v_{t+1}$) nature of price adjustment.

The variable v_t is the deviation of minimized unit costs from its steady state. Suppose this is proportional to output: $v_t = \gamma y_t$.[19] If one further assumes a simple money demand equation of the form $m_t - p_t = y_t$, then

$$\bar{p}_t = \frac{1}{2}\bar{p}_{t-1} + \frac{1}{2}E_t\bar{p}_{t+1} + \gamma(y_t + E_t y_{t+1})$$

$$= \frac{1}{2}\bar{p}_{t-1} + \frac{1}{2}E_t\bar{p}_{t+1} + \gamma(m_t - p_t + E_t m_{t+1} - E_t p_{t+1})$$

$$= \frac{1}{2}\left(\frac{1-\gamma}{1+\gamma}\right)(\bar{p}_{t-1} + E_t\bar{p}_{t+1}) + \left(\frac{\gamma}{1+\gamma}\right)(m_t + E_t m_{t+1}). \tag{6.30}$$

This is a difference equation in $\bar{p}$. It implies that the behavior of prices set during period t will depend on prices set during the previous period, on prices expected to be set during the next period, and on the path of the nominal money supply over the two periods during which $\bar{p}_t$ will be in effect. For the case in which m_t follows a random walk (so that $E_t m_{t+1} = m_t$), the solution for $\bar{p}_t$ is

$$\bar{p}_t = a\bar{p}_{t-1} + (1-a)m_t, \tag{6.31}$$

where $a = (1 - \sqrt{\gamma})/(1 + \sqrt{\gamma})$ is the root less than 1 of $a^2 - 2(1+\gamma)a/(1-\gamma) + 1 = 0$.[20] Since the aggregate price level is an average of prices set at t and $t-1$,

$$p_t = \frac{1}{2}(\bar{p}_t + \bar{p}_{t-1}) = ap_{t-1} + \frac{1}{2}(1-a)(m_t + m_{t-1}). \tag{6.32}$$

Taylor (1979; 1980) demonstrated that a price adjustment equation of the form given by (6.32) is capable of mimicking the dynamic response of U.S. prices.[21] The

---

19. The coefficient γ will depend on the elasticity of labor supply with respect to the real wage. See Chari, Kehoe, and McGrattan (2000).

20. See problem 4 at the end of this chapter.

21. Taylor's actual model was based on nominal wage adjustment rather than price adjustment as presented here.

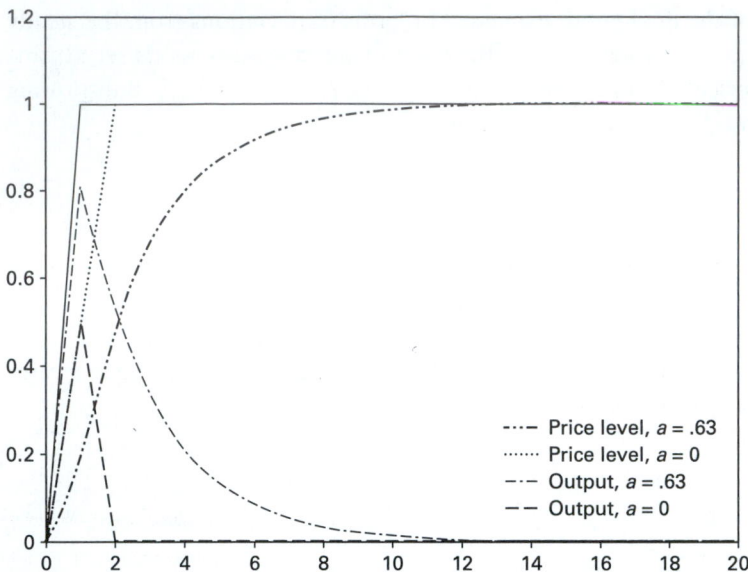

Figure 6.1
Effects of a money shock with staggered price adjustment.

response, however, depends critically on the value of a (which, in turn, depends on γ). Figure 6.1 shows the response of the price level and output for $\gamma = 1$ $(a = 0)$ and $\gamma = 0.05$ $(a = 0.63)$. This latter value is the one that Taylor found matches U.S. data, and, as the figure shows, an unexpected, permanent increase in the nominal money supply produces a rise in output with a slow adjustment back to the baseline, mirrored by a gradual rise in the price level. Though the model assumes that prices are set for only two periods, the money shock leads to a persistent long-lasting effect on output with this value of γ.

Chari, Kehoe, and McGrattan assumed that employment must be consistent with household labor supply choices, and they showed that γ is a function of the parameters of the representative agent's utility function. They argued that a very high labor supply elasticity is required to obtain a value of γ on the order of 0.05. With a low labor supply elasticity, as seems more plausible, γ will be greater than or equal to 1. If $\gamma = 1$, $a = 0$ and the figure suggests the Taylor model is not capable of capturing realistic adjustment to monetary shocks. Ascari (2000) reached similar conclusions in a model that is similar to the framework in Chari, Kehoe, and McGrattan (2000) but that follows Taylor's original work in making wages sticky rather than prices. However, rather than drawing the implication that staggered price (or wage) adjustment is unimportant for price dynamics, the assumption that observed employment is consistent with the labor supply behavior implied by the model of the household can be questioned. Models that interpret observed employment as tracing out a labor supply function typically have difficulty matching other aspects of labor market behavior (Christiano and Eichenbaum 1992b).

Calvo's Model

An alternative model of staggered price adjustment is due to Calvo (1983). He assumed that firms adjust their prices infrequently, and that opportunities to adjust arrive as an exogenous Poisson process. Each period, there is a constant probability $1 - \omega$ that the firm can adjust its price; the expected time between price adjustments is $1/(1 - \omega)$.[22] Because these adjustment opportunities occur randomly, the interval between price changes for an individual firm is a random variable.

The popularity of the Calvo specification is due, in part, to its tractability. This arises from two aspects of the model. First, all firms that adjust their price at time t set the same prices. And since the firms that do not adjust represent a random sample of all firms, the average price of the firms that do not adjust is simply P_{t-1}, last period's average price across all firms. Thus, rather than needing to keep track of the prices of firms that do not adjust, one need only know the average price level in the previous period.

When firm i has an opportunity to reset its price, it will do so to maximize the expected present discounted value of profits,

$$E_t \sum_{j=0}^{\infty} \beta^j \Pi_{t+j}(i) = E_t \sum_{j=0}^{\infty} \beta^j [P_{t+j}(i) - P_{t+j} V_{t+j}] \left[\frac{P_{t+j}}{P_{t+j}(i)}\right]^{1/(1-q)} Y_{t+j}, \qquad (6.33)$$

where V_t is the real marginal cost of production and (6.21), the demand curve faced by the individual firm, has been used. All adjusting firms are the same, so each will choose the same price to maximize profits subject to the assumed process for determining when the firm will next be able to adjust. Let P_t^* denote the optimal price. If only the terms in (6.33) involving the price set at time t are written out, they are

$$[P_t^* - P_t V_t]\left[\frac{P_t}{P_t^*}\right]^{1/(1-q)} Y_t + \omega\beta E_t [P_t^* - P_{t+1} V_{t+1}]\left[\frac{P_{t+1}}{P_t^*}\right]^{1/(1-q)} Y_{t+1}$$

$$+ \omega^2\beta^2 E_t [P_t^* - P_{t+2} V_{t+2}]\left[\frac{P_{t+2}}{P_t^*}\right]^{1/(1-q)} Y_{t+2} + \cdots,$$

---

22. For a firm that can adjust its price, the expected number of periods before adjusting again is one with probability $1 - \omega$, two with probability $\omega(1 - \omega)$, three with probability $\omega^2(1 - \omega)$, etc. Hence, the expected duration between price changes will be

$$(1 - \omega) + 2\omega(1 - \omega) + 3\omega^2(1 - \omega) + \cdots = \frac{1}{1 - \omega}.$$

or

$$\sum_{j=0}^{\infty} \omega^j \beta^j E_t[P_t^* - P_{t+j}V_{t+j}] \left[\frac{P_{t+j}}{P_t^*}\right]^{1/(1-q)} Y_{t+j},$$

since ω^j is the probability that the firm has not adjusted after j periods so that the price set at t still holds in $t + j$. Thus, the first-order condition for the optimal choice of P_t^* requires that

$$\left(\frac{q}{1-q}\right) E_t \sum_{j=0}^{\infty} \omega^j \beta^j \left[\left(\frac{P_t^*}{P_{t+j}}\right) - \left(\frac{1}{q}\right) V_{t+j}\right] \left(\frac{1}{P_t^*}\right) \left(\frac{P_{t+j}}{P_t^*}\right)^{1/(1-q)} Y_{t+j} = 0. \tag{6.34}$$

(6.34) can be rearranged to yield

$$\left(\frac{P_t^*}{P_t}\right) = \left(\frac{1}{q}\right) \frac{E_t \sum_{j=0}^{\infty} \omega^j \beta^j V_{t+j} \left(\frac{P_{t+j}}{P_t}\right)^{1/(1-q)} Y_{t+j}}{E_t \sum_{j=0}^{\infty} \omega^j \beta^j \left(\frac{P_{t+j}}{P_t}\right)^{q/(1-q)} Y_{t+j}}. \tag{6.35}$$

To interpret (6.35), note that if prices are perfectly flexible ($\omega = 0$), then

$$\left(\frac{P_t^*}{P_t}\right) = \left(\frac{1}{q}\right) V_t,$$

and the firm desires to set its real price as a constant markup over real marginal cost. Since all firms set the same price, $P_t^* = P_t$ in an equilibrium with flexible prices and real marginal cost is equal to q. When $\omega > 0$ so that not all firms adjust each period, a firm that can adjust will take into account expected future marginal costs when setting its price. The more rigid prices are (the larger is ω), the more pricing decisions are based on expected future marginal costs since firms expect more time to pass before having another opportunity to adjust.

With a large number of firms, a fraction $1 - \omega$ will actually adjust their price each period, and the aggregate average price level can be expressed as a weighted average of the prices set by those firms that adjust and the average price of the firms that do not adjust. The latter, as previously noted, is P_{t-1}.

The Calvo model of sticky prices is commonly employed in the new Keynesian models that have come to dominate monetary policy analysis; these models form the subject of chapter 8. The chapter 8 appendix shows that the Calvo model, when approximated around a zero average inflation steady-state equilibrium, yields an expression for aggregate inflation of the form

$$\pi_t = \beta E_t \pi_{t+1} + \kappa \hat{v}_t, \tag{6.36}$$

where

$$\kappa = \frac{(1 - \omega)(1 - \beta\omega)}{\omega} \tag{6.37}$$

is an increasing function of the fraction of firms able to adjust each period and $\hat{v}_t$ is real marginal cost, expressed as a percentage deviation around its steady-state value. Equation (6.36) is called the new Keynesian Phillips curve.

Comparing this to the inflation equation from Taylor's model, (6.17), shows them to be quite similar. Current inflation depends on expectations of future inflation and on current output. One difference is that in deriving an inflation equation based on Calvo's specification, expected future inflation has a coefficient equal to the discount factor $\beta < 1$. In deriving an expression for inflation using Taylor's specification, however, discounting was ignored in (6.15), the equation giving the value of the contract wage. A further difference between the Taylor model and the Calvo model was highlighted by Kiley (2002). He showed that Taylor-type staggered adjustment models display less persistence than the Calvo-type partial adjustment model when both are calibrated to produce the same average frequency of price changes. Under the Taylor model, for example, suppose contracts are negotiated every two periods. The average frequency of wage changes is one-half—half of all wages adjust each period—and no wage remains fixed for more than two periods. In contrast, suppose $\omega = 1/2$ in the Calvo model. The expected time between price changes is two periods, so on average, prices are adjusted every two periods. However, many prices will remain fixed for more than two periods. For instance, $\omega^3 = 0.125$ of all prices remain fixed for at least three periods. In general, the Calvo model implies that there is a tail of the distribution of prices that consists of prices that have remained fixed for many periods, whereas the Taylor model implies that no wages remain fixed for longer than the duration of the longest contract.

One attractive aspect of Calvo's model is that it shows how the coefficient on output in the inflation equation depends on the frequency with which prices are adjusted. A rise in ω, which means that the average time between price changes for an individual firm increases, causes κ in (8.17) to decrease. Output movements have a smaller impact on current inflation, holding expected future inflation constant. Because opportunities to adjust prices occur less often, current demand conditions become less important.

6.2.5   State-Dependent Pricing (SDP) Models

The Taylor and Calvo models assumed that pricing decisions were time-dependent. Recent research on nominal price adjustment has stressed the implications of state-dependent pricing (SDP) models of price adjustment. In contrast to the TDP models of Taylor or Calvo, the firms that adjust prices in a given period are not a random sample of all firms. Instead, the firms that choose to adjust will be those for whom adjustment is most profitable. The implications of this important difference can be illustrated through a simple example.

Suppose half of all firms happen to have a price of 1 and half have a price of 3. The aggregate average price is 2. Assume also that the money supply is 2. Now suppose the money supply doubles to 4. Assume that conditional on adjusting, firms would choose a price of 4. If firms are chosen at random to adjust, half the firms with prices equal to 1 and 3 will set their price at 4, while the other half will not adjust. The aggregate price level will now be $0.25 \times 1 + 0.25 \times 3 + 0.5 \times 4 = 3$. Real money balances rise to $4/3 = 1.33$. Now instead of choosing the firms that adjust randomly, suppose it is the firms furthest from the optimal price (4, in this example) that adjust. If there is a small fixed cost of adjusting, all firms with a price of 1 might find it optimal to adjust to 4 while none of the firms with a price of 3 would adjust. The aggregate average price would then be $0.5 \times 3 + 0.5 \times 4 = 3.5$ and real money balances only rise to $4/3.5 = 1.14$. This example emphasizes how the effects of a change in the nominal money supply on the real supply of money can depend critically on whether firms adjust at random, as in the Calvo specification, or based on how far the firm's current price is from the optimal price. The fact that the firms that adjust are more likely to be those furthest from their desired price is called the selection effect by Golosov and Lucas (2007). This effect acts to make the aggregate price level more flexible than might be suggested by simply looking at the fraction of firms that change price.[23]

SDP models allow price behavior to be influenced by an intensive and an extensive margin: after a large shock, those firms that adjust will make, on average, bigger adjustments (this is the intensive margin), *and* more firms will adjust (this is the extensive margin). A number of papers beginning in the 1970s examined the implications of state-dependent pricing models, but the focus here is on the recent generation of SDP models.[24]

As noted earlier, SDP models are generally less tractable than TDP models, thus accounting for their less frequent use. And prior to the availability of microeconomic

23. Caplin and Spulber (1987) were one of the first to demonstrate how the dynamic response of output to money would differ under SDP compared to TDP. They showed that SDP could restore monetary neutrality even in the presence of menu costs. Their model setup was similar to models used in transportation economics to address the following question: If adding traffic to a road increases wear and tear on the road, does average road quality decline with an increase in traffic? If road repairs are done on a fixed schedule (a time-dependent strategy), the answer is yes. If repair work is state-dependent, then an increase in traffic leads to more frequent scheduling of repair work and average quality remains unchanged.

24. Dotsey and King (2005) provided an overview of the aggregate implications of some of the earlier SDP models. Caballero and Engle (2007) argued that it is the presence of an extensive margin, not the selection effect, that accounts for the greater flexibility of the aggregate price level in SDP models.

data on price changes (see section 6.3.1), TDP models were seen as adequate for modeling aggregate phenomena. SDP models are closely related to Ss models of inventory behavior; as long as the firm's price remains in a region close to the optimal price, no adjustment occurs, but whenever the price hits an upper (S) or lower (s) boundary of this region, the firm changes its price. Ss models have proven difficult to aggregate, so SDP models generally impose assumptions on the distribution of adjustment costs or the distribution of shocks to obtain tractable solutions.

Dotsey, King, and Wolman

Dotsey, King, and Wolman (1999) assumed that firms face a cost of price adjustment that is stochastic and differs across firms and time. Each period firms receive a new realization of the cost. Thus, expected costs are the same for all firms, so each firm that does decide to adjust its price will choose the same price. Dotsey, King, and Wolman (DKW) define a vintage j firm as a firm that last adjusted its price j periods ago. Let θ_{jt} be the fraction of firms of vintage j. Since all vintage j firms adjusted at the same time, they all have the same price. Among the firms of vintage j, there will be a critical fixed cost such that all firms with smaller fixed costs adjust and those with larger fixed costs do not. Let α_{jt} be the fraction of vintage j firms that adjust price. Then, in period $t+1$, the fraction of firms that become vintage $j+1$ is equal to $1 - \alpha_{jt}$ times the fraction that were of vintage j in period t:

$$\theta_{j+1,t+1} = (1 - \alpha_{jt})\theta_{jt} \equiv \omega_{jt},$$

and the fraction of all firms that do adjust in period t is equal to

$$\omega_{0t} = \sum_{j=1}^{J} \alpha_{jt}\theta_{jt},$$

where J is the maximum number of periods any firm has not adjusted its price.[25] Prices of each vintage j are weighted by ω_{jt} in forming the aggregate average price level.

Let $v_{j,t}$ be the value function for a firm of vintage j at time t. Then, the value functions for firms that do adjust their price at time t, $v_{0,t}$, takes the form

$$v_{0,t} = \max_{P_t^*} \left\{ [P_t^* - P_t V_t] \left[\frac{P_t}{P_t^*}\right]^{1/(1-q)} Y_t + \beta E_t(1 - \alpha_{1,t+1})v_{1,t+1} \right.$$

$$\left. + \beta E_t \alpha_{1,t+1} v_{0,t+1} - \beta E_t \Xi_{1,t+1} \right\},$$

---

25. In the Calvo model, $\alpha_{jt} = 1 - \omega$ for all j and t, and $J = \infty$. In the Taylor model, J is equal to the length of the longest contract.

where current period profit is written as in (6.33) and $E_t \Xi_{1,t+1}$ is the present value of next period's adjustment costs. Notice that with probability $1 - \alpha_{1,t+1}$ the firm does not adjust at $t + 1$ and so becomes a vintage 1 firm, and with probability $\alpha_{1,t+1}$ the firm does adjust at $t + 1$ and remains a vintage 0 firm.

For nonadjusting firms of vintage j,

$$v_{j,t} = \left\{ [P^*_{t-j} - P_t V_t] \left[\frac{P_t}{P^*_{t-j}} \right]^{1/(1-q)} Y_t + \beta E_t (1 - \alpha_{j+1,t+1}) v_{j+1,t+1} \right.$$

$$\left. + \beta E_t \alpha_{j+1,t+1} v_{0,t+1} - \beta E_t \Xi_{j+1,t+1} \right\}$$

because such firms optimally set their price in period $t - j$.

Suppose $w_t \xi$ is the randomly distributed fixed cost of changing price expressed in terms of labor costs, where w_t is the wage. Then a vintage j firm will change its price if

$$v_{0,t} - v_{jt} \geq w_t \xi.$$

If G is the distribution function of the costs, then the fraction of vintage j firms that change price is just the fraction of firms whose fixed cost realization is less than $(v_{0,t} - v_{jt})/w_t$. Hence,

$$\alpha_{jt} = G\left(\frac{v_{0,t} - v_{jt}}{w_t} \right).$$

If the value of adjusting as measured by $v_{0,t} - v_{jt}$ is high, more firms of the same vintage will pay the fixed cost to adjust. The expected adjustment costs next period for a vintage j firm are equal to the expected value of $w_{t+1} \xi$, conditional on ξ being less than or equal to $(v_{0,t+1} - v_{j+1,t+1})/w_{t+1}$ so that the firm finds it optimal to adjust. Thus,

$$\Xi_{j,t+1} = E_t \left(w_{t+1} \int_0^{G^{-1}(\alpha_{j+1,t+1})} \xi g(\xi)\, dx \right),$$

where $g(\xi) = G'(\xi)$ is the density function of ξ.

If current profits for firms adjusting at time t are denoted by $\Pi_{0,t}$, then the first-order condition for optimal pricing, conditional on adjusting, is

$$\frac{\partial \Pi_{0,t}}{\partial P^*_t} + \beta E_t \left[\frac{\partial (1 - \alpha_{1,t+1}) v_{1,t+1}}{\partial P^*_t} \right] = 0.$$

The impact of P^*_t on current profits is balanced against the effect on future profits, weighted by the probability the firm does not adjust next period. This probability is no longer fixed, as in the Calvo model, but is endogenous.

Dotsey and King (2005) compared the response of the price level and inflation to a monetary shock in the DKW model and in a model with fixed probabilities of adjustment. Interestingly, the two variants display similar responses for the first several periods after the shock. However, as the price level adjusts, more firms now find themselves with prices that are far from the optimal level. In the SDP model of DKW, this leads more firms to change their price, whereas in a Calvo model, the fraction of adjusting firms remains constant.

Firm-Specific Shocks

Most models of price adjustment developed for use in macroeconomics have assumed that firms only face aggregate shocks. This generally implies that all firms that do adjust their price choose the same new price because they all face the same (aggregate) shock. The DKW model features firm-specific shocks to the menu cost, but these shocks only influence whether a firm adjusts, not how much it changes price. In contrast, Golosov and Lucas (2007) and Gertler and Leahy (2008) emphasized the role of idiosyncratic shocks in influencing which firms adjust price and in generating a distribution of prices across firms.

Gertler and Leahy's Ss Model

Gertler and Leahy (2008) developed an Ss model with monopolistically competitive firms located on separate islands, of which there exists a continuum of mass unity. Each island has a continuum of households that can supply labor only on the island on which they live. An island receives a productivity shock with probability $1 - \alpha$. These shocks affect all firms on the island but are independent across islands. There is, however, perfect consumption insurance, so consumption is the same across all islands, and firm profits are distributed to households via lump-sum transfers.

Suppose island z is hit by such a shock. Then, a randomly chosen fraction $1 - \tau$ of the firms on the island disappear. These firms are replaced by new entrants to maintain a constant number of firms on the island. New entrants can optimally set their price. The surviving old firms (there are a fraction τ of such firms) experience independent and identically distributed productivity shocks. These shocks are uniformly distributed.

Gertler and Leahy incorporated two types of fixed costs of adjusting. First, there is a decision cost. If the firm pays this cost, it can then decide whether to adjust its price. The cost can be thought of as capturing the time and effort necessary to evaluate the firm's pricing strategy. If this cost is paid, and the firm decides to adjust its price, then there is a fixed menu cost associated with changing price. Optimal pricing policy takes the form of an Ss rule.

An exact solution is not possible, but an approximate analytical solution can be obtained as a local expansion around a zero inflation steady state. Obtaining a log-linear approximation is difficult because there is a discontinuity in the adjustment of firms near the Ss boundary. For a firm near the top that does not receive an idiosyncratic shock, an aggregate shock of one sign would push it to the barrier and result in an adjustment while the same size aggregate shock with opposite sign would move the firm into the interior of the region of inaction. The role of the decision cost is to deal with this problem. Given the necessity of paying this cost, and if aggregate shocks are also small relative to idiosyncratic shocks, the α fraction of firms that do not receive an idiosyncratic shock do not adjust price. This leads to smooth behavior around the boundaries of the Ss region.

All firms that change their price choose the same markup over real marginal cost, and they do so to ensure that the expected (log) markup is equal to the steady-state markup:

$$E_t \sum_{i=0}^{\infty} (\alpha\beta)^i \ln \mu_{t+i} = \ln \bar{\mu},$$

where $\bar{\mu}$ is the steady-state markup and μ_{t+i} is the actual markup in period $t+i$.[26] Notice that, as in the Calvo model, the future expected markups are discounted by β and the probability of not adjusting α, since only if the firm has not adjusted will future markups be influenced by the current pricing choice.

Aggregating across islands, Gertler and Leahy showed that the economywide inflation rate is given by

$$\pi_t = \beta E_t \pi_{t+1} + \bar{\kappa} \hat{v}_t, \tag{6.38}$$

where $\hat{v}_t$ is, as before, the log deviation of real marginal cost from its steady-state level. The elasticity of inflation with respect to real marginal cost is

$$\bar{\kappa} = \frac{(1-\alpha)(1-\alpha\beta)}{\alpha} \left[\frac{\mu-1}{(1+\varphi)\mu - 1} \right], \tag{6.39}$$

where φ is the inverse of the wage elasticity of labor supply. Comparing (6.38) and (6.39) to (6.36) and (6.37) reveals their close parallel. The first term in (6.39) is identical in form to the marginal cost elasticity of inflation in the Calvo model, with α, the probability that an island (and its firms) do not receive a productivity shock, replacing ω, the probability that a firm does not receive an opportunity to adjust price. The second term in (6.39) arises because of the assumption of local island-specific labor markets in Gertler and Leahy's model; if a similar assumption about the labor market were incorporated into the Calvo model, a similar term would appear in (6.37).

---

26. In terms of the notation employed earlier in the discussion of TDP models, $\mu = 1/q$.

To see how α is related to the probability that a firm adjusts its price, suppose $\ln \mu^H$ and $\ln \mu^L$ are the upper and lower values of the log markup that trigger price adjustment. Assume also that the firm-specific idiosyncratic shocks are uniformly distributed with mean zero and density $1/\phi$. Then, Gertler and Leahy showed,

$$1 - \omega = (1 - \alpha)\left[(1 - \tau) + \tau\left(1 - \frac{\ln \mu^H + \ln \mu^L}{\phi}\right)\right]. \tag{6.40}$$

To understand this equation, note that $1 - \alpha$ is the probability that an island has a productivity shock. Under the assumptions of the model, no firms on the remaining islands change their price. On the islands receiving productivity shocks, a fraction $1 - \tau$ of firms disappear and are replaced. All these new firms set new prices. The remaining τ fraction of firms only adjust if their current markup is above or below the Ss limits given by $\ln \mu^H$ and $\ln \mu^L$. The probability that this occurs is 1 minus the probability that the firm's idiosyncratic shock leaves its markup in the range $\ln \mu_L < \ln \mu_t < \ln \mu^L$. Given the uniform distribution, the probability of this occurring is $(\ln \mu^H + \ln \mu^L)/\phi$. So a fraction

$$\left(1 - \frac{\ln \mu^H + \ln \mu^L}{\phi}\right)$$

of the τ surviving firms choose to change price.

Notice that (6.40) can be rewritten as

$$1 - \omega = (1 - \alpha)\left[1 - \tau\left(\frac{\ln \mu^H + \ln \mu^L}{\phi}\right)\right] < 1 - \alpha,$$

which implies $\omega > \alpha$. This means that $\bar{\kappa} > \kappa$. Inflation will be more sensitive to real marginal cost with state-dependent pricing than implied by Calvo's time-dependent pricing model. In addition, the degree of nominal rigidity in this SDP model is directly related to α, the fraction of islands that do not receive productivity shocks. The variance of aggregate productivity will be $(1 - \alpha)^2$ times the variance of the firm-specific idiosyncratic shocks. Thus, if more sectors in the economy experience aggregate productivity shocks—a decline in α—the degree of nominal rigidity will fall.

6.2.6   Summary on Models of Price Adjustment

The last 20 years have seen an integration of models of sticky prices into general equilibrium models. The workhorse in this area remains the TDP model of Calvo because of its simplicity and ease of aggregation. However, recently a number of tractable SDP models have been developed, and this is an area of active research.

SDP models allow for time variation in the size of price changes, conditional on the firm changing its price (the intensive margin), variation in the number of firms that change their price in a given period (the extensive margin), and variation in the composition of firms that adjust (the selection effect). Costain and Nakov (2008) developed a generalized SDP model that nests both the TDP model of Calvo and the menu cost model of Golosov and Lucas. They did so by assuming the probability that a firm adjusts is a nondecreasing function of the value of adjusting. If this probability is constant, they obtained the Calvo model; if the probability is zero when the value of adjusting is nonpositive and 1 when the value is positive, they obtained the Golosov and Lucas model. They found that the best fit to the microeconomic data is obtained when the degree of state dependence is low.

6.3 Assessing Alternatives

In this section, the microeconomic and aggregate time series evidence on price adjustment and the behavior of inflation is briefly reviewed.

6.3.1 Microeconomic Evidence

One important consequence of the popularity of DSGE models based on sticky prices is that new work has been generated that employs microeconomic data on prices and wages. This work has employed evidence from surveys used to construct consumer price indexes to measure the frequency with which prices adjust. In turn, this evidence provides grounds for evaluating alternative models of price adjustment.

Bils and Klenow (2004) investigated price behavior for the United States for a large fraction of the goods and services that households purchase. They reported that the median duration between price changes is 4.3 months.[27] This median figure masks wide variation in the typical frequency with which prices of different categories of goods and services adjust. At one end, gasoline prices adjusted with high frequency, remaining unchanged for less then a month on average. In contrast, more than a year separated price changes for driver's licenses, vehicle inspections, and coin-operated laundry and dry cleaning.

Based on an analysis of the U.S. data used in the consumer and producer price indexes, Nakamura and Steinsson (2008) presented five facts that they argue characterize price adjustment. First, sales have a significant effect on estimates of the median duration between price changes for items in the U.S. CPI. Excluding price changes associated with sales roughly doubles the estimated median duration be-

---

27. Bils and Klenow focused on the nonshelter component of the consumer price index and weighted individual price durations by the good's expenditure share to obtain this median figure.

tween price changes from around 4.5 months when sales are included to 10 months when they are excluded. Models such as the TDP and SDP models discussed earlier focus on explaining aggregate inflation and ignore the role of sales. Second, one-third of nonsale price changes are price decreases. Third, the frequency of price increases is positively correlated with the inflation rate, whereas the frequency of price decreases and the size of price changes is not correlated with inflation. In fact, Nakamura and Steinsson concluded that most of the variation in the aggregate inflation rate can be accounted for by variations in the frequency of price increases. Fourth, the frequency of price changes follows a seasonal pattern. Price changes are more common during the first quarter of the year. Fifth, the probability that the price of an item changes (the hazard function) declines during the first few months after a change in price. This last fact is inconsistent with the Calvo model, which implies the probability that a firm changes its price is constant, independent of the time since the price was last changed. Nakamura and Steinsson concluded that while facts one through three are consistent with a standard menu cost models of price adjustment, facts four and five are not.

Klenow and Kryvtsov (2008) found, based on U.S. CPI data, somewhat greater frequency of price change (about seven months when sales are excluded) than did Nakamura and Steinsson. They also found that despite the tendency for price changes to be large on average, a significant fraction of the changes are small. This finding is inconsistent with a basic menu cost model with fixed cost of adjustment. Nakamura and Steinsson (2008) reported that the distribution of price change frequency is not symmetric; the average frequency is much higher than the median, suggesting that while many prices change frequently, there are some prices that remain unchanged for sizable periods of time. Klenow and Kryvtsov also found that variations in the size of price changes, rather than variations in the fraction of prices that change, can account for most of the variance of aggregate inflation. As Nakamura and Steinsson argued, this result is consistent with their finding that the variance of aggregate inflation is attributable to changes in the frequency of price increases, since the average size of price changes is a weighted average of the sizes of price increases and decreases with weights equal to the frequency of each type of change. Thus, the average size of price changes increases with an increase in the frequency of price increases or an increase in the average size of price increases.

Klenow and Kryvtsov (2007) compared the ability of the Calvo and Taylor TDP models and the Dotsey, King, and Wolman (DKW) and Golosov and Lucas SDP models to match the empirical evidence from the CPI microeconomic data. Of six microeconomic facts they considered, the Golosov-Lucas model matched all except the presence of many small price changes. The DKW model was able to match this fact because it allows for a stochastic menu cost that varies across firms. Thus, some firms will have small costs and therefore adjust price even when they are already close to the optimal price. However this model is not consistent with three of the other facts (flat hazard rates, size of price change does not increase with duration since last change, and intensive margin accounts for most of the variance of inflation). The Taylor model cannot match the flat hazard rates, nor does it imply that the size of price changes increases with the duration since the last change. This last fact is also not captured by the Calvo model. Surprisingly, this is the only one of the six facts with which the Calvo model, augmented with idiosyncratic firm shocks, is inconsistent. SDP models with idiosyncratic shocks and small menu costs, such as the model of Gertler and Leahy, or DKW augmented with idiosyncratic shocks (Dotsey, King, and Wolman 2006), seem most promising for matching the stylized facts found in the microeconomic evidence.[28]

Hobjin, Ravenna, and Tambalotti (2006) provided a direct test of models that assume price stickiness is attributable to menu costs by using the natural experiment provided by the switch to the euro in January 2002. They found that firms concentrated price changes around the time of the currency switch; prior to the changeover prices did not fully reflect increased marginal costs expected to occur after the adoption of the euro. They showed that a menu cost model augmented to allow for a state-dependent decision on when to adopt the euro successfully captured the behavior of restaurant prices.

While the work examining microeconomic evidence on pricing behavior has helped in assessing alternative models, it is not yet clear which aspects of that evidence are of greatest relevance for understanding macroeconomic phenomena such as the impact of monetary policy on aggregate inflation and real output. The development of microeconomic data sets has, however, greatly expanded our knowledge about the behavior of individual prices.

6.3.2 Evidence on the New Keynesian Phillips Curve

A large body of research has used time series methods to estimate the basic new Keynesian Phillips curve based on the Calvo model of price adjustment. This literature originated with the work of Galí and Gerter (1999) and is surveyed in Galí (2008). Three issues have been the focus of this work: measuring real marginal cost; reconciling time series estimates of the frequency of price adjustment with the microeconomic evidence; and accounting for persistence in the rate of inflation.

---

28. Álvarez et al. (2005) summarized microeconomic evidence from the European Inflation Persistence Network (IPN) project of the European Central Bank. Angeloni et al. (2006) compared this evidence with several models of price adjustment and concluded that "a basic Calvo model (possibly extended to allow for sectors with different degrees of price stickiness) may not be a bad approximation." See also Altissimo, Ehrmann, and Smets (2006) and Dhyne et al. (2006) for a comparison of micro evidence from the Euro area and the United States.

Measuring Marginal Cost

Initial attempts to estimate the new Keynesian Phillips curve (NKPC) equation using aggregate time series data for the United States were not very successful (Galí and Gertler 2000; Sbordone 2001). In fact, when $\hat{v}_t$ was proxied by detrended real GDP, the estimated coefficient on the output gap was small and often negative in quarterly data, although Roberts (1995) found a small positive coefficient using annual data. Galí and Gertler (1999) and Sbordone (2001) argued that detrended output was not the correct measure to enter into the NKPC. According to the basic theory, the appropriate variable is real marginal cost. Hence, one interpretation for the poor results using a standard output gap measure is that it is simply a poor proxy for real marginal cost.

To deal with measuring real marginal cost, Galí and Gertler (1999) noted that in the baseline model, real marginal cost is equal to the real wage divided by the marginal product of labor. With a Cobb-Douglas production function, the marginal product of labor is proportional to its average product. Thus, real marginal cost can be written as

$$\text{MC}_t = \frac{W_t/P_t}{\text{MPL}_t} \propto \frac{W_t/P_t}{Y_t/L_t} = \frac{W_t L_t}{P_t Y_t}.$$

Hence, real marginal cost is proportional to labor's share of total income. Expressed in terms of percent deviations around the steady state, $\hat{v}_t = ls_t$, where ls is the measure of labor's share. Galí and Gertler (2000) and Sbordone (2001) reported evidence in favor of the new Keynesian Phillips curve when labor's share, rather than a standard output gap variable, is used to proxy for real marginal cost. Sbordone (2002) also reported evidence in favor of the implied dependence of inflation on expected future inflation and real marginal cost, as did Neiss and Nelson (2002).

Rudd and Whelan (2005), however, argued that evidence for using labor's share in an inflation equation is weak. In particular, the basic new Keynesian Phillips curve given in (6.36) can be solved forward to yield

$$\pi_t = \beta E_t \pi_{t+1} + \kappa \hat{v}_t = \kappa \sum_{i=0}^{\infty} \beta^i E_t \hat{v}_{t+i}, \tag{6.41}$$

showing that current inflation is proportional to the expected present discounted value of current and future real marginal cost. This means that current inflation should forecast future movements in real marginal cost as, for example, a rise in future real marginal cost that can be forecast should immediately raise current inflation. Rudd and Whelan found that VAR-generated expected discounted future labor share is only very weakly correlated with inflation.

Persistence

While the new Keynesian Phillips curve was derived under the assumption that prices are sticky, the inflation rate is a purely forward-looking variable and is allowed to jump in response to any change in either current or expected future real marginal cost (see (6.41)). Thus, as noted in discussing Chari, Kehoe, and McGrattan (2000), the NKPC is unable to match the persistence inflation displays in actual data (Nelson 1998; Estrella and Fuhrer 2002). For example, suppose real marginal cost follows an exogenous AR(1) process: $\hat{v}_t = \rho\hat{v}_{t-1} + e_t$. To solve for the equilibrium process for inflation using (6.41), assume that $\pi_t = Ax_t$, where A is an unknown parameter. Then $E_t\pi_{t+1} = AE_t\hat{v}_{t+1} = A\rho\hat{v}_t$, and

$$\pi_t = A\hat{v}_t = \beta A\rho\hat{v}_t + \kappa\hat{v}_t \Rightarrow A = \frac{\kappa}{1 - \beta\rho}.$$

If π_t is multiplied by $(1 - \rho L)$, where L is the lag operator, $(1 - \rho L)\pi_t = (1 - \rho L)A\hat{v}_t = Ae_t$, so $\pi_t = \rho\pi_{t-1} + Ae_t$. The dynamics characterizing inflation depend solely on the serial correlation in $\hat{v}_t$ in the form of the parameter ρ. The fact that prices are sticky makes no additional contribution to the resulting dynamic behavior of inflation. In addition, e_t, the innovation to $\hat{v}_t$, has its maximum impact on inflation immediately, with inflation then reverting to its steady-state value at a rate governed by ρ.

In order to capture the inflation persistence found in the data, it is common to augment the basic forward-looking inflation adjustment equation with the addition of lagged inflation, yielding an equation of the form

$$\pi_t = (1 - \phi)\beta E_t\pi_{t+1} + \kappa\hat{v}_t + \phi\pi_{t-1}. \tag{6.42}$$

In this formulation, the parameter ϕ is often described as a measure of the degree of backward-looking behavior in price setting. Fuhrer (1997b) found little role for future inflation once lagged inflation is added to the inflation adjustment equation. Rudebusch (2002a) estimated (6.42) using U.S. data and argued that ϕ is on the order of 0.7, suggesting that inflation is predominantly backward-looking. Both Rudebusch and Fuhrer employed a statistically based measure of the output gap—detrended real GDP.[29]

Galí and Gertler (1999) modified the basic Calvo model of sticky prices to introduce lagged inflation into the Phillips curve. They assumed that a fraction λ of the firms that are allowed to adjust each period simply set $p_{jt} = \bar{\pi}p^*_{t-1}$, where $\bar{\pi}$ is the average inflation rate and p^*_{t-1} is the price chosen by optimizing firms in the previous period. They showed that the inflation adjustment equation then becomes

29. Lindé (2005) also questioned the empirical robustness of the new Keynesian Phillips curve. Galí, Gertler, and López-Salido (2005) responded to the criticisms of both Rudd and Whelan (2005) and Lindé (2005) and argued that forward-looking behavior plays the dominant role in inflation determination.

$$\pi_t = \left(\frac{1}{\delta}\right)[\beta\omega E_t\pi_{t+1} + (1 - \lambda)\bar{\kappa}\hat{v}_t + \lambda\pi_{t-1}] + \varepsilon_t, \tag{6.43}$$

where $\bar{\kappa} = (1 - \omega)(1 - \omega\beta)$ and $\delta = \omega + \lambda[1 - \omega(1 - \beta)]$. Based on U.S. data, their estimate of the coefficient on π_{t-1} is in the range 0.25–0.4, suggesting that the higher weight on lagged inflation obtained when the output gap is used reflects the fact that the gap may be a poor proxy for real marginal cost.[30]

Christiano, Eichenbaum, and Evans (2005) distinguished between firms that re-optimize in setting their price and those that do not. This might capture the idea that the costs of changing prices are those associated with optimization and decision making rather than with actual menu costs. In their formulation, in each period a fraction $1 - \omega$ of all firms optimally set their price. The remaining firms either adjust their price based on the average rate of inflation, so that $p_{jt} = \bar{\pi}p_{jt-1}$, where $\bar{\pi}$ is the average inflation rate, or they adjust based on the most recently observed rate of inflation, so that $p_{jt} = \pi_{t-1}p_{jt-1}$. The first specification leads to (6.36) when the steady-state inflation rate is zero. The second specification results in an inflation adjustment equation of the form

$$\pi_t = \left(\frac{\beta}{1+\beta}\right)E_t\pi_{t+1} + \left(\frac{1}{1+\beta}\right)\pi_{t-1} + \left(\frac{\tilde{\kappa}}{1+\beta}\right)\hat{v}_t. \tag{6.44}$$

The presence of lagged inflation in this equation introduces inertia into the inflation process. Since $\beta \approx 0.99$ in quarterly data, the weights on expected future inflation and lagged inflation in the Christiano, Eichenbaum, and Evans formulation are both about 0.5. Such a value is within the range of estimates obtained by Rudebusch (2002a) and Galí, Gertler, and López-Salido (2001).

Woodford (2003) introduced partial indexation to lagged inflation so that the non-optimizing firms set $p_{jt} = \lambda\pi_{t-1}p_{jt-1}$, for $0 \leq \lambda \leq 1$. The $\lambda = 1$ case corresponds to the model of Christiano, Eichenbaum, and Evans (2005). Woodford showed that the inflation equation takes the form

$$\pi_t - \lambda\pi_{t-1} = \beta(E_t\pi_{t+1} - \lambda\pi_t) + \kappa\hat{v}_t.$$

It has become standard to assume some form of indexation of either prices or wages in empirical new Keynesian models of inflation. For example, indexation is included in the recent generation of DSGE models that are estimated using quarterly data (e.g., Christiano, Eichenbaum, and Evans 2005; Smets and Wouter 2003; Levin et al. 2005; Adolfson, Laseén, Lindé, and Svensson 2008). However, the microeconomic evidence on firm-level pricing behavior offers no support for indexation.

---

30. See also Sbordone (2001).

It is important to note that the standard derivation of the new Keynesian Phillips curve given by (6.41) is based on a linear approximation around a steady state that is characterized by zero inflation. Ascari (2004) showed that the behavior of inflation implied by models with staggered price setting, such as the Calvo model, is significantly affected when trend inflation differs from zero. For example, because of the staggered nature of price adjustment in a Calvo-type model, higher trend inflation leads to a dispersion of relative prices. Since firms have different prices, output levels also differ across firms, and households consume different amounts of the final goods. The presence of diminishing marginal utility or convex costs of production implies that these differences are inefficient, causing steady-state output to decline as steady-state inflation rises.[31] The dynamic behavior of inflation in response to shocks is also influenced (see Ascari and Ropele 2007). However, indexation of the type discussed in this section eliminates the effects of trend inflation by allowing those firms that do not adjust optimally to still reset their prices to reflect the average rate of inflation.

Cogley and Sbordone (2006) combined indexation by nonoptimizing firms with a time-varying trend rate of inflation in a Calvo-type model and showed that the resulting Phillips curve is given by

$$\hat{\pi}_t = \alpha_{1t}(\hat{\pi}_{t-1} - \hat{g}_t^{\bar{\pi}}) + \alpha_{2t}\widehat{mc_t} + \alpha_{3t}\mathrm{E}_t\hat{\pi}_{t+1} + \alpha_{4t}\mathrm{E}_t\sum_{j=2}^{\infty}\phi_{1t}^{j-1}\hat{\pi}_{t+j}, \tag{6.45}$$

where $\hat{\pi}_t$ is log inflation relative to the current trend level, $\hat{g}_t^{\bar{\pi}}$ is the growth rate of the inflation trend, and $\widehat{mc_t}$ is log real marginal cost relative to its steady-state value. Relative to the basic NKPC with a zero trend inflation rate, the coefficients on expectations of future inflation are time-varying, and expectations of inflation more than one period into the future affect current inflation. The time variation of the coefficients occurs because all of them are functions of the (time-varying) trend rate of inflation. Estimating (6.45) using U.S. data, Cogley and Sbordone argued that a purely forward-looking version of their model (i.e., a version without indexation so that $\alpha_{1t} = 0$ and lagged inflation does not appear) can capture short-run inflation dynamics. This success arises, in part, from the high volatility of trend inflation that they estimated. Sbordone (2007) found that if (6.45) with $\alpha_{1t} = 0$ is the true model of inflation but a fixed-coefficient model of the form given by (6.42) is estimated instead, one is likely to conclude, incorrectly, that there is a backward-looking component to inflation.

---

31. The role this dispersion of relative prices has in affecting the welfare cost of fluctuations is discussed in section 8.4.

Rotemberg (2007) offered an alternative explanation for the persistence of observed inflation rates that is consistent with the forward-looking new Keynesian Phillips curve. He assumed that real marginal cost consists of two unobserved components:

$$mc_t = mc_t^P + mc_t^T,$$

where mc is real marginal cost and the two components of mc are each AR(1):

$$mc_t^i = \rho_i mc_{t-1}^i + \varepsilon_t^i \qquad \text{for } i = \{P, T\}.$$

Assume $\rho_P > \rho_T$, so P will denote a more persistent shock and T will denote the more transitory shock. Assume further that the ε^i are uncorrelated at all leads and lags, and the variance of ε^i is σ_i^2. Rotemberg's key insight is that inflation will inherit more of the persistence arising from mc^P and so can actually be more persistent than total marginal cost. Specifically, he showed that the solution for inflation takes the form

$$\pi_t = \left(\frac{\kappa}{1 - \beta\rho_P}\right)mc_t^P + \left(\frac{\kappa}{1 - \beta\rho_T}\right)mc_t^T.$$

Since $\rho_P > \rho_T$, the coefficient on the persistent component of marginal cost is larger than the coefficient on the transitory component. The autocovariance of inflation is more affected than real marginal cost is by the component that is more persistent, so inflation will tend to be more persistent than real marginal cost.

A final explanation for inflation persistence emphasizes deviations from rational expectations. For example, following Roberts (1997), suppose

$$\pi_t = \beta\pi_{t,t+1}^e + \kappa\hat{v}_t,$$

where $\pi_{t,t+1}^e$ is the public's average expectation of π_{t+1} formed at time t. Suppose further that this expectation is a a mixture of rational and backward-looking:

$$\pi_{t,t+1}^e = \alpha E_t \pi_{t+1} + (1 - \alpha)\pi_{t-1}.$$

Then

$$\pi_t = \beta\alpha E_t \pi_{t+1} + \beta(1 - \alpha)\pi_{t-1} + \kappa\hat{v}_t.$$

In this case, the presence of lagged inflation arises because expectations are not fully rational. The deviation from rational expectations is ad hoc, but another possibility is that backward-looking expectations arise because of adaptive learning on the part of the public.

The Degree of Nominal Price Rigidity

A final problem uncovered by structural estimates of the NKPC is that values for ω, the probability that a firm does not adjust its price, were much larger than found in the microeconomic evidence discussion in section 6.3.1. Dennis (2008) reported that estimates of ω have generally been in the range of 0.758 to 0.911. These values are similar to those reported by Eichenbaum and Fisher (2007) and would imply very long durations between price changes. For example, a value of 0.8, which is in the middle of this range, would imply that firms leave prices unchanged for, on average, five quarters, or over one year. As noted earlier, the microeconomic evidence for the United States suggests median durations between price changes closer to two quarters or less, implying $\omega < 0.5$.

The large values of ω obtained in time series estimates of the Phillips curve arise because inflation does not appear to respond strongly to real marginal cost. Since the elasticity of inflation with respect to marginal cost is given by

$$\kappa = \frac{(1 - \omega)(1 - \beta\omega)}{\omega}$$

and β is roughly 0.99 in quarterly data, a small κ can only be made consistent with the theory if ω is large.

To understand the modifications that have been made to the basic model in an attempt to reconcile time series estimates with values of price-change frequency from the microeconomic evidence, some further elements must be incorporated into the model. Chapter 8 embeds the new Keynesian Phillips curve into a general equilibrium setting, so the discussion here is kept brief.

In section 8.3, it is shown that real marginal cost in the basic new Keynesian model can be expressed as

$$\hat{v}_t = (\eta + \sigma)(\hat{y}_t - \hat{y}_t^{flex}),$$

where η is the inverse of the wage elasticity of labor supply, σ is the coefficient of relative risk aversion, and $\hat{y}_t^{flex}$ is the equilibrium output under flexible prices, expressed as a percent deviation around steady-state output. The NKPC can therefore be written in terms of an output gap as

$$\pi_t = \beta E_t \pi_{t+1} + \bar{\kappa}(\hat{y}_t - \hat{y}_t^{flex}),$$

with $\bar{\kappa} \equiv \kappa(\eta + \sigma)$. Notice that the output gap is defined relative to a flexible-price output and need not correspond closely to a standard output gap defined as detrended output. This derivation suggests a small effect of the output gap on inflation (a small $\bar{\kappa}$) can be reconciled with a value of ω around 0.5 if the wage elasticity is large. As output rises, firms need to hire more workers to expand production. This increase in labor demand pushes up real wages and marginal costs, causing inflation to rise. However, if labor supply is highly elastic, then the rise in real wages will be small, marginal cost will not rise significantly, and inflation will not move a lot in response to changes in the output gap. This elasticity is, however, normally thought to be small.

This intuition does suggest, though, that the aggregate evidence could be reconciled with a small ω if a richer production technology were introduced that dampens the impact of output on marginal cost. Three modifications have been explored.

First, variable capital utilization has been introduced (Christiano, Eichenbaum, and Evans 2005). So far, capital has been ignored and only labor was used to produce output. Once capital is introduced and its rate of utilization can vary, then output can increase by utilizing capital more intensely rather than solely by employing more labor. By essentially allowing firms more margins along which to adjust, the effects of output variations on marginal cost are muted.

Second, Sbordone (2002) and Eichenbaum and Fisher (2007) argued that more plausible estimates of ω can be obtained with the introduction of firm-specific capital. To understand the role played by firm-specific capital, consider the situation in the basic Calvo model. Each individual firm takes the aggregate real wage as given. The same would be true for the rental cost of capital if there were an economywide rental market for capital. Consequently, no individual firm takes into account the effect of its output choice on aggregate real factor prices. However, when capital is firm-specific, the firm faces diminishing returns; each firm knows that its marginal costs will rise if it expands production. Faced with an opportunity to adjust price, a firm that would like to raise its price knows that doing so will reduce the demand for its product. The firm will recognize that lower demand, and therefore a lower level of production, will lower its future marginal costs. This acts to mute the firm's desired price increase because price depends on both current and expected future marginal costs. Conversely, a firm considering a cut in price will recognize that this will lead to an increase in the demand it faces, which in turn will require an increase in production and an increase in marginal costs. This anticipated rise in marginal costs will dampen the desired price reduction.

To illustrate this mechanism, suppose the production function for firm i is

$$Y_t(i) = A_t \bar{K}^{1-a} N_t(i)^a.$$

Real marginal cost for the firm is the real wage relative to the marginal product of labor:

$$\mathrm{MC}_t(i) = \frac{W_t}{a A_t \bar{K}^{1-a} N_t(i)^{a-1}} = \frac{W_t N_t(i)}{a Y_t(i)}.$$

From the production function, $N_t(i) = [Y_t(i)/A_t\bar{K}^{1-a}]^{1/a}$, so

$$MC_t(i) = \frac{W_t N_t(i)}{a Y_t(i)} = \left[\frac{W_t Y_t(i)^{(1-a)/a}}{a A_t \bar{K}^{(1-a)/a}}\right].$$

Thus, unlike the basic model, marginal cost now depends on the firm's output and so varies across firms. Marginal cost at firm i relative to aggregate marginal cost can be written, using the demand curve given by (6.21), as

$$\frac{MC_t(i)}{MC_t} = \left(\frac{Y_t(i)}{Y_t}\right)^{(1-a)/a} = \left(\frac{P_t(i)}{P_t}\right)^{(a-1)/a(1-q)},$$

where $1/(1-q)$ is the price elasticity of demand. Hence, in terms of deviations around the steady state,

$$mc_t(i) = mc_t - \left[\frac{1-a}{a(1-q)}\right][p_t(i) - p_t] = mc_t - A[p_t(i) - p_t],$$

where $A = (1-a)/[a(1-q)] > 0$. The inflation adjustment equation becomes

$$\pi_t = \beta E_t \pi_{t+1} + \kappa(1+A)^{-1} mc_t,$$

and the impact of a change in marginal cost on inflation is dampened because $\kappa(1+A)^{-1} < \kappa$.

A third modification of the basic model involves relaxing the standard assumption that firms face a constant elasticity demand curve. If the demand for the firm's output becomes more elastic in response to a price increase, the increase in the firm's desired price when marginal costs rise will be less. Facing a more elastic demand, the firm's optimal relative price declines, so this mutes the degree to which the firm will raise its price.

Eichenbaum and Fisher (2007) argued that by adding indexation and firm-specific capital and dropping the assumption that firms face a constant elasticity of demand, estimated values of ω, the frequency of price changes, are lower than the high values found in the basic Calvo model. In fact, they concluded that for some specifications, the estimated value of ω is consistent with firms' reoptimizing prices every two quarters, a value more in line with microeconomic evidence. However, that evidence refers to the average duration between price changes. In Eichenbaum and Fisher, all firms change prices every period (because of the indexation assumption). Thus, it is not clear how the price change frequency found in the microeconomic data and the reoptimization frequency are related.

Standard models of price adjustment assume that the frequency of price adjustment is the same across all firms in the economy. Carvalho (2006) and Nakamura and Steinsson (2008) considered heterogeneity in this frequency by studying multi-sector economies. When prices adjust at different rates across the sectors, Carvalho showed, in response to a monetary shock most price changes initially occur in sectors characterized by a low degree of nominal rigidity (i.e., in sectors in which prices adjust frequently). As time passes, the speed of adjustment slows, and it is now firms in the sectors with greater nominal rigidity that are the primary adjusters. In addition, if strategic complementarities lead each firm's optimal price to be a function of the prices of other firms, then the price changes of the firms in sectors that adjust rapidly are affected by the presence of more slowly adjusting sectors of the economy. In response to a positive monetary shock, the existence of slow adjusters will cause the early adjusters to limit their price increases. As a result, monetary shocks have longer-lived impacts on the real economy when price adjustment frequencies differ across the economy, relative to an economy in which this frequency is the same for all firms. Carvalho reported that to generate the same dynamic responses to monetary shocks, a model with identical firms needs a frequency of price change that is as much as three times lower than the average frequency in a model with heterogeneous firms.

6.3.3   Sticky Prices versus Sticky Information

Several authors have attempted to test the sticky information Phillips curve (SIPC) model of inflation (see chapter 5) against the sticky price new Keynesian Phillips curve of this chapter. For example, Kiley (2007) estimated the NKPC as well as hybrid versions that incorporate lagged inflation as in (6.43) or (6.44). For the period 1983–2002, he found that a simple sticky price model with one lag of inflation performs reasonably well, as does a sticky information model augmented with one lag of inflation. However, the sticky price model does better than the sticky information version when the number of lags is increased. Thus, both models require ad hoc augmentation to fully account for the behavior of inflation. Kiley argued that the addition of such long lags in inflation might reflect the type of behavior Galí and Gertler (1999) showed led to (6.43). Galí and Gertler assumed that a fraction of firms that could adjust their price simply employed a rule of thumb that called for setting a new price based on lagged information about the optimal price. If this lagged information is assumed to include older information on past optimal prices, one might justify the best-fitting model as one that incorporates sticky prices together with sticky information.

Most macroeconomic models impose the assumption that conditional on the available information set, expectations are rational. Thus, both the SIPC and the NKPC are based on rational expectations, but they differ in terms of the information that is assumed to be available to agents. Coibion (2008) used historical survey measures of inflation forecasts to avoid imposing rational expectations. He found that when the structural parameters of the SIPC are estimated, little evidence of informational stickiness is uncovered. He also found that conditional on the survey forecasts, the SIPC is rejected in favor of the sticky price NKPC.

Klenow and Willis (2007) proposed a reconciliation between microeconomic flexibility and macroeconomic rigidity and set up a model in which firms have price adjustment costs (which will lead to price stickiness) and information costs (information stickiness). The former are introduced to account for the fact that in a given month most prices do not change. Information updating about the aggregate economy occurs every N periods, as in a Taylor adjustment model. This differs from Mankiw and Reis's original sticky information model in which the probability of updating information each period was constant. Klenow and Willis also introduced idiosyncratic firm shocks about which the firm always has full information. Expectations about inflation are assumed to be based on a simple forecasting rule. They found that in microeconomic data from the U.S. CPI, price changes appear to depend on old information in a manner consistent with theories of sticky information.

6.4   Summary

Monetary economists generally agree that the models discussed in chapters 2–4, while useful for examining issues such as the welfare cost of inflation and the optimal inflation tax, need to be modified to account for the short-run effects of monetary factors on the economy. This chapter and chapter 5 reviewed three such modifications: informational frictions, portfolio adjustment frictions, and nominal price adjustment frictions. Most monetary models designed to address short-run monetary issues assume that wages and/or prices do not adjust instantaneously in response to changes in economic conditions. This chapter has examined some standard models of price adjustment, including both time-dependent and state-dependent pricing models. It also briefly discussed some of the microeconomic evidence that has provided new facts against which to judge models of nominal stickiness as well as the time series evidence on sticky price and sticky information models.

6.5   Appendix: A Sticky Wage MIU Model

In section 6.2.1, an MIU model was modified to include one-period nominal wage contracts. The equations characterizing equilibrium in the flexible-price MIU model were given by (6.1)–(6.8). Output was shown to equal

$$y_t - E_{t-1}y_t^* = a(p_t - E_{t-1}p_t) + (1+a)\varepsilon_t, \tag{6.46}$$

where $E_{t-1}y^* = (1 - \alpha)E_{t-1}n_t^* + E_{t-1}e_t$ is the expected equilibrium output under flexible prices, $a = (1 - \alpha)/\alpha$, and

$$y_t^* = \left[\frac{1 + \bar{\eta}}{1 + \bar{\eta} + (1 - \alpha)(\Phi - 1)}\right]e_t = b_2 e_t.$$

The aggregate demand side of this economy consists of (6.4) and (6.6)–(6.8). Making use of the economy's resource constraint, (6.4) can be written as

$$y_t = E_t y_{t+1} - \left(\frac{1}{\Phi}\right)r_t. \tag{6.47}$$

Using the Fisher equation, (6.7), and (6.47), the money demand condition becomes

$$m_t - p_t = y_t - \left(\frac{1}{bi^{ss}}\right)[r_t + E_t p_{t+1} - p_t]$$

$$= y_t - \frac{\Phi}{bi^{ss}}[E_t y_{t+1} - y_t] - \left(\frac{1}{bi^{ss}}\right)(E_t p_{t+1} - p_t).$$

Notice that expected future income affects the demand for money. Higher expected income raises the expected real interest rate for a given level of current output, and this implies lower money demand.

The equations of the model can now be collected:

Aggregate supply: $y_t = b_2 E_{t-1}e_t + a(p_t - E_{t-1}p_t) + (1 + a)\varepsilon_t.$

Aggregate demand: $y_t = E_t y_{t+1} - \left(\frac{1}{\Phi}\right)r_t.$

Money demand: $m_t - p_t = y_t - \frac{\Phi}{bi^{ss}}[E_t y_{t+1} - y_t] - \left(\frac{1}{bi^{ss}}\right)(E_t p_{t+1} - p_t).$

Fisher equation: $i_t = r_t + E_t p_{t+1} - p_t.$

To complete the solution to the model, assume that the productivity shock e_t and the money supply shock s_t are both serially and mutually uncorrelated. Then $E_{t-1}e_t = E_{t-1}y_t^* = 0$. The model reduces to

$$y_t = a(p_t - E_{t-1}p_t) + (1 + a)\varepsilon_t$$

$$m_t - p_t = \left(1 + \frac{\Phi}{bi^{ss}}\right)y_t - \left(\frac{1}{bi^{ss}}\right)(E_t p_{t+1} - p_t)$$

$$m_t = m_{t-1} + s_t.$$

Combining the first and second of these equations,

$$[1 + bi^{ss} + a(bi^{ss} + \Phi)]p_t$$

$$= bi^{ss}m_t + a(bi^{ss} + \Phi)E_{t-1}p_t - (1 + a)(bi^{ss} + \Phi)\varepsilon_t + E_t p_{t+1}. \tag{6.48}$$

Guess a solution of the form $p_t = \gamma_1 m_{t-1} + \gamma_2 s_t + \gamma_3 \varepsilon_t$. Then $E_{t-1}p_t = \gamma_1 m_{t-1}$ and $E_t p_{t+1} = \gamma_1 m_t = \gamma_1 m_{t-1} + \gamma_1 s_t$. Substituting these expressions into (6.48),

$$[1 + bi^{ss} + a(bi^{ss} + \Phi)](\gamma_1 m_{t-1} + \gamma_2 s_t + \gamma_3 \varepsilon_t)$$

$$= bi^{ss}(m_{t-1} + s_t) + a(bi^{ss} + \Phi)\gamma_1 m_{t-1} - (1 + a)(bi^{ss} + \Phi)\varepsilon_t + \gamma_1 m_{t-1} + \gamma_1 s_t.$$

Equating the coefficients on either side, γ_1, γ_2, and γ_3 must satisfy

$$[1 + bi^{ss} + a(bi^{ss} + \Phi)]\gamma_1 = bi^{ss} + a(bi^{ss} + \Phi)\gamma_1 + \gamma_1 \Rightarrow \gamma_1 = 1$$

$$[1 + bi^{ss} + a(bi^{ss} + \Phi)]\gamma_2 = bi^{ss} + \gamma_1 \Rightarrow \gamma_2 = \frac{1 + bi^{ss}}{1 + bi^{ss} + a(bi^{ss} + \Phi)}$$

$$[1 + bi^{ss} + a(bi^{ss} + \Phi)]\gamma_3 = (1 + a)(bi^{ss} + \Phi) \Rightarrow \gamma_3 = -\left[\frac{(1 + a)(bi^{ss} + \Phi)}{1 + bi^{ss} + a(bi^{ss} + \Phi)}\right].$$

To determine the impact of a money shock s_t on output, note that $p_t - E_{t-1}p_t = \gamma_2 s_t + \gamma_3 \varepsilon_t$, so

$$y_t = a(p_t - E_{t-1}p_t) + (1 + a)\varepsilon_t$$

$$= a\gamma_2 s_t + (a\gamma_3 + \alpha^{-1})\varepsilon_t.$$

From the definitions of γ_2 and γ_3,

$$y_t = \left[\frac{a(1 + bi^{ss})}{1 + bi^{ss} + a(bi^{ss} + \Phi)}\right]s_t + (1 + a)\left[\frac{1 + bi^{ss}}{1 + bi^{ss} + a(bi^{ss} + \Phi)}\right]\varepsilon_t.$$

Using the parameter values from section 2.5.4, ($\alpha = 0.36$, $b = 3$, $\Phi = 2$) and a steady-state nominal interest rate of 0.011 (since average money growth, and hence inflation, equals zero), the coefficient on s_t is equal to 0.40. Letting $b \to \infty$ yields (6.14).

6.6   Problems

1. An increase in average inflation lowers the real demand for money. Demonstrate this by using the steady-state version of the model given by (6.1)–(6.7), assuming that the nominal money supply grows at a constant trend rate μ so that $m_t = \mu t$, to show that real money balances $m_t - p_t$ are decreasing in μ.

2. Suppose that the nominal money supply evolves according to $m_t = \mu + \rho_m m_{t-1} + s_t$ for $0 < \rho_m < 1$ and s_t, a white noise control error. If the rest of the economy is characterized by (6.1)–(6.7), solve for the equilibrium expressions for the price level, output, and the nominal rate of interest. What is the effect of a positive money shock $(s_t > 0)$ on the nominal rate? How does this result compare to the $\rho_m = 1$ case discussed in the appendix? Explain.

3. Assume that nominal wages are set for one period but that they can be indexed to the price level:

$$w_t^c = w_t^0 + b(p_t - E_{t-1}p_t),$$

where w^0 is a base wage and b is the indexation parameter $(0 \le b \le 1)$.

a. How does this change modify the aggregate supply equation given by (6.11)?

b. Suppose the demand side of the economy is represented by a simple quantity equation, $m_t - p_t = y_t$, and assume $m_t = v_t$, where v_t, is a mean zero shock. Assume the indexation parameter is set to minimize $E_{t-1}(n_t - E_{t-1}n_t^*)^2$, and show that the optimal degree of wage indexation is increasing in the variance of v and decreasing in the variance of e (Gray 1978).

4. Equation (6.29) was obtained from equation (6.28) by assuming that $R = 1$. Show that in general, if R is constant but $R^{ss} > 1$,

$$\bar{p}_t = \left(\frac{R^{ss}}{1 + R^{ss}}\right)\left[p_t + \frac{1}{R^{ss}}E_t p_{t+1}\right] + \left(\frac{R^{ss}}{1 + R^{ss}}\right)\left[v_t + \frac{1}{R^{ss}}E_t v_{t+1}\right].$$

5. The Chari, Kehoe, and McGrattan (2000) model of price adjustment led to (6.31). Using (6.30), show that the parameter a in (6.31) equals $(1 - \sqrt{\gamma})/(1 + \sqrt{\gamma})$.

6. The basic Taylor model of price level adjustment was derived under the assumption that the nominal wage set in period t remained unchanged for periods t and $t + 1$. Suppose instead that each period t contract specifies a nominal wage x_t^1 for period t and x_t^2 for period $t + 1$. Assume these are given by $x_t^1 = p_t + \kappa y_t$ and $x_t^2 = E_t p_{t+1} + \kappa E_t y_{t+1}$. The aggregate price level at time t is equal to $p_t = \frac{1}{2}(x_t^1 + x_{t-1}^2)$. If aggregate demand is given by $y_t = m_t - p_t$ and $m_t = m_0 + \omega_t$, what is the effect of a money shock ω_t on p_t and y_t? Explain why output shows no persistence after a money shock.

7. Following Rotemberg (1988), suppose the representative firm i sets its price to minimize a quadratic loss function that depends on the difference between the firm's actual log price in period t, p_{it}, and its optimal log price, p_t^*. If the firm can adjust at time t, it will set its price to minimize

$$\frac{1}{2}E_t \sum_{j=0}^{\infty} \beta^j (p_{it+j} - p_{t+j}^*)^2,$$
(6.49)

subject to the assumed process for determining when the firm will next be able to adjust.

a. If the probability of resetting prices each period is $1 - \omega$, as in the Calvo model, and $\hat{p}_t$ denotes the optimal price chosen by all firms that can adjust at time t, show that $\hat{p}_t$ minimizes

$$\frac{1}{2}\sum_{j=0}^{\infty} \omega^j \beta^j E_t(p_{it} - p_{t+j}^*)^2.$$

b. Derive the first-order condition for the optimal choice of $\hat{p}_t$.

c. Using the result from (b), show that

$$\hat{p}_t = (1 - \omega\beta) \sum_{j=0}^{\infty} \omega^j \beta^j E_t p_{t+j}^*.$$
(6.50)

Explain intuitively why the weights on future optimal prices p_{t+j}^* depends on ω.

8. Suppose, as in problem 7, the representative firm i sets its price to minimize a quadratic loss function that depends on the difference between the firm's actual log price in period t, p_{it}, and its optimal log price, p_t^*. The probability of resetting prices each period is $1 - \omega$, as in the Calvo model. If the firm can adjust at time t, it will set its price to minimize

$$\frac{1}{2}E_t \sum_{j=0}^{\infty} \beta^i (p_{it+j} - p_{t+j}^*)^2$$

subject to the assumed process for determining when the firm will next be able to adjust.

a. If $\hat{p}_t$ is the log price chosen by adjusting firms, show that

$$\hat{p}_t = (1 - \omega\beta)p_t^* + \omega\beta E_t\hat{p}_{t+1}.$$

b. Assume the log price target p^* depends on the aggregate log price level and output: $p_t^* = p_t + \gamma y_t + \varepsilon_t$, where ε is a random disturbance to capture other determinants of p^*. The log aggregate price level is $p_t = (1 - \omega)\hat{p}_t + \omega p_{t-1}$. Using this definition and the result in part (a), obtain an expression for aggregate inflation as a function of expected future inflation, output, and ε.

c. Is the impact of output on inflation increasing or decreasing in ω, the measure of the degree of nominal rigidity? Explain.

9. The basic Calvo model assumes that in each period a fraction ω of all firms do not change price. Suppose instead that these firms index their price to last period's inflation, so that for such firms the log price is given by $p_{it} = p_{it-1} + \pi_{t-1}$.

a. What is the first-order condition for $\hat{p}_t$, the price chosen by firms that do adjust optimally in period t?

b. How does this compare to (6.34)?

c. The log aggregate price level becomes

$$p_t = (1 - \omega)\hat{p}_t + \omega(p_{t-1} + \pi_{t-1}).$$

Use this equation with the first-order condition for $\hat{p}_t$ obtained in part (a) to find an expression for the aggregate inflation rate. How is current inflation affected by lagged inflation?

7 Discretionary Policy and Time Inconsistency

7.1 Introduction

Macroeconomic equilibrium depends on both the current and expected future behavior of monetary policy.[1] If policymakers behave according to a systematic rule, the rule can be used to determine rational expectations of future policy actions under the assumption that the central bank continues to behave according to the rule. In principle, one could derive an optimal policy rule by specifying an objective function for the central bank and then determining the values of the parameters in the policy rule that maximize the expected value of the objective function.

But what ensures that the central bank will find it desirable to follow such a rule? Absent enforcement, it may be optimal to deviate from the rule once private agents have made commitments based on the expectation that the rule will be followed. Firms and workers may agree to set nominal wages or prices based on the expectation that monetary policy will be conducted in a particular manner, yet once these wage and price decisions have been made, the central bank may have an incentive to deviate from actions called for under the rule. If deviations from a strict rule are possible—that is, if the policymakers can exercise discretion—agents will need to consider the policymakers' incentive to deviate; they can no longer simply base their expectations on the rule that policymakers say they will follow.

A large literature has focused on the incentives central banks face when actually setting their policy instrument. Following the seminal contribution of Kydland and Prescott (1977), attention has been directed to issues of central bank credibility and the ability to precommit to policies. Absent some means of committing in advance to take specific policy actions, central banks may find that they face incentives to act in ways that are inconsistent with their earlier plans and announcements.

---

1. Illustrations of this dependence are seen in the equilibrium expressions for the price level in the money-in-the-utility function (MIU) and cash-in-advance (CIA) models of chapters 2 and 3 and the discussion of policy in the new Keynesian model of chapter 8.

A policy is *time-consistent* if an action planned at time t for time $t + i$ remains optimal to implement when time $t + i$ actually arrives. The policy can be state-contingent; that is, it can depend on the realization of events that are unknown at time t when the policy is originally planned. But a time-consistent policy is one in which the planned response to new information remains the optimal response once the new information arrives. A policy is *time-inconsistent* if at time $t + i$ it will not be optimal to respond as originally planned. The focus of this chapter is on determining the average level of inflation and how discretion may lead to excessive inflation. The stabilization bias that can arise under discretionary policy regimes when inflation depends on forward-looking expectations is discussed in chapter 8.

The analysis of time inconsistency in monetary policy is important for two reasons. First, it forces one to examine the incentives faced by central banks. The impact of current policy often depends upon the public's expectations, either about current policy or about future policy actions. To predict how policy affects the economy, one needs to understand how expectations will respond, and this understanding can only be achieved if policy behaves in a systematic manner. Just as with private sector behavior, an understanding of systematic behavior by the central bank requires an examination of the incentives the policymaker faces. And by focusing on these incentives, models of time inconsistency have had an important influence as *positive* theories of observed rates of inflation.

Second, if time inconsistency is important, then models that clarify the incentives faced by policymakers and the nature of the decision problems they face are important for the normative task of designing policy-making institutions. For this purpose, monetary economists need models that provide help in understanding how institutional structures affect policy outcomes.

The next section develops a framework, originally due to Barro and Gordon (1983a), that despite its simplicity has proven extremely useful for studying problems of time inconsistency in monetary policy. The discretionary conduct of policy, meaning that the central bank is free at any time to alter its instrument setting, is shown to produce an average inflationary bias; equilibrium inflation exceeds the socially desired rate. This bias arises from a desire for economic expansions above the economy's equilibrium output level (or for unemployment rates below the economy's natural rate) and the inability of the central bank to commit credibly to a low rate of inflation. Section 7.3 examines some of the solutions that have been proposed for overcoming this inflationary bias. Central banks very often seem to be concerned with their reputations; and section 7.3.1 examines how such a concern might reduce or even eliminate the inflation bias. Section 7.3.2 considers the possibility that society or the government might wish to delegate responsibility for monetary policy to a central banker with preferences between employment and inflation fluctuations that differ from those of society as a whole. Since the inflation bias can be viewed as arising because the central bank faces the wrong incentives, a third approach to solving the inflation bias problem is to design mechanisms for creating the right incentives. This approach is discussed in section 7.3.3. Section 7.3.4 considers the role of institutional structures in solving the inflation bias problem arising from discretion. Finally, the role of explicit targeting rules is studied in section 7.3.5.

The models of sections 7.2 and 7.3, with their focus on the inflationary bias that can arise under discretion, have played a major role in the academic literature on inflation. The success of these models as positive theories of inflation—that is, as explanations for the actual historical variations of inflation both over time and across countries—is open to debate. Section 7.4 discusses the empirical importance of the inflation bias in accounting for episodes of inflation.

7.2   Inflation under Discretionary Policy

If inflation is costly (even a little), and if there is no real benefit to having 5 percent inflation on average as opposed to 1 percent inflation or 0 percent inflation, why do we observe average rates of inflation that are consistently positive? Many explanations of positive average rates of inflation have built on the time inconsistency analysis of Kydland and Prescott (1977) and Calvo (1978).[2] The basic insight is that while it may be optimal to achieve a low average inflation rate, such a policy is not time-consistent. If the public were to expect low inflation, the central bank would face an incentive to inflate at a higher rate. Understanding this incentive, and believing that the policymaker will succumb to it, the public correctly anticipates a higher inflation rate. The policymaker then finds it optimal to deliver the inflation rate the public anticipated.

7.2.1   Policy Objectives

To determine the central bank's actions, one needs to specify the preferences of the central bank. It is standard to assume that the central bank's objective function involves output (or employment) and inflation, although the exact manner in which output has been assumed to enter the objective function has taken two different forms. In the formulation of Barro and Gordon (1983b), the central bank's objective is to maximize the expected value of

$$U = \lambda(y - y_n) - \frac{1}{2}\pi^2, \tag{7.1}$$

---

2. For a survey dealing with time inconsistency problems in the design of both monetary and fiscal policies, see Persson and Tabellini (1990). Cukierman (1992) also provided an extensive discussion of the theoretical issues related to the analysis of inflation in models in which time inconsistency plays a critical role. Persson and Tabellini's (1999) survey of political economy covered many of the issues discussed in this chapter. See also Driffill (1988) and Stokey (2003).

where y is output, y_n is the economy's natural rate of output, and π is the inflation rate. More output is preferred to less output with constant marginal utility, so output enters linearly, and inflation is assumed to generate increasing marginal disutility and so enters quadratically. The parameter λ governs the relative weight that the central bank places on output expansions relative to inflation stabilization. Often the desire for greater output is motivated by an appeal to political pressure on monetary policy due to the effects of economic expansions on the reelection prospects of incumbent politicians.[3] Alternatively, distortions due to taxes, monopoly unions, or monopolistic competition may lead y_n to be inefficiently low. For discussions of alternative motivations for this type of loss function, see Cukierman (1992). What will be critical is that the central bank would like to expand output, but it will be able to do so only by creating surprise inflation (see section 7.2.2).

The other standard specification for preferences assumes that the central bank desires to minimize the expected value of a loss function that depends on output and inflation fluctuations. Thus, the *loss function* is quadratic in both output and inflation and takes the form

$$V = \frac{1}{2}\lambda(y - y_n - k)^2 + \frac{1}{2}\pi^2. \tag{7.2}$$

The key aspect of this loss function is the parameter k. The assumption is that the central bank desires to stabilize both output and inflation, inflation around zero but output around $y_n + k$, a level that exceeds the economy's natural rate of output y_n by the constant k.[4] Because the expected value of V involves the variance of output, the loss function (7.2) will generate a role for stabilization policy that is absent when the central bank cares only about the level of output, as in (7.1).

There are several common explanations for a positive k, and these parallel the arguments for the output term in the linear preference function (7.1). Most often, some appeal is made to the presence of imperfect competition, as in the new Keynesian model (see chapter 8), or labor market distortions (e.g., a wage tax) that lead the economy's natural rate of output to be inefficiently low. Attempting to use monetary policy to stabilize output around $y_n + k$ then represents a second-best solution (the first-best would involve eliminating the original distortion). An alternative interpretation is that k arises from political pressure on the central bank. Here the notion is that elected officials have a bias for economic expansions because expansions tend to increase their probability of reelection. The presence of k leads to a third-best out-

---

3. The influence of reelections on the central bank's policy choices was studied by Fratianni, von Hagen, and Waller (1997) and Herrendorf and Neumann (2003).

4. Note that the inflation term in (7.1) and (7.2) can be replaced by $\frac{1}{2}(\pi - \pi^*)^2$ if the monetary authority has a target inflation rate π^* that differs from zero.

come, so the political interpretation motivates institutional reforms designed to minimize political pressures on the central bank.

The two alternative objective functions (7.1) and (7.2) are clearly closely related. Expanding the term involving output in the quadratic loss function, (7.2) can be written as

$$V = -\lambda k(y - y_n) + \frac{1}{2}\pi^2 + \frac{1}{2}\lambda(y - y_n)^2 + \frac{1}{2}\lambda k^2.$$

The first two terms are the same as the linear utility function (with signs reversed because V is a loss function), showing that the assumption of a positive k is equivalent to the presence of a utility gain from output expansions above y_n. In addition, V includes a loss arising from deviations of output around y_n (the $\lambda(y - y_n)^2$ term). This introduces a role for stabilization policies that is absent when the policymaker's preferences are assumed to be strictly linear in output. The final term involving k^2 is simply a constant and so has no effect on the central bank's decisions.[5]

The alternative formulations reflected in (7.1) and (7.2) produce many of the same insights. Following Barro and Gordon (1983b), we will work initially with the function (7.1), which is linear in output. The equilibrium concept in the basic Barro-Gordon model is noncooperative Nash. Given the public's expectations, the central bank's policy choice maximizes its objective function (or equivalently, minimizes its loss function), given the public's expectations. The assumption of rational expectations implicitly defines the loss function for private agents as $L^P = \mathrm{E}(\pi - \pi^e)^2$; given the public's understanding of the central bank's decision problem, their choice of π^e is optimal.

7.2.2   The Economy

The specification of the economy is quite simple and follows the analysis of Barro and Gordon (1983a; 1983b). Aggregate output is given by a Lucas-type aggregate supply function (see chapter 5) of the form

$$y = y_n + a(\pi - \pi^e) + e. \tag{7.3}$$

This can be motivated as arising from the presence of one-period nominal wage contracts set at the beginning of each period based on the public's expectation of the rate

---

5. See Cukierman (1992) for more detailed discussions of alternative motivations that might lead to objective functions of the forms given by either (7.1) or (7.2). In an open-economy framework, Bohn (1991d) showed how the incentives for inflation depend on foreign-held debt denominated in the domestic currency. In chapter 8, the objective function for the central bank is derived as an approximation to the utility of the represented agent. Under certain conditions, such an approximation yields an objective function similar to (7.2).

of inflation. If actual inflation exceeds the expected rate, real wages will be eroded and firms will expand employment. If actual inflation is less than the rate expected, realized real wages will exceed the level expected and employment will be reduced. A critical discussion of this basic aggregate supply relationship can be found in Cukierman (1992, ch. 3).[6]

Recall that the tax distortions of inflation analyzed in chapter 4 were a function of anticipated inflation. Fluctuations in unanticipated inflation caused neutral price level movements, while expected inflation altered nominal interest rates and the opportunity cost of money, leading to tax effects on money holdings, the consumption of cash goods, and the supply of labor. If the costs of inflation arise purely from expected inflation, while surprise inflation generates economic expansions, then a central bank would perceive only benefits from attempting to produce unexpected inflation. Altering the specification of the central bank's objective function in (7.2) or (7.1) to depend only on output and expected inflation would, given (7.3), then imply that the equilibrium inflation rate could be infinite (see Auernheimer 1974; Calvo 1978; and problem 7 at the end of this chapter).

The rest of the model is a simple link between inflation and the policy authority's actual policy instrument:

$$\pi = \Delta m + v, \tag{7.4}$$

where Δm is the growth rate of the money supply (the first difference of the log nominal money supply), assumed to be the central bank's policy instrument, and v is a velocity disturbance. The private sector's expectations are assumed to be determined prior to the central bank's choice of a growth rate for the nominal money supply. Thus, in setting Δm, the central bank will take π^e as given. Also assume that the central bank can observe e (but not v) prior to setting Δm; this assumption generates a role for stabilization policy. Finally, assume e and v are uncorrelated.

The sequence of events is important. First, the private sector sets nominal wages based on its expectations of inflation. Thus, in the first stage, π^e is set. Then the supply shock e is realized. Because expectations have already been determined, they do not respond to the realization of e. Policy can respond, however, and the policy instrument Δm is set after the central bank has observed e. The velocity shock v is then realized, and actual inflation and output are determined.

---

6. If the aggregate supply equation is substituted into the central bank's preference function, both (7.1) and (7.2) can be written in the form $\bar{U}(\pi - \pi^e, \pi, e)$. Thus, the general framework is one in which the central bank's objective function depends on both surprise inflation and actual inflation. In addition to the employment motives mentioned here, one could emphasize the desire for seigniorage as leading to a similar objective function because surprise inflation, by depreciating the real value of both interest-bearing and non-interest-bearing liabilities of the government, produces larger revenue gains for the government than does anticipated inflation (which only erodes non-interest-bearing liabilities).

Several important assumptions have been made here. First, as with most models involving expectations, the exact specification of the information structure is important. Most critically, it is assumed that private agents must commit to nominal wage contracts before the central bank has to set the rate of growth of the nominal money supply. This means that the central bank has the opportunity to surprise the private sector by acting in a manner that differs from what private agents had expected when they locked themselves into nominal contracts. Second, in keeping with the literature based on Barro and Gordon (1983a), it is assumed the central bank sets money growth as its policy instrument. If the main objective is to explain the determinants of average inflation rates, the distinction between money and interest rates as the policy instrument is not critical. Third, the basic model assumes that the central bank can react to realization of the supply shock e while the public commits to wage contracts prior to observing this shock. This informational advantage on the part of the central bank introduces a role for stabilization policy and is meant to capture the fact that policy decisions can be made more frequently than are most wage and price decisions. It means the central bank can respond to economic disturbances before private agents have had the chance to revise nominal contracts.

The assumption that v is observed after Δm is set is not critical. It is easy to show that the central bank will always adjust Δm to offset any observed or forecastable component of the velocity shock, and this is why the rate of inflation itself is often treated as the policy instrument. Output and inflation will only be affected by the component of the velocity disturbance that was unpredictable at the time policy was set.

7.2.3   Equilibrium Inflation

Since the central bank is assumed to act before observing the disturbance v, its objective will be to maximize the expected value of U, where the central bank's expectation is defined over the distribution of v. Substituting (7.3) and (7.4) into the central bank's objective function yields

$$U = \lambda[a(\Delta m + v - \pi^e) + e] - \frac{1}{2}(\Delta m + v)^2.$$

The first-order condition for the optimal choice of Δm, conditional on e and taking π^e as given, is

$$a\lambda - \Delta m = 0,$$

or

$$\Delta m = a\lambda > 0. \tag{7.5}$$

Given this policy, actual inflation will equal $a\lambda + v$. Because private agents are assumed to understand the incentives facing the central bank, that is, they are rational, they use (7.5) in forming their expectations about inflation. With private agents forming expectations prior to observing the velocity shock v, (7.4) and (7.5) imply

$$\pi^e = \mathrm{E}[\Delta m] = a\lambda.$$

Thus, average inflation is fully anticipated. From (7.3), output is $y_n + av + e$ and is independent of the central bank's policy.

When the central bank acts with discretion in setting Δm, equilibrium involves a positive average rate of inflation equal to $a\lambda$. This has no effect on output, since the private sector completely anticipates inflation at this rate ($\pi^e = a\lambda$). The economy suffers from positive average inflation bias, which yields no benefit in terms of greater output. The size of the bias is increasing in the effect of a money surprise on output, a, since this parameter governs the marginal benefit in the form of extra output that can be obtained from an inflation surprise. The larger a is, the greater is the central bank's incentive to inflate. Recognizing this fact, private agents anticipate a higher rate of inflation. The inflation bias is also increasing in the weight the central bank places on its output objective, λ. A small λ implies that the gains from economic expansion are low relative to achieving inflation objectives, so the central bank has less incentive to generate inflation.

Why does the economy end up with positive average inflation even though it confers no benefits and the central bank dislikes inflation? The central bank is acting systematically to maximize the expected value of its objective function, so it weighs the costs and benefits of inflation in setting its policy. At a zero rate of inflation, the marginal benefit of generating a little inflation is positive because, with wages set, the effect of an incremental rise in inflation on output is equal to $a > 0$. The value of this output gain is $a\lambda$. This is illustrated in figure 7.1 by the horizontal line at a height equal to $a\lambda$. The marginal cost of inflation is equal to π. At a planned inflation rate of zero, this marginal cost is zero, so the marginal benefit of inflation exceeds the marginal cost. But the marginal cost rises (linearly) with inflation, as illustrated in the figure. At an expected inflation rate of $a\lambda$, the marginal cost equals the marginal benefit.

Under this discretionary policy outcome, expected utility of the central bank is equal to

$$\mathrm{E}[U^d] = \mathrm{E}\left[\lambda(av + e) - \frac{1}{2}(a\lambda + v)^2\right]$$

$$= -\frac{1}{2}(a^2\lambda^2 + \sigma_v^2),$$

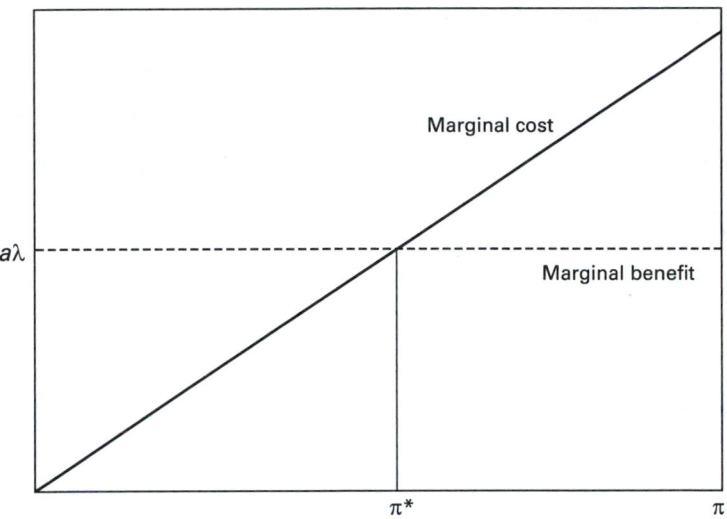

Figure 7.1
Equilibrium inflation under discretion (linear objective function).

where $E[v] = E[e] = 0$ and σ_v^2 is the variance of the random inflation control error v. Expected utility is decreasing in the variance of the random control error v and decreasing in the weight placed on output relative to inflation objectives (λ) because a larger λ increases the average rate of inflation. Although the control error is unavoidable, the loss due to the positive average inflation rate arises from the monetary authority's fruitless attempt to stimulate output.

The outcome under discretion can be contrasted with the situation in which the monetary authority is able to commit to setting money growth always equal to zero: $\Delta m = 0$. In this case, $\pi = v$ and expected utility would equal

$$E[U^c] = E\left[\lambda(av + e) - \frac{1}{2}v^2\right] = -\frac{1}{2}\sigma_v^2 > E[U^d].$$

The central bank (and society, if the central bank's utility is interpreted as a social welfare function) would be better off if it were possible to commit to a policy of zero money growth. Discretion, in this case, generates a cost.

As noted earlier, an alternative specification of the central bank's objectives focuses on the loss associated with output and inflation fluctuations around desired levels. This alternative formulation, given by the loss function (7.2), leads to the same basic conclusions. Discretion will produce an average bias toward positive inflation and lower expected utility. In addition, specifying the loss function so that the central bank cares about output fluctuations means that there will be a potential role for policy to reduce output volatility caused by the supply shock e.

Substituting (7.3) and (7.4) into the quadratic loss function (7.2) yields

$$V = \frac{1}{2}\lambda[a(\Delta m + v - \pi^e) + e - k]^2 + \frac{1}{2}(\Delta m + v)^2.$$

If Δm is chosen after observing the supply shock e, but before observing the velocity shock v, to minimize the expected value of the loss function, the first-order condition for the optimal choice of Δm, conditional on e and taking π^e as given, is

$$a\lambda[a(\Delta m - \pi^e) + e - k] + \Delta m = 0,$$

or

$$\Delta m = \frac{a^2\lambda\pi^e + a\lambda(k - e)}{1 + a^2\lambda}. \tag{7.6}$$

There are two important differences to note in comparing (7.5), the optimal setting for money growth from the model with a linear objective function, to (7.6). First, the aggregate supply shock appears in (7.6); because the central bank wants to minimize the variance of output around its target level, it will make policy conditional on the realization of the supply shock. Thus, an explicit role for stabilization policies arises that will involve trading off some inflation volatility for reduced output volatility. Second, the optimal policy depends on private sector expectations about inflation.

Private agents are assumed to understand the incentives facing the central bank, so they use (7.6) in forming their expectations. However, private agents are atomistic; they do not take into account the effect their choice of expected inflation might have on the central bank's decision.[7] With expectations formed prior to observing the aggregate supply shock, (7.4) and (7.6) imply

$$\pi^e = \mathrm{E}[\Delta m] = \frac{a^2\lambda\pi^e + a\lambda k}{1 + a^2\lambda}.$$

Solving for π^e yields $\pi^e = a\lambda k > 0$. Substituting this back into (7.6) and using (7.4) gives an expression for the equilibrium rate of inflation:

$$\pi^d = \Delta m + v = a\lambda k - \left(\frac{a\lambda}{1 + a^2\lambda}\right)e + v, \tag{7.7}$$

---

7. This assumption is natural in the context of individual firms and workers determining wages and prices. If nominal wages are set in a national bargaining framework, for example by a monopoly union and employer representatives, then it may be more appropriate to assume that wages are set strategically, taking into account the impact of the wage decision on the incentives faced by the central bank. The case of a monopoly union has been analyzed by Tabellini (1988) and Cubitt (1992). See also Cukierman and Lippi (2001).

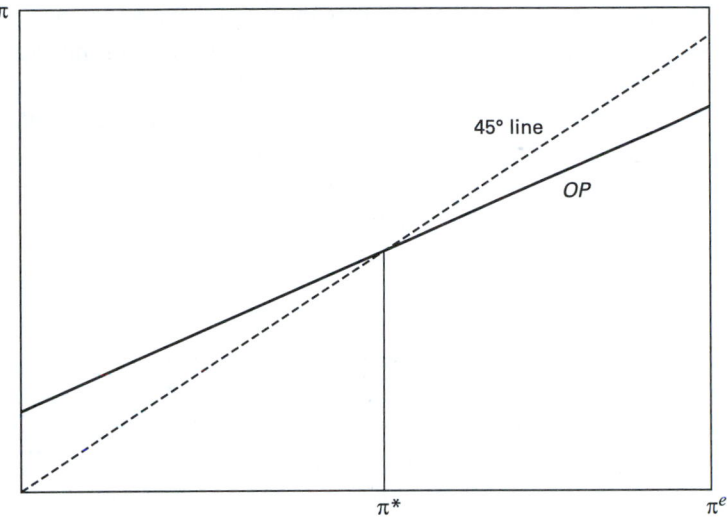

Figure 7.2
Equilibrium inflation under discretion (quadratic loss function).

where the superscript d stands for discretion. Note that the equilibrium when the central bank acts with discretion implies a positive average rate of inflation equal to $a\lambda k$. This has no effect on output because the private sector completely anticipates this rate ($\pi^e = a\lambda k$). The size of the inflation bias is increasing in the distortion (k), the effect of a money surprise on output (a), and the weight the central bank places on its output objective (λ).[8]

If, for the moment, one ignores the random disturbances e and v, the equilibrium with the quadratic loss function can be illustrated using figure 7.2. Equation (7.6) is shown, for $e = 0$, as the straight line OP (for optimal policy), giving the central bank's reaction function for its optimal inflation rate as a function of the public's expected rate of inflation. The slope of this line is $a^2\lambda/(1 + a^2\lambda) < 1$, with intercept $a\lambda k/(1 + a^2\lambda) > 0$. An increase in the expected rate of inflation requires that the central bank increase actual inflation by the same amount in order to achieve the same output effect, but because this action raises the cost associated with inflation, the central bank finds it optimal to raise π by less than the increase in π^e. Hence the slope is less than 1. The positive intercept reflects the fact that if $\pi^e = 0$, the central bank's optimal policy is to set a positive rate of inflation. In equilibrium, expectations of

8. In a model with monetary and fiscal policy authorities, Dixit and Lambertini (2002) showed that if fiscal policy is optimally designed to eliminate the distortions behind k, the central bank's objective function can be reduced to $\frac{1}{2}\lambda(y - y_n)^2 + \frac{1}{2}\pi^2$. This would eliminate the average inflation bias.

private agents must be consistent with the behavior of the central bank. In the absence of any random disturbances, this requires that $\pi^e = \pi$. Thus, equilibrium must lie along the 45° line in figure 7.2.

An increase in k, the measure of the output distortion, shifts the OP line upward and leads to a higher rate of inflation in equilibrium. An increase in a, the impact of an inflation surprise on real output, has two effects. First, it increases the slope of the OP line; by increasing the output effects of an inflation surprise, it raises the marginal benefit to the central bank of more inflation. By increasing the impact of an inflation surprise on output, however, a rise in a reduces the inflation surprise needed to move output to $y_n + k$, and if λ is large, the intercept of OP could actually fall. The net effect of a rise in a, however, is to raise the equilibrium inflation rate (see (7.7), which shows that the equilibrium inflation rate when $e = 0$ is $a\lambda k$, which is increasing in a).

The coefficient on e in (7.7) is negative; a positive supply shock leads to a reduction in money growth and inflation. This response acts to reduce the impact of e on output (the coefficient on e in the output equation becomes $1/(1 + a^2\lambda)$, which is less than 1). The larger the weight on output objectives (λ), the smaller the impact of e on output. In contrast, a central bank that places a larger relative weight on inflation objectives (a small λ) will stabilize output less.

Using (7.7), the loss function under discretion is

$$V^d = \frac{1}{2}\lambda\left[\left(\frac{1}{1+a^2\lambda}\right)e + av - k\right]^2 + \frac{1}{2}\left[a\lambda k - \left(\frac{a\lambda}{1+a^2\lambda}\right)e + v\right]^2. \tag{7.8}$$

The unconditional expectation of this loss is

$$E[V^d] = \frac{1}{2}\lambda(1 + a^2\lambda)k^2 + \frac{1}{2}\left[\left(\frac{\lambda}{1+a^2\lambda}\right)\sigma_e^2 + (1 + a^2\lambda)\sigma_v^2\right], \tag{7.9}$$

where σ_x^2 denotes the variance of x.

Now suppose that the central bank had been able to precommit to a policy rule prior to the formation of private expectations. Because there is a role for stabilization policy in the present case (i.e., the monetary authority would like to respond to the supply shock e), the policy rule will not simply be a fixed growth rate for Δm, as it was in the previous case when the central bank's objective function was a linear function of output. Instead, suppose the central bank is able to commit to a policy rule of the form

$$\Delta m^c = b_0 + b_1 e.$$

In the present linear-quadratic framework, a linear rule such as this will be optimal. Given this rule, $\pi^e = b_0$. Now substituting this into the loss function gives

$$V^c = \frac{1}{2}\lambda[a(b_1 e + v) + e - k]^2 + \frac{1}{2}[b_0 + b_1 e + v]^2. \tag{7.10}$$

Under a commitment policy, the central bank commits itself to particular values of the parameters b_0 and b_1 *prior to* the formation of expectations by the public and *prior to* observing the particular realization of the shock e. Thus, b_0 and b_1 are chosen to minimize the unconditional expectation of the loss function. Solving the minimization problem, the optimal policy under precommitment is

$$\Delta m^c = -\left(\frac{a\lambda}{1 + a^2\lambda}\right)e. \tag{7.11}$$

Note that average inflation under precommitment will be zero ($b_0 = 0$), but the response to the aggregate supply shock is the same as under discretion (see (7.7)). The unconditional expectation of the loss function under precommitment is

$$E[V^c] = \frac{1}{2}\lambda k^2 + \frac{1}{2}\left[\left(\frac{\lambda}{1 + a^2\lambda}\right)\sigma_e^2 + (1 + a^2\lambda)\sigma_v^2\right], \tag{7.12}$$

which is strictly less than the loss under discretion. Comparing (7.9) and (7.12), the cost of discretion is equal to $(a\lambda k)^2/2$, which is simply the loss attributable to the nonzero average rate of inflation.

The inflation bias that arises under discretion occurs for two reasons. First, the central bank has an incentive to inflate once private sector expectations are set. Second, the central bank is unable to precommit to a zero average inflation rate. To see why it cannot commit, suppose the central bank announces that it will deliver zero inflation. If the public believes the announced policy, and therefore $\pi^e = 0$, it is clear from (7.5) or (7.6) that the optimal policy for the central bank to follow would involve setting a positive average money growth rate, and the average inflation rate would be positive. So the central bank's announcement would not be believed in the first place. The central bank cannot believably commit to a zero inflation policy because under such a policy (i.e., if $\pi = \pi^e = 0$) the marginal cost of a little inflation is $\partial\frac{1}{2}\pi^2/\partial\pi = \pi = 0$, while the marginal benefit is $a\lambda > 0$ under the linear objective function formulation or $-a^2\lambda(\pi - \pi^e) + a\lambda k = a\lambda k > 0$ under the quadratic formulation. Because the marginal benefit exceeds the marginal cost, the central bank has an incentive to break its commitment.

Society is clearly worse off under the discretionary policy outcome because it experiences positive average inflation with no systematic improvement in output performance. This result fundamentally alters the long-running debate in economics over rules versus discretion in the conduct of policy. Prior to Kydland and Prescott's analysis of time inconsistency, economists had debated whether monetary policy should be conducted according to a simple rule, such as Milton Friedman's k percent growth rate rule for the nominal supply of money, or whether central banks should have the flexibility to respond with discretion. With the question posed in this form, the answer is clearly that discretion is better. After all, if following a simple rule is optimal, under discretion one could always choose to follow such a rule. Thus, one could do no worse under discretion, and one might do better. But as the Barro-Gordon model illustrates, one might actually do worse under discretion. Restricting the flexibility of monetary policy may result in a superior outcome. To see this, suppose the central bank is forced (somehow) to set $\Delta m = 0$. This avoids any average inflation bias, but it also prevents the central bank from engaging in any stabilization policy. With the loss function given by (7.2), the unconditional expected loss under such a policy rule is $\frac{1}{2}\lambda(\sigma_e^2 + k^2) + \frac{1}{2}(1 + a^2\lambda)\sigma_v^2$. If this is compared to the unconditional expected loss under discretion, $E[V^d]$, given in (7.8), the zero money growth rule will be preferred if

$$\left(\frac{a^2\lambda^2}{1 + a^2\lambda}\right)\sigma_e^2 < (a\lambda k)^2.$$

The left side measures the gains from stabilization policy under discretion; the right side measures the cost of the inflation bias that arises under discretion. If the latter is greater, expected loss is lower if the central bank is forced to follow a fixed money growth rule.

By focusing on the strategic interaction of the central bank's actions and the public's formation of expectations, the Barro-Gordon model provides a simple but rich game-theoretic framework for studying monetary policy outcomes. The approach emphasizes the importance of understanding the incentives faced by the central bank in order to understand policy outcomes. It also helps to highlight the role of credibility, illustrating why central bank promises to reduce inflation may not be believed. The viewpoint provided by models of time inconsistency contrasts sharply with the traditional analysis of policy outcomes as either exogenous or as determined by a rule that implicitly assumes an ability to precommit.

A more formal treatment of the economic structure that could motivate the ad hoc specifications provided by (7.1) or (7.2) and the aggregate supply function (7.3) is contained in Albanesi, Chari, and Christiano (2003). They assumed imperfect competition in the goods market and that a fraction of firms set prices before current period information is revealed. The presence of sticky prices provides the central bank with a means of affecting aggregate output; imperfect competition implies average output is inefficiently low, and this provides the central bank with an incentive to boost output. In addition, Albanesi, Chari, and Christiano introduced the distinction between cash and credit goods (see chapter 3). Cash goods can only be purchased with money. As a consequence, the relative price of cash and credit goods depends on the nominal rate of interest, and inflation alters household choice between these two types of goods. The central bank faces a trade-off—higher inflation that was not anticipated increases welfare by raising output, whereas higher expected inflation lowers welfare by distorting the choice between cash and credit goods. Multiple equilibria can arise in this framework, leading to what Albanesi, Chari, and Christiano described as expectational traps. If the public expects high inflation, the best policy for the central bank is to validate those expectations.

7.3 Solutions to the Inflation Bias

Following Barro and Gordon (1983a), a large literature developed to examine alternative solutions to the inflationary bias under discretion.[9] Because the central bank is assumed to set the inflation rate so that the marginal cost of inflation (given expectations) is equal to the marginal benefit, most solutions alter the basic model to raise the marginal cost of inflation as perceived by the central bank. For example, the first class of solutions incorporates notions of reputation into a repeated-game version of the basic framework. Succumbing to the temptation to inflate today worsens the central bank's reputation for delivering low inflation; as a consequence, the public expects more inflation in the future, and this lowers the expected value of the central bank's objective function. By punishing the central bank, the loss of reputation raises the marginal cost of inflation.

The second class of solutions can also be interpreted in terms of the marginal cost of inflation. Rather than viewing inflation as imposing a reputational cost on the central bank, one could allow the central bank to have preferences that differ from those of society at large so that the marginal cost of inflation as perceived by the central bank is higher. One way to do this is simply to select as the policymaker an individual who places a larger-than-normal weight on achieving low inflation and then give that individual the independence to conduct policy. Another way involves thinking of the policymaker as an executive whose compensation package is structured so as to raise the marginal cost of inflation. Or, if the inflation bias arises from political pressures on the central bank, institutions might be designed to reduce the effect of the current government on the conduct of monetary policy.

Finally, a third class of solutions involves imposing limitations on the central bank's flexibility. The most common such restriction is a targeting rule that requires the central bank to achieve a preset rate of inflation or imposes a cost related to deviations from this target. An analysis of inflation targeting is important because many

---

9. See Persson and Tabellini (1990) for an in-depth discussion of much of this literature. Many of the most important papers are collected in Persson and Tabellini (1994a).

central banks have adopted inflation targeting as a framework for the conduct of policy.[10]

Before considering these solutions, however, it is important to note that the tradition in the monetary policy literature has been to assume that the underlying cause of the bias, the desire for economic expansions captured either by the presence of output in the case of the linear objective function (7.1) or by the parameter k in the quadratic loss function (7.2), is given. Clearly, policies that might eliminate the factors that create a wedge between the economy's equilibrium output and the central bank's desired level would lead to the first-best outcome in the Barro-Gordon model.

7.3.1 Reputation

One potential solution to an inflationary bias is to force the central bank to bear some cost if it deviates from its announced policy of low inflation, thereby raising the marginal cost of inflation as perceived by the central bank. One form such a cost might take is a lost reputation. The central bank might, perhaps through its past behavior, demonstrate that it will deliver zero inflation despite the apparent incentive to inflate. If the central bank then deviates from the low-inflation solution, its credibility is lost and the public expects high inflation in the future. That is, the public employs a trigger strategy. The folk theorem for infinite horizon repeated games (Fudenberg and Maskin 1986) suggests that equilibria exist in which inflation remains below the discretionary equilibrium level as long as the central bank's discount rate is not too high. Hence, as long as the central bank cares enough about the future, a low-inflation equilibrium can be supported.

An alternative approach is to consider situations in which the public may be uncertain about the true preferences of the central bank. In the resulting imperfect information game, the public's expectations concerning inflation must be based on its beliefs about the central bank's preferences or *type*. Based on observed outcomes, these beliefs evolve over time, and central banks may have incentives to affect these beliefs through their actions. A central bank willing to accept some inflation in return for an economic expansion may still find it optimal initially to build a reputation as an anti-inflation central bank.

A Repeated Game

The basic Barro-Gordon model is a one-shot game; even if the central bank's objective is to maximize $E_t \sum_{i=0} \beta^i U_{t+i}$, where U_t is defined by (7.1) and β is a discount factor $(0 < \beta < 1)$, nothing links time t decisions with future periods.[11] Thus, the

---

10. More than 20 countries have adopted inflation targeting. For evaluations of inflation targeting, see Mishkin and Schmidt-Hebbel (2002; 2007); Carare and Stone (2002); Batinit and Laxton (2007); and Walsh (2009).

11. The same clearly applies to the case of a quadratic objective function of the form (7.2).

inflation rate in each period $t + s$ is chosen to maximize the expected value of U_{t+s}, and the discretionary equilibrium of the one-shot game is a noncooperative Nash equilibrium of the repeated game. Barro and Gordon (1983b) evaluated the role of reputation by considering a repeated game in which the choice of inflation at time t can affect expectations about future inflation. They examined whether inflation rates below the one-shot discretionary equilibrium rate can be sustained in a trigger strategy equilibrium.

To illustrate their approach, suppose that the central bank's objective is to maximize the expected present discounted value of (7.1) and that the public behaves in the following manner. If in period $t - 1$ the central bank delivered an inflation rate equal to what the public had expected (i.e., the central bank did not fool them in the previous period), the public expects an inflation rate in period t of $\bar{\pi} < a\lambda$. But if the central bank did fool them, the public expects the inflation rate that would arise under pure discretion, $a\lambda$. The hypothesized behavior of the public is summarized by

$$\pi_t^e = \bar{\pi} < a\lambda \qquad \text{if } \pi_{t-1} = \pi_{t-1}^e$$

$$\pi_t^e = a\lambda \qquad \qquad \text{otherwise.}$$

It is important to note that this trigger strategy involves a one-period punishment. If, after deviating and inflating at a rate that differs from $\bar{\pi}$, the central bank can deliver an inflation rate of $a\lambda$ for one period, the public again expects the lower rate $\bar{\pi}$.[12]

The central bank's objective is to maximize

$$\sum_{i=0}^{\infty} \beta^i E_t(U_{t+i}),$$

where U_t is given by (7.1). Previously, the central bank's actions at time t had no effects in any other period. Consequently, the problem simplified to a sequence of one-period problems, a situation that is no longer true in this repeated game with reputation. Inflation at time t affects expectations at time $t + 1$ and therefore the expected value of U_{t+1}. The question is whether equilibria exist for inflation rates $\bar{\pi}$ that are less than the outcome under pure discretion.

Suppose that the central bank has set $\pi_s = \bar{\pi}$ for all $s < t$. Under the hypothesis about the public's expectations, $\pi_t^e = \bar{\pi}$. What can the central bank gain by deviating from the $\bar{\pi}$ equilibrium? Ignoring any aggregate supply shocks (i.e., $e \equiv 0$), assume

---

12. This type of one-period punishment strategy has little to commend itself in terms of plausibility. It does, however, provide a useful starting point for analyzing a situation in which the central bank might refrain from inflating at the discretionary rate because it recognizes that the public will subsequently expect higher inflation.

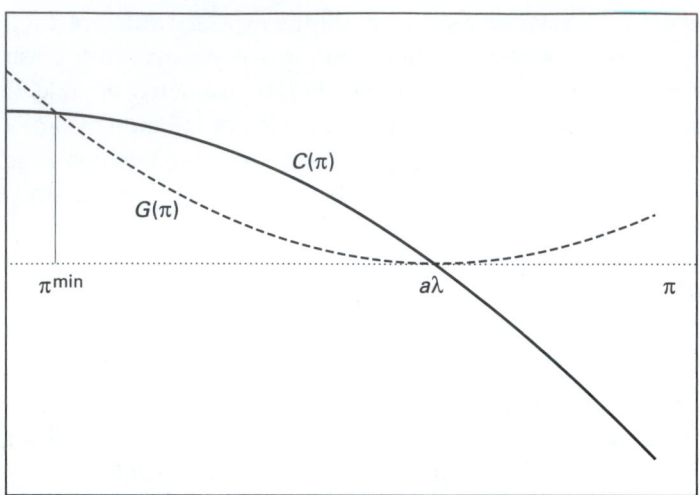

Figure 7.3
Temptation and enforcement.

that the central bank controls inflation directly. Then setting inflation a little above $\bar{\pi}$, say at $\pi_t = \varepsilon > \bar{\pi}$, increases the time t value of the central bank's objective function by

$$\left[a\lambda(\varepsilon - \bar{\pi}) - \frac{1}{2}\varepsilon^2 \right] - \left[-\frac{1}{2}\bar{\pi}^2 \right] = a\lambda(\varepsilon - \bar{\pi}) - \frac{1}{2}(\varepsilon^2 - \bar{\pi}^2).$$

This is maximized for $\varepsilon = a\lambda$, the inflation rate under discretion. So if the central bank deviates, it will set inflation equal to $a\lambda$ and gain

$$G(\bar{\pi}) \equiv a\lambda(a\lambda - \bar{\pi}) - \frac{1}{2}[(a\lambda)^2 - \bar{\pi}^2] = \frac{1}{2}(a\lambda - \bar{\pi})^2 \geq 0.$$

Barro and Gordon referred to this as the *temptation* to cheat. The function $G(\bar{\pi})$ is shown as the dashed line in figure 7.3. It is non-negative for all $\bar{\pi}$ and reaches a minimum at $\bar{\pi} = a\lambda$.

Cheating carries a cost because, in the period following a deviation, the public will punish the central bank by expecting an inflation rate of $a\lambda$. Since $a\lambda$ maximizes the central bank's one-period objective function for any expected rate of inflation, the central bank sets $\pi_{t+1} = a\lambda$. The subsequent loss, relative to the $\bar{\pi}$ inflation path, is given by

$$C(\bar{\pi}) \equiv \beta\left(-\frac{1}{2}\bar{\pi}^2 \right) - \beta\left(-\frac{1}{2}a^2\lambda^2 \right) = \frac{\beta}{2}[(a\lambda)^2 - \bar{\pi}^2]. \tag{7.13}$$

Since the loss occurs in period $t + 1$, multiply it by the central bank's discount factor β. Barro and Gordon referred to this as the *enforcement*. The function $C(\bar{\pi})$ is decreasing for $\bar{\pi} > 0$ and is shown as the solid line in figure 7.3.

The central bank will deviate from the proposed equilibrium if the gain (the temptation) exceeds the loss (the enforcement). Any $\bar{\pi}$ such that $C(\bar{\pi}) \geq G(\bar{\pi})$ can be supported as an equilibrium; with the loss exceeding the gain, the central bank has no incentive to deviate. As shown in figure 7.3, $C(\pi) < G(\pi)$ for inflation rates less than $\pi^{min} \equiv (1 - \beta)a\lambda/(1 + \beta) < a\lambda$. Because $\pi^{min} > 0$, the trigger strategy cannot support the socially optimal, zero inflation outcome. However, any inflation rate in the interval $[\pi^{min}, a\lambda]$ is sustainable. The minimum sustainable inflation rate π^{min} is decreasing in β; the greater the weight the central bank places on the future, the greater the enforcement mechanism provided by the public's expectations and the lower the inflation rate that can be sustained.[13]

This example is a simple illustration of a trigger strategy. The public expects one rate of inflation ($\bar{\pi}$ in this example) as long as the central bank "behaves," and it expects a different, higher rate of inflation if the central bank misbehaves. But how does the public coordinate on this trigger strategy? If the public is atomistic, each member would take the expectations of others as given in forming its own expectations, and the notion of public coordination makes little sense. This problem is even more severe when multiperiod punishment periods are considered, in which the public expects high inflation for some fixed number of period greater than one. Again, how is this expectation determined?

One way to solve the coordination problem is to assume that the central bank plays a game against a monopoly union.[14] With only one agent in the private sector (the union), the issue of atomistic agents coordinating on a trigger strategy no longer arises. Of course, the coordination problem has, in some sense, been solved by simply assuming it away, but it is also the case that many countries do have labor markets that are dominated by national unions and business organizations that negotiate over wages.[15]

The general point, though, is that the reputational solution works because the loss of reputation represents a cost to the central bank. Raising the marginal cost of inflation lowers the equilibrium rate of inflation. If $C(\bar{\pi}) > G(\bar{\pi})$, the central bank will

13. With the central bank's objective given by (7.2), a zero inflation rate can be supported with a one-period punishment trigger strategy of the type considered as long as the central bank places sufficient weight on the future. In particular, zero inflation is an equilibrium if $\beta/(\alpha^2 + \beta) > 1$. See problem 10 at the end of this chapter.

14. Tabellini (1988) studied the case of a monopoly union in the Barro-Gordon framework, although he focused on imperfect information about the central bank's type. See also Cubitt (1992).

15. al-Nowaihi and Levine (1994) provided an interpretation in terms of a game involving successive governments rather than a monopoly union. See also Herrendorf and Lockwood (1997).

not have an incentive to cheat, and inflation at the rate $\bar{\pi}$ can be supported. But suppose the central bank does cheat. Will it be in the interests of a private sector that has somehow coordinated on a trigger strategy to actually punish the central bank? If by punishing the central bank the private sector also punishes itself, the threat to punish may not be credible. If punishment is not credible, the central bank is not deterred from cheating in the first place.

The credibility of trigger strategies in the context of the Barro-Gordon model (with the utility function (7.1)) was examined by al-Nowaihi and Levine (1994). They considered the case of a single monopoly union and showed that if one requires that the punishment hurt the central bank but not the private sector (i.e., consider only equilibria that are renegotiation-proof), then the only equilibrium is the high-inflation discretionary equilibrium. Thus, it would appear that trigger strategies will not support a low-inflation equilibrium.

Requiring that the punishment hurt only the central bank imposes strong restrictions on the possible equilibria. Adopting a weaker notion of renegotiation, al-Nowaihi and Levine introduced the concept of *chisel-proof credibility*[16] by asking, if the central bank cheats just a little, will the public be better off simply acquiescing, or will it be better off punishing? They show that the lowest inflation rate that can be supported in a chisel-proof equilibrium is positive but less than the discretionary rate.

This discussion of trigger strategy equilibria assumed that the trigger was pulled whenever inflation deviated from its optimal value. If inflation differed from $\bar{\pi}$, this outcome revealed to the public that the central bank had cheated. But for such strategies to work, the public must be able to determine whether the central bank cheated. If inflation depends not just on the central bank's policy but also on the outcome of a random disturbance, as in (7.4), then the trigger strategy must be based directly on the central bank's policy instrument rather than on the realized rate of inflation. Simply observing the actual rate of inflation may only reveal the net effects of both the central bank's policy actions and the realizations of a variety of random effects that influence the inflation rate.

This consequence raises a difficulty, one first analyzed by Canzoneri (1985). Suppose that inflation is given by $\pi = \Delta m + v$. In addition, suppose that the central bank has a private, unverifiable forecast of v—call it v^f—and that Δm can be set conditional on v^f. Reputational equilibria will now be harder to sustain. Recall that the trigger strategy equilibrium required that the public punish the central bank whenever the central bank deviated from the low-inflation policy. In the absence of private information, the public can always determine whether the central bank deviated by simply looking at the value of Δm. When the central bank has private infor-

---

16. See also Herrendorf (1995).

mation on the velocity shock, it should adjust Δm to offset v^f. So if the central bank forecasts a negative v, it should raise Δm. Simply observing ex post a high value of Δm, therefore, will not allow the public to determine if the central bank cheated; the central bank can always claim that v^f was negative and that it had not cheated.[17]

Canzoneri showed that a trigger strategy equilibrium can be constructed in which the public assumes that the central bank cheated whenever the implicit forecast error of the central bank is too large. That is, a policy designed to achieve a zero rate of inflation would call for setting $\Delta m = -v^f$, and this might involve a positive rate of money growth. Whenever money growth is too high, that is, whenever $\Delta m > -\bar{v}$ for some $\bar{v}$, the public assumes that the central bank has cheated. The public then expects high inflation in the subsequent period; high expected inflation punishes the central bank. The constant $\bar{v}$ is chosen to ensure that the central bank has no incentive to deviate from the zero inflation policy. This equilibrium leads to a situation in which there are occasional periods of inflation; whenever the central bank's forecast for the random variable v takes on a value such that $\Delta m = -v^f > -\bar{v}$, expected inflation (and actual inflation) rises. One solution to this problem may involve making policy more transparent by establishing targets that allow deviations to be clearly observed by the public. Herrendorf (1999), for example, argued that a fixed exchange rate policy may contribute to credibility because any deviation is immediately apparent. This solves the Canzoneri problem; the public does not need to verify the central bank's private information about velocity. If the central bank has private information on the economy that would call, under the optimal commitment policy, for a change in the exchange rate, a fixed exchange rate regime will limit the flexibility of the central bank to act on this information. Changing the exchange rate would signal to the public that the central bank was attempting to cheat. As a result, a trade-off between credibility and flexibility in conducting stabilization policy can arise.

The basic model of time inconsistency under discretion characterized the equilibrium in terms of a sequence of single-period equilibria that depended only on the current state. In particular, the actions by the private sector in forming expectations did not depend on the past history of policy actions. Chari and Kehoe (1990) introduced the notion of sustainable plans under discretion, where a sustainable plan is a policy that is optimal from the perspective of the policymaker when the impact of the policy on future histories, and the impact of these histories on future private sector decisions, is taken into account. To characterize the set of possible equilibria that are sustainable, Chari and Kehoe followed Abreu (1988) in finding the worst sustainable

---

17. Herrendorf (1999) considered situations in which v has a bounded support $[\underline{v}, \bar{v}]$. If the optimal commitment policy is $\Delta m = 0$, then as long as $\underline{v} \le \pi \le \bar{v}$, the public cannot tell whether the central bank cheated. However, if $\pi > \bar{v}$, the public knows the central bank cheated. Thus, the probability of detection is $\text{Prob}(v > \bar{v} - m)$.

outcome. In the simple Barro-Gordon model, this worst outcome is the one with the average inflation bias that led, in the case of a quadratic loss function, to the expected loss given in (7.9). Ireland (1997a) applied the concept of sustainable equilibrium to study the Barro-Gordon average inflation bias in a well-specified model that allows policies to be ranked according to their implications for the welfare of the representative agent.[18] He showed that if the policymaker places a sufficiently large weight on future outcomes, any inflation rate between a deflation associated with the Friedman rule (a zero nominal rate of interest) and the rate that arises under discretion can be sustained as an equilibrium.

Central Bank Types

In Canzoneri (1985), the central bank has private information about the economy in the form of an unverifiable forecast of an economic disturbance. The public doesn't know what the central bank knows about the economy, and more important, the public cannot ex post verify the central bank's information. An alternative aspect of asymmetric information involves situations in which the public is uncertain about the central bank's true preferences. Backus and Driffill (1985); Barro (1986); Cukierman and Meltzer (1986); Vickers (1986); Tabellini (1988); T. Andersen (1989); Mino and Tsutsui (1990); Cukierman and Liviatan (1991); Cukierman (1992); Garcia de Paso (1993); Drazen and Masson (1994); Ball (1995); Herrendorf (1999); al-Nowaihi and Levine (1996); Briault, Haldane, and King (1996); Nolan and Schaling (1996); and Walsh (2000), among others, studied models in which the public is uncertain about the central bank's type, usually identified either as its preference between output and inflation stabilization or as its ability to commit. In these models, the public must attempt to infer the central bank's type from its policy actions, and equilibria in which central banks may deviate from one-shot optimal policies in order to develop reputations have been studied (for a survey, see Rogoff 1989). In choosing its actions, a central bank must take into account the uncertainty faced by the public, and it may be advantageous for one type of bank to mimic the other type to conceal (possibly only temporarily) its true type from the public.

In one of the earliest reputational models of monetary policy, Backus and Driffill (1985) assumed that governments (or central banks) come in two types: optimizers who always act to maximize the expected present discounted value of a utility function of the form (7.1) and single-minded inflation fighters who always pursue a policy of zero inflation. Alternatively, the inflation fighter types can be described as having access to a precommitment technology. The government in office knows which type it is, but this information is unverifiable by the public. Simply announcing it is a zero

---

18. Kurozumi (2008) examined optimal sustainable monetary policies within the context of a new Keynesian model in which discretionary generates a bias in stabilization policy.

inflation government would not be credible because the public realizes that an optimizing central bank would also announce that it is a strict inflation fighter to induce the public to expect low inflation.[19]

Initially, the public is assumed to have prior beliefs about the current government's type (where these beliefs come from is unspecified, and therefore there will be multiple equilibria, one for each set of initial beliefs). If the government is actually an optimizer and ever chooses to inflate, its identity is revealed, and from then on the public expects the equilibrium inflation rate under discretion. To avoid this outcome, the optimizing government may have an incentive to conceal its true identity by mimicking the zero inflation type, at least for a while. Equilibrium may involve pooling, in which both types behave the same way. In a finite-period game, the optimizer will always inflate in the last period because there is no future gain from further attempts at concealment.

Backus and Driffill solved for the equilibrium in their model by employing the concept of a *sequential equilibrium* (Kreps and Wilson 1982) for a finitely repeated game. Let π_t^d equal the inflation rate for period t set by a zero inflation (a "dry") government, and let π_t^w be the rate set by an optimizing (a "wet") government. Start in the final period T. The zero inflation type always sets $\pi_T^d = 0$, and the optimizing type always inflates in the last period at the discretionary rate $\pi_T^w = a\lambda$. With no further value in investing in a reputation, a wet government just chooses the optimal inflation rate derived from the one-period Barro-Gordon model analyzed earlier.

In periods prior to T, however, the government's policy choice affects its future reputation, and it may therefore benefit a wet government to choose a zero rate of inflation in order to build a reputation as a dry government. Thus, equilibrium may consist of an initial series of periods in which the wet government mimics the dry government, and inflation is zero. For suitable values of the parameters, the sequential equilibrium concept that Backus and Driffill employed also leads to mixed strategies in which the wet government inflates with some probability. So the wet government randomizes; if the outcome calls for it to inflate, the government is revealed as wet, and from then on, inflation is equal to $a\lambda$. If it doesn't inflate, the public updates its beliefs about the government's type using Bayes's rule.

Ball (1995) developed a model of inflation persistence based on the same notion of central bank types used by Backus and Driffill (1985) and Barro (1986). That is, one type, type D, always sets inflation equal to zero, whereas type W acts opportunistically to minimize the expected discounted value of a quadratic loss function of the form

---

19. Vickers (1986) assumed that the types differ with respect to the weight placed on inflation in the loss function. In Tabellini (1988) the "tough" type has $\lambda = 0$ (i.e., no weight on output), while the "weak" type is characterized by a $\lambda > 0$. Cukierman and Liviatan (1991) assumed that the types differ in their ability to commit.

$$L^W = \sum_{i=0}^{\infty} \beta^i [\lambda(y_{t+i} - y_n - k)^2 + \pi_{t+i}^2], \tag{7.14}$$

where $0 < \beta < 1$. To account for shifts in policy, Ball assumed that the central bank type follows a Markov process. If the central bank is of type D in period t, then the probability that the central bank is still type D in period $t+1$ is d; the probability that the bank switches to type W in $t+1$ is $1-d$. Similarly, if the period t central bank is type W, then the $t+1$ central bank is type W with probability w and type D with probability $1-w$.

The specification of the economy is standard, with output a function of inflation surprises and an aggregate supply shock:

$$y_t = y_n + a(\pi_t - \pi_t^e) + e_t. \tag{7.15}$$

To capture the idea that economies are subject to occasional discrete supply shocks, Ball assumed that e takes on only two possible values: 0 with probability $1-q$ and $\bar{e} < 0$ with probability q. If shifts in policy and supply shocks are infrequent, then $1-d$, $1-w$, and q are all small.

The timing in this game has the public forming expectations of inflation; then the supply shock and the central bank type are determined. It is assumed that the realization of e but not of the central bank type is observable. Finally, the central bank sets π. In this game, there are many possible equilibria, depending on how the public is assumed to form its expectations about the central bank type. Ball considered a perfect Nash equilibrium concept in which actions depend only on variables that directly affect current payoffs. Such equilibria are Markov perfect equilibria (Maskin and Tirole 1988) and rule out the types of trigger strategy equilibria considered, for example, by Barro (1986).[20] Ball then showed that such an equilibrium exists and involves the W type setting $\pi = 0$ as long as $e = 0$; if $e = \bar{e}$, the W type inflates at the discretionary rate. Since this reveals the identify of the central bank (i.e., as a type W), inflation remains at the discretionary rate $a\lambda k$ until such time as a type D central bank takes over. At this point, inflation drops to zero, remaining there until a bad supply shock is again realized.[21]

This outcome predicts periodic and persistent bouts of inflation in response to adverse economic disturbances. This prediction for inflation appears to provide a good

---

20. In the trigger strategy equilibria, current actions depend on π_{t-1} even though payoffs do not depend directly on lagged inflation.

21. For this to be an equilibrium, the discount factor must be large but not too large. As in standard reputational models, the type W central bank must place enough weight on the future to be willing to mimic the type D in order to develop a reputation for low inflation. However, if the future receives too much weight, the type W will be unwilling to separate, that is, inflate, when the bad shock occurs. See Ball (1995).

representation of actual inflation experiences, at least in the developed economies over the past 40 years.

One undesirable aspect of the Backus-Driffill framework is its assumption that one government, the dry government, is simply an automaton, always playing zero inflation. While serving a useful purpose in allowing one to characterize how beliefs about type might affect the reputation and behavior of a government that would otherwise like to inflate, the myopic behavior of the dry government is unsatisfactory; such a government might also wish to signal its type to the public or otherwise attempt to differentiate itself from a wet type.

One way a dry government might distinguish itself would be to announce a planned or target rate of inflation and then build credibility by actually delivering on its promises. In the Backus-Driffill model, the dry government could be thought of as always announcing a zero target for inflation, but as Cukierman and Liviatan (1991) noted, even central banks that seem committed to low inflation often set positive inflation targets, and they do so in part because low inflation is not perfectly credible. That is, if the public expects a positive rate of inflation because the central bank's true intentions are unknown, then even a dry central bank may feel the need to partially accommodate these expectations. Doing otherwise would produce a recession.

To model this type of situation, Cukierman and Liviatan assumed that there are two potential government or central bank types, D and W, that differ in their ability to commit. Type D commits to its announced policy; type W cannot precommit. In contrast to Backus and Driffill, Cukierman and Liviatan allowed their central banks to make announcements, and the D type is not simply constrained always to maintain a zero rate of inflation. If the public assigns some prior probability to the central bank's being type W, type D's announcement will not be fully credible. As a result, a type D central bank may find it optimal to announce a positive rate of inflation.

To show the effect on inflation of the public's uncertainty about the type of central bank in office, the basic points can be illustrated within the context of a two-period model. To determine the equilibrium behavior of inflation, one needs to solve the model backward by first considering the equilibrium during the last period.

Assume that both central bank types share a utility function that is linear in output and quadratic in inflation, as given by (7.1). With utility linear in output, stabilization will not play a role, so let output be given by (7.3) with $e \equiv 0$. In the second period, reputation has no further value, so the type W central bank will simply set inflation at the optimal discretionary rate $a\lambda$. To determine $D's$ strategy, however, one needs to consider whether the equilibrium will be a separating, pooling, or mixed-strategy equilibrium. In a separating equilibrium, the behavior of the central bank during the first period reveals its identity; in a pooling equilibrium, both types behave the same way during the first period, so the public will remain uncertain as to the true identity of the bank. A mixed-strategy equilibrium would involve type W mimicking type D, with a positive probability less than 1.

Since a separating equilibrium is a bit simpler to construct, that case is considered first. With first-period behavior revealing the bank's type, the public in period 2 knows the identity of the central bank. Since type D is able to commit, its optimal policy is to announce a zero rate of inflation for period 2. The public, knowing that a type D is truthful, expects a zero inflation rate, and in equilibrium $\pi_2^D = 0$.

In the first period of a separating equilibrium, the public is uncertain about the type of central bank actually in power. Suppose the public assigns an initial probability q to the central bank being type D. In a separating equilibrium in which the W type reveals itself by inflating at a rate that differs from the announced rate, the type W will choose to inflate at the rate $a\lambda$ because this value maximizes its utility function.[22] So if the type D announces π^a, then the public will expect an inflation rate of $\pi_1^e = q\pi^a + (1-q)a\lambda$.[23] The last step to fully characterize the separating equilibrium is to determine the optimal announcement (since the D type actually inflates at the announced rate and the W type inflates at the rate $a\lambda$).

If future utility is discounted at the rate β, the utility of the type D central bank is given by

$$U_{sep}^D = \lambda(y_1 - y_n) - \frac{1}{2}\pi_1^2 + \beta\left[\lambda(y_2 - y_n) - \frac{1}{2}\pi_2^2\right]$$

$$= a\lambda(\pi_1 - \pi_1^e) - \frac{1}{2}\pi_1^2,$$

since, in period 2, $y_2 = y_n$ and $\pi_2^D = 0$. The type D picks first-period inflation subject to $\pi_1 = \pi^a$ and $\pi_1^e = q\pi^a + (1-q)a\lambda$. This yields

$$\pi_1^D = (1-q)a\lambda \le a\lambda.$$

The role of credibility is clearly illustrated in this result. If the central bank were known to be of type D, that is, if $q = 1$, it could announce and deliver a zero rate of inflation. The possibility that the central bank might be of type W, however, forces the D type to actually announce and deliver a positive rate of inflation. The public's uncertainty leads it to expect a positive rate of inflation; the type D central bank could announce and deliver a zero rate of inflation, but doing so would create a recession whose cost outweighs the gain from a lower inflation rate.

---

22. Recall that with the utility function (7.1), the central bank's optimal period 1 inflation rate is independent of the expected rate of inflation.

23. The W type will also announce the same inflation rate as the type D because doing otherwise would immediately raise the public's expectations about first-period inflation and lower type $W's$ utility.

To summarize, in a separating equilibrium, the type W inflates at the rate $a\lambda$ in each period, and the type D inflates at the rate $(1-q)a\lambda$ during the first period and zero during the second period. Since expected inflation in the first period is $q(1-q)a\lambda + (1-q)a\lambda = (1-q^2)a\lambda$, which is less than $a\lambda$ but greater than $(1-q)a\lambda$, output is above y_n if the central bank is actually type W and below y_n if the bank is type D.

What happens in a pooling equilibrium? A pooling equilibrium requires that the W type not only make the same first-period announcement as the D type but also that it pick the same actual inflation rate in period 1 (otherwise, it would reveal itself). In this case, the D type faces period 2 expectations $\pi_2^e = q\pi_2^a + (1-q)a\lambda$.[24] Since this is just like the problem analyzed for the first period of the separating equilibrium, $\pi_2^D = \pi_2^a = (1-q)a\lambda > 0$. The type D inflates at a positive rate in period 2, since its announcement lacks complete credibility. In the first period of a pooling equilibrium, however, things are different. In a pooling equilibrium, the D type knows that the W type will mimic whatever the D type does. And the public knows this also, so both types will inflate at the announced rate of inflation and $\pi_1^e = \pi_1^a$. In this case, with the announcement fully credible, the D type will announce and deliver $\pi_1 = 0$.

To summarize, in the pooling equilibrium, inflation will equal zero in period 1 and either $(1-q)a\lambda$ or $a\lambda$ in period 2, depending on which type is actually in office. In the separating equilibrium, inflation will equal $(1-q)a\lambda$ in period 1 and zero in period 2 if the central bank is of type D, and $a\lambda$ in both periods if the central bank is of type W.

Which equilibrium will occur? If the type W separates by inflating at the rate $a\lambda$ during period 1, its utility will be $a\lambda[a\lambda - (1-q^2)a\lambda] - \frac{1}{2}(a\lambda)^2 - \beta\frac{1}{2}(a\lambda)^2$, or

$$U_{sep}^W = (a\lambda)^2 \left[q^2 - \frac{1}{2}(1+\beta) \right].$$

If the type W deviates from the separating equilibrium and mimics type D by only inflating at the rate $(1-q)a\lambda$ during period 1, it will achieve a utility payoff of $a\lambda[(1-q)a\lambda - (1-q^2)a\lambda] - \frac{1}{2}[(1-q)a\lambda]^2 + \beta a\lambda(a\lambda - 0) - \beta\frac{1}{2}(a\lambda)^2$, or

$$U_m^W = \frac{1}{2}(a\lambda)^2(q^2 - 1 + \beta),$$

---

24. In the pooling equilibrium, first-period outcomes do not reveal any information about the identity of the central bank type, so the public continues to assess the probability of a type D as equal to q. This would not be the case if the equilibrium involved the W type following a mixed strategy in which it inflates in period 1 with probability $p < 1$. In a sequential Bayesian equilibrium, the public updates the probability of a D type on the basis of the period 1 outcomes using Bayes's rule.

because mimicking fools the public into expecting zero inflation in period 2. Type W will separate if and only if $U_{sep}^W > U_m^W$, which occurs when

$$\beta < q^2/2 \equiv \underline{\beta}. \tag{7.16}$$

Thus, the separating equilibrium occurs if the public places a high initial probability on the central bank's being type D (q is large). In this case, the type D is able to set a low first-period rate of inflation and the W type does not find it worthwhile to mimic. Only if the type W places a large weight on being able to engineer a surprise inflation in period 2 (i.e., β is large) would deviating from the separating equilibrium be profitable.[25]

Suppose $\beta \geq \underline{\beta}$; will pooling emerge? Not necessarily. If the type W pools, its utility payoff will be

$$a\lambda[0] - \frac{1}{2}[0]^2 + \beta a\lambda[a\lambda - \pi_2^e] - \beta\frac{1}{2}(a\lambda)^2$$

or, since $\pi_2^e = q\pi_2^a + (1-q)a\lambda = (1-q^2)a\lambda$,

$$U_p^W = \beta(a\lambda)^2\left(q^2 - \frac{1}{2}\right).$$

If the type W deviates from the pooling equilibrium, it will generate an output expansion in period 1, but by revealing its identity, period 2 inflation is fully anticipated and output equals y_n. Thus, deviating gives the type W a payoff of $a\lambda[a\lambda] - \frac{1}{2}[a\lambda]^2 + \beta a\lambda[0] - \beta\frac{1}{2}[a\lambda]^2$, or

$$U_{dev}^W = \frac{1}{2}(a\lambda)^2(1-\beta).$$

By comparing the incentive for W to deviate from a pooling equilibrium, the pooling outcome is an equilibrium whenever

$$\beta > \frac{1}{2q^2} \equiv \bar{\beta} \tag{7.17}$$

since in this case $U_p^W > U_{dev}^W$. If β is large enough, meaning $\beta > 1/(2q^2)$, type W places enough weight on the future that it is willing to forgo the temptation to inflate immediately, and zero inflation is the equilibrium in period 1. Of course, in period 2,

---

25. Walsh (2000) showed that a separating equilibrium is less likely if inflation is determined by the type of forward-looking new Keynesian Phillips curves discussed in chapter 6. When current inflation depends on expected future inflation, a type W whose identity is revealed in the the first period suffers an immediate rise in inflation as expected future inflation rises.

there is no further value in maintaining a reputation, so type W inflates at the rate $a\lambda$. Equation (7.17) shows that the critical cutoff value for β depends on q, the prior probability the public assigns to a type D setting policy. A larger q makes pooling an equilibrium for more values of β, so that even less patient type W banks will find it advantageous to not deviate from the pooling equilibrium. If q is large, then the public thinks it likely that the central bank is a type D. This leads them to expect low inflation in period 2, so the output gains of inflating at the rate $a\lambda$ will be large. By pooling during period 1, a type W can then benefit from causing a large expansion in period 2. If the type W deviates and reveals its type during period 1, the first-period output gain is independent of q.[26] So a rise in q leaves the period 1 advantage of deviating unchanged while increasing the gain from waiting until period 2 to inflate.

Comparing (7.16) and (7.17) shows that $\underline{\beta} < \bar{\beta}$, so there will be a range of values for the discount factor for which neither the separating nor the pooling outcomes will be an equilibrium. For β in this range, there will be mixed-strategy equilibria (see Cukierman and Liviatan 1991).

This model reveals how public uncertainty about the intentions of the central bank affects the equilibrium inflation rate. In both the separating equilibrium and the mixed-strategy equilibrium, the type D central bank inflates in the first period even though it is (by assumption) capable of commitment and always delivers on its announcements.

The formulation of Cukierman and Liviatan provides a nice illustration of the role that announcements can play in influencing the conduct of policy. It also illustrates why central banks might be required to make announcements about their inflation plans. The type D central bank is clearly better off making announcements; as long as $q > 0$, making an announcement allows the type D to influence expectations and reduce the first-period inflation rate (this occurs in the separating and pooling equilibria and also in mixed-strategy equilibria). Even when there may be incentives to manipulate announcements, they can serve to constrain the subsequent conduct of policy. They may also convey information about the economy if the central bank has private and unverifiable information such as its own internal forecast of economic conditions.[27]

7.3.2   Preferences

An alternative approach to solving the inflationary bias of discretion focuses directly on the preferences of the central bank. This branch of the literature has closer connections with the extensive empirical work that has found, at least for the

---

26. This is because expected inflation equals zero during the first period of a pooling equilibrium. Consequently, the output expansion of inflating at the rate $a\lambda$ is $a(a\lambda - 0) = a^2\lambda$, which is independent of q.

27. See Persson and Tabellini (1993); Muscatelli (1999); and Walsh (1999).

industrialized economies, that average inflation rates across countries are negatively correlated with measures of the degree to which a central bank is independent of the political authorities.[28] If the central bank is independent, then one can begin to think of the preferences of the central bank as differing from those of the elected government. And if they can differ, then one can ask how they might differ and how the government, through its appointment process, might influence the preferences of the central bank(er).

Rogoff (1985b) was the first to analyze explicitly the issue of the optimal preferences of the central banker.[29] He did so in terms of the relative weight the central banker places on the inflation objective. In the objective function (7.2), λ measures the weight on output relative to a weight normalized to 1 on inflation objectives. Rogoff concluded that the government should appoint as central banker someone who places greater relative weight on the inflation objective than does society (the government) as a whole. That is, the central banker should have preferences that are of the form given by (7.2) but with a weight on inflation of $1 + \delta > 1$. Rogoff characterized such a central banker as more *conservative* than society as a whole. This is usefully described as *weight conservatism* (Svensson 1997b) because there are other interpretations of conservatism; for example, the central bank might have a target inflation rate that is lower than that of the government. In most of the literature, however, *conservative* is interpreted in terms of the weight placed on inflation objectives relative to output objectives.

The intuition behind Rogoff's result is easily understood by referring to (7.7), which showed the inflation rate under discretion for the quadratic loss function (7.2). If the central banker conducting monetary policy has a loss function that differs from (7.2) only by placing weight $1 + \delta$ on inflation rather than 1, then inflation under discretion will equal

$$\pi^d(\delta) = \Delta m + v = \frac{a\lambda k}{1 + \delta} - \left(\frac{a\lambda}{1 + \delta + a^2\lambda} \right) e + v. \tag{7.18}$$

The equilibrium inflation rate is a function δ. Two effects are at work. First, the average inflation bias is reduced, since $1 + \delta > 1$. This tends to reduce the social loss function (the loss function with weight 1 on inflation and λ on output). But the coef-

28. The empirical literature on central bank independence and inflation and other macroeconomic outcomes is large. See Cukierman (1998) for an excellent treatment. I surveyed this literature in previous editions (see section 8.5 of the second edition). That material is now available at ⟨http://people.ucsc.edu/~walshc/mtp3e/⟩.

29. Interestingly, Barro and Gordon recognized that outcomes could be improved under discretion by distorting the central banker's preferences so that "there is a divergence in preferences between the principal (society) and its agent (the policymaker)" (Barro and Gordon 1983a, 607, n. 19). This insight is also relevant for the contracting approach (see section 7.3.3).

ficient on the aggregate supply shock is also reduced; stabilization policy is distorted, and the central bank responds too little to e. As a consequence, output fluctuates more than is socially optimal in response to supply shocks. The first effect (lower average inflation) makes it optimal to appoint a central banker who places more weight on inflation than does society; this is usually interpreted to mean that society should appoint a conservative to head the central bank. But the second effect (less output stabilization) limits how conservative the central banker should be.

Using (7.18), one can evaluate the government's loss function V as a function of δ. By then minimizing the government's expected loss function with respect to δ, one can find the *optimal preferences* for a central banker. The expected value of the government's objective function is

$$
E[V] = \frac{1}{2} E(\lambda \{a[\pi^d(\delta) - \pi^e] + e - k\}^2 + [\pi^d(\delta)]^2)
$$

$$
= \frac{1}{2} \left[\lambda k^2 + \lambda \left(\frac{1+\delta}{1+\delta+a^2\lambda} \right)^2 \sigma_e^2 + a^2 \lambda \sigma_v^2 \right]
$$

$$
+ \frac{1}{2} \left[\left(\frac{a\lambda k}{1+\delta} \right)^2 + \left(\frac{a\lambda}{1+\delta+a^2\lambda} \right)^2 \sigma_e^2 + \sigma_v^2 \right],
$$

where (7.18) is used to replace π^e with $a\lambda k/(1+\delta)$ under the assumption that the public knows δ when forming its expectations. Minimizing this expression with respect to δ yields, after some manipulation, the following condition that must be satisfied by the optimal value of δ:

$$
\delta = \left(\frac{k^2}{\sigma_e^2} \right) \left(\frac{1+\delta+a^2\lambda}{1+\delta} \right)^3 \equiv g(\delta). \tag{7.19}
$$

The function $g(\delta)$ is shown in figure 7.4.[30] Equation (7.19) is satisfied where $g(\delta)$ crosses the 45° line. Since $g(0) > 0$ and $\lim_{\delta \to \infty} g(\delta) = k^2/\sigma_e^2 > 0$, the intersection always occurs in the range $\delta \in (0, \infty]$; given the trade-off between distorting the response of policy to aggregate supply shocks and reducing the average inflation bias, it is always optimal to appoint a central banker who places more weight ($\delta > 0$) on inflation objectives than the government itself does.

Rogoff's solution is often characterized as involving the appointment of a conservative to head an independent central bank. The concept of *independence* means that,

---

30. See Eijffinger, Hoeberichts, and Schaling (1995) for a discussion of this graphical representation of the determinants of the optimal degree of conservatism. Eijffinger and Schaling (1995) extended the framework to an open-economy context.

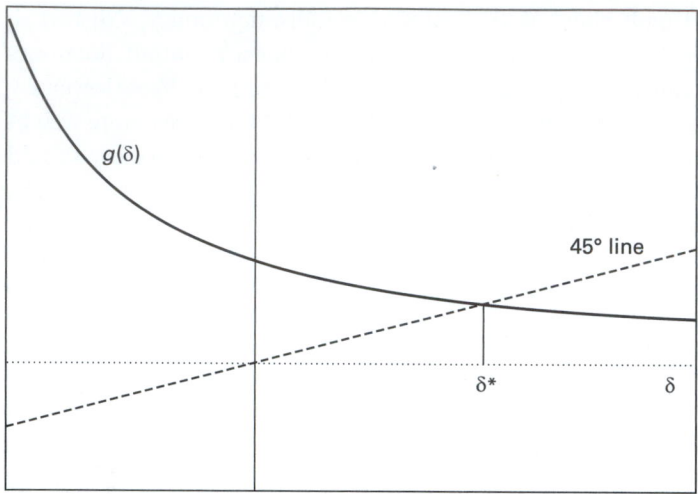

Figure 7.4
Optimal degree of conservatism.

once appointed, the central banker is able to set policy without interference or restriction and will do so to minimize his own assessment of social costs. Thus, the inflation bias problem is solved partly through delegation; the government delegates responsibility for monetary policy to an independent central bank. The benefit of this independence is lower average inflation; the cost depends on the realization of the aggregate supply shock. If shocks are small, the gain in terms of low inflation clearly dominates the distortion in stabilization policy; if shocks are large, the costs associated with the stabilization distortion can dominate the gain from low inflation.[31]

Lohmann (1992) showed that the government can do even better if it appoints a weight-conservative central banker but limits the central bank's independence. If the aggregate supply shock turns out to be too large, the government overrides the central banker, where the critical size determining what is too large is determined endogenously as a function of the costs of overriding. The knowledge that the government can override also affects the way the central banker responds to shocks that are less than the threshold level that triggers an override. By responding more actively to large shocks, the central banker is able to extend the range of shocks over which she maintains independence.

31. Since society is better off appointing a conservative, the expected gain from low inflation exceeds the expected stabilization cost, however.

Rogoff's solution highlights a trade-off; one can reduce the bias but only at the cost of distorting stabilization policy. One implication is that countries with central banks that place a high weight on inflation objectives should have, on average, lower inflation, but they should also experience greater output variance. The variance of output is equal to

$$\left(\frac{1+\delta}{1+\delta+a^2\lambda}\right)^2 \sigma_e^2 + a^2\sigma_v^2,$$

and this is increasing in δ. Highly independent central banks are presumed to place more weight on achieving low inflation, and a large literature has investigated the finding that measures of central bank independence are negatively correlated with average inflation, at least for the industrialized economies (see Cukierman 1992; Eijffinger and de Haan 1996). Alesina and Summers (1993) showed, however, that such measures do not appear to be correlated with the variance of real output. This runs counter to the implications of the Rogoff model.

Solving the inflationary bias of discretionary policy through the appointment of a conservative central banker raises several issues. First, how does the government identify the preference parameter δ? Second, how does it commit to a δ? Once expectations are set, the government has an incentive to fire the conservative central banker and appoint a replacement who shares the government's preferences. Finally, the focus on preferences, as opposed to incentives, clouds the model's implications for institutional structure and design. Should institutions be designed to generate appropriate incentives for policymakers? Or does good policy simply require putting the right people in charge?

7.3.3 Contracts

The problems that occur under discretion arise because central banks respond optimally to the incentive structure they face, but the incentives are wrong. This perspective suggests that rather than relying on the central bank having the right preferences, one might try to affect the incentives the central bank faces. But this requires first determining what incentives central banks *should* face.

The appropriate perspective for addressing such issues is provided by the principal agent literature.[32] A key insight that motivated the large literature on the analysis of the time inconsistency of optimal plans was the recognition that central banks respond to the incentives they face. These incentives may be shaped by the institutional structure within which policy is conducted. For example, as has been noted, Lohmann showed how policy is affected when the central banker knows that the government

---

32. This section draws heavily on Walsh (1995c). See also Persson and Tabellini (1993) and Waller (1995).

will override if the economy is subject to a disturbance that is too large. Rogoff (1985b, 1180) argued that targeting rules might be enforced by making the monetary authority's budget depend on adherence to the rule. In a similar vein, Garfinkel and Oh (1993) suggested that a targeting rule might be enforced by legislation punishing the monetary authority if it fails to achieve the target. Such institutional aspects of the central bank's structure and its relationship with the government can be thought of as representing a *contract* between the government and the monetary authority. The conduct of monetary policy is then affected by the contract the government offers to the central bank.

The government's (or perhaps society's) problem can be viewed as that of designing an optimal incentive structure for the central bank. Following Walsh (1995c), the most convenient way to determine an optimal incentive structure is to assume that the government can offer the head of the central bank a state-contingent wage contract. Such a contract allows one to derive explicitly the manner in which the bank's incentives should depend on the state of the economy. While there are numerous reasons to question the effectiveness and implementability of such employment contracts in the context of monetary policy determination, a (possibly) state-contingent wage contract for the central banker represents a useful fiction for deriving the optimal incentive structure with which the central bank should be faced and provides a convenient starting point for the analysis of optimal central bank incentives.[33]

The basic structure of the model is identical to that used earlier, consisting of an aggregate supply relationship given by (7.3), a link between money growth and inflation given by (7.4), and an objective function that depends on output fluctuations and inflation variability, as in (7.2). The private sector's expectations are assumed to be determined prior to the central bank's choice of a growth rate for the nominal money supply. Thus, in setting Δm, the central bank will take π^e as given. Assume that the central bank can observe the supply shock e prior to setting Δm because this will generate a role for stabilization policy. The disturbance v in the link between money growth and inflation is realized after the central bank sets Δm. Finally, assume that e and v are uncorrelated.

Monetary policy is conducted by an independent central bank that shares the government's preferences, V, but that also receives a monetary transfer payment from the government. This payment can be thought of either as the direct income of the central banker or as the budget of the central bank. Or the transfer payment can be viewed more broadly as reflecting legislated performance objectives for the central bank. Let t represent the transfer to the central bank, and assume that the central bank's utility is given by

---

33. Walsh (2002) demonstrated that a dismissal rule can, in some circumstances, substitute for a state-contingent wage contract in affecting the central bank's incentives.

U $= t - V$.

That is, the central bank cares about both the transfer it receives and the social loss generated by inflation and output fluctuations. The central bank sets Δm to maximize the expected value of **U**, conditional on the realization of e. The problem faced by the government (the principal) is to design a transfer function t that induces the central bank to choose $\Delta m = \Delta m^c(e)$, where Δm^c is the socially optimal commitment policy. As already noted, the optimal commitment policy in this framework is $\Delta m^c(e) = -a\lambda e/(1 + a^2\lambda)$ (see (7.11)).

   If the government can verify e ex post, there are clearly many contracts that would achieve the desired result. For example, any contract that imposes a large penalty on the central bank if Δm deviates from Δm^c will ensure that Δm^c is chosen. However, the difficulty of determining both the possible states of nature ex ante and the actual realization of shocks ex post makes such contracts infeasible. This task is particularly difficult if the central bank must respond to a forecast of e, since its internal forecast might be difficult to verify ex post, leading to the problems of private information highlighted by Canzoneri's (1985) analysis. Therefore, consider a transfer function $t(\pi)$ that makes the government's payment to the central bank contingent on the observed rate of inflation. The transfer function implements the optimal policy $\pi^c(e) = \Delta m^c(e) + v$ if π^c maximizes $E^{cb}[t(\pi(e)) - V]$ for all e, where $E^{cb}[\ ]$ denotes the central bank's expectation conditional on e.

   The first-order condition for the central bank's problem can be solved for $\Delta m^{cb}(e)$, the optimal discretionary policy:

$$\Delta m^{cb}(e) = \frac{a\lambda k}{1 + a^2\lambda} + \left(\frac{a^2\lambda}{1 + a^2\lambda}\right)\pi^e + \frac{E^{cb}(t')}{1 + a^2\lambda} - \left(\frac{a\lambda}{1 + a^2\lambda}\right)e, \qquad (7.20)$$

where $t' = \partial t(\pi)/\partial\pi$. The last term in (7.20) shows that the optimal discretionary policy response to the supply shock is equal to the response under the optimal commitment policy Δm^c. This is important because it implies that the government's objective will be to design a contract that eliminates the inflationary bias while leaving the central bank free to respond with discretion to e. Taking expectations of (7.20) and letting $E[\ ]$ denote the public's expectation, one obtains

$$E[\Delta m^{cb}(e)] = \pi^e = a\lambda k + E[t'(\pi)].$$

When this is substituted back into (7.20),

$$\Delta m^{cb}(e) = a\lambda k + E[t'(\pi(e))] - \frac{E[t'] - E^{cb}[t']}{1 + a^2\lambda} - \frac{a\lambda}{1 + a^2\lambda}e.$$

Setting $\Delta m^{cb}(e)$ equal to the optimal commitment policy $\Delta m^c(e)$ for all e requires that the first three terms vanish. They will vanish if $t(\pi)$ satisfies

$$t' = \frac{\partial t}{\partial \pi} = -a\lambda k.$$

The optimal commitment policy can therefore be implemented by the linear transfer function

$$t = t_0 - a\lambda k\pi.$$

The constant t_0 is set to ensure that the expected return to the central bank is sufficient to ensure its participation.[34] Presenting the central bank with this incentive contract achieves the dual objectives of eliminating the inflationary bias while still ensuring optimal stabilization policy in response to the central bank's private information about the aggregate supply shock.

Why does the transfer function take such a simple linear form? Recall that the time-consistent policy under discretion resulted in an inflationary bias of $a\lambda k$. The key insight is that this is constant; it does not vary with the realization of the aggregate supply shock. Therefore, the incentive structure for the central bank just needs to raise the marginal cost of inflation (from the perspective of the central bank) by a constant amount; that is what the linear transfer function does. Because the bias is independent of the realization of the underlying state of nature, it is not necessary for the government to actually verify the state, and so the presence of private information about the state of the economy on the part of the central bank does not affect the ability of the linear contract to support the optimal policy. This case contrasts sharply with the one in which reputation is relied upon to achieve low average inflation (Canzoneri 1985).

One interpretation of the linear inflation contract result is that it simply points out that the Barro-Gordon framework is too simple to adequately capture important aspects of monetary policy design. In this view, there really is a trade-off between credibility and flexibility, and the fact that this trade-off can be made to disappear so easily represents a methodological criticism of the Barro-Gordon model.[35] Several authors have explored modifications to the Barro-Gordon model that allow this trade-off to be reintroduced. They do so by making the inflation bias state-dependent. In this way, the linear contract, which raises the marginal cost of inflation by a constant amount for all state realizations, cannot achieve the socially optimal

---

34. This is known as the *individual rationality constraint*. Since $\partial\pi/\partial m = 1$, a contract of the form $t_0 - akm$ based on the observed rate of money growth would also work. Chortareas and Miller (2007) analyzed the case in which the government also cares about the cost of the contract.

35. This argument is made by Canzoneri, Nolan, and Yates (1997).

commitment policy. If the penalty cannot be made state-contingent, then average inflation can be eliminated, but inflation will remain too volatile. For example, Walsh (1995b), Canzoneri, Nolan, and Yates (1997), and Herrendorf and Lockwood (1997) introduced a state-contingent bias by modifying the basic model structure. Walsh assumed that there exists a flexible wage sector in addition to a nominal wage contract sector. Herrendorf and Lockwood assumed that labor market participants can observe a signal that reveals information about aggregate supply shocks prior to forming nominal wage contracts. Canzoneri, Nolan, and Yates assumed that the central bank has an interest rate–smoothing objective. Herrendorf and Lockwood (1997) and Muscatelli (1998) showed that when the inflation bias is state-contingent rather than constant, as in the Barro-Gordon model, there can be a role for a linear inflation contract, as in Walsh (1995c), *and* a conservative central banker, as in Rogoff (1985b). Schellekens (2002) considered delegation to a central bank with preferences that are generalized from the standard quadratic form. He examined the connection between optimal conservatism and cautionary policy arising from model uncertainty.

Chortareas and Miller (2003) showed that the linear inflation contract would not fully offset the inflation bias when the government cares about the cost of the contract, costs that were ignored by Walsh (1995c).[36] However, as Chortareas and Miller (2007) demonstrated, the original linear inflation contract remains optimal if the government must ensure that the central bank's participation constraint is satisfied, even when the government also cares about the costs of the contract. Intuitively, with a linear inflation contract of the form $a + b\pi$, the government can always set b to generate the correct incentives for the central bank (since the value of the constant term a does not alter the first-order conditions of the central bank's optimality conditions). Then a can be set to minimize the cost of the contract to the government, where this minimum cost is determined by the central bank's outside opportunity.

The contracting approach was developed further in Persson and Tabellini (1993). Walsh (1995b; 2002) showed how the properties of a linear inflation contract can be mimicked by a dismissal rule under which the central banker is fired if inflation ever rises above a critical level. Lockwood (1997), Jonsson (1995; 1997), and Svensson (1997b) showed how linear inflation contracts are affected when the inflation bias is time-dependent because of persistence in the unemployment process. *Persistence* means that a surprise expansion in period t reduces unemployment (increases output) in period t but also leads to lower expected unemployment in periods $t + 1$, $t + 2$, and so on. Thus, the benefits of a surprise inflation are larger, leading to a higher average inflation rate under discretionary policy. The bias at time t, though, will

36. See also Candel-Sánchez and Campoy-Miñarroy (2004).

depend on the unemployment rate at $t - 1$, since, with persistence, unemployment at $t - 1$ affects the average unemployment rate expected for period t. Therefore, the inflation bias will be time-varying. The simple linear contract with a fixed weight on inflation will no longer be optimal if the inflation bias is state-dependent. However, a state-contingent contract can support the optimal commitment policy.

Like the Rogoff conservative central banker solution, the contracting solution *relocates* the commitment problem that gives rise to the inflation bias in the first place.[37] H. Jensen (1997) showed how the ability of an incentive contract for the central banker to solve an inflation bias is weakened when the government can undo the contract ex post. In the case of a conservative central banker, the proposed solution assumes that the government cannot commit to a specific inflation policy but can commit to the appointment of an agent with specific preferences. In the contracting case, the government is assumed to be able to commit to a specific contract. Both of these assumptions are plausible; relocating the commitment problem is often a means of solving the problem. Confirmation processes, together with long terms of office, can reveal the appointee's preferences and ensure that policy is actually conducted by the appointed agent. Incentives called for in the contracting approach can similarly be thought of as aspects of the institutional structure and may therefore be more difficult to change than actual policy instrument settings.

As al-Nowaihi and Levine (1996) argued, relocation can allow the government to commit credibly to a contract or to a particular appointee if the process is public. If contract renegotiations or the firing of the central banker are publicly observable, then it may be in the interest of the government to forgo any short-term incentive to renegotiate in order to develop a reputation as a government that can commit. Thus, the transparency of any renegotiation serves to support a low-inflation equilibrium; relocating the time inconsistency problem can solve it.[38]

The type of policy transparency emphasized by al-Nowaihi and Levine characterizes the policy process established under the 1989 central banking reform in New Zealand. There the government and the Reserve Bank establish short-run inflation targets under a Policy Targets Agreement (PTA). The PTA can be renegotiated, and once current economic disturbances have been observed, both the government and the Reserve Bank have incentives to renegotiate the target (Walsh 1995b). Because this renegotiation must be public, however, reputational considerations may sustain an equilibrium in which the targets are not renegotiated. Publicly assigning an infla-

---

37. McCallum (1995; 1997c) emphasized the relocation issue with respect to the contracting approach. A similar criticism applies to the conservative central banker solution.

38. See also Herrendorf (1995; 1998), who developed a similar point using inflation targeting, and Walsh (2002), who showed that the government will find it advantageous to carry out a dismissal rule policy under which the central banker is fired if inflation exceeds a critical level.

tion target to the central bank may also replicate the optimal incentives called for under the linear inflation contract (Svensson 1997b).

Dixit and Jensen (2001) extended the contracting approach to the case of a monetary union in which member governments offer the common central bank incentive contracts designed to influence monetary policy. They showed that if the central bank cares about the incentives it receives and about the unionwide inflation rate, the central bank implements a policy that leads to average inflation that is too low and stable. The central bank implements a weighted average of each member country's desired policy only if the central bank cares only about the contract incentives. Hence, mandating that the central bank achieve price stability would result in a deflationary bias under discretion.

Athey, Chari, and Kehoe (2005) reexamined the optimal delegation of monetary policy by employing mechanism design theory in an environment similar to the one studied originally by Canzoneri (1985) in which the central bank has private information. They showed that under certain conditions, the optimal scheme involves an inflation cap—a maximum inflation rate the central bank is allowed to choose. The greater the time inconsistency problem, the lower is the cap. If the central bank has little private information, then the optimal design calls for giving no discretion to the central bank.

7.3.4   Institutions

One interpretation of the contracting approach is that the incentive structures might be embedded in the institutional structure of the central bank. If institutions are costly to change, then institutional reforms designed to raise the costs of inflation can serve as commitment devices. Incorporating a price stability objective directly into the central bank's charter legislation, for example, might raise the implicit penalty (in terms of institutional embarrassment) the central bank would suffer if it failed to control inflation. Most discussions of the role of institutional structure and inflation have, however, focused on the effects of alternative structures on the extent to which political pressures affect the conduct of monetary policy.

A starting point for such a focus is Alesina's model of policy in a two-party system.[39] Suppose there is uncertainty about the outcome of an approaching election, and suppose the parties differ in their economic policies, so that inflation in the post-election period will depend on which party wins the election. Let the parties be denoted A and B. The inflation rate expected if party A wins the election is π^A; inflation under party B will be π^B. Assume $\pi^A > \pi^B$. If the probability that party A wins the election is q, then expected inflation prior to the election will be $\pi^e = q\pi^A +$

---

39. For a discussion of this model, see Alesina (1987); Alesina and Sachs (1988); Alesina and Roubini (1992; 1997); and Drazen (2000).

$(1 - q)\pi^B$. Since q is between 0 and 1, expected inflation falls in the interval $[\pi^B, \pi^A]$. If postelection output is equal to $y = a(\pi - \pi^e)$, where π is actual inflation, then the election of party A will generate an economic expansion (since $\pi^A - \pi^e = (1 - q)(\pi^A - \pi^B) > 0$), whereas the election of party B will lead to an economic contraction $(\pi^B - \pi^e = q(\pi^B - \pi^A) < 0)$.

This very simple framework provides an explanation for a political business cycle that arises because of policy differences between parties and electoral uncertainty. Because parties are assumed to exploit monetary policy to get their desired inflation rate, and because election outcomes cannot be predicted with certainty, inflation surprises will occur after an election. Alesina and Sachs (1988) provided evidence for this theory based on U.S. data, and Alesina and Roubini (1992) examined OECD countries. Faust and Irons (1996), however, concluded that there is little evidence from the United States to support the hypothesis that political effects generate monetary policy surprises.

Waller (1989; 1992) showed how the process used to appoint members of the central bank's policy board can influence the degree to which partisan political factors are translated into monetary policy outcomes. If policy is set by a board whose members serve overlapping but noncoincident terms, the effect of policy shifts resulting from changes in government is reduced. In a two-party system in which nominees forwarded by the party in power are subject to confirmation by the out-of-power party, the party in power will nominate increasingly moderate candidates as elections near. Increasing the length of terms of office for central bank board members also reduces the role of partisanship in monetary policy making.[40] Waller and Walsh (1996) considered a partisan model of monetary policy. They focused on the implications for output of the degree of partisanship in the appointment process and the term length of the central banker. Similarly, Alesina and Gatti (1995) showed that electorally induced business cycles can be reduced if political parties jointly appoint the central banker.

While most work has focused on the appointment of political nominees to the policy board, the Federal Reserve's policy board (the FOMC) includes both political appointees (the governors) and nonappointed members (the regional bank presidents).[41] Faust (1996) provided an explanation for this structure by developing an overlapping-generations model in which inflation has distributional effects. If monetary policy is set by majority vote, excessive inflation results as the (larger) young generation attempts to transfer wealth from the old generation. If policy is delegated

---

40. See also Havrilesky and Gildea (1992) and Garcia de Paso (1994). For some empirical evidence in support of these models, see Mixon and Gibson (2002).

41. Havrilesky and Gildea (1991; 1995) argued that the voting behavior of regional bank presidents and board governors differs, with regional bank presidents tending to be tougher on inflation; this conclusion was disputed by Tootell (1991).

to a board consisting of one representative from the young generation and one from the old, the inflationary bias is eliminated. Faust argued that the structure of the FOMC takes its shape because of the advantages of delegating to a board in which the relative balance of different political constituencies differs from that of the voting public as a whole.

Who makes policy and who appoints the policymakers can affect policy outcomes, but institutional design also includes mechanisms for accountability, and these can affect policy as well. Minford (1995), in fact, argued that democratic elections can enforce low-inflation outcomes if voters punish governments that succumb to the temptation to inflate, and Lippi (1997) developed a model in which rational voters choose a weight-conservative central banker. O'Flaherty (1990) showed how finite term lengths can ensure accountability, and Walsh (1995b) showed that the type of dismissal rule incorporated into New Zealand's Reserve Bank Act of 1989 can partially mimic an optimal contract.

The launch of the European Central Bank in 2000 helped to focus attention on the role institutions and their formal structure play in affecting policy outcomes. Because the individual member countries in a monetary union may face different economic conditions, disagreements about the common central bank's policies may arise. Dixit (2000) used a principal agent approach to study policy determination in a monetary union. With a single central bank determining monetary policy for a union of countries, the central bank is the agent of many principals. Each principal may try to influence policy outcomes, and the central bank may need to appease its principals to avoid noncooperative outcomes.

Dixit showed that the central bank's decision problem must take into account the individual incentive compatibility constraints that require all principals to accept a continuation of the policy the central bank chooses. For example, if one country has an large adverse shock, the central bank may have to raise inflation above the optimal commitment level to ensure the continued participation in the union of the affected country. When the incentive constraint binds, policy will diverge from the full-commitment case in order to secure the continued participation of the union members. Dixit showed that when countries are hit by different shocks, it is the incentive constraint of the worst-hit country that is binding—policy must shade toward what that country would want. If the costs of overturning the central bank's policy (and thereby reverting to the discretionary equilibrium) are high enough, there will be some range of asymmetric shocks within which it is possible to sustain the full-commitment policy.

7.3.5   Targeting Rules

The contracting approach focuses on the incentive structure faced by the central bank; once the incentives are correct, complete flexibility in the actual conduct of policy is allowed. This allows the central bank to respond to new and possibly unverifiable information. An alternative approach acts to reduce the problems arising from discretion by *restricting* policy flexibility. The gold standard or a fixed exchange rate regime are examples of situations in which policy flexibility is deliberately limited; Milton Friedman's proposal that the Fed be required to maintain a constant growth rate of the money supply is another famous example. A wide variety of rules designed to restrict the flexibility of the central bank have been proposed and analyzed. The cost of reduced flexibility depends on the nature of the economic disturbances affecting the economy and the original scope for stabilization policies in the first place, and the gain from reducing flexibility takes the form of a lower average inflation rate.

Targeting rules are rules under which the central bank is judged in part on its ability to achieve a prespecified value for some macroeconomic variable. Inflation targeting is currently the most commonly discussed form of targeting, and some form of inflation targeting has been adopted in over 20 developed and developing economies.[42] Fixed or target zone exchange rate systems also can be interpreted as targeting regimes. The central bank's ability to respond to economic disturbances, or to succumb to the temptation to inflate, is limited by the need to maintain an exchange rate target. When the lack of credibility is a problem for the central bank, committing to maintaining a fixed nominal exchange rate against a low-inflation country can serve to import credibility. Giavazzi and Pagano (1988) provided an analysis of the advantages of "tying one's hands" by committing to a fixed exchange rate.

Flexible Targeting Rules

Suppose the central bank cares about output and inflation stabilization but is, in addition, penalized for deviations of actual inflation from a target level.[43] In other words, the central bank's objective is to minimize

$$V^{cb} = \frac{1}{2}\lambda E_t(y_t - y_n - k)^2 + \frac{1}{2}E_t(\pi_t - \pi^*)^2 + \frac{1}{2}hE_t(\pi_t - \pi^T)^2, \qquad (7.21)$$

where this differs from (7.2) in that π^* now denotes the socially optimal inflation rate (which may differ from zero), and the last term represents the penalty related to deviations from the target inflation rate π^T. The parameter h measures the weight placed on deviations from the target inflation rate. Targeting rules of this form are known as

42. In addition to the references cited earlier, see Ammer and Freeman (1995); Haldane (1995); McCallum (1997a); Mishkin and Posen (1997); Bernanke et al. (1998); and the papers in Leiderman and Svensson (1995) and Lowe (1997) for discussions of inflation targeting. Walsh (2009) contains an extensive list of references on the topic. See also section 8.4.6.

43. The central bank might be required to report on its success or failure in achieving the target, with target misses punished by public censoring and embarrassment or by some more formal dismissal procedure.

flexible targeting rules. They do not require that the central bank hit its target exactly; instead, one can view the last term as representing a penalty suffered by the central bank based on how large the deviation from the target turns out to be. This type of targeting rule allows the central bank to trade off achieving its inflation target for achieving more desired values of its other goals.

The rest of the model consists of an aggregate supply function and a link between the policy instrument, the growth rate of money, and inflation:

$$y_t = y_n + a(\pi_t - \pi^e) + e_t$$

and

$$\pi_t = \Delta m_t + v_t,$$

where v is a velocity disturbance. It is assumed that the public's expectations are formed prior to observing either e or v, but the central bank can observe e (but not v) before setting Δm.

Before deriving the policy followed by the central bank, note that the socially optimal commitment policy is given by[44]

$$\Delta m_t^S = \pi^* - \left(\frac{a\lambda}{1 + a^2\lambda}\right)e_t. \tag{7.22}$$

Now consider policy under discretion. Using the aggregate supply function and the link between inflation and money growth, the loss function (7.21) can be written as

$$V^{cb} = \frac{1}{2}\lambda E[a(\Delta m + v - \pi^e) + e - k]^2 + \frac{1}{2}E(\Delta m + v - \pi^*)^2 + \frac{1}{2}hE(\Delta m + v - \pi^T)^2.$$

The first-order condition for the optimal choice of Δm, taking expectations as given, is

$$a^2\lambda(\Delta m - \pi^e) + a\lambda(e - k) + (\Delta m - \pi^*) + h(\Delta m - \pi^T) = 0.$$

Solving yields

$$\Delta m = \frac{a^2\lambda\pi^e - a\lambda e + a\lambda k + \pi^* + h\pi^T}{1 + h + a^2\lambda}. \tag{7.23}$$

---

44. This is obtained by substituting the commitment policy $\Delta m = b_0 + b_1 e$ into the social objective function

$$\frac{1}{2}[\lambda E(y - y_n - k)^2 + E(\pi - \pi^*)^2]$$

and minimizing the unconditional expectation with respect to b_0 and b_1.

Assuming rational expectations, $\pi^e = \Delta m^e = (a\lambda k + \pi^* + h\pi^T)/(1+h)$ because the public forms expectations prior to knowing e. Substituting this result into (7.23) yields the time-consistent money growth rate:

$$\Delta m^T = \frac{a\lambda k + \pi^* + h\pi^T}{1+h} - \left(\frac{a\lambda}{1+h+a^2\lambda}\right)e$$

$$= \pi^* + \frac{a\lambda k}{1+h} + \frac{h(\pi^T - \pi^*)}{1+h} - \left(\frac{a\lambda}{1+h+a^2\lambda}\right)e. \tag{7.24}$$

If the target inflation rate is equal to the socially optimal inflation rate ($\pi^T = \pi^*$), (7.24) reduces to

$$\Delta m^T = \pi^* + \frac{a\lambda k}{1+h} - \left(\frac{a\lambda}{1+h+a^2\lambda}\right)e. \tag{7.25}$$

Setting $h = 0$ yields the time-consistent discretionary solution *without* targeting:

$$\Delta m^{NT} = \pi^* + a\lambda k - \left(\frac{a\lambda}{1+a^2\lambda}\right)e, \tag{7.26}$$

with the inflation bias equal to $a\lambda k$.

Comparing (7.22), (7.25), and (7.26) reveals that the targeting penalty reduces the inflation bias from $a\lambda k$ to $a\lambda k/(1+h)$. The targeting requirement imposes an additional cost on the central bank if it allows inflation to deviate too much from π^T; this raises the marginal cost of inflation and reduces the time-consistent inflation rate. The cost of this reduction in the average inflation bias is the distortion that targeting introduces into the central bank's response to the aggregate supply shock e. Under pure discretion, the central bank responds optimally to e (note that the coefficient on the supply shock is the same in (7.26) as in (7.22)), but the presence of a targeting rule distorts the response to e. Comparing (7.25) with (7.22) shows that the central bank will respond too little to the supply shock (the coefficient falls from $a\lambda/(1+a^2\lambda)$ to $a\lambda/(1+h+a^2\lambda)$).

This trade-off between bias reduction and stabilization response was seen earlier in discussing Rogoff's model.[45] Note that if $\pi^T = \pi^*$, the central bank's objective function can be written as

$$V^{cb} = \frac{1}{2}\lambda E(y_t - y_n - k)^2 + \frac{1}{2}(1+h)E(\pi - \pi^*)^2. \tag{7.27}$$

---

45. Canzoneri (1985); Garfinkel and Oh (1993); and Garcia de Paso (1993; 1994) considered multiperiod targeting rules as solutions to this trade-off between stabilization and inflation bias. Defining money growth or inflation targets as averages over several periods restricts average inflation while allowing the central bank more flexibility in each period to respond to shocks.

It is apparent from (7.27) that the parameter h plays exactly the same role that Rogoff's degree of conservatism played. From the analysis of Rogoff's model, the optimal value of h is positive, so the total weight placed on the inflation objective exceeds society's weight, which is equal to 1. A flexible inflation target, interpreted here as a value for h that is positive, leads to an outcome that dominates pure discretion.[46]

The connection between an inflation targeting rule and Rogoff's conservative central banker approach has just been highlighted. Svensson (1997b) showed that a similar connection exists between inflation targeting and the optimal linear inflation contract. Svensson demonstrated that the optimal linear inflation contract can be implemented if the central bank is required to target an inflation rate π^T that is actually less than the socially optimal rate of inflation. To see how this result is obtained, let $H = 1 + h$, replace π^* with π^T in (7.27), and expand the resulting second term so that the expression becomes

$$V^{cb} = \frac{1}{2}\lambda E(y_t - y_n - k)^2 + \frac{1}{2}HE(\pi - \pi^* + \pi^* - \pi^T)^2$$

$$= \frac{1}{2}\lambda E(y_t - y_n - k)^2 + \frac{1}{2}HE(\pi - \pi^*)^2 + DE(\pi - \pi^*) + C,$$

where $D = H(\pi^* - \pi^T)$ and $C = \frac{1}{2}H(\pi^* - \pi^T)^2$. Since C is a constant, it does not affect the central bank's behavior. Notice that V^{cb} is equal to $V + \frac{1}{2}hE(\pi - \pi^*)^2 + DE(\pi - \pi^*) + C$. This is exactly equivalent to the incentive structure established under the optimal linear inflation contract if and only if $h = 0$ and $D = a\lambda k$. The condition $h = 0$ is achieved if the central banker is not weight-conservative but instead shares society's preferences (so $H = 1$); the condition $D = a\lambda k$ is then achieved if

$$\pi^T = \pi^* - a\lambda k < \pi^*.$$

Thus, the optimal linear contract can be implemented by assigning to the central bank an inflation target that is actually below the rate that is socially preferred. But at the same time, policy should be assigned to an agent who has the same preferences between inflation and output stabilization as society in general.

Strict Targeting Rules

The preceding analysis considered a flexible targeting rule. The central bank was penalized for deviations of π around a targeted level but was not required to achieve the target precisely. This flexibility allowed the central bank to trade off the objective

---

46. That is, of course, unless h is too large.

of meeting the target against achieving its other objectives. Often, however, targeting is analyzed in terms of strict targets; the central bank is required to achieve a specific target outcome regardless of the implications for its other objectives. For an early analysis of strict targeting regimes, see Aizenman and Frankel (1986).

As an example, consider a strict money growth rate target under which the central bank is required to set the growth rate of the money supply equal to some constant:[47]

$$\Delta m = \Delta m^T.$$

Since the desired rate of inflation is π^*, it makes sense to set $\Delta m^T = \pi^*$, and the public will set $\pi^e = \pi^*$. With this rule in place, the social loss function can be evaluated. If social loss is given by

$$V = \frac{1}{2}\lambda E_t(y_t - y_n - k)^2 + \frac{1}{2}E_t(\pi_t - \pi^*)^2,$$

then under a strict money growth rate target it takes the value

$$V(\Delta m^T) = \frac{1}{2}[\lambda k^2 + \lambda\sigma_e^2 + (1 + a^2\lambda)\sigma_v^2].$$

Recall that under pure discretion the expected value of the loss function was, from (7.9),

$$V^d = \frac{1}{2}\lambda(1 + a^2\lambda)k^2 + \frac{1}{2}\left[\left(\frac{\lambda}{1 + a^2\lambda}\right)\sigma_e^2 + (1 + a^2\lambda)\sigma_v^2\right].$$

Comparing these two, one obtains

$$V(\Delta m^T) - V^d = -\frac{1}{2}(a\lambda k)^2 + \frac{1}{2}\left(\frac{a^2\lambda^2}{1 + a^2\lambda}\right)\sigma_e^2.$$

Notice that this can be either positive or negative. It is more likely to be negative (implying that the strict money growth rate target is superior to discretion) if the underlying inflationary bias under discretion, $a\lambda k$, is large. Since the strict targeting rule ensures that average inflation is π^*, it eliminates any inflationary bias, so the gain is larger, the larger the bias that arises under discretion. However, discretion is more likely to be preferred to the strict rule when σ_e^2 is large. The strict targeting rule eliminates any stabilization role for monetary policy. The cost of doing so will depend on

---

47. Alternatively, the targeting rule could require the central bank to minimize $E(\Delta m - \Delta m^T)^2$. However, this occurs if the central bank sets policy such that $E(\Delta m) = \Delta m^T$. If Δm is controlled exactly, this is equivalent to $\Delta m = \Delta m^T$.

the variance of supply shocks. Eliminating the central bank's flexibility to respond to economic disturbances increases welfare if

$$k > \sigma_e \sqrt{\frac{1}{1 + a^2 \lambda}}.$$

If σ_e^2 is large, pure discretion, even with its inflationary bias, may still be the preferred policy (Flood and Isard 1988).

Another alternative targeting rule that has often been proposed focuses on nominal income (e.g., Hall and Mankiw 1994). If $y - y_n$ is interpreted as the percentage output deviation from trend, one can approximate a nominal income rule as requiring that

$$(y - y_n) + \pi = g^*,$$

where g^* is the target growth rate for nominal income. Since the equilibrium growth rate of $y - y_n$ is zero (because it is a deviation from trend) and the desired rate of inflation is π^*, one should set $g^* = 0 + \pi^* = \pi^*$. Under this rule, expected inflation is $\pi^e = g^* - \mathrm{E}(y - y_n) = g^* - 0 = g^* = \pi^*$. Aggregate output is given by

$$y = y_n + a(\pi - \pi^e) + e = y_n + a(y_n - y) + e \Rightarrow y - y_n = \left(\frac{1}{1 + a}\right)e,$$

since $\pi = g^* - (y - y_n) = \pi^e - (y - y_n)$ under the proposed rule. A positive supply shock that causes output to rise will induce a contraction designed to reduce the inflation rate to maintain a constant rate of nominal income growth. The decline in inflation (which is unanticipated because it was induced by the shock e) acts to reduce output and partially offset the initial rise. With the specification used here, exactly $a/(1 + a)$ of the effect of e is offset. Substituting this result into the policy rule implies that $\pi = \pi^* - e/(1 + a)$.

Using these results, the expected value of the social loss function is

$$V(g^*) = \frac{1}{2} \lambda k^2 + \frac{1}{2} \left[\frac{1 + \lambda}{(1 + a)^2} \right] \sigma_e^2.$$

In the present model, nominal income targeting stabilizes real output more than pure discretion (and the optimal commitment policy) if $a\lambda < 1$. In this example, it is assumed that the central bank could control nominal income growth exactly. If, as is more realistic, this is not the case, a term due to control errors will also appear in the expected value of the loss function.

Nominal income targeting imposes a particular trade-off between real income growth and inflation in response to aggregate supply disturbances. The social loss function does not weigh output fluctuations and inflation fluctuations equally (unless $\lambda = 1$), but nominal income targeting does. Nevertheless, nominal income targeting is often proposed as a "reasonably good rule for the conduct of monetary policy" (Hall and Mankiw 1994). For analyses of nominal income targeting, see Bean (1983); Frankel and Chinn (1995); McCallum (1988); Taylor (1985); and West (1986). Targeting rules in new Keynesian models are discussed in section 8.4.6.

The analysis of targeting rules has much in common with the analysis of monetary policy operating procedures (see chapter 11). Targeting rules limit the flexibility of the central bank to respond as economic conditions change. Thus, the manner in which disturbances will affect real output and inflation will be affected by the choice of targeting rule. For example, a strict inflation or price level rule forces real output to absorb all the effects of an aggregate productivity disturbance. Under a nominal income rule, such disturbances are allowed to affect both real output and the price level. As with operating procedures, the relative desirability of alternative rules will depend both on the objective function and on the relative variances of different types of disturbances.

7.4   Is the Inflation Bias Important?

Despite the large academic literature that has focused on the inflationary bias of discretionary monetary policy, some have questioned whether this whole approach has anything to do with explaining actual episodes of inflation. Do these models provide useful frameworks for positive theories of inflation? Since monetary models generally imply that the behavior of real output should be the same whether the average inflation rate is zero or 10 percent, the very fact that most economies have consistently experienced average inflation rates well above zero for extended periods of time might be taken as evidence for the existence of an inflation bias.[48] However, earlier chapters examined theories of inflation based on optimal tax considerations that might imply nonzero average rates of inflation, although few argue that tax considerations alone could account for the level of inflation observed during the 1970s in most industrialized economies (or for the observed variations in inflation). There are several reasons for questioning the empirical relevance of time inconsistency as a factor in monetary policy. Some economists have argued that time inconsistency just isn't a problem. For example, Taylor (1983) pointed out that society finds solutions to these sorts of problems in many other areas (patent law, for example) and that there is no reason to suppose that the problem is particularly severe in the monetary

---

48. While most monetary models do not display superneutrality (so that inflation does affect real variables even in the steady state), most policy-oriented models satisfy a natural rate property in that average values of real variables such as output are assumed to be independent of monetary policy.

policy arena.[49] Others, such as Blinder and Rudd (2008), attributed the rise in inflation during the 1970s to supply shocks rather than to any inherent bias of discretionary policies. Institutional solutions, such as separating responsibility for monetary
policy from the direct control of elected political officials, may reduce or even eliminate the underlying bias toward expansion that leads to excessively high average inflation under discretion.[50]

McCallum (1995; 1997c) argued that central banks can be trusted not to succumb
to the incentive to inflate because they know that succumbing leads to a bad equilibrium. But such a view ignores the basic problem; even central banks that want to do
the right thing may face the choice of either inflating or causing a recession. In such
circumstances, the best policy may not be to cause a recession. For example, consider
Cukierman and Liviatan's type D policymaker. Such a policymaker is capable of
committing to and delivering on a zero inflation policy, but if the public assigns
some probability to the possibility that a type W might be in office, even the type D
ends up inflating. If central banks were to define their objectives in terms of stabilizing output around the economy's natural rate (i.e., $k \equiv 0$), then there would be no
inflationary bias; central banks would deliver the socially optimal policy. However,
this corresponds to a situation in which there is no bias, not to one in which an incentive to inflate exists but the central bank resists it.

An alternative criticism of the time inconsistency literature questions the underlying assumption that the central bank cannot commit. Blinder (1995), for example,
argued that the inherent lags between a policy action and its effect on inflation and
output serve as a commitment technology. Inflation in period t is determined by policy actions taken in earlier periods, so if the public knows past policy actions, the
central bank can never produce a surprise inflation. The presence of lags does serve
as a commitment device. If outcomes today are entirely determined by actions taken
earlier, the central bank is clearly committed; nothing it can do will affect today's
outcome. And few would disagree that monetary policy acts with a (long) lag. But
appealing to lags solves the time inconsistency problem by eliminating *any* real
effects of monetary policy. That is, there is no incentive to inflate because expansionary monetary policy does not affect real output or unemployment. If this were the
case, central banks could costlessly disinflate; seeing a shift in policy, private agents
could revise all nominal wages and prices before any real effects occurred.

If monetary policy does have real effects, even if these occur with a lag, the inflationary bias under discretion will reappear. In the models that have been used in the

49. As Taylor (1983) put it, "In the Barro-Gordon inflation-unemployment model, the superiority of the
zero inflation policy is just as obvious to people as the well-recognized patent problem is in the real world.
It is therefore difficult to see why the zero inflation policy would not be adopted in such a world" (125).

50. For material from the second edition surveying the empirical literature on central bank institutional
structure and macroeconomic outcomes, see ⟨http://people.ucsc.edu/~walshc/mtp3e/MTP3e/⟩.

time inconsistency literature, monetary policy affects real output through its effect on inflation, more specifically, by creating inflation surprises. The empirical evidence from most countries, however, indicates that policy actions affect output before inflation is affected.[51] Policy actions can be observed long before the effects on inflation occur. But for this to represent a commitment technology that can overcome the time inconsistency problem requires that the observability of policy eliminate its ability to affect real output. It is the ability of monetary policy to generate real output effects that leads to the inflationary bias under discretion, and the incentive toward expansionary policies exists as long as monetary policy can influence real output. The fact that the costs of an expansion in terms of higher inflation only occur later actually increases the incentive for expansion if the central bank discounts the future.

There has been relatively little empirical work testing directly for the inflation bias. One relevant piece of evidence is provided by D. Romer (1993). He argued that the average inflation bias should depend on the degree to which an economy is open. A monetary expansion produces a real depreciation, raising the price of foreign imports. This increases inflation as measured by the consumer price index, raising the inflationary cost of the monetary expansion.[52] As a result, a given output expansion caused by an unanticipated rise in the domestic price level brings with it a larger inflation cost in terms of an increase in consumer price inflation. In addition, the output gain from such an expansion will be reduced if domestic firms use imported intermediate goods or if nominal wages are indexed. In terms of the basic model, this could be interpreted either as a lowering of the benefits of expansion relative to the costs of inflation or as a reduction in the output effects of unanticipated inflation. Consequently, the weight on output, λ, should be smaller (or the weight on inflation larger) in more open economies, and the coefficient of the supply curve, a, should be smaller. Since the inflation bias is increasing in $a\lambda$ (see, e.g., equation (7.7)), the average inflation rate should be lower in more open economies.

Romer tested these implications using data on 114 countries for the post-1973 period. Using the import share as a measure of openness, he found the predicted negative association between openness and average inflation. The empirical results,

---

51. Kiley (1996) presents evidence for the United States, Canada, Great Britain, France, and Germany.

52. That is, output depends on domestic price inflation π_d and is given by

$$y = y_n + \alpha(\pi_d - \pi_d^e),$$

and consumer price inflation is equal to

$$\pi_{cpi} = \theta\pi_d + (1 - \theta)s,$$

where s is the rate of change of the nominal exchange rate and θ is the share of domestic output in the consumer price index.

however, do not hold for the OECD economies. For the highly industrialized, high-income countries, openness is unrelated to average inflation.[53]

Temple (2002) examined the link between inflation and the slope of the Phillips curve linking inflation and output (represented by the value of the parameter a in (7.3) and found little evidence that a is smaller in more open economies. To account for Romer's finding that openness is associated with lower inflation, he suggested that inflation may be more costly in open economies because it is associated with greater real exchange rate variability. In this case, the parameter λ would be smaller in a more open economy because the central bank places relatively more weight on inflation objectives. As a result, average inflation would be lower in open economies, as Romer found.

Ireland (1999) argued that the behavior of inflation in the United States is consistent with the Barro-Gordon model if one allows for time variation in the natural rate of unemployment. Ireland assumed that the central bank's objective is to minimize

$$V = \frac{1}{2}\lambda(u - ku_n)^2 + \frac{1}{2}\pi^2,$$

where u is the unemployment rate and u_n is the natural rate of unemployment. It is assumed that $k < 1$ so that the central bank attempts to target an unemployment rate below the economy's natural rate. Ireland assumed that u_n is unobservable but varies over time and is subject to permanent stochastic shifts. As a result, the average inflation rate varies with these shifts in u_n; when u_n rises, average inflation also rises (see problem 9). Ireland found support for a long-run (cointegrating) relationship between unemployment and inflation in the United States. However, this is driven by the rise in inflation in the 1970s that coincided with the rise in the natural rate of unemployment as the baby boom generation entered the labor force. Whether the latter was the cause of the former is more difficult to determine, and Europe in the 1990s certainly experienced a rise in average unemployment rates with a fall rather than an increase in average inflation.

A serious criticism of explanations of actual inflation episodes based on the Barro-Gordon approach relates to the assumption that the central bank and the public understand that there is no long-run trade-off between inflation and unemployment. The standard aggregate supply curve, relating output movements to inflation surprises, implies that the behavior of real output (and unemployment) will be independent of the average rate of inflation. However, many central banks in the 1960s and

---

53. Terra (1998) argued that Romer's results were driven by the countries in his sample that are severely indebted. However, Romer (1998) noted in reply that the relationship between indebtedness and the openness-inflation correlation disappears when one controls for central bank independence. This suggests that both indebtedness and inflation are more severe in countries that have not solved the policy commitment problem.

into the 1970s did not accept this as an accurate description of the economy. Phillips curves were viewed as offering a menu of inflation-unemployment combinations from which policymakers could choose. Actual inflation may have reflected policymakers' misconceptions about the economy rather than their attempts to engineer surprise inflations that would not be anticipated by the public. For example, Romer and Romer (2002) attributed policy mistakes and high inflation in the United States during the late 1960s and the 1970s to the use of a wrong model. Specifically, they argued that policymakers during the 1960s believed the Phillips curve offered a permanent trade-off between average unemployment and average inflation. They then argued that once inflation had reached high levels, policymakers came to believe that inflation was insensitive to recessions, implying that the cost of reducing inflation would be extremely high. Thus, inflation was allowed to rise and policymakers delayed reducing it because they based decisions on models that are now viewed as incorrect.

These criticisms, while suggesting that the simple models of time inconsistency may not account for all observed inflation, do not mean that time inconsistency issues are unimportant. Explaining actual inflationary experiences will certainly involve consideration of the incentives faced by policymakers and the interaction of the factors such as uncertainty over policy preferences, responses to shocks, and a bias toward expansions that play a key role in models of discretionary policy.[54] So the issues that are central to the time inconsistency literature do seem relevant for understanding the conduct of monetary policy. At the same time, important considerations faced by central banks are absent from the basic models generally used in the literature. For example, the models have implications for average inflation rates but usually do not explain variations in average inflation over longer time periods.[55] Yet one of the most important characteristics of inflation during the past 40 years in the developed economies is that it has varied; it was low in the 1950s and early 1960s, much higher in the 1970s, and lower again in the mid-1980s and 1990s. Thus, average inflation changes, but it also displays a high degree of persistence.

This persistence does not arise in the models examined so far. Reputational models can display a type of inflation persistence; inflation may remain low in a pooling equilibrium; then, once the high-inflation central bank reveals itself, the inflation rate jumps and remains at a higher level. But this description does not seem to cap-

---

54. And in reputational solutions, observed inflation may remain low for extended periods of time even though the factors highlighted in the time inconsistency literature play an important role in determining the equilibrium.

55. Potential sources of shifts in the discretionary average rate of inflation would be changes in labor market structure that affect the output effects of inflation (the a parameter in the basic model), shifts in the relative importance of output expansions or output stabilization in the policymaker's objective functions (the λ parameter), or changes in the percentage gap between the economy's natural rate of output (unemployment) and the socially desired level (the parameter k).

ture the manner in which a high degree of persistence is displayed in the response of actual inflation to economic shocks that, in principle, should cause only one-time price level effects. For example, consider a negative supply shock. When the central bank is concerned with stabilizing real output, such a shock leads to a rise in the inflation rate. This reaction seems consistent with the early 1970s, when the worldwide oil price shock is generally viewed as being responsible for the rise in inflation. In the models considered in previous sections, the rise in inflation lasts only one period. The shock may have a permanent effect on the price level, but it cannot account for persistence in the inflation rate. Ball (1991; 1995) argued, however, that inflation results from an adverse shock and that once inflation increases, it remains high for some time. Eventually, policy shifts do bring inflation back down. Models of unemployment persistence based on labor market hysteresis, such as those developed by Lockwood and Philippopoulos (1994), Jonsson (1995), Lockwood (1997), and Svensson (1997b), also imply some inflation persistence. A shock that raises unemployment now also raises expected unemployment in the future. This increases the incentive to generate an expansion and so leads to a rise in inflation both now and in the future. But these models imply that inflation gradually returns to its long-run average, so they cannot account for the shifts in policy that often seem to characterize disinflations.

One model that does display such shifts was discussed earlier. Ball (1995) accounted for shifts in policy by assuming that the central bank type can change between a zero inflation type and an optimizing type according to a Markov process. With imperfect information, the public must attempt to infer the current central bank's type from inflation outcomes. The wet type mimics the zero inflation type until an adverse disturbance occurs. If such a shock occurs and the central bank is a wet type, inflation rises. This increase reveals the central bank's type, so the public expects positive inflation, and in equilibrium, inflation remains high until a dry type takes over. As a result, the model predicts the type of periodic and persistent bouts of inflation that seem to have characterized inflation in many developed economies. The model of Albanesi, Chari, and Christiano (2003) displays multiple equilibria and so can account for shifts between low- and high-inflation equilibria.

A number of authors have suggested that central banks now understand the dangers of having an overly ambitious output target and consequently now target the output gap $y_t - y_n$; in other words, $k = 0$. With the standard quadratic loss function, the inflation bias under discretion is zero when $k = 0$. Cukierman (2002), however, showed that an inflation bias reemerges if central bank preferences are asymmetric. He argued that central banks are not indifferent between $y_t - y_n > 0$ and $y_t - y_n < 0$ even if the deviations are of equal magnitude. A central bank that views a 1 percent fall in output below y_n as more costly than a 1 percent rise above y_n will tend to err in the direction of an overly expansionary policy. As a result, an average inflation bias reemerges even though $k = 0$. Ruge-Murcia (2003a), in contrast, considered the case of a central bank with an inflation target and asymmetric preferences over target misses. He showed that if the central bank prefers undershooting its target rather than overshooting it, average inflation will tend to be less than the target inflation rate.

Ruge-Murcia (2003b) nested both Cukierman's asymmetric preferences and the standard quadratic preferences of the Barro-Gordon model into a model he was able to take to the data. He did so by specifying preferences over inflation and unemployment by the following mixture of a quadratic function in inflation and a linex function in unemployment:

$$L_t = \frac{1}{2}(\pi_t - \pi^*)^2 + \left(\frac{\phi}{\gamma^2}\right)\{\exp[\gamma(u_t - u_t^*)] - \gamma(u_t - u_t^*) - 1\},$$

where π^* is a constant inflation target and u_t^* is the policymaker's desired rate of unemployment. For $\gamma > 0$, positive deviations of unemployment above target are viewed as more costly than negative deviations. If $u_t^* = kE_{t-1}u_t^n$, where u_t^n is the natural rate of unemployment and $0 < k < 1$, Ruge-Murcia showed, the Barro-Gordon model is obtained by letting $\gamma \to 0$ and a version similar to Cukierman's asymmetric preferences is obtained when $\gamma > 0$ and $k = 1$, that is, when the target unemployment rate equals the natural rate. In the standard Barro-Gordon model, the inflation bias would disappear when $k = 1$. Using U.S. data, Ruge-Murcia found that the Barro-Gordon model is rejected, but Cukierman's model is not, suggesting that a stronger aversion to unemployment rate increases relative to unemployment rate decreases may have been important in generating the observed pattern of inflation in the United States.

Cukierman and Gerlach (2003) also found support for the importance of asymmetric preferences. They showed that if central banks are uncertain about economic developments and have asymmetric preferences over output, average inflation should be positively correlated with the volatility of output. They found evidence supporting this implication from a cross-section of 22 OECD countries.

Finally, in an important contribution, Sargent (1999) studied the case of a central bank in a Barro-Gordon world that must learn about the structure of the economy. Initially, if the central bank believes it faces a Phillips curve trade-off between output and inflation, it will attempt to expand the economy. The equilibrium involves the standard inflation bias. As new data reveal to the central bank that the Phillips curve is vertical and that it has not gained an output expansion despite the inflation, the equilibrium can switch to a zero inflation path. However, the apparent conquest of inflation is temporary, and the equilibrium can alternate between periods of high inflation and periods of low inflation.

In testing for the role of the biases arising under time inconsistency on actual inflation, it is important to keep in mind that observed inflation is an equilibrium outcome, and a low observed inflation rate need not imply the absence of time inconsistency problems. As noted in the discussion of reputational models, equilibrium may involve pooling in which even an opportunistic central bank delivers low inflation, at least for a while.

7.5 Summary

Many countries experience, for long periods of time, average inflation rates that clearly exceed what would seem to be reasonable estimates of the socially desired inflation rate. The time inconsistency literature originated as a positive attempt to explain this observation. In the process, the approach made important methodological contributions to monetary policy analysis by emphasizing the need to treat central banks as responding to the incentives they face.

The factors emphasized in this chapter—central bank preferences, the short-run real effects of surprise inflation, the rate at which the central bank discounts the future, the effects of political influences on the central bank—are quite different from the factors that received prominence in the optimal taxation models of inflation of chapter 4. Although a large number of empirical studies of the industrialized economies have found that indices of central bank political independence are negatively related to average inflation, evidence also suggests the importance of financing considerations.

Perhaps the most important contribution of the literature on time inconsistency, however, has been to provide theoretical frameworks for thinking formally about credibility issues, on the one hand, and the role of institutions and political factors, on the other, in influencing policy choices. By emphasizing the interactions of the incentives faced by policymakers, the structure of information about the economy and about the central bank's preferences, and the public's beliefs, the models examined in this chapter provide a critical set of insights that have influenced the recent debates over rules, discretion, and the design of monetary policy institutions.

7.6 Problems

1. Consider the following simple economy. Output is given by

$$y_t = \bar{y} + a(\pi_t - \pi_t^e) + e_t,$$

where y is output, π is inflation, π^e is expected inflation, and e is a productivity shock. Private sector expectations are formed before observing e, and the central bank can act after observing e. Suppose the central bank controls inflation and does so to minimize

$$L_t = \left(\frac{1}{2}\right)[(\pi_t - \pi^*)^2 + \lambda(y_t - y^*)^2],$$

where $y^* > \bar{y}$.

a. Solve for the rational-expectations equilibrium for inflation and output if the central bank acts with discretion.

b. Solve for the rational-expectations equilibrium for inflation and output under the optimal commitment policy.

c. Explain (in words) how the inflation bias under discretion depends on a, λ, and $y^* - \bar{y}$.

2. Suppose output is given by

$$y_t = \bar{y} + a(\pi_t - \pi_t^e) + e_t,$$

where y is output, π is inflation, π^e is expected inflation, and e is a productivity shock. Private sector expectations are formed *after* receiving a signal v on the productivity shock, where

$$v_t = e_t + n_t,$$

and n_t is white noise. Let σ_x^2 denote the variance of x and the public's forecast of e_t conditional on v_t is sv_t, where $s = \sigma_e^2/(\sigma_e^2 + \sigma_n^2)$. The central bank can act after observing e. Suppose the central bank controls inflation and does so to minimize

$$L_t = \left(\frac{1}{2}\right)[(\pi_t - \pi^*)^2 + \lambda(y_t - y^*)^2],$$

where $y^* > \bar{y}$.

a. Solve for the rational-expectations equilibrium for inflation and output if the central bank acts with discretion. How does the central bank's reaction to e_t depend on how noisy the public's signal is, as measured by σ_n^2?

b. Solve for the rational-expectations equilibrium for inflation and output under the optimal commitment policy. How does the central bank's reaction to e_t depend on how noisy the public's signal is, as measured by σ_n^2?

c. Calculate expected loss under discretion and under commitment. Does σ_n^2 influence the expected gains from commitment? Explain.

3. Suppose the central bank dislikes inflation variability around a target level π^*. It also prefers to keep unemployment stable around an unemployment target u^*. These objectives can be represented in terms of minimizing

$$V = \lambda(u - u^*)^2 + \frac{1}{2}(\pi - \pi^*)^2,$$

where π is the inflation rate and u is the unemployment rate. The economy is described by

$$u = u_n - a(\pi - \pi^e) + v,$$

where u_n is the natural rate of unemployment and π^e is expected inflation. Expectations are formed by the public before observing the disturbance v. The central bank can set inflation after observing v. Assume $u^* < u_n$.

a. What is the equilibrium rate of inflation under discretion? What is the equilibrium unemployment rate?

b. Is equilibrium unemployment under discretion affected by u^*? Explain.

c. Is equilibrium inflation under discretion affected by u^*? Explain.

d. How is equilibrium inflation under discretion affected by v? Explain.

e. What is the equilibrium rate of inflation under commitment? What is the equilibrium unemployment rate under commitment? How are they affected by u^*? Explain.

4. Suppose an economy is characterized by the following three equations:

$$\pi = \pi^e + ay + e$$

$$y = -br + u$$

$$\Delta m - \pi = -di + y + v,$$

where the first equation is an aggregate supply function written in the form of an expectations-augmented Phillips curve, the second is an IS or aggregate demand relationship, and the third is a money demand equation, where Δm denotes the growth rate of the nominal money supply. The real interest rate is denoted by r and the nominal rate by i, with $i = r + \pi^e$. Let the central bank implement policy by setting i to minimize the expected value of $\frac{1}{2}[\lambda(y - k)^2 + \pi^2]$, where $k > 0$. Assume that the policy authority has forecasts e^f, u^f, and v^f of the shocks but that the public forms its expectations prior to the setting of i and without any information on the shocks.

a. Assume that the central bank can commit to a policy of the form $i = c_0 + c_1 e^f + c_2 u^f + c_3 v^f$ prior to knowing any of the realizations of the shocks. Derive the optimal commitment policy (i.e., the optimal values of c_0, c_1, c_2, and c_3).

b. Derive the time-consistent equilibrium under discretion. How does the nominal interest rate compare to the case under commitment? What is the average inflation rate?

5. Verify that the optimal commitment rule that minimizes the unconditional expected value of the loss function given by (7.10) is $\Delta m^c = -a\lambda e/(1 + a^2\lambda)$.

6. Suppose the central bank acts under discretion to minimize the expected value of (7.2). The central bank can observe e prior to setting Δm, but v is observed only after policy is set. Assume, however, that e and v are correlated and that the expected value of v, conditional on e, is $E[v|e] = qe$, where $q = \sigma_{v,e}/\sigma_e^2$ and $\sigma_{v,e}$ is the covariance between e and v.

a. Find the optimal policy under discretion. Explain how policy depends on q.

b. What is the equilibrium rate of inflation? Does it depend on q?

7. Since the tax distortions of inflation are related to expected inflation, suppose the loss function (7.2) is replaced by

$$L = \lambda(y - y_n - k)^2 + (\pi^e)^2,$$

where $y = y_n + a(\pi - \pi^e)$. How is figure 7.2 modified by this change in the central bank's loss function? Is there an equilibrium inflation rate? Explain.

8. (Based on Jonsson 1995 and Svensson 1997b) Suppose (7.3) is modified to incorporate persistence in the output process:

$$y_t = (1 - \theta)y_n + \theta y_{t-1} + a(\pi_t - \pi_t^e) + e; \qquad 0 < \theta < 1.$$

Suppose the policymaker has a two-period horizon with objective function given by

$$L = \min E[L_t + \beta L_{t+1}],$$

where $L_i = \frac{1}{2}[\lambda(y_i - y_n - k)^2 + \pi_i^2]$.

a. Derive the optimal commitment policy.

b. Derive the optimal policy under discretion without commitment.

c. How does the presence of persistence ($\theta > 0$) affect the inflation bias?

9. Suppose the central bank's objective is to minimize

$$V = \frac{1}{2}\lambda(u - ku_n)^2 + \frac{1}{2}\pi^2,$$

where u is the unemployment rate and u_n is the natural rate of unemployment, with $k < 1$. If the economy is described by

$$u = u_n - a(\pi - \pi^e),$$

what is the equilibrium rate of inflation under discretion? How does a fall in u_n affect the equilibrium rate of inflation?

10. Suppose that the private sector forms expectations according to

$$\pi_t^e = \pi^* \qquad \text{if } \pi_{t-1} = \pi_{t-1}^e$$

$$\pi_t^e = a\lambda k \qquad \text{otherwise.}$$

If the central bank's objective function is the discounted present value of the single-period loss function given by (7.2), and its discount rate is β, what is the minimum value of π^* that can be sustained in equilibrium?

11. (Based on Cukierman and Liviatan 1991) Assume that there are two central bank types with common preferences given by (7.1), but type D always delivers what it announces, whereas type W acts opportunistically. Assume that output is given by (7.3), with $e \equiv 0$. Using a two-period framework, show how output behaves under each type in (a) a pooling equilibrium and (b) a separating equilibrium. Are there any values of β such that welfare is higher if a type W central bank is setting policy?

12. Suppose there are two possible policymaker types: a commitment type (C) whose announced target represents a commitment, and an opportunistic type (O) who is not necessarily bound by the target. The objective of both types is to maximize

$$A(\pi_1 - \pi_1^e) - \frac{\pi_1^2}{2} + \beta\left[A(\pi_2 - \pi_2^e) - \frac{\pi_2^2}{2}\right], \tag{7.28}$$

where π_j and π_j^e, $j = 1, 2$ are actual and expected inflation in period j respectively, $0 \le \beta \le 1$ is a discount factor, and A is a positive parameter. Assume that the type in office in the first period remains in office also in the second period. The public does not know which type is in office but believes, at the beginning of period 1, that the probability that a preannounced inflation target has been issued by type C is $0 \le p_1 \le 1$ (this is the first-period reputation of policymakers). The timing of moves within each period is as follows. First, the policymaker in office announces the inflation target for that period. Then inflationary expectations are formed. Following that, the policymaker picks the actual rate of inflation.

a. Derive the policy plans of each of the two types, when in office, in the second period. What is the intuition underlying your answer?

b. Let p_2 be the reputation of policymakers at the beginning of the second period. Find (and motivate) an expression for the public's (rational) expectation of inflation for that period.

c. Derive the policy plans of each of the two types, when in office, in the first period, and explain your results intuitively.

d. What is the relationship between second- and first-period reputations in equilibrium? Why?

e. How does the discount factor, β, affect the rates of inflation planned by each of the two types in the first period? Why?

13. Assume that nominal wages are set at the start of each period but that wages are partially indexed against inflation. Suppose w^c is the contract nominal wage and the actual nominal wage is $w = w^c + \kappa(p_t - p_{t-1})$, where κ is the indexation parameter. Show how indexation affects the equilibrium rate of inflation under pure discretion. What is the effect on average inflation of an increase in κ? Explain.

14. (Beetsma and Jensen 1998) Suppose the social loss function is equal to

$$V^s = \frac{1}{2}E[\lambda(y - y_n - k)^2 + \pi^2],$$

and the central bank's loss function is given by

$$V^{cb} = \frac{1}{2}E[(\lambda - \theta)(y - y_n - k)^2 + (1 + \theta)(\pi - \pi^T)^2] + t\pi,$$

where θ is a mean zero stochastic shock to the central bank's preferences, π^T is an inflation target assigned by the government, and $t\pi$ is a linear inflation contract with t a parameter chosen by the government. Assume that the private sector forms expectations before observing θ. Let $y = y_n + (\pi - \pi^e) + e$ and $\pi = \Delta m + v$. Finally, assume that θ and the supply shock e are uncorrelated.

a. Suppose the government only assigns an inflation target (so $t = 0$). What is the optimal value for π^T?

b. Suppose the government only assigns a linear inflation contract (so $\pi^T = 0$). What is the optimal value for t?

c. Is the expected social loss lower under the inflation target arrangement or the inflation contract arrangement?

8 New Keynesian Monetary Economics

8.1 Introduction

In the 1970s, 1980s, and early 1990s, models used for monetary policy analysis combined the assumption of nominal rigidity with a simple structure that linked the quantity of money to aggregate spending. Although the theoretical foundations of these models were weak, the approach proved remarkably useful in addressing a wide range of monetary policy topics.[1] Today, the standard approach in monetary economics and monetary policy analysis incorporates nominal wage or price rigidity into a dynamic stochastic general equilibrium (DSGE) framework that is based on optimizing behavior by the agents in the model.

These modern DSGE models with nominal frictions are commonly labeled *new Keynesian models* because, like older versions of models in the Keynesian tradition, aggregate demand plays a central role in determining output in the short run, and there is a presumption that some fluctuations both can be and should be dampened by countercylical monetary or fiscal policy.[2] Early examples of models with these properties include those of Yun (1996); Goodfriend and King (1998); Rotemberg and Woodford (1995; 1998); and McCallum and Nelson (1999). Galí (2002) discusses the derivation of the model's equilibrium conditions, and book-length treatments of the new Keynesian model are provided by Woodford (2003a) and Galí (2008).

The first section of this chapter shows how a basic money-in-the-utility function (MIU) model, combined with the assumption of monopolistically competitive goods markets and price stickiness, can form the basis for a simple linear new Keynesian model.[3] The model is a consistent general equilibrium model in which all agents face well-defined decision problems and behave optimally, given the environment in

---

1. Chapter 7 provided a taste of the many interesting insights obtained from these models.

2. Goodfriend and King (1998) proposed the name "the new neoclassical synthesis" to emphasize the connection with neoclassical rather than Keynesian traditions.

3. See chapter 2 for a discussion of money-in-the-utility function (MIU) models.

which they find themselves. To obtain a canonical new Keynesian model, three key modifications will be made to the MIU model of chapter 2. First, endogenous variations in the capital stock are ignored. This follows McCallum and Nelson (1999), who showed that, at least for the United States, there is little relationship between the capital stock and output at business cycle frequencies. Endogenous capital stock dynamics play a key role in equilibrium business cycle models in the real business cycle tradition, but as Cogley and Nason (1995) showed, the response of investment and the capital stock to productivity shocks actually contributes little to the dynamics implied by such models. For simplicity, then, the capital stock will be ignored.[4]

Second, the single final good in the MIU model is replaced by a continuum of differentiated goods produced by monopolistically competitive firms. These firms face constraints on their ability to adjust prices, thus introducing nominal price stickiness into the model. In the basic model, nominal wages will be allowed to fluctuate freely, although section 8.3.6 explores the implications of assuming that both prices and wages are sticky.

Third, monetary policy is represented by a rule for setting the nominal rate of interest. Most central banks today use a short-term nominal interest rate as their instrument for implementing monetary policy. The nominal quantity of money is then endogenously determined to achieve the desired nominal interest rate. Important issues are involved in choosing between money supply policy procedures and interest rate procedures; these are discussed in chapter 11.

These three modifications yield a new Keynesian framework that is consistent with optimizing behavior by private agents and incorporates nominal rigidities yet is simple enough to use for exploring a number of policy issues. It can be linked directly to the more traditional aggregate supply-demand (AS-IS-LM) model that long served as one of the workhorses for monetary policy analysis and is still common in most undergraduate texts. Once the basic framework has been developed, section 8.4 considers optimal policy as well as a variety of policy issues.

8.2 The Basic Model

The model consists of households and firms. Households supply labor, purchase goods for consumption, and hold money and bonds, and firms hire labor and produce and sell differentiated products in monopolistically competitive goods markets. The basic model of monopolistic competition is drawn from Dixit and Stiglitz (1977).

---

4. However, Dotsey and King (2001) and Christiano, Eichenbaum, and Evans (2005) emphasized the importance of variable capital utilization for understanding the behavior of inflation. Firm-specific capital in a new Keynesian framework was analyzed by Altig et al. (2005).

The model of price stickiness is taken from Calvo (1983).[5] Each firm sets the price of the good it produces, but not all firms reset their price in each period. Households and firms behave optimally; households maximize the expected present value of utility, and firms maximize profits. There is also a central bank that controls the nominal rate of interest. Initially, the central bank, in contrast to households and firms, is not assumed to behave optimally; optimal policy is explored in section 8.4.

8.2.1 Households

The preferences of the representative household are defined over a composite consumption good C_t, real money balances M_t/P_t, and the time devoted to market employment N_t. Households maximize the expected present discounted value of utility:

$$E_t \sum_{i=0}^{\infty} \beta^i \left[\frac{C_{t+i}^{1-\sigma}}{1-\sigma} + \frac{\gamma}{1-b} \left(\frac{M_{t+i}}{P_{t+i}} \right)^{1-b} - \chi \frac{N_{t+i}^{1+\eta}}{1+\eta} \right]. \tag{8.1}$$

The composite consumption good consists of differentiated products produced by monopolistically competitive final goods producers (firms). There is a continuum of such firms of measure 1, and firm j produces good c_j. The composite consumption good that enters the household's utility function is defined as

$$C_t = \left[\int_0^1 c_{jt}^{(\theta-1)/\theta} \, dj \right]^{\theta/(\theta-1)}, \qquad \theta > 1. \tag{8.2}$$

The household's decision problem can be dealt with in two stages. First, regardless of the level of C_t the household decides on, it will always be optimal to purchase the combination of individual goods that minimizes the cost of achieving this level of the composite good. Second, given the cost of achieving any given level of C_t, the household chooses C_t, N_t, and M_t optimally.

Dealing first with the problem of minimizing the cost of buying C_t, the household's decision problem is

$$\min_{c_{jt}} \int_0^1 p_{jt} c_{jt} \, dj$$

subject to

$$\left[\int_0^1 c_{jt}^{(\theta-1)/\theta} \, dj \right]^{\theta/(\theta-1)} \geq C_t, \tag{8.3}$$

---

5. See section 6.2.3.

where p_{jt} is the price of good j. Letting ψ_t be the Lagrangian multiplier on the constraint, the first-order condition for good j is

$$p_{jt} - \psi_t \left[\int_0^1 c_{jt}^{(\theta-1)/\theta} \, dj \right]^{1/(\theta-1)} c_{jt}^{-1/\theta} = 0.$$

Rearranging, $c_{jt} = (p_{jt}/\psi_t)^{-\theta} C_t$. From the definition of the composite level of consumption (8.2), this implies

$$C_t = \left[\int_0^1 \left[\left(\frac{p_{jt}}{\psi_t} \right)^{-\theta} C_t \right]^{(\theta-1)/\theta} dj \right]^{\theta/(\theta-1)} = \left(\frac{1}{\psi_t} \right)^{-\theta} \left[\int_0^1 p_{jt}^{1-\theta} \, dj \right]^{\theta/(\theta-1)} C_t.$$

Solving for ψ_t,

$$\psi_t = \left[\int_0^1 p_{jt}^{1-\theta} \, dj \right]^{1/(1-\theta)} \equiv P_t. \tag{8.4}$$

The Lagrangian multiplier is the appropriately aggregated price index for consumption. The demand for good j can then be written as

$$c_{jt} = \left(\frac{p_{jt}}{P_t} \right)^{-\theta} C_t. \tag{8.5}$$

The price elasticity of demand for good j is equal to θ. As $\theta \to \infty$, the individual goods become closer and closer substitutes, and consequently individual firms will have less market power.

   Given the definition of the aggregate price index in (8.4), the budget constraint of the household is, in real terms,

$$C_t + \frac{M_t}{P_t} + \frac{B_t}{P_t} = \left(\frac{W_t}{P_t} \right) N_t + \frac{M_{t-1}}{P_t} + (1 + i_{t-1}) \left(\frac{B_{t-1}}{P_t} \right) + \Pi_t, \tag{8.6}$$

where M_t (B_t) is the household's nominal holdings of money (one-period bonds). Bonds pay a nominal rate of interest i_t. Real profits received from firms are equal to Π_t.

   In the second stage of the household's decision problem, consumption, labor supply, money, and bond holdings are chosen to maximize (8.1) subject to (8.6). This leads to the following conditions, which, in addition to the budget constraint, must hold in equilibrium:

$$C_t^{-\sigma} = \beta(1 + i_t) E_t \left(\frac{P_t}{P_{t+1}} \right) C_{t+1}^{-\sigma} \tag{8.7}$$

$$\frac{\gamma \left(\frac{M_t}{P_t}\right)^{-b}}{C_t^{-\sigma}} = \frac{i_t}{1 + i_t} \tag{8.8}$$

$$\frac{\chi N_t^{\eta}}{C_t^{-\sigma}} = \frac{W_t}{P_t}. \tag{8.9}$$

These conditions represent the Euler condition for the optimal intertemporal allocation of consumption, the intratemporal optimality condition setting the marginal rate of substitution between money and consumption equal to the opportunity cost of holding money, and the intratemporal optimality condition setting the marginal rate of substitution between leisure and consumption equal to the real wage.[6]

8.2.2   Firms

Firms maximize profits, subject to three constraints. The first is the production function summarizing the available technology. For simplicity, capital is ignored, so output is a function solely of labor input N_{jt} and an aggregate productivity disturbance Z_t:

$$c_{jt} = Z_t N_{jt}, \qquad E(Z_t) = 1,$$

where constant returns to scale have been assumed. The second constraint on the firm is the demand curve each firm faces. This is given by (8.5). The third constraint is that in each period some firms are not able to adjust their price. The specific model of price stickiness used here is due to Calvo (1983). Each period, the firms that adjust their price are randomly selected, and a fraction $1 - \omega$ of all firms adjust while the remaining ω fraction do not adjust. The parameter ω is a measure of the degree of nominal rigidity; a larger ω implies that fewer firms adjust each period and that the expected time between price changes is longer. Those firms that do adjust their price at time t do so to maximize the expected discounted value of current and future profits. Profits at some future date $t + s$ are affected by the choice of price at time t only if the firm has not received another opportunity to adjust between t and $t + s$. The probability of this is ω^s.[7]

Before analyzing the firm's pricing decision, consider its cost minimization problem, which involves minimizing $W_t N_{jt}$ subject to producing $c_{jt} = Z_t N_{jt}$. This problem can be written, in real terms, as

---

6. See chapter 2 for further discussion of these first-order conditions in an MIU model.

7. In this formulation, the degree of nominal rigidity, as measured by ω, is constant, and the probability that a firm has adjusted its price is a function of time, not of the current state. State-dependent pricing models were discussed in section 6.2.5.

$$\min_{N_t} \left(\frac{W_t}{P_t} \right) N_t + \varphi_t (c_{jt} - Z_t N_{jt}),$$

where φ_t is equal to the firm's real marginal cost. The first-order condition implies

$$\varphi_t = \frac{W_t/P_t}{Z_t}. \tag{8.10}$$

The firm's pricing decision problem then involves picking p_{jt} to maximize

$$E_t \sum_{i=0}^{\infty} \omega^i \Delta_{i,t+i} \left[\left(\frac{p_{jt}}{P_{t+i}} \right) c_{jt+i} - \varphi_{t+i} c_{jt+i} \right],$$

where the discount factor $\Delta_{i,t+i}$ is given by $\beta^i (C_{t+i}/C_t)^{-\sigma}$. Using the demand curve (8.5) to eliminate c_{jt}, this objective function can be written as

$$E_t \sum_{i=0}^{\infty} \omega^i \Delta_{i,t+i} \left[\left(\frac{p_{jt}}{P_{t+i}} \right)^{1-\theta} - \varphi_{t+i} \left(\frac{p_{jt}}{P_{t+i}} \right)^{-\theta} \right] C_{t+i}.$$

While individual firms produce differentiated products, they all have the same production technology and face demand curves with constant and equal demand elasticities. In other words, they are essentially identical except that they may have set their current price at different dates in the past. However, all firms adjusting in period t face the same problem, so all adjusting firms will set the same price. Let p_t^* be the optimal price chosen by all firms adjusting at time t. The first-order condition for the optimal choice of p_t^* is

$$E_t \sum_{i=0}^{\infty} \omega^i \Delta_{i,t+i} \left[(1-\theta) \left(\frac{p_t^*}{P_{t+i}} \right) + \theta \varphi_{t+i} \right] \left(\frac{1}{p_t^*} \right) \left(\frac{p_t^*}{P_{t+i}} \right)^{-\theta} C_{t+i} = 0. \tag{8.11}$$

Using the definition of $\Delta_{i,t+i}$, (8.11) can be rearranged to yield

$$\left(\frac{p_t^*}{P_t} \right) = \left(\frac{\theta}{\theta-1} \right) \frac{E_t \sum_{i=0}^{\infty} \omega^i \beta^i C_{t+i}^{1-\sigma} \varphi_{t+i} \left(\frac{P_{t+i}}{P_t} \right)^{\theta}}{E_t \sum_{i=0}^{\infty} \omega^i \beta^i C_{t+i}^{1-\sigma} \left(\frac{P_{t+i}}{P_t} \right)^{\theta-1}}. \tag{8.12}$$

Consider the case in which all firms are able to adjust their price every period ($\omega = 0$). When $\omega = 0$, (8.12) reduces to

$$\left(\frac{p_t^*}{P_t} \right) = \left(\frac{\theta}{\theta-1} \right) \varphi_t = \mu \varphi_t. \tag{8.13}$$

Each firm sets its price p_t^* equal to a markup $\mu > 1$ over its nominal marginal cost $P_t\varphi_t$. This is the standard result in a model of monopolistic competition. Because price exceeds marginal cost, output will be inefficiently low. When prices are flexible, all firms charge the same price. In this case, $p_t^* = P_t$ and $\varphi_t = 1/\mu$. Using the definition of real marginal cost, this means $W_t/P_t = Z_t/\mu < Z_t$ in a flexible-price equilibrium. However, the real wage must also equal the marginal rate of substitution between leisure and consumption to be consistent with household optimization. This condition implies, from (8.9), that

$$\frac{\chi N_t^\eta}{C_t^{-\sigma}} = \frac{W_t}{P_t} = \frac{Z_t}{\mu}. \tag{8.14}$$

Goods market clearing and the production function imply that $C_t = Y_t$ and $N_t = Y_t/Z_t$. Using these conditions in (8.14), and letting Y_t^f denote equilibrium output under flexible prices, Y_t^f is given by

$$Y_t^f = \left(\frac{1}{\chi\mu}\right)^{1/(\sigma+\eta)} Z_t^{(1+\eta)/(\sigma+\eta)}. \tag{8.15}$$

When prices are flexible, output is a function of the aggregate productivity shock, reflecting the fact that in the absence of sticky prices, the new Keynesian model reduces to a real business cycle model.

When prices are sticky ($\omega > 0$), output can differ from the flexible-price equilibrium level. Because a firm will not adjust its price every period, (8.12) shows it must take into account expected future marginal cost as well as current marginal cost whenever it has an opportunity to adjust its price.

The aggregate price index is an average of the price charged by the fraction $1 - \omega$ of firms setting their price in period t and the average of the remaining fraction ω of all firms that do not change their price in period t. However, because the adjusting firms were selected randomly from among all firms, the average price of the non-adjusters is just the average price of all firms that prevailed in period $t - 1$. Thus, from (8.4), the average price in period t satisfies

$$P_t^{1-\theta} = (1 - \omega)(p_t^*)^{1-\theta} + \omega P_{t-1}^{1-\theta}. \tag{8.16}$$

To summarize, (8.7)–(8.10), (8.12), (8.14), and (8.16) represent a system in C_t, N_t, M/P_t, Y_t, φ_t, P_t, p_t^*, W_t/P_t, and i_t that can be combined with the aggregate production function, $Y_t = Z_t N_t$, and a specification of monetary policy to determine the economy's equilibrium.

8.3   A Linearized New Keynesian Model

One reason for the popularity of the new Keynesian model is that it allows for a simple linear representation in terms of an inflation adjustment equation, or Phillips curve, and an output and real interest rate relationship that corresponds to the IS curve of undergraduate macroeconomics. To derive this linearized version of the model, let $\hat{x}_t$ denote the percentage deviation of a variable X_t around its steady state and let the superscript f denote the flexible-price equilibrium. The equilibrium conditions in the model will be linearized around a steady state in which the inflation rate is zero.

8.3.1   The Linearized Phillips Curve

Equations (8.12) and (8.16) can be approximated around a zero average inflation, steady-state equilibrium to obtain an expression for aggregate inflation (see section 8.6.1 of the chapter appendix) of the form

$$\pi_t = \beta E_t \pi_{t+1} + \tilde{\kappa} \hat{\varphi}_t, \tag{8.17}$$

where

$$\tilde{\kappa} = \frac{(1-\omega)(1-\beta\omega)}{\omega}$$

is an increasing function of the fraction of firms able to adjust each period and $\hat{\varphi}_t$ is real marginal cost, expressed as a percentage deviation around its steady-state value.[8]

Equation (8.17) is often referred to as the *new Keynesian Phillips curve*. Unlike more traditional Phillips curve equations, the new Keynesian Phillips curve implies that real marginal cost is the correct driving variable for the inflation process. It also implies that the inflation process is forward-looking, with current inflation a function of expected future inflation. When a firm sets its price, it must be concerned with inflation in the future because it may be unable to adjust its price for several periods. Solving (8.17) forward,

$$\pi_t = \tilde{\kappa} \sum_{i=0}^{\infty} \beta^i E_t \hat{\varphi}_{t+i},$$

which shows that inflation is a function of the present discounted value of current and future real marginal costs.

---

8. Ascari (2004) showed that the behavior of inflation in the Calvo model can be significantly affected if steady-state inflation is not zero.

The new Keynesian Phillips curve also differs from traditional Phillips curves in having been derived explicitly from a model of optimizing behavior on the part of price setters, conditional on the assumed economic environment (monopolistic competition, constant elasticity demand curves, and randomly arriving opportunities to adjust prices). This derivation reveals how $\tilde{\kappa}$, the impact of real marginal cost on inflation, depends on the structural parameters β and ω. An increase in β means that the firm gives more weight to future expected profits. As a consequence, $\tilde{\kappa}$ declines; inflation is less sensitive to current marginal costs. Increased price rigidity (a rise in ω) reduces $\tilde{\kappa}$; with opportunities to adjust arriving less frequently, the firm places less weight on current marginal cost (and more on expected future marginal costs) when it does adjust its price.

Equation (8.17) implies that inflation depends on real marginal cost and not directly on a measure of the gap between actual output and some measure of potential output or on a measure of unemployment relative to the natural rate, as is typical in traditional Phillips curves.[9] However, real marginal costs can be related to an output gap measure. The firm's real marginal cost is equal to the real wage it faces divided by the marginal product of labor (see (8.10)). In a flexible-price equilibrium, all firms set the same price, so (8.13) implies that real marginal cost will equal its steady-state value of $1/\mu$. Because nominal wages have been assumed to be completely flexible, the real wage must, according to (8.9), equal the marginal rate of substitution between leisure and consumption. Expressed in terms of percentage deviations around the steady state, (8.9) implies that $\hat{w}_t - \hat{p}_t = \eta \hat{n}_t + \sigma \hat{y}_t$. Recalling that $\hat{c}_t = \hat{y}_t$ and $\hat{y}_t = \hat{n}_t + \hat{z}_t$, the percentage deviation of real marginal cost around its steady-state value is

$$\hat{\varphi}_t = (\hat{w}_t - \hat{p}_t) - (\hat{y}_t - \hat{n}_t)$$

$$= (\sigma + \eta)\left[\hat{y}_t - \left(\frac{1+\eta}{\sigma+\eta}\right)\hat{z}_t\right].$$

To interpret the term involving $\hat{z}_t$, linearize (8.15) giving flexible-price output to obtain

$$\hat{y}_t^f = \left(\frac{1+\eta}{\sigma+\eta}\right)\hat{z}_t. \tag{8.18}$$

Thus, (8.18) can be used to express real marginal cost as

$$\hat{\varphi}_t = \gamma(\hat{y}_t - \hat{y}_t^f), \tag{8.19}$$

---

9. See Ravenna and Walsh (2008) and Blanchard and Gali (2008) for models of labor market frictions that relate inflation to unemployment.

where $\gamma = \sigma + \eta$. Using this result, the inflation adjustment equation (8.17) becomes

$$\pi_t = \beta E_t \pi_{t+1} + \kappa x_t, \tag{8.20}$$

where $\kappa = \gamma \tilde{\kappa} = \gamma(1 - \omega)(1 - \beta\omega)/\omega$ and $x_t \equiv \hat{y}_t - \hat{y}_t^f$ is the gap between actual output and flexible-price equilibrium output.

The preceding assumed that firms face constant returns to scale. If, instead, each firm's production function is $c_{jt} = Z_t N_{jt}^a$, where $0 < a \le 1$, then the results must be modified slightly. When $a < 1$, firms with different production levels will face different marginal costs, and real marginal cost for firm j will equal

$$\varphi_{jt} = \frac{W_t/P_t}{a Z_t N_{jt}^{a-1}} = \frac{W_t/P_t}{a c_{jt}/N_{jt}}.$$

Linearizing this expression for firm $j's$ real marginal cost and using the production function yields

$$\hat{\varphi}_{jt} = (\hat{w}_t - \hat{p}_t) - (\hat{c}_{jt} - \hat{n}_{jt}) = (\hat{w}_t - \hat{p}_t) - \left(\frac{a-1}{a}\right)\hat{c}_{jt} - \left(\frac{1}{a}\right)\hat{z}_t. \tag{8.21}$$

Marginal cost for the individual firm can be related to average marginal cost, $\varphi_t = (W_t/P_t)/(a C_t/N_t)$, where

$$N_t = \int_0^1 N_{jt}\, dj = \int_0^1 \left(\frac{c_{jt}}{Z_t}\right)^{1/a} dj = \left(\frac{C_t}{Z_t}\right)^{1/a} \int_0^1 \left(\frac{p_{jt}}{P_t}\right)^{-\theta/a} dj.$$

When this last expression is linearized around a zero inflation steady state, the final term involving the dispersion of relative prices turns out to be of second order,[10] so one obtains

$$\hat{n}_t = \left(\frac{1}{a}\right)(\hat{c}_t - \hat{z}_t)$$

and

$$\hat{\varphi}_t = (\hat{w}_t - \hat{p}_t) - (\hat{c}_t - \hat{n}_t) = (\hat{w}_t - \hat{p}_t) - \left(\frac{a-1}{a}\right)\hat{c}_t - \left(\frac{1}{a}\right)\hat{z}_t. \tag{8.22}$$

Subtracting (8.22) from (8.21) gives

---

10. When linearized, the last term becomes

$$-\left(\frac{\theta}{a}\right)\int(\hat{p}_{jt} - \hat{p}_t)\, dj,$$

but to a first-order approximation, $\int \hat{p}_{jt}\, dj = \hat{p}_t$, so the price dispersion term is approximately equal to zero.

$$\hat{\varphi}_{jt} - \hat{\varphi}_t = -\left(\frac{a-1}{a}\right)(\hat{c}_{jt} - \hat{c}_t).$$

Finally, employing the demand relationship (8.5) to express $\hat{c}_{jt} - \hat{c}_t$ in terms of relative prices,

$$\hat{\varphi}_{jt} = \hat{\varphi}_t - \left[\frac{\theta(1-a)}{a}\right](\hat{p}_{jt} - \hat{p}_t).$$

Firms with relatively high prices (and therefore low output) will have relatively low real marginal costs. In the case of constant returns to scale ($a = 1$), all firms face the same marginal cost. Sbordone (2002) and Galí, Gertler, and López-Salido (2001) showed that when $a < 1$, the new Keynesian inflation adjustment equation becomes[11]

$$\pi_t = \beta E_t \pi_{t+1} + \tilde{\kappa}\left[\frac{a}{a+\theta(1-a)}\right]\hat{\varphi}_t.$$

In addition, the labor market equilibrium condition under flexible prices becomes

$$\frac{W_t}{P_t} = \frac{aZ_t N_t^{a-1}}{\mu} = \frac{\chi N_t^{\eta}}{C_t^{-\sigma}},$$

which implies flexible-price output is

$$\hat{y}_t^f = \left[\frac{1+\eta}{1+\eta+a(\sigma-1)}\right]\hat{z}_t.$$

When $a = 1$, this reduces to (8.18).

8.3.2 The Linearized IS Curve

Equation (8.20) relates output to inflation in the form of the deviation around the level of output that would occur in the absence of nominal price rigidity. It forms one of the two key components of an optimizing model that can be used for monetary policy analysis. The other component is a linearized version of the household's Euler condition, (8.7). Because consumption is equal to output in this model (there is no government or investment because capital has been ignored), (8.7) can be approximated around the zero inflation steady state as[12]

$$\hat{y}_t = E_t \hat{y}_{t+1} - \left(\frac{1}{\sigma}\right)(\hat{\imath}_t - E_t \pi_{t+1}), \tag{8.23}$$

---

11. See the chapter appendix for further details on the derivation.
12. See the chapter 2 appendix for details on linearizing the Euler condition; $\hat{c}_t = \hat{y}_t$ is used in (8.23).

where $\hat{\imath}_t$ is the deviation of the nominal interest rate from its steady-state value. Expressing this in terms of the output gap $x_t = \hat{y}_t - \hat{y}_t^f$,

$$x_t = E_t x_{t+1} - \left(\frac{1}{\sigma}\right)(\hat{\imath}_t - E_t \pi_{t+1}) + u_t, \tag{8.24}$$

where $u_t \equiv E_t \hat{y}_{t+1}^f - \hat{y}_t^f$ depends only on the exogenous productivity disturbance (see (8.18)). Combining (8.24) with (8.20) gives a simple two-equation, forward-looking, rational-expectations model for inflation and the output gap measure x_t, once the behavior of the nominal rate of interest is specified.[13] This two-equation model consists of the equilibrium conditions for a well-specified general equilibrium model. The equations appear broadly similar, however, to the types of aggregate demand and aggregate supply equations commonly found in intermediate-level macroeconomics textbooks. Equation (8.24) represents the demand side of the economy (an expectational, forward-looking IS curve), and the new Keynesian Phillips curve (8.20) corresponds to the supply side. In fact, both equations are derived from optimization problems, with (8.24) based on the Euler condition for the representative household's decision problem and (8.20) derived from the optimal pricing decisions of individual firms.

There is a long tradition of using two-equation, aggregate demand–aggregate supply (AD-AS) models in intermediate-level macroeconomic and monetary policy analysis. Models in the AD-AS tradition are often criticized as "starting from curves" rather than starting from the primitive tastes and technology from which behavioral relationships can be derived, given maximizing behavior and a market structure (Sargent 1982). This criticism does not apply to (8.24) and (8.20). The parameters appearing in these two equations are explicit functions of the underlying structural parameters of the production and utility functions and the assumed process for price adjustment.[14] And (8.24) and (8.20) contain expectations of future variables; the absence of this type of forward-looking behavior is a critical shortcoming of older AD-AS frameworks. The importance of incorporating a role for future income was emphasized by Kerr and King (1996).

Equations (8.24) and (8.20) contain three variables: the output gap, inflation, and the nominal interest rate. The model can be closed by assuming that the central bank implements monetary policy through control of the nominal interest rate.[15] Alternatively, if the central bank implements monetary policy by setting a path for the nom-

---

13. With the nominal interest rate treated as the monetary policy instrument, (8.8) simply determines the real quantity of money in equilibrium.

14. The process for price adjustment, however, has not been derived from the underlying structure of the economic environment.

15. Important issues of price level determinacy arise under interest rate–setting policies (see chapter 11).

inal supply of money, (8.24) and (8.20), together with the linearized version of (8.8), determine x_t, π_t, and $\hat{\imath}_t$.[16]

8.3.3 Uniqueness of the Equilibrium

If a policy rule for the nominal interest rate is added to the model, this must be done with care to ensure that the policy rule does not render the system unstable or introduce multiple equilibria. For example, suppose monetary policy is represented by the following purely exogenous process for $\hat{\imath}_t$:

$$\hat{\imath}_t = v_t, \tag{8.25}$$

where v_t is a stationary stochastic process. Combining (8.25) with (8.24) and (8.20), the resulting system of equations can be written as

$$\begin{bmatrix} 1 & \sigma^{-1} \\ 0 & \beta \end{bmatrix} \begin{bmatrix} E_t x_{t+1} \\ E_t \pi_{t+1} \end{bmatrix} = \begin{bmatrix} 1 & 0 \\ -\kappa & 1 \end{bmatrix} \begin{bmatrix} x_t \\ \pi_t \end{bmatrix} + \begin{bmatrix} \sigma^{-1} v_t - u_t \\ 0 \end{bmatrix}.$$

Premultiplying both sides by the inverse of the matrix on the left produces

$$\begin{bmatrix} E_t x_{t+1} \\ E_t \pi_{t+1} \end{bmatrix} = M \begin{bmatrix} x_t \\ \pi_t \end{bmatrix} + \begin{bmatrix} \sigma^{-1} v_t - u_t \\ 0 \end{bmatrix}, \tag{8.26}$$

where

$$M = \begin{bmatrix} 1 + \frac{\kappa}{\sigma\beta} & -\frac{1}{\sigma\beta} \\ -\frac{\kappa}{\beta} & \frac{1}{\beta} \end{bmatrix}.$$

Equation (8.26) has a unique stationary solution for the output gap and inflation if and only if the number of eigenvalues of M outside the unit circle is equal to the number of forward-looking variables, in this case, two (Blanchard and Kahn 1980). However, only the largest eigenvalue of this matrix is outside the unit circle, implying that multiple bounded equilibria exist and that the equilibrium is locally indeterminate. Stationary sunspot equilibria are possible.

This example illustrates that an exogenous policy rule—one that does not respond to the endogenous variables x and π—introduces the possibility of multiple equilibria. To understand why, consider what would happen if expected inflation were to rise. Since (8.25) does not allow for any endogenous feedback from this rise in expected inflation to the nominal interest rate, the real interest rate must fall. This decline in the real interest rate is expansionary, and the output gap increases. The rise

---

16. An alternative approach (see section 8.4) specifies an objective function for the monetary authority and then derives the policymaker's decision rule for setting the nominal interest rate.

in output increases actual inflation, according to (8.20). Thus, a change in expected inflation, even if due to factors unrelated to the fundamentals of inflation, can set off a self-fulfilling change in actual inflation.

This discussion suggests that a policy that raised the nominal interest rate when inflation rose, and raised $\hat{\imath}_t$ enough to increase the real interest rate so that the output gap fell, would be sufficient to ensure a unique equilibrium. For example, suppose the nominal interest rate responds to inflation according to the rule

$$\hat{\imath}_t = \delta\pi_t + v_t. \tag{8.27}$$

Combining (8.27) with (8.24) and (8.20), $\hat{\imath}_t$ can be eliminated, and the resulting system is written as

$$\begin{bmatrix} E_t x_{t+1} \\ E_t \pi_{t+1} \end{bmatrix} = N \begin{bmatrix} x_t \\ \pi_t \end{bmatrix} + \begin{bmatrix} \sigma^{-1} v_t - u_t \\ 0 \end{bmatrix}, \tag{8.28}$$

where

$$N = \begin{bmatrix} 1 + \frac{\kappa}{\sigma\beta} & \frac{\beta\delta-1}{\sigma\beta} \\ -\frac{\kappa}{\beta} & \frac{1}{\beta} \end{bmatrix}.$$

Bullard and Mitra (2002) showed that a unique stationary equilibrium exists as long as $\delta > 1$.[17] Setting $\delta > 1$ is referred to as the *Taylor principle*, because John Taylor was the first to stress the importance of interest rate rules that called for responding more than one-for-one to changes in inflation.

Suppose that instead of reacting solely to inflation, as in (8.27), the central bank responds to both inflation and the output gap according to

$$\hat{\imath}_t = \delta_\pi \pi_t + \delta_x x_t + v_t.$$

This type of policy rule is called a *Taylor rule* (Taylor 1993a), and variants of it have been shown to provide a reasonable empirical description of the policy behavior of many central banks (Clarida, Galí, and Gertler 2000).[18] With this policy rule, Bullard and Mitra (2002) showed that the condition necessary to ensure that the economy has a unique stationary equilibrium becomes

---

17. If the nominal interest rate is adjusted in response to expected future inflation (rather than current inflation), multiple solutions again become possible if $\hat{\imath}_t$ responds too strongly to $E_t\hat{\pi}_{t+1}$. See Clarida, Galí, and Gertler (2000).

18. Sometimes the term *Taylor rule* is reserved for the case in which $\delta_\pi = 1.5$ and $\delta_x = 0.5$ when inflation and the interest rate are expressed at annual rates. These are the values Taylor (1993a) found matched the behavior of the federal funds rates rate during the Greenspan period.

$$\kappa(\delta_\pi - 1) + (1 - \beta)\delta_x > 0. \tag{8.29}$$

Determinacy now depends on both the policy parameters δ_π and δ_x. A policy that failed to raise the nominal interest rate sufficiently when inflation rose would lead to a rise in aggregate demand and output. This rise in x could produce a rise in the real interest rate that served to contract spending if δ_x were large. Thus, a policy rule with $\delta_\pi < 1$ could still be consistent with a unique stationary equilibrium. At a quarterly frequency, however, β is about 0.99, so δ_x would need to be very large to offset a value of δ_π much below 1.

The Taylor principle is an important policy lesson that has emerged from the new Keynesian model. It has been argued that the failure of central banks such as the Federal Reserve to respond sufficiently strongly to inflation during the 1970s provides an explanation for the rise in inflation experiences at the time (Lubik and Schorfheide 2004). Further, Orphanides (2001) argued that estimated Taylor rules for the Federal Reserve are sensitive to whether real-time data are used, and he found a much weaker response to inflation in the 1987–1999 period based on real-time data.[19] Because the Taylor principle is based on the mapping from policy response coefficients to eigenvalues in the state space representation of the model, one would expect that the exact restrictions the policy responses must satisfy to ensure determinacy will depend on the specification of the model. Two aspects of the model have been explored that lead to significant modifications of the Taylor principle.

First, Ascari and Ropele (2007) and Kiley (2007b) found that the Taylor rule can be insufficient to ensure determinacy when trend inflation is positive rather than zero as assumed when obtaining the standard linearized new Keynesian inflation equation. For example, Coibion and Gorodnichenko (2008) showed, in a calibrated model, that the central bank's response to inflation would need to be over ten-to-one to ensure determinacy if steady-state inflation exceeded 6 percent. However, many models assume some form of indexation (see chapter 6), and for these models the Taylor principle would continue to hold even in the face of a positive steady-state rate of inflation.

Second, the Taylor principle can be significantly affected when interest rates have direct effects on real marginal cost. Such an effect, usually referred to as the cost channel of monetary policy, is common in models in which firms need to finance wage payments, as in Christiano, Eichenbaum, and Evans (2005) or Ravenna and Walsh (2006), or in which search frictions in the labor market introduce an intertemporal aspect to the firm's labor demand condition (Ravenna and Walsh 2008). For

---

19. Other papers employing real-time data to estimate policy rules include Rudebusch (2006) for the United States and Papell, Molodtsova, and Nikolsko-Rzhevskyy (2008) for the United States and Germany.

example, Llosa and Tuesta (2006), for a model with a cost channel, and Kurozumi and Van Zandwedge (2008), for a model with search and matching frictions in the labor market, found that satisfying the standard Taylor principle of responding more than one-for-one to inflation need not ensure determinacy.

Finally, note that if v_t and u_t are zero for all t, the solution to (8.28) would be $\pi_t = x_t = 0$ for all t. In this case, the parameter δ in the policy rule (8.27) could not be identified. As Cochrane (2007) emphasized, determinacy relies on assumptions about how the central bank would respond to movements of inflation out of equilibrium. Estimated Taylor rules may not reveal how policy would react in circumstances that are not observed.

8.3.4 The Monetary Transmission Mechanism

The model consisting of (8.24) and (8.20) assumes that the impact of monetary policy on output and inflation operates through the real rate of interest. As long as the central bank is able to affect the real interest rate through its control of the nominal interest rate, monetary policy can affect real output. Changes in the real interest rate alter the optimal time path of consumption. An increase in the real rate of interest, for instance, leads households to attempt to postpone consumption. Current consumption falls relative to future consumption.[20]

Figure 8.1 illustrates the impact of a monetary policy shock (an increase in the nominal interest rate) in the model consisting of (8.24), (8.20), and the policy rule (8.27). The parameter values used in constructing the figure are $\beta = 0.99$, $\sigma = \eta = 1$, $\delta = 1.5$, and $\omega = 0.8$. In addition, the policy shock v_t in the policy rule is assumed to follow an AR(1) process given by $v_t = \rho_v v_{t-1} + \varepsilon_t$, with $\rho_v = 0.5$. The rise in the nominal rate causes inflation and the output gap to fall immediately. This reflects the forward-looking nature of both variables. In fact, all the persistence displayed by the responses arises from the serial correlation introduced into the process for the monetary shock v_t. If $\rho_v = 0$, all variables return to their steady-state values in the period after the shock.[21]

To emphasize the interest rate as the primary channel through which monetary influences affect output, it is convenient to express the output gap as a function of an *interest rate gap*, the gap between the current interest rate and the interest rate consistent with the flexible-price equilibrium. For example, let $\hat{r}_t \equiv \hat{i}_t - E_t\pi_{t+1}$ be the real interest rate, and write (8.24) as

---

20. Estrella and Fuhrer (2002) noted that the forward-looking Euler equation implies counterfactual dynamics; (8.24) implies that $E_t\hat{c}_{t+1} - \hat{c}_t = \sigma^{-1}(\hat{i}_t - E_t\pi_{t+1})$, so that a rise in the real interest rate means that consumption must *increase* from t to $t + 1$.

21. See Galí (2002) for a discussion of the monetary transmission mechanism incorporated in the basic new Keynesian model.

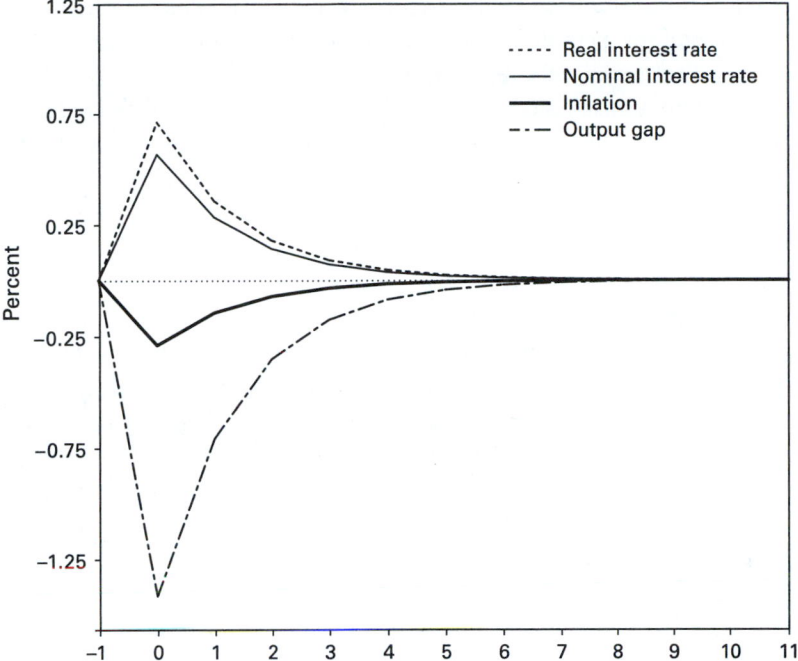

Figure 8.1
Response of output, inflation, and real interest rate to a policy shock in the new Keynesian model.

$$x_t = \mathrm{E}_t x_{t+1} - \left(\frac{1}{\sigma}\right)(\hat{r}_t - \tilde{r}_t),$$

where $\tilde{r}_t \equiv \sigma u_t$. Woodford (2000) labeled $\tilde{r}_t$ the *Wicksellian real interest rate*. It is the interest rate consistent with output equaling the flexible-price equilibrium level. If $\hat{r}_t = \tilde{r}_t$ for all t, then $x_t = 0$ and output is kept equal to the level that would arise in the absence of nominal rigidities. The interest rate gap $\hat{r}_t - \tilde{r}_t$ then summarizes the effects on the actual equilibrium that are due to nominal rigidities.[22]

The presence of expected future output in (8.24) implies that the future path of the one-period real interest rate matters for current demand. To see this, recursively solve (8.24) forward to yield

$$x_t = -\left(\frac{1}{\sigma}\right) \sum_{i=0}^{\infty} \mathrm{E}_t(\hat{r}_{t+i} - \tilde{r}_{t+i}).$$

22. Neiss and Nelson (2001) used a structural model to estimate the real interest rate gap $\hat{r}_t - \tilde{r}_t$ and found that it has value as a predictor of inflation.

Changes in the one-period rate that are persistent will influence expectations of future interest rates. Therefore, persistent changes should have stronger effects on x_t than more temporary changes in real interest rates.

The basic interest rate transmission mechanism for monetary policy could be extended to include effects on investment spending if capital were reintroduced into the model (Christiano, Eichenbaum, and Evans 2005; Dotsey and King 2001). Increases in the real interest rate would reduce the demand for capital and lead to a fall in investment spending. In the case of both investment and consumption, monetary policy effects are transmitted through interest rates.

In addition to these interest rate channels, monetary policy is often thought to affect the economy either indirectly through credit channels or directly through the quantity of money. Real money holdings represent part of household wealth; an increase in real balances should induce an increase in consumption spending through a wealth effect. This channel is often called the *Pigou effect* and was viewed as generating a channel through which price level declines during a depression would eventually increase real balances and household wealth sufficiently to restore consumption spending. During the Keynesian/monetarist debates of the 1960s and early 1970s, some monetarists argued for a direct wealth effect that linked changes in the money supply directly to aggregate demand (Patinkin 1965). The effect of money on aggregate demand operating through interest rate effects was viewed as a Keynesian interpretation of the transmission mechanism, whereas most monetarists argued that changes in monetary policy lead to substitution effects over a broader range of assets than Keynesians normally considered. Since wealth effects are likely to be small at business cycle frequencies, most simple models used for policy analysis ignore them.[23]

Direct effects of the quantity of money are not present in the model used here; the quantity of money appears in neither (8.24) nor (8.20). The underlying model was derived from an MIU model, and the absence of money in (8.24) and (8.20) results from the assumption that the utility function is separable (see (8.1)). If utility is not separable, then changes in the real quantity of money alter the marginal utility of consumption. This would affect the model specification in two ways. First, the real money stock would appear in the household's Euler condition and therefore in (8.24). Second, to replace real marginal cost with a measure of the output gap in (8.20), the real wage was equated to the marginal rate of substitution between leisure and consumption, and this would also involve real money balances if utility were nonseparable (see problem 7 at the end of this chapter). Thus, the absence of money constitutes a special case. However, McCallum and Nelson (1999) and Woodford

---

23. For an analysis of the real balance effect, see Ireland (2001b).

(2001b) argued that the effects arising with nonseparable utility are quite small, so that little is lost by assuming separability. Ireland (2001c) finds little evidence for nonseparable preferences in a model estimated on U.S. data.

The quantity of money is not totally absent from the underlying model, since (8.8) also must hold in equilibrium. Linearizing this equation around the steady state yields[24]

$$\hat{m}_t - \hat{p}_t = \left(\frac{1}{bi^{ss}}\right)(\sigma\hat{y}_t - \hat{\imath}_t). \tag{8.30}$$

Given the nominal interest rate chosen by the monetary policy authority, this equation determines the nominal quantity of money. Alternatively, if the policymaker sets the nominal quantity of money, then (8.20), (8.24), and (8.30) must all be used to solve jointly for x_t, π_t, and $\hat{\imath}_t$.

Chapter 10 discusses the role of credit channels in the monetary transmission process.

8.3.5 Adding Economic Disturbances

As the model consisting of (8.20) and (8.24) stands, there are no underlying non-policy disturbances that might generate movements in either the output gap or inflation other than the productivity disturbance that affects the flexible-price output level. It is common, however, to include in these equations stochastic disturbances arising from other sources.

Suppose the representative household's utility from consumption is subject to random shocks that alter the marginal utility of consumption. Specifically, let the utility function in (8.1) be modified to include a taste shock ψ:

$$E_t \sum_{i=0}^{\infty} \beta^i \left[\frac{(\psi_{t+i} C_{t+i})^{1-\sigma}}{1-\sigma} + \frac{\gamma}{1-b}\left(\frac{M_{t+i}}{P_{t+i}}\right)^{1-b} - \chi\frac{N_{t+i}^{1+\eta}}{1+\eta} \right]. \tag{8.31}$$

The Euler condition (8.7) becomes

$$\psi_t^{1-\sigma} C_t^{-\sigma} = \beta(1+i_t)E_t(P_t/P_{t+1})(\psi_{t+1}^{1-\sigma} C_{t+1}^{-\sigma}),$$

which, when linearized around the zero inflation steady state yields

$$\hat{c}_t = E_t\hat{c}_{t+1} - \left(\frac{1}{\sigma}\right)(\hat{\imath}_t - E_t\pi_{t+1}) + \left(\frac{\sigma - 1}{\sigma}\right)(E_t\psi_{t+1} - \psi_t). \tag{8.32}$$

---

24. See the chapter 2 appendix.

If, in addition to consumption by households, the government purchases final output G_t, the goods market equilibrium condition becomes $Y_t = C_t + G_t$. When this is expressed in terms of percentage deviations around the steady state, one obtains

$$\hat{y}_t = \left(\frac{C}{Y}\right)^{ss} \hat{c}_t + \left(\frac{G}{Y}\right)^{ss} \hat{g}_t.$$

Using this equation to eliminate $\hat{c}_t$ from (8.32) and then replacing $\hat{y}_t$ with $x_t + \hat{y}_t^f$ yields an expression for the output gap $(\hat{y}_t - \hat{y}_t^f)$,

$$x_t = \mathrm{E}_t x_{t+1} - \tilde{\sigma}^{-1}(\hat{\imath}_t - \mathrm{E}_t \pi_{t+1}) + \xi_t, \tag{8.33}$$

where $\tilde{\sigma}^{-1} = \sigma^{-1}(C/Y)^{ss}$ and

$$\xi_t \equiv \left(\frac{\sigma-1}{\sigma}\right)\left(\frac{C}{Y}\right)^{ss}(\mathrm{E}_t\psi_{t+1} - \psi_t) - \left(\frac{G}{Y}\right)^{ss}(\mathrm{E}_t\hat{g}_{t+1} - \hat{g}_t) + (\mathrm{E}_t\hat{y}_{t+1}^f - \hat{y}_t^f).$$

Equation (8.33) represents the Euler condition consistent with the representative household's intertemporal optimality condition linking consumption levels over time. It is also consistent with the resource constraint $Y_t = C_t + G_t$. The disturbance term arises from taste shocks that alter the marginal utility of consumption, shifts in government purchases, and shifts in the flexible-price equilibrium output. In each case, it is expected changes in ψ, g, and $\hat{y}^f$ that matter. For example, an expected rise in government purchases implies that future consumption must fall. This reduces current consumption.

The source of a disturbance term in the inflation adjustment equation is both more critical for policy analysis and more controversial (section 8.4 takes up policy analysis). It is easy to see why exogenous shifts in (8.20) can have important implications for policy. Two commonly assumed objectives of monetary policy are to maintain a low and stable average rate of inflation and to stabilize output around full employment. These two objectives are often viewed as presenting central banks with a tradeoff. A supply shock, such as an increase in oil prices, increases inflation and reduces output. To keep inflation from rising calls for contractionary policies that would exacerbate the decline in output; stabilizing output calls for expansionary policies that would worsen inflation. However, if the output objective is interpreted as meaning that output should be stabilized around its flexible-price equilibrium level, then (8.20) implies that the central bank can always achieve a zero output gap (i.e., keep output at its flexible-price equilibrium level) and simultaneously keep inflation equal to zero. Solving (8.20) forward yields

$$\pi_t = \kappa \sum_{i=0}^{\infty} \beta^i \mathrm{E}_t x_{t+i}.$$

By keeping current and expected future output equal to the flexible-price equilibrium level, $E_t \hat{x}_{t+i} = 0$ for all i, and inflation remains equal to zero. Blanchard and Galí (2007) described this as the "divine coincidence." However, if an error term is added to the inflation adjustment equation so that

$$\pi_t = \beta E_t \pi_{t+1} + \kappa x_t + e_t, \tag{8.34}$$

then

$$\pi_t = \kappa \sum_{i=0}^{\infty} \beta^i E_t x_{t+i} + \sum_{i=0}^{\infty} \beta^i E_t e_{t+i}.$$

As long as $\sum_{i=0}^{\infty} \beta^i E_t e_{t+i} \neq 0$, maintaining $\sum_{i=0}^{\infty} \beta^i E_t x_{t+i} = 0$ is not sufficient to ensure that inflation always remains equal to zero. A trade-off between stabilizing output and stabilizing inflation can arise. Disturbance terms in the inflation adjustment equation are often called *cost shocks* or *inflation shocks*. Since these shocks ultimately affect only the price level, they are also called *price shocks*.

Clarida, Galí, and Gertler (2001) suggested one means of introducing a stochastic shock into the inflation adjustment equation. They added a stochastic *wage markup* to represent deviations between the real wage and the marginal rate of substitution between leisure and consumption. Thus, the labor supply condition (8.9) becomes

$$\left(\frac{\chi N_t^{\eta}}{C_t^{-\sigma}} \right) e^{\mu_t^w} = \frac{W_t}{P_t},$$

where μ_t^w is a random disturbance.[25] This could arise from shifts in tastes that affect the marginal utility of leisure. Or, if labor markets are imperfectly competitive, it could arise from stochastic shifts in the markup of wages over the marginal rate of substitution (Clarida, Galí, and Gertler 2002). Having linearized around the steady state, one obtains

$$\eta \hat{n}_t + \sigma \hat{c}_t + \mu_t^w = \hat{w}_t - \hat{p}_t. \tag{8.35}$$

The real marginal cost variable becomes

---

25. With the utility function given in (8.31), this becomes

$$\left(\frac{\chi N_t^{\eta}}{C_t^{-\sigma}} \right) \left(\frac{e^{\mu_t^w}}{\psi_t^{1-\sigma}} \right) = \frac{W_t}{P_t},$$

showing that μ_t^w affects the labor market condition in a manner similar to a taste shock.

$$\varphi_t = (\eta \hat{n}_t + \sigma \hat{c}_t) - (\hat{y}_t - \hat{n}_t) + \mu_t^w,$$

and this suggests that the inflation adjustment equation becomes

$$\pi_t = \beta \mathrm{E}_t \pi_{t+1} + \gamma \tilde{\kappa} x_t + \tilde{\kappa} \mu_t^w. \tag{8.36}$$

In this formulation, μ_t^w is the source of inflation shocks.

Although this approach appears to provide an explanation for a disturbance term to appear in the inflation adjustment equation, if μ_t^w reflects taste shocks that alter the marginal rate of substitution between leisure and consumption, then μ_t^w also affects the flexible-price equilibrium level of output. The same would be true if μ_t^w were a markup due to imperfect competition in the labor market. Thus, if the output gap variable in the inflation adjustment equation is correctly measured as the deviation of output from the flexible-price equilibrium level, μ_t^w no longer has a separate, independent impact on π_t.

Benigno and Woodford (2005) showed that a cost shock arises in the presence of stochastic variation in the gap between the welfare-maximizing level of output and the flexible-price equilibrium level of output. In the model developed so far, only two distortions are present, one due to monopolistic competition and one due to nominal price stickiness. The first distortion implies that the flexible-price output level is below the efficient output level even when prices are flexible. However, this wedge is constant, so when the model is linearized, percent deviations of the flexible-price output and the efficient output around their respective steady-state values are equal. If there are time-varying distortions such as would arise with stochastic variation in distortionary taxes, then fluctuations in the two output concepts will differ. In this case, if x_t^w is the percent deviation of the welfare-maximizing output level around its steady state (the welfare gap),

$$x_t = x_t^w + \delta_t,$$

where δ_t represents these stochastic distortions. Since policymakers would be concerned with stabilizing fluctuations in x_t^w, the relevant constraint the policymaker will face is obtained by rewriting the Phillips curve (8.20) as

$$\pi_t = \beta \mathrm{E}_t \pi_{t+1} + \kappa x_t = \beta \mathrm{E}_t \pi_{t+1} + \kappa x_t^w + \kappa \delta_t. \tag{8.37}$$

In this formulation, δ_t acts as a cost shock; stabilizing inflation in the face of nonzero realizations of δ cannot be achieved without creating volatility in the welfare gap x_t^w. One implication of (8.37) is that the variance of the cost shock will depend on κ^2. Thus, if the degree of price rigidity is high, implying that κ is small, cost shocks will also be less volatile (see Walsh 2005a; 2005b).

Recent models, particularly those designed to be taken to the data, introduce a disturbance in the inflation equation by assuming that individual firms face random variation in the price elasticity of demand, that is, θ_t becomes time-varying (see 8.13). This modification raises similar issues to those arising with the introduction of a stochastic wage markup.

8.3.6   Sticky Wages and Prices

Erceg, Henderson, and Levin (2000) employed the Calvo specification to incorporate sticky wages *and* sticky prices into an optimizing framework.[26] The goods market side of their model is identical in structure to the one developed in section 8.3.2. However, they assumed that in the labor market individual households supply differentiated labor services; firms combine these labor services to produce output. Output is given by a standard production function, $F(N_t, K_t)$, but the labor aggregate is a composite function of the individual types of labor services:

$$N_t = \left[\int_0^1 n_{jt}^{(\gamma-1)/\gamma} \, dj \right]^{\gamma/(\gamma-1)}, \qquad \gamma > 1,$$

where n_{jt} is the labor from household j that the firm employs. With this specification, households face a demand for their labor services that depends on the wage they set relative to the aggregate wage rate. Erceg, Henderson, and Levin assumed that a randomly drawn fraction of households optimally set their wage each period, just as the models of price stickiness assume that only a fraction of firms adjust their price each period (see also Christiano, Eichenbaum, and Evans 2005; Sbordone 2001).

The model of inflation adjustment based on the Calvo specification implies that inflation depends on real marginal cost. In terms of deviations from the flexible-price equilibrium, real marginal cost equals the gap between the real wage (ω) and the marginal product of labor (mpl). Similarly, wage inflation (when linearized around a zero inflation steady state) responds to a gap variable, but this time the appropriate gap depends on a comparison between the real wage and the household's marginal rate of substitution between leisure and consumption. With flexible wages, as in the earlier sections where only prices were assumed to be sticky, workers are always on their labor supply curves; nominal wages can adjust to ensure that the real wage equals the marginal rate of substitution between leisure and consumption (mrs). When nominal wages are also sticky, however, ω_t and mrs_t can differ. If $\omega_t < mrs_t$, workers will want to raise their nominal wage when the opportunity to adjust arises. Letting π_t^w denote the rate of nominal wage inflation, Erceg, Henderson, and Levin showed that

---

26. Other models incorporating both wage and price stickiness include those of Guerrieri (2000); Ravenna (2000); Christiano, Eichenbaum, and Evans (2001); and Sbordone (2001; 2002). This is now standard in models being taken to the data.

$$\pi_t^w = \beta E_t \pi_{t+1}^w + \kappa^w (mrs_t - \omega_t). \tag{8.38}$$

From the definition of the real wage,

$$\omega_t = \omega_{t-1} + \pi_t^w - \pi_t. \tag{8.39}$$

Equations (8.38) and (8.39), when combined with the new Keynesian Phillips curve in which inflation depends on $\omega_t - mpl_t$, constitute the inflation adjustment block of an optimizing model with both wage and price rigidities.

8.4 Monetary Policy Analysis in New Keynesian Models

During the ten years after its introduction, the new Keynesian model became the standard framework for monetary policy analysis. Clarida, Galí, and Gertler (1999), Woodford (2003a), McCallum and Nelson (1999), and Svensson and Woodford (1999; 2005), among others, popularized this simple model for use in monetary policy analysis. Galí (2002) and Galí and Gertler (2007) discussed some of the model's implications for monetary policy, and Galí (2008) provided an excellent treatment of the model and its implications for policy.

As noted in section 8.3, the basic new Keynesian model takes the form

$$x_t = E_t x_{t+1} - \left(\frac{1}{\sigma}\right)(i_t - E_t \pi_{t+1}) + u_t \tag{8.40}$$

and

$$\pi_t = \beta E_t \pi_{t+1} + \kappa x_t + e_t, \tag{8.41}$$

where x is the output gap, defined as output relative to the equilibrium level of output under flexible prices, i is the nominal rate of interest, and π is the inflation rate. All variables are expressed as percentage deviations around their steady-state values. The demand disturbance u can arise from taste shocks to the preferences of the representative household, fluctuations in the flexible-price equilibrium output level, or shocks to government purchases of goods and services. The e shock is a *cost shock*. In this section, (8.40) and (8.41) are used to address issues of monetary policy design.

8.4.1 Policy Objectives

Given the economic environment that leads to (8.40) and (8.41), what are the appropriate objectives of the central bank? There is a long history in monetary policy analysis of assuming that the central bank is concerned with minimizing a quadratic loss function that depends on output and inflation. Models that assume this were discussed in chapter 7. Although such an assumption is plausible, it is ultimately ad hoc. In the new Keynesian model, the description of the economy is based on an approximation to a fully specified general equilibrium model. Can one therefore develop a policy objective function that can be interpreted as an approximation to the utility of the representative household? Put differently, can one draw insights from the general equilibrium foundations of (8.40) and (8.41) to determine the basic objectives central banks should pursue? Woodford (2003a), building on earlier work by Rotemberg and Woodford (1998), provided the most detailed analysis of the link between a welfare criterion derived as an approximation to the utility of the representative agent and the types of quadratic loss functions common in the older literature.

Woodford assumed that there is a continuum of differentiated goods c_{it} defined on the interval $[0, 1]$ and that the representative household derives utility from consuming a composite of these individual goods. The composite consumption good is defined as

$$Y_t = C_t = \left[\int_0^1 c_{jt}^{(\theta-1)/\theta} \, dj \right]^{\theta/(\theta-1)}. \tag{8.42}$$

In addition, each household produces one of these individual goods and experiences disutility from production. Suppose labor effort is proportional to output. Woodford assumed that the period utility of the representative agent is then

$$V_t = U(Y_t, z_t) - \int_0^1 v(c_{jt}, z_t) \, dj, \tag{8.43}$$

where $v(c_{jt}, z_t)$ is the disutility of producing good c_{jt}, and z_t is a vector of exogenous shocks.[27] Woodford demonstrated that deviations of the expected discounted utility of the representative agent around the level of steady-state utility can be approximated by

$$E_t \sum_{i=0}^{\infty} \beta^i V_{t+i} \approx -\Omega E_t \sum_{i=0}^{\infty} \beta^i [\pi_{t+i}^2 + \lambda(x_{t+i} - x^*)^2] + \text{t.i.p.}, \tag{8.44}$$

where t.i.p. indicates terms independent of policy. The derivation of (8.44) and the values of Ω and λ are given in section 8.6.2 of the chapter appendix. In (8.44), x_t is the gap between output and the output level that would arise under flexible prices, and x^* is the gap between the steady-state efficient level of output (in the absence of the monopolistic distortions) and the actual steady-state level of output.

---

27. Woodford considered a cashless economy, so real money balances do not appear in the utility function as they did in (8.1).

Equation (8.44) looks like the standard quadratic loss function employed in
chapter 7 to represent the objectives of the monetary policy authority. There are,
however, two critical differences. First, the output gap is measured relative to equilibrium output under flexible prices. In the traditional literature the output variable was
more commonly interpreted as output relative to trend or output relative to the natural rate of output, which in turn was often defined as output in the absence of price
surprises (see section 6.2.1).

A second difference between (8.44) and a standard quadratic loss function arises
from the reason inflation variability enters the loss function. When prices are sticky,
and firms do not all adjust simultaneously, inflation results in an inefficient dispersion
of relative prices and production among individual producers. The representative
household's utility depends on its consumption of a composite good; faced with a
dispersion of prices for the differentiated goods produced in the economy, the household buys more of the relatively cheaper goods and less of the relatively more expensive goods. Because of diminishing marginal utility, the increase in utility derived
from consuming more of some goods is less than the loss in utility due to consuming
less of the more expensive goods. Hence, price dispersion reduces utility. Similarly,
if one assumes diminishing returns to labor in the production process rather than
constant returns to scale, dispersion on the production side will also be costly. The
increased cost of producing more of some goods is greater than the cost saving from
reducing production of other goods. For these reasons, price dispersion reduces utility, and when each firm does not adjust its price every period, price dispersion is
caused by inflation. These welfare costs can be eliminated under a zero inflation
policy.

In chapter 7, the efficiency distortion represented by x^* was used to motivate an
overly ambitious output target in the central bank's objective function. The presence
of $x^* > 0$ implies that a central bank acting under discretion to maximize (8.44)
would produce a positive average inflation bias. However, with average rates of inflation in the major industrialized economies remaining low during the 1990s, many
authors now simply assume that $x^* = 0$. In this case, the central bank is concerned
with stabilizing the output gap x_t, and no average inflation bias arises.[28] If tax subsidies can be used to offset the distortions associated with monopolistic competition,
one could assign fiscal policy the task of ensuring that $x^* = 0$. In this case, the central
bank has no incentive to create inflationary expansions, and average inflation will be
zero under discretion. Dixit and Lambertini (2002) showed that when both the monetary and fiscal authorities are acting optimally, the fiscal authority will use its tax

---

28. In addition, the inflation equation was derived by linearizing around a zero inflation steady state. It
would thus be inappropriate to use it to study situations in which the average is positive.

instruments to set $x^* = 0$, and the central bank then ensures that inflation remains equal to zero.

In the context of the linear-quadratic model, (8.44) represents a second-order approximation to the welfare of the representative agent around the steady state. Expanding the period loss function,

$$\pi_{t+i}^2 + \lambda(x_{t+i} - x^*)^2 = \pi_{t+i}^2 + \lambda x_{t+i}^2 - 2\lambda x^* x_{t+i} + \lambda(x^*)^2.$$

Employing a first-order approximation for the structural equations will be adequate for evaluating the π_{t+i}^2 and x_{t+i}^2 terms, because any higher-order terms in the structural equations would become of order greater than 2 when squared. However, this is not the case for the $2\lambda x^* x_{t+i}$ term, which is linear in x_{t+i}. Hence, to approximate this correctly to the required degree of accuracy would require second-order approximations to the structural equations rather than the linear approximations derived in (8.40) and (8.41). Thus, assume the fiscal authority employs a subsidy to undo the distortion arising from imperfect competition so that $x^* = 0$. In this case, the linear approximations to the structural equations will allow correct evaluation of the second-order approximation to welfare. See Benigno and Woodford (2005) for a discussion of optimal policy when $x^* > 0$.

8.4.2   Policy Trade-offs

The basic new Keynesian inflation adjustment equation given by (8.20) did not include a disturbance term, such as the e_t that was added to (8.41). The absence of e implies that there is no conflict between a policy designed to maintain inflation at zero and a policy designed to keep the output gap equal to zero. If $x_{t+i} = 0$ for all $i \geq 0$, then $\pi_{t+i} = 0$. In this case, a central bank that wants to maximize the expected utility of the representative household will ensure that output is kept equal to the flexible-price equilibrium level of output. This also guarantees that inflation is equal to zero, thereby eliminating the costly dispersion of relative prices that arises with inflation. When firms do not need to adjust their prices, the fact that prices are sticky is no longer relevant. Thus, a key implication of the basic new Keynesian model is that price stability is the appropriate objective of monetary policy.[29]

The optimality of zero inflation conflicts with the Friedman rule for optimal inflation. M. Friedman (1969) concluded that the optimal inflation rate must be negative to make the nominal rate of interest zero (see chapter 4). The reason a different conclusion is reached here is the absence of any explicit role for money when the utility approximation given by (8.44) is derived. In general, zero inflation still generates

---

29. Notice that the conclusion that price stability is optimal is independent of the degree of nominal rigidity (see Adao, Correia, and Teles 1999).

a monetary distortion. With zero inflation, the nominal rate of interest will be positive and the private opportunity cost of holding money will exceed the social cost of producing it. A. Khan, King, and Wolman (2000) and Adao, Correia, and Teles (2003) considered models that integrate nominal rigidities and the Friedman distortion. Khan, King, and Wolman introduced money into a sticky price model by assuming the presence of cash and credit goods, with money required to purchase cash goods. If prices are flexible, it is optimal to have a rate of deflation such that the nominal interest rate is zero. If prices are sticky, price stability is optimal in the absence of the cash-in-advance (CIA) constraint. With both sticky prices and the monetary inefficiency associated with a positive nominal interest rate, the optimal rate of inflation is less than zero but greater than the rate that yields a zero nominal interest rate. Khan, King, and Wolman conducted simulations in a calibrated version of their model and found that the relative price distortion dominates the Friedman monetary inefficiency. Thus, the optimal policy is close to the policy that maintains price stability.

In the baseline model with no monetary distortion and with $x^* = 0$, the optimality of price stability is a reflection of the presence of only one nominal rigidity. The welfare costs of a single nominal rigidity can be eliminated using the single instrument provided by monetary policy. As discussed in section 8.3.6, Erceg, Henderson, and Levin (2000) introduced nominal wage stickiness into the basic new Keynesian framework as a second nominal rigidity. Nominal wage inflation with staggered adjustment of wages causes distortions of relative wages and reduces welfare. Erceg, Henderson, and Levin showed that in this case the approximation to the welfare of the representative agent will include a term in wage inflation as well as the inflation and output gap terms appearing in (8.44). Wage stability is desirable because it eliminates dispersion of hours worked across households. With two distortions—sticky prices and sticky wages—the single instrument of monetary policy cannot simultaneously offset both distortions. With sticky prices but flexible wages, the real wage can adjust efficiently in the face of productivity shocks, and monetary policy should maintain price stability. With sticky wages and flexible prices, the real wage can still adjust efficiently to ensure that labor market equilibrium is maintained in the face of productivity shocks, and monetary policy should maintain nominal wage stability. If both wages and prices are sticky, a policy that stabilizes either prices or wages will not allow the real wage to move so as to keep output equal to the flexible-price output. Productivity shocks will lead to movements in the output gap, and the monetary authority will be forced to trade off stabilizing inflation, wage inflation, and the output gap.

Galí, Gertler, and López-Salido (2002) defined the *inefficiency gap* as the gap between the household's marginal rate of substitution between leisure and consumption (mrs_t) and the marginal product of labor (mpl_t). This inefficiency gap can be divided into two parts: the wedge between the real wage and the marginal rate of substitution, labeled the *wage markup*, and the wedge between the real wage and the marginal product of labor, labeled the *price markup*. Based on U.S. data, they concluded that the wage markup accounts for most of the time series variation in the inefficiency gap. Levin et al. (2006) estimated a new Keynesian general equilibrium model with both price and wage stickiness. They found that the welfare costs of nominal rigidity are primarily generated by wage stickiness rather than by price stickiness. This finding is consistent with Christiano, Eichenbaum, and Evans (2005), who concluded that a model with flexible prices and sticky wages does better at fitting impulse responses estimated on U.S. data than a sticky price–flexible wage version of their model. Sbordone (2001) also suggested that nominal wage rigidity is more important empirically than price rigidity. Huang and Liu (2002) argued that wage stickiness is more important than price stickiness for generating output persistence.

In contrast, Goodfriend and King (2001) argued that the long-term nature of employment relationships reduces the effects of nominal wage rigidity on real resource allocations. Models that incorporate the intertemporal nature of employment relationships based on search and matching models of unemployment include Walsh (2003a; 2005b); Trigari (2009); Krause, López-Salido, and Lubik (2007); Thomas (2008); Ravenna and Walsh (2008); and Sala, Söderström, and Trigari (2008).

8.4.3 Optimal Commitment and Discretion

Suppose the central bank attempts to minimize a quadratic loss function such as (8.44), defined in terms of inflation and output relative to the flexible-price equilibrium.[30] Assume that the steady-state gap between output and its efficient value is zero (i.e., $x^* = 0$). In this case, the central bank's loss function takes the form

$$L_t = \left(\frac{1}{2}\right) \mathrm{E}_t \sum_{i=0}^{\infty} \beta^i (\pi_{t+i}^2 + \lambda x_{t+i}^2). \tag{8.45}$$

Two alternative policy regimes can be considered (see chapter 7). In a discretionary regime, the central bank behaves optimally in each period, taking as given the current state of the economy and private sector expectations. Given that the public knows that the central bank optimizes each period, any promises the central bank makes about future inflation will not be credible—the public knows that whatever may have been promised in the past, the central bank will do what is optimal at the time it sets policy. The alternative regime is one of commitment. In a commitment regime, the central bank can make credible promises about what it will do in the

---

30. Svensson (1999b; 1999d) argued that there is widespread agreement among policymakers and academics that inflation stability and output gap stability are the appropriate objectives of monetary policy.

future. By promising to take certain actions in the future, the central bank can influence the public's expectations about future inflation. When forward-looking expectations play a role, as in (8.41), discretion will lead to what is known as a *stabilization bias*.

Commitment

A central bank able to precommit chooses a path for current and future inflation and the output gap to minimize the loss function (8.45) subject to the expectational IS curve (8.40) and the inflation adjustment equation (8.41). Let θ_{t+i} and ψ_{t+i} denote the Lagrangian multipliers associated with the period $t+i$ IS curve and the inflation adjustment equation. The central bank's objective is to pick i_{t+i}, π_{t+i}, and x_{t+i} to minimize

$$E_t \sum_{i=0}^{\infty} \beta^i \left\{ \left(\frac{1}{2}\right)(\pi_{t+i}^2 + \lambda x_{t+i}^2) + \theta_{t+i}[x_{t+i} - x_{t+i+1} + \sigma^{-1}(i_{t+i} - \pi_{t+i+1}) - u_{t+i}] \right.$$
$$\left. + \psi_{t+i}(\pi_{t+i} - \beta\pi_{t+i+1} - \kappa x_{t+i} - e_{t+i}) \right\}.$$

The first-order condition for i_{t+i} takes the form

$$\sigma^{-1} E_t(\theta_{t+i}) = 0, \qquad i \geq 0.$$

Hence, $E_t \theta_{t+i} = 0$ for all $i \geq 0$. This result implies that (8.40) imposes no real constraint on the central bank as long as there are no restrictions on, or costs associated with, varying the nominal interest rate. Given the central bank's optimal choices for the output gap and inflation, (8.40) will simply determine the setting for i_t necessary to achieve the desired value of x_t. For that reason, it is often more convenient to treat x_t as if it were the central bank's policy instrument.

Setting $E_t \theta_{t+i} = 0$, the remaining first-order conditions for π_{t+i} and x_{t+i} can be written as

$$\pi_t + \psi_t = 0 \tag{8.46}$$

$$E_t(\pi_{t+i} + \psi_{t+i} - \psi_{t+i-1}) = 0, \qquad i \geq 1 \tag{8.47}$$

$$E_t(\lambda x_{t+i} - \kappa \psi_{t+i}) = 0, \qquad i \geq 0. \tag{8.48}$$

Equations (8.46) and (8.47) reveal the dynamic inconsistency that characterizes the optimal precommitment policy. At time t, the central bank sets $\pi_t = -\psi_t$ and promises to set $\pi_{t+1} = -(\psi_{t+1} - \psi_t)$. But when period $t+1$ arrives, a central bank that reoptimizes will again obtain $\pi_{t+1} = -\psi_{t+1}$ as its optimal setting for inflation. That is, the first-order condition (8.46) updated to $t+1$ will reappear.

An alternative definition of an optimal precommitment policy requires that the central bank implement conditions (8.47) and (8.48) for all periods, including the current period. Woodford (2003a; 2003b) has labeled this the *timeless perspective* approach to precommitment. One can think of such a policy as having been chosen in the distant past, and the current values of the inflation rate and output gap are the values chosen from that earlier perspective to satisfy the two conditions (8.47) and (8.48). McCallum and Nelson (2000b) provided further discussion of the timeless perspective and argued that this approach agrees with the one commonly used in many studies of precommitment policies.

Combining (8.47) and (8.48), under the timeless perspective optimal commitment policy inflation and the output gap satisfy

$$\pi_{t+i} = -\left(\frac{\lambda}{\kappa}\right)(x_{t+i} - x_{t+i-1}) \tag{8.49}$$

for all $i \geq 0$. Using this equation to eliminate inflation from (8.41) and rearranging, one obtains

$$\left(1 + \beta + \frac{\kappa^2}{\lambda}\right)x_t = \beta E_t x_{t+1} + x_{t-1} - \frac{\kappa}{\lambda}e_t. \tag{8.50}$$

The solution to this expectational difference equation for x_t will be of the form $x_t = a_x x_{t-1} + b_x e_t$. To determine the coefficients a_x and b_x, note that if $e_t = \rho e_{t-1} + \varepsilon_t$, the proposed solution implies $E_t x_{t+1} = a_x x_t + b_x \rho e_t = a_x^2 x_{t-1} + (a_x + \rho)b_x e_t$. Substituting this into (8.50) and equating coefficients, the parameter a_x is the solution less than 1 of the quadratic equation

$$\beta a_x^2 - \left(1 + \beta + \frac{\kappa^2}{\lambda}\right)a_x + 1 = 0,$$

and b_x is given by

$$b_x = -\left\{\frac{\kappa}{\lambda[1 + \beta(1 - \rho - a_x)] + \kappa^2}\right\}.$$

From (8.49), equilibrium inflation under the timeless perspective policy is

$$\pi_t = \left(\frac{\lambda}{\kappa}\right)(1 - a_x)x_{t-1} + \left[\frac{\lambda}{\lambda[1 + \beta(1 - \rho - a_x)] + \kappa^2}\right]e_t. \tag{8.51}$$

Woodford (2003b) stressed that even if $\rho = 0$, so that there is no natural source of persistence in the model itself, $a_x > 0$ and the precommitment policy introduces inertia into the output gap and inflation processes. Because the central bank responds to the lagged output gap (see (8.49)), past movements in the gap continue to affect current inflation. This commitment to inertia implies that the central bank's actions at date t allow it to influence expected future inflation. Doing so leads to a better trade-off between gap and inflation variability than would arise if policy did not react to the lagged gap. Equation (8.41) implies that the inflation impact of a positive cost shock, for example, can be stabilized at a lower output cost if the central bank can induce a fall in expected future inflation. Such a fall in expected inflation is achieved when the central bank follows (8.49).

A condition for policy such as (8.49) that is derived from the central bank's first-order conditions and only involves variables that appear in the objective function (in this case, inflation and the output gap) is generally called a *targeting rule* (e.g., Svensson and Woodford 2005). It represents a relationship among the targeted variables that the central bank should maintain, because doing so is consistent with the first-order conditions from its policy problem.

Because the timeless perspective commitment policy is not the solution to the policy problem under optimal commitment, the policy rule given by (8.49) may be dominated by other policy rules. For instance, it may be dominated by the optimal discretion policy (see next section). Under the timeless perspective, inflation as given by (8.49) is the same function each period of the current and lagged output gap; the policy displays the property of continuation in the sense that the policy implemented in any period continues the plan to which it was optimal to commit in an earlier period. Blake (2001); Damjanovic, Damjanovic, and Nolan (2008); and C. Jensen and McCallum (2008) considered *optimal* continuation policies that require that the policy instrument, in this case x_t, be a time-invariant function, as under the timeless perspective, but rather than ignoring the first-period conditions, as is done under the timeless perspective, they focused on the optimal unconditional continuation policy to which the central bank should commit. This policy minimizes the unconditional expectation of the objective function, so that the Lagrangian for the policy problem becomes

$$\tilde{E}\mathcal{L} = \tilde{E}\left\{ E_t \sum_{i=0}^{\infty} \beta^i \left[\frac{1}{2}(\pi_{t+i}^2 + \lambda x_{t+i}^2) + \theta_{t+i}(\pi_{t+i} - \beta E_t \pi_{t+i+1} - \kappa x_{t+i} - e_{t+i}) \right] \right\},$$

where $\tilde{E}$ denotes the unconditional expectations operator. Because

$$\tilde{E}E_t \theta_{t+i} \pi_{t+i+1} = \tilde{E}\theta_{t-1}\pi_t,$$

the unconditional Lagrangian can be expressed as

$$\tilde{E}\mathcal{L} = \left(\frac{1}{1-\beta}\right)\tilde{E}\left\{ \left[\frac{1}{2}(\pi_t^2 + \lambda x_t^2) + \theta_t \pi_t - \beta \theta_{t-1}\pi_t - \kappa \theta_t x_t - \theta_t e_t \right] \right\}.$$

The first-order conditions then become

$$\pi_t + \theta_t - \beta\theta_{t-1} = 0 \tag{8.52}$$

$$\lambda x_t - \kappa\theta_t = 0.$$

Combining these to eliminate the Lagrangian multiplier yields the optimal unconditional continuation policy:

$$\pi_t = -\left(\frac{\lambda}{\kappa}\right)(x_{t+i} - \beta x_{t+i-1}). \tag{8.53}$$

Comparing this to (8.49) shows that rather than giving full weight to past output gaps, the optimal unconditional continuation policy discounts the past slightly (recall $\beta \approx 0.99$).

Discretion

When the central bank operates with discretion, it acts each period to minimize the loss function (8.45) subject to the inflation adjustment equation (8.41). Because the decisions of the central bank at date t do not bind it at any future dates, the central bank is unable to affect the private sector's expectations about future inflation. Thus, the decision problem of the central bank becomes the single-period problem of minimizing $\pi_t^2 + \lambda x_t^2$ subject to the inflation adjustment equation (8.41).

The first-order condition for this problem is

$$\kappa\pi_t + \lambda x_t = 0. \tag{8.54}$$

Equation (8.54) is the optimal targeting rule under discretion. Notice that by combining (8.46) with (8.48) evaluated at time t, one obtains (8.54); thus, the central bank's first-order condition relating inflation and the output gap at time t is the same under discretion or under the fully optimal precommitment policy (but not under the timeless perspective policy). The differences appear in subsequent periods. For $t+1$, under discretion $\kappa\pi_{t+1} + \lambda x_{t+1} = 0$, whereas under precommitment (from (8.47) and (8.48)), $\kappa\pi_{t+1} + \lambda(x_{t+1} - x_t) = 0$.

The equilibrium expressions for inflation and the output gap under discretion can be obtained by using (8.54) to eliminate inflation from the inflation adjustment equation. This yields

$$\left(1 + \frac{\kappa^2}{\lambda}\right)x_t = \beta E_t x_{t+1} - \left(\frac{\kappa}{\lambda}\right)e_t. \tag{8.55}$$

Guessing a solution of the form $x_t = \delta e_t$, so that $E_t x_{t+1} = \delta\rho e_t$, one obtains

$$\delta = -\left[\frac{\kappa}{\lambda(1 - \beta\rho) + \kappa^2}\right].$$

Equation (8.54) implies that equilibrium inflation under optimal discretion is

$$\pi_t = -\left(\frac{\lambda}{\kappa}\right)x_t = \left[\frac{\lambda}{\lambda(1-\beta\rho)+\kappa^2}\right]e_t. \tag{8.56}$$

According to (8.56) the unconditional expected value of inflation is zero; there is no average inflation bias under discretion. However, there is a stabilization bias in that the response of inflation to a cost shock under discretion differs from the response under commitment. This can be seen by comparing (8.56) to (8.51).

Discretion versus Commitment

The impact of a cost shock on inflation and the output gap under the timeless perspective optimal precommitment policy and optimal discretionary policy can be obtained by calibrating (8.41) and (8.49) and solving them numerically. Four unknown parameters appear in the model: β, κ, λ, and ρ. The discount factor, β, is set equal to 0.99, appropriate for interpreting the time interval as one quarter. A weight on output fluctuations of $\lambda = 0.25$ is used. This value is also used by H. Jensen (2002) and McCallum and Nelson (2000b).[31] The parameter κ captures both the impact of a change in real marginal cost on inflation and the co-movement of real marginal cost and the output gap and is set equal to 0.05. McCallum and Nelson reported that the empirical evidence is consistent with a value of κ in the range $[0.01, 0.05]$. Roberts (1995) reported higher values; his estimate of the coefficient on the output gap is about 0.3 when inflation is measured at an annual rate, so this translates into a value for κ of 0.075 for inflation at quarterly rates. Jensen used a baseline value of $\kappa = 0.1$, whereas Walsh (2003b) used 0.05.

The solid lines in figures 8.2 and 8.3 show the response of the output gap and inflation to a transitory, one standard deviation cost push shock under the optimal precommitment policy.[32] Despite the fact that the shock itself has no persistence, the output gap displays strong positive serial correlation. By keeping output below potential (a negative output gap) for several periods into the future after a positive cost shock, the central bank is able to lower expectations of future inflation. A fall in $E_t\pi_{t+1}$ at the time of the positive inflation shock improves the trade-off between inflation and output gap stabilization faced by the central bank.

Outcomes under optimal discretion are shown by the dashed lines in the figures. There is no inertia under discretion; both the output gap and inflation return to their steady-state values in the period after the shock occurs. The difference in the stabilization response under commitment and discretion is the stabilization bias due to discretion. The intuition behind the suboptimality of discretion can be seen by con-

---

31. If (8.45) is interpreted as an approximation to the welfare of the representative agent, the implied value of λ would be much smaller.

32. The programs used to obtain these figures are available at ⟨http://people.ucsc.edu/~walshc/mtp3e/⟩.

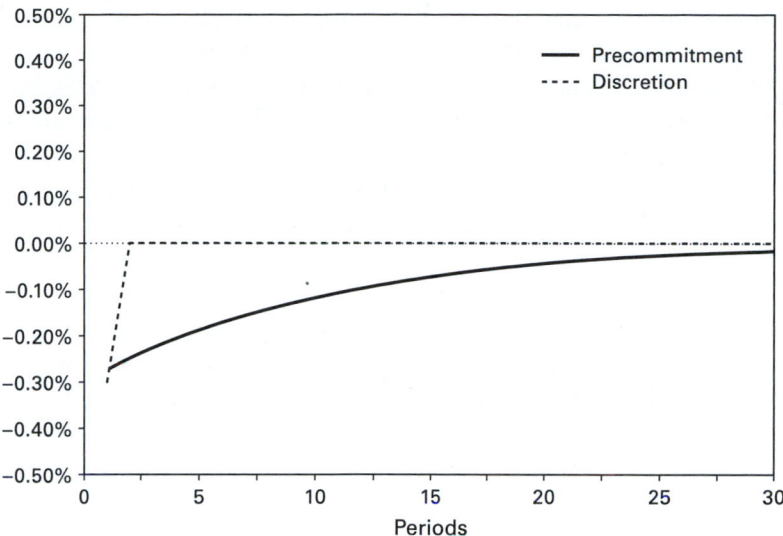

Figure 8.2
Response of output gap to a cost shock: timeless precommitment and pure discretion.

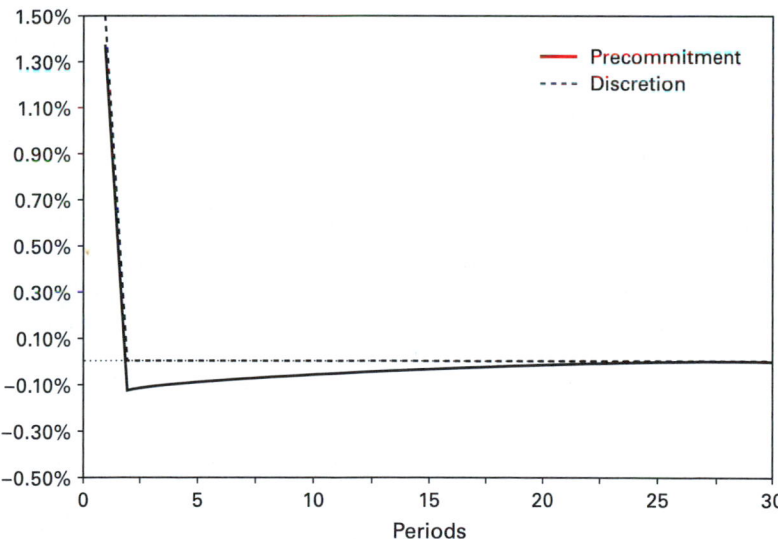

Figure 8.3
Response of inflation to a cost shock: timeless precommitment and pure discretion.

sidering the inflation adjustment equation given by (8.41). Under discretion, the central bank's only tool for offsetting the effects on inflation of a cost shock is the output gap. In the face of a positive realization of e_t, x_t must fall to help stabilize inflation. Under commitment, however, the central bank has two instruments; it can affect both x_t and $E_t \pi_{t+1}$. By creating expectations of a deflation at $t + 1$, the reduction in the output gap does not need to be as large. Of course, under commitment a promise of future deflation must be honored, so actually inflation falls below the baseline beginning in period $t + 1$ (see figure 8.3). Consistent with producing a deflation, the output gap remains negative for several periods.

The analysis so far has focused on the goal variables, inflation and the output gap. Using (8.40), the associated setting for the interest rate can be derived. For example, under optimal discretion, the output gap is given by

$$x_t = - \left[\frac{\kappa}{\lambda(1 - \beta\rho) + \kappa^2} \right] e_t,$$

and inflation is given by (8.56). Using these to evaluate $E_t x_{t+1}$ and $E_t \pi_{t+1}$ and then solving for i_t from (8.40) yields

$$i_t = E_t \pi_{t+1} + \sigma(E_t x_{t+1} - x_t + u_t)$$

$$= \left[\frac{\lambda\rho + (1 - \rho)\sigma\kappa}{\lambda(1 - \beta\rho) + \kappa^2} \right] e_t + \sigma u_t. \tag{8.57}$$

Equation (8.57) is the reduced-form solution for the nominal rate of interest. The nominal interest rate is adjusted to offset completely the impact of the demand disturbance u_t on the output gap. As a result, it affects neither inflation nor the output gap. Section 8.3.3 illustrated how a policy that commits to a rule that calls for responding to the exogenous shocks renders the new Keynesian model's equilibrium indeterminate. Thus, it is important to recognize that (8.57) describes the *equilibrium* behavior of the nominal interest rate under optimal discretion; (8.57) is not an instrument rule (see Svensson and Woodford 1999).

8.4.4 Commitment to a Rule

In the Barro-Gordon model (examined in chapter 7) optimal commitment was interpreted as commitment to a policy that was a (linear) function of the state variables. In the present model, consisting of (8.40) and (8.41), the only state variable is the current realization of the cost shock e_t. Suppose then that the central bank can commit to a rule of the form[33]

---

33. This commitment does not raise the same uniqueness of an equilibrium problem that would arise under a commitment to an instrument rule of the form $i_t = b_i e_t$. See problem 9 at the end of this chapter.

$$x_t = b_x e_t. \tag{8.58}$$

What is the optimal value of b_x? With x_t given by (8.58), inflation satisfies

$$\pi_t = \beta E_t \pi_{t+1} + \kappa b_x e_t + e_t,$$

and the solution to this expectational difference equation is[34]

$$\pi_t = b_\pi e_t, \qquad b_\pi = \frac{1 + \kappa b_x}{1 - \beta\rho}. \tag{8.59}$$

Using (8.58) and (8.59), the loss function can now be written as

$$\left(\frac{1}{2}\right) E_t \sum_{i=0}^{\infty} \beta^i (\pi_{t+i}^2 + \lambda x_{t+i}^2) = \left(\frac{1}{2}\right) \sum_{i=0}^{\infty} \beta^i \left[\left(\frac{1 + \kappa b_x}{1 - \beta\rho}\right)^2 + \lambda b_x^2\right] e_t^2.$$

This is minimized when

$$b_x = -\left[\frac{\kappa}{\lambda(1 - \beta\rho)^2 + \kappa^2}\right].$$

Using this solution for b_x in (8.59), equilibrium inflation is given by

$$\pi_t = \left(\frac{1 + \kappa b_x}{1 - \beta\rho}\right) e_t = \left[\frac{\lambda(1 - \beta\rho)}{\lambda(1 - \beta\rho)^2 + \kappa^2}\right] e_t. \tag{8.60}$$

Comparing the solution for inflation under optimal discretion, given by (8.56), and the solution under commitment to a simple rule, given by (8.60), one notes that they are identical if the cost shock is serially uncorrelated ($\rho = 0$). If $0 < \rho < 1$, there is a stabilization bias under discretion relative to the case of committing to a simple rule.

Clarida, Galí, and Gertler (1999) argued that this stabilization bias provides a rationale for appointing a Rogoff-conservative central banker—a central bank that puts more weight on inflation objectives than is reflected in the social loss function—when $\rho > 0$, even though in the present context there is no average inflation bias.[35] A

---

34. To verify this is the solution, note that

$$\pi_t = \beta E_t \pi_{t+1} + \kappa b_x e_t + e_t = \beta b_\pi \rho e_t + \kappa b_x e_t + e_t$$

$$= [\beta b_\pi \rho + \kappa b_x + 1] e_t,$$

so that $b_\pi = \beta b_\pi \rho + \kappa b_x + 1 = (\kappa b_x + 1)/(1 - \beta\rho)$.

35. Rogoff (1985) proposed appointing a conservative central banker as a way to solve the average inflation bias that can arise under discretionary policies (see chapter 7). There is no average inflation bias in the present model because it is assumed that $x^* = 0$, ensuring that the central bank's loss function depends on output only through the gap between actual output and flexible-price equilibrium output.

Rogoff-conservative central banker places a weight $\hat{\lambda} < \lambda$ on output gap fluctuations (see section 7.3.2). In a discretionary environment with such a central banker, (8.56) implies that inflation will equal

$$\pi_t = \left[\frac{\hat{\lambda}}{\hat{\lambda}(1 - \beta\rho) + \kappa^2}\right] e_t.$$

Comparing this with (8.60) reveals that if a central banker is appointed for whom $\hat{\lambda} = \lambda(1 - \beta\rho) < \lambda$, the discretionary solution will coincide with the outcome under commitment to the optimal simple rule. Such a central banker stabilizes inflation more under discretion than would be the case if the relative weight placed on output gap and inflation stability were equal to the weight in the social loss function, λ. Because the public knows inflation will respond less to a cost shock, future expected inflation rises less in the face of a positive e_t shock. As a consequence, current inflation can be stabilized, with a smaller fall in the output gap. The inflation-output trade-off is improved.

Recall, however, that the notion of commitment used here is actually suboptimal. As noted earlier, fully optimal commitment leads to inertial behavior in that future inflation depends not on the output gap but on the change in the gap.

8.4.5 Endogenous Persistence

Empirical research on inflation (see section 6.3.2) has generally found that when lagged inflation is added to (8.41), its coefficient is statistically and economically significant. If lagged inflation affects current inflation, then even under discretion the central bank faces a dynamic optimization problem; decisions that affect current inflation also affect future inflation, and this intertemporal link must be taken into account by the central bank when setting current policy. Svensson (1999d) and Vestin (2006) illustrated how the linear-quadratic structure of the problem allows one to solve for the optimal discretionary policy in the face of endogenous persistence.

To analyze the effects introduced when inflation depends on both expected future inflation and lagged inflation, suppose (8.41) is replaced by

$$\pi_t = (1 - \phi)\beta E_t \pi_{t+1} + \phi\pi_{t-1} + \kappa x_t + e_t. \tag{8.61}$$

The coefficient ϕ measures the degree of backward-looking behavior exhibited by inflation.[36] If the central bank's objective is to minimize the loss function given by

---

36. Galí and Gertler (1999), Woodford (2003), and Christiano, Eichenbaum, and Evans (2005) developed inflation adjustment equations in which lagged inflation appears by assuming that some fraction of firms do not reset their prices optimally (see section 6.3.2).

(8.45), the policy problem under discretion can be written in terms of the value function defined by

$$V(\pi_{t-1}, e_t) = \min_{\pi_t, x_t} \left\{ \left(\frac{1}{2}\right)(\pi_t^2 + \lambda x_t^2) + \beta E_t V(\pi_t, e_{t+1}) \right.$$

$$\left. + \theta_t[\pi_t - (1 - \phi)\beta E_t \pi_{t+1} - \phi \pi_{t-1} - \kappa x_t - e_t] \right\}. \tag{8.62}$$

The value function depends on lagged inflation because it is an endogenous state variable.

Because the objective function is quadratic and the constraints are linear, the value function will be quadratic, and one can hypothesize that it takes the form

$$V(\pi_{t-1}, e_t) = a_0 + a_1 e_t + \frac{1}{2}a_2 e_t^2 + a_3 e_t \pi_{t-1} + a_4 \pi_{t-1} + \frac{1}{2}a_5 \pi_{t-1}^2. \tag{8.63}$$

As Vestin demonstrated, this guess is only needed to evaluate $E_t V_\pi(\pi_t, e_{t+1})$, and $E_t V_\pi(\pi_t, e_{t+1}) = a_3 E_t e_{t+1} + a_4 + a_5 \pi_t$. If one assumes that the cost shock is serially uncorrelated, $E_t e_{t+1} = 0$ and, as a consequence, the only unknown coefficients in (8.63) that will play a role are a_4 and a_5.

The solution for inflation will take the form

$$\pi_t = b_1 e_t + b_2 \pi_{t-1}. \tag{8.64}$$

Using this proposed solution, one obtains $E_t \pi_{t+1} = b_2 \pi_t$. This expression for expected future inflation can be substituted into (8.61) to yield

$$\pi_t = \frac{\kappa x_t + \phi \pi_{t-1} + e_t}{1 - (1 - \phi)\beta b_2}, \tag{8.65}$$

which implies $\partial \pi_t / \partial x_t = \kappa / [1 - (1 - \phi)\beta b_2]$.

Collecting these results, the first-order condition for the optimal choice of x_t by a central bank whose decision problem is given by (8.62) is

$$\left[\frac{\kappa}{1 - (1 - \phi)\beta b_2}\right][\pi_t + \beta E_t V_\pi(\pi_t, e_{t+1})] + \lambda x_t = 0. \tag{8.66}$$

Using (8.65) to eliminate x_t from (8.66) and recalling that $E_t V_\pi(\pi_t, e_{t+1}) = a_4 + a_5 \pi_t$, one obtains

$$\pi_t = \left[\frac{\Psi}{\kappa^2(1 + \beta a_5) + \lambda \Psi^2}\right]\left[\lambda \phi \pi_{t-1} + \lambda e_t - \left(\frac{\beta \kappa^2}{\Psi}\right)a_4\right], \tag{8.67}$$

where $\Psi \equiv 1 - (1 - \phi)\beta b_2$.

From the envelope theorem and (8.66),

$$V_\pi(\pi_{t-1}, e_t) = a_3 e_t + a_4 + a_5 \pi_{t-1}$$

$$= \left[\frac{\phi}{1 - (1 - \phi)\beta b_2}\right][\pi_t + E_t V_\pi(\pi_t, e_{t+1})] = -\left(\frac{\lambda\phi}{\kappa}\right)x_t.$$

Again using (8.65) to eliminate x_t,

$$V_\pi(\pi_{t-1}, e_t) = -\left(\frac{\lambda\phi}{\kappa}\right)\left[\frac{\Psi\pi_t - \phi\pi_{t-1} - e_t}{\kappa}\right]$$

$$= -\left(\frac{\lambda\phi}{\kappa}\right)\left[\frac{(\Psi b_2 - \phi)\pi_{t-1} + (\Psi b_1 - 1)e_t}{\kappa}\right]. \tag{8.68}$$

However, (8.63) implies that

$$V_\pi(\pi_{t-1}, e_t) = a_3 e_t + a_4 + a_5 \pi_{t-1}.$$

Comparing this with (8.68) reveals that $a_4 = 0$,

$$a_3 = \lambda\phi\left(\frac{1 - \Psi b_1}{\kappa^2}\right)$$

and

$$a_5 = \lambda\phi\left(\frac{\phi - \Psi b_2}{\kappa^2}\right).$$

Finally, substitute these results into (8.67) to obtain

$$\pi_t = \left[\frac{\Psi}{\kappa^2 + \beta\lambda\phi(\phi - \Psi b_2) + \lambda\Psi^2}\right][\lambda\phi\pi_{t-1} + \lambda e_t].$$

Equating coefficients with (8.64),

$$b_1 = \left[\frac{\lambda\Psi}{\kappa^2 + \beta\lambda\phi(\phi - \Psi b_2) + \lambda\Psi^2}\right]$$

and

$$b_2 = \left[\frac{\lambda\Psi\phi}{\kappa^2 + \beta\lambda\phi(\phi - \Psi b_2) + \lambda\Psi^2}\right]. \tag{8.69}$$

Because Ψ also depends on the unknown parameter b_2, (8.69) does not yield a con-venient analytic solution. To gain insights into the effects of backward-looking

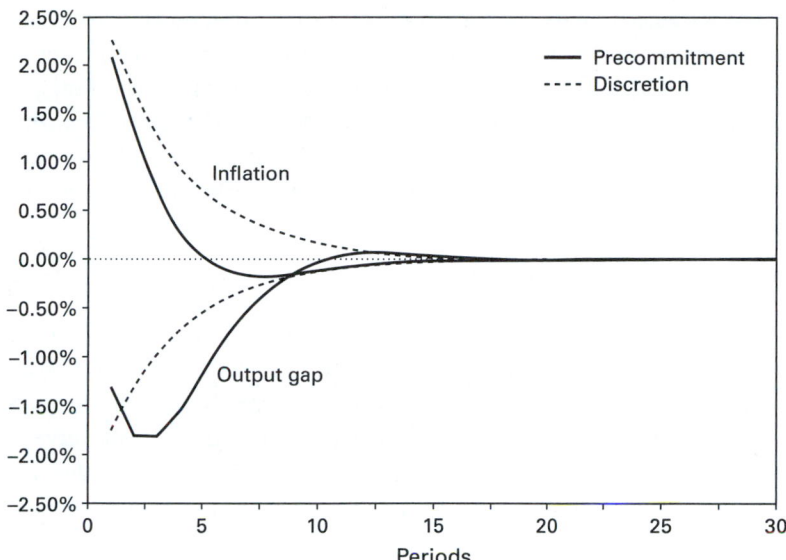

Figure 8.4
Responses to a cost shock with endogenous persistence ($\phi = 0.5$).

aspects of inflation, it is useful to employ numerical techniques. This is done to generate figure 8.4, which shows the response of the output gap and inflation under optimal discretion when $\phi = 0.5$. Also shown for comparison are the responses under the optimal commitment policy. Both the output gap and inflation display more persistence than when $\phi = 0$ (see figures 8.2 and 8.3), and inflation returns to zero more slowly under discretion.

It is insightful to consider explicitly the first-order conditions for the optimal policy problem under commitment. Adopting the timeless perspective, maximizing (8.45) subject to (8.61) leads to the following first-order conditions:

$$\pi_t = (1 - \phi)\beta E_t \pi_{t+1} + \phi \pi_{t-1} + \kappa x_t + e_t$$

$$\pi_t + \psi_t - (1 - \phi)\psi_{t-1} - \beta \phi E_t \psi_{t+1} = 0$$

$$\lambda x_t - \kappa \psi_t = 0,$$

where ψ_t is the Lagrangian multiplier associated with (8.61). Eliminating this multiplier, the optimal targeting rule becomes

$$\pi_t = -\left(\frac{\lambda}{\kappa}\right)[x_t - (1 - \phi)x_{t-1} - \beta \phi E_t x_{t+1}]. \tag{8.70}$$

As noted earlier, the presence of forward-looking expectations in the new Keynesian Phillips curve led optimal policy to be backward-looking by introducing inertia through the appearance of x_{t-1} in the optimal targeting rule. The presence of lagged inflation in the inflation adjustment equation when $\phi > 0$ leads policy to be forward-looking through the role of $E_t x_{t+1}$ in the targeting rule. This illustrates a key aspect of policy design; when policy affects the economy with a lag, policymakers must be forward-looking.

8.4.6 Targeting Regimes and Instrument Rules

The analysis of optimal policy contained in section 8.4.3 specified an objective function for the central bank. The central bank was assumed to behave optimally, given its objective function and the constraints imposed on its choices by the structure of the economy. A policy regime in which the central bank is assigned an objective is commonly described as a *targeting regime*. A targeting regime is defined by (1) the variables in the central bank's loss function (the objectives), and (2) the weights assigned to these objectives, with policy implemented under discretion to minimize the expected discounted value of the loss function.[37] Targeting rules were also discussed in section 7.3.5 in the context of solving the inflation bias that can arise under discretion.

Perhaps the most widely discussed targeting regime is inflation targeting (Bernanke and Mishkin 1997; Svensson 1997a; 1997b; 1999b; 1999c; 1999d; Svensson and Woodford 1999). Experiences with inflation targeting are analyzed by Ammer and Freeman (1995); Bernanke et al. (1998); Mishkin and Schmidt-Hebbel (2001); Amato and Gerlach (2002); and the papers in Leiderman and Svensson (1995). Mishkin and Schmidt-Hebbel had identified 19 countries as inflation targeters by 2001, with New Zealand, in 1990, being the first country to have adopted formal targets for inflation. By 2008, there were 26 inflation targeters. Some of the lessons from the experiences with inflation targeting are discussed in Walsh (2009).

This section also briefly discusses instrument rules. These constitute an alternative approach to policy that assumes the central bank can commit to a simple feedback rule for its policy instrument. The best known of such rules is the Taylor rule (Taylor 1993a).

Inflation Targeting

Inflation targeting has been characterized in a variety of ways in the academic literature, and it has been implemented in different ways in the countries that have adopted

---

37. This definition of a targeting regime is consistent with that of Svensson (1999b), who stated, "By a targeting rule, I mean, at the most general level, the assignment of a particular loss function to be minimized" (617). An alternative interpretation of a targeting regime is that it is a rule for adjusting the policy instrument in the face of deviations between the current (or expected) value of the targeted variable and its target level (see, e.g., McCallum 1990a and the references he cites). H. Jensen (2002) and Rudebusch (2002a) illustrated these two alternative interpretations of targeting.

inflation targeting as a framework for monetary policy. In general, the announce-ment of a formal target for inflation is a key component, and this is often accompa-nied by publication of the central bank's inflation forecasts. An inflation targeting regime can be viewed as the assignment to the central bank of an objective function of the form

$$L_t^{IT} = \left(\frac{1}{2}\right) E_t \sum_{i=0}^{\infty} \beta^i [(\pi_{t+i} - \pi^T)^2 + \lambda_{IT} x_{t+i}^2],\tag{8.71}$$

where π^T is the target inflation rate and λ_{IT} is the weight assigned to achieving the output gap objective relative to the inflation objective. λ_{IT} may differ from the weight placed on output gap stabilization in the social loss function (8.45). As long as $\lambda_{IT} > 0$, specifying inflation targeting in terms of the loss function (8.71) assumes that the central bank is concerned with output stabilization as well as inflation stabi-lization.[38] An inflation targeting regime in which $\lambda_{IT} > 0$ is described as a flexible in-flation targeting regime.

In the policy problems analyzed so far, the central bank's choice of its instrument i_t allows it to affect both output and inflation immediately. This absence of any lag between the time a policy action is taken and the time it affects output and inflation is unrealistic. If policy decisions taken in period t only affect future output and infla-tion, then the central bank must rely on forecasts of future output and inflation when making its policy choices. In analyzing the case of such policy lags, Svensson (1997a) and Svensson and Woodford (1999) emphasized the role of inflation forecast target-ing. To illustrate the role of forecasts in the policy process, suppose the central bank must set i_t prior to observing any time t information. This assumption implies that the central bank cannot respond to time t shocks contemporaneously; information about shocks occurring in period t will affect the central bank's choice of i_{t+1} and, as a consequence, x_{t+1} and π_{t+1} can be affected. The model is otherwise given by (8.40) and (8.41) as before, with the additional assumption that the cost shock fol-lows an AR(1) process: $e_t = \rho e_{t-1} + \varepsilon_t$. Assume that the demand shock in (8.40) is serially uncorrelated. The central bank's objective is to choose i_t to minimize

$$\left(\frac{1}{2}\right) E_{t-1} \sum_{i=0}^{\infty} \beta^i [(\pi_{t+i} - \pi^T)^2 + \lambda_{IT} x_{t+i}^2],$$

where the subscript on the expectations operator is now $t - 1$ to reflect the informa-tion available to the central bank when it sets policy. The choice of i_t is subject to the

---

38. This is the terminology used in section 7.3.5 for inflation targeting with the loss function (8.71).

constraints represented by (8.40) and (8.41). Taking expectations based on the central bank's information, these two equations can be written as

$$
E_{t-1}x_t = E_{t-1}x_{t+1} - \left(\frac{1}{\sigma}\right)(i_t - E_{t-1}\pi_{t+1})
\tag{8.72}
$$

and

$$
E_{t-1}\pi_t = \beta E_{t-1}\pi_{t+1} + \kappa E_{t-1}x_t + \rho e_{t-1}.
\tag{8.73}
$$

Under discretion, the first-order condition for the central bank's choice of i_t implies that

$$
E_{t-1}[\kappa(\pi_t - \pi^T) + \lambda x_t] = 0.
\tag{8.74}
$$

Rearranging this first-order condition yields

$$
E_{t-1}x_t = -\left(\frac{\kappa}{\lambda}\right)E_{t-1}(\pi_t - \pi^T).
$$

Thus, if the central bank forecasts that period t inflation will exceed its target rate of inflation, it should adjust policy to ensure that the forecast of the output gap is negative.

Svensson and Woodford (1999) provided a detailed discussion of inflation forecast targeting, focusing on the implications for the determinacy of equilibrium under different specifications of the policy decision process. The possibility of multiple equilibria becomes particularly relevant if the central bank bases its own forecasts on private sector forecasts, which are in turn based on expectations about the central bank's actions.

Other Targeting Regimes

Inflation targeting is just one example of a policy targeting regime. A number of alternative targeting regimes have been analyzed in the literature. These include price level targeting (Dittmar, Gavin, and Kydland 1999; Svensson 1999c; Vestin 2006); nominal income growth targeting (H. Jensen 2002); hybrid price level–inflation targeting (Batini and Yates 2001); average inflation targeting (Nessén and Vestin 2000); and regimes based on the change in the output gap or its quasi-difference (C. Jensen and McCallum 2002; Walsh 2002). In each case, it is assumed that given the assigned loss function, the central bank chooses policy under discretion. The optimal values for the parameters in the assigned loss function, for example, the value of λ_{IT} in (8.71), are chosen to minimize the unconditional expectation of the social loss function (8.45).

The importance of forward-looking expectations in affecting policy choice is well illustrated by work on price level targeting. The traditional view argued that attempts to stabilize the price level, as opposed to the inflation rate, would generate undesirable levels of output variability. A positive cost shock that raised the price level would require a deflation to bring the price level back on target, and this deflation would be costly. However, as figure 8.3 shows, an optimal commitment policy that focuses on output and inflation stability also induces a deflation after a positive cost shock. By reducing $E_t\pi_{t+1}$, such a policy achieves a better trade-off between inflation variability and output variability. The deflation generated under a discretionary policy concerned with output and price level stability might actually come closer to the commitment policy outcomes than discretionary inflation targeting would. Using a basic new Keynesian model, Vestin (2006) showed that this intuition is correct. In fact, when inflation is given by (8.41) and the cost shock is serially uncorrelated, price level targeting can replicate the timeless precommitment solution exactly if the central bank is assigned the loss function $p_t^2 + \lambda_{PL}x_t^2$, where λ_{PL} differs from the weight λ in the social loss function.

H. Jensen (2002) showed that a nominal income growth targeting regime can also dominate inflation targeting. Walsh (2003b) added lagged inflation to the inflation adjustment equation and showed that the advantages of price level targeting over inflation targeting decline as the weight on lagged inflation increases. Walsh analyzed discretionary outcomes when the central bank targets inflation and the change in the output gap (a *speed limit policy*). Introducing the change in the gap induces inertial behavior similar to that obtained under precommitment. For empirically relevant values of the weight on lagged inflation (ϕ in the range 0.3 to 0.7), speed limit policies dominate price level targeting, inflation targeting, and nominal income growth targeting. For ϕ below 0.3, price level targeting does best. Svensson and Woodford (1999) considered interest rate–smoothing objectives as a means of introducing into discretionary policy the inertia that is optimal under commitment.

Instrument Rules

The approach to policy analysis adopted in the preceding sections starts with a specification of the central bank's objective function and then derives the optimal setting for the policy instrument. An alternative approach specifies an instrument rule directly. The best known of such instrument rules is the Taylor rule (Taylor 1993a). Taylor showed that the behavior of the federal funds interest rate in the United States from the mid-1980s through 1992 (when Taylor was writing) could be fairly well matched by a simple rule of the form

$$i_t = \pi_t + 0.5x_t + 0.5(\pi_t - \pi^T) + r^*,$$

where π^T was the target level of average inflation (Taylor assumed it to be 2 percent) and r^* was the equilibrium real rate of interest (Taylor assumed that this too was equal to 2 percent). The Taylor rule for general coefficients is often written

$$i_t = r^* + \pi^T + \alpha_x x_t + \alpha_\pi (\pi_t - \pi^T). \tag{8.75}$$

The nominal interest rate deviates from the level consistent with the economy's equilibrium real rate and the target inflation rate if the output gap is nonzero or if inflation deviates from target. A positive output gap leads to a rise in the nominal rate, as does a deviation of actual inflation above target. With Taylor's original coefficients, $\alpha_\pi = 1.5$, so the nominal rate is changed more than one-for-one with deviations of inflation from target. Thus, the rule satisfies the Taylor principle (see section 8.3.3); a greater than one-for-one reaction of i_t ensures that the economy has a unique stationary rational-expectations equilibrium. Lansing and Trehan (2001) explored conditions under which the Taylor rule emerges as the fully optimal instrument rule under discretionary policy.

A large literature has estimated Taylor rules or similar simple rules for a variety of countries and time periods. For example, Clarida, Galí, and Gertler (2000) did so for the Federal Reserve, the Bundesbank, and the Bank of Japan. In their specification, however, actual inflation is replaced by expected future inflation so that the central bank is assumed to be forward-looking in setting policy. Estimates for the United States under different Federal Reserve chairmen were reported by Judd and Rudebusch (1997). In general, the basic Taylor rule, when supplemented by the addition of the lagged nominal interest rate, does quite well in matching the actual behavior of the policy interest rate. However, Orphanides (2000) found that when estimated using the data on the output gap and inflation actually available at the time policy actions were taken (i.e., using real-time data), the Taylor rule does much more poorly in matching the U.S. funds rate. Clarida, Galí, and Gertler (2000) found that the Fed moved the funds rate less than one-for-one during the period 1960–1979, thereby violating the Taylor principle. In a further example of the importance of using real-time data, however, Perez (2001) found that when the Fed's reaction function is reestimated for this earlier period using real-time data, the coefficient on inflation is greater than 1. Lubik and Schorfheide (2004) estimated a complete, dynamic stochastic general equilibrium (DSGE) new Keynesian model of the U.S. economy and found evidence that Federal Reserve policy has been consistent with determinacy since 1982. However, their estimates suggested policy was not consistent with determinacy prior to 1979.

When a policy interest rate such as the federal funds rate in the United States is regressed on inflation and output gap variables, the lagged value of the interest rate normally enters with a statistically significant and large coefficient. The interpretation of this coefficient on the lagged interest rate has been the subject of debate. One interpretation is that it reflects inertial behavior of the sort discussed in section 8.4.3 that would arise under an optimal precommitment policy. It has also been interpreted to mean that central banks adjust gradually toward a desired interest rate level. For example, suppose that i_t^* is the central bank's desired value for its policy instrument, but it wants to avoid large changes in interest rates. Such an interest rate–smoothing objective might arise from a desire for financial market stability. If the central bank adjusts i_t gradually toward i_t^*, then the behavior of i_t may be captured by a partial adjustment model of the form

$$i_t = i_{t-1} + \theta(i_t^* - i_{t-1}) = (1 - \theta)i_{t-1} + \theta i_t^*. \tag{8.76}$$

The estimated coefficient on i_{t-1} provides an estimate of $1 - \theta$. Values close to 1 imply that θ is small; each period the central bank closes only a small fraction of the gap between its policy rate and its desired value.

The view that central banks adjust slowly has been criticized. Sack (2000) and Rudebusch (2002b) argued that the presence of a lagged interest rate in estimated instrument rules is not evidence that the Fed acts gradually. Sack attributed the Fed's behavior to parameter uncertainty that leads the Fed to adjust the funds rate less aggressively than would be optimal in the absence of parameter uncertainty. Rudebusch argued that imperfect information about the degree of persistence in economic disturbances induces behavior by the Fed that appears to reflect gradual adjustment. He noted that if the Fed followed a rule such as (8.76), future changes in the funds rate would be predictable, but evidence from forward interest rates does not support the presence of predictable changes. Similarly, Lansing (2002) showed that the appearance of interest rate smoothing can arise if the Fed uses real-time data to update its estimate of trend output each period. When final data are used to estimate a policy instrument rule, the serial correlation present in the Fed's real-time errors in measuring trend output will be correlated with lagged interest rates, creating the illusion of interest rate–smoothing behavior by the Fed.

8.4.7   Model Uncertainty

Up to this point, the analysis has assumed that the central bank knows the true model of the economy with certainty. Fluctuations in output and inflation arose only from disturbances that took the form of additive errors. In this case, the linear-quadratic framework results in certainty equivalence holding; the central bank's actions depend on its expectations of future variables but not on the uncertainty associated with those expectations. When error terms enter multiplicatively, as occurs, for example, when the model's parameters are not known with certainty, equivalence will not hold. Brainard (1967) provided the classic analysis of multiplicative uncertainty. He showed that when there is uncertainty about the impact a policy instrument has on the economy, it will be optimal to respond more cautiously than would be the case in the absence of uncertainty.

Brainard's basic conclusion can be illustrated with a simple example. Suppose the inflation adjustment equation given by (8.41) is modified to take the following form:

$$\pi_t = \beta E_t \pi_{t+1} + \kappa_t x_t + e_t, \tag{8.77}$$

where $\kappa_t = \bar{\kappa} + v_t$ and v_t is a white noise stochastic process. In this formulation, the central bank is uncertain about the true impact of the gap x_t on inflation. For example, the central bank may have an estimate of the coefficient on x_t in the inflation equation, but there is some uncertainty associated with this estimate. The central bank's best guess of this coefficient is $\bar{\kappa}$, and the central bank must choose its policy before observing the actual realization of v_t.

To analyze the effect that uncertainty about the coefficient has on optimal policy, assume that policy is conducted with discretion and the central bank's loss function is

$$L = \frac{1}{2} E_t(\pi_t^2 + \lambda x_t^2).$$

In addition, assume that the cost shock e_t is serially uncorrelated.

Under discretion, the central bank takes $E_t \pi_{t+1}$ as given, and the first-order condition for the optimal choice of x_t is

$$E_t(\pi_t \kappa_t + \lambda x_t) = 0.$$

Since all stochastic disturbances have been assumed to be serially uncorrelated, expected inflation will be zero, so (8.77) can be used to rewrite the first-order condition as

$$E_t[(\kappa_t x_t + e_t)\kappa_t + \lambda x_t] = (\bar{\kappa}^2 + \sigma_v^2)x_t + \bar{\kappa}e_t + \lambda x_t = 0.$$

Solving for x_t, one obtains

$$x_t = -\left(\frac{\bar{\kappa}}{\lambda + \bar{\kappa}^2 + \sigma_v^2}\right)e_t. \tag{8.78}$$

Equation (8.78) can be compared to the optimal discretionary response to the cost shock when there is no parameter uncertainty. In this case, $\sigma_v^2 = 0$ and

$$x_t = -\left(\frac{\bar{\kappa}}{\lambda + \bar{\kappa}^2}\right)e_t.$$

The presence of multiplicative parameter uncertainty ($\sigma_v^2 > 0$) reduces the impact of e_t on x_t. As uncertainty increases, it becomes optimal to respond less to e_t, that is, to behave more cautiously in setting policy.

Using (8.78) in the inflation adjustment equation (8.77),

$$\pi_t = \kappa_t x_t + e_t = \left(\frac{\lambda + \sigma_v^2 - \bar{\kappa}(\kappa_t - \bar{\kappa})}{\lambda + \bar{\kappa}^2 + \sigma_v^2}\right) e_t = \left(\frac{\lambda + \sigma_v^2 - \bar{\kappa} v_t}{\lambda + \bar{\kappa}^2 + \sigma_v^2}\right) e_t.$$

Since it is assumed that the two disturbances v_t and e_t are uncorrelated, the unconditional variance of inflation is increasing in σ_v^2. In the presence of multiplicative uncertainty of the type modeled here, equilibrium output is stabilized more and inflation less in the face of cost shocks. The reason for this result is straightforward. With a quadratic loss function, the additional inflation variability induced by the variance in κ_t is proportional to x_t. Reducing the variability of x_t helps to offset the impact of v_t on the variance of inflation. It is optimal to respond more cautiously, thereby reducing the variance of x_t but at the cost of greater inflation variability.

Brainard's basic result—multiplicative uncertainty leads to caution—is intuitively appealing, but it is not a general result. For example, Söderström (2002) examined a model in which there are lagged variables whose coefficients are subject to random shocks. He showed that in this case, optimal policy reacts more aggressively. For example, suppose current inflation depends on lagged inflation, but the impact of π_{t-1} on π_t is uncertain. The effect this coefficient uncertainty has on the variance of π_t depends on the variability of π_{t-1}. If the central bank fails to stabilize current inflation, it increases the variance of inflation in the following period. It can be optimal to respond more aggressively to stabilize inflation, thereby reducing the impact the coefficient uncertainty has on the unconditional variance of inflation.

Some studies have combined the notion of parameter uncertainty with models of learning to examine the implications for monetary policy (Sargent 1999). Wieland (2000a; 2000b) examined the trade-off between control and estimation that can arise under model uncertainty. A central bank may find it optimal to experiment, changing policy to generate observations that can help it learn about the true structure of the economy.

Another aspect of model uncertainty is measurement error or the inability to observe some relevant variables. For example, the flexible-price equilibrium level of output is needed to measure the gap variable x_t, but it is not directly observable. Svensson and Woodford (2003; 2004) provided a general treatment of optimal policy when the central bank's problem involves both an estimation problem (determining the true state of the economy such as the value of the output gap) and a control policy (setting the nominal interest rate to affect the output gap and inflation). In a

linear-quadratic framework in which private agents and the central bank have the
same information, these two problems can be dealt with separately. Orphanides
(2000) emphasized the role the productivity slowdown played during the 1970s in
causing the Fed to overestimate potential output.[39] Svensson and Williams (2008)
developed a general approach for dealing with a variety of sources of model and
data uncertainty.

Finally, the approach adopted in section 8.4.1 derived policy objectives from an
approximation to the welfare of the representative agent. The nature of this approximation, however, will depend on the underlying model structure. For example,
Steinsson (2000) showed that in the Galí and Gertler (1999) hybrid inflation model,
in which lagged inflation appears in the inflation adjustment equation, the loss function also includes a term in the squared change in inflation. Woodford (2003a) found
that if price adjustment is characterized by partial indexation to lagged inflation,
so that the inflation adjustment equation involves $\pi_t - \gamma\pi_{t-1}$ and $E_t(\pi_{t+1} - \gamma\pi_t)$ (see
section 6.3.2), the period loss function includes $(\pi_t - \gamma\pi_{t-1})^2$ rather than π_t^2. Thus,
uncertainty about the underlying model will also translate into uncertainty about
the appropriate objectives of monetary policy because policy objectives cannot be
defined independently of the model that defines the costs of economic fluctuations
(see Walsh 2005a).

8.5   Summary

This chapter has reviewed the basic new Keynesian model that has come to dominate
modern macroeconomics, particularly for addressing monetary policy issues. The
basic model is a dynamic stochastic general equilibrium model based on optimizing
households, with firms operating in an environment of monopolistic competition and
facing limited ability to adjust their prices. The staggered overlapping process of
price adjustment apparent in the microeconomic evidence (see chapter 6) is captured
through the use of the Calvo mechanism. The details would differ slightly if alternative models of price stickiness were employed, but the basic model structure would
not change. This structure consists of two parts. The first is an expectational IS curve
derived from the Euler condition describing the first-order condition implied by intertemporal optimization on the part of the representative household. The second is a
Phillips curve relationship linking inflation to an output gap measure. The model is
closed by adding a specification for policy.

39. See also Levin, Wieland, and Williams (1999); Ehrmann and Smets (2001); and Orphanides and
Williams (2002).

The model provides insights into the costs of inflation in generating an inefficient dispersion of relative prices. A model-consistent objective function for policy, derived as a second-order approximation to the welfare of the representative agent, calls for stabilizing inflation volatility as well as volatility in the gap between output and the output level that would arise under flexible prices.

The new Keynesian approach emphasizes the role of forward-looking expectations. The presence of forward-looking expectations implies that expectations about future policy actions play an important role, and a central bank that can influence these expectations, as assumed under a policy regime of commitment, can do better than one that sets policy in a discretionary manner.

8.6 Appendix

This appendix provides details on the derivation of the linear new Keynesian Phillips curve and on the approximation to the welfare of the representative household.

8.6.1 The New Keynesian Phillips Curve

In this section, (8.12) and (8.16) are used to obtain an expression for the deviations of the inflation rate around its steady-state level. Assume that the steady state involves a zero rate of inflation. Let $Q_t = p_t^*/P_t$ be the relative price chosen by all firms that adjust their price in period t. The steady-state value of Q_t is $Q = 1$; this is also the value Q_t equals when all firms are able to adjust every period. Dividing (8.16) by P_t, one obtains $1 = (1 - \omega)Q_t^{1-\theta} + \omega(P_{t-1}/P_t)^{1-\theta}$. Expressed in terms of percentage deviations around the zero inflation steady state, this becomes

$$0 = (1 - \omega)\hat{q}_t - \omega\pi_t \Rightarrow \hat{q}_t = \left(\frac{\omega}{1 - \omega}\right)\pi_t. \tag{8.79}$$

To obtain an approximation to (8.12), note that it can be written as

$$\left[\mathrm{E}_t \sum_{i=0}^{\infty} \omega^i \beta^i C_{t+i}^{1-\sigma} \left(\frac{P_{t+i}}{P_t}\right)^{\theta-1}\right] Q_t = \mu \left[\mathrm{E}_t \sum_{i=0}^{\infty} \omega^i \beta^i C_{t+i}^{1-\sigma} \varphi_{t+i} \left(\frac{P_{t+i}}{P_t}\right)^{\theta}\right]. \tag{8.80}$$

The left side of (8.80) is approximated by

$$\left(\frac{C^{1-\sigma}}{1 - \omega\beta}\right) + \left(\frac{C^{1-\sigma}}{1 - \omega\beta}\right)\hat{q}_t + C^{1-\sigma} \sum_{i=0}^{\infty} \omega^i \beta^i [(1 - \sigma)\mathrm{E}_t \hat{c}_{t+i} + (\theta - 1)(\mathrm{E}_t \hat{p}_{t+i} - \hat{p}_t)].$$

The right side is approximated by

$$\mu\left\{\left(\frac{C^{1-\sigma}}{1-\omega\beta}\right)\varphi + \varphi C^{1-\sigma}\sum_{i=0}^{\infty}\omega^i\beta^i[E_t\hat{\varphi}_{t+i} + (1-\sigma)E_t\hat{c}_{t+i} + \theta(E_t\hat{p}_{t+i} - \hat{p}_t)]\right\}.$$

Setting these two expressions equal and noting that $\mu\varphi = 1$ yields

$$\left(\frac{1}{1-\omega\beta}\right)\hat{q}_t + \sum_{i=0}^{\infty}\omega^i\beta^i[(1-\sigma)E_t\hat{c}_{t+i} + (\theta-1)(E_t\hat{p}_{t+i} - \hat{p}_t)]$$

$$= \sum_{i=0}^{\infty}\omega^i\beta^i[E_t\hat{\varphi}_{t+i} + (1-\sigma)E_t\hat{c}_{t+i} + \theta(E_t\hat{p}_{t+i} - \hat{p}_t)].$$

Canceling terms that appear on both sides of this equation leaves

$$\left(\frac{1}{1-\omega\beta}\right)\hat{q}_t = \sum_{i=0}^{\infty}\omega^i\beta^i(E_t\hat{\varphi}_{t+i} + E_t\hat{p}_{t+i} - \hat{p}_t),$$

or

$$\left(\frac{1}{1-\omega\beta}\right)\hat{q}_t = \sum_{i=0}^{\infty}\omega^i\beta^i(E_t\hat{\varphi}_{t+i} + E_t\hat{p}_{t+i}) - \left(\frac{1}{1-\omega\beta}\right)\hat{p}_t.$$

Multiplying by $1 - \omega\beta$ and adding $\hat{p}_t$ to both sides yields

$$\hat{q}_t + \hat{p}_t = (1-\omega\beta)\sum_{i=0}^{\infty}\omega^i\beta^i(E_t\hat{\varphi}_{t+i} + E_t\hat{p}_{t+i}).$$

The left side is the optimal nominal price $\hat{p}_t^* = \hat{q}_t + \hat{p}_t$, and this is set equal to the expected discounted value of future nominal marginal costs. This equation can be rewritten as $\hat{q}_t + \hat{p}_t = (1-\omega\beta)(\hat{\varphi}_t + \hat{p}_t) + \omega\beta(E_t\hat{q}_{t+1} + E_t\hat{p}_{t+1})$. Rearranging this expression yields

$$\hat{q}_t = (1-\omega\beta)\hat{\varphi}_t + \omega\beta(E_t\hat{q}_{t+1} + E_t\hat{p}_{t+1} - \hat{p}_t)$$

$$= (1-\omega\beta)\hat{\varphi}_t + \omega\beta(E_t\hat{q}_{t+1} + E_t\pi_{t+1}).$$

Now using (8.79) to eliminate $\hat{q}_t$, one obtains

$$\left(\frac{\omega}{1-\omega}\right)\pi_t = (1-\omega\beta)\hat{\varphi}_t + \omega\beta\left[\left(\frac{\omega}{1-\omega}\right)E_t\pi_{t+1} + E_t\pi_{t+1}\right]$$

$$= (1-\omega\beta)\hat{\varphi}_t + \omega\beta\left(\frac{1}{1-\omega}\right)E_t\pi_{t+1}.$$

Multiplying both sides by $(1 - \omega)/\omega$ produces the forward-looking new Keynesian Phillips curve:

$$\pi_t = \tilde{\kappa}\hat{\varphi}_t + \beta E_t \pi_{t+1},$$

where

$$\tilde{\kappa} = \frac{(1 - \omega)(1 - \omega\beta)}{\omega}.$$

When production is subject to diminishing returns to scale, firm-specific marginal cost may differ from average marginal cost. Let $A = \theta(1 - a)/a$. All firms adjusting at time t set their relative price such that

$$\hat{q}_t + \hat{p}_t = (1 - \omega\beta) \sum_{i=0}^{\infty} \omega^i \beta^i (E_t \hat{\varphi}_{jt+i} + E_t \hat{p}_{t+i})$$

$$= (1 - \omega\beta) \sum_{i=0}^{\infty} \omega^i \beta^i [E_t \hat{\varphi}_{t+i} - A(\hat{q}_t + \hat{p}_t - E_t \hat{p}_{t+i}) + E_t \hat{p}_{t+i}].$$

This equation can be rewritten as

$$\hat{q}_t + \hat{p}_t = (1 - \omega\beta)(\hat{\varphi}_t - A\hat{q}_t + \hat{p}_t)$$

$$+ \omega\beta(1 - \omega\beta) \sum_{i=0}^{\infty} \omega^i \beta^i [E_t \hat{\varphi}_{t+1+i} - A(\hat{q}_t + \hat{p}_t - E_t \hat{p}_{t+1+i}) + E_t \hat{p}_{t+1+i}].$$

By rearranging this equation, and recalling that $\hat{q}_t = \omega\pi_t/(1 - \omega)$, one obtains

$$\left(\frac{\omega}{1 - \omega}\right)(1 + A)\pi_t = (1 - \omega\beta)\hat{\varphi}_t + \omega\beta(1 + A)\left[\left(\frac{\omega}{1 - \omega}\right)E_t\pi_{t+1} + E_t\pi_{t+1}\right]$$

$$= (1 - \omega\beta)\hat{\varphi}_t + \omega\beta(1 + A)\left(\frac{1}{1 - \omega}\right)E_t\pi_{t+1}.$$

Multiplying both sides by $(1 - \omega)/\omega(1 + A)$ produces

$$\pi_t = \beta E_t \pi_{t+1} + \left(\frac{\tilde{\kappa}}{1 + A}\right)\hat{\varphi}_t.$$

8.6.2 Approximating Utility

In this section, details on the derivation of (8.44) are provided. The analysis is based on Woodford (2003). To derive an approximation to the representative agent's utility, it is necessary to first introduce some additional notation. For any variable X_t, let $\bar{X}$ be its steady-state value, let X_t^* be its efficient level (if relevant), and let $\tilde{X}_t = X_t - \bar{X}$ be the deviation of X_t around the steady state. Let $\hat{X}_t = \log(X_t/\bar{X})$ be the log deviation of X_t around its steady-state value. Using a second-order Taylor approximation, the variables $\tilde{X}_t$ and $\hat{X}_t$ can be related as

$$\tilde{X}_t = X_t - \bar{X} = \bar{X}\left(\frac{X_t}{\bar{X}} - 1\right) \approx \bar{X}\left(\hat{X}_t + \frac{1}{2}\hat{X}_t^2\right). \tag{8.81}$$

Employing this notation, one can develop a second-order approximation to the utility of the representative household.

The first term on the right side of (8.43) is the utility from consumption. This can be approximated around the steady state as

$$U(Y_t, z_t) \approx U(\bar{Y}, 0) + U_Y \tilde{Y}_t + U_z z_t + \frac{1}{2} U_{YY} \tilde{Y}_t^2 + U_{Y,z} z_t \tilde{Y}_t + \frac{1}{2} z_t' U_{z,z} z_t. \tag{8.82}$$

Using (8.81), and ignoring terms of order 3 or higher, such as $\hat{Y}_t^i$ for $i > 2$ and $z_t \hat{Y}_t^2$, (8.82) becomes

$$U(Y_t, z_t) \approx U(\bar{Y}, 0) + U_Y \bar{Y}\left(\hat{Y}_t + \frac{1}{2}\hat{Y}_t^2\right) + U_z z_t + \frac{1}{2} U_{YY} \bar{Y}^2 \hat{Y}_t^2$$

$$+ U_{Y,z} z_t \bar{Y} \hat{Y}_t + \frac{1}{2} z_t' U_{z,z} z_t$$

$$= U_Y \bar{Y}\left[\hat{Y}_t + \frac{1}{2}\left(1 + \frac{U_{YY}}{U_Y}\bar{Y}\right)\hat{Y}_t^2 + \frac{U_{Y,z}}{U_Y} z_t \hat{Y}_t\right] + \text{t.i.p.},$$

where t.i.p. are terms independent of policy. The choice of terms to include in t.i.p. is based on the implication of the new Keynesian model that the steady state is independent of monetary policy. To simplify the approximation, define

$$\sigma = -\frac{U_{YY}\bar{Y}}{U_Y}$$

as the coefficient of relative risk aversion, and let

$$\phi_t = -\frac{U_{Y,z}}{U_{YY}\bar{Y}} z_t.$$

Then the approximation for $U(Y, z)$ becomes

$$U(Y_t, z_t) \approx U_Y \overline{Y} \left[\hat{Y}_t + \frac{1}{2}(1 - \sigma)\hat{Y}_t^2 + \sigma\phi_t \hat{Y}_t \right] + \text{t.i.p.}$$

Next, analyze the second term on the right in (8.43), the term arising from the disutility of work. Expanding this around the steady state yields

$$v(c_{jt}, z_t) \approx v(\overline{Y}, 0) + v_c \tilde{c}_{jt} + v_z z_t + \frac{1}{2} v_{cc} \tilde{c}_{jt}^2 + v_{c,z} z_t \tilde{c}_{jt} + \frac{1}{2} z_t' v_{zz} z_t.$$

By approximating $\tilde{c}_{jt}$ with $\overline{Y}\left(\hat{c}_{jt} + \frac{1}{2}\hat{c}_{jt}^2\right)$, one obtains

$$v(c_{jt}, z_t) \approx v_c \overline{Y} \left(\hat{c}_{jt} + \frac{1}{2}\hat{c}_{jt}^2 + \frac{1}{2}\frac{v_{cc}\overline{Y}}{v_c}\hat{c}_{jt}^2 + \frac{v_{c,z}}{v_c} z_t \hat{c}_{jt} \right) + \text{t.i.p.}$$

This last equation can be written as

$$v(c_{jt}, z_t) \approx v_c \overline{Y} \left[\hat{c}_{jt} + \frac{1}{2}\left(1 + \frac{v_{cc}\overline{Y}}{v_c} \right)\hat{c}_{jt}^2 + \frac{v_{c,z}}{v_c} z_t \hat{c}_{jt} \right] + \text{t.i.p.}$$

$$= v_c \overline{Y} \left[\hat{c}_{jt} + \frac{1}{2}(1 + \eta)\hat{c}_{jt}^2 - \eta q_t \hat{c}_{jt} \right] + \text{t.i.p.},$$

where

$$\eta = \frac{v_{cc}\overline{Y}}{v_c}$$

and

$$q_t = -\frac{v_{c,z}}{v_{cc}\overline{Y}} z_t.$$

To proceed further, recall the model of monopolistic competition underlying the new Keynesian framework. In a model of perfect competition, the household producer of good i would equate the marginal rate of substitution between leisure and consumption to the real wage, or $v_c/U_Y = 1$, since the implicit production function is $c_{jt} = n_{jt}$. In the presence of monopolistic competition, $v_c/U_Y = (\theta - 1)/\theta$ is 1 over the markup. Define $\Phi = 1/\theta$. Then $v_c/U_Y = 1 - \Phi$. If the distortion created by monopolistic competition is small, terms such as $\Phi\hat{c}_{jt}^2$ and $\Phi q_t \hat{c}_{jt}$ will be of third order, and

$$v(c_{jt}, z_t) \approx U_Y \overline{Y} \left[(1 - \Phi)\hat{c}_{jt} + \frac{1}{2}(1 + \eta)\hat{c}_{jt}^2 - \eta q_t \hat{c}_{jt} \right] + \text{t.i.p.}$$

Integrating over all goods, and using the relationship $\hat{Y} \approx E_j \hat{c}_{jt} + \frac{1}{2}(1 - \theta^{-1})var_j \hat{c}_{jt}$,

$$\int_0^1 v(\hat{c}_{jt}, z_t)\, dj \approx U_Y \bar{Y} \left\{ (1 - \Phi) E_j \hat{c}_{jt} + \frac{1}{2}(1 + \eta)[(E_j \hat{c}_{jt})^2 + var_j \hat{c}_{jt}] - \eta q_t E_j \hat{c}_{jt} \right\} + \text{t.i.p.}$$

$$= U_Y \bar{Y} \left[(1 - \Phi - \eta q_t) \hat{Y}_t + \frac{1}{2}(1 + \eta) \hat{Y}_t^2 + \frac{1}{2}(\theta^{-1} + \eta) var_j \hat{c}_{jt} \right] + \text{t.i.p.},$$

where terms such as $var_j \hat{c}_{jt}^4$ and $\hat{c}_{jt} var_j \hat{c}_{jt}$ are set equal to zero.

Bringing together the results for the utility of consumption and the disutility of work,

$$V \approx U_Y \bar{Y} \left[\hat{Y}_t + \frac{1}{2}(1 - \sigma) \hat{Y}_t^2 + \sigma \phi_t \hat{Y}_t \right]$$

$$- U_Y \bar{Y} \left[(1 - \Phi - \eta q_t) \hat{Y}_t + \frac{1}{2}(1 + \eta) \hat{Y}_t^2 + \frac{1}{2}(\theta^{-1} + \eta) var_j \hat{c}_{jt} \right] + \text{t.i.p.}$$

$$= U_Y \bar{Y} \left[(\Phi + \sigma \phi_t + \eta q_t) \hat{Y}_t - \frac{1}{2}(\sigma + \eta) \hat{Y}_t^2 - \frac{1}{2}(\theta^{-1} + \eta) var_j \hat{c}_{jt} \right] + \text{t.i.p.}$$

To gain insight into this expression for utility, it is useful to derive the equilibrium output level under flexible prices. In a flexible-price equilibrium, the marginal product of labor equals the markup arising from monopolistic competition times the marginal rate of substitution between leisure and consumption. Given the specification of the composite consumption good in (8.42), the markup equals $\theta/(\theta - 1)$. Thus, in the flexible-price equilibrium,

$$\left(\frac{\theta}{\theta - 1} \right) \frac{v_c}{U_Y} = 1.$$

Multiply both sides of this expression by U_Y and log-linearizing the result reveals that the flexible-price output level $\hat{Y}_t^f$ satisfies

$$\left(\frac{\theta}{\theta - 1} \right) [v_c(\bar{Y}, 0) + v_{cc} \bar{Y} \hat{Y}_t^f + v_{c,z} \hat{z}_t] = U_Y + U_{YY} \bar{Y} \hat{Y}_t^f + U_{Y,z} \hat{z}_t.$$

Dividing both sides by $U_Y = \theta v_c(\bar{Y}, 0)/(\theta - 1)$,

$$\frac{v_{cc} \bar{Y} \hat{Y}_t^f + v_{c,z} \hat{z}_t}{v_c(\bar{Y}, 0)} = \frac{U_{YY} \bar{Y} \hat{Y}_t^f + U_{Y,z} \hat{z}_t}{U_Y},$$

or

$$\eta \hat{Y}_t^f - \eta q_t = -\sigma \hat{Y}_t^f + \sigma \phi_t.$$

Solving for $\hat{Y}_t^f$,

$$\hat{Y}_t^f = \left(\frac{\sigma\phi_t + \eta q_t}{\sigma + \eta}\right).$$

The utility approximation can now be written as

$$V \approx -\left(\frac{1}{2}\right)(\sigma + \eta)U_c\overline{Y}\left[\hat{Y}_t^2 - 2\left(\frac{\Phi + \sigma\phi_t + \eta q_t}{\sigma + \eta}\right)\hat{Y}_t + \left(\frac{\theta^{-1} + \eta}{\sigma + \eta}\right)var_j\hat{c}_{jt}\right] + \text{t.i.p.}$$

$$= -\left(\frac{1}{2}\right)(\sigma + \eta)U_c\overline{Y}\left[(x_t - x^*)^2 + \left(\frac{\theta^{-1} + \eta}{\sigma + \eta}\right)var_j\hat{c}_{jt}\right] + \text{t.i.p.},$$

where

$$x_t \equiv \hat{Y}_t - \hat{Y}_t^f$$

is the gap between output and the flexible-price equilibrium output, and

$$x^* \equiv \frac{\Phi}{\sigma + \eta}.$$

Letting $\overline{Y}^*$ be the steady-state efficient level of output, x^* is equal to $\log(\overline{Y}^*/\overline{Y})$ and is a measure of the distortion created by the presence of monopolistic competition.

The next step in obtaining an approximation to the utility of the representative agent involves expressing the variance of $\hat{c}_{jt}$ in terms of the dispersion of prices across individual firms.

With the assumed utility function, the demand for good i satisfies $\hat{c}_{jt} = [p_{jt}/P_t]^{-\theta}Y_t$. Taking logs,

$$\log \hat{c}_{jt} = \log Y_t - \theta(\log p_{jt} - \log P_t),$$

so

$$var_i \log \hat{c}_{jt} = \theta^2 var_i \log p_{jt}.$$

Hence, one can evaluate alternative policies using as the welfare criterion

$$-\frac{1}{2}\overline{Y}U_c[(\sigma + \eta)(x_t - x^*)^2 + (\theta^{-1} + \eta)\theta^2 var_j \log p_{jt}]. \tag{8.83}$$

The last step in the approximation process is to relate $var_j \log p_{jt}$ to the average inflation rate across all firms. To do so, recall that the price adjustment mechanism involves a randomly chosen fraction $1 - \omega$ of all firms optimally adjusting price each period. Define $\bar{P}_t \equiv E_j \log p_{jt}$ and $\Delta_t \equiv var_j \log p_{jt}$. Then, since $var_j \bar{P}_{t-1} = 0$,

$$\Delta_t = var_j[\log p_{jt} - \bar{P}_{t-1}]$$

$$= E_j[\log p_{jt} - \bar{P}_{t-1}]^2 - [E_j \log p_{jt} - \bar{P}_{t-1}]^2$$

$$= \omega E_j[\log p_{jt-1} - \bar{P}_{t-1}]^2 + (1 - \omega)(\log p_t^* - \bar{P}_{t-1})^2 - (\bar{P}_t - \bar{P}_{t-1})^2,$$

where p_t^* is the price set at time t by the fraction $1 - \omega$ of firms that reset their price. Given that $\bar{P}_t = (1 - \omega) \log p_t^* + \omega \bar{P}_{t-1}$,

$$\log p_t^* - \bar{P}_{t-1} = \left(\frac{1}{1 - \omega}\right)(\bar{P}_t - \bar{P}_{t-1}).$$

Using this result,

$$\Delta_t = \omega \Delta_{t-1} + \left(\frac{\omega}{1 - \omega}\right)(\bar{P}_t - \bar{P}_{t-1})^2$$

$$\approx \omega \Delta_{t-1} + \left(\frac{\omega}{1 - \omega}\right)\pi_t^2.$$

This implies

$$E_t \sum_{i=0}^{\infty} \beta^i \Delta_{t+i} = \left[\frac{\omega}{(1 - \omega)(1 - \omega\beta)}\right] E_t \sum_{i=0}^{\infty} \beta^i \pi_{t+i}^2 + \text{t.i.p.},$$

where the terms independent of policy include the initial degree of price dispersion.

Combining this with (8.83), the present discounted value of the utility of the representative household can be approximated by

$$E_t \sum_{i=0}^{\infty} \beta^i V_{t+i} \approx -\Omega E_t \sum_{i=0}^{\infty} \beta^i [\pi_{t+i}^2 + \lambda(x_{t+i} - x^*)^2],$$

where

$$\Omega = \frac{1}{2} U_Y \bar{Y} \left[\frac{\omega}{(1 - \omega)(1 - \omega\beta)}\right](\theta^{-1} + \eta)\theta^2$$

and

$$\lambda = \left[\frac{(1 - \omega)(1 - \omega\beta)}{\omega}\right]\frac{(\sigma + \eta)}{(1 + \eta\theta)\theta}.$$

8.7 Problems

1. Consider a simple forward-looking model of the form

$$x_t = E_t x_{t+1} - \sigma^{-1}(i_t - E_t \pi_{t+1}) + u_t,$$

$$\pi_t = \beta E_t \pi_{t+1} + \kappa x_t + e_t.$$

Suppose policy reacts to the output gap:

$$i_t = \delta x_t.$$

Write this system in the form given by (8.26). Are there values of δ that ensure a unique stationary equilibrium? Are there values that do not?

2. Consider the model given by

$$x_t = E_t x_{t+1} - \sigma^{-1}(i_t - E_t \pi_{t+1})$$

$$\pi_t = \beta E_t \pi_{t+1} + \kappa x_t.$$

Suppose policy sets the nominal interest rate according to a policy rule of the form

$$i_t = \phi_1 E_t \pi_{t+1}$$

for the nominal rate of interest.

a. Write this system in the form $E_t z_{t+1} = M z_t + \eta_t$, where $z_t = [x_t, \pi_t]'$.

b. For $\beta = 0.99$, $\kappa = 0.05$, and $\sigma = 1.5$, plot the absolute values of the two eigenvalues of M as a function of $\phi_1 > 0$.

c. Are there values of ϕ_1 for which the economy does not have a unique stationary equilibrium?

3. Assume the utility of the representative agent is given by

$$\frac{C_t^{1-\sigma}}{1-\sigma} - \frac{\xi_t N_t^{1+\eta}}{1+\eta}.$$

The aggregate production function is $Y_t = Z_t N_t$. The notation is C is consumption, ξ is a stochastic shock to tastes, N is time spent working, Y is output, and Z is an aggregate productivity disturbance; σ and η are constants. The stochastic variable ξ has a mean of 1.

a. Derive the household's first-order condition for labor supply. Show how labor supply depends on the taste shock, and explain how a positive realization of ξ would affect labor supply.

b. Derive an expression for the flexible-price equilibrium output $\hat{y}_t^f$ for this economy.

c. Does the taste shock affect the flexible-price equilibrium? If it does, explain how and why.

d. The household's Euler condition for optimal consumption choice (expressed in terms of the output gap and in percent deviations around the steady state) can be written as

$$x_t = E_t x_{t+1} - \left(\frac{1}{\sigma}\right)(i_t - E_t \pi_{t+1} - r_t^n).$$

How does r^n depend on the behavior of the flexible-price equilibrium output? Does it depend on the taste shock ξ? Explain intuitively whether a positive realization of ξ raises, lowers, or leaves unchanged the flexible-price equilibrium real interest rate.

4. Suppose the economy is characterized by

$$x_t = E_t x_{t+1} - \left(\frac{1}{\sigma}\right)(i_t - E_t \pi_{t+1} - r_t^n)$$

and

$$\pi_t = \beta E_t \pi_{t+1} + \kappa x_t.$$

What problems might arise if the central bank decides to set its interest rate instrument according to the rule $i_t = r_t^n$?

5. Suppose the economy is described by the basic new Keynesian model consisting of

$$x_t = E_t x_{t+1} - \sigma^{-1}(i_t - E_t \pi_{t+1})$$

$$\pi_t = \beta E_t \pi_{t+1} + \kappa x_t$$

$$i_t = \phi_\pi \pi_t + \phi_x x_t.$$

a. If $\phi_x = 0$, explain intuitively why $\phi_\pi > 1$ is needed to ensure that the equilibrium will be unique.

b. If both ϕ_π and ϕ_x are non-negative, the condition given by (8.29) implies that the economy can still have a unique stable equilibrium even when

$$1 - \frac{(1-\beta)\phi_x}{\kappa} < \phi_\pi < 1.$$

Explain intuitively why some values of $\phi_\pi < 1$ are still consistent with uniqueness when $\phi_x > 0$.

6. Assume the utility of the representative agent is given by

$$\frac{C_t^{1-\sigma}}{1-\sigma} - \frac{(1+\xi_t)N_t^{1+\eta}}{1+\eta}.$$

The aggregate production function is $Y_t = Z_t N_t$. The notation is C is consumption, ξ is a stochastic shock to tastes, N is time spent working, Y is output, and $Z_t = (1+z_t)$ is a stochastic aggregate productivity disturbance; σ and η are constants. Both ξ and z have zero means. Assume a standard model of monopolistic competition with Calvo pricing.

a. Assuming a zero steady-state rate of inflation, the inflation adjustment equation can be written as

$$\pi_t = \beta E_t \pi_{t+1} + \kappa \mu_t,$$

where μ_t is real marginal cost (expressed as a percent deviation around the steady state). Derive an expression for μ_t in terms of an output gap.

b. Does the taste shock affect the output gap? Does it affect inflation? Explain.

7. Assume the utility of the representative agent is given by

$$\frac{C_t^{1-\sigma}\left(\frac{M_t}{P_t}\right)^{1-b}}{1-\sigma} - \frac{N_t^{1+\eta}}{1+\eta}.$$

The aggregate production function is $Y_t = Z_t N_t^a$.

a. Show that the household's first-order condition for labor supply takes the form

$$\eta \hat{n}_t + \sigma \hat{c}_t - \mu_t^w = \hat{w}_t - \hat{p}_t,$$

where $\mu_t^w = (1-b)(\hat{m}_t - \hat{p}_t)$.

b. Derive an expression for the flexible-price equilibrium output $\hat{y}_t^f$ and the output gap $x_t = \hat{y}_t - \hat{y}_t^f$.

c. Does money affect the flexible-price equilibrium? Does the nominal interest rate? Explain.

8. Suppose the economy is characterized by (8.40) and (8.41), and let the cost shock be given by $e_t = \rho e_{t-1} + \varepsilon_t$. The central bank's loss function is (8.45). Assume that the central bank can commit to a policy rule of the form $\pi_t = \gamma e_t$.

a. What is the optimal value of γ?

b. Find the expression for equilibrium output gap under this policy.

9. In section 8.4.4, the case of commitment to a rule of the form $x_t = b_x e_t$ was ana-lyzed. Does a unique stationary rational-expectations equilibrium exist under such a commitment? Suppose instead that the central bank commits to the rule $i_t = b_i e_t$ for some constant b_i. Does a unique stationary rational-expectations equilibrium exist under such a commitment? Explain why the two cases differ.

10. Suppose the economy's inflation rate is described by the following equation (all variables expressed as percentage deviations around a zero inflation steady state):

$$\pi_t = \beta E_t \pi_{t+1} + \kappa x_t + e_t,$$

where x_t is the gap between output and the flexible-price equilibrium output level, and e_t is a cost shock. Assume that

$$e_t = \rho_e e_{t-1} + \varepsilon_t,$$

where ψ and ε are white noise processes. The central bank sets the nominal interest rate i_t to minimize

$$\frac{1}{2} E_t \left[\sum_{i=0}^{\infty} \beta^i (\pi_{t+i}^2 + \lambda x_{t+i}^2) \right].$$

a. Derive the first-order conditions linking inflation and the output gap for the *fully* optimal commitment policy.

b. Explain why the first-order condition for time t differs from the first-order condi-tion for $t + i$ for $i > 0$.

c. What is meant by a commitment policy that is optimal from a timeless perspec-tive? (Explain in words.)

d. What is the first-order condition linking inflation and the output gap that the cen-tral bank follows under an optimal commitment policy from a timeless perspective?

e. Explain why, under commitment, the central bank promises a deflation in the period after a positive cost shock (assume the cost shock is serially uncorrelated).

11. Explain why inflation is costly in a new Keynesian model.

12. Suppose the economy is described by the following log-linearized system:

$$x_t = E_t x_{t+1} - \left(\frac{1}{\sigma}\right)(i_t - E_t \pi_{t+1}) + E_t(z_{t+1} - z_t) + u_t$$

$$\pi_t = \beta E_t \pi_{t+1} + \kappa x_t + e_t,$$

where u_t is a demand shock, z_t is a productivity shock, and e_t is a cost shock. Assume that

$$u_t = \rho_u u_{t-1} + \xi_t$$

$$z_t = \rho_z z_{t-1} + \psi_t$$

$$e_t = \rho_e e_{t-1} + \varepsilon_t,$$

where ξ, ψ, and ε are white noise processes. The central bank sets the nominal interest rate i_t to minimize

$$\left(\frac{1}{2}\right) E_t \left[\sum_{i=0}^{\infty} \beta^i (\pi_{t+i}^2 + \lambda x_{t+i}^2)\right].$$

a. Derive the optimal time-consistent policy for the discretionary central banker. Write the first-order conditions and the reduced-form solutions for x_t and π_t.

b. Derive the interest rate feedback rule implied by the optimal discretionary policy.

c. Show that under the optimal policy, nominal interest rates are increased enough to raise the real interest rate in response to a rise in expected inflation.

d. How will x_t and π_t move in response to a demand shock? A productivity shock?

13. Suppose the central bank cares about inflation variability, output gap variablility, and interest rate variability. The objective of the central bank is to minimize

$$\left(\frac{1}{2}\right) E_t \sum_{i=0}^{\infty} \beta^i [\pi_{t+i}^2 + \lambda_x x_{t+i}^2 + \lambda_i (i_{t+i} - i^*)^2].$$

The structure of the economy is given by

$$\pi_t = \beta E_t \pi_{t+1} + \kappa x_t + e_t$$

$$x_t = E_t x_{t+1} - \left(\frac{1}{\sigma}\right)(i_t - E_t \pi_{t+1} - r_t),$$

where e and r are exogenous stochastic shocks. Let ψ_t denote the Lagrangian multiplier on the Phillips curve, and let θ_t be the multipler on the IS curve.

a. Derive the first-order conditions for the optimal policy of the central bank under discretion.

b. Show that θ is nonzero if $\lambda_i > 0$. Explain the economics behind this result.

c. Derive the first-order conditions for the fully optimal commitment policy. How do these differ from the conditions you found in (a)?

d. Derive the first-order conditions for the optimal commitment policy from a timeless perspective. How do these differ from the conditions you found in (c)?

14. Consider a basic new Keynesian model with Calvo adjustment of prices and flexible nominal wages.

a. In this model, inflation volatility reduces the welfare of the representative agent. Explain why.

b. In the absence of cost shocks, optimal policy would ensure that inflation and the output gap both remain equal to zero. What does this imply for the behavior of output? Why can output fluctuate efficiently despite sticky prices?

c. Suppose both prices and nominal wages are sticky (assume a Calvo model for wages). Will volatility in the rate of wage inflation be welfare reducing? Explain.

d. Are zero inflation and a zero output gap still feasible? Explain.

15. A key issue in the analysis of policy trade-offs is the source of the stochastic shocks in the model. Consider two examples: (1) The utility function takes the form

$$\frac{C_t^{1-\sigma}}{1-\sigma} - \chi\frac{N_t^{1+\eta_t}}{1+\eta_t},$$

where η_t is stochastic. (2) There is a labor tax τ_t such that the after-tax wage is $(1-\tau_t)W_t$. Assume a standard model of monopolistic competition.

a. Derive the condition for labor market equilibrium under flexible prices for each of the two cases.

b. Linearize the conditions found in part (a), and for each case, derive the flexible-price equilibrium output in terms of percent deviations from the steady state. Clearly state any assumptions you need to make on the η and τ processes or about other aspects of the model.

c. Assume sticky prices, as in the Calvo model. Express real marginal cost in terms of an output gap.

d. Does either η_t or τ_t appear as a cost shock?

e. Do you think either η_t or τ_t causes a wedge between the flexible-price output level and the efficient output level?

16. Suppose inflation adjustment is given by (8.61). The central bank's objective is to minimize

$$\left(\frac{1}{2}\right)E_t\sum_{i=0}^{\infty}\beta^i(\pi_{t+i}^2 + \lambda x_{t+i}^2)$$

subject to (8.61). Use the programs available from Paul Söderlind's web site, ⟨http://www.hhs.se/personal/Psoderlind/Software/Software.htm⟩, to answer this question.

a. Calculate the response of the output gap and inflation to a serially uncorrelated positive cost shock for $\phi = 0, 0.25, 0.5, 0.75$, and 1 under the optimal discretionary policy.

b. Now do the same for the optimal commitment policy.

c. Discuss how the differences between commitment and discretion depend on ϕ, the weight on lagged inflation in the inflation adjustment equation.

17. Suppose

$$\pi_t - \gamma\pi_{t-1} = \beta(E_t\pi_{t+1} - \gamma\pi_t) + \kappa x_t + e_t$$

$$e_t = 0.25e_{t-1} + \varepsilon_t,$$

and the period loss function is

$$L_t = (\pi_t - \gamma\pi_{t-1})^2 + 0.25x_t^2.$$

a. Analytically find the optimal targeting rule under discretion.

b. Analytically find the optimal targeting rule under commitment (timeless perspective).

c. How do the volatilities of inflation and the output gap depend on the value of γ? Explain.

d. How does the unconditional expected value of the loss function depend on γ? Explain.

18. Suppose the inflation equation contains lagged inflation:

$$\pi_t = (1 - \phi)\beta E_t\pi_{t+1} + \phi\pi_{t-1} + \kappa x_t + e_t.$$

a. Show that the optimal commitment policy from a timeless perspective is

$$\pi_t + (\lambda/\kappa)[x_t - (1 - \phi)x_{t-1} - \beta\phi E_t x_{t+1}] = 0.$$

b. Show that the unconditional optimal commitment policy takes the form

$$\pi_t + (\lambda/\kappa)[x_t - \beta(1 - \phi)x_{t-1} - \phi E_t x_{t+1}] = 0.$$

19. The following model has been estimated by Lindé (2002), although the values here are from Svensson and Williams (2005):

$$\pi_t = 0.4908 E_t\pi_{t+1} + (1 - 0.4908)\pi_{t-1} + 0.0081 y_t + \varepsilon_t^\pi$$

$$y_t = 0.4408 E_t y_{t+1} + (1 - 0.4408)[1.1778 y_{t-1} + (1 - 1.1778)y_{t-2}]$$

$$- 0.0048(i_t - E_t\pi_{t+1}) + \varepsilon_t^y$$

$$i_t = (1 - 0.9557 + 0.0673)(1.3474\pi_t + 0.7948y_t) + 0.9557i_{t-1} - 0.0673i_{t-2} + \varepsilon_t^i$$

with $\sigma_\pi = 0.5923$, $\sigma_y = 0.4126$, and $\sigma_i = 0.9918$.

a. Write this system in the form $E_t z_{t+1} = M z_t + \eta_t$ for appropriately defined vectors z and η.

b. Using the programs available at $\langle$http://people.ucsc.edu/~walshc/mtp3e/$\rangle$, plot the impulse response functions showing how inflation and the output gap respond to each of the three shocks.

c. How are the impulse responses affected if the coefficient on inflation in the policy rule is reduced from 1.3474 to 1.1?

9 Money and the Open Economy

9.1 Introduction

The analysis in earlier chapters was conducted in the context of a closed economy. Many useful insights into monetary phenomena can be obtained while abstracting from the linkages that tie different economies together, but clearly many issues do require an open-economy framework if they are to be adequately addressed. New channels through which monetary factors can influence the economy arise in open economies. Exchange rate movements, for example, play an important role in the transmission process that links monetary disturbances to output and inflation movements. Open economies face the possibility of economic disturbances that originate in other countries, and this raises questions of monetary policy design that are absent in a closed-economy environment. Should policy respond to exchange rate movements? Should monetary policy be used to stabilize exchange rates? Should national monetary policies be coordinated?

This chapter begins with a two-country model based on Obstfeld and Rogoff (1995; 1996). The two-country model has the advantage of capturing some of the important linkages between economies while still maintaining a degree of simplicity and tractability. Because an open economy is linked to other economies, policy actions in one economy have the potential to affect other economies. Spillovers can occur. And policy actions in one country will depend on the response of monetary policy in the other. Often, because of these spillovers, countries attempt to coordinate their policy actions. The role of policy coordination is examined in section 9.3.

Section 9.4 considers the case of a *small open economy*. In the open-economy literature, a small open economy denotes an economy that is too small to affect world prices, interest rates, or economic activity. Since many countries really are small relative to the world economy, the small-open-economy model provides a framework that is relevant for studying many policy issues.

The analyses of policy coordination and the small open economy are conducted using models in which behavioral relationships are specified directly rather than derived from underlying assumptions about the behavior of individuals and firms. As a result, the frameworks are of limited use for conducting normative analysis because they are unable to make predictions about the welfare of the agents in the model. This is one reason for beginning the discussion of the open economy with the Obstfeld-Rogoff model. It is based explicitly on the assumption of optimizing agents and therefore offers a natural metric—in the form of the utility of the representative agent—for addressing normative policy questions. The chapter ends by returning, in section 9.5, to a class of models based on optimizing agents and nominal rigidities. These models are the open-economy counterparts of the new Keynesian model of chapter 8.

9.2   The Obstfeld-Rogoff Two-Country Model

Obstfeld and Rogoff (1995; 1996) examined the linkages between two economies within a framework that combines three fundamental building blocks. The first is an emphasis on intertemporal decisions by individual agents; foreign trade and asset exchange open up avenues for transferring resources over time that are not available in a closed economy. A temporary positive productivity shock that raises current output relative to future output induces individuals to increase consumption both now and in the future as they try to smooth the path of consumption. Since domestic consumption rises less than domestic output, the economy increases its net exports, thereby accumulating claims against future foreign output. These claims can be used to maintain higher consumption in the future after the temporary productivity increase has ended. The trade balance therefore plays an important role in facilitating the intertemporal transfer of resources.

Monopolistic competition in the goods market is the second building block of the Obstfeld-Rogoff model. This by itself has no implications for the effects of monetary disturbances, but it does set the stage for the third aspect of their model, sticky prices. These basic building have already been discussed, so the focus here is on the new aspects introduced by open-economy considerations. Detailed derivations of the various components of the model are provided in the chapter appendix (section 9.7). It will simplify the exposition to deal with a nonstochastic model in order to highlight the new factors that arise in the open-economy context.

Each of the two countries is populated by a continuum of agents, indexed by $z \in [0, 1]$, who are monopolistic producers of differentiated goods. Agents $z \in [0, n]$ reside in the home country, and agents $z \in (n, 1]$ reside in the foreign country. Thus, n provides an index of the relative sizes of the two countries. If the countries are of equal size, $n = \frac{1}{2}$. Foreign variables are denoted by a superscript asterisk $(*)$.

The present discounted value of lifetime utility of a domestic resident j is

$$U^j = \sum_{t=0}^{\infty} \beta^t \left[\log C_t^j + b \log \frac{M_t^j}{P_t} - \frac{k}{2} Y_t(j)^2 \right], \tag{9.1}$$

where C_t^j is agent $j's$ period t consumption of the composite consumption good, defined by

$$C_t^j = \left[\int_0^1 C_t^j(z)^q \right]^{1/q}, \qquad 0 < q < 1, \tag{9.2}$$

and consumption by agent j of good z is $C_t^j(z)$, $z \in [0, 1]$. The aggregate domestic price deflator P is defined as

$$P_t = \left[\int_0^1 P_t(z)^{q/(q-1)} \right]^{(q-1)/q}. \tag{9.3}$$

This price index P depends on the prices of all goods consumed by domestic residents (the limits of integration run from 0 to 1). It incorporates prices of both domestically produced goods $\{P(z) \text{ for } z \in [0, n]\}$ and foreign-produced goods $\{P(z) \text{ for } z \in (n, 1]\}$. Thus, P corresponds to a consumer price index concept of the price level, not a GDP price deflator that would include only the prices of domestically produced goods.

Utility also depends on the agent's holdings of real money balances. Agents are assumed to hold only their domestic currency, so M_t^j/P_t appears in the utility function (9.1). Since agent j is the producer of good j, the effort of producing output $Y_t(j)$ generates disutility. A similar utility function is assumed for residents of the foreign country:

$$U^{*j} = \sum_{t=0}^{\infty} \beta^t \left[\log C_t^{*j} + b \log \frac{M_t^{*j}}{P_t^*} - \frac{k}{2} Y_t^*(j)^2 \right],$$

where C^{*j} and P^* are defined analogously to C^j and P.

Agent j will pick consumption, money holdings, holdings of internationally traded bonds, and output of good j to maximize utility subject to the budget constraint

$$P_t C_t^j + M_t^j + P_t T_t + P_t B_t^j \leq P_t(j) Y_t(j) + R_{t-1} P_t B_{t-1}^j + M_{t-1}^j.$$

The gross real rate of interest is denoted R, and T represents real taxes minus transfers. Bonds purchased at time $t - 1$, B_{t-1}^j, yield a gross real return R_{t-1}. As in the analysis in chapter 2, the role of T is to allow for variations in the nominal supply of money, with $P_t T_t = (M_t - M_{t-1})$. Dividing the budget constraint by P_t, one obtains

$$C_t^j + \frac{M_t^j}{P_t} + T_t + B_t^j \leq \left[\frac{P_t(j)}{P_t}\right] Y_t(j) + R_{t-1} B_{t-1}^j + \left(\frac{1}{1+\pi_t}\right) \frac{M_{t-1}^j}{P_{t-1}}, \tag{9.4}$$

where π_t is the inflation rate from $t-1$ to t. To complete the description of the agent's decision problem, one needs to specify the demand for the good the agent produces. This specification is provided in chapter appendix section 9.7.1, where it is shown that the following necessary first-order conditions can be derived from the individual consumer/producer's decision problem:

$$C_{t+1}^j = \beta R_t C_t^j \tag{9.5}$$

$$k Y_t(j) = q \left(\frac{1}{C_t^j}\right) \left(\frac{Y_t(j)}{C_t^w}\right)^{q-1} \tag{9.6}$$

$$\frac{M_t^j}{P_t} = b C_t^j \left(\frac{1+i_t}{i_t}\right), \tag{9.7}$$

together with the budget constraint (9.4) and the transversality condition

$$\lim_{i \to \infty} \prod_{s=0}^{i} R_{t+s-1}^{-1} \left(B_{t+i}^j + \frac{M_{t+i}^j}{P_{t+i}}\right) = 0.$$

In these expressions, i_t is the nominal rate of interest, defined as $R_t(1 + \pi_{t+1}) - 1$. In (9.6), $C_t^w \equiv nC_t + (1-n)C_t^*$ is world consumption, where $C_t = \int_0^n C_t^j \, dj$ and $C_t^* = \int_n^1 C_t^j \, dj$ equal total home and foreign consumption.

Equation (9.5) is a standard Euler condition for the optimal consumption path. Equation (9.6) states that the ratio of the marginal disutility of work to the marginal utility of consumption must equal the marginal product of labor.[1] Equation (9.7) is the familiar condition for the demand for real balances of the domestic currency, requiring that the ratio of the marginal utility of money to the marginal utility of consumption equal $i_t/(1+i_t)$. Similar expressions hold for the foreign consumer and producer.

Let S_t denote the nominal exchange rate between the two currencies, defined as the price of foreign currency in terms of domestic currency. A rise in S_t means that the price of foreign currency has risen in terms of domestic currency; consequently, a

---

1. See (9.107) in the appendix.

unit of domestic currency buys fewer units of foreign currency. So a rise in S_t corresponds to a fall in the value of the domestic currency.

The exchange rate between goods produced domestically and goods produced in the foreign economy will also play an important role. The law of one price requires that good z sell for the same price in both the home and foreign countries when expressed in a common currency.[2] This requires

$$P_t(z) = S_t P_t^*(z).$$

It follows from the definitions of the home and foreign price levels that

$$P_t = S_t P_t^*. \tag{9.8}$$

Any equilibrium must satisfy the first-order conditions for the agent's decision problem, the law of one price, and the following additional market-clearing conditions:

Goods market clearing: $C_t^w = n \left[\dfrac{P_t(h)}{P_t} \right] Y_t(h) + (1 - n) \left[\dfrac{P_t^*(f)}{P_t^*} \right] Y_t^*(f) \equiv Y_t^w,$

where $P(h)$ and $Y(h)$ are the price and output of the representative home good (and similarly for $P^*(f)$ and $Y^*(f)$), and

Bond market clearing: $nB_t + (1 - n)B_t^* = 0.$

From the structure of the model, it should be clear that one-time proportional changes in the nominal home money supply, all domestic prices, and the nominal exchange rate leave the equilibrium for all real variables unaffected—the model displays monetary neutrality. An increase in M accompanied by a proportional decline in the value of home money in terms of goods (i.e., a proportional rise in all $P(j)$) and a decline in the value of M in terms of M^* (i.e., a proportional rise in S) leaves equilibrium consumption and output in both countries, together with prices in the foreign country, unchanged.

In the steady state, the model's budget constraint (9.4) becomes

$$C = \frac{P(h)}{P} Y(h) + (R - 1)B, \tag{9.9}$$

---

2. While the law of one price is intuitively appealing and provides a convenient means of linking the prices $P(j)$ and $P^*(j)$ to the nominal exchange rate, it may be a poor empirical approximation. In a study of prices in different U.S. cities, Parsley and Wei (1996) found rates of price convergence to be faster than in cross-country comparisons, and they concluded that tradable-goods prices converge quickly. Even so, the half-life of a price difference among U.S. cities for tradables is estimated to be on the order of 12–15 months. See section 9.5.3.

where B is the steady-state real stock of bonds held by the home country. For the foreign country,

$$C^* = \frac{P(f)}{P} Y(f) - (R - 1)\left(\frac{n}{1 - n}\right)B. \tag{9.10}$$

These two equations imply that real consumption equals real income (the real value of output plus income from net asset holdings) in the steady state.

9.2.1   The Linear Approximation

It will be helpful to develop a linear approximation to the basic Obstfeld-Rogoff model in terms of percentage deviations around the steady state. This serves to make the linkages between the two economies clear and provides a base of comparison when, in the following section, a more traditional open-economy model is considered that is not directly derived from the assumption of optimizing agents. Using lowercase letters to denote percentage deviations around the steady state, the equilibrium conditions can be expressed as

$$p_t = np_t(h) + (1 - n)[s_t + p_t^*(f)] \tag{9.11}$$

$$p_t^* = n[p_t(h) - s_t] + (1 - n)p_t^*(f) \tag{9.12}$$

$$y_t = \frac{1}{1 - q}[p_t - p_t(h)] + c_t^w \tag{9.13}$$

$$y_t^* = \frac{1}{1 - q}[p_t^* - p_t^*(f)] + c_t^w \tag{9.14}$$

$$nc_t + (1 - n)c_t^* = c_t^w \tag{9.15}$$

$$c_{t+1} = c_t + r_t \tag{9.16}$$

$$c_{t+1}^* = c_t^* + r_t \tag{9.17}$$

$$(2 - q)y_t = (1 - q)c_t^w - c_t \tag{9.18}$$

$$(2 - q)y_t^* = (1 - q)c_t^w - c_t^* \tag{9.19}$$

$$m_t - p_t = c_t - \delta(r_t + \pi_{t+1}) \tag{9.20}$$

$$m_t^* - p_t^* = c_t^* - \delta(r_t + \pi_{t+1}^*), \tag{9.21}$$

where $\delta = \beta/(\overline{\Pi} - \beta)$ and $\overline{\Pi}$ is 1 plus the steady-state rate of inflation (assumed to be equal in both economies). Equations (9.11) and (9.12) express the domestic and foreign price levels as weighted averages of the prices of home- and foreign-produced goods expressed in a common currency. The weights depend on the relative sizes of the two countries as measured by n. Equations (9.13) and (9.14) are derived from (9.99) of the appendix and give the demand for each country's output as a function of world consumption and relative price. Increases in world consumption (c^w) increase the demand for the output of both countries, and demand also depends on a relative price variable. Home country demand, for example, falls as the price of home production $p(h)$ rises relative to the home price level. Equation (9.15) defines world consumption as the weighted average of consumption in the two countries.

Equations (9.16)–(9.21) are from the individual agent's first-order conditions (9.5), (9.6), and (9.7). The first two of these equations are simply the Euler condition for the optimal intertemporal allocation of consumption; the change in consumption is equal to the real rate of return. Equations (9.18) and (9.19) are implied by optimal production decisions. Finally, (9.20) and (9.21) give the real demand for home and foreign money as functions of consumption and nominal interest rates. Although both countries face the same real interest rate r_t, nominal interest rates may differ if inflation rates differ between the two countries.

The equilibrium path of home and foreign production (y_t, y_t^*), home, domestic, and world consumption (c_t, c_t^*, c_t^w), prices and the nominal exchange rate ($p_t(h), p_t, p_t^*(f), p_t^*, s_t$), and the real interest rate (r_t) must be consistent with these equilibrium conditions.[3] Note that subtracting (9.12) from (9.11) implies

$$s_t = p_t - p_t^*, \tag{9.22}$$

and the addition of n times (9.13) and $(1 - n)$ times (9.14) yields the goods market–clearing relationship equating world production to world consumption: $ny_t + (1 - n)y_t^* = c_t^w$.

9.2.2   Equilibrium with Flexible Prices

The linear version of the two-country model serves to highlight the channels that link open economies. With this framework, the role of money when prices are perfectly flexible is discussed first. As in the closed-economy case, the real equilibrium is independent of monetary phenomena when prices can move flexibly to offset changes in

---

3. Equations (9.20)–(9.21) differ somewhat from Obstfeld and Rogoff's specification because of differences in the methods used to obtain linear approximations. See Obstfeld and Rogoff (1996, ch. 10).

the nominal supply of money.[4] Prices and the nominal exchange rate will depend on the behavior of the money supplies in the two countries, and the adjustment of the nominal exchange rate becomes part of the equilibrating mechanism that insulates real output and consumption from monetary effects.

The assumption of a common capital market, implying that consumers in both countries face the same real interest rate, means, from the Euler conditions (9.16) and (9.17), that $c_{t+1} - c^*_{t+1} = c_t - c^*_t$; any difference in relative consumption is permanent. And world consumption c^w is the relevant scale variable for demand facing both home and domestic producers.

Monetary Dichotomy

With prices and the nominal exchange rate free to adjust immediately in the face of changes in either the home or foreign money supply, the model displays the classic dichotomy discussed in section 6.2.1 under which the equilibrium values of all real variables can be determined independently of the money supply and money demand factors. To see this, define the two relative price variables $\chi_t \equiv p_t(h) - p_t$ and $\chi^*_t \equiv p^*_t(f) - p^*_t$. Equations (9.11) and (9.12) imply that

$$n\chi_t + (1-n)\chi^*_t = 0,$$

and (9.13) and (9.14) can be rewritten as

$$y_t = -\frac{\chi_t}{1-q} + c^w_t$$

$$y^*_t = -\frac{\chi^*_t}{1-q} + c^w_t.$$

These equations, together with (9.15)–(9.19), suffice to determine the real equilibrium. The money demand equations (9.20) and (9.21) determine the price paths, and (9.22) determines the equilibrium nominal exchange rate given these price paths. Thus, an important implication of this model is that monetary policy (defined as changes in nominal money supplies) has no short-run effects on the real interest rate, output, or consumption in either country. Rather, only nominal interest rates, prices, and the nominal exchange rate are affected by variations in the nominal money stock. One-time changes in m produce proportional changes in p, $p(h)$, and s.

---

4. Recall from the discussion in chapter 2 that the dynamic adjustment outside the steady state is independent of money when utility is log-separable, as assumed in (9.1). This result would also characterize this open-economy model if it were modified to incorporate stochastic uncertainty due to productivity and money growth rate disturbances.

Equation (9.20) shows that inflation affects the real demand for money. Changes in nominal money growth rates produce changes in the inflation rate and nominal interest rates, thereby affecting the opportunity cost of holding money and, in equilibrium, the real stock of money. The price level and the nominal exchange rate jump to ensure that the real supply of money is equal to the new real demand for money.

Equation (9.21) can be subtracted from (9.20), yielding

$$m_t - m_t^* - (p_t - p_t^*) = (c_t - c_t^*) - \delta(\pi_{t+1} - \pi_{t+1}^*),$$

which, using (9.22), implies[5]

$$m_t - m_t^* - s_t = (c_t - c_t^*) - \delta(s_{t+1} - s_t). \tag{9.23}$$

Solving this forward for the nominal exchange rate, the no-bubbles solution is

$$s_t = \frac{1}{1+\delta} \sum_{i=0}^{\infty} \left(\frac{\delta}{1+\delta}\right)^i [(m_{t+i} - m_{t+i}^*) - (c_{t+i} - c_{t+i}^*)]. \tag{9.24}$$

Since (9.16) and (9.17) imply that $c_{t+i} - c_{t+i}^* = c_t - c_t^*$, the expression for the nominal exchange rate can be rewritten as

$$s_t = -(c_t - c_t^*) + \frac{1}{1+\delta} \sum_{i=0}^{\infty} \left(\frac{\delta}{1+\delta}\right)^i (m_{t+i} - m_{t+i}^*).$$

The current nominal exchange rate depends on the current and future path of the nominal money supplies in the two countries and on consumption differentials. The exchange rate measures the price of one money in terms of the other, and as (9.24) shows, this depends on the relative supplies of the two monies. An increase in one country's money supply relative to the other's depreciates that country's exchange rate. From the standard steady-state condition that $\beta R^{ss} = 1$ and the definition of δ as $\beta/(\overline{\Pi} - \beta)$, the discount factor in (9.24), $\delta/(1+\delta)$, is equal to $\beta/\overline{\Pi} = 1/R^{ss}\overline{\Pi} = 1/(1 + i^{ss})$. Future nominal money supply differentials are discounted by the steady-state nominal rate of interest. Because agents are forward-looking in their decision making, it is only the present discounted value of the relative money supplies that matters. In other words, the nominal exchange rate depends on a measure of the permanent money supply differential. Letting $x_{t+i} \equiv (m_{t+i} - m_{t+i}^*) - (c_{t+i} - c_{t+i}^*)$, the equilibrium condition for the nominal exchange rate can be written as

---

5. This uses the fact that $\pi_{t+1} - \pi_{t+1}^* = (p_{t+1} - p_{t+1}^*) - (p_t - p_t^*) = s_{t+1} - s_t$.

$$s_t = \frac{1}{1+\delta}\sum_{i=0}^{\infty}\left(\frac{\delta}{1+\delta}\right)^i x_{t+i} = \frac{1}{1+\delta}x_t + \frac{\delta}{1+\delta}\sum_{i=0}^{\infty}\left(\frac{\delta}{1+\delta}\right)^i x_{t+1+i}$$

$$= \frac{1}{1+\delta}x_t + \frac{\delta}{1+\delta}s_{t+1}.$$

Rearranging and using (9.24) yields

$$s_{t+1} - s_t = -\frac{1}{\delta}(x_t - s_t)$$

$$= -\frac{1}{\delta}\left[(m_t - m_t^*) - \frac{1}{1+\delta}\sum_{i=0}^{\infty}\left(\frac{\delta}{1+\delta}\right)^i (m_{t+1+i} - m_{t+1+i}^*)\right].$$

Analogously to Friedman's permanent income concept, the term

$$\frac{1}{1+\delta}\sum_{i=0}^{\infty}\left(\frac{\delta}{1+\delta}\right)^i (m_{t+1+i} - m_{t+1+i}^*)$$

can be interpreted as the permanent money supply differential. If the current value of $m - m^*$ is high relative to the permanent value of this differential, the nominal exchange rate will fall (the home currency will appreciate). If s_t reflects the permanent money supply differential at time t, and m_t is temporarily high relative to m_t^*, then the permanent differential will be lower beginning in period $t+1$. As a result, the home currency appreciates.

An explicit solution for the nominal exchange rate can be obtained if specific processes for the nominal money supplies are assumed. To take a very simple case, suppose m and m^* each follow constant, deterministic growth paths given by

$$m_t = m_0 + \mu t$$

and

$$m_t^* = m_0^* + \mu^* t.$$

Strictly speaking, (9.24) applies only to deviations around the steady state and not to money supply processes that include deterministic trends. However, it is very common to specify (9.20) and (9.21), which were used to derive (9.24), in terms of the log levels of the variables, perhaps adding a constant to represent steady-state levels. The advantage of interpreting (9.24) as holding for the log levels of the variables is that one can then use it to analyze shifts in the trend growth paths of the nominal money supplies, rather than just deviations around the trend. It is important to keep in mind, however, that the underlying representative-agent model implies that the interest rate coefficients in the money demand equations are functions of the steady-state rate of inflation. Assume this is the same in both countries, implying that the δ parameter is the same as well. The assumption of common coefficients in two-country models is common, and it is maintained in the following examples. The limitations of doing so should be kept in mind.

Then (9.24) implies

$$
s_t = -(c_t - c_t^*) + \frac{1}{1+\delta} \sum_{i=0}^{\infty} \left(\frac{\delta}{1+\delta} \right)^i [m_0 - m_0^* + (\mu - \mu^*)(t + i)]
$$

$$
= s_0 + (\mu - \mu^*)t - (c_t - c_t^*),
$$

where $s_0 = m_0 - m_0^* + \delta(\mu - \mu^*).$[6] In this case, the nominal exchange rate has a deterministic trend equal to the difference in the trend of money growth rates in the two economies (also equal to the inflation rate differentials since $\pi = \mu$ and $\pi^* = \mu^*$). If domestic money growth exceeds foreign money growth ($\mu > \mu^*$), s will rise over time to reflect the falling value of the home currency relative to the foreign currency.

Uncovered Interest Parity

Real rates of return in the two countries have been assumed to be equal, so the Euler conditions for the optimal consumption paths (9.16) and (9.17) imply the same expected consumption growth in each economy. It follows from the equality of real returns that nominal interest rates must satisfy $i_t - \pi_{t+1} = r_t = i_t^* - \pi_{t+1}^*$, and this means, using (9.22), that

$$
i_t - i_t^* = \pi_{t+1} - \pi_{t+1}^* = s_{t+1} - s_t.
$$

The nominal interest rate differential is equal to the actual change in the exchange rate in a perfect-foresight equilibrium. This equality would not hold in the presence of uncertainty because variables dated $t + 1$ would need to be replaced with their expected values, conditional on the information available at time t. In this case,

$$
E_t s_{t+1} - s_t = i_t - i_t^*, \tag{9.25}
$$

and nominal interest rate differentials would reflect expected exchange rate changes. If the home country has a higher nominal interest rate in equilibrium, its currency must be expected to depreciate (s must be expected to rise) to equalize real returns across the two countries.

---

6. This uses the fact that $\sum_{i=0}^{\infty} ib^i = b/(1 - b)^2$ for $|b| < 1$.

This condition, known as *uncovered nominal interest parity*, links interest rates and exchange rate expectations in different economies if their financial markets are integrated. Under rational expectations, the actual exchange rate at $t + 1$ can be written as equal to the expectation of the future exchange rate plus a forecast error φ_t uncorrelated with $E_t s_{t+1}$: $s_{t+1} = E_t s_{t+1} + \varphi_t$. Uncovered interest parity then implies

$$s_{t+1} - s_t = i_t - i_t^* + \varphi_{t+1}.$$

The ex post observed change in the exchange rate between times t and $t + 1$ is equal to the interest rate differential at time t plus a random mean zero forecast error. Since this forecast error will, under rational expectations, be uncorrelated with information, such as i_t and i_t^*, that is known at time t, one can recast uncovered interest parity in the form of a regression equation:

$$s_{t+1} - s_t = a + b(i_t - i_t^*) + \varphi_{t+1}, \tag{9.26}$$

with the null hypothesis of uncovered interest parity implying that $a = 0$ and $b = 1$. Unfortunately, the evidence rejects this hypothesis.[7] In fact, estimated values of b are often negative.

One interpretation of these rejections is that the error term in an equation such as (9.26) is not simply due to forecast errors. Suppose, more realistically, that (9.25) does not hold exactly:

$$E_t s_{t+1} - s_t = i_t - i_t^* + v_t,$$

where v_t captures factors such as risk premiums that would lead to divergences between real returns in the two countries. In this case, the error term in the regression of $s_{t+1} - s_t$ on $i_t - i_t^*$ becomes $v_t + \varphi_{t+1}$. If v_t and $i_t - i_t^*$ are correlated, ordinary least-squares estimates of the parameter b in (9.26) will be biased and inconsistent.

Correlation between v and $i - i^*$ might arise if monetary policies are implemented in a manner that leads the nominal interest rate differential to respond to the current exchange rate. For example, suppose that the monetary authority in each country tends to tighten policy whenever its currency depreciates. This could occur if the monetary authorities are concerned with inflation; depreciation raises the domestic currency price of foreign goods and raises the domestic price level. To keep the example simple for illustrative purposes, suppose that as a result of such a policy, the nominal interest rate differential is given by

7. For a summary of the evidence, see Froot and Thaler (1990). See also McCallum (1994a); Eichenbaum and Evans (1995); and Schlagenhauf and Wrase (1995).

$$i_t - i_t^* = \mu s_t + u_t, \qquad \mu > 0,$$

where u_t captures any other factors affecting the interest rate differential.[8] Assume u is an exogenous white noise process. Substituting this into the uncovered interest parity condition yields

$$E_t s_{t+1} = (1 + \mu)s_t + u_t + v_t, \tag{9.27}$$

the solution to which is[9]

$$s_t = - \left(\frac{1}{1 + \mu} \right)(u_t + v_t).$$

Since this solution implies that $E_t s_{t+1} = -E_t(u_{t+1} + v_{t+1})/(1+\mu) = 0$, the interest parity condition is then given by

$$E_t s_{t+1} - s_t = \left(\frac{1}{1 + \mu} \right)(u_t + v_t) = i_t - i_t^* + v_t$$

or $i_t - i_t^* = (u_t - \mu v_t)/(1 + \mu)$.

What does this imply for tests of uncovered interest parity? From the solution for $s_t, s_{t+1} - s_t = -(u_{t+1} - u_t + v_{t+1} - v_t)/(1+\mu)$. The probability limit of the interest rate coefficient in the regression of $s_{t+1} - s_t$ on $i_t - i_t^*$ is equal to

$$\frac{cov(s_{t+1} - s_t, i_t - i_t^*)}{var(i_t - i_t^*)} = \frac{\frac{1}{(1+\mu)^2}(\sigma_u^2 - \mu\sigma_v^2)}{\frac{1}{(1+\mu)^2}(\sigma_u^2 + \mu^2\sigma_v^2)} = \frac{\sigma_u^2 - \mu\sigma_v^2}{\sigma_u^2 + \mu^2\sigma_v^2},$$

which will not generally equal 1, the standard null in tests of interest parity. If $u \equiv 0$, the probability limit of the regression coefficient is $-1/\mu$. That is, the regression estimate uncovers the policy parameter μ. Not only would a regression of the change in the exchange rate on the interest differential not yield the value of 1 predicted by the uncovered interest parity condition but the estimate would be negative.

McCallum (1994a) developed more fully the argument that rejections of uncovered interest parity may arise because standard tests compound the parity condition with the manner in which monetary policy is conducted. Although uncovered interest parity is implied by the model independently of the manner in which policy is

---

8. The rationale for such a policy is clearly not motivated within the context of a model with perfectly flexible prices in which monetary policy has no real effects. The general point is to illustrate how empirical relationships such as (9.26) can depend on the conduct of policy.

9. From (9.27), the equilibrium exchange rate process must satisfy $E_t s_{t+1} = (1 + \mu)s_t + u_t + v_t$, so that the state variables are u_t and v_t. Following McCallum (1983a), the minimal state solution takes the form $s_t = b_0 + b_1(u_t + v_t)$. This implies that $E_t s_{t+1} = b_0$. So the interest parity condition becomes $b_0 = (1 + \mu)(b_0 + b_1(u_t + v_t)) + u_t + v_t$, which will hold for all realizations of u and v if $b_0 = 0$ and $b_1 = -1/(1 + \mu)$.

conducted, the outcomes of statistical tests may in fact be dependent on the behavior of monetary policy because policy may influence the time series properties of the nominal interest rate differential.

As noted earlier, tests of interest parity often report negative regression coefficients on the interest rate differential in (9.26). This finding is also consistent with the empirical evidence reported by Eichenbaum and Evans (1995). They estimated the impact of monetary shocks on nominal and real exchange rates and interest rate differentials between the United States and France, Germany, Italy, Japan, and the United Kingdom. A contractionary U.S. monetary policy shock leads to a persistent nominal and real appreciation of the dollar and a fall in $i_t^* - i_t + s_{t+1} - s_t$, where i is the U.S. interest rate and i^* is the foreign rate. Uncovered interest parity implies that this expression should have expected value equal to zero, yet it remains predictably low for several months. Rather than leading to an expected depreciation that offsets the rise in i, excess returns on U.S. dollar securities remain high for several months following a contractionary U.S. monetary policy shock.[10]

9.2.3 Sticky Prices

Just as was the case with the closed economy, flexible-price models of the open economy appear unable to replicate the size and persistence of monetary shocks on real variables. And just as with closed-economy models, this can be remedied by the introduction of nominal rigidities. Obstfeld and Rogoff (1996, ch. 10) provided an analysis of their basic two-country model under the assumption that prices are set one period in advance.[11] The presence of nominal rigidities leads to real effects of monetary disturbances through the channels discussed in chapter 6, but in an open economy new channels through which monetary disturbances have real effects are now also present.

Suppose $p(h)$, the domestic currency price of domestically produced goods, is set one period in advance and fixed for one period. A similar assumption is made for the foreign currency price of foreign-produced goods, $p^*(f)$. Although $p(h)$ and $p^*(f)$ are preset, the aggregate price indices in each country will fluctuate with the nominal exchange rate according to (9.11) and (9.12). Nominal depreciation, for example, raises the domestic price index p by increasing the domestic currency price of foreign-produced goods. This introduces a new channel, one absent in a closed economy, through which monetary disturbances can have an immediate impact on the

---

10. Eichenbaum and Evans measured monetary policy shocks in a variety of ways (VAR innovations to nonborrowed reserves relative to total reserves, VAR innovations to the federal funds rate, and Romer and Romer's 1989 measures of policy shifts). However, the identification scheme used in their VARs assumes that policy does not respond contemporaneously to the real exchange rate. This means that the specific illustrative policy response to the exchange rate that led to (9.27) is ruled out by their framework.

11. They also considered the case in which nominal wages are preset.

price level. Recall that in the closed economy, there is no distinction between the price of domestic output and the general price level. Nominal price rigidities imply that the price level cannot adjust immediately to monetary disturbances. Exchange rate movements alter the domestic currency price of foreign goods, allowing the consumer price index to move in response to such disturbances even in the presence of nominal rigidities.

Now suppose that in period t the home country's money supply rises unexpectedly relative to that of the foreign country.[12] Under Obstfeld and Rogoff's simplifying assumption that prices adjust completely after one period, both economies return to their steady state one period after the change in m. But during the one period in which product prices are preset, real output and consumptions levels will be affected.[13] And these real effects mean that the home country may run a current account surplus or deficit in response to the change in m. This effect on the current account alters the net asset positions of the two economies and can affect the new steady-state equilibrium.

Interpreting the model consisting of (9.11)–(9.21) as applying to deviations around the initial steady state, the Euler conditions (9.16) and (9.17) imply that $c_{t+1} - c_{t+1}^* = c_t - c_t^*$. Since the economies are in the new steady state after one period (i.e., in $t+1$), $c_{t+1} - c_{t+1}^* \equiv C$ is the steady-state consumption differential between the two countries. But since $c_t - c_t^* = c_{t+1} - c_{t+1}^* = C$ also, this relationship implies that relative consumption in the two economies immediately jumps in period t to the new steady-state value. Equation (9.23), which expresses relative money demands in the two economies, can then be written $m_t - m_t^* - s_t = C - \delta(s_{t+1} - s_t)$. Solving this equation forward for the nominal exchange rate (assuming no bubbles),

$$s_t = \frac{1}{1+\delta} \sum_{i=0}^{\infty} \left(\frac{\delta}{1+\delta} \right)^i (m_{t+i} - m_{t+i}^* - C).$$

If the change in $m_t - m_t^*$ is a permanent one-time change, one can let $\Omega \equiv m - m^*$ without time subscripts denote this permanent change. The equilibrium exchange rate is then equal to

$$s_t = \frac{1}{1+\delta} \sum_{i=0}^{\infty} \left(\frac{\delta}{1+\delta} \right)^i (\Omega - C) = \Omega - C. \tag{9.28}$$

---

12. An unexpected change is inconsistent with the assumption of perfect foresight implicit in the nonstochastic version of the model derived earlier. However, the linear approximation will continue to hold under uncertainty if future variables are replaced with their mathematical expectation.

13. In a situation in which the economies are initially in a steady state, the preset values for $p(h)$ and $p^*(f)$ will equal zero.

Since $\Omega - C$ is a constant, (9.28) implies that the exchange rate jumps immediately to its new steady state following a permanent change in relative nominal money supplies. If relative consumption levels do not adjust (i.e., if $C = 0$), then the permanent change in s is just equal to the relative change in nominal money supplies Ω. An increase in m relative to m^* (i.e., $\Omega > 0$) produces a depreciation of the home country currency. If $C \neq 0$, then changes in relative consumption affect the relative demand for money from (9.20) and (9.21). For example, if $C > 0$, consumption as well as money demand in the home country is higher than initially. Equilibrium between home money supply and home money demand can be restored with a smaller increase in the home price level. Since $p(h)$ and $p^*(f)$ are fixed for one period, the increase in p necessary to maintain real money demand and real money supply equal is generated by a depreciation (a rise in s). The larger the rise in home consumption, the larger the rise in real money demand and the smaller the necessary rise in s. This is just what (9.28) says.

Although the impact of a change in $m - m^*$ on the exchange rate, given C, has been determined, the real consumption differential is itself endogenous. To determine C requires several steps. First, the linear approximation to the current account relates the home country's accumulation of net assets to the excess of its real income over its consumption: $b = y_t + [p_t(h) - p_t] - c_t = y_t - (1 - n)s_t - c_t$, where $p_t(h) - p_t = -(1 - n)s_t$ follows from (9.11) and the fact that $p_t(h)$ is fixed (and equal to zero) during period t. Similarly, for the foreign economy, $-nb/(1 - n) = y_t^* + ns_t - c_t^*$. Together, these imply

$$\frac{b}{1 - n} = (y_t - y_t^*) - (c_t - c_t^*) - s_t. \tag{9.29}$$

From (9.13) and (9.14), $y_t - y_t^* = s_t/(1 - q)$, so (9.29) becomes

$$\frac{b}{1 - n} = \left(\frac{q}{1 - q}\right)s_t - (c_t - c_t^*) = \left(\frac{q}{1 - q}\right)s_t - C, \tag{9.30}$$

where the definition of C is used as the consumption differential.

The last step is to use the steady-state relationship between consumption, income, and asset holdings given by (9.9) and (9.10) to eliminate b in (9.30) by expressing it in terms of the exchange rate and consumption differences. In the steady state, b is constant and current accounts are zero, so consumption equals real income inclusive of asset income. In terms of the linear approximation, (9.9) and (9.10) become

$$c = rb + y + [p(h) - p] = rb + y - (1 - n)[s + p^*(f) - p(h)] \tag{9.31}$$

and

$$c^* = -\left(\frac{n}{1-n}\right)rb + y^* + n[s + p^*(f) - p(h)].$$ (9.32)

From the steady-state labor-leisure choice linking output and consumption given in (9.18) and (9.19), $(2-q)(y-y^*) = -(c-c^*)$, and from the link between relative prices and demand from (9.13) and (9.14), $y - y^* = [s + p^*(f) - p(h)]/(1-q)$. Using these relationships, one can now subtract (9.32) from (9.31), yielding

$$\mathcal{C} = \left(\frac{1}{1-n}\right)rb + (y - y^*) - [s + p^*(f) - p(h)]$$

$$= \left(\frac{1}{1-n}\right)rb + q(y - y^*)$$

$$= \left(\frac{1}{1-n}\right)rb + \left(\frac{q}{q-2}\right)\mathcal{C}.$$

Finally, this yields

$$b = \left(\frac{1-n}{r}\right)\left(\frac{2}{2-q}\right)\mathcal{C}.$$ (9.33)

Substituting (9.33) into (9.30), $[2/(2-q)]\mathcal{C}/r = qs_t/(1-q) - \mathcal{C}$. Solving for s in terms of $\mathcal{C}$,

$$s_t = \psi\mathcal{C},$$ (9.34)

where $\psi = (1-q)[1 + 2/r(2-q)]/q > 0$. But from (9.28), $s_t = \Omega - \mathcal{C}$, so $\psi\mathcal{C} = \Omega - \mathcal{C}$. It follows that the consumption differential is $\mathcal{C} = \Omega/(1+\psi)$. The equilibrium nominal exchange rate adjustment to a permanent change in the home country's nominal money supply is then given by

$$s_t = \left(\frac{\psi}{1+\psi}\right)\Omega < \Omega.$$

With $\psi > 0$, the domestic monetary expansion leads to a depreciation that is less than proportional to the increase in m. This induces an expansion in domestic production and consumption. Consumption rises by less than income, so the home country runs a current account surplus and accumulates assets that represent claims against the future income of the foreign country. This allows the home country to maintain higher consumption forever. As noted, consumption levels jump immediately to their new steady state with $\mathcal{C} = \Omega/(1+\psi) > 0$.

The two-country model employed in this section has the advantage of being based on the clearly specified decision problems faced by agents in the model. As a consequence, the responses of consumption, output, interest rates, and the exchange rate are consistent with optimizing behavior. Unanticipated monetary disturbances can have a permanent impact on real consumption levels and welfare when prices are preset. These effects arise because the output effects of a monetary surprise alter each country's current account, thereby altering their relative asset positions. A monetary expansion in the home country, for instance, produces a currency depreciation and a rise in the domestic price level p. This, in turn, induces a temporary expansion in output in the home country (see (9.13)). With consumption determined on the basis of permanent income, consumption rises less than output, leading the home country to run a trade surplus as the excess of output over domestic consumption is exported. As payment for these exports, the home country receives claims against the future output of the foreign country. Home consumption does rise, even though the increase in output lasts only one period, as the home country's permanent income has risen by the annuity value of its claim on future foreign output.

A domestic monetary expansion leads to permanently higher real consumption for domestic residents; welfare is increased. This observation suggests that each country has an incentive to engage in a monetary expansion. However, a joint proportionate expansion of each country's money supply leaves $m - m^*$ unchanged. There are then no exchange rate effects, and relative consumption levels do not change. After one period, when prices fully adjust, a proportional change in $p(h)$ and $p^*(f)$ returns both economies to the initial equilibrium. But since output is inefficiently low because monopolistic competition is present, the one-period rise in output does increase welfare in both countries. Both countries have an incentive to expand their money supplies, either individually or in a coordinated fashion.

This analysis involved changes in money supplies that were unexpected. If they had been anticipated, the level at which price setters would set individual goods prices would have incorporated expectations of money supply changes. As noted in chapter 5, fully anticipated changes in the nominal money supply will not have the real effects that unexpected changes do. As noted in chapter 7, the incentive to create surprise expansions can, in equilibrium, lead to steady inflation without the welfare gains an unanticipated expansion would bring.

Unanticipated permanent changes in the money supply can have permanent effects on the international distribution of wealth in the Obstfeld-Rogoff model when there are nominal rigidities. Corsetti and Presenti (2001) developed a two-country model with microeconomic foundations similar to those in the Obstfeld-Rogoff model but in which preferences are specified so that changes in national money supplies do not cause wealth redistributions. Corsetti and Presenti assumed the elasticity of output supply with respect to relative prices and the elasticity of substitution between the home-produced and foreign-produced goods are both equal to 1. Thus, an increase in the relative price of the foreign good (a decline in the terms of trade) lowers the purchasing power of domestic agents but also leads to a rise in the demand for domestic goods that increases nominal incomes. These two effects cancel, leaving the current account and international lending and borrowing unaffected. By eliminating current account effects, the Corsetti-Presenti model allows for a tractable closed-form solution with one-period nominal wage rigidity and permits determination of the impact of policy changes on welfare.

A large literature has studied open-economy models that are explicitly based on optimizing behavior by firms and households but that also incorporate nominal rigidities. Besides the work of Obstfeld and Rogoff (1995; 1996) and Corsetti and Presenti (2001), examples include Betts and Devereux (2000); Obstfeld and Rogoff (2000); Benigno and Benigno (2001); Corsetti and Presenti (2002); and Kollmann (2001). Lane (2001) and Engel (2002) provided surveys of the "new open economy macroeconomics."

9.3   Policy Coordination

An important issue facing economies linked by trade and capital flows is the role to be played by policy coordination. Monetary policy actions by one country will affect other countries, leading to spillover effects that open the possibility of gains from policy coordination. As demonstrated in the previous section, the real effects of an unanticipated change in the nominal money supply in the two-country model depend on how $m - m^*$ is affected. A rise in m, holding m^* unchanged, will produce home country depreciation, shifting world demand toward the home country's output. With preset prices and output demand determined, the exchange rate movement represents an important channel through which a monetary expansion affects domestic output. If both monetary authorities attempt to generate output expansions by increasing their money supplies, this exchange rate channel will not operate because the exchange rate depends on relative money supplies. Thus, the impact of an unanticipated change in m depends critically on the behavior of m^*.

This dependence raises the issue of whether there are gains from coordinating monetary policy. Hamada (1976) is closely identified with the basic approach that has been used to analyze policy coordination, and this section develops a version of his framework. Canzoneri and Henderson (1989) provided an extensive discussion of monetary policy coordination issues; a survey was provided by Currie and Levine (1991).

Consider a model with two economies. Assume that each economy's policy authority can choose its inflation rate and that because of nominal rigidities, monetary policy can have real effects in the short run. In this context, a complete specification of policy behavior is more complicated than in a closed-economy setting; one must specify how each national policy authority interacts strategically with the other policy authority. Two possibilities are considered. Coordinated policy is considered first, meaning that inflation rates in the two economies are chosen jointly to maximize a weighted sum of the objective functions of the two policy authorities. Noncoordinated policy is considered second, with the policy authorities interacting in a Nash equilibrium. In this setting, each policy authority sets its own inflation rate to maximize its objective function, taking as given the inflation rate in the other economy. These clearly are not the only possibilities. One economy may act as a Stackelberg leader, recognizing the impact its choice has on the inflation rate set by the other economy. Reputational considerations along the lines studied in chapter 7 can also be incorporated into the analysis (see Canzoneri and Henderson 1989).

9.3.1   The Basic Model

The two-country model is specified as a linear system in log deviations around a steady state and represents an extension to the open-economy environment of the sticky wage AS-IS model (see chapter 6). The LM relationship is dispensed with by assuming that the monetary policy authorities in the two countries set the inflation rate directly. An asterisk will denote the foreign economy, and ρ will be the real exchange rate, defined as the relative price of home and foreign output, expressed in terms of the home currency; a rise in ρ represents a real depreciation for the home economy. If s is the nominal exchange rate and $p(h)$ and $p^*(f)$ are the prices of home and foreign output, then $\rho = s + p^*(f) - p(h)$. The model should be viewed as an approximation that is appropriate when nominal wages are set in advance so that unanticipated movements in inflation affect real output. In addition to aggregate supply and demand relationships for each economy, an interest parity condition links the real interest rate differential to anticipated changes in the real exchange rate:

$$y_t = -b_1\rho_t + b_2(\pi_t - \mathrm{E}_{t-1}\pi_t) + e_t \tag{9.35}$$

$$y_t^* = b_1\rho_t + b_2(\pi_t^* - \mathrm{E}_{t-1}\pi_t^*) + e_t^* \tag{9.36}$$

$$y_t = a_1\rho_t - a_2r_t + a_3y_t^* + u_t \tag{9.37}$$

$$y_t^* = -a_1\rho_t - a_2r_t^* + a_3y_t + u_t^* \tag{9.38}$$

$$\rho_t = r_t^* - r_t + \mathrm{E}_t\rho_{t+1}. \tag{9.39}$$

Equations (9.35) and (9.36) relate output to inflation surprises and the real exchange rate. A real exchange rate depreciation reduces home aggregate supply by raising the price of imported materials and by raising consumer prices relative to producer prices. This latter effect increases the real wage in terms of producer prices. Equations (9.37) and (9.38) make demand in each country an increasing function of output in the other to reflect spillover effects that arise as an increase in output in one country raises demand for the goods produced by the other. A rise in ρ_t (a real domestic depreciation) makes domestically produced goods less expensive relative to foreign goods and shifts demand away from foreign output and toward home output.

To simplify the analysis, the inflation rate is treated as the choice variable of the policymaker. An alternative approach to treating inflation as the policy variable would be to specify money demand relationships for each country and then take the nominal money supply as the policy instrument. This would complicate the analysis without offering any new insights.

A third approach would be to replace r_t with $i_t - E_t\pi_{t+1}$, where i_t is the nominal interest rate, and treat i_t as the policy instrument. An advantage of this approach is that it more closely reflects the way most central banks actually implement policy. Because a number of new issues arise under nominal interest rate policies (see section 8.3.3), policy is interpreted as choosing the rate of inflation in order to focus, in this section, on the role of policy coordination. Finally, a further simplification is reflected in the assumption that the parameters (the a_i' and b_i') are the same in the two countries.

Demand (u_t, u_t^*) and supply (e_t, e_t^*) shocks are included to introduce a role for stabilization policy. These disturbances are assumed to be mean zero serially uncorrelated processes, but here they are allowed to be correlated to distinguish between common shocks that affect both economies and asymmetric shocks that originate in a single economy.

Equation (9.39) is an uncovered interest rate parity condition. Rewritten in the form $r_t = r_t^* + E_t\rho_{t+1} - \rho_t$, it implies that the home country real interest rate will exceed the foreign real rate if the home country is expected to experience a real depreciation.

Evaluating outcomes under coordinated and noncoordinated policies requires some assumption about the objective functions of the policymakers. In models built more explicitly on the behavior of optimizing agents, alternative policies could be ranked according to their implications for the utility of the agents in the economies. Here a common approach is followed in which polices are evaluated on the basis of loss functions that depend on output variability and inflation variability:

$$V_t = \sum_{i=0}^{\infty} \beta^i (\lambda y_{t+i}^2 + \pi_{t+i}^2) \tag{9.40}$$

$$V_t^* = \sum_{i=0}^{\infty} \beta^i [\lambda (y_{t+i}^*)^2 + (\pi_{t+i}^*)^2]. \tag{9.41}$$

The parameter β is a discount factor between 0 and 1. The weight attached to output fluctuations relative to inflation fluctuations is λ. These objective functions are ad hoc, but they capture the idea that policymakers prefer to minimize output fluctuations around the steady state and fluctuations of inflation.[14] Objective functions of this basic form have played a major role in the analysis of policy. They reflect the assumption that steady-state output will be independent of monetary policy, so policy should focus on minimizing fluctuations around the steady state, not on the level of output.

The model can be solved to yield expressions for equilibrium output in each economy and for the real exchange rate. To obtain the real exchange rate, first subtract foreign aggregate demand (9.38) from domestic aggregate demand (9.37), using the interest parity condition (9.39) to eliminate $r_t - r_t^*$. This process yields an expression for $y_t - y_t^*$. Next, subtract foreign aggregate supply (9.36) from domestic aggregate supply (9.35) to yield a second expression for $y_t - y_t^*$. Equating these two expressions and solving for the equilibrium real exchange rate leads to the following:

$$\rho_t = \frac{1}{B}\{b_2(1+a_3)[(\pi_t - \mathrm{E}_{t-1}\pi_t) - (\pi_t^* - \mathrm{E}_{t-1}\pi_t^*)]$$

$$+ (1+a_3)(e_t - e_t^*) - (u_t - u_t^*) + a_2\mathrm{E}_t\rho_{t+1}\}, \tag{9.42}$$

where $B \equiv 2a_1 + a_2 + 2b_1(1+a_3) > 0$. An unanticipated rise in domestic inflation relative to unanticipated foreign inflation or in e_t relative to e_t^* will increase domestic output supply relative to foreign output. Equilibrium requires a decline in the relative price of domestic output; the real exchange rate rises (depreciates), shifting demand toward domestic output. If the domestic aggregate demand shock exceeds the foreign shock, $u_t - u_t^* > 0$, the relative price of domestic output must rise (ρ must fall) to shift demand toward foreign output. A rise in the expected future exchange rate also leads to a rise in the current equilibrium ρ. If ρ were to increase by the same amount as the rise in $\mathrm{E}_t\rho_{t+1}$, the interest differential $r_t - r_t^*$ would be left unchanged, but the higher ρ would, from (9.35) and (9.36), lower domestic supply relative to foreign supply. So ρ rises by less than the increase in $\mathrm{E}_t\rho_{t+1}$ to maintain goods market equilibrium.[15]

---

14. The steady-state values of y and y^* are zero by definition. The assumption that the policy loss functions depend on the variance of output around its steady-state level, and not on some higher output target, is critical for the determination of average inflation. Chapter 7 deals extensively with the time inconsistency issues that arise when policymakers target a level of output that exceeds the economy's equilibrium level.

15. The coefficient on $\mathrm{E}_t\rho_{t+1}$, a_2/B is less than 1 in absolute value.

Notice that (9.42) can be written as $\rho_t = A\mathrm{E}_t\rho_{t+1} + v_t$, where $0 < A < 1$ and v_t is white noise, since the disturbances are assumed to be serially uncorrelated and the same will be true of the inflation forecast errors under rational expectations. It follows that $\mathrm{E}_t\rho_{t+1} = 0$ in any no-bubbles solution. The expected future real exchange rate would be nonzero if either the aggregate demand or aggregate supply shocks were serially correlated.

Now the expression for the equilibrium real exchange rate can be substituted into the aggregate supply relationships (9.35) and (9.36) to yield

$$y_t = b_2 A_1(\pi_t - \mathrm{E}_{t-1}\pi_t) + b_2 A_2(\pi_t^* - \mathrm{E}_{t-1}\pi_t^*)$$

$$- a_2 A_3 \mathrm{E}_t\rho_{t+1} + A_1 e_t + A_2 e_t^* + A_3(u_t - u_t^*) \tag{9.43}$$

$$y_t^* = b_2 A_2(\pi_t - \mathrm{E}_{t-1}\pi_t) + b_2 A_1(\pi_t^* - \mathrm{E}_{t-1}\pi_t^*)$$

$$+ a_2 A_3 \mathrm{E}_t\rho_{t+1} + A_2 e_t + A_1 e_t^* - A_3(u_t - u_t^*). \tag{9.44}$$

The A_i parameters are given by

$$A_1 = \frac{2a_1 + a_2 + b_1(1 + a_3)}{B} > 0$$

$$A_2 = \frac{b_1(1 + a_3)}{B} > 0$$

$$A_3 = \frac{b_1}{B} > 0.$$

Equations (9.43) and (9.44) reveal the spillover effects through which the inflation choice of one economy affects the other economy when $b_2 A_2 \neq 0$. An increase in inflation in the home economy (assuming it is unanticipated) leads to a real depreciation. This occurs because unanticipated inflation leads to a home output expansion (see (9.35)). Equilibrium requires a rise in demand for home country production. In the closed economy, this occurs through a fall in the real interest rate. In the open economy, an additional channel of adjustment arises from the role of the real exchange rate. Given that $\mathrm{E}_t\rho_{t+1} = 0$, the interest parity condition (9.39) becomes $\rho_t = r_t^* - r_t$, so for given r_t^*, the fall in r_t requires a rise in ρ_t (a real depreciation), which also serves to raise home demand.

The rise in ρ_t represents a real appreciation for the foreign economy, and this raises consumer price wages relative to producer price wages and increases aggregate output in the foreign economy (see (9.36)). As a result, an expansion in the home country produces an economic expansion in the foreign country. But as (9.42) shows, a surprise inflation by both countries leaves the real exchange rate unaffected. It is this link that opens the possibility that outcomes will depend on the extent to which the two countries coordinate their policies.

9.3.2   Equilibrium with Coordination

To focus on the implications of policy coordination, attention is restricted to the case of a common aggregate supply shock, common in the sense that it affects both countries. That is, suppose $e_t = e_t^* \equiv \varepsilon_t$, where ε_t is the common disturbance. For the rest of this section, assume $u \equiv u^* \equiv 0$, so that ε represents the only disturbance.

In solving for equilibrium outcomes under alternative policy interactions, the objective functions (9.40) and (9.41) simplify to a sequence of one-period problems (the problem is a static one with no link between periods). Assuming that the policy authority is able to set the inflation rate after observing the supply shock ε_t, the decision problem under a coordinated policy is

$$\min_{\pi,\pi^*}\left\{\frac{1}{2}[\lambda y_t^2 + \pi_t^2] + \frac{1}{2}[\lambda(y_t^*)^2 + (\pi_t^*)^2]\right\}$$

subject to (9.43) and (9.44).[16] The first-order conditions are

$$0 = \lambda b_2 A_1 y_t + \pi_t + \lambda b_2 A_2 y_t^*$$

$$= (1 + \lambda b_2^2 A_1^2 + \lambda b_2^2 A_2^2)\pi_t + 2\lambda b_2^2 A_1 A_2 \pi_t^* + \lambda b_2 \varepsilon_t$$

$$0 = \lambda b_2 A_2 y_t + \lambda b_2 A_1 y_t^* + \pi_t^*$$

$$= (1 + \lambda b_2^2 A_1^2 + \lambda b_2^2 A_2^2)\pi_t^* + 2\lambda b_2^2 A_1 A_2 \pi_t + \lambda b_2 \varepsilon_t,$$

which used the fact that $A_1 + A_2 = 1$ and the result that the first-order conditions imply $E_{t-1}\pi_t = E_{t-1}\pi_t^* = 0$.[17] Solving these two equations yields the equilibrium inflation rates under coordination:

$$\pi_{c,t} = \pi_{c,t}^* = -\left(\frac{\lambda b_2}{1 + \lambda b_2^2}\right)\varepsilon_t \equiv -\theta_c \varepsilon_t. \tag{9.45}$$

16. In defining the objective function under coordinated policy, it is assumed that each country's utility receives equal weight.

17. Writing out the first-order condition for π_t in full, $0 = \pi_t + \lambda b_2^2 (A_1^2 + A_2^2)(\pi_t - E_{t-1}\pi_t) + 2\lambda b_2^2 A_1 A_2 (\pi_t^* - E_{t-1}\pi_t^*) + 2\lambda b_2 \varepsilon_t$. Taking expectations conditional on time $t-1$ information (i.e., prior to the realization of ε_t), one obtains $E_{t-1}\pi_t = 0$.

Both countries maintain equal inflation rates. In response to an adverse supply shock $(\varepsilon < 0)$, inflation in both countries rises to offset partially the decline in output. Substituting (9.45) into the expressions for output and the equilibrium real exchange rate,

$$y_{c,t} = y_{c,t}^* = \left(\frac{1}{1 + \lambda b_2^2}\right)\varepsilon_t < \varepsilon_t$$

and

$$p_t = 0.$$

The policy response acts to offset partially the output effects of the supply shock. The larger the weight placed on output in the loss function (λ), the larger the inflation response and the more output is stabilized. Because both economies respond symmetrically, the real exchange rate is left unaffected.[18]

9.3.3   Equilibrium without Coordination

When policy is not coordinated, some assumption must be made about the nature of the strategic interaction between the two separate policy authorities. One natural case to consider corresponds to a Nash equilibrium; the policy authorities choose inflation to minimize loss, taking as given the inflation rate in the other economy. An alternative case arises when one country behaves as a Stackelberg leader, taking into account how the other policy authority will respond to the leader's choice of inflation. The Nash case is analyzed, and the Stackelberg case is studied as a problem at the end of the chapter.

The home policy authority picks inflation to minimize $\lambda y_t^2 + \pi_t^2$, taking π_t^* as given. The first-order condition is

$$0 = \lambda b_2 A_1 y_t + \pi_t$$

$$= (1 + \lambda b_2^2 A_1^2)\pi_t + \lambda b_2^2 A_1 A_2 \pi_t^* + \lambda b_2 A_1 \varepsilon_t,$$

so that the home country's reaction function is

$$\pi_t = -\left(\frac{\lambda b_2^2 A_1 A_2}{1 + \lambda b_2^2 A_1^2}\right)\pi_t^* - \left(\frac{\lambda b_2 A_1}{1 + b_2^2 A_1^2}\right)\varepsilon_t. \tag{9.46a}$$

A rise in the foreign country's inflation rate is expansionary for the domestic economy (see (9.43)). The domestic policy authority lowers domestic inflation to partially

---

18. This would not be the case in response to an asymmetric supply shock. See problem 4 at the end of this chapter.

stabilize domestic output. A parallel treatment of the foreign country policy authority's decision problem leads to the reaction function

$$\pi_t^* = -\left(\frac{\lambda b_2^2 A_1 A_2}{1 + \lambda b_2^2 A_1^2}\right)\pi_t - \left(\frac{\lambda b_2 A_1}{1 + \lambda b_2^2 A_1^2}\right)\varepsilon_t. \tag{9.47}$$

Jointly solving these two reaction functions for the Nash equilibrium inflation rates yields

$$\pi_{N,t} = \pi_{N,t}^* = -\left(\frac{\lambda b_2 A_1}{1 + \lambda b_2^2 A_1}\right)\varepsilon_t \equiv -\theta_N \varepsilon_t. \tag{9.48}$$

How does stabilization policy with noncoordinated policies compare with the coordinated policy response given in (9.45)? Since $A_1 < 1$,

$$|\theta_N| < |\theta_c|.$$

Policy responds less to the aggregate supply shock in the absence of coordination, and as a result, output fluctuates more:

$$y_{N,t} = y_{N,t}^* = \left(\frac{1}{1 + \lambda b_2^2 A_1}\right)\varepsilon_t > \left(\frac{1}{1 + \lambda b_2^2}\right)\varepsilon_t.$$

Because output and inflation responses are symmetric in the Nash equilibrium, the real exchange rate does not respond to ε_t.

Why does policy respond less in the absence of coordination? For each individual policymaker, the perceived marginal output gain from more inflation when there is an adverse realization of ε reflects the two channels through which inflation affects output. First, surprise inflation directly increases real output because of the assumption of nominal rigidities. This direct effect is given by the term $b_2(\pi_t - E_{t-1}\pi_t)$ in (9.35). Second, for given foreign inflation, a rise in home inflation leads to a real depreciation (see (9.42)) and, again from (9.35), the rise in ρ_t acts to lower output, reducing the net impact of inflation on output. With π^* treated as given, the exchange rate channel implies that a larger inflation increase is necessary to offset the output effects of an adverse supply shock. Since inflation is costly, the optimal policy response involves a smaller inflation response and less output stabilization. With a coordinated policy, the decision problem faced by the policy authority recognizes that a symmetric increase in inflation in both countries leaves the real exchange rate unaffected. With inflation perceived to have a larger marginal impact on output, the optimal response is to stabilize more.

The loss functions of the two countries can be evaluated under the alternative policy regimes (coordination and noncoordination). Because the two countries have been specified symmetrically, the value of the loss function will be the same for each. For the domestic economy, the expected loss when policies are coordinated is equal to

$$L^c = \frac{1}{2} \left(\frac{1}{1 + \lambda b_2^2} \right) \lambda \sigma_\varepsilon^2.$$

When policies are determined in a Nash noncooperative equilibrium,

$$L^N = \frac{1}{2} \left[\frac{1 + \lambda b_2^2 A_1^2}{(1 + \lambda b_2^2 A_1)^2} \right] \lambda \sigma_\varepsilon^2.$$

Because $0 < A_1 < 1$, it follows that $L^c < L^N$; coordination achieves a better outcome than occurs in the Nash equilibrium.

This example appears to imply that coordination will always dominate noncoordination. It is important to recall that the only source of disturbance was a common aggregate supply shock. The case of asymmetric shocks is addressed in problem 4 at the end of this chapter. But even when there are only common shocks, coordination need not always be superior. Rogoff (1985a) provided a counterexample. His argument is based on a model in which optimal policy is time-inconsistent (see chapter 7) but one can briefly describe the intuition behind Rogoff's results. A coordinated monetary expansion leads to a larger short-run real output expansion because it avoids changes in the real exchange rate. But this fact increases the incentive to engineer a surprise monetary expansion if the policymakers believe the natural rate of output is too low. Wage and price setters will anticipate this tactic, together with the associated higher inflation. Equilibrium involves higher inflation, but because it has been anticipated, output (which depends on inflation surprises) does not increase. Consequently, coordination leads to better stabilization but higher average inflation. If the costs of the latter are high enough, noncoordination can dominate coordination.

The discussion of policy coordination serves to illustrate several important aspects of open-economy monetary economics. First, the real exchange rate is the relative price of output in the two countries, so it plays an important role in equilibrating relative demand and supply in the two countries. Second, foreign shocks matter for the domestic economy; both aggregate supply shocks and aggregate demand shocks originating in the foreign economy affect output in the domestic economy. As (9.43) and (9.44) show, however, the model implies that common demand shocks that leave $u - u^*$ unaffected have no effect on output levels or the real exchange rate. Since these shocks do affect demand in each country, a common demand shock raises real interest rates in each country. Third, policy coordination can matter.

Although the two-country model of this section is useful, it has several omissions that may limit the insights to be gained from its use. First, the aggregate demand and aggregate supply relationships are not derived explicitly within an optimizing framework. As noted in chapter 8 and in the Obstfeld-Rogoff model, expectations of future income will play a role when consumption is determined by forward-looking, rational economic agents. Second, there is no role for current account imbalances to affect equilibrium through their effects on foreign asset holdings. Third, no distinction has been drawn between the price of domestic output and the price index relevant for domestic residents. The loss function for the policymaker may depend on consumer price inflation. Fourth, the inflation rate was treated as the instrument of policy, directly controllable by the central bank. Finally, the model, like the Obstfeld-Rogoff example, assumed one-period nominal contracts. Such a formulation fails to capture the persistence that generally characterizes actual inflation and the lags between changes in policy and the resulting changes in output and inflation.

9.4 The Small Open Economy

A two-country model provides a useful framework for examining policy interactions in an environment in which developments in one economy affect the other. For many economies, however, domestic developments have little or no impact on other economies. Decisions about policy can, in this case, treat foreign interest rates, output levels, and inflation as exogenous because the domestic economy is small relative to the rest of the world. The small open economy is a useful construct for analyzing issues when developments in the country of interest are unlikely to influence other economies.

In the small-open-economy case, the model of the previous section simplifies to become

$$y_t = -b_1\rho_t + b_2(p_t - E_{t-1}p_t) + e_t \tag{9.49}$$

$$y_t = a_1\rho_t - a_2r_t + u_t \tag{9.50}$$

$$\rho_t = r_t^* - r_t + E_t\rho_{t+1}. \tag{9.51}$$

The real exchange rate ρ is equal to $s + p^* - p$, where s is the nominal exchange rate, and p^* and p are the prices of foreign and domestic output, all expressed in log terms. The aggregate supply relationship has been written in terms of the unanticipated price level rather than unanticipated inflation.[19] The dependence of output on price surprises arises from the presence of nominal wage and price rigidities. With foreign income and consumption exogenous, the impact of world consumption on the domestic economy can be viewed as one of the factors giving rise to the disturbance term u_t.

---

19. Since $p_t - E_{t-1}p_t = p_t - p_{t-1} - (E_{t-1}p_t - p_{t-1}) = \pi_t - E_{t-1}\pi_t$, the two formulations are equivalent.

Consumer prices in the domestic economy are defined as

$$q_t = hp_t + (1 - h)(s_t + p_t^*), \tag{9.52}$$

where h is the share of domestic output in the consumer price index, and the Fisher relationship links the real rate of interest appearing in (9.50) and (9.51) with the nominal interest rate,

$$r_t = i_t - E_t p_{t+1} + p_t. \tag{9.53}$$

Uncovered interest parity links nominal interest rates. Since i^* will be exogenous from the perspective of the small open economy, (9.51) can be written as

$$i_t = E_t s_{t+1} - s_t + i_t^*, \tag{9.54}$$

where $i^* = r^* + E_t p_{t+1}^* - p_t^*$. Finally, real money demand is assumed to be given by

$$m_t - q_t = y_t - ci_t + v_t. \tag{9.55}$$

Notice that the basic structure of the model, like the closed-economy models of chapter 6 based on wage and/or price rigidities, displays the classical dichotomy between the real and monetary sectors if wages are flexible. That is, if wages adjust completely to equate labor demand and labor supply, the price surprise term in (9.49) disappears.[20] In this case, (9.49)–(9.51) constitute a three-equation system for real output, the real interest rate, and the real exchange rate. Using the interest parity condition to eliminate r_t from the aggregate demand relationship, and setting the resulting expression for output equal to aggregate supply, yields the following equation for the equilibrium real exchange rate in the absence of nominal rigidities:

$$(a_1 + a_2 + b_1)p_t = a_2(r_t^* + E_t p_{t+1}) + e_t - u_t.$$

This can be solved forward for p_t:

$$p_t = \sum_{i=0}^{\infty} d^i E_t \left(\frac{a_2 r_{t+i}^* + e_{t+i} - u_{t+i}}{a_1 + a_2 + b_1} \right)$$

$$= d \sum_{i=0}^{\infty} d^i E_t r_{t+i}^* + \frac{e_t - u_t}{a_1 + a_2 + b_1},$$

---

20. Recall from chapter 6 that the assumption behind an aggregate supply function such as (9.49) is that nominal wages are set in advance on the basis of expectations of the price level, and actual employment is determined by firms on the basis of realized real wages (and therefore on the actual price level).

where $d \equiv a_2/(a_1 + a_2 + b_1) < 1$ and the second equals sign follows from the assumption that e and u are serially uncorrelated processes. The real exchange rate responds to excess supply for domestic output; if $e_t - u_t > 0$, a real depreciation increases aggregate demand and lowers aggregate supply to restore goods market equilibrium.

The monetary sector consists of (9.52)–(9.55), plus the definition of the nominal exchange rate as $s_t = p_t - p_t^* + p_t$. When wages and prices are flexible, these determine the two price levels p (the price of domestic output) and q (the consumer price index). From the Fisher equation, the money demand equation, and the definition of q_t,

$$m_t - p_t = y_t + (1 - h)\rho_t - c(r_t + E_t p_{t+1} - p_t) + v_t.$$

Because the real values are exogenous with respect to the monetary sector when there are no nominal rigidities, this equation can be solved for the equilibrium value of p_t:

$$p_t = \left(\frac{1}{1+c}\right) \sum_{i=0}^{\infty} \left(\frac{c}{1+c}\right)^i E_t(m_{t+i} - z_{t+i} - v_{t+i}),$$

where $z_{t+i} \equiv y_{t+i} + (1 - h)\rho_{t+i} - cr_{t+i}$. The equilibrium p_t depends not just on the current money supply but also on the expected future path of m. Since (9.52) implies $p_t = q_t - (1 - h)\rho_t$, the equilibrium behavior of the domestic consumer price index q_t follows from the solutions for p_t and ρ_t.

When nominal wages are set in advance, the classical dichotomy no longer holds. With $p_t - E_{t-1}p_t$ affecting the real wage, employment, and output, any disturbance in the monetary sector that was unanticipated will affect output, the real interest rate, and the real exchange rate. Since the model does not incorporate any mechanism to generate real persistence, these effects last only for one period.

With nominal wage rigidity, monetary policy affects real aggregate demand through both interest rate and exchange rate channels. As can be seen from (9.50), these two variables appear in the combination $a_1\rho_t - a_2r_t$. For this reason, the interest rate and exchange rate are often combined to create a *monetary conditions index*; in the context of the present model, this index would be equal to $r_t - a_1\rho_t/a_2$. Variations in the real interest rate and real exchange rate that leave this linear combination unchanged would be neutral in their impact on aggregate demand because the reduction in domestic aggregate demand caused by a higher real interest rate would be offset by a depreciation in the real exchange rate.

9.4.1   Flexible Exchange Rates

Suppose that nominal wages are set in advance, but the nominal exchange rate is free to adjust flexibly in the face of economic disturbances. In addition, assume that monetary policy is implemented through control of the nominal money supply. In this case, the model consisting of (9.49)–(9.54) can be reduced to two equations involving the price level, the nominal exchange rate, and the nominal money supply (see the chapter appendix for details). Equilibrium will depend on expectations of the period $t+1$ exchange rate, and the response of the economy to current policy actions may depend on how these expectations are affected.

To determine how the exchange rate and the price level respond to monetary shocks, assume a specific process for the nominal money supply. To allow for a distinction between transitory and permanent monetary shocks, assume

$$m_t = \mu + m_{t-1} + \varphi_t - \gamma \varphi_{t-1}, \qquad 0 \le \gamma \le 1, \tag{9.56}$$

where φ is a serially uncorrelated white noise process. If $\gamma = 0$, m_t follows a random walk with drift μ; innovations φ have a permanent impact on the level of m. If $\gamma = 1$, the money supply is white noise around a deterministic trend. If $0 < \gamma < 1$, a fraction $(1 - \gamma)$ of the innovation has a permanent effect on the level of the money supply.

To analyze the impact of foreign price shocks on the home country, let

$$p_t^* = \pi^* + p_{t-1}^* + \phi_t, \tag{9.57}$$

where ϕ is a random white noise disturbance. This allows for a constant average foreign inflation rate of π^* with permanent shifts in the price path due to the realizations of ϕ.

Using the method of undetermined coefficients, the following solutions for p_t and s_t are consistent with (9.49)–(9.54) and with rational expectations (see appendix):

$$p_t = k_0 + m_{t-1} + \frac{B_2[1 + c(1 - \gamma)]}{K} \varphi_t - \gamma \varphi_{t-1}$$

$$+ \frac{[(A_2 - B_2)u_t - A_2 e_t - B_2 v_t]}{K} \tag{9.58}$$

$$s_t = d_0 + m_{t-1} - p_{t-1}^* - \phi_t - \frac{B_1[1 + c(1 - \gamma)]}{K} \varphi_t$$

$$- \gamma \varphi_{t-1} + \frac{[(B_1 - A_1)u_t + A_1 e_t + B_1 v_t]}{K}, \tag{9.59}$$

where $A_1 = h - a_1 - a_2$, $A_2 = 1 + c - A_1 > 0$, $B_1 = -(a_1 + a_2 + b_1 + b_2) < 0$, $B_2 = a_1 + a_2 + b_1 > 0$, and $K = -[(1 + c)B_1 + b_2 A_1]$. The constant k_0 is given by

$$k_0 = (1 + c)\mu + \left[c - \frac{a_2(1 - h - b_1)}{a_1 + b_1} \right] r^*,$$

and $d_0 = k_0 - \pi^*$.

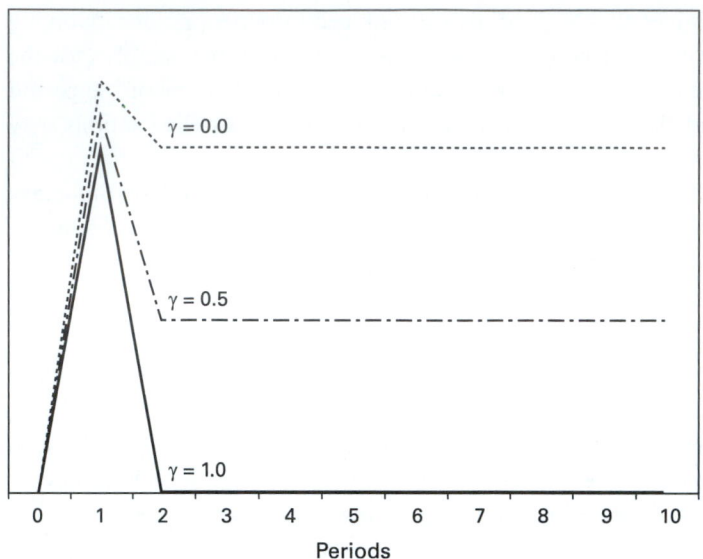

Figure 9.1
Response of nominal exchange rate to a monetary shock.

Of particular note is the way a flexible exchange rate insulates the domestic economy from the foreign price shock ϕ. Neither p^*_{t-1} nor ϕ_t affects the domestic price level under a flexible exchange rate system (see (9.58)). Instead, (9.59) shows how they move the nominal exchange rate to maintain the domestic currency price of foreign goods, $s + p^*$, unchanged. This insulates the real exchange rate and domestic output from fluctuations in the foreign price level.

With $B_2[1 + c(1 - \gamma)]/K > 0$ and $-B_1[1 + c(1 - \gamma)]/K > 0$, a positive monetary shock increases the equilibrium price level and the nominal exchange rate. That is, the domestic currency depreciates in response to a positive money shock. The effect is offset partially the following period if $\gamma > 0$. The shape of the exchange rate response to a monetary shock is shown in figure 9.1 for different values of γ.

The $\gamma < 1$ cases in figure 9.1 illustrate Dornbusch's (1976) overshooting result. To the extent that the rise in m is permanent (i.e., $\gamma < 1$), the price level and the nominal exchange rate eventually rise proportionately. With one-period nominal rigidities, this occurs in period 2. A rise in the nominal money supply that increases the real supply of money reduces the nominal interest rate to restore money market equilibrium. From the interest parity condition, the domestic nominal rate can fall only if the exchange rate is expected to fall. Yet the exchange rate will be higher than its initial value in period 2, so to generate an expectation of a fall, s must rise more than proportionately to the permanent rise in m. It is then expected to fall from period 1 to period 2; the nominal rate overshoots its new long-run value.

The Dornbusch overshooting result stands in contrast to Obstfeld and Rogoff's conclusion, derived in section 9.2.3, that a permanent change in the nominal money supply does not lead to overshooting. Instead, the nominal exchange rate jumps immediately to its new long-run level. This difference results from the ad hoc nature of aggregate demand in the model of this section. In the Obstfeld-Rogoff model, consumption is derived from the decision problem of the representative agent, with the Euler condition for consumption linking consumption choices over time. The desire to smooth consumption implies that consumption immediately jumps to its new equilibrium level. As a result, exchange rate overshooting is eliminated in the basic Obstfeld-Rogoff model.

One implication of the overshooting hypothesis is that exchange rate movements should follow a predictable or forecastable pattern in response to monetary shocks. A positive monetary shock leads to an immediate depreciation followed by an appreciation. The path of adjustment will depend on the extent of nominal rigidities in the economy because these influence the speed with which the economy adjusts in response to shocks. Such a predictable pattern is not clearly evident in the data. In fact, nominal exchange rates display close to random walk behavior over short time periods (Meese and Rogoff 1983). In a VAR-based study of exchange rate responses to U.S. monetary shocks, Eichenbaum and Evans (1995) did not find evidence of overshooting, but they did find sustained and predictable exchange rate movements following monetary policy shocks. A monetary contraction produces a small initial appreciation, with the effect growing so that the dollar appreciates for some time. However, in a study based on more direct measurement of policy changes, Bonser-Neal, Roley, and Sellon (1998) found general support for the overshooting hypothesis. They measured policy changes by using data on changes in the Federal Reserve's target for the federal funds rate, rather than the actual funds rate, and restricted attention to time periods during which the funds rate was the Fed's policy instrument.

9.4.2 Fixed Exchange Rates

Under a system of fixed exchange rates, the monetary authority is committed to using its policy instrument to maintain a constant nominal exchange rate. This commitment requires that the monetary authority stand ready to buy or sell domestic currency for foreign exchange to maintain the fixed exchange rate. When it is necessary to sell foreign exchange, such a policy will be unsustainable if the domestic central bank's reserves of foreign exchange are expected to go to zero. Such expectations can produce speculative attacks on the currency.[21] The analysis here considers only

---

21. See Krugman (1979) and Garber and Svensson (1995).

the case of a sustainable fixed rate. And to draw the sharpest contrast with the flexible exchange rate regime, it is assumed that the exchange rate is pegged. In practice,
most fixed exchange rate regimes allow rates to fluctuate within narrow bands.[22]

Normalizing the fixed rate at $s_t = 0$ for all t, the real exchange rate equals $p_t^* - p_t$.
Assuming the foreign price level follows (9.57), the basic model becomes

$$y_t = -b_1(p_t^* - p_t) + b_2(p_t - E_{t-1}p_t) + e_t$$

$$y_t = a_1(p_t^* - p_t) - a_2 r_t + u_t$$

$$r_t = r^* + \pi^* - (E_t p_{t+1} - p_t).$$

The nominal interest rate has been eliminated, since the interest parity condition and
the fixed exchange rate assumption imply that $i = r^* + \pi^*$. These three equations can
be solved for the price level, output, and the domestic real interest rate. The money
demand condition plays no role because m must endogenously adjust to maintain the
fixed exchange rate.

Solving for p_t,

$$p_t = \frac{(a_1 + b_1)p_t^* - a_2(r^* + \pi^*) + a_2 E_t p_{t+1} + b_2 E_{t-1}p_t + u_t - e_t}{a_1 + a_2 + b_1 + b_2}.$$

Using the method of undetermined coefficients, one obtains

$$p_t = p_t^* - \frac{a_2 r^*}{a_1 + b_1} + \frac{u_t - e_t - b_2 \phi_t}{a_1 + a_2 + b_1 + b_2}. \tag{9.60}$$

Comparing (9.60) to (9.58) reveals some of the major differences between the fixed
and flexible exchange rate systems. Under fixed exchange rates, the average domestic
rate of inflation must equal the foreign inflation rate: $E(p_{t+1} - p_t) = E(p_{t+1}^* - p_t^*) =
\pi^*$. The foreign price level and foreign price shocks (ϕ) affect domestic prices and
output under the fixed rate system. But domestic disturbances to money demand or
supply (φ and v) have no price level or output effects. This situation is in contrast to
the case under flexible exchange rates and is one reason that high-inflation economies
often attempt to fix their exchange rates with low-inflation countries. But when world
inflation is high, a country can maintain lower domestic inflation only by allowing its
nominal exchange rate to adjust.

The effects on real output of aggregate demand and supply disturbances also depend on the nature of the exchange rate system. Under flexible exchange rates, a

---

22. Exchange rate behavior under a target zone system was first analyzed by Krugman (1991).

positive aggregate demand shock increases prices and real output. Goods market equilibrium requires a rise in the real interest rate and a real appreciation. By serving to equilibrate the goods market and partially offset the rise in aggregate demand following a positive realization of u, the exchange rate movement helps stabilize aggregate output. As a result, the effect of u on y is smaller under flexible exchange rates than under fixed exchange rates.[23]

The choice of exchange rate regime influences the manner in which economic disturbances affect the small open economy. Although the model examined here does not provide an internal welfare criterion (such as the utility of the representative agent in the economy), such models have often been supplemented with loss functions depending on output or inflation volatility (see section 9.3), which are then used to rank alternative exchange rate regimes. Based on such measures, the choice of an exchange rate regime should depend on the relative importance of various disturbances. If volatility of foreign prices is of major concern, a flexible exchange rate will serve to insulate the domestic economy from real exchange rate fluctuations that would otherwise affect domestic output and prices. If domestic monetary instability is a source of economic fluctuations, a fixed exchange rate system provides an automatic monetary response to offset such disturbances.

The role of economic disturbances in the choice of a policy regime is an important topic of study in monetary policy analysis. It figures most prominently in discussion of the choice between using an interest rate or a monetary aggregate as the instrument of monetary policy (see chapter 11).

9.5   Open-Economy Models with Optimizing Agents and Nominal Rigidities

Chapter 8 developed a dynamic general equilibrium model based on optimizing households and firms but in which prices were sticky. This model could be summarized in terms of an expectational IS curve relating aggregate output to expected future output and the real interest rate, and an inflation adjustment relationship, in which current inflation was a function of expected future inflation and real marginal cost. Real marginal cost was a function of output relative to the flexible-price equilibrium level of output. The model was closed by assuming that the monetary authority determined the nominal rate of interest. A number of authors have extended the basic new Keynesian framework to the open-economy context. Examples include McCallum and Nelson (2000a); Clarida, Galí, and Gertler (2001; 2002); Gertler, Gilchrist, and Natalucci (2001); and Monacelli (2005). See also Galí and Monacelli (2005) and Galí (2008, ch. 7). Lubik and Schorfheide (2007); Adolfson, Laseén,

---

23. This is consistent with the estimates for Japan reported in Hutchison and Walsh (1992). Obstfeld (1985) discusses the insulation properties of exchange rate systems.

Lindé, and Villani (2007a; 2008), and Adolfson, Laseén, Lindé, and Svensson (2008) provided examples of an estimated DSGE model for policy analysis based on the framework discussed in this section. Lubik and Schorfheide (2006) jointly estimated a two-country open economy DSGE model with nominal rigidities using U.S. and euro area data. These models differ from the models discussed in section 9.2.3 in that an inflation adjustment model based on Calvo (1983) replaces the assumption of one-period nominal rigidity. This section develops an example of an open-economy new Keynesian model.

9.5.1   A Model of the Small Open Economy

Suppose there are two countries. The home country is denoted by the superscript h, and the foreign country by the superscript f. The countries share the same preferences and technologies. Both produce traded consumption goods that are imperfect substitutes in utility. The foreign country is a stand-in for the rest of the world, and the home country is small relative to the foreign country.

Households
Households consume a CES composite of home and foreign goods, defined as

$$C_t = [(1-\gamma)^{1/a}(C_t^h)^{(a-1)/a} + \gamma^{1/a}(C_t^f)^{(a-1)/a}]^{a/(a-1)} \tag{9.61}$$

for $a > 1$. As in chapter 8, assume C^h (and C^f) are Dixit-Stiglitz aggregates of differentiated goods produced by domestic (and foreign) firms. The domestic household's relative demand for C^h and C^f will depend on their relative prices. Let P_t^h (P_t^f) be the average price of domestically (foreign) produced consumption goods. The problem of minimizing the cost $P_t^h C_t^h + P_t^f C_t^f$ of achieving a given level of C_t yields the first-order conditions

$$P_t^h = \lambda_t[(1-\gamma)^{1/a}(C_t^h)^{(a-1)/a} + \gamma^{1/a}(C_t^f)^{(a-1)/a}]^{1/(a-1)}(1-\gamma)^{1/a}(C_t^h)^{-1/a}$$

$$P_t^f = \lambda_t[(1-\gamma)^{1/a}(C_t^h)^{(a-1)/a} + \gamma^{1/a}(C_t^f)^{(a-1)/a}]^{1/(a-1)}\gamma^{1/a}(C_t^f)^{-1/a},$$

where λ is the Lagrangian multiplier on the constraint. Using (9.61), these first-order conditions can be written as

$$P_t^h = \lambda_t C_t^{1/a}(1-\gamma)^{1/a}(C_t^h)^{-1/a} \Rightarrow C_t^h = (1-\gamma)\left(\frac{P_t^h}{\lambda_t}\right)^{-a} C_t$$

$$P_t^f = \lambda_t C_t^{1/a}\gamma^{1/a}(C_t^f)^{-1/a} \Rightarrow C_t^f = \gamma\left(\frac{P_t^f}{\lambda_t}\right)^{-a} C_t.$$

These equations imply in turn that the home country's relative demand for home- and foreign-produced goods depends on their relative price:

$$\frac{C_t^h}{C_t^f} = \left(\frac{1-\gamma}{\gamma}\right)\left(\frac{P_t^h}{P_t^f}\right)^{-a}. \tag{9.62}$$

Substituting the solutions for C_t^h and C_t^f into the definition of the aggregate consumption bundle yields

$$C_t = \left[(1-\gamma)\left(\frac{P_t^h}{\lambda_t}\right)^{1-a} + \gamma\left(\frac{P_t^f}{\lambda_t}\right)^{1-a}\right]^{a/(a-1)} C_t.$$

Dividing both sides by C_t and solving for λ_t yields

$$\lambda_t = [(1-\gamma)(P_t^h)^{1-a} + \gamma(P_t^f)^{1-a}]^{1/(1-a)} \equiv P_t^c \tag{9.63}$$

as the aggregate (consumer) price index.

Household utility depends on its consumption of the composite good and on its labor supply. Assume that

$$U(C_t, N_t) = \frac{C_t^{1-\sigma}}{1-\sigma} - \frac{N_t^{1+\eta}}{1+\eta}. \tag{9.64}$$

Intertemporal optimization implies the standard Euler condition,

$$C_t^{-\sigma} = \beta E_t R_t \left(\frac{P_t^c}{P_{t+1}^c}\right) C_{t+1}^{-\sigma}, \tag{9.65}$$

where R_t is the (gross) nominal rate of interest, and the optimal labor-leisure choice requires that the marginal rate of substitution between leisure and consumption equal the real wage. This last condition takes the form

$$\frac{N_t^\eta}{C_t^{-\sigma}} = \frac{W_t}{P_t^c}, \tag{9.66}$$

where W_t is the nominal wage.

Assume that the law of one price holds. This implies that

$$P_t^f = S_t P_t^*, \tag{9.67}$$

where P_t^* is the foreign currency price of foreign-produced goods and S_t is the nominal exchange rate (price of foreign currency in terms of domestic currency). For simplicity, assume that all foreign goods sell for the price P_t^f. This specification assumes complete exchange rate pass-through; given P_t^*, a 1 percent change in the exchange rate produces a 1 percent change in the domestic currency price of foreign produced goods P_t^f. Given the law of one price, the price levels in the domestic and foreign countries are linked by

$$P_t^c = S_t P_t^{c*}.$$

For the rest of the world, the distinction between the CPI and the price of domestic production is ignored, so $P_t^{c*} = P_t^*$.[24]

It will be useful to define the terms of trade and the real exchange rate. The terms of trade equal the relative price of foreign and domestic goods:

$$\Delta_t \equiv \frac{P_t^f}{P_t^h} = \frac{S_t P_t^*}{P_t^h}. \tag{9.68}$$

The real exchange rate is the price of foreign-produced goods (in terms of domestic currency) relative to the home country's consumer price index:

$$Q_t = \frac{S_t P_t^*}{P_t^c} = \left(\frac{P_t^h}{P_t^c}\right)\Delta_t. \tag{9.69}$$

As was the case with the new Keynesian model of chapter 8, the focus will be on percentage deviations around the steady state. Let lowercase letters denote percentage deviation around the steady state of the corresponding uppercase letter. Then (9.68) and (9.69) can be expressed as

$$\delta_t = s_t + p_t^* - p_t^h$$

and

$$q_t = s_t + p_t^* - p_t^c.$$

Using the definition of the terms of trade in (9.63),

$$p_t^c = (1 - \gamma)p_t^h + \gamma p_t^f = p_t^h + \gamma\delta_t. \tag{9.70}$$

Equations (9.61), (9.62), (9.65), and (9.66) can be written as

---

24. That is, the rest of the world is large relative to the home country, so changes in the price of home-produced goods have little impact on the consumer price index for the rest of the world.

$$c_t = (1 - \gamma)c_t^h + \gamma c_t^f \tag{9.71}$$

$$c_t^f = -a\delta_t + c_t^h \tag{9.72}$$

$$c_t = E_t c_{t+1} - \left(\frac{1}{\sigma}\right)(i_t - E_t \pi_{t+1}^c - \rho), \tag{9.73}$$

where $\rho = \beta^{-1} - 1$ and

$$\eta n_t + \sigma c_t = w_t - p_t^h - \gamma\delta_t, \tag{9.74}$$

where $\pi_t^c = p_t^c - p_{t-1}^c$. Combining (9.71) and (9.72), $c_t = c_t^h - \gamma a\delta_t$. Defining inflation in the prices of domestically produced goods as $\pi_t^h = p_t^h - p_{t-1}^h$, inflation in the consumer price index equals

$$\pi_t^c = p_t^c - p_{t-1}^c = \pi_t^h + \gamma(\delta_t - \delta_{t-1}). \tag{9.75}$$

Note that the real interest rate is defined in terms of consumer price inflation π_t^c. In turn, this measure of inflation depends on the rate of inflation of domestically produced goods π_t^h and the rate of change in the terms of trade.

Clarida, Galí, and Gertler (2001) added a stochastic *wage markup* μ_t^w to (9.74) to represent deviations from the marginal rate of substitution between leisure and consumption:

$$\eta n_t + \sigma c_t + \mu_t^w = w_t - p_t^h - \gamma\delta_t. \tag{9.76}$$

They motivated this markup as arising from the monopoly power of labor suppliers who set wages as a markup over the marginal rate of substitution. The markup was then assumed to be subject to exogenous stochastic variation.

International Risk Sharing
It is assumed that agents in both economies have access to a complete set of internationally traded securities. The time t home currency price of a bond that pays off one unit of the domestic currency at time $t+1$ is R_t^{-1}, and the Euler condition given by (9.65) can be written as

$$\beta E_t \left(\frac{P_t^c}{P_{t+1}^c}\right)\left(\frac{C_{t+1}}{C_t}\right)^{-\sigma} = \frac{1}{R_t}. \tag{9.77}$$

Since residents in the rest of the world also have access to these same financial securities, intertemporal optimization implies

$$\frac{C_t^{*-\sigma}}{S_t P_t^*} = \beta E_t \left(\frac{R_t}{S_{t+1} P_{t+1}^*} \right) C_{t+1}^{*-\sigma}.$$

The left side of this expression shows the marginal utility cost at time t of using $1/S_t$ units of the foreign currency (worth $1/P_t^*$ each in terms of consumption goods) to obtain one unit of the domestic currency. This is invested in the domestic bond, yielding at time $t+1$ a gross return R_t. This can be converted into R_t/S_{t+1} units of foreign currency, worth $R_t/(S_{t+1}P_{t+1}^*)$ in terms of foreign consumption, yielding expected utility of $E_t(R_t/S_{t+1}P_{t+1}^*)C_{t+1}^{*-\sigma}$. Thus, the right side is the marginal benefit in terms of utility from this financial transaction. Since this payout occurs at time $t+1$, it must be discounted at the rate β to compare to the cost of purchasing the financial asset. Along the optimal path, the marginal costs and benefits are equal. Rearranging,

$$\beta E_t \left(\frac{P_t^*}{P_{t+1}^*} \right) \left(\frac{S_t}{S_{t+1}} \right) \left(\frac{C_{t+1}^*}{C_t^*} \right)^{-\sigma} = \frac{1}{R_t}.$$

Using the law of one price and the definition of the real exchange rate, this condition can be written as

$$\beta E_t \left(\frac{P_t^c}{P_{t+1}^c} \right) \left(\frac{Q_t}{Q_{t+1}} \right) \left(\frac{C_{t+1}^*}{C_t^*} \right)^{-\sigma} = \frac{1}{R_t}.$$

Hence,

$$\beta E_t \left(\frac{P_t^c}{P_{t+1}^c} \right) \left(\frac{C_{t+1}}{C_t} \right)^{-\sigma} = \left(\frac{1}{R_t} \right) = \beta E_t \left(\frac{P_t^c}{P_{t+1}^c} \right) \left(\frac{Q_t}{Q_{t+1}} \right) \left(\frac{C_{t+1}^*}{C_t^*} \right)^{-\sigma},$$

which implies

$$C_t = \phi Q_t^{1/\sigma} C_t^*, \tag{9.78}$$

where ϕ is a constant of proportionality. For convenience, adopt $\phi = 1$ as a normalization. This is consistent with a symmetric initial condition with zero net foreign asset holdings. In terms of a first-order linear approximation around the steady state,

$$c_t = c_t^* + \left(\frac{1}{\sigma} \right) q_t = c_t^* + \left(\frac{1-\gamma}{\sigma} \right) \delta_t. \tag{9.79}$$

This last equation employs the fact that

$$q_t = s_t + p_t^* - p_t^c = \delta_t + p_t^h - p_t^c = (1-\gamma)\delta_t. \tag{9.80}$$

Uncovered Interest Parity

If R_t^* is the foreign interest rate, then

$$\beta E_t \left(\frac{P_t^*}{P_{t+1}^*}\right) \left(\frac{C_{t+1}^*}{C_t^*}\right)^{-\sigma} = \frac{1}{R_t^*}.$$

Linearizing this condition yields

$$\sigma(E_t c_{t+1}^* - c_t^*) = r_t^* - E_t \pi_{t+1}^*,$$

and doing the same for (9.77) implies

$$\sigma(E_t c_{t+1} - c_t) = r_t - E_t \pi_{t+1}^c.$$

Using (9.79),

$$(r_t - E_t \pi_{t+1}^c) - (r_t^* - E_t \pi_{t+1}^*) = \sigma(E_t c_{t+1} - c_t) - \sigma(E_t c_{t+1}^* - c_t^*)$$

$$= E_t q_{t+1} - q_t.$$

Subtracting the inflation terms from each side and using the definition of the real exchange rate yields the condition for uncovered interest parity:

$$r_t = r_t^* + E_t(s_{t+1} - s_t).$$

The domestic nominal interest rate is equal to the foreign (rest of the world) nominal interest rate plus the expected rate of depreciation in the domestic currency.

The uncovered interest rate parity condition can also be expressed in real terms by subtracting inflation in domestic produced goods prices and using the definition of the terms of trade:

$$r_t - E_t \pi_{t+1}^h = \rho_t^* + (E_t \delta_{t+1} - \delta_t), \tag{9.81}$$

where $\rho^* \equiv r_t^* - E_t \pi_{t+1}^*$.

Domestic Firms

The analysis of domestic firms parallels the approach followed in chapter 8.

In each period, there is a fixed probability $1 - \omega$ that the firm can adjust its price. When it can adjust, it does so to maximize the expected discounted value of profits. Each domestic firm faces the identical production function,

$$Y_t^h = e^{\varepsilon_t} N_t,$$

and a constant elasticity demand curve for its output. The firm's real marginal cost is equal to

$$MC_t = \frac{W_t/P_t^h}{e^{\varepsilon_t}},$$

where W_t/P_t^h is the real product wage and e^{ε_t} is the marginal product of labor. In terms of percentage deviations around the steady state, this expression becomes

$$mc_t = w_t - p_t^h - \varepsilon_t. \tag{9.82}$$

Following the derivation of chapter 8, the inflation rate for the price index of domestically produced goods is

$$\pi_t^h = \beta E_t \pi_{t+1}^h + \kappa mc_t, \tag{9.83}$$

where $\kappa = (1 - \omega)(1 - \beta\omega)/\omega$. Combining (9.83) with (9.75),

$$\pi_t^c = \beta E_t \pi_{t+1}^c + \kappa mc_t - \beta\gamma(E_t\delta_{t+1} - \delta_t) + \gamma(\delta_t - \delta_{t-1}). \tag{9.84}$$

Inflation, as measured by the consumer price index, depends on expected future inflation and real marginal cost, the same two factors that appeared in the closed-economy inflation adjustment equation. The difference in the open economy is that given real marginal cost, inflation in the consumer price index can be affected by current and expected future changes in the terms of trade. A rise in the terms of trade $(\delta_t - \delta_{t-1} > 0)$ implies an increase in the relative price of foreign goods. Because foreign goods prices are included in the consumer price index (see (9.70)), a rise in their relative prices increases consumer price inflation. An expected future rise in the terms of trade reduces current consumer price inflation because for a given $E_t\pi_{t+1}^c$, this rise in the terms of trade must imply a fall in expected future domestic goods inflation and therefore a fall in current domestic goods inflation.

The Foreign Country

To keep the analysis simple, it was assumed that the foreign country is large relative to the home country. This is taken to mean that it is unnecessary to distinguish between consumer price inflation and domestic inflation in the foreign country and that domestic output and consumption are equal. Trade does take place, however, and so goods produced in the home country are sold to domestic residents and to foreigners. Let c_t^{h*} be the foreign country's consumption of the domestically produced good (as a percentage deviation from the steady state). The foreign country's demand for the home country's output depends on the terms of trade. Assuming that foreign households have the same preferences as those of the home country (so the demand elasticity is the same),

$$C_t^{h*} = \gamma \Delta_t^a Y_t^f,$$

or

$$c_t^{h*} = a\delta_t + y_t^f, \tag{9.85}$$

where y_t^f is foreign income (in terms of the percent deviation from the steady state). The Euler condition for foreign country households implies

$$y_t^* = E_t y_{t+1}^* - \left(\frac{1}{\sigma}\right)(i_t^f - E_t \pi_{t+1}^*),$$

or

$$\rho_t^* \equiv i_t^* - E_t \pi_{t+1}^* = \sigma(E_t y_{t+1}^* - y_t^*). \tag{9.86}$$

Equilibrium Conditions

The conditions for each market that need to be satisfied in equilibrium can now be collected.

Equilibrium requires that domestic production equal the consumption of the domestically produced good. Since the domestic good is consumed by both domestic residents and by residents of the rest of the world, equilibrium requires that

$$Y_t = (1 - \gamma)\left(\frac{P_t^h}{P_t^c}\right)^{-a} C_t + \gamma\left(\frac{P_t^h}{S_t P_t^*}\right)^{-a} Y_t^*.$$

Using the earlier result that $C_t = Q_t^{1/\sigma} C_t^* = Q_t^{1/\sigma} Y_t^*$ to eliminate Y_t^*, and employing the definition of the real exchange rate as $Q_t = S_t P_t^*/P_t^c$, the goods market equilibrium condition can be written as

$$Y_t = \left(\frac{P_t^h}{P_t^c}\right)^{-a} [(1 - \gamma) + \gamma Q_t^{a-1/\sigma}] C_t.$$

Taking a first-order linear approximation of this equation around the steady state yields[25]

$$y_t = c_t + \left(\frac{\gamma w}{\sigma}\right)\delta_t, \tag{9.87}$$

where $w = a\sigma + (a\sigma - 1)(1 - \gamma)$.

---

25. This makes use of the fact that in the steady state, $Q = 1$, so $Y = (P^h/P^c)^{-a}C$, and of the definition of the terms of trade, which implies $p_t^h - p_t^c = -\gamma\delta_t$.

Since $c_t^* = y_t^*$, and from (9.79) and (9.80), $c_t = c_t^* + \left(\frac{1}{\sigma}\right)q_t = c_t^* + \left(\frac{1-\gamma}{\sigma}\right)\delta_t$, (9.87) can be written as

$$y_t = c_t + \left(\frac{\gamma w}{\sigma}\right)\delta_t = c_t^* + \left(\frac{1-\gamma}{\sigma} + \frac{\gamma w}{\sigma}\right)\delta_t$$

$$= y_t^* + \left(\frac{1}{\sigma_\gamma}\right)\delta_t, \tag{9.88}$$

where $\sigma_\gamma \equiv \sigma/[1 - \gamma(1 - w)]$.

These results can be used in the Euler condition (9.73) to obtain the small-open-economy version of the expectational IS relations. Starting with the Euler condition, use (9.87) to replace consumption with $y_t - \left(\frac{\gamma w}{\sigma}\right)\delta_t$, yielding

$$y_t = E_t y_{t+1} - \left(\frac{1}{\sigma}\right)(i_t - E_t \pi_{t+1}^c - \rho) - \left(\frac{\gamma w}{\sigma}\right)(E_t \delta_{t+1} - \delta_t).$$

Because $E_t \pi_{t+1}^c = E_t \pi_{t+1}^h + \gamma E_t \Delta\delta_{t+1}$ (see (9.75)),

$$y_t = E_t y_{t+1} - \left(\frac{1}{\sigma}\right)(i_t - E_t \pi_{t+1}^h - \rho) + \frac{\gamma}{\sigma}(1 - w)(E_t \delta_{t+1} - \delta_t).$$

Equation (9.88) implies $(E_t \delta_{t+1} - \delta_t) = \sigma_\gamma [E_t(y_{t+1} - y_t) - (E_t y_{t+1}^* - y_t^*)]$, and using this expression to eliminate the expected change in the terms of trade from the Euler condition yields

$$y_t = E_t y_{t+1} - \left(\frac{1}{\sigma_\gamma}\right)(i_t - E_t \pi_{t+1}^h - \rho^*), \tag{9.89}$$

where

$$\rho^* \equiv \rho - \sigma_\gamma \gamma (1 - w)(E_t y_{t+1}^* - y_t^*).$$

Equation (9.89) is the small-open-economy equivalent to the closed-economy expectational IS curve. There are two primary differences between the open- and closed-economy versions of this relationship. First, the elasticity of demand with respect to the real interest rate is no longer equal to the elasticity of intertemporal substitution, $1/\sigma$. Instead, it equals $1/\sigma_\gamma = [1 - \gamma(1 - w)]/\sigma$. From the definition of w,

$$\sigma_\gamma = \frac{\sigma}{1 - \gamma^2[1 - a\sigma]},$$

which depends on the openness of the economy through γ (the larger γ is, the smaller the share of home-produced goods in the consumption bundle of domestic residents) and a, the price elasticity of demand for home-produced and foreign-produced goods.

Inflation Adjustment

To determine the rate of inflation of domestically produced goods, (9.82) and (9.83) imply

$$\pi_t^h = \beta E_t \pi_{t+1}^h + \kappa(w_t - p_t^h - \varepsilon_t).$$

The real consumption wage is $w_t - p_t^c$, and this is related to the real product wage $w_t - p_t^h$ by the terms of trade: $p_t^c = p_t^h + \gamma\delta_t$. Since households equate the real consumption wage to the marginal rate of substitution between leisure and consumption, (9.66) implies that

$$\eta n_t + \sigma c_t = w_t - p_t^c = w_t - p_t^h - \gamma\delta_t.$$

Hence, real marginal cost is $w_t - p_t^h - \varepsilon_t = \eta n_t + \sigma c_t + \gamma\delta_t - \varepsilon_t$. Now use (9.87) and (9.88) to eliminate consumption and the terms of trade to obtain an expression for real marginal cost solely in terms of domestic output and foreign variables:

$$\pi_t^h = \beta E_t \pi_{t+1}^h + \kappa[(\eta + \sigma_\gamma) y_t - (\sigma - \sigma_\gamma) y_t^* - (1+\eta)\varepsilon_t],$$

or

$$\pi_t^h = \beta E_t \pi_{t+1}^h + \kappa(\eta + \sigma_\gamma)(y_t - \tilde{y}_t), \tag{9.90}$$

where $\tilde{y}_t \equiv [(\sigma - \sigma_\gamma) y_t^* - (1+\eta)\varepsilon_t]/(\eta + \sigma_\gamma)$.

Notice that because ρ^* and $\tilde{y}_t$ depend only on exogenous shocks or foreign variables, (9.89) and (9.90) constitute a two-equation model for domestic output and inflation once a specification for monetary policy in terms of the nominal rate of interest has been added.

Clarida, Galí, and Gertler (2002) relaxed the assumption that the foreign country is large and examined the role of policy coordination. To carry out this examination, assume that both countries are subject to nominal price rigidities. In this case, (9.88) is modified to

$$\tilde{x}_t = \tilde{x}_t^f + \left(\frac{1}{\sigma_\gamma}\right)\tilde{\delta}_t,$$

where $\tilde{\delta}_t$, $\tilde{x}_t$ and $\tilde{x}_t^f$ are defined as gaps relative to the outcome when prices are flexible in *both* countries. Using this equation to derive real marginal cost, Clarida, Galí, and Gertler found that

$$\pi_t^h = \beta E_t \pi_{t+1}^h + \kappa\tilde{x}_t + \kappa\tilde{x}_t^f$$

for domestic goods inflation in the home country, with inflation in the foreign country satisfying a similar equation. The spillover effect of the output gap on inflation in the other country gives rise, in general, to gains from policy coordination.

9.5.2 The Relationship to the Closed-Economy NK Model

The small-open-economy model consisting of (9.89) and (9.90) is identical in form to the closed-economy new Keynesian model of chapter 8. Output satisfies an Euler condition with the real interest rate defined in terms of domestically produced goods, and inflation of domestically produced goods is forward-looking and depends on an output gap measure. The parameters in these relationships differ from those in the close-economy model because they depend on factors related to the openness of the economy.

To further draw the parallel with the closed-economy model, define the output gap as

$$x_t \equiv y_t - \tilde{y}_t. \tag{9.91}$$

Then rewrite (9.89) and (9.90) as

$$x_t = E_t x_{t+1} - \left(\frac{1}{\sigma_y}\right)(i_t - E_t \pi_{t+1}^h - \tilde{\rho}_t) \tag{9.92}$$

$$\pi_t^h = \beta E_t \pi_{t+1}^h + \kappa(\eta + \sigma_y) x_t, \tag{9.93}$$

where

$$\tilde{\rho}_t = \rho^* + \sigma_y E_t(\tilde{y}_{t+1} - \tilde{y}_t). \tag{9.94}$$

Thus, the small-open-economy model has been reduced to a form that exactly parallels that of the closed-economy model *if* one can show that the output gap $x_t = y_t - \tilde{y}_t$ is the gap between output and the flexible-price equilibrium price. That is, one needs to show that with flexible prices, $\tilde{y}_t$ is the equilibrium output.

The flexible-price equilibrium output is defined as the output level consistent with real marginal cost equaling its constant steady-state value. Since

$$mc_t = (\eta + \sigma_y)y_t + (\sigma - \sigma_y)y_t^* - (1 + \eta)\varepsilon_t,$$

it follows that the flexible-price output is

$$y_t^{flex} = \frac{(\sigma_y - \sigma)y_t^* + (1 + \eta)\varepsilon_t}{\eta + \sigma_y},$$

which is the definition assigned earlier to $\tilde{y}_t$. Hence, x_t is the flexible-price output gap, just as it was in the closed-economy new Keynesian model.

Equations (9.93) and (9.92) are, as Clarida, Galí, and Gertler (2001; 2002) emphasized, isomorphic to the closed-economy new Keynesian model.[26] The parallel is exact if the central bank's objective can be represented as minimizing a quadratic form of the output gap as defined in (9.91) and the inflation rate of domestically produced goods π_t^h. In this case, the central bank's policy involves minimizing

$$E_t \sum_{i=0}^{\infty} \beta^i [(\pi_{t+i}^h)^2 + \lambda x_{t+i}^2] \qquad (9.95)$$

subject to (9.93) and (9.92). This is exactly equivalent to the closed-economy policy problem studied in chapter 8, and so all the conclusions about policy reached there would apply without modification to the small open economy. The critical requirement is that the inflation rate appearing in the central bank's objective function must be π^h and not the inflation rate in consumer prices π^c. If π^c is the relevant objective of the central bank (and most inflation-targeting central banks in small open economies define their targets in terms of consumer price inflation), then (9.93) and (9.92) are not sufficient to determine either optimal policy or the economy's equilibrium. Thus, an important issue for the analysis of monetary policy in the context of an open economy is determining the price index that is the appropriate objective of policy.

Optimal Policy in the Small Open Economy
As demonstrated in the previous section, the analysis of optimal monetary policy in the small open economy would be equivalent to that in the closed economy if the central bank's objectives were given by (9.95). In the absence of cost shocks to the inflation equation for domestic goods prices, optimal policy would involve stabilizing the domestic price index.

The basic intuition for such a policy carries over from the case of the closed economy. If tax subsidies have dealt with the distortions associated with monopolistic competition, then the role of monetary policy should be to eliminate the distortions created by sticky prices. The central bank can eliminate these distortions by stabilizing prices, and since the sticky prices are the prices of domestically produced goods, the optimal policy would stabilize domestic prices.

Unfortunately, as Galí and Monacelli (2005) discussed, this intuition is not correct in general. Even if the distortion arising from the markup is offset by fiscal subsidies,

---

26. McCallum and Nelson (2000b) also developed a model that can be reduced to a version isomorphic to the closed-economy new Keynesian model. See problem 9 at the end of this chapter.

there remains an additional factor present in the open-economy context that leads to a distortion and implies the flexible-price equilibrium is not fully efficient. Because foreign-produced and domestically produced goods are imperfect substitutes, the central bank faces an incentive to affect the terms of trade. This is welfare-improving and would cause the optimal policy to deviate from price stability.[27]

9.5.3 Imperfect Pass-Through

The isomporphism between the open and closed versions of the basic new Keynesian model is a consequence of continuing to incorporate only a single nominal rigidity. Prices were assumed to be sticky, but nominal wages were assumed to be flexible. In addition, only the prices of domestically produced goods were taken to be sticky. The home country prices of foreign-produced goods were taken to be perfectly flexible; they moved one-for-one with the nominal exchange rate (see (9.67)).

Adolfson (2001), Corsetti and Presenti (2002), and Monacelli (2005) provided examples of models that allow for incomplete pass-through. When pass-through is incomplete, the law of one price no longer holds. The law of one price allows the domestic currency price of foreign goods, p_t^f, to be expressed as $s_t + p_t^*$, where s_t is the nominal exchange rate and p_t^* is the foreign currency price of foreign goods (all expressed as percentage deviations from their steady-state values). The terms of trade are then equal to $s_t + p_t^* - p_t^h$. With incomplete pass-though, however, p_t^f and $s_t + p_t^*$ can differ.

Following Monacelli (2005), the real exchange rate q_t can be written as[28]

$$q_t = s_t + p_t^* - p_t^c = \psi_t + (1 - \gamma)\delta_t,$$

where $\psi_t = s_t + p_t^* - p_t^f$ measures the deviation from the law of one price. In the model of the previous section, the law of one price held, so ψ_t was identically equal to zero. Suppose pass-through is incomplete because of nominal rigidity in the price of imports, with only a fraction of importers adjusting their price each period, as in a standard Calvo-type model of price adjustment. Then the variable ψ_t represents the marginal cost of importers, and the rate of inflation in the average domestic currency price of foreign imports takes the form

$$\pi_t^f = \beta E_t \pi_{t+1}^f + \kappa^f \psi_t,$$

where $\pi_t^f = p_t^f - p_{t-1}^f$ and the parameter κ^f depends on the fraction of import prices that adjust each period.

---

27. See Corsetti and Presenti (2001). Benigno and Benigno (2003) considered this issue in a two-country model.

28. This uses (9.70), which defines the consumer price index as $(1 - \gamma)p_t^h + \gamma p_t^f$ and the definition of the terms of trade, $\delta_t = p_t^f - p_t^h$.

Letting z_t^o denote the flexible-price equilibrium value of a variable z_t, Monacelli (2005) showed that with imperfect pass-through, the output gap can be written as

$$x_t = \left(\frac{1+w}{\sigma}\right)(\delta_t - \delta_t^o) + \left[\frac{1+\gamma(\sigma a - 1)}{\sigma}\right](\psi_t - \psi_t^o),$$

where $w = \gamma(\sigma a - 1)(2 - \gamma)$ as before. The real marginal cost of domestic firms can then be expressed as

$$mc_t - mc_t^o = \left(\frac{\sigma}{1+w} + \eta\right)x_t + \left[1 - \frac{1+\gamma(\sigma a - 1)}{1+w}\right](\psi_t - \psi_t^o).$$

Inflation in domestic producer prices is equal to

$$\pi_t^h = \beta E_t \pi_{t+1}^h + \kappa(mc_t - mc_t^o).$$

Thus, deviations from the law of one price, as measured by $\psi_t - \psi_t^o$, directly affect inflation through their impact on marginal cost.

Imperfect pass-through represents a second nominal rigidity when combined with the assumption of sticky prices. Not surprisingly, therefore, it introduces policy trade-offs, much as the addition of sticky wages did in the basic new Keynesian model of chapter 8. Both the output gap and deviations from the law of one price affect real marginal cost and, as a result, inflation. Stabilizing inflation in the face of a movement in $\psi_t - \psi_t^o$ requires that the output gap be allowed to fluctuate; stabilizing the output gap in the face of a movement in $\psi_t - \psi_t^o$ requires that inflation fluctuate. With two sources of nominal rigidity—sticky prices and imperfect pass-through—the central bank cannot undo the effects of both distortions with a single policy instrument.

9.6 Summary

This chapter has reviewed various models that are useful for studying aspects of open-economy monetary economics. A two-country model whose equilibrium conditions were consistent with optimizing agents was presented. This model, based on the work of Obstfeld and Rogoff, preserved the classical dichotomy between real and monetary factors when prices and wages are assumed to be perfectly flexible. In this case, the price level and the nominal exchange rate could be expressed simply in terms of the current and expected future paths of the nominal money supplies in the two countries.

Two primary lessons are that new channels by which monetary factors affect the economy are present in an open economy, and the choice of exchange rate regime has important implications for the role of monetary policy. With sticky nominal wages, monetary factors have important short-run effects on the real exchange rate. Exchange rate movements alter the relative price of the domestic good and the foreign good, affecting aggregate demand and supply. In addition, consumer prices, because they are indices of domestic currency prices of domestically produced and foreign-produced goods, respond to exchange rate movements.[29] The impact of exchange rate movements on consumer price inflation suggests that monetary policy may have more rapid effects on inflation in more open economies.

Unlike the analysis of the closed economy, the Obstfeld-Rogoff model implies that monetary-induced output movements would have persistent real effects by altering the distribution of wealth between economies. In general, standard open-economy frameworks used for policy analysis assume that the real effects of monetary policy arise only in the short run and are due to nominal rigidities. Over time, as wages and prices adjust, real output, real interest rates, and the real exchange rate return to equilibrium levels that are independent of monetary policy. This long-run neutrality means that these models, like their closed-economy counterparts, imply that the long-run effects of monetary policy fall on prices, inflation, nominal interest rates, and the nominal exchange rate. In the short run, however, monetary policy can have important effects on the manner in which real output and the real exchange rate fluctuate around their longer-run equilibrium values.

The final section of the chapter reviewed some extensions of new Keynesian models to open-economy settings. In these models, households and firms are optimizing agents, but nominal rigidities lead to a staggered adjustment of prices over time. In some cases, these models result in reduced-form equations for the output gap and inflation that are identical in form to the closed-economy equivalents. However, as in closed-economy models, policy trade-offs are significantly affected with the addition of multiple sources of nominal rigidity. The model of imperfect pass-through provides one empirically relevant example of a nominal rigidity that is absent in the closed economy. As with models of the closed economy, empirical work with DSGE open-economy models such as Adolfson, Laseén, Lindé, and Villani (2007a; 2008) incorporate multiple sources of nominal (and real) frictions into the basic model structure reviewed in this chapter.

9.7 Appendix

9.7.1 The Obstfeld-Rogoff Model

This appendix provides a derivation of some of the components of the Obstfeld-Rogoff (1995; 1996) model.

---

29. Duguay (1994) provides evidence on these channels in the case of Canada.

Individual Product Demand

The demand functions faced by individual producers are obtained as the solution to the following problem:

$$\max \left[\int_0^1 c(z)^q \, dz \right]^{1/q} \quad \text{subject to} \quad \int_0^1 p(z)c(z) \, dz = Z$$

for a given total expenditure Z. Letting θ denote the Lagrangian multiplier associated with the budget constraint, the first-order conditions imply, for all z,

$$c(z)^{q-1} \left[\int_0^1 c(z)^q \, dz \right]^{1/q-1} = \theta p(z).$$

For any two goods z and z', therefore, $[c(z)/c(z')]^{q-1} = p(z)/p(z')$, or

$$c(z) = c(z') \left[\frac{p(z')}{p(z)} \right]^{1/(1-q)}.$$

If this expression is substituted into the budget constraint, one obtains

$$\int_0^1 p(z)c(z') \left[\frac{p(z')}{p(z)} \right]^{1/(1-q)} dz = c(z')p(z')^{1/(1-q)} \left[\int_0^1 p(z)^{q/(q-1)} \, dz \right] = Z. \tag{9.96}$$

Using the definition of P given in (9.3), both sides of (9.96) can be divided by P to yield

$$\frac{c(z')p(z')^{1/(1-q)} [\int_0^1 p(z)^{q/(q-1)} \, dz]}{[\int_0^1 p(z)^{q/(q-1)} \, dz]^{(q-1)/q}} = \frac{Z}{P}.$$

This can be simplified to

$$c(z') \left[\frac{p(z')}{P} \right]^{1/(1-q)} = \frac{Z}{P} \quad \text{or} \quad c(z') = \left[\frac{p(z')}{P} \right]^{1/(q-1)} C, \tag{9.97}$$

where $C = \frac{Z}{P}$ is total real consumption of the composite good. Equation (9.97) implies that the demand for good z by agent j is equal to $c^j(z) = [p(z)/P]^{1/(q-1)}C^j$, so the world demand for product z will be equal to

$$y_t^d(z) \equiv n \left[\frac{p_t(z)}{P_t} \right]^{1/(q-1)} C_t + (1-n) \left[\frac{p_t^*(z)}{P_t^*} \right]^{1/(q-1)} C_t^*$$

$$= \left[\frac{p_t(z)}{P_t} \right]^{1/(q-1)} C_t^w, \tag{9.98}$$

where $C^w = nC + (1-n)C^*$ is world real consumption. Notice that the law of one price is used here because it implies that the relative price for good z is the same for home and foreign consumers: $p(z)/P = Sp^*(z)/SP^* = p^*(z)/P^*$. Finally, note that (9.98) implies

$$p_t(z) = P_t \left[\frac{y_t^d(z)}{C_t^w} \right]^{q-1}.$$

(9.99)

The Individual's Decision Problem

Each individual begins period t with existing asset holdings B_{t-1}^j and M_{t-1}^j and chooses how much of good j to produce (subject to the world demand function for good j), how much to consume, and what levels of real bonds and money to hold. These choices are made to maximize utility given by (9.1) and subject to the following budget constraint:

$$C_t^j + B_t^j + \frac{M_t^j}{P_t} \leq \frac{p_t(j)y_t(j)}{P_t} + R_{t-1}B_{t-1}^j + \frac{M_{t-1}^j}{P_t} + \tau_t,$$

where τ_t is the real net transfer from the government and R_t is the real gross rate of return. From (9.99), agent's $j's$ real income from producing $y(j)$ will be equal to $y(j)^q (C_t^w)^{1-q}$, so the budget constraint can be written as

$$C_t^j + B_t^j + \frac{M_t^j}{P_t} = y_t(j)^q (C_t^w)^{1-q} + R_{t-1}B_{t-1}^j + \frac{M_{t-1}^j}{P_t} + \tau_t.$$

(9.100)

The value function for the individual's decision problem is

$$V(B_{t-1}^j, M_{t-1}^j) = \max \left\{ \log C_t^j + b \log \frac{M_t^j}{P_t} - \frac{k}{2} y_t(j)^2 + \beta V(B_t^j, M_t^j) \right\},$$

where the maximization is subject to (9.100). Letting λ denote the Lagrangian multiplier associate with the budget constraint, first-order conditions are

$$\frac{1}{C_t^j} - \lambda_t = 0$$

(9.101)

$$\frac{b}{M_t^j} + \beta V_2(B_t^j, M_t^j) - \frac{\lambda_t}{P_t} = 0$$

(9.102)

$$-k y_t(j) + \lambda_t q y_t(j)^{q-1} (C_t^w)^{1-q} = 0$$

(9.103)

$$\beta V_1(B_t^j, M_t^j) - \lambda_t = 0$$

(9.104)

$$V_1(B_{t-1}^j, M_{t-1}^j) = \lambda_t R_{t-1} \tag{9.105}$$

$$V_2(B_{t-1}^j, M_{t-1}^j) = \frac{\lambda_t}{P_t}. \tag{9.106}$$

There is also the transversality condition $\lim_{i \to \infty} \prod_{k=0}^i R_{t+s-1}(B_{t+i}^j + M_{t+i}^j/P_{t+i}) = 0$.

These first-order conditions lead to the standard Euler condition for consumption with log utility:

$$C_{t+1}^j = \beta R_t C_t^j,$$

which is obtained using (9.101), (9.104), and (9.105). Equations (9.103) and (9.101) imply that the optimal production level the individual chooses satisfies

$$y_t(j)^{2-q} = \frac{q}{k} \frac{(C_t^w)^{1-q}}{C_t^j}. \tag{9.107}$$

Equation (9.102) yields an expression for the real demand for money,

$$\frac{M_t^j}{P_t} = bC_t^j \left(\frac{1+i_t}{i_t} \right),$$

where $(1 + i_t) = R_{t+1} P_{t+1}/P_t$ is the gross nominal rate of interest from period t to $t+1$. This expression should look familiar from chapter 2.

9.7.2 The Small-Open-Economy Model

This appendix employs the method of undetermined coefficients to obtain the equilibrium exchange rate and price level processes consistent with (9.49)–(9.57). The equations of the model are repeated here, where the real exchange rate p_t has been replaced by $s_t + p_t^* - p_t$, r_t by $r^* - (s_t + p_t^* - p_t) + E_t(s_{t+1} + p_{t+1}^* - p_{t+1})$, i_t by $i_t^* + E_t s_{t+1} - s_t$, and q_t by $p_t + (1-h)(s_t + p_t^* - p_t)$:

$$y_t = -b_1(s_t + p_t^* - p_t) + b_2(p_t - E_{t-1}p_t) + e_t \tag{9.108}$$

$$y_t = a_1(s_t + p_t^* - p_t) - a_2[r^* - (s_t + p_t^* - p_t) + E_t(s_{t+1} + p_{t+1}^* - p_{t+1})] + u_t \tag{9.109}$$

$$m_t - [p_t + (1-h)(s_t + p_t^* - p_t)] = y_t - c(i_t^* + E_t s_{t+1} - s_t) + v_t \tag{9.110}$$

$$m_t = \mu + m_{t-1} + \varphi_t - \gamma\varphi_{t-1}, \qquad 0 \leq \gamma \leq 1 \tag{9.111}$$

$$p_t^* = \pi^* + p_{t-1}^* + \phi_t. \tag{9.112}$$

Substituting the aggregate demand relationship (9.109), the money supply process (9.111), and the foreign price process (9.112) into the money demand equation (9.110) yields, after some rearrangement,

$$A_1 p_t + A_2 s_t = C_0 + \mu + m_{t-1} + \varphi_t - \gamma \varphi_{t-1}$$

$$- (1 - h + a_1)(p_{t-1}^* + \phi_t) - a_2 E_t p_{t+1}$$

$$+ (a_2 + c) E_t s_{t+1} - u_t - v_t, \tag{9.113}$$

where $A_1 = h - a_1 - a_2$, $A_2 = 1 - h + a_1 + a_2 + c > 0$ and $C_0 = (c + a_2)r^* - (1 - h + a_1 - a_2 - c)\pi^*$. In deriving (9.113), two additional results have been used: from (9.112), $E_t p_{t+1}^* = 2\pi^* + p_{t-1}^* + \phi_t$, and $i_t^* = r^* + E_t p_{t+1}^* - p_t^* = r^* + \pi^*$.

Using the aggregate supply and demand relationships (9.108) and (9.109),

$$B_1 p_t + B_2 s_t = -b_2 E_{t-1} p_t + a_2 (E_t s_{t+1} - E_t p_{t+1}) - (a_1 + b_1)\pi^*$$

$$+ a_2(r^* + \pi^*) + e_t - u_t - (a_1 + b_1)(p_{t-1}^* + \phi_t), \tag{9.114}$$

where $B_1 = -(a_1 + a_2 + b_1 + b_2) < 0$, and $B_2 = a_1 + a_2 + b_1 > 0$.

The state variables at time t are m_{t-1}, p_t^* and the various random disturbances. To rule out possible bubble solutions, follow McCallum (1983a) and hypothesize minimum state variable solutions of the form:[30]

$$p_t = k_0 + m_{t-1} + k_1 p_{t-1}^* + k_2 \varphi_t + k_3 \varphi_{t-1} + k_4 u_t + k_5 e_t + k_6 v_t + k_7 \phi_t$$

$$s_t = d_0 + m_{t-1} + d_1 p_{t-1}^* + d_2 \varphi_t + d_3 \varphi_{t-1} + d_4 u_t + d_5 e_t + d_6 v_t + d_7 \phi_t.$$

These imply

$$E_{t-1} p_t = k_0 + m_{t-1} + k_1 p_{t-1}^* + k_3 \varphi_{t-1}$$

$$E_t p_{t+1} = k_0 + m_t + k_1 p_t^* + k_3 \varphi_t$$

$$= k_0 + \mu + m_{t-1} + (1 + k_3)\varphi_t - \gamma \varphi_{t-1} + k_1(\pi^* + p_{t-1}^* + \phi_t)$$

and

$$E_t s_{t+1} = d_0 + \mu + m_{t-1} + (1 + d_3)\varphi_t - \gamma \varphi_{t-1} + d_1(\pi^* + p_{t-1}^* + \phi_t).$$

---

30. The coefficient on m_{t-1} is set equal to 1 in these trial solutions. It is easy to verify that this assumption is in fact correct.

These expressions for p_t and s_t, together with those for the various expectations of p and s, can be substituted into (9.113) and (9.114). These then yield a pair of equations that must be satisfied by each pair (k_i, d_i). For example, the coefficients on p_{t-1}^* in (9.113) and (9.114) must satisfy

$$A_1 k_1 + A_2 d_1 = -(1 - h + a_1) - a_2 k_1 + (a_2 + c) d_1$$

and

$$B_1 k_1 + B_2 d_1 = a_2 (d_1 - k_1) - b_2 k_1 - (a_1 + b_1).$$

Using the definitions of A_i and B_i to cancel terms, the second equation implies that $d_1 = k_1 - 1$. Substituting this into the first equation yields $k_1 = 0$. Therefore, the solution pair is $(k_1, d_1) = (0, 1)$. Repeating this process yields the values for (k_i, d_i) reported in (9.58) and (9.59).

9.8 Problems

1. Suppose $m_t = m_0 + \gamma m_{t-1}$ and $m_t^* = m_0^* + \gamma^* m_{t-1}^*$. Use (9.24) to show how the behavior of the nominal exchange rate under flexible prices depends on the degree of serial correlation exhibited by the home and foreign money supplies.

2. In the model of section 9.3 used to study policy coordination, aggregate demand shocks were set equal to zero in order to focus on a common aggregate supply shock. Suppose instead that the aggregate supply shocks are zero, and the demand shocks are given by $u \equiv x + \phi$ and $u^* \equiv x + \phi^*$, so that x represents a common demand shock and ϕ and ϕ^* are uncorrelated country-specific demand shocks. Derive policy outcomes under coordinated and (Nash) noncoordinated policy setting. Is there a role for policy coordination in the face of demand shocks? Explain.

3. Continuing with the same model as in the previous question, how are real interest rates affected by a common aggregate demand shock?

4. Policy coordination with asymmetric supply shocks. Continuing with the same model as in the previous two questions, assume that there are no demand shocks but that the supply shocks e and e^* are uncorrelated. Derive policy outcomes under coordinated and uncoordinated policy settings. Does coordination or noncoordination lead to a greater inflation response to supply shocks? Explain.

5. Assume that the home country policymaker acts as a Stackelberg leader and recognizes that foreign inflation will be given by (9.47). How does this change in the nature of the strategic interaction affect the home country's response to disturbances?

6. In a small open economy with perfectly flexible nominal wages, the text showed that the real exchange rate and domestic price level were given by

$$p_t = \sum_{i=0}^{\infty} d^i E_t \left(\frac{a_2 r_{t+i}^* + e_{t+i} - u_{t+i}}{a_1 + a_2 + b_1} \right)$$

and

$$p_t = \left(\frac{1}{1+c} \right) \sum_{i=0}^{\infty} \left(\frac{c}{1+c} \right)^i E_t (m_{t+i} - z_{t+i} - v_{t+i}),$$

where $z_{t+i} \equiv y_{t+i} + (1-h)p_{t+i} - cr_{t+i}$. Assume that $r^* = 0$ for all t and that e, u, and $z + v$ all follow first-order autoregressive processes (e.g., $e_t = \rho_e e_{t-1} + x_{e,t}$ for x_e white noise). Let the nominal money supply be given by

$$m_t = g_1 e_{t-1} + g_2 u_{t-1} + g_3 (z_{t-1} + v_{t-1}).$$

Find equilibrium expressions for the real exchange rate, the nominal exchange rate, and the consumer price index. What values of the parameters g_1, g_2, and g_3 minimize fluctuations in s_t? in q_t? in p_t? Are there any conflicts between stabilizing the exchange rate (real or nominal) and stabilizing the consumer price index?

7. Equation (9.42) for the equilibrium real exchange rate in the two-country model of section 9.3.1 takes the form $p_t = A E_t p_{t+1} + v_t$. Suppose $v_t = \gamma v_{t-1} + \psi_t$, where ψ_t is a mean zero white noise process. Suppose the solution for p_t is of the form $p_t = b v_t$. Find the value of b. How does it depend on γ?

8. Section 9.5.1 demonstrated how a simple open-economy model with nominal price stickiness could be expressed in a form that paralleled the closed-economy new Keynesian model of chapter 8. Would this same conclusion result in a model of sticky wages with flexible prices? What if both wages and prices were sticky?

9. McCallum and Nelson (2000a) proposed a new Keynesian open-economy model in which imported goods are only used as inputs into the production of the domestic good and households consumer only the domestically produced good. If e_t is the nominal exchange rate, and s_t is the real exchange rate, the model can be summarized by the following equations:

$$c_t = E_t c_{t+1} - b_1 [R_t - E_t \pi_{t+1} - r_t]$$

$$im_t = y_t - \sigma s_t$$

$$ep_t = y_t^* + \sigma^* s_t$$

$$s_t = e_t - p_t + p_t^*$$

$$R_t = R_t^* + E_t e_{t+1} - e_t,$$

$$y_t = (1 - \alpha)(n_t + \varepsilon_t) + \alpha im_t$$

$$\pi_t = \beta E_t \pi_{t+1} + \kappa x_t,$$

where im_t denotes imports, ep_t denotes exports, and all variables are expressed relative to their flexible-price equivalents. Foreign variables are denoted by $*$. The linearized production function is

$$y_t = (1 - \alpha)(n_t + \varepsilon_t) + \alpha im_t,$$

and the goods market equilibrium condition takes the form

$$y_t = \omega_1 c_t + \omega_2 g_t + \omega_3 ep_t.$$

Show that this open-economy model can be reduced to two equations corresponding to the IS relationship and the Phillips curve that, when combined with a specification of monetary policy, could be solved for the equilibrium output gap and inflation rate. How does the interest elasticity of the output gap depend on the openness of the economy?

10. Assume the utility function of the representative household in a small open economy is

$$U = E_0 \sum_{t=0}^{\infty} \beta^t \left\{ \ln(C_t) - \frac{N_t^{1+\eta}}{1+\eta} + \frac{a_m}{1-\gamma_m} \left(\frac{M_t}{P_t} \right)^{1-\gamma_m} \right\},$$

where C is total consumption, N is labor supply, and M/P is real money holdings. C_t is defined by (9.61), and utility is maximized subject to the sequence of constraints given by

$$P_t C_t + M_t + e_t \frac{1}{1+i_t^*} B_t^* + \frac{1}{1+i_t} B_t \le W_t N_t + M_{t-1} + e_t B_{t-1}^* + B_{t-1} + \Pi_t - \tau_t.$$

Let P_t^h (P_t^f) be the average price of domestic- (foreign-) produced consumption goods.

a. Derive the first-order conditions for the household's problem.

b. Show that the choice of home-produced consumption goods relative to foreign-produced consumption goods depends on the terms of trade. Why is it not a function of the real exchange rate?

c. Derive an expression for the price index P_t.

11. Using the first-order conditions derived in question 10a, derive the Euler equations and obtain the uncovered interest rate parity condition. Can you provide economic intuition to explain this equation.

10 Financial Markets and Monetary Policy

10.1 Introduction

Central banks in the major industrialized economies implement policy by intervening in the money market to achieve a target level for a short-term interest rate.[1] The focus in this chapter is on the role of financial markets and the linkages between the interest rate affected directly by monetary policy and the broad range of market interest rates and credit conditions that affect investment and consumption spending.

After consideration of price level determinacy and liquidity traps in section 10.2, the term structure of interest rates and the relationship between short-term and long-term interest rates are discussed in section 10.3. Recent work has linked the term structure models commonly used in the finance literature to the types of macroeconomic models commonly used to investigate monetary policy issues. These models are the topic of section 10.4. If, however, credit markets are imperfect, interest rates (i.e., prices) may not be sufficient to capture the impact of monetary policy on the economy. Instead, there may be credit effects that arise when frictions are present in financial markets. Section 10.5 examines these frictions and their implications for macroeconomic equilibrium and the impact of monetary policy. Section 10.6 concludes by providing a brief review of the evidence on whether credit matters.

10.2 Interest Rates and Monetary Policy

This section explores three issues: (1) the connection between interest rate policies and price level determinacy (in chapter 8, the new Keynesian model was used to explore issues of determinacy, but this related to the existence of a unique rational-expectations equilibrium for the inflation rate, not the price level); (2) interest rate policies in flexible-price general equilibrium models; and (3) the implications of liquidity traps.

---

1. Monetary policy operating procedures are discussed in chapter 11.

10.2.1   Interest Rate Rules and the Price Level

Monetary policy can affect nominal rates, both in the short run and in the long run, but the Fisher relationship links the real rate, expected inflation, and the nominal rate of interest. Targets for nominal interest rates and inflation cannot be independently chosen, and controlling the nominal interest rate has important implications for the behavior of the aggregate price level.

In section 6.2.1, a simple model with one-period sticky wages was developed that could be expressed in the following form:

$$y_t = y^c + a(p_t - E_{t-1}p_t) + e_t \tag{10.1}$$

$$y_t = \alpha_0 - \alpha_1 r_t + u_t \tag{10.2}$$

$$m_t - p_t = y_t - ci_t + v_t \tag{10.3}$$

$$i_t = r_t + (E_t p_{t+1} - p_t), \tag{10.4}$$

where y, m, and p are the natural logs of output, the money stock, and the price level, and r and i are the real and nominal rates of interest. Although central banks may closely control the nominal rate i, it is the expected real rate of interest r that influences consumption and investment decisions and therefore aggregate demand.[2] This distinction has important implications for the feasibility of an interest targeting rule.

Suppose that the central bank conducts policy by pegging the nominal interest rate at some targeted value:

$$i_t = i^T. \tag{10.5}$$

Under an interest rate peg, the basic aggregate demand and supply system given by (10.1), (10.2), and (10.4) become

$$y_t = y^c + a(p_t - E_{t-1}p_t) + e_t \tag{10.6}$$

$$y_t = \alpha_0 - \alpha_1 r_t + u_t \tag{10.7}$$

$$i^T = r_t + (E_t p_{t+1} - p_t). \tag{10.8}$$

The money demand equation, (10.3), is no longer relevant because the central bank must allow the nominal money stock to adjust to the level of money demand at the targeted interest rate and the equilibrium level of output.

---

2. Term structure considerations are postponed until section 10.3.

Note that the price level only appears in the form of an expectation error (i.e., as $p_t - E_{t-1}p_t$ in the aggregate supply equation) or as an expected rate of change (i.e., as $E_t p_{t+1} - p_t$ in the Fisher equation). This structure implies that the price *level* is indeterminate. That is, if the sequence $\{p_{t+i}^*\}_{i=0}^{\infty}$ is an equilibrium, so is any sequence $\{\hat{p}_{t+i}\}_{i=0}^{\infty}$ where $\hat{p}$ differs from p^* by any constant κ: $\hat{p}_t = p_t^* + \kappa$ for all t. Since κ is an arbitrary constant, $p_t^* - E_{t-1}p_t^* = \hat{p}_t - E_{t-1}\hat{p}_t$; hence, y_t is the same under either price sequence. From (10.7), the equilibrium real interest rate is equal to $(\alpha_0 - y_t + u_t)/\alpha_1$, so it too is the same. With expected inflation the same under either price sequence, the only restriction on the price path is that the expected rate of inflation be such that $i^T = (\alpha_0 - y_t + u_t)/\alpha_1 + E_t p_{t+1}^* - p_t^*$.

The indeterminacy of the price level is perhaps even more apparent if (10.6)–(10.8) are rewritten explicitly in terms of the rate of inflation. By adding ap_{t-1} and subtracting it from the supply function, the equilibrium conditions become

$$y_t = y^c + a(\pi_t - E_{t-1}\pi_t) + e_t$$

$$y_t = \alpha_0 - \alpha_1 r_t + u_t$$

$$i^T = r_t + E_t \pi_{t+1}.$$

These three equations can be solved for output, the real rate of interest, and the rate of inflation. Since the price level does not appear, it is formally indeterminate.[3] In a forward-looking model, an interest rate peg would also leave the inflation rate indeterminate (see chapter 8).

As stressed by McCallum (1986), the issue of indeterminacy differs from the problem of multiple equilibria. The latter involves situations in which multiple equilibrium price paths are consistent with a given path for the nominal supply of money. One example of such a multiplicity of equilibria is the model of hyperinflation studied in chapter 4. With indeterminacy, neither the price level nor the nominal supply of money is determined by the equilibrium conditions of the model. If the demand for real money balances is given by (10.3), then the price sequence p^* is associated with the sequence $m_t^* = p_t^* + y_t - ci_t^T + v_t$, while $\hat{p}$ is associated with $\hat{m}_t = \hat{p}_t + y_t - ci_t^T + v_t = m^* + \kappa$. The price sequences p^* and $\hat{p}$ will be associated with different paths for the nominal money stock.

Intuitively, if all agents expect the price level to be 10 percent higher permanently, such an expectation is completely self-fulfilling. To peg the nominal rate of interest,

---

3. Employing McCallum's (1983a) minimum state solution method, the equilibrium inflation rate is $\pi_t = i^T + (y^c - \alpha_0)/\alpha_1 + (u_t - e_t)/a$ when u and e are serially uncorrelated and the target nominal interest rate is expected to remain constant. In this case, $E_t \pi_{t+1} = i^T + (y^c - \alpha_0)/\alpha_1$, so permanent changes in the target rate i^T do not affect the real interest rate: $r_t = i^T - E_t \pi_{t+1} = -(y^c - \alpha_0)/\alpha_1$.

the central bank simply lets the nominal money supply jump by 10 percent. This stands in contrast to the case in which the central bank controls the nominal quantity of money; a jump of 10 percent in the price level would reduce the real quantity of money, thereby disturbing the initial equilibrium. Under a rule such as (10.5), which has the policymaker pegging the nominal interest rate, the central bank lets the nominal quantity of money adjust as the price level does, leaving the real quantity unchanged.[4]

Price level indeterminacy is often noted as a potential problem with pure interest rate pegs; if private agents don't care about the absolute price level—and under pure interest rate control, neither does the central bank—nothing pins down the price level. Simply pegging the nominal interest rate does not provide a *nominal anchor* to pin down the price level. However, this problem will not arise if the central bank's behavior does depend on a nominal quantity such as the nominal money supply.

For example, suppose the nominal money supply (or a narrow reserve aggregate) is the actual instrument used to affect control of the interest rate, and assume it is adjusted in response to interest rate movements (Canzoneri, Henderson, and Rogoff 1983; McCallum 1986):

$$m_t = \mu_0 + m_{t-1} + \mu(i_t - i^T). \tag{10.9}$$

Under this policy rule, the monetary authority adjusts the nominal money supply growth rate, $m_t - m_{t-1}$, in response to deviations of the nominal interest rate from its target value. If i_t fluctuates randomly around the target i^T, then the average rate of money growth will be μ_0. As $\mu \to \infty$, the variance of the nominal rate around the targeted value i^T will shrink to zero, but the price level can remain determinate (see problem 1 at the end of this chapter).

The nominal money stock is $I(1)$ under the policy rule given by (10.9). That is, m_t is nonstationary and integrated of order 1. This property of m causes the price level to be nonstationary also.[5] One implication is that the error variance of price level forecasts increases with the forecast horizon.

As McCallum (1986) demonstrated, a different equilibrium describing the stochastic behavior of the nominal interest rate and the price level is obtained if the money supply process takes the trend stationary form

$$m_t = \mu' + \mu_0 t + \mu(i_t - i^T) \tag{10.10}$$

---

4. See Patinkin (1965) for an early discussion of price level indeterminacy and Schmitt-Grohé and Uribe (2000a) for a more recent discussion.

5. In contrast, the nominal interest rate is stationary because both the real rate of interest and the inflation rate (and therefore expected inflation) are stationary.

even though (10.10) and (10.9) both imply that the average growth rate of money will equal μ_0 (see problem 2). With the money supply process (10.10), the equilibrium price level is trend stationary, and the forecast error variance does not increase without limit as the forecast horizon increases.

It is not surprising that (10.9) and (10.10) lead to different solutions for the price level. Under (10.9), the nominal money supply is a nontrend stationary process; random target misses have permanent effects on the future level of the money supply and therefore on the future price level. In contrast, (10.10) implies that the nominal money supply is trend stationary. Deviations of money from the deterministic growth path $\mu' + \mu_0 t$ are temporary, so the price level is also trend stationary.

This discussion leads to two conclusions. First, monetary policy can be implemented to reduce fluctuations in the nominal interest rate without leading to price level indeterminacy. Canzoneri, Henderson, and Rogoff (1983) and McCallum (1986) showed that by adjusting the money supply aggressively in response to interest rate movements, a central bank can reduce the variance of the nominal rate around its target level while leaving the price level determinate. However, the level at which the nominal rate can be set is determined by the growth rate of the nominal money supply because the latter equals the expected rate of inflation. The choice of μ_0 determines the feasible value of i^T (or equivalently, the choice of i^T determines μ_0). Targets for the nominal interest rate and rate of inflation cannot be independently determined.

Second, the underlying behavior of the nominal money supply is not uniquely determined by the assumption that the nominal rate is to be fixed at i^T; this target can be achieved with different money supply processes. And the different processes for m will lead to different behaviors of the price level. A complete description of policy, even under a nominal interest rate targeting policy, requires a specification of the underlying money supply process.

10.2.2 Interest Rate Policies in General Equilibrium

The analysis in the previous section employed a model that was not derived directly from the assumption of optimizing behavior on the part of the agents in the economy. Among authors employing general equilibrium representative agent models to study interest rate policies are Carlstrom and Fuerst (1995; 1997) and Woodford (1999b). Carlstrom and Fuerst addressed welfare issues associated with interest rate policies. They employed a cash-in-advance (CIA) framework in which consumption must be financed from nominal money balances. As noted in chapter 3, a positive nominal interest rate represents a distorting tax on consumption, affecting the household's choice between cash goods (i.e., consumption) and credit goods (i.e., investment and leisure). Introducing one-period price stickiness into their model, Carlstrom and Fuerst (1997) concluded that a constant nominal interest rate eliminates the distortion on capital accumulation, an interest rate peg Pareto-dominates a fixed money rule, and for any interest rate peg, there exists a money growth process that replicates the real equilibrium in the flexible-price version of their model. That is, an appropriate movement in the nominal money growth rate can undo the effects of the one-period price stickiness.

To illustrate the basic issues in a simple manner, consider the following five equilibrium conditions for a basic CIA economy with a positive nominal interest rate:

$$\frac{u_{c,t}}{1+i_t} = \beta E_t R_t \left(\frac{u_{c,t+1}}{1+i_{t+1}} \right)$$

$$\frac{u_{l,t}}{u_{c,t}} = \frac{\text{MPL}_t}{1+i_t}$$

$$R_t = 1 + E_t(\text{MPK}_{t+1})$$

$$m_t = \frac{M_t}{P_t} = c_t$$

$$1 + i_{t+1} = E_t \left(\frac{R_t P_{t+1}}{P_t} \right),$$

where $u_{c,t}$ is the marginal utility of consumption at time t, β is the subjective rate of time preference, R_t is 1 plus the real rate of return, $u_{l,t}$ is the marginal utility of leisure at time t, i_t is the nominal interest rate, MPL_t (MPK_t) is the marginal product of labor (capital), P_t is the price level, and m_t is the level of *real* money balances. The first of these five equations can be derived from a basic CIA model by recalling that $u_{c,t} = (1+i_t)\lambda_t$, where λ_t is the time t marginal value of wealth. (This assumes asset markets open before goods markets; see chapter 3.) Since $\lambda_t = \beta E_t R_t \lambda_{t+1}$ (see (3.26)), it follows that $u_{c,t}/(1+i_t) = \lambda_t = \beta E_t R_t u_{c,t+1}/(1+i_{t+1})$. The second equation equates the marginal rate of substitution between leisure and wealth to the marginal product of labor, again using the result that $\lambda_t = u_{c,t}/(1+i_t)$. The third equation is the definition of the real return on capital. The fourth equation is the binding CIA constraint that determines the demand for money as a function of the level of consumption. The final equation is simply the Fisher relationship linking nominal and real returns. The fourth and fifth equations of this system, as Woodford (1999b) emphasized, are traditionally interpreted as determining the price level and the nominal interest rate for an exogenous nominal money supply process. The model could be completed by adding the production function and the economywide resource constraint.

Rebelo and Xie (1999) argued that this CIA economy will replicate the behavior of a nonmonetary real economy under any nominal interest rate peg. To demonstrate the conditions under which their result holds, assume that the nominal interest rate is pegged at a value $\bar{\imath}$ for all t. Under an interest rate peg, the first two equations of the basic CIA model become

$$\frac{u_{c,t}}{1+\bar{\imath}} = \beta E_t R_t \left(\frac{u_{c,t}}{1+\bar{\imath}} \right) \Rightarrow u_{c,t} = \beta E_t R_t u_{c,t+1}$$

and

$$\frac{u_{l,t}}{u_{c,t}} = \frac{\mathrm{MPL}_t}{1+\bar{\imath}}.$$

The Euler condition is now identical to the form obtained in a real, nonmonetary economy, an economy not facing a CIA constraint.[6] The level at which the nominal interest rate is pegged only appears in the labor market equilibrium condition. Thus, Rebelo and Xie concluded that if labor supply is inelastic, the equilibrium with an interest rate peg is the same as the equilibrium in the corresponding nonmonetary real economy. Any equilibrium of the purely real economy can be achieved by a CIA model with a nominal interest rate peg if labor supply is inelastic. If labor supply is elastic, however, the choice of $\bar{\imath}$ does have effects on the real equilibrium.

   Under an interest rate peg, the price level process must satisfy

$$E_t \left(\frac{R_t P_{t+1}}{P_t} \right) = 1 + \bar{\imath},$$

and the nominal money supply must satisfy

$$M_t = P_t c_t.$$

These requirements do not, however, uniquely determine the nominal money supply process. For example, suppose the utility of consumption is $\ln c_t$. Then $u_{c,t} = 1/c_t$, and the Euler condition under an interest rate peg can be written as

$$\frac{1}{c_t} = \frac{P_t}{M_t} = \beta E_t R_t \left(\frac{P_{t+1}}{M_{t+1}} \right).$$

Rearranging this equation yields

$$1 = \beta E_t R_t \left(\frac{P_{t+1}}{P_t} \frac{M_t}{M_{t+1}} \right).$$

---

6. If output follows an exogenous process and all output is perishable, equilibrium requires that c_t equal output; the Euler condition then determines the real rate of return.

If this equation is linearized around the steady state, one obtains

$$r_t + E_t\pi_{t+1} - E_t\mu_{t+1} = \bar{\imath} - E_t\mu_{t+1} = 0,$$

where $E_t\mu_{t+1}$ is the expected growth rate of money. In this formulation, while real money balances are determined $(m_t = c_t)$, there are many nominal money supply processes consistent with equilibrium, as long as they all generate the same expected rate of nominal money growth.

The price level is indeterminate under such an interest rate–pegging policy (see section 10.2.1). However, assuming that P_t is predetermined because of price level stickiness still allows the money demand equation and the Fisher equation to determine P_{t+1} and m_t (and so the implied nominal supply of money) without affecting the real equilibrium determined by the Euler condition. In that sense, Carlstrom and Fuerst (1997) concluded that there exists a path for the nominal money supply in the face of price stickiness that leads to the same real equilibrium under an interest rate peg as would occur with a flexible price level.

Carlstrom and Fuerst (1995) provided some simulation evidence to suggest that nominal interest rate pegs dominate constant money growth rate policies. While this suggests that a constant nominal interest rate peg is desirable within the context of their model, Carlstrom and Fuerst did not explicitly derive the optimal policy. Instead, their argument was based on quite different grounds than the traditional Poole (1970) argument for an interest rate–oriented policy.[7] In Poole's analysis, stabilizing the interest rate served to insulate the real economy from purely financial disturbances. In contrast, Carlstrom and Fuerst appealed to standard tax-smoothing arguments to speculate, based on intertemporal tax considerations, that an interest rate peg might be optimal (see chapter 4).

The tax-smoothing argument for an interest rate peg is suggestive, but it is unlikely to be robust in the face of financial market disturbances. For example, in an analysis of optimal policy defined as money growth rate control, Ireland (1996) introduced a stochastic velocity shock by assuming the CIA constraint applies to only a time-varying fraction v_t of all consumption. In this case, the CIA constraint takes the form $P_t v_t c_t \le Q_t$, where Q_t is the nominal quantity out of which cash goods must be purchased. It is straightforward to show that the Euler condition must be modified in this case to become

$$\frac{u_c(c_t)}{1 + v_t i_t} = \beta E_t R_t \left(\frac{u_c(c_{t+1})}{1 + v_{t+1} i_{t+1}} \right).$$

---

7. See chapter 11 for a discussion of Poole's analysis of the choice of monetary policy operating procedures.

If $v_t \equiv 1$, the case considered by Carlstrom and Fuerst is obtained. If v_t is random, eliminating the intertemporal distortion requires that $v_t i_t$ be pegged and that the nominal interest rate vary over time to offset the stochastic fluctuations in v_t. The introduction of a stochastic velocity disturbance suggests that an interest rate peg would not be optimal.

10.2.3 Liquidity Traps

In a standard money-in-the-utility function (MIU) model, the Euler condition and the Fisher equation can be combined and written as $u_{c,t}/(1+i_t) = \beta E_t P_t u_{c,t+1}/P_{t+1}$ or, in the absence of uncertainty,

$$\frac{P_t(1+i_t)}{P_{t+1}} = \frac{u_{c,t}}{\beta u_{c,t+1}} \equiv z_t. \tag{10.11}$$

Following Woodford (2000), an interest rate policy can be written as

$$1 + i_t = \phi(P_t, z_t).$$

The function $\phi(P_t, z_t)$ specifies the setting for the policy instrument (the nominal rate i_t) as a function of the current price level and the variable z_t, which captures the real factors that determine the marginal utility of consumption. Woodford labels policies of this form *Wicksellian policies*. Under such a policy, equilibrium, if it exists, is a sequence for the price level that satisfies (10.11). Using the policy rule in (10.11), this equilibrium condition becomes

$$P_t \phi(P_t, z_t) = P_{t+1} z_t. \tag{10.12}$$

Equilibrium conditions such as (10.12) were used to illustrate how a monetary economy may have multiple equilibria (see chapters 2 and 4). The nominal quantity of money was assumed to be fixed, and it was demonstrated that there existed multiple price paths consistent with equilibrium. Suppose P^* is the stationary solution to (10.12): $P^* \phi(P^*, z) = P^* z$, where, for simplicity, z_t is treated as constant. Initial price levels greater than P^* are consistent with a perfect-foresight equilibrium. Along price paths originating above P^*, hyperinflations occurred, with real money balances shrinking toward zero. These equilibrium paths involve rising inflation and an increasing nominal interest rate. Because the opportunity cost of holding money rises, the demand for real money balances falls, so that equilibrium between money demand and supply is maintained.

When the price path originates at a value less than P^*, the argument was made that such price paths, involving explosive deflations, could be ruled out as perfect-foresight equilibria. With real money balances going to infinity, the transversality condition for the representative agent's optimization problem would eventually be violated (see section 2.2.1).

Benhabib, Schmitt-Grohé, and Uribe (2001a; 2001b; 2002) and Schmitt-Grohé, and Uribe (2000b) argued that deflationary paths originating from initial price levels less than P^* cannot be ruled out. Their argument was based on the observation that the nominal rate of interest cannot fall below zero. Explosive deflations would eventually force the nominal interest rate to zero, but the nominal rate is then prevented from falling further. They argued that simple and seemingly reasonable monetary policy rules, rules that follow the Taylor principle and change the nominal interest rate more than one-for-one in response to changes in inflation (see chapter 8) may actually lead to macroeconomic instability that would force the economy into a liquidity trap—a situation of zero nominal interest rates.

To illustrate this possibility, rewrite the equilibrium condition (10.11) as

$$1 + i_t = \left(\frac{P_{t+1}}{P_t}\right) z,$$

where the real factors summarized by z that determine the real interest rate are taken to be constant. Taking logs of both sides, this equilibrium relationship can be approximated by

$$i_t = \pi_{t+1} + \log(z).$$

Now suppose the central bank follows an interest rate rule of the form

$$i_t = r^* + \pi^* + \delta(\pi_t - \pi^*), \tag{10.13}$$

where π^* is the central bank's target inflation rate and $r^* \equiv \log(z)$ is the equilibrium rate rate. This policy rule can be viewed as a simple form of the Taylor rule. The Taylor principle calls for ensuring that the nominal interest rate responds more than one-for-one to changes in inflation: $\delta > 1$.

If these two equations are combined, the equilibrium process for the inflation rate becomes

$$\pi_{t+1} = \pi^* + \delta(\pi_t - \pi^*),$$

which is unstable for $\delta > 1$, that is, for policy rules following the Taylor principle. The dynamics of the model are illustrated in figure 10.1. A stationary equilibrium exists with inflation equal to π^*. However, for inflation rates that start out below the target rate π^*, π declines. If the rate of deflation is bounded below by the zero bound on nominal interest rates, however, the economy converges to a zero nominal rate liquidity trap. The resulting equilibrium at π^{**} is stable.

This simple example has expected future inflation depend on current inflation through the assumed policy rule. Standard stability arguments in the presence of

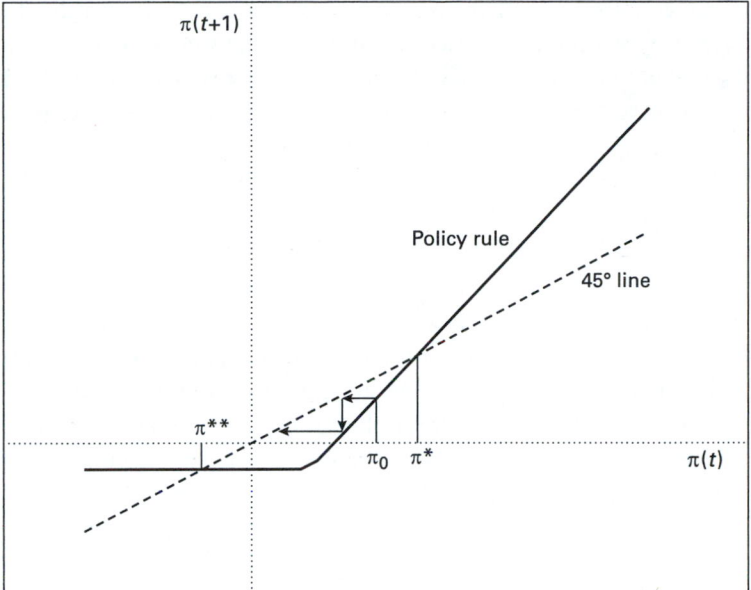

Figure 10.1
Dynamics of a liquidity trap.

forward-looking jump variables rely on notions of saddle-path stability in which the inflation rate would jump to put the economy on a stable path converging to the unique stationary steady state. In the present context, this would involve current inflation jumping immediately to equal π^*, the unique value consistent with a stationary equilibrium. That is, the only perfect-foresight stationary equilibrium in a neighborhood of π^* is that associated with inflation equal to the target rate π^*. In contrast, in a neighborhood around the deflationary equilibrium π^{**}, there are many equilibrium paths consistent with a perfect-foresight equilibrium. Given this nonuniqueness or indeterminacy, sunspot equilibria are possible. If inflation starts out just to the left of π^*, the central bank cuts the nominal rate in an attempt to lower the real rate and stimulate the economy. But instead, this policy reaction simply generates expectations of lower inflation, causing actual inflation to decline further. Expressed in terms of the quantity of money, the lower nominal rate increases the demand for real money balances, forcing a fall in the price level and pushing the economy into a deflationary equilibrium.

Solutions
How can the economy get out of a liquidity trap? First, it is worth noting that, in general, optimal monetary policy in the absence of nominal rigidities requires that

the nominal interest rate equal zero. Rather than being a bad outcome, converging to a zero nominal interest rate is optimal because it eliminates the wedge between the private and social opportunity costs of money. If, however, for reasons not specified in the simple model used here, the liquidity trap equilibrium is a bad outcome, then one must question the assumption that the policymaker follows an ad hoc nonoptimal decision rule such as (10.13).

Suggestions for getting out of a liquidity trap have involved both fiscal and monetary policies. Suppose fiscal policy is non-Ricardian.[8] The government could promise to run huge deficits whenever the inflation rate gets too low (Benhabib, Schmitt-Grohé, and Uribe 2002). According to the fiscal theory of the price level, this action, by increasing the government's total stock of nominal debt, would increase the equilibrium price level. This policy would rule out the low-inflation equilibrium by producing expectations of higher inflation whenever inflation becomes too low.

Ireland (2001b) departed from the standard representative agent framework to show that a traditional *real balance effect* can eliminate liquidity traps.[9] In his model, there are two overlapping generations. In the liquidity trap, nominal interest rates are zero, and the demand for real money balances is indeterminate. As a consequence, variations in the nominal stock of money may not affect the price level—there is a real indeterminacy (of real money balances). However, in a steady state with a zero nominal interest rate, prices are falling, so the nominal stock of money must also decline to keep real balances constant. This requires taxing the young to reduce the money supply. With population growth, Ricardian equivalence does not hold. The future taxes necessary to reduce M will be paid, in part, by future generations, so the present discounted value of these taxes to the current generation is less than the value of their money holdings. In this environment, money is wealth, and aggregate demand depends on the real stock of money. This uniquely determines the level of real balances in equilibrium. But if M/P is uniquely determined, then varying M must always affect P, even in the liquidity trap.

If the central bank can conduct open market operations in an asset that is an imperfect substitute for money, monetary policy can still affect inflation, even in a liquidity trap. McCallum (2000) and Svensson (2001), for example, argued that a central bank can generate inflation by depreciating its currency, and Goodfriend (2000) considered the effects of open market operations in long-term bonds. By increasing the equilibrium price level, and thereby causing private agents to expect a positive rate of inflation, such policies can prevent nominal interest rates from falling to zero.

8. Under a non-Ricardian fiscal policy, the government's intertemporal budget constraint holds only at the equilibrium price level (see chapter 4).

9. See also McCallum (2000).

Our simple model used to illutrate a liquidity trap ignored the real side of the economy. In practice, the zero lower bound on the nominal interest rate can create serious problems when the equilibrium real interest rate becomes negative. Since the real interest rate is $i_t - E_t\pi_{t+1}$, if the nominal interest rate set by the central bank has been reduced to zero, expectations of deflation act to raise the real interest. When the central bank has an explicit (positive) target for inflation as under an inflation targeting regime, the likelihood that the public will expected deflation may be reduced. Price level targeting may be even more effective, since under such a policy any actual fall in the price level must be offset by above average inflation to bring the price level back to target. In this way, a regime of price level targeting may generate higher expectations of future inflation, thereby lowering the real interest rate even when the current policy rate is at zero. Price level targeting was analyzed by Svensson (1999d) and Vestin (2006).[10] Eggertsson and Woodford (2003) empahsized the importance of commitments to future policies and found that a history-dependent price level targeting rule can implement optimal policy even in a liquidity trap.

10.3   The Term Structure of Interest Rates

The distinction between real and nominal rates of interest is critical for understanding monetary policy issues, but another important distinction is that between short-term and long-term interest rates. Changes in the short-term interest rate that serves as the operational target for implementing monetary policy will affect aggregate spending decisions only if longer-term real rates of interest are affected. While the use of an interest rate–oriented policy reduces the importance of money demand in the transmission of policy actions to the real economy, it raises to prominence the role played by the term structure of interest rates.

The exposition here builds on the expectations theory of the term structure. For a systematic discussion of the theory of the term structure, see Cox, Ingersoll, and Ross (1985); Shiller (1990); or Campbell and Shiller (1991). Under the expectations hypothesis of the term structure, long-term nominal interest rates depend on expectations of future nominal short-term interest rates. These future short-term rates will be functions of monetary policy, so expectations about future policy play an important role in determining the shape of the term structure.

10.3.1   The Expectations Theory of the Term Structure

Under the expectations theory of the term structure, the n-period interest rate equals an average of the current short-term rate and the future short-term rates expected to

---

10. See section 8.4.6, for an analysis of alternative targeting regimes in new Keynesian models.

hold over the n-period horizon. For example, if $i_{n,t}$ is the nominal yield to maturity at time t on an n-period discount bond, and i_t is the one-period rate, the pure expectations hypothesis in the absence of uncertainty would imply that[11]

$$(1 + i_{n,t})^n = \prod_{i=0}^{n-1}(1 + i_{t+i}).$$

This condition ensures that the holding period yield on the n-period bond is equal to the yield from holding a sequence of one-period bonds. Taking logs of both sides and recalling that $\ln(1 + x) \approx x$ for small x yields a common approximation:

$$i_{n,t} = \frac{1}{n}\sum_{i=0}^{n-1} i_{t+i}.$$

Since an n-period bond becomes an $n-1$ period bond after one period, these two relationships can also be written as

$$(1 + i_{n,t})^n = (1 + i_t)(1 + i_{n-1,t+1})^{n-1}$$

and

$$i_{n,t} = \left(\frac{1}{n}\right)i_t + \left(\frac{n-1}{n}\right)i_{n-1,t+1}.$$

These conditions will not hold exactly under conditions of uncertainty for two reasons. First, if risk-neutral investors equate expected one-period returns, then the one-period rate $1 + i_t$ will equal $E_t(1 + i_{n,t})^n/(1 + i_{n-1,t+1})^{n-1}$, which, from Jensen's inequality, is not the same as $(1 + i_{n,t})^n = (1 + i_t)E_t(1 + i_{n-1,t+1})^{n-1}$.[12] Second, Jensen's inequality implies that $\ln E_t(1 + i_{n-1,t+1})$ is not the same as $E_t \ln(1 + i_{n-1,t+1})$.

These two issues are ignored, however, to illustrate the basic linkages between the term structure of interest rates and monetary policy. It is sufficient to simplify further by dealing only with one- and two-period interest rates. Letting $I_t \equiv i_{2,t}$ be the two-period rate (the long-term interest rate), the term structure equation becomes

$$(1 + I_t)^2 = (1 + i_t)(1 + E_t i_{t+1}), \tag{10.14}$$

---

11. A constant risk premium could easily be incorporated. A time-varying risk premium is added to the analysis in section 10.3.2.

12. Suppose $P_{n,t}$ is the time t price of an n-period discount bond. Then $P_{n,t}^{-1} = (1 + i_{n,t})^n$. Since at time $t + 1$ this becomes an $n-1$ period bond, the one-period gross return is

$$E_t P_{n-1,t+1}/P_{n,t} = E_t(1 + i_{n,t})^n/(1 + i_{n-1,t})^{n-1}.$$

and this is approximated as

$$I_t = \frac{1}{2}(i_t + \mathrm{E}_t i_{t+1}). \tag{10.15}$$

The critical implication of this relationship for monetary policy is that the current structure of interest rates will depend on current short-term rates *and* on market expectations of future short rates. Since the short rate is affected by monetary policy, I_t will depend on expectations about future policy.

The one-period ahead forward rate is defined as

$$f_t^1 = \frac{(1 + I_t)^2}{1 + i_t} - 1.$$

If the pure expectations hypothesis of the term structure holds, (10.14) implies that f_t^1 is equal to the market's expectation of the future one-period rate. Hence, forward rates derived from the term structure are often used to gain information on expectations of future interest rates (see Dahlquist and Svensson 1996; Söderlind and Svensson 1997; Rudebusch 2002b).

Equation (10.15) has a direct and testable empirical implication. Subtracting i_t from both sides, the equation can be rewritten as

$$I_t - i_t = \frac{1}{2}(\mathrm{E}_t i_{t+1} - i_t).$$

If the current two-period rate is greater than the one-period rate (i.e., $I_t - i_t > 0$), then agents must expect the one-period rate to rise ($\mathrm{E}_t i_{t+1} > i_t$). Because one can always write $i_{t+1} = \mathrm{E}_t i_{t+1} + (i_{t+1} - \mathrm{E}_t i_{t+1})$, it follows that

$$\frac{1}{2}(i_{t+1} - i_t) = I_t - i_t + \frac{1}{2}(i_{t+1} - \mathrm{E}_t i_{t+1})$$

$$= a + b(I_t - i_t) + \theta_{t+1}, \tag{10.16}$$

where $a = 0$, $b = 1$, and $\theta_{t+1} = \frac{1}{2}(i_{t+1} - \mathrm{E}_t i_{t+1})$ is the error the private sector makes in forecasting the future short-term interest rate. Under the assumption of rational expectations, θ_{t+1} will be uncorrelated with information available at time t. In this case, (10.16) forms a regression equation that can be estimated consistently by least-squares. Unfortunately, estimates of such equations usually reject the joint hypothesis that $a = 0$ and $b = 1$, generally obtaining point estimates of b significantly less than 1. Some of this empirical evidence is summarized in Rudebusch (1995, table 1) and McCallum (1994b, table 1). In section 10.3.2, the observed relationship between long and short rates, as well as the way in which interest rates react to monetary policy, is shown to depend on the manner in which policy is conducted.

10.3.2 Policy and the Term Structure

In this section, a simple model illustrates how the behavior of nominal interest rates depends on the money supply process. Consider the following model:

$$R_t = q_t \tag{10.17}$$

$$R_t = \frac{1}{2}[i_t - E_t\pi_{t+1} + E_t(i_{t+1} - \pi_{t+2})] \tag{10.18}$$

$$m_t - p_t = -ai_t + v_t \tag{10.19}$$

$$m_t = \gamma m_{t-1} + \varphi_t, \qquad 0 < \gamma < 1, \tag{10.20}$$

where $\pi_t = p_t - p_{t-1}$. This model incorporates the assumption that output and the long-term (in this case, two-period) real interest rate are exogenous, with the gross long-term real rate R_t equal to a stochastic mean zero random variable q_t. R_t is equal to the average of the current real short-term rate $i_t - E_t\pi_{t+1}$ and the expected future real short-term rate $E_t(i_{t+1} - \pi_{t+2})$. The real demand for money is decreasing in the nominal short-term interest rate and is subject to a random shock v_t. Finally, the nominal money supply is assumed to follow a first-order autoregressive process, subject to a control error φ_t. Note that this process implies that $E_t m_{t+1} = \gamma m_t$.

By using (10.19) to eliminate i_t and $E_t i_{t+1}$ from (10.18), this system of four equations implies that the equilibrium process for the price level must satisfy the following expectations difference equation:

$$2aq_t = (1 + a)p_t + E_t p_{t+1} - aE_t p_{t+2} - (1 + \gamma)m_t + v_t. \tag{10.21}$$

To find the solution for the short-term interest rate, one can employ the method of undetermined coefficients. Since the relevant state variables in (10.21) are m_t, q_t, and v_t, it is possible to guess a solution of the form

$$p_t = b_1 m_t + b_2 q_t + b_3 v_t.$$

This implies that $E_t p_{t+1} = b_1 \gamma m_t$ and $E_t p_{t+2} = b_1 E_t m_{t+2} = b_1 \gamma^2 m_t$. Using these in (10.21), the equilibrium solution for the price level is

$$p_t = \left[\frac{1}{1 + a(1 - \gamma)}\right]m_t + \left(\frac{1}{1 + a}\right)(2aq_t - v_t). \tag{10.22}$$

From the money demand equation, $i_t = (v_t + p_t - m_t)/a$, so, given the equilibrium process for p_t,

$$i_t = -\left[\frac{1-\gamma}{1+a(1-\gamma)}\right]m_t + \left(\frac{1}{1+a}\right)(2q_t + v_t),\tag{10.23}$$

and the two-period nominal rate is

$$I_t = \frac{1}{2}(i_t + E_t i_{t+1})$$

$$= \frac{1}{2}\left\{-\left[\frac{1-\gamma^2}{1+a(1-\gamma)}\right]m_t + \left(\frac{1}{1+a}\right)(2q_t + v_t)\right\}.\tag{10.24}$$

Equation (10.24) illustrates how the long-term rate depends on the money supply process, where this process is characterized in this example by the parameter γ.

From (10.24), the impact of an innovation to m_t (i.e., a φ shock) on the current long rate is equal to

$$-\frac{1}{2}\left[\frac{1-\gamma^2}{1+a(1-\gamma)}\right] < 0,$$

which depends on the parameter γ. The greater the degree of serial correlation in the money supply process (the larger is γ), the smaller the effect in absolute value on i_t of a change in m_t. The effect of a money innovation on the slope of the term structure, $I_t - i_t$, is equal to $\frac{1}{2}(1-\gamma)^2/[1+a(1-\gamma)]$, and this also depends on γ. High persistence in the money supply process produces a flatter term structure. To take the extreme case, suppose $\gamma = 1$; the nominal money supply follows a random walk with innovation φ_t. An innovation implies a permanent change in the *level* of the money supply. This causes a proportionate change in the price level (the coefficient on m_t in (10.22) is equal to 1 if $\gamma = 1$), but there is no impact on the expected rate of inflation. With the real rate exogenous, the nominal interest rate adjusts only in response to changes in expected inflation, so with $\gamma = 1$, changes in m have no effect on the nominal interest rate. If $\gamma < 1$, an unexpected increase in m causes the expectation of a subsequent decline in m and p. It is this expectation of a deflation that lowers the nominal rate of interest.

Similarly, the impact of real interest rate disturbances on nominal rates will depend on the money supply process if policy responds to real disturbances. If, for example, the money supply process is modified to become $m_t = m_{t-1} + \psi q_{t-1} + \varphi_t$, so that the growth rate of m_t depends on the real rate shock, it can be shown that the equilibrium short-term rate is

$$i_t = \left(\frac{2+\psi}{1+a}\right)q_t + \left(\frac{1}{1+a}\right)v_t.$$

If $\psi > 0$, an increase in the real rate $(q > 0)$ induces an increase in the nominal money supply the following period. This increase implies that the money supply is expected to grow $(E_t m_{t+1} - m_t = \psi q_t > 0)$, so expected inflation rises. This increases the positive impact of q_t on the short-term nominal rate.

These results are illustrative, showing how interest rate responses depend on expectations of the future money supply and consequently on the systematic behavior of m. The exact mechanism highlighted in these examples requires that a monetary innovation (i.e., $\varphi > 0$) generate an expected deflation in order for nominal rates to decline, since the real rate has been treated as exogenous.

The dependence of interest rates and the term structure on monetary policy implies that the results of empirical studies of the term structure should depend on the operating procedures followed by the central bank. McCallum (1994b), Rudebusch (1995), Fuhrer (1996), and Balduzzi et al. (1998) examined the connection between the Fed's tendency to target interest rates, the dynamics of short-term interest rates, and empirical tests of the expectations model of the term structure.

This dependence can be seen most easily by employing a setup similar to that used by McCallum. Consider the following two-period model of nominal interest rates in which, as before, I is the two-period rate and i is the one-period rate:

$$I_t = \frac{1}{2}(i_t + E_t i_{t+1}) + \xi_t, \tag{10.25}$$

where ξ is a random variable that represents a time-varying term premium. Equation (10.15) implied that the pure expectations model of the term structure holds exactly, without error; the term premium ξ introduced in (10.25) allows for a stochastic deviation from the exact form of the expectations hypothesis. Variation in risk factors might account for the presence of ξ. Suppose further that the term premium is serially correlated:

$$\xi_t = \rho \xi_{t-1} + \eta_t, \tag{10.26}$$

where η_t is a white noise process.

If $\varepsilon_{t+1} = i_{t+1} - E_t i_{t+1}$ is the expectational error in forecasting the future one-period rate, (10.25) implies that

$$\frac{1}{2}(i_{t+1} - i_t) = I_t - i_t - \xi_t + \frac{1}{2}\varepsilon_{t+1}, \tag{10.27}$$

which is usually interpreted to mean that the slope coefficient in a regression of one-half the change in the short rate on the spread between the long rate and the short rate should equal 1. It was previously noted that actual estimates of this slope coefficient have generally been much less than 1 and have even been negative.

The final aspect of the model is a description of the behavior of the central bank. Since many central banks use the short-term interest rate as their operational policy instrument, and since they often engage in interest rate smoothing, McCallum assumed that $i_t = i_{t-1} + \mu(I_t - i_t) + \zeta_t.$[13] However, problems of multiple equilibria may arise when policy responds to forward-looking variables such as I_t (see Bernanke and Woodford 1997 and problem 6). To avoid this possibility, assume that policy adjusts the short-term rate according to

$$i_t = i_{t-1} - \mu \xi_t + \zeta_t, \tag{10.28}$$

where ζ_t is a white noise process and $|\mu| < 1$. According to (10.28), a rise in the risk premium in the long-term rate induces a policy response that lowers the short rate. Exogenous changes in risk that alter the term structure might also affect consumption or investment spending, leading the central bank to lower short-term interest rates to counter the contractionary effects of a positive realization of ξ_t. Because no real explanation has been given for ξ or why policy might respond to it, it important to keep in mind that this is only an illustrative example that will serve to suggest how policy behavior might affect the term structure.

Equations (10.25)–(10.28) form a simple model that can be used to study how policy responses to the term structure risk premium (i.e., μ) affect the observed relationship between short-term and long-term interest rates. From (10.28), $E_t i_{t+1} = i_t - \mu\rho\xi_t$, so

$$I_t = \frac{1}{2}(i_t + E_t i_{t+1}) + \xi_t = i_t + \left(1 - \frac{\mu\rho}{2}\right)\xi_t.$$

This implies that

$$\left(1 - \frac{\mu\rho}{2}\right)^{-1}(I_t - i_t) = \xi_t.$$

Using this result, (10.27) can be written as

$$\frac{1}{2}(i_{t+1} - i_t) = I_t - i_t - \left(1 - \frac{\mu\rho}{2}\right)^{-1}(I_t - i_t) + \frac{1}{2}\varepsilon_{t+1},$$

or

$$\frac{1}{2}(i_{t+1} - i_t) = -\left(\frac{\mu\rho}{2 - \mu\rho}\right)(I_t - i_t) + \frac{1}{2}\varepsilon_{t+1}, \tag{10.29}$$

13. McCallum actually allows the coefficient on i_{t-1} in (10.28) to differ from 1.

so that one would expect the regression coefficient on $I_t - i_t$ to be $-\mu\rho/(2 - \mu\rho)$ and not 1. In other words, the estimated slope of the term structure, even when the expectations model is correct, will depend on the serial correlation properties of the term premium (ρ) and on the policy response to the spread between long and short rates (μ). The problem arises even though (10.27) implies that $\frac{1}{2}(i_{t+1} - i_t) = a + b(I_t - i_t) + x_{t+1}$, with $a = 0$ and $b = 1$, because the error term x_{t+1} is equal to $-\xi_t + \frac{1}{2}\varepsilon_{t+1}$; since this is correlated with $I_t - i_t$, ordinary least-squares is an inconsistent estimator of b.

The important lesson of McCallum's analysis was that observed term structure relationships can be affected by the way monetary policy is conducted. McCallum assumed policy responded to the slope of the term structure, which in his model reflected variations in the risk premium. Cochrane and Piazzesi (2002) found evidence that the interest rate–setting behavior of the Federal Reserve has been affected by both long-term interest rates and by the slope of the yield curve. If the former reflects long-term inflation expectations and the latter helps forecast real economic activity, then this behavior would be broadly consistent with the Taylor rule (see chapter 8). Gallmeyer, Hollifield, and Zin (2005) provided a more modern treatment of McCallum's results in the context of models that allow for endogenous variation in risk premiums.[14] They showed how the policy behavior assumed by McCallum can be reconciled with Taylor rule representations of monetary policy. Ravenna and Seppälä (2007a) showed how a new Keynesian model can account for rejections of the expectations model of the term structure, and McGough, Rudebusch, Williams (2005) considered monetary policy rules that respond to long-term interest rates.

Rather than employing an equation such as (10.28) to represent policy behavior, Rudebusch (1995) used data from periods of funds rate targeting (1974–1979 and 1984–1992) to estimate a model of the Federal Reserve's target for the funds rate. He was then able to simulate the implied behavior of the term structure, using the expectations hypothesis to link funds rate behavior to the behavior of longer-term interest rates. He found that the manner in which the Fed adjusted its target can account for the failure of the spread between long and short rates to have much predictive content for changes in long rates, at least at horizons of 3 to 12 months (that is, for the failure to obtain a coefficient of 1, or even a significant coefficient, in a regression of $\frac{1}{2}(i_{t+1} - i_t)$ on $(I_t - i_t)$). Thus, if the three-month rate exceeds the funds rate, (10.16) would appear to predict a rise in the funds rate. As Rudebusch demonstrated, the Fed tends to set its target for the funds rate at a level it expects to maintain. In this case, any spread between the funds rate and other rates has no implications for future changes in the funds rate (in terms of 10.28, $\mu \approx 0$). Only as new information becomes available might the target funds rate change.

---

14. These models are discussed in section 10.4.

Fuhrer (1996) provided further evidence on the relationship between the Fed's policy rule and the behavior of long-term interest rates. He estimated time-varying parameters of a policy reaction rule for the funds rate consistent with observed long-term rates. Agents are assumed to use the current parameter values of the policy rule to forecast future short rates.[15] Fuhrer argued that the parameters he obtained are consistent with general views on the evolution of the Fed's reaction function. Balduzzi et al. (1998) found that during the 1989–1996 period of federal funds rate targeting in the United States, the term structure was consistent with a regime in which changes in the target for the funds rate occurred infrequently but were partially predictable. In a related literature, Mankiw and Miron (1986) and Mankiw, Miron, and Weil (1987) studied how the founding of the Federal Reserve affected the seasonal behavior of interest rates (see also Fisher and Wohar 1990; Angelini 1994a; 1994b; Mankiw, Miron, and Weil 1994).

10.3.3   Expected Inflation and the Term Structure

The term structure plays an important role as an indicator of inflationary expectations. Since market interest rates are the sum of an expected real return and an expected inflation premium, the nominal interest rate on an n-period bond can be expressed as

$$i_t^n = \frac{1}{n} \sum_{i=0}^{n} \mathrm{E}_t r_{t+i} + \frac{1}{n} \mathrm{E}_t \bar{\pi}_{t+n},$$

where $\mathrm{E}_t r_{t+i}$ is the one-period real rate expected at time t to prevail at $t+i$, and $\mathrm{E}_t \bar{\pi}_{t+n} \equiv \mathrm{E}_t p_{t+n} - p_t$ is the expected change in log price from t to $t+n$. If real rates are stationary around a constant value $\bar{r}$, then $\frac{1}{n} \sum_{i=0}^{n} \mathrm{E}_t r_{t+i} \approx \bar{r}$ and

$$i_t^n \approx \bar{r} + \frac{1}{n} \mathrm{E}_t \bar{\pi}_{t+n}.$$

In this case, fluctuations in the long rate will be caused mainly by variations in expected inflation. Based on a study of interest rates on nominal and indexed government bonds in the United Kingdom, Barr and Campbell (1997) concluded that "almost 80 percent of the movement in long-term nominal rates appears to be due to changes in expected long-term inflation." For this reason, increases in long-term nominal rates of interest are often interpreted as signaling an increase in expected inflation.

---

15. As Fuhrer noted, this behavior is not fully rational because agents presumably learn that the policy rule changes over time. However, the time-varying parameters approximately follow a random walk process, so using the current values to forecast future policy does not introduce large systematic errors.

When both nominal bonds and bonds whose returns are indexed to inflation are traded, a comparison of the returns on the two assets will provide information about the expected rate of inflation. However, if there are time-varying inflation risk premiums, this comparison may make it difficult to tell whether the different interest rates on the nominal bond and the real indexed bond are reflecting changes in expected inflation or changes in the risk premium. Ravenna and Seppälä (2007b), using a new Keynesian model calibrated to U.S. data, found that inflation risk premiums are small and not highly volatile. Thus, indexed bonds can be used to extract information about expected inflation.

A policy-induced rise in short rates that is accompanied by a decline in long rates would be interpreted as meaning that the contractionary policy (the rise in short rates) is expected to lower future inflation, thereby lowering nominal long-term interest rates and future short-term rates. Conversely, a cut in the short-run policy rate accompanied by a rise in long rates would provide evidence that the central bank was following an inflationary policy. Goodfriend (1993) provided an interpretation of U.S. monetary policy in the period 1979–1992 based on the notion that long-term interest rates provide important information on market inflation expectations.

Buttiglione, Del Giovane, and Tristani (1998) examined the impact of policy rate changes on forward rates in OECD countries. Under the hypothesis that changes in monetary policy do not affect the expected real interest rate far in the future, changes in the forward rates implied by the term structure should reflect the impact of the policy change on expected future inflation. The forward interest rate on a one-period discount bond n periods in the future can be derived from the rates on n and $n+1$ period bonds and is equal to

$$f_t^n = \frac{(1 + i_{n+1,t})^{n+1}}{(1 + i_{n,t})^n} - 1 \approx (n+1)i_{n+1,t} - ni_{n,t}.$$

Thus, if long-term expected real rates are constant, then for large n, $f_t^n \approx \bar{r} + E_t\bar{\pi}_{t+n+1} - E_t\bar{\pi}_{t+n} = \bar{r} + E_t(p_{t+n+1} - p_{t+n})$ or $f_t^n \approx \bar{r} + E_t\pi_{t+n+1}$. The forward rate then provides a direct estimate of future expected rates of inflation.[16] Interestingly, Buttiglione, Del Giovane, and Tristani found that a contractionary shift in policy (a rise in the short-term policy interest rate) lowered forward rates for some countries and raised them for others. The response of forward rates was closely related to a country's average inflation rate; for low-inflation countries, a policy action that increased short-term rates was estimated to lower forward rates. This response is consistent with the hypothesis that the increases in the short rate represented a cred-

---

16. Söderlind and Svensson (1997) provided a survey of techniques for estimating market expectations from the term structure.

ible policy expected to reduce inflation. In countries with high-inflation experiences, increases in short rates were not associated with decreases in forward rates.

A key maintained hypothesis in the view that movements in interest rates reveal information about inflation expectations is that the Fisher hypothesis, the hypothesis that nominal interest rates will incorporate a premium for expected inflation, holds. Suppose that the real rate is stationary around an average value of $\bar{r}$. Then, since $i_t = r_t + \pi_{t+1}^e = r_t + \pi_{t+1} + e_{t+1}$, where e_{t+1} is the inflation forecast error (which is stationary under rational expectations), the ex post real rate $i_t - \pi_{t+1}$ is stationary. Thus, if the nominal interest rate and the inflation rate are nonstationary, they must be cointegrated under the Fisher hypothesis. This is the sense in which long-term movements in inflation should be reflected in the nominal interest rate. Mishkin (1992) adopted this cointegrating interpretation of the Fisher relationship to test for the presence of a long-term relationship between inflation and nominal interest rates in the United States. If over a particular time period neither i nor π is integrated of order 1 but instead are both stationary, there is no real meaning to the statement that permanent shifts in the level of inflation should cause similar movements in nominal rates because such permanent shifts have not occurred. If either i or π is $I(1)$, they should both be $I(1)$, and they should be cointegrated. Mishkin found the evidence to be consistent with the Fisher relationship.

10.4 Macrofinance

A recent literature has developed that identifies the latent factors employed in finance models of the term structure to macroeconomic variables such as inflation, real economic activity, and monetary policy. The term structure is represented using affine no-arbitrage models, as in Dai and Singleton (2000). The unobserved latent variables that determine bond prices in these models are linked to macroeconomic variables, either through nonstructural statistical models such as a VAR (e.g., Ang and Piazzesi 2003) or by using a new Keynesian model to represent macroeconomic and monetary policy outcomes (e.g., Rudebusch and Wu 2007; 2008). Diebold, Piazzesi, and Rudebusch (2005) provided an overview of this research area and discussed some of the issues that arise in linking finance models and macroeconomic models.

Suppose there are two latent (unobserved) factors that determine bond prices.[17] Following Rudebusch and Wu (2007), denote these factors by L_t and S_t and assume they follow a VAR process given by

$$F_t \equiv \begin{bmatrix} L_t \\ S_t \end{bmatrix} = \rho \begin{bmatrix} L_{t-1} \\ S_{t-1} \end{bmatrix} + \Sigma e_t = \rho F_{t-1} + \Sigma e_t, \tag{10.30}$$

17. Rudebusch and Wu (2008) found that two-factor models are rich enough to fit the data adequately.

where e_t is independently and identically distributed as a normal mean zero unit variance process, where Σ is a 2×2 nonsingular matrix. Assume further that one can write the short-term interest rate i_t as a function of the two factors. Specifically,

$$i_t = \delta_0 + \delta_1 F_t. \tag{10.31}$$

Finally, assume the prices of risk associated with each factor are linear functions of the two factors, so that if $\Lambda_{i,t}$ is the price of risk associated with conditional volatility of factor i,

$$\Lambda_t = \begin{bmatrix} \Lambda_{L,t} \\ \Lambda_{S,t} \end{bmatrix} = \lambda_0 + \lambda_1 F_t. \tag{10.32}$$

If i_t is the return on a one-period bond, than the structure given by (10.30)–(10.32), together with the assumption that no-arbitrage opportunities exist, allows one to price longer-term bonds. In particular, if $b_{j,t}$ is the log price of a j-period nominal bond, one can show that

$$b_{j,t} = \bar{A}_j + \bar{B}_j F_t,$$

where

$$\bar{A}_1 = -\delta_0; \quad \bar{B}_1 = -\delta_1,$$

and for $j = 2, \ldots, J$,

$$\bar{A}_{j+1} - \bar{A}_j = \bar{B}_j(-\Sigma\lambda_0) + \frac{1}{2}\bar{B}_j\Sigma\Sigma'\bar{B}_j + \bar{A}_1$$

$$\bar{B}_{j+1} = \bar{B}_j(\rho - \Sigma\lambda_1) + \bar{B}_1.$$

Empirical research aimed at estimating this type of no-arbitrage model generally finds that one factor affects yields at all maturities and so is called the level factor, whereas the other factor affects short and long rates differently and so is called the slope factor.

The macrofinance literature has attempted to identify the level and slope factors with macroeconomic factors. For example, in new Keynesian models, the short-term interest rate is often represented in terms of a Taylor rule of the form

$$i_t = r^* + \pi_t^T + a_\pi(\pi_t - \pi_t^T) + a_x x_t,$$

where π_t^T is the central bank's inflation target and x_t is the output gap. In this case, changes in the inflation target should affect nominal interest rates at all maturities by altering inflation expectations. Thus, it would seem to be a prime candidate for the level factor. The slope factor might then be capturing the central bank's policy actions intended to stabilize the economy in the short run. Thus, one could model the factors explicitly in terms of the policy behavior of the central bank.[18]

Of course, this approach requires that the behavior of inflation, the inflation target, and the output gap also be modeled. As noted, Ang and Piazzesi (2003) represented the behavior of the macroeconomic variables using a VAR representation. They grouped variables into a set related to inflation and a set related to real activity. By then using the principal component from each group, they obtained the two factors that determine the term structure. Macroeconomic factors are found to explain movements of short- and medium-term interest rates but little of the long-term interest rate. Rudebusch and Wu (2008) employed a simplified new Keynesian model to model the behavior of macroeconomic variables, and Rudebusch and Wu (2007) argued that shifts in the pricing of risk associated with the Fed's inflation target can account for shifts in the behavior of the term structure in the United States.

In new Keynesian models and other structural macroeconomic models, the consumption Euler equation linking the marginal utility of current consumption to the discounted real return and future marginal utilities plays a key role in linking real economic activity and real interest rates. However, the interest rate appearing in this equation is normally identified with the real policy rate controlled by the central bank. As Canzoneri, Cumby, and Diba (2007) showed, monetary tightening (a rise in the policy rate) is typically associated with a decline in future consumption growth, yet standard specifications of the Euler condition would imply that a decline in expected consumption growth should be associated with a fall in the real interest rate.[19]

10.5 Financial Frictions in Credit Markets

Money has traditionally played a special role in macroeconomics and monetary theory because of the relationship between the nominal stock of money and the aggregate price level. The importance of money for understanding the determination of the general level of prices and average inflation rates, however, does not necessarily

---

18. McCallum (1994b) (see section 10.3.2) can be viewed as an early attempt to link the term structure to the behavior of monetary policy. Ballmeyer, Hollifield, and Zin (2007) provided an explicit analysis of the role of the policy rule in a no-arbitrage model of the term structure.

19. With standard log preferences, the linearized Euler equation (see chapter 8) is

$$c_t = E_t c_{t+1} - \left(\frac{1}{\sigma}\right) r_t,$$

so expected consumption growth $E_t c_{t+1} - c_t = \left(\frac{1}{\sigma}\right) r_t$ and the real interest rate are positively related. Canzoneri, Cumby, and Diba (2007) showed how this relationship is affected by habit persistence (a common component of new Keynesian models), but they argued that habit persistence does not fully reconcil the Euler equation with the empirical effects of a monetary policy contraction.

imply that the stock of money is the key variable that links the real and financial sectors or the most appropriate indicator of the short-run influence of financial factors on the economy. Many economists have argued that monetary policy has direct effects on aggregate spending that do not operate through traditional interest rate or exchange rate channels, and a large literature has focused on credit markets as playing a critical role in the transmission of monetary policy actions to the real economy.

The *credit view* stresses the distinct role played by financial assets and liabilities. Rather than aggregate all nonmoney financial assets into a single category called *bonds*, the credit view argues that macroeconomic models need to distinguish between different nonmonetary assets, either along the dimension of bank versus nonbank sources of funds or, more generally, internal versus external financing. The credit view also highlights heterogeneity among borrowers, stressing that some borrowers may be more vulnerable to changes in credit conditions than others. Finally, investment may be sensitive to variables such as net worth or cash flow if agency costs associated with imperfect information or costly monitoring create a wedge between the cost of internal and external funds. A rise in interest rates may have a much stronger contractionary impact on the economy if balance sheets are already weak, introducing the possibility that nonlinearities in the impact of monetary policy may be important.

The credit channel also operates when shifts in monetary policy alter either the efficiency of financial markets in matching borrowers and lenders or the extent to which borrowers face rationing in credit markets so that aggregate spending is influenced by liquidity constraints. There are several definitions of nonprice credit rationing. Jaffee and Russell (1976) defined credit rationing as existing when at the quoted interest rate the lender supplies a smaller loan than the borrower demands. Jaffee and Stiglitz (1990), however, pointed out that this practice represents standard price rationing; larger loans will normally be accompanied by a higher default rate and therefore carry a higher interest rate. Instead, Jaffee and Stiglitz characterized "pure credit rationing" as occurring when, among a group of agents (firms or individuals) who appear to be identical, some receive loans and others do not. Stiglitz and Weiss (1981) defined equilibrium credit rationing as being present whenever "either (a) among loan applicants who appear to be identical some receive a loan and others do not, and the rejected applicants would not receive a loan even if they offered to pay a higher interest rate; or (b) there are identifiable groups of individuals in the population who, with a given supply of credit, are unable to obtain loans at any interest rate, even though with a larger supply of credit, they would" (394–395). The critical aspect of this definition is that at the market equilibrium interest rate there is an unsatisfied demand for loans that cannot be eliminated through higher interest rates. Rejected loan applicants cannot succeed in getting a loan by offering to pay a higher interest rate.

It is important to recognize that credit rationing is sufficient but not necessary for a credit channel to exist. A theme of Gertler (1988), Bernanke and Gertler (1989), and Bernanke (1993) was that agency costs in credit markets will vary countercyclically; a monetary tightening that raises interest rates and generates a real economic slowdown will cause firm balance sheets to deteriorate, raising agency costs and lowering the efficiency of credit allocation. Changes in credit conditions are not reflected solely in interest rate levels. Thus, the general issue is to understand how credit market imperfections affect the macroeconomic equilibrium and the channels through which monetary policy actions are transmitted to the real economy.

The main focus here is on credit markets for firms undertaking investment projects. This approach is chosen primarily for convenience; the theoretical models may also be applied to the consumer loan market, and there is evidence that a significant fraction of households behave as if they faced liquidity constraints that link consumption spending more closely to current income than would be predicted by forward-looking models of consumption.[20]

The role of credit effects in the transmission of monetary policy arises as a result of imperfect information between parties in credit relationships. The information that each party to a credit transaction brings to the exchange will have important implications for the nature of credit contracts, the ability of credit markets to match borrowers and lenders efficiently, and the role played by the rate of interest in allocating credit among borrowers. The nature of credit markets can lead to distinct roles for different types of lenders (e.g., bank versus nonbank) and different types of borrowers (e.g., small firms versus large firms).

Critical to the presence of a distinct credit channel is the presence of imperfections in financial markets. The first task, then, is to review theories of credit market imperfections based on adverse selection, moral hazard, monitoring costs and agency costs; this is done in sections 10.5.1–10.5.4. These theories help to explain many of the distinctive features of financial markets, from collateral to debt contracts to the possibility of credit rationing. This material provides the microfoundations for the macroeconomic analysis of credit channels in section 10.5.5. Section 10.6 reviews the empirical evidence on the role played by credit channels in the transmission of monetary policy actions.

10.5.1   Adverse Selection

Jaffee and Russell (1976) analyzed a credit market model in which there are two types of borrowers, "honest" ones who always repay and "dishonest" ones who

---

20. Empirical evidence on consumption and liquidity constraints can be found in Campbell and Mankiw (1989; 1991), who provided estimates of the fraction of liquidity-constrained households for a number of OECD countries.

repay only if it is in their interest to do so. Ex ante the two types appear identical to lenders. Default is assumed to impose a cost on the defaulter, and dishonest borrowers default whenever the loan repayment amount exceeds the cost of default. By assuming a distribution of default costs across the population of borrowers, Jaffee and Russell showed that the fraction of borrowers who default is increasing in the loan amount.[21] In a pooling equilibrium, lenders offer the same loan contract (interest rate and amount) to all borrowers because they are unable to distinguish between the two types.[22] If lenders operate with constant returns to scale, if there is free entry, and if funds are available to lenders at an exogenously given opportunity cost, then the equilibrium loan rate must satisfy a zero profit condition for lenders. Since the expected return on a loan is less than or equal to the interest rate charged, the actual interest rate on loans must equal or exceed the opportunity cost of funds to the lenders.[23]

The effects of borrower heterogeneity and imperfect information on credit market equilibria can be illustrated following Stiglitz and Weiss (1981). The lender's expected return on a loan is a function of the interest rate charged and the probability that the loan will be repaid, but individual borrowers differ in their probabilities of repayment. Suppose borrowers come in two types. Type G repays with probability q_g; type B repays with probability $q_b < q_g$. If lenders can observe the borrower's type, each type will be charged a different interest rate to reflect the differing repayment probabilities. If the supply of credit is perfectly elastic at the opportunity cost of r, and lenders are risk-neutral and able to lend to a large number of borrowers so that the law of large numbers holds, then all type G borrowers can borrow at an interest rate of r/q_g, whereas type B borrowers borrow at $r/q_b > r/q_g$. At these interest rates, the lender's expected return from lending to either type of borrower is equal to the lender's opportunity cost of r. No credit rationing occurs; riskier borrowers are simply charged higher interest rates.

Now suppose the lender cannot observe the borrower's type. It may be the case that changes in the terms of a loan (interest rate, collateral, amount) affect the mix of borrower types the lender attracts. If increases in the loan interest rate shift the mix of borrowers, raising the fraction of type B borrowers, the expected return to the lender might actually decline with higher loan rates because of adverse selection. In this case, further increases in the loan rate would lower the lender's expected prof-

21. See Smith (1983) for a general equilibrium version of Jaffee and Russell's model using an overlapping-generations framework.

22. This ignores the possibility of separating equilibrium in which the lender offers two contracts and the borrowers (truthfully) signal their type by the contract they choose.

23. If the probability of default was zero, the constant-returns-to-scale assumption with free entry would ensure that lenders charge an interest rate on loans equal to the opportunity cost of funds. If default rates are positive, then the expected return on a loan is less than the actual interest rate charged, and the loan interest rate must be greater than the opportunity cost of funds.

its, even if an excess demand for loans remains. The intuition is similar to that of Akerlof's market for lemons (Akerlof 1970). Assume that a fraction g of all borrowers are of type G. Suppose the lender charges an interest rate of r_l such that $gq_gr_l + (1 - g)q_br_l = r$, or $r_l = r/[gq_g + (1 - g)q_b]$. At this loan rate, the lender earns the required return of r if borrowers are drawn randomly from the population. But at this rate, the pool of borrowers is no longer the same as in the population at large. Since $r/q_g < r_l < r/q_b$, the lender is more likely to attract type B borrowers, and the lender's expected return would be less than r.

Loans are, however, characterized by more than just their interest rate. For example, suppose a loan is characterized by its interest rate r_l, the loan amount L, and the collateral the lender requires C. The probability that the loan will be repaid depends on the (risky) return yielded by the borrower's project. If the project return is R, then the lender is repaid if

$$L(1 + r_l) < R + C.$$

If $L(1 + r_l) > R + C$, the borrower defaults and the lender receives $R + C$.

Suppose the return R is $R' + x$ with probability $\frac{1}{2}$ and $R' - x$ with probability $\frac{1}{2}$. The expected return is R', and the variance is x^2. An increase in x represents a mean preserving spread in the return disturbance and corresponds to an increase in the project's risk. Assume that $R' - x < (1 + r_l)L - C$ so that the borrower must default when the bad outcome occurs. If the project pays off $R' + x$, the borrower receives $R' + x - (1 + r_l)L$; if the bad outcome occurs, the borrower receives $-C$, that is, any collateral is lost. The expected profit to the borrower is

$$E\pi^B = \frac{1}{2}[R' + x - (1 + r_l)L] - \frac{1}{2}C.$$

Define

$$x^*(r_l, L, C) \equiv (1 + r_l)L + C - R'. \tag{10.33}$$

Expected profits for the borrower are positive for all $x > x^*$. This critical cutoff value of x is increasing in r_l. Recall that increases in x imply an increase in the project's risk, as measured by the variance of returns. An increase in the loan rate r_l increases x^*, and this implies that some borrowers with less risky projects will find it unprofitable to borrow if the loan rate rises, while borrowers with riskier projects will still find it worthwhile to borrow. Because the borrower can lose no more than his collateral in the bad state, expected profits are a convex function of the project's return and therefore increase with an increase in risk (for a constant mean return).

While the expected return to the firm is increasing in risk, as measured by x, the lender's return is decreasing in x. To see this point, note that the lender's expected profit is

$$E\pi^L = \frac{1}{2}[(1 + r_l)L] + \frac{1}{2}[C + R' - x] - (1 + r)L,$$

where r is the opportunity cost of funds to the lender. The lender's expected profit decreases with x. Because the lender receives a fixed amount in the good state, the lender's expected return is a concave function of the project's return and therefore decreases with an increase in risk.

Now suppose there are two groups of borrowers, those with $x = x_g$ and those with $x = x_b$, with $x_g < x_b$. Type x_g borrowers have lower-risk projects. From (10.33), if the loan rate r_l is low enough such that $x_b > x_g \geq x^*(r_l, L, C)$, then both types will find it profitable to borrow. If each type is equally likely, the lender's expected return is

$$E\pi^L = \frac{1}{4}[(1 + r_l)L + C + R' - x_g] + \frac{1}{4}[(1 + r_l)L + C + R' - x_b] - (1 + r)L$$

$$= \frac{1}{2}[(1 + r_l)L + C + R'] - \frac{1}{4}(x_g + x_b) - (1 + r)L, \qquad x^*(r_l, L, C) \leq x_g,$$

which is increasing in r_l. But as soon as r_l increases to the point where $x^*(r_l, L, C) = x_g$, any further increase causes all x_g types to stop borrowing. Only x_b types will still find it profitable to borrow, and the lender's expected profit falls to

$$E\pi^L = \frac{1}{2}[(1 + r_l)L + C + R'] - \frac{1}{2}x_b - (1 + r)L, \qquad x_g \leq x^*(r_l, L, C) \leq x_b.$$

As a result, the lender's expected profit as a function of the loan rate is increasing for $x^*(r_l, L, C) \leq x_g$ and then falls discretely at $1 + r_l = [x_g - C + R']/L$ as all low-risk types exit the market. This is illustrated in figure 10.2, where r^* denotes the loan rate that tips the composition of the pool of borrowers. For loan rates between r_1 and r^*, both types borrow and the lender's expected profit is positive. Expected profits are again positive for loan rates above r_2, but in this region only x_b types borrow.

The existence of a local maximum in the lender's profit function at r^* introduces the possibility that credit rationing will occur in equilibrium. Suppose at r^* there remains an excess demand for loans. Type x_g would not be willing to borrow at a rate above r^*, but type x_b would. If the lender responds to the excess demand by raising the loan rate, expected profits fall. Equilibrium may involve a loan rate of r^*, with some potential borrowers being rationed.[24] Thus, adverse selection provides one rationale for a lender's profit function that is not monotonic in the loan rate. Equi-

---

24. As figure 10.2 suggests, if the demand for loans is strong enough, the lender may be able to raise the loan rate sufficiently so that expected profits do rise.

Lender's
expected profit

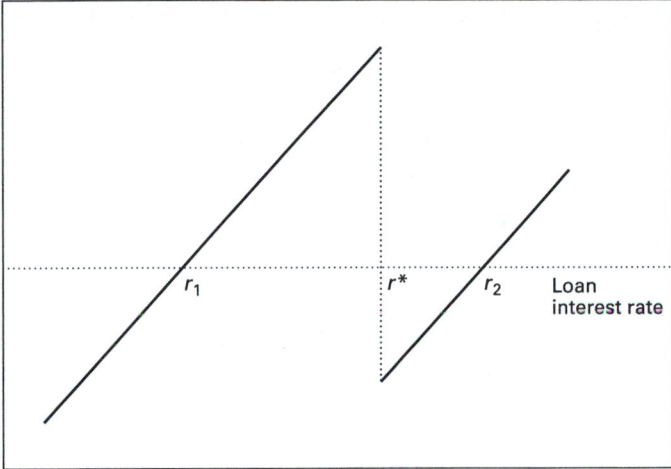

Figure 10.2
Expected loan profit with adverse selection.

librium credit rationing may exist because lenders find it unprofitable to raise the interest rate on loans even in the face of an excess demand for loans.

10.5.2   Moral Hazard

Moral hazard can arise in credit markets when the borrower's behavior is influenced by the terms of the loan contract. In the model of the previous section, the borrower decided whether to borrow, but the project's return was exogenous. Borrowers differed in terms of the underlying riskiness of their projects, and adverse selection occurred as loan rate changes affected the pool of borrowers. Suppose instead that each borrower can choose between several projects of differing risk. If the lender cannot monitor this choice, a moral hazard problem arises. The lender's expected return may not be monotonic in the interest rate charged on the loans. Higher loan rates lead the borrower to invest in riskier projects, lowering the expected return to the lender.

  To illustrate this situation, again following Stiglitz and Weiss (1981), suppose the borrower can invest either in project A, which pays off R^a in the good state and 0 in the bad state, or in project B, which pays off $R^b > R^a$ in the good state and 0 in the bad state. Suppose the probability of success for project A is p^a and p^b for project B, with $p^a > p^b$. Project B is the riskier project. Further, assume the expected payoff from A is higher: $p^a R^a > p^b R^b$. By investing in A, the borrower's expected return is

$$E\pi^A = p^a[R^a - (1+r_l)L] - (1-p^a)C,$$

where the borrower loses collateral C if the project fails. The expected return from project B is

$$E\pi^B = p^b[R^b - (1+r_l)L] - (1-p^b)C.$$

The expected returns on the two projects depend on the interest rate on the loan r_l. It is straightforward to show that

$$E\pi^A > E\pi^B$$

if and only if

$$\frac{p^a R^a - p^b R^b}{p^a - p^b} > (1+r_l)L - C.$$

The left side of this condition is independent of the loan rate, but the right side is increasing in r_l. Define r_l^* as the loan rate at which the expected returns to the borrower from the two projects are equal. This occurs when

$$(1+r_l^*)L - C = \frac{p^a R^a - p^b R^b}{p^a - p^b}.$$

For loan rates less than r_l^*, the borrower will prefer to invest in project A; for loan rates above r_l^*, the riskier project B is preferred. The expected payment to the lender, therefore, will be $p^a(1+r_l)L + (1-p^a)C$ if $r_l < r_l^*$, and $p^b(1+r_l)L + (1-p^b)C$ for $r_l > r_l^*$. Since

$$p^a(1+r_l^*)L + (1-p^a)C > p^b(1+r_l^*)L + (1-p^b)C, \tag{10.34}$$

the lender's profits fall as the loan rate rises above r^*; the lender's profits are not monotonic in the loan rate.[25] Just as in the example of the previous section, this leads to the possibility that credit rationing may characterize the loan market's equilibrium.

10.5.3   Monitoring Costs

The previous analysis illustrated how debt contracts in the presence of adverse selection or moral hazard could lead to credit rationing as an equilibrium phenomenon.

---

25. To see this, note that using the definition of r_l^* implies that the left side of (10.34) is equal to $p^a[(1+r_l^*)L - C] = p^a((p^a R^a - p^b R^b)/(p^a - p^b))$, and the right side is equal to $p^b[(1+r_l^*)L - C] = p^b((p^a R^a - p^b R^b)/(p^a - p^b))$. The direction of the inequality follows because $p^a > p^b$.

One limitation of the discussion, however, was the treatment of the nature of the loan contract—repayment equal to a fixed interest rate times the loan amount in some states of nature, zero or a predetermined collateral amount in others—as exogenous. Williamson (1986; 1987a; 1987b) illustrated how debt contracts and credit rationing can arise, even in the absence of adverse selection or moral hazard problems, if lenders must incur costs to monitor borrowers.[26] The intuition behind his result is straightforward. Suppose the lender can observe the borrower's project outcome only at some positive cost. Any repayment schedule that ties the borrower's payment to the project outcome would require that the monitoring cost be incurred; otherwise, the borrower always has an incentive to underreport the success of the project. Expected monitoring costs can be reduced if the borrower is monitored only in some states of nature. If the borrower reports a low project outcome and defaults on the loan, the lender incurs the monitoring cost to verify the truth of the report. If the borrower reports a good project outcome and repays the loan, the lender does not need to incur the monitoring cost.

Following Williamson (1987a), assume there are two types of agents, borrowers and lenders. Lenders are risk-neutral and have access to funds at an opportunity cost of r. Each lender takes r as given and offers contracts to borrowers that yield, to the lender, an expected return of r. Assume there are two periods. In period 1, lenders offer contracts to borrowers who have access to a risky investment project that yields a payoff in period 2 of $x \in [0, \bar{x}]$. The return x is a random variable, drawn from a distribution known to both borrowers and lenders. The actual realization is observed costlessly by the borrower; the lender can observe it by first paying a cost of c. This assumption captures the idea that borrowers are likely to have better information about their own projects than do lenders. Lenders can obtain this information by monitoring the project, but such monitoring is costly.

In period 2, after observing x, the borrower reports the project outcome to the lender. Let this report be x^s. While x^s must be in $[0, \bar{x}]$, it need not equal the true x, since the borrower will have an incentive to misreport if doing so is in the borrower's own interest. By choice of normalization, projects require an initial resource investment of 1 unit. Although borrowers have access to an investment project, assume they have no resources of their own, so to invest they must obtain resources from lenders.

Suppose that monitoring occurs whenever $x^s \in S \subset [0, \bar{x}]$. Otherwise, the lender does not monitor. Denote by $R(x)$ the payment from the borrower to the lender if $x^s \in S$ and monitoring takes place. Because the lender monitors and therefore observes x, the repayment can be made a function of the actual x. The return to the lender net of monitoring costs is $R(x) - c$. If the reported value $x^s \notin S$, then no

---

26. Townsend (1979) provided the first analysis of optimal contracts when it is costly to verify the state.

monitoring occurs and the borrower pays $K(x^s)$ to the lender. This payment can only depend on the signal, not the true realization of x, since the lender cannot verify the latter. In this case, the return to the lender is simply $K(x^s)$. Whatever the actual value of $x^s \notin S$, the borrower will report the value that results in the smallest payment to the lender; hence, if monitoring does not occur, the payment to the lender must be equal to a constant, $\bar{K}$.[27] Since all loans are for 1 unit, $\bar{K} - 1$ is the interest rate on the loan when $x^s \notin S$.

If the reported signal is in S, then monitoring occurs so that the lender can learn the true value of x. The borrower will report x^s in S only if it is in her best interest, that is, reporting $x^s \in S$ must be incentive-compatible. For this to be the case, the net return to the borrower when $x^s \in S$, equal to $x - R(x)$, must exceed the return from reporting a signal not in S, $x - \bar{K}$. That is, incentive compatibility requires that

$$x - R(x) > x - \bar{K} \quad \text{or} \quad \bar{K} > R(x) \quad \text{for all } x^s \in S.$$

The borrower will report a signal that leads to monitoring only if $R(x) < \bar{K}$ and will report a signal not in S (so that no monitoring occurs) if $R(x) \geq \bar{K}$.

The optimal contract is a payment schedule $R(x)$ and a value $\bar{K}$ that maximizes the borrower's expected return, subject to the constraint that the lender's expected return be at least equal to the opportunity cost r. Letting $\Pr[x < y]$ denote the probability that x is less than y, the expected return to the borrower can be written as the expected return conditional on monitoring occurring, times the probability that $R(x) < \bar{K}$, plus the expected return conditional on no monitoring occurring, times the probability that $R(x) \geq \bar{K}$:

$$\mathrm{E}[R^b] \equiv \mathrm{E}[x - R(x)|R(x) < \bar{K}] \Pr[R(x) < \bar{K}] + \mathrm{E}[x - \bar{K}|R(x) \geq \bar{K}] \Pr[R(x) \geq \bar{K}]. \tag{10.35}$$

The optimal loan contract maximizes this expected return subject to the constraint that the lender's expected return be at least r:

$$\mathrm{E}[R(x) - c|R(x) < \bar{K}] \Pr[R(x) < \bar{K}] + \bar{K} \Pr[R(x) \geq \bar{K}] \geq r. \tag{10.36}$$

The solution to this problem, and therefore the optimal loan contract, has $R(x) = x$. In other words, if the borrower reports a signal that leads the lender to monitor, then the lender takes the entire actual project return. This result corresponds to a loan default in which the lender takes over the project, incurs the monitoring cost c (which in this case can be thought of as a liquidation cost), and ends up with $x - c$. If the project earns a sufficient return, that is, $R(x) = x \geq \bar{K}$, then the

---

27. That is, suppose x_1 and x_2 are project return realizations such that the borrower would report x_1^s and $x_2^s \notin S$. If reporting x_1^s results in a larger payment to the lender, the borrower would always report x_2^s.

borrower pays the lender the fixed amount $\bar{K}$. Since $\bar{K}$ is independent of the realization of x, no monitoring is necessary. The presence of monitoring costs and imperfect information leads to the endogenous determination of the optimal loan contract.

The proof that $R(x) = x$ whenever monitoring takes place is straightforward. In equilibrium, the constraint given by (10.36) will be satisfied with equality. Otherwise, the payment to the lender could be reduced in some states, which would increase the expected return to the borrower. Hence,

$$E[R(x) - c|R(x) < \bar{K}] \Pr[R(x) < \bar{K}] + \bar{K} \Pr[R(x) \geq \bar{K}] = r.$$

Any contract that called for $R(x) < x$ for some realizations of x could be replaced by another contract that increases repayment slightly when monitoring occurs but lowers $\bar{K}$ to decrease the range of x for which monitoring actually takes place. This can be done such that the lender's expected profit is unchanged.[28] Using the constraint for the lender's expected return, the expected return to the borrower can be written as

$$\begin{aligned}
E[R^b] &= E[x - R(x)|R(x) < \bar{K}] \Pr[R(x) < \bar{K}] + \{E[x|R(x) \geq \bar{K}] - \bar{K}\} \Pr[R(x) \geq \bar{K}] \\
&= E[x - R(x)|R(x) < \bar{K}] \Pr[R(x) < \bar{K}] + E[x|R(x) \geq \bar{K}] \Pr[R(x) \geq \bar{K}] \\
&\quad - \{r - E[R(x) - c|R(x) < \bar{K}] \Pr[R(x) < \bar{K}]\} \\
&= E[x - c|R(x) < \bar{K}] \Pr[R(x) < \bar{K}] + E[x|R(x) \geq \bar{K}] \Pr[R(x) \geq \bar{K}] - r \\
&= E[x] - c \Pr[R(x) < \bar{K}] - r,
\end{aligned} \tag{10.37}$$

where $\Pr[R(x) < \bar{K}]$ is the probability that monitoring occurs. Equation (10.37) shows that the expected return to the borrower is decreasing in $\bar{K}$. Any contract that lowers $\bar{K}$ and reduces the probability of monitoring while leaving the lender with an expected return of r will be strictly preferred by the borrower. Such a contract can be constructed if $R(x) < x$.[29]

To make the example more specific, suppose x is uniformly distributed on $[0, \bar{x}]$. The expected return to the lender is equal to

$$\int_0^{\bar{K}} (x - c) \frac{1}{\bar{x}} dx + \int_{\bar{K}}^{\bar{x}} \bar{K} \frac{1}{\bar{x}} dx.$$

28. $R(x) > x$ is ruled out by the assumption that the borrower has no other resources. If $R(x) < x$ for some x for which monitoring occurs, then the new contract, which increases $R(x)$ in those states, increases $R(x) - c$ when monitoring does occur. For a given $\bar{K}$, this increases $E[R(x) - c|R(x) < \bar{K}]$, making the lender's expected profit greater than r. Since $\bar{K}$ is then lowered, monitoring occurs in fewer states, thereby reducing the lender's expected profit so that it again equals r.

29. One implication of (10.37) is that the borrower bears the cost of monitoring; the expected return to the borrower is equal to the total expected project return net of the opportunity cost of funds (r) and expected monitoring costs ($c \Pr[R(x) < \bar{K}]$).

The first term is the expected return to the lender if the borrower defaults, an outcome that occurs whenever $x < \bar{K}$; the probability of this outcome is $\bar{K}/\bar{x}$. The second term is the fixed payment received by the lender whenever $x \geq \bar{K}$, an outcome that occurs with probability $[\bar{x} - \bar{K}]/\bar{x}$. Evaluating the expected return and equating it to r yields the following condition to determine $\bar{K}$:

$$\left[\frac{1}{2}\left(\frac{\bar{K}^2}{\bar{x}}\right) - c\left(\frac{\bar{K}}{\bar{x}}\right)\right] + \bar{K}\left[1 - \left(\frac{\bar{K}}{\bar{x}}\right)\right] = r.$$

If $(\bar{x} - c)^2 > 2\bar{x}r$, this quadratic has two real solutions, one less than $\bar{x} - c$ and one greater than $\bar{x} - c$.[30] However, the effect of $\bar{K}$ on the lender's expected return is

$$\frac{\bar{K}}{\bar{x}} - \frac{c}{\bar{x}} + \left(1 - \frac{2\bar{K}}{\bar{x}}\right) = 1 - \frac{c + \bar{K}}{\bar{x}},$$

which becomes negative for $\bar{K} > \bar{x} - c$. This means that when the loan repayment amount is large, further increases in the contracted repayment would actually lower the lender's expected return; loan contracts with less monitoring (a lower $\bar{K}$) would be preferred by both borrower and lender; $\bar{K} > \bar{x} - c$ cannot be an equilibrium.

When the lender's expected profits are no longer monotonic in the loan interest rate but can actually decrease at higher interest rates, the possibility exists of an equilibrium in which some borrowers face credit rationing. In a nonrationing equilibrium, all borrowers receive loans.[31] The expected rate of return r is determined by the condition that loan demand equal loan supply, and the gross interest rate on loans, $\bar{K}$, is less than $\bar{x} - c$. In a credit rationing equilibrium, $\bar{K} = \bar{x} - c$, and not all potential borrowers receive loans. Even though there are unsatisfied potential borrowers, the interest rate on loans will not rise because the lenders' expected profits are decreasing in the loan rate when $\bar{K} > \bar{x} - c$. Even though all potential borrowers were assumed to be identical ex ante, some receive loans while others do not. The ones that do not get loans would be willing to borrow at an interest rate above the market rate, yet no lenders are willing to lend.

Williamson's model illustrates that neither adverse selection nor moral hazard is necessary for rationing to characterize credit markets. The presence of monitoring costs can account for both the general form of loan contracts in which monitoring

---

30. These are given by

$$\bar{x} - c \pm \sqrt{(\bar{x} - c)^2 - 2\bar{x}r}.$$

31. A complete specification of the model requires assumptions on the number of (potential) borrowers and lenders that ensures an upward-sloping supply curve of funds. See Williamson (1987a) for details on one such specfication.

occurs only when the borrower defaults—in which case the lender takes over the entire project's return—and for rationing to arise in some equilibria.

10.5.4 Agency Costs

Adverse selection, moral hazard, and monitoring costs all arise as important factors in any relationship in which a principal delegates decision-making authority to an agent. In credit markets, the lender delegates to a borrower control over resources. The inability to monitor the borrower's actions or to share the borrower's information gives rise to agency costs. Bernanke and Gertler (1989) and Gertler (1988) emphasized the role of agency costs that make external funding sources more expensive for firms than internal sources. As a consequence, a firm's balance sheet plays a role in affecting the cost of finance. In recessions, internal sources of funds decline, forcing firms to turn to external sources. But the deterioration of the firm's balance sheet worsens the agency problems and increases the cost of external funds, thereby further contracting investment spending and contributing to the recession. Thus, credit conditions can play a role in amplifying the impact of other shocks to the economy and affecting their propagation throughout the economy and through time.

In the model of Bernanke and Gertler (1989), firms are assumed to be able to observe the outcome of their own investment projects costlessly; others must incur a monitoring cost to observe project outcomes. Firms and lenders are assumed to be risk-neutral. Firms are indexed by efficiency type ω, distributed uniformly on $[0, 1]$. More efficient types (ones with low ω) need to invest fewer inputs in a given project. Projects themselves require inputs of $x(\omega)$, yielding gross payoff κ_1 with probability π_1, and $\kappa_2 > \kappa_1$ with probability $\pi_2 = 1 - \pi_1$. The function $x(.)$ is increasing in ω. The expected project return, $\pi_1\kappa_1 + \pi_2\kappa_2$, will be denoted κ. The realized outcome of a particular project can be observed costlessly by the firm undertaking the project and at cost c by others. Firms are assumed to have internal sources of financing equal to S; S is assumed to be less than $x(0)$, so that even the most efficient firm must borrow to undertake a project. Finally, let r denote the opportunity cost of funds to lenders; firms that do not undertake a project also receive this rate on their funds.[32]

If lenders could observe project outcomes costlessly, equilibrium would involve lenders' financing all projects whose expected payoff exceeds their opportunity cost of rx. Thus, all firms whose ω is less than a critical value ω^* defined by

$$\kappa - rx(\omega^*) = 0$$

would receive loans. Firms with $\omega < \omega^*$ borrow $B \equiv x(\omega) - S$.

---

32. Bernanke and Gertler developed a general equilibrium model; here a partial equilibrium version is described to focus on the role played by credit market imperfections in investment decisions.

With imperfect information, the firm clearly has an incentive to always announce that the bad outcome, κ_1, occurred. It will never pay for the lender to incur the monitoring cost if the firm announces κ_2. Let p be the probability that the firm is audited (i.e., the lender pays the monitoring cost to observe the true outcome) when the firm announces κ_1. Let P_1^a be the payment to the firm when κ_1 is announced and auditing takes place, P_1 the payment when κ_1 is announced and no auditing occurs, and P_2 the payment if κ_2 is announced. The optimal lending contract must maximize the expected payoff to the firm, subject to several constraints. First, the lender's expected return must be at least as great as her opportunity cost rB. Second, the firm must have no incentive to report the bad state when in fact the good state occurred. Third, even in the bad state, limited liability requires that P_1^a and P_1 be non-negative. The optimal contract is characterized by the values of $\{p, P_1^a, P_1, P_2\}$ that solve

$$\max \ \pi_1[pP_1^a + (1 - p)P_1] + \pi_2 P_2$$

subject to

$$\pi_1[\kappa_1 - p(P_1^a + c) - (1 - p)P_1] + \pi_2[\kappa_2 - P_2] \geq rB \tag{10.38}$$

$$P_2 \geq (1 - p)(\kappa_2 - \kappa_1 + P_1) \tag{10.39}$$

$$P_1^a \geq 0 \tag{10.40}$$

$$P_1 \geq 0 \tag{10.41}$$

and $0 \leq p \leq 1$.

Only the constraint given by (10.39) may require comment. The left side is the firm's income in the good state. The right side gives the firm's income if the good state occurs but the firm reports the bad state. After reporting the bad state, the firm is audited with probability p. So with probability $1 - p$ the firm is not audited, turns over $\kappa_1 - P_1$ to the lender. But the firm now gets to keep the amount $\kappa_2 - \kappa_1$ because, by assumption, the good state had actually occurred. If (10.39) is satisfied, the firm has no incentive to conceal the truth in announcing the project outcome.

Assuming an interior solution, the first-order necessary conditions for this problem are

$$\pi_1[(P_1^a - P_1) + \mu_1(P_1 - P_1^a - c)] + \mu_2(\kappa_2 - \kappa_1 + P_1) = 0 \tag{10.42}$$

$$\pi_1 p(1 - \mu_1) + \mu_3 = 0 \tag{10.43}$$

$$\pi_1(1 - p)(1 - \mu_1) - \mu_2(1 - p) + \mu_4 = 0 \tag{10.44}$$

$$\pi_2(1 - \mu_1) + \mu_2 = 0, \tag{10.45}$$

where the μ_i are the (non-negative) Lagrangian multipliers associated with the constraints (10.38)–(10.41).

Since $\mu_3 \geq 0$, (10.43) implies that $\mu_1 \geq 1$. This means the constraint on the lender's return (10.38) holds with equality. With $\pi_1[\kappa_1 - p(P_1^a + c) - (1 - p)P_1] + \pi_2[\kappa_2 - P_2] - r(x - S) = 0$, this can be added to the objective function, yielding an equivalent problem that the optimal contract solves, given by $\max[\pi_1(\kappa_1 - pc) + \pi_2\kappa_2]$, subject to (10.39) and the non-negative constraints on P_1^a and P_1. However, $\pi_1(\kappa_1 - pc) + \pi_2\kappa_2 = \kappa - \pi_1pc$, and with κ an exogenous parameter, this new problem is equivalent to minimizing expected auditing costs π_1pc.

If the return to the lender, rB, is less than the project return even in the bad state κ_1, then no auditing is ever necessary and $p = 0$. Agency costs are therefore zero whenever $\kappa_1 \geq rB$. Recall that the amount borrowed, B, was equal to $x(\omega) - S$, where S represented the firm's internal funds invested in the project, so the no-agency-cost condition can be written

$$S \geq x(\omega) - \frac{\kappa_1}{r} \equiv S^*(\omega).$$

Any type ω with internal funds greater than or equal to $S^*(\omega)$ can always repay the lender, so no auditing on the project is required. When $S < S^*(\omega)$, a situation Bernanke and Gertler labeled as one of *incomplete collateralization*, constraints (10.38)–(10.41) all hold with equality. Since auditing is costly, the optimal auditing probability is just high enough to ensure that the firm truthfully reports the good state when it occurs. From the incentive constraint (10.39), $P_2 = (1 - p)(\kappa_2 - \kappa_1)$ since $P_1 = P_1^a = 0$ (the firm keeps nothing in the bad state). Substituting this into the lender's required return condition (10.38),

$$p = \frac{r[x(\omega) - S] - \kappa_1}{\pi_2(\kappa_2 - \kappa_1) - \pi_1c}.$$

The auditing probability is decreasing in the return in the good state (κ_2) and the firm's own contribution S. If the firm invests little in the project and borrows more, then the firm receives less of the project's return in the good state, increasing its incentive to falsely claim that the bad state occurred. To remove this incentive, the probability of auditing must rise.

Bernanke and Gertler characterized the expected costs of project auditing, π_1pc, as the *agency costs due to asymmetric information*. As they showed, some firms with intermediate values of ω (i.e., neither the most nor the least efficient) will find that the investment project is not worth undertaking if they have only low levels of internal funds to invest. The probability of auditing that lenders would require makes agency costs too high to justify the investment. If the firm had a higher level of internal funds, it would undertake the project. Even though the opportunity costs of funds r and the project inputs x and returns (κ_1 and κ_2) have not changed, variations in S can alter the number of projects undertaken. This illustrates how investment levels may depend on the firm's internal sources of financing. Agency costs drive a wedge between the costs of internal and external funds, so investment decisions will depend on variables such as cash flow that would not play a role if information were perfect. Since a recession will worsen firms' balance sheets, reducing the availability of internal funds, the resulting rise in agency costs and the reduction in investment may serve to amplify the initial cause of a recession.

10.5.5   Macroeconomic Implications

The presence of credit market imperfections can play a role in determining how the economy responds to economic disturbances and how these disturbances are propagated throughout the economy and over time. Various partial equilibrium models have provided insights into how imperfect information and costly state verification affect the nature of credit market equilibria. The next step is to embed these partial equilibrium models of the credit market within a general equilibrium macroeconomic model so that the qualitative and quantitative importance of credit channels can be assessed. As Bernanke, Gertler, and Gilchrist (1996) discussed, there are difficulties in taking this step. For one, distributional issues are critical. Private sector borrowing and lending do not occur in a representative-agent world, so agents must differ in ways that give rise to borrowers and lenders. And both the source of credit and the characteristics of the borrower matter, so not all borrowers and not all lenders are alike. Changes in the distribution of wealth or the distribution of cash flow can affect the ability of agents to obtain credit. Incorporating heterogeneity among agents in a tractable general equilibrium model can lead to new complexities when the nature of debt and financial contracts in the model economy should be derived from the characteristics of the basic technology and informational assumptions of the model environment.

General Equilibrium Models

Two early examples of general equilibrium models designed to highlight the role of credit factors are due to Williamson (1987b) and Bernanke and Gertler (1989). In these models, credit markets play an important role in determining how the economy responds to a real productivity shock. Williamson embedded his model of financial intermediation with costly monitoring (see section 10.5.3) in a dynamic general equilibrium model. In response to shocks to the riskiness of investment, credit rationing increases, loans from intermediaries fall, and investment declines. The decline in investment reduces future output and contributes to the propagation of the initial shock. Bernanke and Gertler (1989) incorporated the model of costly state verification reviewed in section 10.5.4 into a general equilibrium framework in which shocks to productivity drive the business cycle dynamics. A positive productivity shock increases the income of the owners of the production technology; this rise in their net worth lowers agency costs associated with external financing of investment projects, allowing for increased investment. This serves to propagate the shock through time.

Kiyotaki and Moore (1997) developed a model that illustrates the role of net worth and credit constraints on equilibrium output. In their model economy, there are two types of agents. One group, called *farmers*, can combine their own labor with land to produce output. They can borrow to purchase additional land but face credit constraints in so doing. These constraints arise because a farmer's labor input is assumed to be critical to production—once a farmer starts producing, no one else can replace him—and the farmer is assumed to be unable to precommit to work. Thus, if any creditor attempts to extract too much from a farmer, the farmer can simply walk away from the land, leaving the creditor with only the value of the land; all current production is lost. The inability to precommit to work plays a role similar to the assumption of cost state verification; in this case, the creditor is unable to monitor the farmer to ensure that he continues to work. As a result, the farmer's ability to borrow will be limited by the collateral value of his land.

Letting k_t denote the quantity of land cultivated by farmers, output by farmers is produced according to a linear technology:

$$y_{t+1}^f = (a + c)k_t,$$

where ck_t is nonmarketable output ("bruised fruit" in the farmer analogy) that can be consumed by the farmer.

The creditors in Kiyotaki and Moore's model are called *gatherers*. They too can use land to produce output, employing a technology characterized by decreasing returns to scale. The output of gatherers is

$$y_{t+1}^g = G(\bar{k} - k_t); \qquad G' \geq 0; \ G'' \leq 0,$$

where $\bar{k}$ is the total fixed stock of land, so $\bar{k} - k_t$ is the land cultivated by gatherers.

Utility of both farmers and gatherers is assumed to be linear in consumption, although gatherers are assumed to discount the future more. Because of the linear utility, and the assumption that labor generates no disutility, the socially efficient allocation of the fixed stock of land between the two types of agents would ensure that the marginal product of land is equalized between the two production technologies, or

$$G'(\bar{k} - k^*) = a + c, \tag{10.46}$$

where k^* is the efficient amount of land allocated to farmers.

Consider the market equilibrium. Taking the gatherers first, given that they are not credit-constrained and have linear utility, the real rate of interest will simply equal the inverse of their subjective rate of time preference: $R = 1/\beta$.[33] Again exploiting the unconstrained nature of the gatherers' decision, the value of a unit of land, q_t, must satisfy

$$q_t = \beta[G'(\bar{k} - k_t) + q_{t+1}].$$

The present value of a unit of land is just equal to the discounted marginal return G' plus its resale value at time $t + 1$. Since $\beta = R^{-1}$, this condition can be rewritten as

$$\frac{1}{R} G'(\bar{k} - k_t) = q_t - \frac{q_{t+1}}{R} \equiv u_t. \tag{10.47}$$

The variable u_t will play an important role in the farmers' decision problem. To interpret it, q_{t+1}/R is the present value of land in period $t + 1$. This represents the collateralized value of a unit of land; a creditor who lends q_{t+1}/R or less against a piece of land is sure of being repaid. The price of a unit of land at time t is q_t, so u_t is the difference between the cost of the land and the amount that can be borrowed against the land. It thus represents the downpayment a farmer will need to make in order to purchase more land.

Kiyotaki and Moore constructed the basic parameters of their model to ensure that farmers will wish to consume only their nonmarketable output (ck_{t-1}). Farmers then use the proceeds of their marketable output plus new loans minus repayment of old loans (including interest) to purchase more land. However, the maximum a farmer can borrow will be the collateralized value of the land, equal to $q_{t+1}k_t/R$. Hence, if b_t is the farmer's debt,

$$b_t \leq \frac{q_{t+1}k_t}{R}. \tag{10.48}$$

This can be shown to be a binding constraint in equilibrium, and the change in the farmer's land holdings will be

$$q_t(k_t - k_{t-1}) = ak_{t-1} + \frac{q_{t+1}k_t}{R} - Rb_{t-1},$$

where b_{t-1} is debt incurred in the previous period. Rearranging,

---

33. The standard Euler condition for optimal consumption requires that $u_c(t) = \beta R u_c(t + 1)$, where $u_c(s)$ is the marginal utility of consumption at date s. With linear utility, $u_c(t) = u_c(t + 1) = h$ for some constant h. Hence, $h = \beta R h$ or $R = 1/\beta$.

$$k_t = \frac{(a + q_t)k_{t-1} - Rb_{t-1}}{u_t}.$$ (10.49)

The numerator of this expression represents the farmer's net worth—current output plus land holdings minus existing debt. With u_t equal to the required down payment per unit of land, the farmer invests his entire net worth in purchasing new land.

To verify that the borrowing constraint is binding, it is necessary to show that the farmer always finds it optimal to use all marketable output to purchase additional land (after repaying outstanding loans). Suppose instead that the farmer consumes a unit of output over and above ck_{t-1}. This yields marginal utility u_c (a constant by the assumption of linear utility), but by reducing the farmer's land in period t by $1/u_t$, this additional consumption costs

$$u_c \left[\beta_f \frac{c}{u_t} + \beta_f^2 \left(\frac{a}{u_t} \left(\frac{c}{u_{t+1}} + \beta_f \left(\frac{a}{u_{t+1}} \left(\frac{c}{u_{t+2}} + \cdots \right) \cdots \right) \cdots \right) \cdots \right) \right]$$

since the $1/u_t$ units of land purchased at time t would have yielded additional consumption c/u_t plus marketable output a/u_t that could have been used to purchase more land that would have yielded c/u_{t+1} in consumption, and so on. Each of these future consumption additions must be discounted back to time t using the farmer's discount rate β_f. It will be demonstrated subsequently that the steady-state value of u will be a. Making this substitution, the farmer will always prefer to use marketable output to purchase land if

$$1 < \left[\beta_f \frac{c}{a} + \beta_f^2 \left(\frac{a}{a} \left(\frac{c}{a} + \beta_f \left(\frac{a}{a} \left(\frac{c}{a} + \cdots \right) \cdots \right) \cdots \right) \cdots \right) \right] = \frac{\beta_f}{1 - \beta_f} \frac{c}{a},$$

or

$$\frac{a + c}{a} > \frac{1}{\beta_f} > R.$$ (10.50)

Kiyotaki and Moore assumed that c is large enough to ensure that this condition holds. This means farmers would always like to postpone consumption and will borrow as much as possible to purchase land. Hence, the borrowing constraint will bind.

Equation (10.49) can be written as $u_t k_t = (a + q_t)k_{t-1} - Rb_{t-1}$. But $Rb_{t-1} = q_t k_{t-1}$ from (10.48), so $u_t k_t = a k_{t-1}$. Now using (10.47) to eliminate u_t, the capital stock held by farmers satisfies the following difference equation:

$$\frac{1}{R} G'(\bar{k} - k_t)k_t = a k_{t-1}.$$ (10.51)

Assuming standard restrictions on the gatherers' production function, (10.51) defines a convergent path for the land held by farmers.[34] The steady-state value of k is then given as the solution k^{ss} to

$$\frac{1}{R} G'(\bar{k} - k^{ss}) = a. \tag{10.52}$$

Multiplying through by R, $G'(\bar{k} - k^{ss}) = Ra$. From (10.47) this implies

$$u^{ss} = a.$$

Equation (10.52) can be compared with (10.46), which gives the condition for an efficient allocation of land between farmers and gatherers. The efficient allocation of land to farmers, k^*, was such that $G'(\bar{k} - k^*) = a + c > Ra = G'(\bar{k} - k^{ss})$, where the inequality sign is implied by (10.50). Since the marginal product of gatherers' output is positive but declines with the amount of land held by gatherers, it follows that $k^{ss} < k^*$. The market equilibrium is characterized by too little land in the hands of farmers. As a consequence, aggregate output is too low.

Using the definition of u, the steady-state price of land is equal to $q^{ss} = Ra/(R-1)$, and steady-state debt is equal to $b^{ss} = q^{ss}k^{ss}/R = ak^{ss}/(R-1)$. The farmer's debt repayments each period are then equal to $Rb^{ss} = [R/(R-1)]ak^{ss} > ak^{ss}$.

Kiyotaki and Moore extended this basic model to allow for reproducible capital and were able to study the dynamics of the more general model. The simple version, though, allows the key channels through which credit affects the economy's equilibrium to be highlighted. First, output is inefficiently low because of borrowing restrictions; even though farmers have access to a technology that at the steady state is more productive than that of gatherers, they cannot obtain the credit necessary to purchase additional land. Second, the ability of farmers to obtain credit is limited by their net worth. Equation (10.49) shows how the borrowing constraint makes land holdings at time t dependent on net worth (marketable output plus the value of existing land holdings minus debt). Third, land purchases by farmers will depend on asset prices. A fall in the value of land that is expected to persist (so q_t and q_{t+1} both fall) reduces the farmers' net worth and demand for land. This follows from (10.49), which can be written as $k_t = (q_t k_{t-1}/u_t) + (ak_{t-1} - Rb_{t-1})/u_t$. A proportional fall in q_t and q_{t+1} leaves the first term, $q_t k_{t-1}/u_t$, unchanged. The second term increases in absolute value, but at the steady state, $Rb > ak$, so this term is negative. Thus, farmers' net worth declines with a fall in land prices.

These mechanisms capture the financial accelerator effects, as can be seen by considering the effects of an unexpected but transitory productivity shock. Suppose the

---

34. As long as $G'(\bar{k} - k)$ is monotonically increasing in k, $G'(\bar{k}) < a$, and $G'(0) > a$, there will be a single stable equilibirum.

output of both farmers and gatherers increases unexpectedly at time t. If the economy was initially at the steady state, then if Δ is the productivity increase for farmers, (10.49) implies

$$u(k_t)k_t = (a + \Delta a + q_t - q^{ss})k^{ss}, \tag{10.53}$$

since $q^{ss}k^{ss} = Rb^{ss}$ from the borrowing constraint, and the required downpayment u is written as a function of k.[35] Two factors are at work in determining the impact of the productivity shock on the farmers' demand for land. First, because marketable output rises by Δak^{ss}, this directly increases farmers' demand for land. Second, the term $(q_t - q^{ss})k^{ss}$ represents a capital gain on existing holdings of land. Both factors act to increase farmers' net worth and their demand for land.

One way to highlight the dynamics is to examine a linear approximation to (10.53) around the steady state. Letting e denote the elasticity of the user cost of land $u(k)$ with respect to k, the left side of (10.53) can be approximated by

$$ak^{ss}[1 + (1 + e)\hat{k}],$$

using the fact that $u(k^{ss}) = a$ and letting $\hat{x}$ denote the percentage deviation of a variable x around the steady state.[36] The right side is approximated by

$$(a + \Delta a + q^{ss}\hat{q}_t)k^{ss}.$$

Equating these two and using the steady-state result that $q^{ss} = Ra/(R-1)$ yields

$$(1 + e)\hat{k} = \Delta + \frac{R}{R-1}\hat{q}_t. \tag{10.54}$$

The capital gain effect on farmers' land purchases is, as Kiyotaki and Moore emphasized, scaled up by $R/(R-1) > 1$ because farmers are able to leverage their net worth. This factor can be quite large; if $R = 1.05$, the coefficient on $\hat{q}_t$ is 21.

The asset price effects of the temporary productivity shock reinforce the original disturbance. These effects also generate a channel for persistence. When more land is purchased in period t, the initial rise in aggregate output persists.[37]

Agency Costs and General Equilibrium

Carlstrom and Fuerst (1997) embedded a model of agency costs based on Bernanke and Gertler (1989) in a general equilibrium framework that can be used to investigate

---

35. Recall that $u_t = G'(\bar{k} - k_t)/R$, from (10.47).

36. The elasticity e is equal to $[u'(k^{ss})k^{ss}]/u(k^{ss}) = u'(k^{ss})k^{ss}/a$, where u' denotes the derivative of u with respect to k. Since u is increasing in $\bar{k} - k$, $u' < 0$.

37. Recall that at the margin, farmers are more productive than gatherers; a shift of land from gatherers to farmers raises total output.

the model's qualitative and quantitative implications. In particular, they studied the way agency costs arising from costly state verification affect the impact that shocks to net worth have on the economy.[38]

In their model, entrepreneurs borrow external funds in an intraperiod loan market to invest in a project that is subject to idiosyncratic productivity shocks. Suppose entrepreneur j has a net worth of n_j and borrows $i_j - n_j$. The project return is $\omega_j i_j$, where ω_j is the idiosyncratic productivity shock. Entrepreneurs have private information about this shock, whereas lenders can observe it only by incurring a cost. If the interest rate on the loan to entrepreneur j is r_j^k, then the borrower defaults if

$$\omega_j < \frac{(1 + r_j^k)(i_j - n_j)}{i_j} \equiv \bar{\omega}_j.$$

If the realization of ω_j is less than $\bar{\omega}_j$, the entrepreneur's resources, $\omega_j i_j$, are less than the amount needed to repay the loan, $(1 + r_j^k)(i_j - n_j)$. If default occurs, the lender monitors the project at a cost μi_j.

Carlstrom and Fuerst derived the optimal loan contract between entrepreneurs and lenders and showed that it is characterized by i_j and $\bar{\omega}_j$. Given these two parameters, the loan interest rate is

$$1 + r_j^k = \frac{\bar{\omega}_j i_j}{i_j - n_j}.$$

Suppose the distribution function of ω_j is $\Phi(\omega_j)$. The probability of default is $\Phi(\bar{\omega}_j)$. Let q denote the end-of-period price of capital. If the entrepreneur does not default, she receives $q\omega_j i_j - (1 + r_j^k)(i_j - n_j)$. If the borrower defaults, she receives nothing. If $f(\bar{\omega})$ is defined as the fraction of expected net capital output received by the entrepreneur, then

$$qi_j f(\bar{\omega}_j) \equiv q \left\{ \int_{\bar{\omega}}^{\infty} \omega i_j \Phi(d\omega) - [1 - \Phi(\bar{\omega}_j)](1 + r_j^k)(i_j - n_j) \right\}$$

$$= qi_j \left\{ \int_{\bar{\omega}}^{\infty} \omega \Phi(d\omega) - [1 - \Phi(\bar{\omega}_j)]\bar{\omega}_j \right\}. \tag{10.55}$$

The expected income of the lender is

$$q \left\{ \int_0^{\bar{\omega}} \omega i_j \Phi(d\omega) - \mu i_j \Phi(\bar{\omega}_j) + [1 - \Phi(\bar{\omega}_j)](1 + r_j^k)(i_j - n_j) \right\}.$$

---

38. See also Kocherlakota (2000).

If $g(\bar{\omega}_j)$ is defined as the fraction of expected net capital output received by the lender, then

$$qi_j g(\bar{\omega}_j) \equiv qi_j \left\{ \int_0^{\bar{\omega}} \omega\Phi(d\omega) - \mu\Phi(\bar{\omega}_j) + [1 - \Phi(\bar{\omega}_j)]\bar{\omega}_j \right\}. \tag{10.56}$$

By adding together (10.55) and (10.56), one finds that

$$f(\bar{\omega}_j) + g(\bar{\omega}_j) = 1 - \mu\Phi(\bar{\omega}_j) < 1. \tag{10.57}$$

Hence, the total expected income to the entrepreneur and the lender is less than the total expected project return (the fractions sum to less than 1) because of the expected monitoring costs.

The optimal lending contract maximizes $qif(\bar{\omega})$ subject to

$$qig(\bar{\omega}) \geq i - n \tag{10.58}$$

and

$$qif(\bar{\omega}) \geq n,$$

where, for convenience, the j notation has been dropped. The first constraint reflects the assumption that these are intraperiod loans, so the lender just needs to be indifferent between lending and retaining funds. The second constraint must hold if the entrepreneur is to participate; it ensures that the expected payout to the entrepreneur is greater than the net worth the entrepreneur invests in the project. Carlstrom and Fuerst showed that this second constraint always holds, so it will be ignored in the following. Using (10.57), the optimal loan contract solves

$$\max_{i,\bar{\omega}}\{qif(\bar{\omega}) + \lambda[qi(1 - \mu\Phi - f(\bar{\omega})) - i + n]\}.$$

The first-order conditions for i and $\bar{\omega}$ are

$$qf(\bar{\omega}) + \lambda[q(1 - \mu\Phi - f(\bar{\omega})) - 1] = 0 \tag{10.59}$$

and

$$qif'(\bar{\omega}) - \lambda qi(\mu\phi + f'(\bar{\omega})) = 0,$$

where $\phi = \Phi'$ is the density function for ω. Solving this second equation for λ,

$$\lambda\left[1 + \frac{\mu\phi(\bar{\omega})}{f'(\bar{\omega})}\right] = 1. \tag{10.60}$$

Now multiplying both sides of (10.59) by $[1 + \mu\phi(\bar{\omega})/f'(\bar{\omega})]$ and using (10.60) yields, after some rearrangement,

$$q\left[1 - \mu\Phi + \mu\phi(\bar{\omega})\frac{f(\bar{\omega})}{f'(\bar{\omega})}\right] = 1. \tag{10.61}$$

Finally, from the constraint (10.58),

$$qig(\bar{\omega}) = i - n. \tag{10.62}$$

Equation (10.61) determines $\bar{\omega}$ as a function of the price of capital q, the distribution of the shocks, and the cost of monitoring. All three of these factors are the same for all entrepreneurs, so all borrowers face the same $\bar{\omega}$, justifying the dropping of the j subscript. Writing $\bar{\omega} = \bar{\omega}(q)$, investment i can be expressed using (10.62) as a function of q and n:

$$i(q, n) = \left[\frac{1}{1 - qg(\bar{\omega}(q))}\right]n. \tag{10.63}$$

Expected capital output is

$$I^s(q, n) = i(q, n)[1 - \mu\Phi(\bar{\omega})]. \tag{10.64}$$

The optimal contract has been derived while taking the price of capital, q, as given. In a general equilibrium analysis, this price must also be determined. To complete the model specification, assume that firms produce output using a standard neoclassical production function employing labor and capital:

$$Y_t = \theta_t F(K_t, H_t),$$

where θ_t is an aggregate productivity shock. Factor markets are competitive. Households supply labor and rent capital to firms. If households wish to accumulate more capital, they can purchase investment goods at the price q_t from a mutual fund that lends to entrepreneurs. These entrepreneurs then create capital goods using the project technology just described and end the period by making their consumption decision.[39] This last choice then determines the net worth entrepreneurs carry into the following period.

If net worth is constant, Carlstrom and Fuerst showed, their general equilibrium model can be mapped into a standard real business cycle model with capital adjust-

---

39. Carlstrom and Fuerst assumed that entrepreneurs discount the future more heavily than households and that their utility is linear. The Euler condition for entrepreneurs is

$$q_t = \beta\gamma E_t[q_{t+1}(1 - \delta) + F_K(t + 1)]\left[\frac{q_{t+1}f(\bar{\omega}_{t+1})}{1 - q_{t+1}g(\bar{\omega}_{t+1})}\right], \qquad 0 < \gamma < 1,$$

where the first term on the right side is the return to capital and the second term is the additional return on internal funds.

ment costs. They argued that agency costs therefore provide a means of endogenizing adjustment costs. Because net worth is not constant in their model, however, variations in entrepreneur net worth can serve to propagate shocks over time. For example, a positive productivity shock increases the demand for capital, and this pushes up the price of capital. By increasing entrepreneurs' net worth, the rise in the price of capital increases the production of capital (see (10.64)). By boosting the return on internal funds, the rise in the price of capital also induces entrepreneurs to reduce their own consumption to build up additional net worth. The endogenous response of net worth causes investment to display a hump-shaped response to an aggregate productivity shock. This type of response is more consistent with empirical evidence than is the response predicted by a standard real-business-cycle model in which the maximum impact of a productivity shock on investment occurs in the initial period.

Agency Costs and Sticky Prices

In chapter 6, it was emphasized that nominal rigidities play an important role in transmitting monetary policy disturbances to the real economy. Bernanke, Gertler, and Gilchrist (1999) combined nominal rigidities with an agency cost model to explore the interactions between credit market factors and price stickiness. They developed a tractable framework by employing a model with three types of agents: households, entrepreneurs, and retailers. Entrepreneurs borrow to purchase capital. Costly state verification in the Bernanke, Gertler, and Gilchrist model implies that investment will depend positively on entrepreneurs' net worth, just as it did in the Carlstrom and Fuerst (1997) model (see (10.63)). Entrepreneurs use capital and labor to produce wholesale goods. These wholesale goods are sold in a competitive goods market to retailers. Retailers use wholesale goods to produce differentiated consumer goods that are sold to households. Wholesale prices are flexible, but retail prices are sticky. This model exhibits a financial accelerator (Bernanke, Gertler, and Gilchrist 1996); movements in asset prices affect net worth and amplify the impact of an initial shock to the economy.

Sticky price adjustment in the retail sector is modeled following Calvo (see chapter 6) so that in each period there is a fixed probability that the individual retail firm can adjust its price. When a firm does adjust, it sets its price optimally. As a result, the rate of inflation of retail prices is a function of expected future inflation and given by real marginal cost in the retail sector. Since retail firms simply purchase wholesale goods at the competitive wholesale price P_t^w and resell these goods to households, real marginal cost for retailers is just the ratio of wholesale to retail prices.

Bernanke, Gertler, and Gilchrist (1999) calibrated a log-linearized version of their model to study the role the financial accelerator plays in propagating the impact of a monetary policy shock. They found that it increases the real impact of a policy shock. A positive nominal interest rate shock reduces the demand for capital, and this lowers the price of capital. The decline in the value of capital lowers entrepreneurs' net worth. As a consequence, the finance premium demanded by lenders rises, and this further reduces investment demand. Thus, a multiplier effect operates to amplify the initial impact of the interest rate rise. The contraction in the wholesale sector lowers wholesale prices relative to sticky retail prices. The retail price markup increases, reducing retail price inflation.

The financial crisis of 2007–2009 has led to a rapidly growing literature that incorporates financial frictions, often based on the Bernanke, Gertler, and Gilchrist (1999) approach, in models with nominal rigidities designed to address monetary policy issues. For example, in a model without capital, Demirel (2007) assumed firms must borrow to finance inputs into the production process. Christiano, Motto, and Rostagno (2007) embedded the Bernanke-Gertler-Gilchrist model of agency costs in a DSGE model with sticky wages and prices, which they then fit to U.S. and euro area data. De Fiore and Tristani (2008) developed a model with sticky prices and costly state verification that leads to agency costs because firms must borrow to finance their wage payments. Cúrdia and Woodford (2008) allowed for interest rates paid by borrowers and received by savers to differ. They found that the optimal Taylor rule calls for responding to credit spreads. Monacelli (2008) added financial frictions by incorporating the presence of collateral constraints on borrowing by the household sector. In the context of open-economy models, Gertler, Gilchrist, and Natalucci (2007) embedded the financial accelerator into a model of a small open economy to study the role of exchange rate regimes. They found that financial frictions play a significant role in accounting for output declines in the face of an exogenous rise in the country's risk premium.

10.6 Does Credit Matter?

Given the global recession triggered by the financial crisis beginning in the United States in 2007, the question of whether credit matters seems to be easily answered with a resounding yes. However, the role of credit and its importance for understanding macroeconomic fluctuations has historically been a source of controversy. If credit channels are important for the monetary transmission process, then evolution in financial markets due to changes in regulations or financial innovations will change the manner in which monetary policy affects the real economy. This also implies that the level of real interest rates may not provide a sufficient indicator of the stance of monetary policy. And credit shocks may have played an independent role in creating economic fluctuations. In this section, the empirical evidence on the credit channel is reviewed. The coverage is selective; a number of surveys discuss (and extend) the empirical work in the area (Gertler 1988; Gertler and Gilchrist 1993; Ramey 1993; Kashyap and Stein 1994; Hubbard 1995; Bernanke, Gertler, and Gilchrist 1996).

In an influential article, Bernanke (1983) provided evidence consistent with an important role for nonmonetary financial factors in accounting for the severity of the Great Depression in the United States. After controlling for unexpected money growth, he found that proxies for the financial crises of the early 1930s contributed significantly to explaining the growth rate of industrial production in his regression analysis.[40] If pure monetary causes were responsible for the decline in output during the Depression, the other measures of financial disruptions should not add explanatory power to the regression.

As Bernanke noted, his evidence is "not inconsistent" with the proposition that the financial crisis in the United States represented a distinct nonmonetary channel through which real output was affected during the Depression. The evidence is not conclusive, however; an alternative hypothesis is simply that the Depression itself was the result of nonmonetary factors (or at least factors not captured by unanticipated money growth) and that these factors caused output to decline, businesses to fail, and banks to close. By controlling only for unanticipated money growth, Bernanke's measures of financial crisis may only have been picking up the effects of the underlying nonmonetary causes of the Depression. Still, Bernanke's results offered support for the notion that the massive bank failures of the 1930s in the United States were not simply a sideshow but were at least partially responsible for the output declines.

Attempts to isolate a special role for credit in more normal business cycle periods have been plagued by what are essentially similar identification problems. Are movements in credit aggregates a reflection of shifts in demand resulting from effects operating through the traditional money channel, or do they reflect supply factors that constitute a distinct credit channel? Most macroeconomic variables behave similarly under either a money view or a credit view, so distinguishing between the two views based on time series evidence is difficult. For example, under the traditional money channel view, a contractionary shift in monetary policy raises interest rates and reduces investment spending. The decline in investment is associated with a decline in credit demand, so quantity measures of both bank and nonbank financing should fall. The competing theories are not sufficiently powerful to permit sharp predictions about the timing of interest rate, money, credit, and output movements that would allow the alternative views to be tested. As a consequence, much of the empirical work has focused on compositional effects, seeking to determine whether there are differential impacts of interest rate and credit movements that might distinguish between the alternative views.

---

40. Bernanke employed the real change in the deposits at failing banks and the real change in the liabilities of failing businesses as measures of the financial crises.

10.6.1 The Bank Lending Channel

Discussions of the credit channel often distinguish between a *bank lending channel* and a broader financial accelerator mechanism.[41] The bank lending channel emphasizes the special nature of bank credit and the role of banks in the economy's financial structure. In the bank lending view, banks play a particularly critical role in the transmission of monetary policy actions to the real economy. Policy actions that affect the reserve positions of banks will generate adjustments in interest rates and in the components of the banking sector's balance sheet. Traditional models of the monetary transmission mechanism focus on the impact of these interest rate changes on money demand and on consumption and investment decisions by households and firms. The ultimate effects on bank deposits and the supply of money are reflected in adjustments to the liability side of the banking sector's balance sheet.

The effects on banking sector reserves and interest rates also influence the supply of bank credit, the asset side of the balance sheet. If banks cannot offset a decline in reserves by adjusting securities holdings or raising funds through issuing nonreservable liabilities (such as CDs in the United States), bank lending must contract. If banking lending is *special* in the sense that bank borrowers do not have close substitutes for obtaining funds, variation in the availability of bank lending may have an independent impact on aggregate spending. Key, then, to the bank lending channel is the lack of close substitutes for deposit liabilities on the liability side of the banking sector's balance sheet and the lack of close substitutes for bank credit on the part of borrowers.

Imperfect information plays an important role in credit markets, and bank credit may be special, that is, have no close substitutes, because of information advantages banks have in providing both transactions services and credit to businesses. Small firms in particular may have difficulty obtaining funding from nonbank sources, so a contraction in bank lending will force these firms to contract their activities.

Banks play an important role in discussions of the monetary transmission mechanism, but the traditional approach stresses the role of bank liabilities as part of the money supply. Part of the reason for the continued focus on the liabilities side is the lack of convincing empirical evidence that bank lending plays a distinct role in the transmission process through which monetary policy affects the real economy. As C. Romer and Romer (1990b) summarized this literature, "A large body of recent theoretical work argues that the Federal Reserve's leverage over the economy may stem as much from the distinctive properties of the loans that banks make as from the unique characteristics of the transaction deposits that they receive. . . . Examining

41. A variety of excellent surveys and overviews of the credit channel is available. These include Gertler (1988); Bernanke (1993); Gertler and Gilchrist (1993); Ramey (1993); Kashyap and Stein (1994); Bernanke and Gertler (1995); Cecchetti (1995); Hubbard (1995); and Bernanke, Gertler, and Gilchrist (1999).

the behavior of financial variables and real output in a series of episodes of restrictive monetary policy, we are unable to find any support for this view" (196–197).

One of the first attempts to test for a distinct bank lending channel was that of S. King (1986). He found that monetary aggregates were better predictors of future output than were bank loans. More recently, Romer and Romer (1990b) and Ramey (1993) reached similar conclusions. Unfortunately, existing theories are usually not rich enough to provide sharp predictions about timing patterns that are critical for drawing conclusions from evidence on the predictive content of macroeconomic variables. This is particularly true when behavior depends on forward-looking expectations. Anticipations of future output movements can lead to portfolio and financing readjustments that will affect the lead-lag relationship between credit measures and output. Because a decline in output may be associated with inventory buildups, the demand for short-term credit can initially rise, and the existence of loan commitments will limit the ability of banks to alter their loan portfolios quickly. These factors make money credit and output timing patterns difficult to interpret.

In part, Romer and Romer's negative assessment reflects the difficult identification problem mentioned earlier. A policy-induced contraction of bank reserves will lead to a fall in both bank liabilities (deposits) and bank assets (loans and securities). With both sides of the banking sector's balance sheet shrinking, it is clearly difficult to know whether to attribute a subsequent decline in output to the money channel, the credit channel, or both.[42] Kashyap, Stein, and Wilcox (1993) addressed this problem by examining the composition of credit between bank and nonbank sources. Under the money view, a contractionary policy raises interest rates, lowering aggregate demand and the total demand for credit. Consequently, all measures of outstanding credit should decline. Under the bank lending view, the contractionary policy has a distinct effect in reducing the supply of bank credit. With bank credit less available, borrowers will attempt to substitute other sources of credit, and the relative demand for nonbank credit should rise. Thus, the composition of credit should change if the bank lending view is valid, with bank credit falling more in response to contractionary monetary policy than other forms of credit.

Kashyap, Stein, and Wilcox did find evidence for the bank lending channel when they examined aggregate U.S. data on bank versus nonbank sources of finance, the latter measured by the stock of outstanding commercial paper. Using the Romer and Romer (1990a) dates to identify contractionary shifts in monetary policy,[43] Kashyap,

42. The identification problems are not quite so severe in attempting to estimate the role of credit supply versus credit demand shocks on the economy. A contractionary bank credit supply shock would generally lower loan quantity and raise loan interest rates; a contraction in loan quantity caused by a demand shock would lower loan interest rates.

43. C. Romer and Romer (1990a) based their dating of monetary policy shifts on a reading of FOMC documents. See chapter 1.

Stein, and Wilcox found that the financing mix shifts away from bank loans following a monetary contraction. However, this occurs primarily because of a rise in commercial paper issuance, not a contraction in bank lending. Den Haan, Summer, and Yamashiro (2007) find that commercial lending at banks actually increases following a contractionary monetary policy shock.

Evidence based on aggregate credit measures can be problematic, however, if borrowers are heterogeneous in their sensitivity to the business cycle and in the types of credit they use. For example, the sales of small firms fluctuate more over the business cycle than those of large firms, and small firms are more reliant on bank credit than large firms that have greater access to the commercial paper market. Contractionary monetary policy that causes both small and large firms to reduce their demand for credit will cause aggregate bank lending to fall relative to nonbank financing as small firms contract more than large firms. This could account for the behavior of the debt mix even in the absence of any bank lending channel. Oliner and Rudebusch (1995; 1996b) argued that this is exactly what happens. Using disaggregate data on large and small firms, they showed that in response to a monetary contraction, there is no significant effect on the mix of bank/nonbank credit used by either small or large firms. Instead, the movement in the aggregate debt mix arises because of a general shift of short-term debt away from small firms and toward large firms. They concluded that the evidence does not support the bank lending channel as an important part of the transmission process of monetary policy. Similar conclusions were reached by Gertler and Gilchrist (1994) in an analysis also based on disaggregated data.

While the bank lending channel as part of the monetary policy transmission process may not be operative, it might still be the case that shifts in bank loan supply are a cause of economic fluctuations. In the United States, the 1989–1992 period generated a renewed interest in credit channels and monetary policy.[44] An unusually large decline in bank lending and stories, particularly from New England, of firms facing difficulty borrowing led many to seek evidence that credit markets played an independent role in contributing to the 1990–1991 recession. One difficulty in attempting to isolate the impact of credit supply disturbances is the need to separate movements caused by a shift in credit supply from movements due to changes in credit demand.

Walsh and Wilcox (1995) estimated a monthly VAR in which bank loan supply shocks are identified with innovations in the prime lending rate. They showed that their estimated loan supply innovations are related to changes in bank capital ratios,

---

44. See, for example, Bernanke and Lown (1992); the papers collected in Federal Reserve Bank of New York (1994); and Peek and Rosengren (1995).

changes in required reserves, and the imposition of credit controls. This provides some evidence that the innovations are actually picking up factors that affect the supply of bank loans. While prime rate shocks are estimated to lower loan quantity and output, they were not found to play a major causal role in U.S. business cycles, although their role was somewhat atypically large during the 1990–1991 recession.

10.6.2 The Broad Credit Channel

The broad credit channel is not restricted to the bank lending channel. Credit market imperfections may characterize all credit markets, influencing the nature of financial contracts, raising the possibility of equilibria with rationing, and creating a wedge between the costs of internal and external financing. This wedge arises because of agency costs associated with information asymmetries and the inability of lenders to monitor borrowers costlessly. As a result, cash flow and net worth become important in affecting the cost and availability of finance and the level of investment spending. A recession that weakens a firm's sources of internal finance can generate a *financial accelerator* effect; the firm is forced to rely more on higher-cost external funds just at the time the decline in internal finance drives up the relative cost of external funds. Contractionary monetary policy that produces an economic slowdown will reduce firm cash flow and profits. If this policy increases the external finance premium, there will be further contractionary effects on spending. In this way, the credit channel can serve to propagate and amplify an initial monetary contraction.

Financial accelerator effects can arise from the adjustment of asset prices to contractionary monetary policy. Borrowers may be limited in the amount they can borrow by the value of their assets that can serve as collateral. A rise in interest rates that lowers asset prices reduces the market value of borrowers' collateral. This reduction in value may then force some firms to reduce investment spending as their ability to borrow declines. The evidence in support of a broad credit channel was surveyed by Bernanke, Gertler, and Gilchrist (1996), who concluded, "We now have fairly strong evidence—at least for the case of firms—that downturns differentially affect both the access to credit and the real economic activity of high-agency-cost borrowers" (14).

Hubbard (1995) and Bernanke, Gertler, and Gilchrist (1996) listed three empirical implications of the broad credit channel. First, external finance is more expensive for borrowers than internal finance. This should apply particularly to uncollateralized external finance. Second, because the cost differential between internal and external finance arises from agency costs, the gap should depend inversely on the borrower's net worth. A fall in net worth raises the cost of external finance. Third, adverse shocks to net worth should reduce borrowers' access to finance, thereby reducing their investment, employment, and production levels.

If, as emphasized under the broad credit channel, agency costs increase during recessions and in response to contractionary monetary policy, then the share of credit going to low-agency-cost borrowers should rise. Bernanke, Gertler, and Gilchrist characterized this as the *flight to quality*. Aggregate data are likely to be of limited usefulness in testing such a hypothesis because most data on credit stocks and flows are not constructed based on the characteristics of the borrowers. Because small firms presumably are subject to higher agency costs than large firms, much of the evidence for a broad credit channel has been sought by looking for differences in the behavior of large and small firms in the face of monetary contractions.

Gertler and Gilchrist (1994) documented that small firms do behave differently than large firms over the business cycle, being much more sensitive to cyclical fluctuations. Kashyap, Lamont, and Stein (1994) found that inventory investment by firms without access to public bond markets appears to be affected by liquidity constraints.[45] Oliner and Rudebusch (1996a) assessed the role of financial factors by examining the behavior of small and large firms in response to changes in monetary policy. Interest rate increases in response to a monetary contraction lower asset values and the value of collateral, increasing the cost of external funds relative to internal funds. Since agency problems are likely to be more severe for small firms than for large firms, the linkage between internal sources of funds and investment spending should be particularly strong for small firms after a monetary contraction. Oliner and Rudebusch did find that the impact of cash flow on investment increases for small firms, but not for large firms, when monetary policy tightens.

10.7 Summary

This chapter has examined a number of issues related to financial markets and monetary policy, including the question of price level determinacy with interest rate pegs, the role of the term structure of interest rates, and imperfect information in credit markets. The economics of imperfect information provides numerous insights into the structure of credit markets. Credit market imperfections commonly lead to situations in which the lender's expected profits are not monotonic in the interest rate charged on a loan; expected profits initially rise with the loan rate but can then reach a maximum before declining. Thus, equilibrium may be characterized by credit rationing: excess demand fails to induce lenders to raise the loan rate because doing so lowers their expected profits. Perhaps more important, balance sheets matter. Variations in borrowers' net worth affect their ability to gain credit. A recession

---

45. They focused on the 1981–1982 recession in the United States, a recession typically attributed to tight monetary policy.

that lowers cash flows or a decline in asset prices that lowers net worth will reduce credit availability and increase the wedge between the costs of external and internal finance. The resulting impact on aggregate demand can generate a financial accelerator effect.

In general, skepticism surrounds the existence and importance of the credit channel, or at least it did before the financial crisis of 2007–2009. Certainly the previous evidence on the empirical importance of a distinct bank lending channel for monetary policy was mixed. Although periods of monetary contraction are followed by a fall in bank credit relative to open market credit, this may reflect simple composition effects and not a bank lending channel. The access to managed liabilities also suggests that variations in banking sector reserves caused by changes in monetary policy will affect bank lending mainly through traditional interest rate channels. The evidence for a broad credit channel or for financial accelerator effects is more favorable. Recessions are associated with a flight to quality. Small firms, a group likely to face large agency costs in obtaining external financing, are affected more severely during recessions. Net worth and cash flow do seem to affect investment, inventory, and production decisions.

10.8   Problems

1. For the model of (10.1)–(10.4) and the policy rule (10.9), find the rational-expectations equilibrium expression for the price level as a function of m_{t-1} and the model shocks. Verify that i_t fluctuates randomly around the target i^T, $\mu \to \infty$, and the variance of the nominal rate around the targeted value i^T will shrink to zero, but the price level can remain determinate. (Hint: The model can be solved using the method of undetermined coefficients. See Sheffrin 1983; McCallum 1989; or Attfield, Demery, and Duck 1991.)

2. Redo problem (10.1) using the policy rule (10.10) instead of (10.9).

3. Suppose (10.1) is replaced by a Taylor sticky price adjustment model of the type studied in chapter 6. Is the price level still indeterminate under the policy rule (10.5)? What if prices adjust according to the Calvo sticky price model?

4. Suppose the money supply process in (10.20) is replaced with

$$m_t = \gamma m_{t-1} + \sigma q_{t-1} + \phi_t$$

so that the policymaker is assumed to respond with a lag to the real rate shock, with the parameter σ viewed as a policy choice. Thus, policy involves a choice of γ and σ, with the parameter σ capturing the systematic response of policy to real interest rate shocks. Show how the effect of q_t on the one- and two-period nominal interest rates depends on σ. Explain why the absolute value of the impact of q_t on the spread between the long and short rates increases with σ.

5. Suppose the money supply process in (10.20) is replaced with

$$m_t = m_{t-1} + \xi_t - \gamma \xi_{t-1}.$$

Does i_t depend on γ? Does I_t? Explain.

6. (McCallum 1994a) Suppose the central bank adjusts the short-term rate i_t in respond to the slope of the term structure: $i_t = i_{t-1} + \lambda(I_t - i_t) + \zeta_t$, where ζ is a white noise process and $|\lambda| < 1$ and I_t is the two-period rate.

a. If the long-term rate is given by (10.25) and $\xi_t = \rho \xi_{t-1} + u_t$, show that the short-term rate must satisfy $(1 + \lambda)i_t = i_{t-1} + \frac{\lambda}{2}(i_t + E_t i_{t+1}) + \lambda \xi_t + \zeta_t$.

b. Now suppose the solution for i_t is of the form

$$i_t = \phi_0 + \phi_1 i_{t-1} + \phi_2 \xi_t + \phi_3 \zeta_t.$$

Assuming that private agents can observe the contemporaneous values of the two shocks ξ_t and ζ_t, show that

$$i_t = i_{t-1} + \frac{\lambda}{1 - \frac{\lambda \rho}{2}} \xi_t + \zeta_t$$

and

$$i_t = \frac{2}{\lambda} i_{t-1} + \frac{2}{1 - \rho} \xi_t + \frac{2}{\lambda} \zeta_t$$

are both consistent with equilibrium but that the second of these solutions implies explosive behavior of the short rate.

11 Monetary Policy Operating Procedures

11.1 Introduction

Previous chapters treated the nominal money supply, the nominal interest rate, or even inflation as the variable directly controlled by the monetary policymaker. This approach ignores the actual problems surrounding policy implementation. Central banks do not directly control the nominal money supply, inflation, or long-term interest rates likely to be most relevant for aggregate spending. Instead, narrow reserve aggregates, such as the monetary base, or very short-term interest rates, such as the federal funds rate in the United States, are the variables over which the central bank can exercise close control. Yet previous chapters have not discussed the specific relationship between short-term interest rates, other reserve aggregates such as non-borrowed reserves or the monetary base, and the broader monetary aggregates such as $M1$ or $M2$. And there has been no discussion of the factors that might explain why many central banks choose to use a short-term interest rate rather than a monetary aggregate as their policy instrument. These issues are addressed in this chapter.

The actual implementation of monetary policy involves a variety of rules, traditions, and practices, and these collectively are called *operating procedures*. Operating procedures differ according to the actual instrument the central bank uses in its daily conduct of policy, the operating target whose control is achieved over short horizons (e.g., a short-term interest rate versus a reserve aggregate), the conditions under which the instruments and operating targets are automatically adjusted in light of economic developments, the information about policy and the types of announcements the monetary authority might make, its choice of variables for which it establishes targets (e.g., money supply growth or the inflation rate), and whether these targets are formal or informal.

The objective in examining monetary policy operating procedures is to understand what instruments are actually under the control of the monetary authority, the factors that determine the optimal instrument choice, and how the choice of instrument affects the manner in which short-term interest rates, reserve aggregates, or the money stock might reflect policy actions and nonpolicy disturbances. After discussing the role of instruments and goals, the chapter examines the factors that determine the optimal choice of an operating procedure and the relationship between the choice of operating procedure and the response of the market for bank reserves to various economic disturbances. Then, a model of a channel system for setting interest rates is presented. The chapter concludes with a brief history of the Fed's operating procedures.

11.2   From Instruments to Goals

Discussions of monetary policy implementation focus on *instruments, operating targets, intermediate targets*, and *policy goals*. Instruments are the variables directly controlled by the central bank. These typically include an interest rate charged on reserves borrowed from the central bank, the reserve requirement ratios that determine the level of reserves banks must hold against their deposit liabilities, and the composition of the central bank's own balance sheet (its holdings of government securities, for example). The instruments of policy are manipulated to achieve a pre-specified value of an operating target, typically some measure of bank reserves (total reserves, borrowed reserves, or nonborrowed reserves—the difference between total and borrowed reserves), or a very short-term rate of interest, usually an overnight interbank rate (the federal funds rate in the case of the United States).

Goals such as inflation or deviations of unemployment from the natural rate are the ultimate variables of interest to policymakers; instruments are the actual variables under their direct control. Intermediate target variables fall between operating targets and goals in the sequence of links that run from policy instruments to real economic activity and inflation. Because observations on some or all of the goal variables are usually obtained less frequently than are data on interest rates, exchange rates, or monetary aggregates, the behavior of these latter variables can often provide the central bank with information about economic developments that will affect the goal variables. For example, faster than expected money growth may signal that real output is expanding more rapidly than was previously thought. The central bank might change its operating target (e.g., raise the interbank rate or contract reserves) to keep the money growth rate on a path believed to be consistent with achieving its policy goals. In this case, money growth serves as an intermediate target variable. Under inflation targeting policies, the inflation forecast plays the role of an intermediate target (Svensson and Woodford 2005).

Instruments, operating targets, intermediate targets, and goals have been described in a sequence running from the instruments directly controlled by the central bank to goals, the ultimate objectives of policy. Actually, policy design operates in the reverse fashion: from the goals of policy, to the values of the intermediate targets consistent with the goals, to the values of the operating targets needed to achieve the intermediate targets, and finally to the instrument settings that yield the desired values of the operating targets (Tinbergen 1956). In earlier chapters, inflation and the money supply were sometimes treated as policy instruments, ignoring the linkages from reserve markets to interest rates to banking sector behavior to aggregate demand. Similarly, it is often useful to ignore reserve market behavior and treat an operating target variable, such as the overnight interbank interest rate or a reserve aggregate, as the policy instrument. Since these two variables can be controlled closely over short time horizons, they are often also described as *policy instruments*.

11.3   The Instrument Choice Problem

If the monetary policy authority can choose between employing an interest rate or a monetary aggregate as its policy instrument, which should it choose? The classic analysis of this question is due to Poole (1970). He showed how the stochastic structure of the economy—the nature and relative importance of different types of disturbances—would determine the optimal choice of instrument.

11.3.1   Poole's Analysis

Suppose the central bank must set policy before observing the current disturbances to the goods and money markets, and assume that information on interest rates, but not output, is immediately available. This informational assumption reflects a situation in which the central bank can observe market interest rates essentially continuously, but data on inflation and output might be available only monthly or quarterly. In such an environment, the central bank will be unable to determine from a movement in market interest rates the exact nature of any economic disturbances. To make a simple parallel with a model of supply and demand, observing a rise in price does not indicate whether there has been a positive shock to the demand curve or a negative shock to the supply curve. Only by observing both price and quantity can these two alternatives be distinguished because a demand shift would be associated with a rise in both price and quantity, whereas a supply shift would be associated with a rise in price and a decline in quantity. At the macroeconomic level, an increase in the interest rate could be due to expanding aggregate demand (which might call for contractionary monetary policy to stabilize output) or an exogenous shift in money demand (which might call for letting the money supply expand). With imperfect information about economic developments, it will be impossible to determine the source of shocks that have caused interest rates to move.

Poole asked, in this environment, whether the central bank should try to hold market interest rates constant or hold a monetary quantity constant while allowing interest rates to move. And he assumed that the objective of policy was to stabilize real output, so he answered the question by comparing the variance of output implied by the two alternative policies.

Poole treated the price level as fixed; to highlight his basic results, the same is done here. Since the instrument choice problem primarily relates to the decision to hold either a market rate or a monetary quantity constant over a fairly short period of time (say, the time between policy board meetings), ignoring price level effects is not unreasonable as a starting point for the analysis. Poole's result can be derived in a simple model given in log terms by

$$y_t = -\alpha i_t + u_t \tag{11.1}$$

$$m_t = y_t - c i_t + v_t. \tag{11.2}$$

Equation (11.1) represents an aggregate demand relationship in which output is a decreasing function of the interest rate; demand also depends on an exogenous disturbance u_t with variance σ_u^2. Equation (11.2) gives the demand for money as a decreasing function of the interest rate and an increasing function of output. Money demand is subject to a random shock v_t with variance σ_v^2. Equilibrium requires that the demand for money equal the supply of money m_t. For simplicity, u and v are treated as mean zero serially and mutually uncorrelated processes. These two equations represent a simple IS-LM model of output determination, given a fixed price level.[1]

The final aspect of the model is a specification of the policymaker's objective, assumed to be the minimization of the variance of output deviations:

$$E[y_t]^2, \tag{11.3}$$

where all variables have been normalized so that the economy's equilibrium level of output in the absence of shocks is $y = 0$.

The timing is as follows: the central bank sets either i_t or m_t at the start of the period, then the stochastic shocks u_t and v_t occur, determining the values of the endogenous variables (either y_t and i_t if m_t is the policy instrument, or y_t and m_t if i_t is the policy instrument).

When the money stock is the policy instrument, (11.1) and (11.2) can be solved jointly for equilibrium output:

$$y_t = \frac{\alpha m_t + c u_t - \alpha v_t}{\alpha + c}.$$

---

1. Note that the price level has been normalized to equal 1 so that the log of the price level is zero; $p = 0$. The income elasticity of money demand has also been set equal to 1.

Then, setting m_t such that $E[y_t] = 0$,[2] one obtains $y_t = (cu_t - \alpha v_t)/(\alpha + c)$. Hence, the value of the objective function under a money supply procedure is

$$E_m[y_t]^2 = \frac{c^2 \sigma_u^2 + \alpha^2 \sigma_v^2}{(\alpha + c)^2}, \tag{11.4}$$

where it is assumed that u and v are uncorrelated.

Under the alternative policy, i_t is the policy instrument, and (11.1) can be solved directly for output. That is, the money market condition is no longer needed, although it will determine the level of m_t necessary to ensure money market equilibrium. By fixing the rate of interest, the central bank lets the money stock adjust endogenously to equal the level of money demand given by the interest rate and the level of income. Setting i_t such that $E[y_t] = 0$, output will equal u_t and

$$E_i[y_t]^2 = \sigma_u^2. \tag{11.5}$$

The two alternative policy choices can be evaluated by comparing the variance of output implied by each. The interest rate operating procedure is preferred to the money supply operating procedure if and only if

$$E_i[y_t]^2 < E_m[y_t]^2,$$

and, from (11.4) and (11.5), this condition is satisfied if and only if

$$\sigma_v^2 > \left(1 + \frac{2c}{\alpha}\right) \sigma_u^2. \tag{11.6}$$

Thus, an interest rate procedure is more likely to be preferred when the variance of money demand disturbances is larger, the LM curve is steeper (the slope of the LM curve is $1/c$), and the IS curve is flatter (the slope of the IS curve is $-1/\alpha$). A money supply procedure will be preferred if the variance of aggregate demand shocks (σ_u^2) is large, the LM curve is flat, or the IS curve is steep.[3]

If only aggregate demand shocks are present (i.e., $\sigma_v^2 = 0$), a money rule leads to a smaller variance for output. Under a money rule, a positive IS shock leads to an increase in the interest rate. This acts to reduce aggregate spending, thereby partially offsetting the original shock. Since the adjustment of i acts automatically to stabilize output, preventing this interest rate adjustment by fixing i leads to larger output

---

2. This just requires $m = 0$ because of the normalization.

3. In the context of an open economy in which the IS relationship is $y_t = -\alpha_1 i_t + \alpha_2 s_t + u_t$, where s_t is the exchange rate, Poole's conclusions go through without modification if the central bank's choice is expressed not in terms of i_t but in terms of the monetary conditions index $i_t - (\alpha_2/\alpha_1)s_t$.

fluctuations. If only money demand shocks are present, (i.e., $\sigma_u^2 = 0$), output can be stabilized perfectly under an interest rate rule. Under a money rule, money demand shocks cause the interest rate to move to maintain money market equilibrium; these interest rate movements then lead to output fluctuations. With both types of shocks occurring, the comparison of the two policy rules depends on the relative variances of u and v as well as on the slopes of the IS and the LM curves, as shown by (11.6).

This framework is quite simple and ignores many important factors. To take just one example, no central bank has direct control over the money supply. Instead, control can be exercised over a narrow monetary aggregate such as the monetary base, and variations in this aggregate are then associated with variations in broader measures of the money supply. To see how the basic framework can be modified to distinguish between the base as a policy instrument and the money supply, suppose the two are linked by

$$m_t = b_t + hi_t + \omega_t, \tag{11.7}$$

where b is the (log) monetary base, and the money multiplier ($m_t - b_t$ in log terms) is assumed to be an increasing function of the rate of interest (i.e., $h > 0$). In addition, ω_t is a random money multiplier disturbance. Equation (11.7) could arise under a fractional reserve system in which excess reserves are a decreasing function of the rate of interest.[4] Under an interest rate procedure, (11.7) is irrelevant for output determination, so $E_i(y_t)^2 = \sigma_u^2$, as before. But now, under a monetary base operating procedure,

$$y_t = \frac{(c+h)u_t - \alpha v_t + \alpha \omega_t}{\alpha + c + h}$$

and

$$E_b(y_t)^2 = \left(\frac{1}{\alpha + c + h}\right)^2 [(c+h)^2 \sigma_u^2 + \alpha^2(\sigma_v^2 + \sigma_\omega^2)].$$

The interest rate procedure is preferred over the monetary base procedure if and only if

$$\sigma_v^2 + \sigma_\omega^2 > \left[1 + \frac{2(c+h)}{\alpha}\right]\sigma_u^2.$$

Because ω shocks do not affect output under an interest rate procedure, the presence of money multiplier disturbances makes a base rule less attractive and makes it more

---

4. See, for example, Modigliani, Rasche, and Cooper (1970) or McCallum and Hoehn (1983).

likely that an interest rate procedure will lead to a smaller output variance. This simple extension reinforces the basic message of Poole's analysis; increased financial sector volatility (money demand or money multiplier shocks in the model used here) increases the desirability of an interest rate policy procedure over a monetary aggregate procedure. If money demand is viewed as highly unstable and difficult to predict over short time horizons, greater output stability can be achieved by stabilizing interest rates, letting monetary aggregates fluctuate. If, however, the main source of short-run instability arises from aggregate spending, a policy that stabilizes a monetary aggregate will lead to greater output stability.

This analysis is based on the realistic assumption that policy is unable to identify and respond directly to underlying disturbances. Instead, policy is implemented by fixing, at least over some short time interval, the value of an operating target or policy instrument. As additional information about the economy is obtained, the appropriate level at which to fix the policy instrument changes. So the critical issue is not so much which variable is used as a policy instrument but how that instrument should be adjusted in light of new but imperfect information about economic developments.

Poole's basic model ignores such factors as inflation, expectations, and aggregate supply disturbances. These factors and many others have been incorporated into models examining the choice between operating procedures based on an interest rate or a monetary aggregate (e.g., see Canzoneri, Henderson, and Rogoff 1983). B. Friedman (1990) contains a useful and comprehensive survey. In addition, as Friedman stressed, the appropriate definition of the policymaker's objective function is unlikely to be simply the variance of output once inflation is included in the model. The choice of instrument is an endogenous decision of the policymaker and is therefore dependent on the objectives of monetary policy.

This dependence is highlighted in the analysis of Collard and Dellas (2005). They employed a new Keynesian model of the type studied in chapter 8 in which households optimally choose consumption and firms maximize profit subject to a restriction on the frequency with which they can change prices, as in the model of Calvo (1983).[5] Two policy rules are considered. One is a fixed growth rate for the nominal quantity of money. The second is an interest rate rule that is close to a nominal interest rate peg. The rule does allow a long-run response to inflation that slightly exceeds 1 to ensure determinacy of the rational-expectations equilibrium (see section 8.3.3). Unlike Poole's original analysis, in which an ad hoc loss function was used to evaluate policies, Collard and Dellas ranked each rule according to its effect on the welfare of the representative agent. In a calibrated version of their model, they found that the

---

5. Collard and Dellas included capital in their model and allowed firms to index prices to nominal growth.

relative ranking of the rules can differ from the ones obtained in Poole's analysis. For example, a fiscal policy shock acts to raise nominal interest rates, so the interest rate rule must allow the money supply to expand to prevent the nominal rate from rising. This represented a procyclical policy in Poole's framework, and made the interest rate rule less desirable than the money rule. However, in the new Keynesian and other neoclassical frameworks, a rise in government spending reduces consumption, so the interest rate rule turns out to be countercyclical with respect to consumption. By stabilizing consumption (which enters the welfare function), the interest rate rule could actually dominate the money rule for some values of the calibrated parameters. In response to a positive money demand shock, a money rule causes consumption and output to fall. However, this induces a negative correlation between consumption and leisure that can actually stabilize utility. Thus, depending on parameter values, a money rule may outperform an interest rate rule in the face of money demand shocks. Ireland (2000) evaluated a money rule and an interest rate rule estimated from post-1980 Federal Reserve behavior. He found that an estimated policy rule dominates a fixed money growth rule. The general lesson to be drawn is that the objectives used to evaluate alternative policy rules and the parameter values used to calibrate the model can be critical to the results.

11.3.2 Policy Rules and Information

The alternative policies considered in the previous section can be viewed as special cases of the following policy rule:[6]

$$b_t = \mu i_t. \tag{11.8}$$

According to (11.8), the monetary authority adjusts the base, its actual instrument, in response to interest rate movements. The parameter μ, both its sign and its magnitude, determine how the base is varied by the central bank as interest rates vary. If $\mu = 0$, then $b_t = 0$ and one has the case of a monetary base operating procedure in which b is fixed (at zero by normalization) and is not adjusted in response to interest rate movements. If $\mu = -h$, then (11.7) implies that $m_t = \omega_t$ and one has the case of a money supply operating procedure in which the base is automatically adjusted to keep m_t equal to zero on average; the actual value of m_t varies as a result of the control error ω_t. In this case, b_t is the policy instrument and m_t is the operating target. Equation (11.8) is called a *policy rule* or an *instrument rule* in that it provides a description of how the policy instrument is set.

---

6. Recall that constants are normalized in equations such as (11.8) to be zero. More generally, there might be a rule of the form $b_t = b_0 + \mu(i_t - \mathrm{E}i_t)$, where b_0 is a constant and $\mathrm{E}i_t$ is the expected value of i_t. Issues of price level indeterminacy can arise if the average value of b_t is not tied down (as it is in this case by b_0); see chapter 10.

Combining (11.8) with (11.1) and (11.2),

$$i_t = \frac{v_t - \omega_t + u_t}{\alpha + c + \mu + h},$$ (11.9)

so that large values of μ reduce the variance of the interest rate. As $\mu \to \infty$, an interest rate operating procedure is approximated in which i_t is set equal to a fixed value (zero by normalization). By representing policy in terms of the policy rule and then characterizing policy in terms of the choice of a value for μ, one can consider intermediate cases to the extreme alternatives considered in section 11.3.1.

Substituting (11.9) into (11.1), output is given by

$$y_t = \frac{(c + \mu + h)u_t - \alpha(v_t - \omega_t)}{\alpha + c + \mu + h}.$$

From this expression, the variance of output can be calculated:

$$\sigma_y^2 = \frac{(c + \mu + h)^2 \sigma_u^2 + \alpha^2(\sigma_v^2 + \sigma_\omega^2)}{(\alpha + c + \mu + h)^2}.$$

Minimizing with respect to μ, the optimal policy rule (in the sense of minimizing the variance of output) is given by

$$\mu^* = -\left[c + h - \frac{\alpha(\sigma_v^2 + \sigma_\omega^2)}{\sigma_u^2}\right].$$ (11.10)

In general, neither the interest rate ($\mu \to \infty$) nor the base ($\mu = 0$) nor the money supply ($\mu = -h$) operating procedures will be optimal. Instead, as Poole (1970) demonstrated, the way policy (in the form of the setting for b_t) should respond to interest rate movements will depend on the relative variances of the three underlying economic disturbances.

To understand the role these variances play, suppose first that $v \equiv \omega \equiv 0$ so that $\sigma_v^2 = \sigma_\omega^2 = 0$; there are no shifts in either money demand or money supply, given the base. In this environment, the basic Poole analysis concludes that a base rule dominates an interest rate rule. Equation (11.10) shows that the central bank should reduce b_t when the interest rate rises (i.e., $b_t = -(c + h)i_t$). With interest rate movements signaling aggregate demand shifts (since u_t is the only source of disturbance), a rise in the interest rate indicates that $u_t > 0$. A policy designed to stabilize output should reduce m_t; this decline in m_t can be achieved by reducing the base. Rather than "leaning against the wind" to offset the interest rate rise, the central bank should engage in a contractionary policy that pushes i_t up even further.

When σ_v^2 and σ_ω^2 are positive, interest rate increases may now be the result of an increase in money demand or a decrease in money supply. Since the appropriate response to a positive money demand shock or a negative money supply shock is to increase the monetary base and offset the interest rate rise (i.e., it *is* appropriate to lean against the wind), $\mu^* > -(c+h)$; it will become optimal to actually increase the base as $\sigma_v^2 + \sigma_\omega^2$ becomes sufficiently large.

The value for the policy rule parameter in (11.10) can also be interpreted in terms of a signal extraction problem faced by the policy authority. Recall that the basic assumption in the Poole analysis was that the policymaker could observe and react to the interest rate, but perhaps because of information lags, the current values of output and the underlying disturbances could not be observed. Suppose instead that the shocks u, v, and e are observed, and the central bank can respond to them. That is, suppose the policy rule could take the form $b_t = \mu_u u_t + \mu_v v_t + \mu_\omega \omega_t$ for some parameters μ_u, μ_v, and μ_ω. If this policy rule is substituted into (11.1) and (11.2), one obtains

$$y_t = \frac{(c+h+\alpha\mu_u)u_t - \alpha(1-\mu_v)v_t + \alpha(1+\mu_\omega)\omega_t}{\alpha+c+h}.$$

In this case, which corresponds to a situation of perfect information about the basic shocks, it is clear that the variance of output can be minimized if $\mu_u = -(c+h)/\alpha$, $\mu_v = 1$ and $\mu_\omega = -1$.

If the policymaker cannot observe the underlying shocks, then policy will need to be set on the basis of forecasts of these disturbances. Given the linear structure of the model and the quadratic form of the objective, the optimal policy can be written $b_t = \mu_u \hat{u}_t + \mu_v \hat{v}_t + \mu_\omega \hat{\omega}_t = -[(c+h)/\alpha]\hat{u}_t + \hat{v}_t - \hat{\omega}_t$, where $\hat{u}_t$, $\hat{v}_t$, and $\hat{\omega}_t$ are the forecasts of the shocks.[7] In the Poole framework, the central bank observes the interest rate and can set policy conditional on i_t. Thus, the forecasts of shocks will depend on i_t and will take the form $\hat{u}_t = \delta_u i_t$, $\hat{v}_t = \delta_v i_t$, and $\hat{\omega}_t = \delta_\omega i_t$. The policy rule can then be written as

$$b_t = -\left(\frac{c+h}{\alpha}\right)\hat{u}_t + \hat{v}_t - \hat{\omega}_t = \left(-\frac{c+h}{\alpha}\delta_u + \delta_v - \delta_\omega\right)i_t. \tag{11.11}$$

Using this policy rule to solve for the equilibrium interest rate, determining the $\delta_i's$ from the assumption that forecasts are equal to the projections of the shocks on i_t, it is straightforward to verify that the coefficient on i_t in the policy rule (11.11) is equal to the value μ^* given in (11.10).[8] Thus, the optimal policy response to observed

---

7. The linear quadratic structure of the policy problem implies certainty equivalence holds. Under certainty equivalence, optimal policy depends only on the expected values of the disturbances.

8. See problem 5 at the end of this chapter.

interest rate movements represents an optimal response to the central bank's forecasts of the underlying economic disturbances.

11.3.3   Intermediate Targets

The previous section showed how the optimal response coefficients in the policy rule could be related to the central bank's forecast of the underlying disturbances. This interpretation of the policy rule parameter is important because it captures a very general way of thinking about policy. When the central bank faces imperfect information about the shocks to the economy, it should respond based on its best forecasts of these shocks.[9] In the present example, the only information variable available was the interest rate, so forecasts of the underlying shocks were based on i. In more general settings, information on other variables may be available on a frequent basis, and this should also be used in forecasting the sources of economic disturbances. Examples of such information variables include (besides market interest rates) exchange rates, commodity prices, and asset prices.[10]

Because the central bank must respond to partial and incomplete information about the true state of the economy, monetary policy is often formulated in practice in terms of intermediate targets. Intermediate targets are variables whose behavior provides information useful in forecasting the goal variables.[11] Deviations in the intermediate targets from their expected paths indicate a likely deviation of a goal variable from its target and signal the need for a policy adjustment. For example, if money growth, which is observed weekly, is closely related to subsequent inflation, which is observed only monthly, then faster than expected money growth signals the need to tighten policy. When action is taken to keep the intermediate target variable equal to its target, the hope is that policy will be adjusted automatically to keep the goal variables close to their targets as well.[12]

To see the role of intermediate targets in a very simple framework, consider the following aggregate supply, aggregate demand, and money demand system, expressed in terms of the rate of inflation:

9. Brainard (1967) showed that this statement is no longer true when there is uncertainty about the model parameters in additional to the additive uncertainty considered here. Parameter uncertainty may make it optimal to adjust less than completely. See section 8.4.7.

10. As discussed in chapter 1, commodity prices eliminate the price puzzle in VAR estimates of monetary policy effects because of the informational role they appear to play.

11. See Kareken, Muench, and Wallace (1973) and B. Friedman (1975; 1977b; 1990) for early treatments of the informational role of intermediate targets. More recently, Svensson (1997a; 1999b) stressed the role of inflation forecasts as an intermediate target. Bernanke and Woodford (1997) showed, however, how multiple equilibria may arise if policy is based on private sector forecasts, which are, in turn, based on expectations of future policy.

12. B. Friedman (1990) and McCallum (1990b) provided discussions of the intermediate target problem.

$$y_t = a(\pi_t - E_{t-1}\pi_t) + z_t \tag{11.12}$$

$$y_t = -\alpha(i_t - E_t\pi_{t+1}) + u_t \tag{11.13}$$

$$m_t - p_t = m_t - \pi_t - p_{t-1} = y_t - ci_t + v_t. \tag{11.14}$$

Equation (11.12) is a standard Lucas supply curve; (11.13) gives aggregate demand as a decreasing function of the expected real interest rate; and (11.14) is a simple money demand relationship. Assume that each of the three disturbances z, u, and v follows a first-order autoregressive process:

$$z_t = \rho_z z_{t-1} + e_t$$

$$u_t = \rho_u u_{t-1} + \varphi_t$$

$$v_t = \rho_v v_{t-1} + \psi_t,$$

where $-1 < \rho_i < 1$ for $i = z, u, v$. The innovations e, φ, and ψ are assumed to be mean zero serially and mutually uncorrelated processes. The interest rate i is taken to be the policy instrument.

Suppose that the monetary authority's objective is to minimize the expected squared deviations of the inflation rate around a target level π^*. Hence, i_t is chosen to minimize[13]

$$V = \frac{1}{2}E(\pi_t - \pi^*)^2. \tag{11.15}$$

To complete the model, one must specify the information structure. Suppose that i_t must be set before observing e_t, φ_t, or ψ_t but that y_{t-1}, π_{t-1}, and m_{t-1} (and therefore p_{t-1}, z_{t-1}, u_{t-1}, and v_{t-1}) are known when i_t is set. The optimal setting for the policy instrument can be found by solving for the equilibrium price level in terms of the policy instrument and then evaluating the loss function given by (11.15).

Solving the model is simplified by recognizing that i_t will always be set to ensure that the expected value of inflation equals the target value π^*.[14] Actual inflation will

---

13. Note that for this example the loss function in output deviations is replaced with one involving only inflation stabilization objectives. As is clear from (11.12), stabilizing inflation to minimize unexpected movements in π is consistent with minimizing output variability if there are no supply disturbances ($z \equiv 0$). If the loss function depends on output and inflation variability and there are supply shocks, the optimal policy will depend on the relative weight placed on these two objectives.

14. The first-order condition for the optimal choice of i_t is

$$\frac{\partial V}{\partial i_t} = E(\pi_t - \pi^*)\frac{\partial \pi_t}{\partial i_t} = 0,$$

implying $E\pi_t = \pi^*$.

differ from π^* because policy cannot respond to offset the effects of the shocks to aggregate supply, aggregate demand, or money demand, but policy will offset any expected effects of lagged disturbances to ensure that $E_{t-1}\pi_t = E_t\pi_{t+1} = \pi^*$. Using this result, (11.12) can be used to eliminate y_t from (11.13) to yield

$$\pi_t = \frac{(a+\alpha)\pi^* - \alpha i_t + u_t - z_t}{a}.\tag{11.16}$$

Equation (11.16) shows that, under an interest rate policy, π_t is independent of v_t and the parameters of the money demand function. If the policymaker had full information on u_t and z_t, the optimal policy would be to set the interest rate equal to $i_t^* = \pi^* + (1/\alpha)(u_t - z_t)$ since this would yield $\pi_t = \pi^*$. If policy must be set prior to observing the realization of the shocks at time t, the optimal policy can be obtained by taking expectations of (11.16), conditional on time $t-1$ information, yielding the optimal setting for i_t:

$$\hat{\imath} = \pi^* + \left(\frac{1}{\alpha}\right)(\rho_u u_{t-1} - \rho_z z_{t-1}).\tag{11.17}$$

Substituting (11.17) into (11.16) shows that the actual inflation rate under this policy is equal to[15]

$$\pi_t(\hat{\imath}) = \pi^* + \frac{\varphi_t - e_t}{a},\tag{11.18}$$

and the value of the loss function is equal to

$$V(\hat{\imath}) = \frac{1}{2}\left(\frac{1}{a}\right)^2 (\sigma_\varphi^2 + \sigma_e^2),$$

where σ_x^2 denotes the variance of a random variable x.

An alternative approach to setting policy in this example would be to derive the money supply consistent with achieving the target inflation rate π^* and then to set the interest rate to achieve this level of m_t. Using (11.14) to eliminate i_t from (11.13),

$$y_t = \left(\frac{\alpha}{\alpha+c}\right)(m_t - \pi_t - p_{t-1} - v_t) + \left(\frac{c}{\alpha+c}\right)(u_t + \alpha\pi^*).$$

Using the aggregate supply relationship (11.12), the equilibrium inflation rate is

---

15. Note that under this policy, $E_{t-1}\pi_t = \pi^*$, as assumed.

$$\pi_t = \pi^* + \frac{1}{a}\left[\left(\frac{\alpha}{\alpha+c}\right)(m_t - \pi_t - p_{t-1} - v_t) + \left(\frac{c}{\alpha+c}\right)(u_t + \alpha\pi^*) - z_t\right]$$

$$= \frac{[a(\alpha+c) + \alpha c]\pi^* + \alpha(m_t - p_{t-1} - v_t) + cu_t - (\alpha+c)z_t}{a(\alpha+c) + \alpha}.$$

The value of m_t consistent with $\pi_t = \pi^*$ is therefore

$$m_t^* = (1-c)\pi^* + p_{t-1} - \left(\frac{c}{\alpha}\right)u_t + \left(1+\frac{c}{\alpha}\right)z_t + v_t.$$

If the money supply must be set before observing the time t shocks, the optimal target for m is

$$\hat{m}_t \equiv (1-c)\pi^* + p_{t-1} - \left(\frac{c}{\alpha}\right)\rho_u u_{t-1} + \left(1+\frac{c}{\alpha}\right)\rho_z z_{t-1} + \rho_v v_{t-1}. \qquad (11.19)$$

As can be easily verified, the interest rate consistent with achieving the targeted money supply $\hat{m}_t$ is just $\hat{\imath}_t$, given by (11.17). Thus, an equivalent procedure for deriving the policy that minimizes the loss function is to first calculate the value of the money supply consistent with the target for π and then to set i equal to the value that achieves the targeted money supply.

Now suppose the policymaker can observe m_t and respond to it. Under the policy that sets i_t equal to $\hat{\imath}$, (11.14) implies that the actual money supply will equal $m_t = \pi_t(\hat{\imath}) + p_{t-1} + y_t(\hat{\imath}) - c\hat{\imath}_t + v_t$, which can be written as[16]

$$m_t(\hat{\imath}) = \hat{m}_t - \left(\frac{1}{a}\right)e_t + \left(1 + \frac{1}{a}\right)\varphi_t + \psi_t. \qquad (11.20)$$

Observing how m_t deviates from $\hat{m}_t$ reveals information about the shocks, and this information can be used to adjust the interest rate to keep inflation closer to target. For example, suppose aggregate demand shocks (φ) are the only source of uncertainty (i.e., $e \equiv \psi \equiv 0$). A positive aggregate demand shock ($\varphi > 0$) will, for a given nominal interest rate, increase output and inflation, both of which contribute to an increase in nominal money demand. Under a policy of keeping i fixed, the policy-

---

16. Substitute the solution (11.18) into the aggregate supply function to yield $y(\hat{\imath}_t) = \varphi_t - e_t + z_t = \varphi_t + \rho_z z_{t-1}$. Using this result in (11.17) and (11.18) in (11.14),

$$m(\hat{\imath}_t) = \pi^* + \frac{\varphi_t - e_t}{a} + p_{t-1} + \varphi_t + \rho_z z_{t-1} - c\hat{\imath}_t + v_t$$

$$= \pi^* + \left(\frac{\varphi_t - e_t}{a}\right) + p_{t-1} + \varphi_t + \rho_z z_{t-1} - c\left[\pi^* + \frac{\rho_u u_{t-1} - \rho_z z_{t-1}}{\alpha}\right] + v_t.$$

Collecting terms and using (11.18) yields (11.20).

maker automatically allows reserves to increase, letting m rise in response to the increased demand for money. Thus, an increase in m_t above $\hat{m}_t$ would signal that the nominal interest rate should be increased to offset the demand shock. Responding to the money supply to keep m_t equal to the targeted value $\hat{m}_t$ would achieve the ultimate goal of keeping the inflation rate equal to π^*. This is an example of an intermediate targeting policy; the nominal money supply serves as an intermediate target, and by adjusting policy to achieve the intermediate target, policy is also better able to achieve the target for the goal variable π_t.

Problems arise, however, when there are several potential sources of economic disturbances. Then it can be the case that the impact on the goal variable of a disturbance would be exacerbated by attempts to keep the intermediate target variable on target. For example, a positive realization of the money demand shock ψ_t does not require a change in i_t to maintain inflation on target.[17] But (11.20) shows that a positive money demand shock causes m_t to rise above the target value $m_t(\hat{\imath})$. Under a policy of adjusting i to keep m close to its target, the nominal interest rate would be raised, causing π to deviate from π^*. Responding to keep m on target will not produce the appropriate policy for keeping π on target.

Automatically adjusting the nominal interest rate to ensure that m_t always equals its target $\hat{m}_t$ requires that the nominal interest rate equal[18]

$$i_t^T = \hat{\imath}_t + \frac{(1+a)\varphi_t - e_t + a\psi_t}{ac + \alpha(1+a)}. \tag{11.21}$$

In this case, inflation is equal to

$$\pi_t(i_t^T) = \pi^* + \left(\frac{1}{a}\right)[-\alpha(i_t^T - \hat{\imath}) + \varphi_t - e_t]$$

$$= \pi^* + \frac{c\varphi_t - (\alpha + c)e_t - \alpha\psi_t}{ac + \alpha(1+a)}.$$

Comparing this expression for inflation to $\pi_t(\hat{\imath}_t)$ from (11.18), the value obtained when information on the money supply is not used, one can see that the impact of an aggregate demand shock, φ, on the price level is reduced to $(c/[ac + \alpha(1+a)] < 1/a)$; because a positive φ shock tends to raise money demand, the interest rate must be increased to offset the effects on the money supply to keep m on target. This inter-

---

17. Equation (11.18) shows that inflation is independent of v_t.

18. Note that this discussion does not assume that the realizations of the individual disturbances can be observed by the policymaker; as long as m_t is observed, i_t can be adjusted to ensure that $m_t = \hat{m}_t$, and this results in i being given by (11.21). Equation (11.21) is obtained by solving (11.12)–(11.14) for m_t as a function of i_t and the various disturbances. Setting this expression equal to $\hat{m}_t$ yields the required value of i_t^T.

est rate increase acts to offset partially the impact of a demand shock on inflation. The impact of an aggregate supply shock (e) under an intermediate money targeting policy is also decreased. However, money demand shocks, ψ, now affect inflation, something they did not do under a policy of keeping i equal to $\hat{\imath}$; a positive ψ tends to increase m above target. If i is increased to offset this shock, inflation will fall below target.

The value of the loss function under the money targeting procedure is

$$V(i_t^T) = \frac{1}{2}\left(\frac{1}{ac + \alpha(1+a)}\right)^2 [c^2\sigma_\varphi^2 + (\alpha + c)^2\sigma_e^2 + \alpha^2\sigma_\psi^2].$$

Comparing this to $V(\hat{\imath})$, the improvement from employing an intermediate targeting procedure in which the policy instrument is adjusted to keep the money supply on target will be decreasing in the variance of money demand shocks, σ_ψ^2. As long as this variance is not too large, the intermediate targeting procedure will do better than a policy of simply keeping the nominal rate equal to $\hat{\imath}$. If this variance is too large, the intermediate targeting procedure will do worse.

An intermediate targeting procedure represents a rule for adjusting the policy instrument to a specific linear combination of the new information contained in movements of the intermediate target. Using (11.20) and (11.21), the policy adjustment can be written as

$$i_t^T - \hat{\imath} = \left[\frac{a}{ac + \alpha(1+a)}\right][m_t(\hat{\imath}) - \hat{m}]$$

$$= \mu^T[m_t(\hat{\imath}) - \hat{m}].$$

In other words, if the money supply realized under the initial policy setting ($m_t(\hat{\imath})$) deviates from its expected level ($\hat{m}$), the policy instrument is adjusted. Because the money supply will deviate from target due to φ and e shocks, which do call for a policy adjustment, as well as ψ shocks, which do not call for any change in policy, an *optimal* adjustment to the new information in money supply movements would depend on the relative likelihood that movements in m are caused by the various possible shocks. An intermediate targeting rule, by adjusting to deviations of money from target in a manner that does not take into account whether fluctuations in m are more likely to be due to φ or e or ψ shocks, represents an inefficient use of the information in m.

To derive the optimal policy response to fluctuations in the nominal money supply, let

$$i_t - \hat{\imath} = \mu(m_t - \hat{m})$$

$$= \mu x_t, \tag{11.22}$$

where $x_t = (1 + a^{-1})\varphi_t - a^{-1}e_t + \psi_t$ is the new information obtained from observing m_t.[19] Under an intermediate targeting rule, the monetary authority would adjust its policy instrument to minimize deviations of the intermediate target from the value consistent with achieving the ultimate policy target, in this case an inflation rate of π^*. But under a policy that optimally uses the information in the intermediate target variable, μ will be chosen to minimize $E(\pi_t - \pi^*)^2$, not $E(m_t - \hat{m})^2$. Using (11.22) in (11.16), one finds that the value of μ that minimizes the loss function is

$$\mu^* = \frac{1}{\alpha}\left[\frac{a(1 + a)\sigma_\varphi^2 + a\sigma_e^2}{(1 + a)^2\sigma_\varphi^2 + \sigma_e^2 + a^2\sigma_\psi^2}\right].$$

This is a messy expression, but some intuition for it can be gained by recognizing that if the policymaker could observe the underlying shocks, (11.16) implies that the optimal policy would set the nominal interest rate i equal to $\hat{i} + (1/\alpha)(\varphi_t - e_t)$. The policymaker cannot observe φ_t or e_t, but information that can be used to estimate them is available from observing the deviation of money from its target. As already shown, observing m_t provides information on the linear combination of the underlying shocks given by x_t. Letting $E^x[\ ]$ denote expectations conditional on x, the policy instrument should be adjusted according to

$$i(x_t) = \hat{i} + \frac{1}{\alpha}(E^x\varphi_t - E^x e_t). \tag{11.23}$$

Evaluating these expectations gives

$$E^x\varphi_t = \left[\frac{a(1 + a)\sigma_\varphi^2}{(1 + a)^2\sigma_\varphi^2 + \sigma_e^2 + a^2\sigma_\psi^2}\right]x_t$$

---

19. The expression for x_t is obtained by solving (11.12)–(11.14) for m_t as a function of the interest rate, yielding

$$m_t = \pi_t + p_{t-1} + y_t - ci_t + v_t = \left[\pi^* + \frac{y_t - z_t}{a}\right] + p_{t-1} + y_t - ci_t + v_t,$$

or

$$m_t = \left[\pi^* + \frac{-\alpha i_t + \alpha\pi^* + u_t - z_t}{a}\right] + p_{t-1} + [-\alpha i_t + \alpha\pi^* + u_t] - ci_t + v_t$$

$$= (1 + \alpha(1 + a^{-1}))\pi^* + p_{t-1} - (c + \alpha(1 + a^{-1}))i_t - a^{-1}z_t + (1 + a^{-1})u_t + v_t,$$

so that, conditional on i_t,

$$m_t - E_{t-1}m_t = -a^{-1}e_t + (1 + a^{-1})\varphi_t + \psi_t \equiv x_t.$$

and

$$\mathrm{E}^x e_t = \left[\frac{-a\sigma_e^2}{(1+a)^2\sigma_\varphi^2 + \sigma_e^2 + a^2\sigma_\psi^2}\right] x_t.$$

Substituting these expressions into (11.23) yields

$$i(z_t) = \hat{i} + \left(\frac{1}{\alpha}\right)\left[\frac{a(1+a)\sigma_\varphi^2 + a\sigma_e^2}{(1+a)^2\sigma_\varphi^2 + \sigma_e^2 + a^2\sigma_\psi^2}\right] x_t$$

$$= \hat{i} + \mu^* x_t.$$

Under this policy, the information in the intermediate target is used optimally. As a result, the loss function is reduced relative to a policy that adjusts i to keep the money supply always equal to its target:

$$V^* \leq V(i^T),$$

where V^* is the loss function under the policy that adjusts i according to $\mu^* z_t$.

As long as money demand shocks are not too large, an intermediate targeting procedure does better than following a policy rule that fails to respond at all to new information. The intermediate targeting rule does worse, however, than a rule that optimally responds to the new information. This point was first made by Kareken, Muench, and Wallace (1973) and B. Friedman (1975).

Despite the general inefficiency of intermediate targeting procedures, central banks often implement policy as if they were following an intermediate targeting procedure. During the 1970s, there was strong support in the United States for using money growth as an intermediate target. Support faded in the 1980s, when money demand because significantly more difficult to predict.[20] The Bundesbank (prior to being superseded by the European Central Bank) and the Swiss National Bank continued to formulate policy in terms of money growth rates that can be interpreted as intermediate targets, and money formed one of the pillars in the two-pillar strategy of the European Central Bank.[21] Other central banks seem to use the nominal exchange rate as an intermediate target. Today, many central banks have shifted to using inflation itself as an intermediate target.

20. B. Friedman and Kuttner (1996) examined the behavior of the Fed during the era of monetary targeting.

21. Laubach and Posen (1997) argued that the targets were used to signal policy intentions rather than serving as strict intermediate targets. See Beck and Wieland (2007) on the role of money in the ECB's strategy.

Intermediate targets provide a simple framework for responding automatically to economic disturbances. The model of this section can be used to evaluate desirable properties that characterize good intermediate targets. The critical condition is that σ_ψ^2 be small. Since ψ_t represents the innovation or shock to the money demand equation, intermediate monetary targeting will work best if money demand is relatively predictable. Often this has not been the case. The unpredictability of money demand is an important reason that most central banks moved away from using monetary targeting during the 1980s. The shock ψ can also be interpreted as arising from control errors. For example, assuming that the monetary base was the policy instrument, unpredictable fluctuations in the link between the base and the monetary aggregate being targeted (corresponding to the ω disturbance in 11.7) would reduce the value of an intermediate targeting procedure. Controllability is therefore a desirable property of an intermediate target.

Lags in the relationship between the policy instrument, the intermediate target, and the final goal variable represent an additional important consideration. The presence of lags introduces no new fundamental issues; as the simple framework shows, targeting an intermediate variable allows policy to respond to new information, either because the intermediate target variable is observed contemporaneously (as in the example) or because it helps to forecast future values of the goal variable. In either case, adjusting policy to achieve the intermediate target forces policy to respond to new information is a manner that is generally suboptimal. But this inefficiency will be smaller if the intermediate target is relatively easily controllable (i.e., σ_ψ^2 is small) yet is highly correlated with the variable of ultimate interest (i.e., σ_φ^2 and σ_e^2 are large), so that a deviation of the intermediate variable from its target provides a clear signal that the goal variable has deviated from its target. For central banks that target inflation, the inflation forecast serves as an intermediate target. An efficient forecast is based on all available information and should be highly correlated with the variable of ultimate interest (future inflation). Svensson and Woodford (2005) discussed the implementation of optimal policies through the use of inflation forecasts.

11.3.4 Real Effects of Operating Procedures

The traditional analysis of operating procedures focuses on volatility; the operating procedure adopted by the central bank affects the way disturbances influence the variability of output, prices, real interest rates, and monetary aggregates. The average values of these variables, however, is treated as independent of the choice of operating procedure. Canzoneri and Dellas (1998) showed that the choice of procedure can have a sizable effect on the average level of the real rate of interest by affecting the variability of aggregate consumption.

The standard Euler condition relates the current marginal utility of consumption to the expected real return and the future marginal utility of consumption:

$$u_c(c_t) = \beta R_{ft} \mathrm{E}_t u_c(c_{t+1}),$$

where β is the discount factor, R_{ft} is the gross risk-free real rate of return, and $u_c(c_t)$ is the marginal utility of consumption at time t. The right side of this expression can be written as

$$\beta R_{ft} \mathrm{E}_t u_c(c_{t+1}) \approx \beta R_{ft} u_c(\mathrm{E}_t c_{t+1}) + \frac{1}{2} \beta R_{ft} u_{ccc}(\mathrm{E}_t c_{t+1}) \, \mathrm{Var}_t(c_{t+1}),$$

where u_{ccc} is the third derivative of the utility function and $\mathrm{Var}_t(c_{t+1})$ is the conditional variance of c_{t+1}. If the variance of consumption differs under alternative monetary policy operating procedures, then either the marginal utility of consumption must adjust (i.e., consumption will change) or the risk-free real return must change. Because the expected real interest rate can be expressed as the sum of the risk-free rate and a risk premium, average real interest rates will be affected if the central bank's operating procedure affects R_{ft} or the risk premium.

Canzoneri and Dellas developed a general equilibrium model with nominal wage rigidity and simulated the model under alternative operating procedures (interest rate targeting, money targeting, and nominal income targeting). They found that real interest rates, on average, are highest under a nominal interest rate targeting procedure. To understand why, suppose the economy is subject to money demand shocks. Under a procedure that fixes the nominal money supply, such shocks induce a positive correlation between consumption (output) and inflation. This generates a negative risk premium (when consumption is lower than expected, the ex post real return is high because inflation is lower than expected). A nominal interest rate procedure accommodates money demand shocks and so results in a higher average risk premium. By calibrating their model and conducting simulations, Canzoneri and Dellas concluded that the choice of operating procedure can have a significant effect on average real interest rates.

11.4 Operating Procedures and Policy Measures

Understanding a central bank's operating procedures is important for two reasons. First, it is important in empirical work to distinguish between endogenous responses to developments in the economy and exogenous shifts in policy. Whether movements in a monetary aggregate or a short-term interest rate are predominantly endogenous responses to disturbances unrelated to policy shifts or are exogenous shifts in policy will depend on the nature of the procedures used to implement policy. Thus, some understanding of operating procedures is required for empirical investigations of the impact of monetary policy.

Second, operating procedures, by affecting the automatic adjustment of interest rates and monetary aggregates to economic disturbances, can have implications for the macroeconomic equilibrium. For example, operating procedures that lead the monetary authority to smooth interest rate movements can introduce a unit root into the price level,[22] and in the models examined in chapters 2 and 3, the economy's response to productivity shocks was shown to depend on how the money supply was adjusted (although the effects were small).

Analyses of operating procedures are based on the market for bank reserves. In the United States, this is the federal funds market. The focus in this section is on the United States and the behavior of the Federal Reserve; similar issues arise in the analysis of monetary policy in other countries, although institutional details can vary considerably. Discussions of operating procedures in major OECD countries can be found in Batten et al. (1990); Bernanke and Mishkin (1993); Morton and Wood (1993); Kasman (1993); Borio (1997); and the Bank for International Settlements (2007).

11.4.1   Money Multipliers

Theoretical models of monetary economies often provide little guidance to how the quantity of money appearing in the theory should be related to empirical measures of the money supply. If m is viewed as the quantity of the means of payment used in the conduct of exchange, then cash, demand deposits, and other checkable deposits should be included in the empirical correspondence.[23] If m is viewed as a variable set by the policy authority, then an aggregate such as the monetary base, which represents the liabilities of the central bank and so can be directly controlled, would be more appropriate. The *monetary base* is equal to the sum of the reserve holdings of the banking sector and the currency held by the nonbank public.[24] These are liabilities of the central bank and can be affected by open market operations. Most policy discussions, however, focus on broader monetary aggregates, but these are not the direct instruments of monetary policy. A traditional approach to understanding the linkages between a potential instrument such as the monetary base and the various measures of the money supply is to express broader measures of money as the product of the monetary base and a money multiplier. Changes in the money supply can then be decomposed into those resulting from changes in the base and those resulting

---

22. See Goodfriend (1987) and Van Hoose (1989).

23. Whether these difference components of money should simply be added together, as they are in monetary aggregates such as $M1$ and $M2$, or weighted to reflect their differing degree of liquidity is a separate issue. Barnett (1980) argued for the use of divisia indices of monetary aggregates. See also Spindt (1985).

24. There are two commonly used data series on the U.S. monetary base—one produced by the Board of Governors of the Federal Reserve System and one by the Federal Reserve Bank of St. Louis. The two series treat vault cash and the adjustment for changes in reserve requirements differently.

from changes in the multiplier. The multiplier is developed using definitional relationships, combined with some simple behavioral assumptions.

Denoting total reserves by TR and currency by C, the monetary base MB is given by

$$MB = TR + C.$$

In the United States, currency represents close to 90 percent of the base. Aggregates such as the monetary base and total reserves are of interest because of their close connection to the actual instruments central banks can control and their relationship to broader measures of the money supply. A central bank can control the monetary base through open market operations. By purchasing securities, the central bank can increase the supply of bank reserves and the base. Securities sales reduce the base.[25]

In the United States, the monetary aggregate $M1$ is equal to currency in the hands of the public plus demand deposits and other checkable deposits. If the deposit component is denoted D and there is a reserve requirement ratio of rr against all such deposits, then

$$MB = RR + ER + C = (rr + ex + c)D,$$

where total reserves have been divided into required reserves (RR) and excess reserves (ER), and where $ex = ER/D$ is the ratio of excess reserves to deposits that banks choose to hold and $c = C/D$ is the currency-to-deposit ratio. Then

$$M1 = D + C = (1 + c)D = \left(\frac{1+c}{rr + ex + c}\right)MB. \qquad (11.24)$$

Equation (11.24) is a very simple example of money multiplier analysis; a broad monetary aggregate such as $M1$ is expressed as a multiplier, in this case $(1 + c)/(rr + ex + c)$, times the monetary base. Changes in the monetary base translate into changes in broader measures of the money supply, given the ratios rr, ex, and c. Of course, the ratios rr, ex, and c need not remain constant as MB changes. The ratio ex is determined by bank decisions and the Fed's policies on discount lending, and c is determined by the decisions of the public concerning the level of cash they wish to hold relative to deposits. The usefulness of this money multiplier framework was illustrated by M. Friedman and Schwartz (1963b), who employed it to organize their study of the causes of changes in the money supply.

In terms of an analysis of the market for bank reserves and operating procedures, the most important ratio appearing in (11.24) is ex, the excess reserve ratio. Since tra-

---

25. In the United States, daily Fed interventions are chiefly designed to smooth temporary fluctuations and are conducted mainly through repurchase and sale-purchase agreements rather than outright purchases or sales.

ditionally reserves earned no interest,[26] banks faced an opportunity cost in holding excess reserves. As market interest rates rise, banks will tend to hold a lower average level of excess reserves. This drop in *ex* will work to increase $M1$. This implies that, holding the base constant, fluctuations in market interest rates will induce movements in the money supply.

11.4.2   The Reserve Market

Traditional models of the reserve market generally have a very simple structure; reserve demand and reserve supply interact to determine the funds rate.[27] In the United States, the federal funds rate is the interest rate banks in need of reserves pay to borrow reserves from banks with surplus reserves. The Federal Reserve can use open market operations to affect the supply of reserves, and it is by intervening in the reserve market that the Fed attempts to affect the money supply, market interest rates, and ultimately economic activity and inflation.

Models of the demand for reserves model bank reserve holdings as arising from the need to meet reserve requirements and settlement payments in the interbank market. Banks balance the opportunity cost of holding reserves in excess of their needs against the cost of being forced to borrow in the face of a reserve shortfall. When payment flows are random, the optimal level of reserves will depend on the variability of shocks to the level of the bank's reserve holdings. The first model to incorporate these elements is due to Poole (1968). Recent examples include Furfine (2000); Furfine and Stehem (1998); and Heller and Lengwiler (2003), who allow banks to balance liquidity costs against the cost of liquidity management. Hamilton (1996) provided a model that emphasizes the microstructure of the reserve market, and Bartolini, Bertola, and Prati (2002) developed a model designed to capture the day-to-day operations of the reserve market when the central bank targets the funds rate. The way reserve market variables (various reserve aggregates and the funds rate) respond to disturbances depends on the operating procedure followed by the Fed. One objective of a model of the reserve market is to disentangle movements in reserves and the funds rate that are due to nonpolicy sources from those caused by exogenous policy actions.

Traditional models of the U.S. reserve market typically assumed that reserves earned zero interest and that the discount rate at which reserves could be borrowed from the Fed was below the funds rate. To prevent banks from exploiting the profit

---

26. This statement is not true of all countries. For example, in New Zealand, reserves earn an interest rate set 300 basis points below the seven-day market rate. As noted in the following section, the Federal Reserve began paying interest on reserves in October 2008.

27. In the United States, the development of the modern reserves market dates from the mid-1960s. See Meulendyke (1998).

opportunity available when the rate paid on borrowed funds was below the rate to be obtained by lending funds, discount borrowing was rationed through nonprice mechanisms that limited a bank's ability to borrow. Such models have become less relevant as many central banks, including the Fed, pay interest on reserves and impose penalty rates on borrowing that allow central banks to eliminate nonprice mechanisms for limiting borrowing. For example, the Federal Reserve established a penalty borrowing rate in 2003[28] and began paying interest on reserve balances on October 6, 2008.[29] In addition, the use of sweep accounts has reduced the level of required reserves, and in some countries banks are not required to hold reserves. These institutional changes have led to new models of the reserve market to study the determination of the overnight interbank interest rate, models that focus on banks' need to hold reserves because of the volatility of payment balances rather than to meet reserve requirements. Furfine (2000), for example, stated that banks active in the payment system might send and receive payments that total more than 30 times their reserve balance on a typical day. Thus, section 11.4.3 presents a simple model that incorporates stochastic variability in bank reserve balances, interest on reserves, and a penalty rate on reserves borrowed from the central bank. The following section, however, begins with a traditional model.

A Traditional Model of the Reserve Market

The demand for reserves will depend on the costs of reserves and on any factors that influence money demand—aggregate income, for example. In order to focus on the very short-run determination of reserve aggregates and the funds rate, factors such as aggregate income and prices are simply treated as part of the error term in the total reserve demand relationship, resulting in

$$\mathrm{TR}^d = -ai^f + v^d, \tag{11.25}$$

where TR^d represents total reserve demand, i^f is the funds rate (the rate at which a bank can borrow reserves in the private market), and v^d is a demand disturbance.

---

28. The Federal Reserve set the discount rate 100 basis points above the federal funds rate target beginning on January 6, 2003. This spread was maintained at this level until early 2007. (It was reduced to 75 basis points on June 30, 2005, but increased back to 100 basis points the following month.) From August 17, 2007, the spread was cut to 50 basis points and then was reduced further to 25 basis points on March 18, 2008.

29. Authority for the Federal Reserve to pay interest was originally scheduled to come into effect in 2011 but accelerated authority was granted as part of the Emergency Economic Stabilization Act of 2008. This act's primary purpose was to establish the Troubled Asset Relief Program (TARP). Coincidentally, an earlier major change in Fed operating procedures also took place on an October 6. On this date in 1979, the Volcker Fed shifted to a reserve aggregates operating procedure that saw interest rates rise significantly as the Fed moved to bring inflation down. For a discussion of monetary policy implementation when interest is paid on reserves, see Goodfriend (2002).

This disturbance will reflect variations in income or other factors that produce fluctuations in deposit demand. One interpretation of (11.25) is that it represents a relationship between the innovations in total reserve demand and the funds rate after the lagged effects of all other factors have been removed. For example, Bernanke and Mihov (1998) attempted to identify policy shocks by focusing on the relationships among the innovations to reserve demand, reserve supply, and the funds rate obtained as the residuals from a VAR model of reserve market variables. They characterized alternative operating procedures in terms of the parameters linking these innovations.[30]

The total supply of reserves held by the banking system can be expressed as the sum of the reserves that banks have borrowed from the Federal Reserve System plus nonborrowed reserves:

$$TR_t^s = BR_t + NBR_t.$$

The Federal Reserve can control the stock of nonborrowed reserves through open market operations; by buying or selling government securities, the Fed affects the stock of nonborrowed reserves. For example, a purchase of government debt by the Fed raises the stock of nonborrowed reserves when the Fed pays for its purchase by crediting the reserve account of the seller's bank with the amount of the purchase. Open market sales of government debt by the Fed reduce the stock of nonborrowed reserves. So the Fed can, even over relatively short time horizons, exercise close control over the stock of nonborrowed reserves.

The stock of borrowed reserves depends on the behavior of private banks and on their decisions about borrowing from the Fed (borrowing from the discount window). Bank demand for borrowed reserves will depend on the opportunity cost of borrowing from the Fed (the discount rate) and the cost of borrowing reserves in the federal funds market (the federal funds rate). An increase in the funds rate relative to the discount rate makes borrowing from the Fed more attractive and leads to an increase in bank borrowing. The elasticity of borrowing with respect to the spread between the funds rate and the discount rate will depend on the Fed's management of the discount window. Traditionally, the Fed maintained the discount rate below the federal funds rate. This created an incentive for banks to borrow reserves at the discount rate and then lend these reserves at the higher market interest rates. To prevent banks from exploiting this arbitrage opportunity, the Fed used nonprice methods to ration bank borrowing. Nonprice rationing affects the degree to which banks

---

30. Kasa and Popper (1995) employed a similar approach to study monetary policy in Japan. Leeper, Sims, and Zha (1996) developed a more general formulation of the links between reserve market variables in an identified VAR framework.

turn to the discount window to borrow as the incentive to do so, the spread between the funds rate and the discount rate, widens. Banks must weigh the benefits of borrowing reserves in a particular week against the possible cost in terms of reduced future access to the discount window. Banks reduce their current borrowing if they expect the funds rate to be higher in the future because they prefer to preserve their future access to the discount window, timing their borrowing for periods when the funds rate is high. This type of intertemporal substitution also occurs because required reserves in the United States are based on an average over a two-week maintenance period; except for the last day of the maintenance period, banks have an incentive to hold reserves on days they are least costly. Therefore, borrowing decisions depend on the expected future funds rate as well as on the current funds rate, and this can be represented by a simple demand function of the form

$$BR_t = b_1(i_t^f - i_t^d) - b_2 E_t(i_{t+1}^f - i_{t+1}^d) + v_t^b, \tag{11.26}$$

where i^d is the discount rate (a policy variable) and v^b is a borrowing disturbance.

In 2003 the Fed changed the way it administers the discount window. Under the new procedures, the discount rate would be set above the federal funds rate. Banks that qualify for *primary credit* could borrow at a rate 1 percent above the funds rate; *secondary credit* would be available at a rate of 1.5 percent above the funds rate. By converting the discount rate into a penalty rate, the arbitrage opportunity created when the discount rate is below the funds rate and the need for nonprice rationing at the discount window are eliminated. Because much of the empirical work on the U.S. reserve market was based on data from periods when the discount rate was kept below the funds rate, the model of this section assumes that $i^f > i^d$. The case of a penalty rate is discussed in section 11.4.3.

The simplest versions of a reserve market model often postulate a borrowing function of the form

$$BR_t = b(i_t^f - i_t^d) + v_t^b. \tag{11.27}$$

The manner in which an innovation in the funds rate affects borrowings, given by the coefficient b in (11.27), will vary depending on how such a funds rate innovation affects expectations of future funds rate levels. Suppose, for example, that borrowings are actually given by (11.26) and that policy results in the funds rate following the process $i_t^f = \rho i_{t-1}^f + \xi_t$. Then $E_t i_{t+1}^f = \rho i_t^f$ and, from (11.26), $BR_t = b i_t^f$, where $b = b_1 - \rho b_2$.[31] A change in operating procedures that leads the funds rate to be more highly serially correlated (increases ρ) will reduce the response of borrowings

31. For simplicity, this ignores the discount rate i^d for the moment.

to the funds rate–discount rate spread.[32] Relationships such as (11.27) can assist understanding of the linkages that affect the correlations among reserve market variables for a given operating procedure, but one should not expect the parameter values to remain constant across operating procedures.

To complete the reserve market model, the Fed's behavior in setting nonborrowed reserves must be specified. To consider a variety of different operating procedures, assume the Fed can respond contemporaneously to the various disturbances to the reserve market, so that nonborrowed reserves are given by

$$\mathrm{NBR}_t = \phi^d v_t^d + \phi^b v_t^b + v_t^s, \tag{11.28}$$

where v^s is a *monetary policy shock*. Different operating procedures will be characterized by alternative values of the parameters ϕ^d and ϕ^b.[33]

Equilibrium in the reserve market requires that total reserve demand equal total reserve supply. This condition is stated as

$$\mathrm{TR}_t^d = \mathrm{BR}_t + \mathrm{NBR}_t. \tag{11.29}$$

If a month is the unit of observation, reserve market disturbances are likely to have no contemporaneous effect on real output or the aggregate price level.[34] Using this identifying restriction, Bernanke and Mihov (1998) obtained estimates of the innovations to TR, BR, i^f, and NBR from a VAR system that also includes GDP, the GDP deflator, and an index of commodity prices but in which the reserve market variables are ordered last.[35] Whether any of these VAR residuals can be interpreted directly as a measure of the policy shock v^s will depend on the particular operating procedure being used. For example, if $\phi^d = \phi^b = 0$, (11.28) implies that $\mathrm{NBR} = v^s$; this corresponds to a situation in which the Fed does not allow nonborrowed reserves to be affected by disturbances to total reserve demand or to borrowed reserves, so the innovation to nonborrowed reserves can be interpreted directly as a policy shock.

---

32. Goodfriend (1983) provided a formal model of borrowed reserves; see also Waller (1990). For a discussion of how alternative operating procedures affect the relationship between the funds rate and reserve aggregates, see Walsh (1982). Attempts to estimate the borrowings function can be found in Peristiani (1991) and Pearce (1993).

33. Note that ϕ^d and ϕ^b correspond to ϕ in (1.9), since they reflect the impact of nonpolicy originating disturbances on the policy variable NBR.

34. Referring to the discussion in section 1.3.4, this assumption corresponds to setting $\theta = 0$ to identify VAR innovations.

35. The commodity price index is included to eliminate the price puzzle discussed in chapter 1. This creates a potential problem for Bernanke and Mihov's identification scheme, since forward-looking variables such as asset prices, interest rates, and commodity prices may respond immediately to policy shocks. See the discussion of this issue in Leeper, Sims, and Zha (1996), who distinguished between policy, banking sector, production, and information variables.

Under such an operating procedure, using nonborrowed reserve innovations (i.e., NBR) as the measure of monetary policy, as in Christiano and Eichenbaum (1992a), is correct. However, if either ϕ^d or ϕ^b differs from zero, NBR will reflect nonpolicy shocks as well as policy shocks.

Substituting (11.25), (11.27), and (11.28) into the equilibrium condition (11.29) and solving for the innovation in the funds rate yields

$$i_t^f = \left(\frac{b}{a+b}\right)i_t^d - \left(\frac{1}{a+b}\right)[v_t^s + (1+\phi^b)v_t^b - (1-\phi^d)v_t^d]. \tag{11.30}$$

The reduced-form expressions for the innovations to borrowed and total reserves are then found to be

$$\mathrm{BR}_t = -\left(\frac{ab}{a+b}\right)i_t^d - \left(\frac{1}{a+b}\right)[bv_t^s - (a-b\phi^b)v_t^b - b(1-\phi^d)v_t^d] \tag{11.31}$$

$$\mathrm{TR}_t = -\left(\frac{ab}{a+b}\right)i_t^d + \left(\frac{1}{a+b}\right)[av_t^s + a(1+\phi^b)v_t^b + (b+a\phi^d)v_t^d]. \tag{11.32}$$

How does the Fed's operating procedure affect the interpretation of movements in nonborrowed reserves, borrowed reserves, and the federal funds rate as measures of monetary policy shocks? Under a federal funds rate operating procedure, the Fed offsets total reserve demand and borrowing demand disturbances so that they do not affect the funds rate. According to (11.30), this policy requires that $\phi^b = -1$ and $\phi^d = 1$. In other words, a shock to borrowed reserves leads to an equal but opposite movement in nonborrowed reserves to keep the funds rate (and total reserves) unchanged (see 11.28), whereas a shock to total reserve demand leads to an equal change in reserve supply through the adjustment of nonborrowed reserves. The innovation in nonborrowed reserves is equal to $v^s - v^b + v^d$ and so does not reflect solely exogenous policy shocks.

Under a nonborrowed reserve procedure, $\phi^b = 0$ and $\phi^d = 0$ as innovations to nonborrowed reserves reflect policy shocks. In this case, (11.30) becomes

$$i_t^f = \left(\frac{b}{a+b}\right)i_t^d - \left(\frac{1}{a+b}\right)(v_t^s + v_t^b - v_t^d), \tag{11.33}$$

so innovations in the funds rate reflect both policy changes and disturbances to reserve demand and the demand for borrowed reserves. In fact, if v^d arises from shocks to money demand that lead to increases in measured monetary aggregates, innovations to the funds rate can be positively correlated with innovations to broader monetary aggregates. Positive innovations in an aggregate such as $M1$ would then appear to increase the funds rate, a phenomenon found in the VAR evidence reported in chapter 1.

Table 11.1
Parameters under Alternative Operating Procedures

| | Operating Procedure | | | |
	Funds Rate	Nonborrowed	Borrowed	Total
ϕ^d	1	0	1	$-\frac{b}{a}$
ϕ^b	-1	0	$\frac{a}{b}$	-1

From (11.31), a borrowed reserves policy corresponds to $\phi^d = 1$ and $\phi^b = a/b$, since adjusting nonborrowed reserves in this manner insulates borrowed reserves from nonpolicy shocks. That is, nonborrowed reserves are fully adjusted to accommodate fluctuations in total reserve demand. Under a borrowed reserves procedure, innovations to the funds rate are, from (11.30),

$$i_t^f = \left(\frac{b}{a+b}\right)i_t^d - \left(\frac{1}{a+b}\right)\left[v_t^s + \left(1 + \frac{a}{b}\right)v_t^b\right],$$

so the funds rate reflects both policy and borrowing disturbances.

Table 11.1 summarizes the values of ϕ^d and ϕ^b that correspond to different operating procedures.

In general, the innovations in the observed variables can be written (ignoring discount rate innovations) as

$$\begin{bmatrix} i_t^f \\ \mathrm{BR}_t \\ \mathrm{NBR}_t \end{bmatrix} \equiv u_t = \begin{bmatrix} -\frac{1}{a+b} & -\frac{1+\phi^b}{a+b} & \frac{1-\phi^d}{a+b} \\ -\frac{b}{a+b} & \frac{a-b\phi^b}{a+b} & \frac{b(1-\phi^d)}{a+b} \\ 1 & \phi^b & \phi^d \end{bmatrix} \begin{bmatrix} v_t^s \\ v_t^b \\ v_t^d \end{bmatrix} \equiv Av_t. \tag{11.34}$$

By inverting the matrix A, one can solve for the underlying shocks, the vector v, in terms of the observed innovations u: $v = A^{-1}u$. This operation produces

$$\begin{bmatrix} v_t^s \\ v_t^b \\ v_t^d \end{bmatrix} = \begin{bmatrix} b\phi^b - a\phi^d & -(\phi^d + \phi^b) & 1 - \phi^d \\ -b & 1 & 0 \\ a & 1 & 1 \end{bmatrix} \begin{bmatrix} i_t^f \\ \mathrm{BR}_t \\ \mathrm{NBR}_t \end{bmatrix}.$$

Hence,

$$v_t^s = (b\phi^b - a\phi^d)i_t^f - (\phi^d + \phi^b)\mathrm{BR}_t + (1 - \phi^d)\mathrm{NBR}_t, \tag{11.35}$$

so that the policy shock can be recovered as a specific linear combination of the innovations to the funds rate, borrowed reserves, and nonborrowed reserves. From the parameter values in table 11.1, the following relationship holds between the policy shock and the VAR residuals:

Funds rate procedure: $v_t^s = -(b+a)i_t^f$

Nonborrowed reserve procedure: $v_t^s = \text{NBR}_t$

Borrowed reserve procedure: $v_t^s = -\left(1 + \dfrac{a}{b}\right)\text{BR}_t$

Total reserve procedure: $v_t^s = \left(1 + \dfrac{a}{b}\right)\text{TR}_t$

Policy shock cannot generally be identified with innovations in any one of the reserve market variables. Only for specific values of the parameters ϕ^d and ϕ^b, that is, for specific operating procedures, might the policy shock be recoverable from the innovation to just one of the reserve market variables.

Reserve Market Responses

This section uses the basic reserve market model to discuss how various disturbances affect reserve quantities and the funds rate under alternative operating procedures. Figure 11.1 illustrates reserve market equilibrium between total reserve demand and supply. For values of the funds rate less than the discount rate, reserve supply is vertical and equal to nonborrowed reserves. With the discount rate serving as a penalty

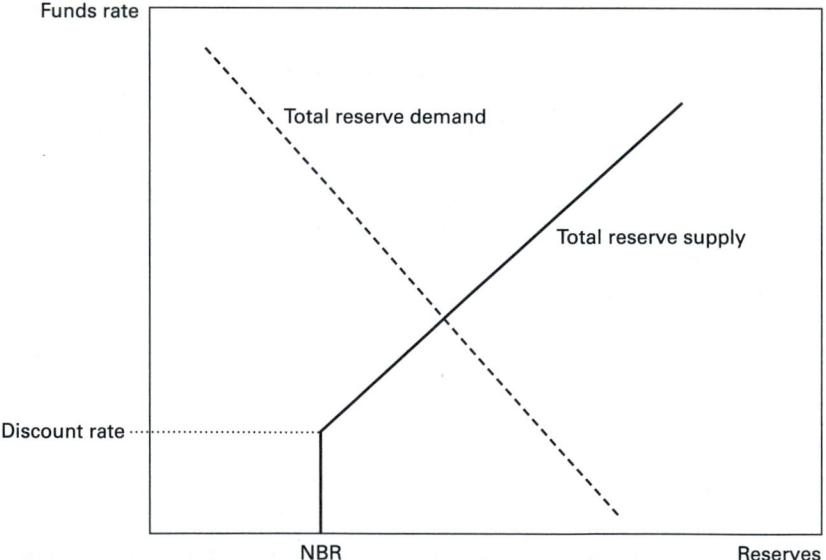

Figure 11.1
The reserve market.

rate, borrowed reserves fall to zero in this range, so that total reserve supply is just NBR. As the funds rate increases above the discount rate, borrowings become positive (see (11.27)) and the total supply of reserves increases. Total reserve demand is decreasing in the funds rate according to (11.25).

Consider first a positive realization of the policy shock v^s. The effects on i^f, BR, and NBR can be found from the first column of the matrix A in (11.34). The policy shock increases nonborrowed reserves (think of it as initiating an open market purchase that increases banking sector reserve assets). In figure 11.1, the reserve supply curve shifts to the right horizontally by the amount of the increase in NBR. Given the borrowed reserves and total reserve demand functions, this increase in reserve supply causes the funds rate to fall. Bank borrowing from the Fed decreases because the relative cost of borrowed reserves $(i^d - i^f)$ has risen, partially offsetting some of the increase in total reserve supply.[36] A policy shock is associated with an increase in total reserves, a fall in the funds rate, and a fall in borrowed reserves.

It is the response to nonpolicy disturbances that will differ, depending on the operating procedures (see the second and third columns of the matrix A; the elements of these columns depend on the ϕ^j parameters). Suppose there is a positive disturbance to total reserve demand, $v^d > 0$. This shifts total reserve demand to the right. In the absence of any policy response (i.e., if $\phi^d = 0$), the funds rate increases. This increase reduces total reserve demand (if $a > 0$), offsetting to some degree the initial increase in reserve demand. The rise in the funds rate induces an increase in reserve supply as banks increase their borrowing from the Fed. Under a funds rate operating procedure, however, $\phi^d = 1$; the Fed lets nonborrowed reserves rise by the full amount of the rise in reserve demand to prevent the funds rate from rising. Both reserve demand and reserve supply shift to the right by the amount of the disturbance to reserve demand, and the new equilibrium is at an unchanged funds rate. Thus, total reserve demand shocks are completely accommodated under a funds rate procedure. If the positive reserve demand shock originated from an increase in the demand for bank deposits as a result of an economic expansion, a funds rate procedure automatically accommodates the increase in money demand and has the potential to produce procyclical movements of money and output.[37]

In contrast, under a total reserves operating procedure, the Fed would adjust nonborrowed reserves to prevent v^d from affecting total reserves. From (11.32), this requires that $\phi^d = -b/a$; nonborrowed reserves must be reduced in response to a

---

36. This analysis assumes that the discount rate has not changed; the Fed could, for example, change the discount rate to keep $i^f - i^d$ constant and keep borrowed reserves unchanged. Since the total supply of reserves has increased, the funds rate must fall, so this would require a cut in the discount rate.

37. Since operating procedures have been defined in terms of the innovations to reserves and the funds rate, nothing has been said about the extent to which the funds rate might be adjusted in subsequent periods to offset movements in reserve demand induced by output or inflation.

Table 11.2
Response to a Positive Reserve Demand Shock

	Operating Procedure			
	FF	BR	NBR	TR
Funds rate	0	0	+	+
Total reserves	+	+	+	0
Nonborrowed reserves	+	+	0	−
Borrowed reserves	0	0	+	+

positive realization of v^d. It is not sufficient just to hold nonborrowed reserves constant; the rise in the funds rate caused by the rise in total reserve demand will induce an endogenous rise in reserve supply as banks increase their borrowing from the Fed. To offset this, nonborrowed reserves are reduced. Thus, while a funds rate procedure offsets none of the impact of a reserve demand shock on total reserves, a total reserve procedure offsets all of it.

Under a nonborrowed reserves procedure, $\phi^d = 0$; hence, a positive shock to reserve demand raises the funds rate and borrowed reserves. Total reserves rise by $-ai^f + v^d = [b/(a + b)]v^d < v^d$. So reserves do rise (in contrast to the case under a total reserves procedure) but by less than under a funds rate procedure.

Finally, under a borrowed reserves procedure, a positive shock to total reserve demand will, by increasing the funds rate, also tend to increase bank borrowing. To hold borrowed reserves constant, the Fed must prevent the funds rate from rising (i.e., it must keep $i^f = 0$; see (11.27)). This objective requires letting nonborrowed reserves rise. So in the face of shocks to total reserve demand, a funds rate operating procedure and a borrowed reserves procedure lead to the same response. As (11.33) shows, however, a borrowed reserves operating procedure is an inefficient procedure for controlling the funds rate in that it allows disturbances to the borrowing function (i.e., v^b shocks) to affect the funds rate. These results are summarized in table 11.2.

Now suppose there is a positive shock to bank borrowing; $v^b > 0$. The increase in borrowed reserves, by increasing total reserves, will lower the funds rate. Under a funds rate procedure, the Fed prevents this outcome by reducing nonborrowed reserves ($\phi^b = -1$) to fully neutralize the effect of v^b on the total reserve supply. The same response would occur under a total reserves operating procedure. In contrast, under a nonborrowed reserves procedure, $\phi^b = 0$, so the increase in borrowed reserves also increases total reserve supply, and the funds rate must decline to clear the reserve market. These results are summarized in table 11.3.

Following Bernanke and Mihov, ϕ^d and ϕ^b characterize different operating procedures. However, the parameters a and b in the total reserve demand (11.25) and the borrowed reserves (11.27) relationships may also vary under difference operating

Table 11.3
Response to a Positive Shock to Borrowed Reserves

	Operating Procedure			
	FF	BR	NBR	TR
Funds rate	0	−	−	0
Total reserves	0	+	+	0
Nonborrowed reserves	−	+	0	−
Borrowed reserves	+	0	+	+

procedures. For example, models of bank borrowing from the discount window (e.g., Goodfriend 1983) imply that the slope of the borrowing function should depend on the operating procedure being employed.[38] Evidence supporting this hypothesis is reported in Pearce (1993). As noted earlier, the coefficient b should depend on the time series process that characterizes the funds rate. If changes in the funds rate are very persistent, b will tend to be smaller than under a procedure that leads to more transitory changes in the funds rate.

While the focus has been on the reserve market, it is important to keep in mind that the purpose of reserve market intervention by the Fed is not to affect the funds rate or reserve measures themselves. The Fed's objective is to influence its policy goal variables, such as the rate of inflation. The simple money multiplier framework discussed earlier provides a link between the reserve market and other factors affecting the supply of money. The observed quantities of the broader monetary aggregates then reflect the interaction of the supply of and demand for money. Movements in the funds rate are linked to longer-term interest rates through the term structure (see chapter 10).

11.4.3   A Simple Model of a Channel System

Several central banks (e.g., Australia, Canada, New Zealand, Sweden, and Switzerland, all of whom, with the exception of Switzerland, are inflation targeters) employ a corridor or channel system for interest rate control. In a channel system, the central bank sets lower and upper bounds for the interest rate. The upper bound is provided by the penalty rate on reserve borrowing because no bank will borrow in the private market if the interest rate exceeds the rate at which reserves can be obtained from the central bank. The lower bound is provided by the interest rate paid on reserves because no bank would lend in the private market if the interest rate is less than the rate received on reserves. Under a channel system, the central bank's target interest

---

38. See (11.26) and the discussion after (11.27). Some of the implications of Goodfriend's model are examined in Walsh (1990).

rate may not provide a complete description of policy because, conditional on the target rate, the spread between the interest rate paid on reserves and the penalty borrowing rate can affect bank behavior. A channel system can also allow the central bank to alter the market interest rate without altering the level of reserves (see Woodford 2001c).

The simplest form of channel system is one in which there are no reserve requirements; the central bank pays an interest rate $i^* - s_1$ on any reserve balances and charges a rate $i^* + s_2$ on any bank reserve overdrafts (i.e., it lends reserves at the rate $i^* + s_2$ to any bank that has a negative reserve balance at the central bank). The central bank's target interest rate is i^*. Assume, as Whitesell (2006) does, that the central bank sets a symmetric window around i^* with $s_1 = s_2 = s$.[39] Assume further that loans from the central bank are perfect substitutes for funds obtained in the private market, and overnight balances with the central bank are perfect substitutes for lending in the private market. These assumptions ensure that no bank will borrow in the private market if the interest on such loans exceeds $i^* + s$ or lend to another bank if the private market interest rate is less than $i^* - s$. The willingness of the central bank to pay a fixed rate on balances and to lend automatically at a fixed rate is called a standing facility. Hence, if i is the private market interbank rate,

$$i^* - s \leq i \leq i^* + s.$$

The rate i is constrained to remain within the corridor established by the spread s. Hence, this type of system is also called a corridor system.[40]

The Bank's Decision Problem

Assume bank balances are subject to stochastic fluctuations. Let T be the expected value of the bank's end-of-day balances, and let actual end-of-day balances be $T + \varepsilon$, where ε is a mean zero random variable with continuous distribution function $F(.)$. The model presumes that the realization of ε occurs after the interbank market closes. The representative bank chooses T to balance two costs. First, if it sets T too high, it is likely to end the day with a positive reserve balance that earns $i^* - s$ rather than the rate i that could have been obtained by lending to another bank. Hence, the opportunity cost of holding positive end-of-day balances relative to lending them out is $i - (i^* - s)$. Second, if T is set too low, the bank may end the day with a negative

---

39. Berentsen and Monnet (2008) developed a model in which money demand is motivated by the assumption that goods market transactions are anonymous. They derived the optimal spread and noted that the impact of monetary policy is characterized by both the target interest rate and the spread between borrowing and lending rates from the central bank's standing facility.

40. Whitesell (2006) noted that between June 2003 and June 2004, the Fed's target for the federal funds rate was 1 percent and it charged a 2 percent penalty rate on discount window borrowing. Since the Fed did not pay interest on reserves at the time, the Fed was essentially using a symmetric channel system wth $i^* = 1$ percent and $s = 1$ percent.

balance and need to borrow from the central bank at the rate $i^* + s$ rather than from another bank at the rate i. Hence, the opportunity cost of ending the day with an overdraft and borrowing from central bank is $i^* + s - i$. The bank will choose T to minimize the expected sum of these two costs, subject to the probability distribution of the stochastic process ε.[41]

The problem of a risk-neutral bank is to pick T to minimize

$$\int_{-T}^{\infty} (i - i^* + s)(T + \varepsilon)\, dF(\varepsilon) - \int_{-\infty}^{-T} (i^* + s - i)(T + \varepsilon)\, dF(\varepsilon).$$

The first term is the opportunity cost of ending the day with positive balances. This occurs whenever $\varepsilon > -T$. The second term is the opportunity cost of borrowing from the central bank, and this occurs whenever $\varepsilon < -T$. The first-order condition for the optimal choice of T is

$$(i - i^* + s) \int_{-T}^{\infty} dF(\varepsilon) - (i^* + s - i) \int_{-\infty}^{-T} dF(\varepsilon) = 0.$$

This can be expressed as $(i - i^* + s)[1 - F(-T^*)] - (i^* + s - i)F(-T^*) = 0$, where T^* is the optimal level of planned reserve balances, or

$$T^* = -F^{-1}\left(\frac{1}{2} + \frac{i - i^*}{2s}\right). \tag{11.36}$$

If the market rate equals the target rate, $i = i^*$, then $T^* = -F^{-1}(1/2)$, so if the distribution function F is symmetric, $T^* = 0$. However, if the net supply of clearing balances differs from zero, the market rate will differ from i^*. For example, if the net supply is $\bar{T}$, then market equilibrium requires that $T^* = \bar{T}$ and

$$i = i^* - s[1 - 2F(-\bar{T})], \tag{11.37}$$

so that $i^* - s \leq i \leq i^* + s$, showing that the private market rate i remains in the corridor defined by the target rate and the spread. In the case of New Zealand, for example, net settlement cash is quite small and s is equal to 25 basis points. Thus, with $\bar{T}$ small but positive, $F(-\bar{T})$ is slightly less than $1/2$, and i will be slightly below i^*.

Figure 11.2 illustrates the demand for reserves given by (11.36) when ε is normally distributed, the target interest rate is 3 percent, and s is equal to 50 basis points. The supply of reserves when $\bar{T} = 0$ is given by the solid line at 2.5 percent up to the net

---

41. Reserve management problems are essentially equivalent to inventory management problems. When sales and/or production are stochastic, the optimal level of inventories balances the costs of stocking out versus the cost of carrying unsold goods.

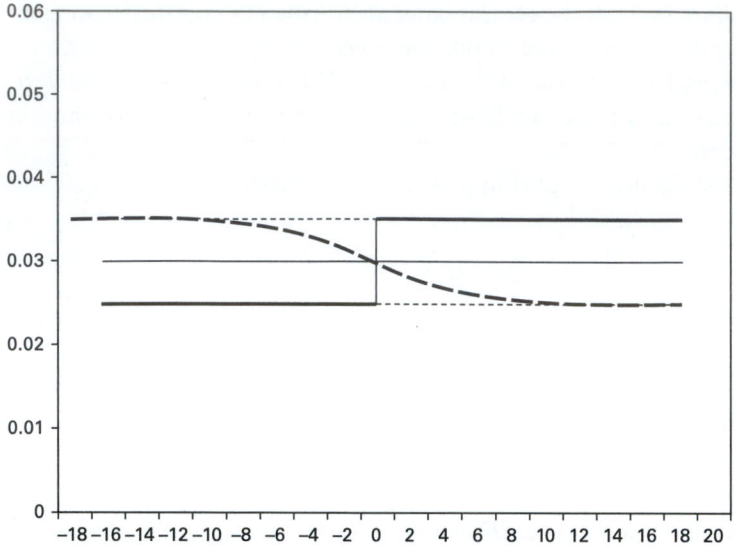

Figure 11.2
Reserve market equilibrium under a channel system with a target rate of 3 percent, a symmetric spread of ± 50 basis points, and zero net supply of settlement balances. The demand curve for reserves is downward-sloping within the corridor defined by $i^* - s$ and $i^* + s$.

balance of zero and then it jumps up to the penalty rate of 3.5 percent. Equilibrium occurs where the demand curve cuts the supply curve, and the interest rate is equal to the target rate. The figure illustrates the case of a zero net settlement balance, but the same argument would apply for any positive level; the supply curve would simply shift to the right. If the central bank were unable to control reserve supply exactly due to random variation, then the overnight rate might end up slightly above or below the actual target i^* (see Woodford 2001c on both points).

An interesting implication of (11.37) is that the central bank can affect the equilibrium market rate without altering the supply of settlement balances. It can do so by simply announcing a change in its target rate i^* without altering $\bar{T}$. Guthrie and Wright (2000) characterized the Reserve Bank of New Zealand as employing "open mouth" operations rather than open market operations to affect the market rate. The ability of the central bank in a channel system to affect the market without engaging in open market operations that affect the supply of reserves is in marked contrast to the tradition model of the reserve market.

The model of a channel system assumes that borrowing from the private market and borrowing from the central bank are perfect substitutes, so i can never rise above $i^* + s$. Similarly, lending to another bank and leaving deposits at the central bank are assumed to be perfect substitutes, so i can never fall below $i^* - s$. In practice, these various options are not equivalent. For example, in the U.S. interbank market, loans are generally unsecured and central bank (Fed) borrowings are collateralized, so the two are not perfect substitutes. In this case, the cost of borrowing from the central bank would be $i^* + s$ *plus* the cost of collateral (see Berentsen and Monnet 2008). Since private lending is unsecured, it is riskier than holding a riskless account balance at the central bank. So the opportunity cost of having overnight balances with the central bank is $(i - r) - (i^* - s)$, where r is a risk premium. In addition, not all banks may have access to the central bank's standing facilities. For example, according to Whitesell (2006), only 60 percent of U.S. depository institutions have completed the paper work necessary to borrow at the discount window. The Bank of Canada and the Bank of England limit access to certain institutions, and the ECB and Bank of England pay interest on reserves only if banks shift funds out of reserve accounts and into special deposit accounts each day.

Channel systems are becoming increasingly common. When reserve holdings by banks are small, as a result either of innovations that reduce the level of required reserves or because reserve requirements have been eliminated, channel systems provide an operating procedure for controlling the overnight bank rate. Open market operations are still necessary to offset random fluctuations in the stock of reserves, but these operations are not used to control interest rate levels as under traditional models of operating procedures.

11.5   A Brief History of Fed Operating Procedures

In the United States, the operating procedures employed by the Fed have changed over time. This fact implies that the manner in which the reserve market has responded to disturbances has varied and that the appropriate measure of policy shocks has also changed.

Fed operating procedures have been discussed by various authors,[42] and major studies of operating procedures have been undertaken by the Federal Reserve (Federal Reserve System 1981; Goodfriend and Small 1993). Over the past 30 years in the United States, most monetary economists have identified four different regimes, each defined according to the basic operating procedure the Fed followed. Chronologically, these correspond to periods of funds rate, nonborrowed reserves, borrowed reserves, and funds rate operating procedures, although in no case did the Fed's behavior reflect pure examples of any one type.[43]

---

42. Examples include Walsh (1990); Goodfriend (1991; 1993); Strongin (1995); Meulendyke (1998); and the references they cite.

43. From 1975 to 1993, the Fed announced targets for various monetary aggregates, and these played a role as intermediate targets during some periods; see B. Friedman and Kuttner (1996).

11.5.1 1972–1979

The first period dates from the end of the Bretton Woods exchange rate system in the early 1970s to October 6, 1979. The Fed is usually described as having followed a federal funds rate operating procedure during this period. Under such a policy, the Fed allowed nonborrowed reserves to adjust automatically to stabilize the funds rate within a narrow band around its target level. Thus, a shock to total reserve demand that in the absence of a policy response would have led to an increase in both the funds rate and borrowed reserves was offset by open market purchases that expanded nonborrowed reserves sufficiently to prevent the funds rate from rising (i.e., $\phi^d = 1$). As a result, expansions in reserve demand were fully accommodated by increases in reserve supply.[44]

A funds rate operating procedure only implies that shocks to the funds rate are offset initially; the targeted funds rate could, in principle, respond strongly beginning in period $t + 1$. However, the funds rate operating procedure came under intense criticism during the 1970s because of the Fed's tendency to stabilize interest rates for longer periods of time. Such interest rate–smoothing behavior can have important implications for price level behavior (Goodfriend 1987). Because a rise in the price level will increase the nominal demand for bank deposits as private agents attempt to maintain their real money holdings, periods of inflation will lead to increases in the nominal demand for bank reserves. If the central bank holds nonborrowed reserves fixed, the rising demand for reserves pushes up interest rates, thereby moderating the rise in money demand and real economic activity. If the central bank instead attempts to prevent interest rates from rising, it must allow the reserve supply to expand to accommodate the rising demand for reserves. Thus, interest rate–stabilizing policies can automatically accommodate increases in the price level, contributing to ongoing inflation. Under some circumstances, an interest rate policy can even render the price level indeterminate; an arbitrary change in the price level produces a proportionate change in nominal money demand, which the central bank automatically accommodates to keep interest rates from changing. Since market interest rates incorporate a premium for expected inflation, an increase in expected inflation would, under a policy of stabilizing market interest rates, also be automatically accommodated.

Recall from the reserve-market model that under a funds rate procedure, nonborrowed reserves are automatically adjusted to offset the impact on the funds rate

---

44. While the discussion here focuses on reserve market adjustments, changes in the funds rate target then lead to changes in market interest rates. For evidence, see Cook and Hahn (1989); Rudebusch (1995); or Roley and Sellon (1996). International evidence on the response of market interest rates to changes in the short-run interest rate used to implement policy can be found in Buttiglione, Del Giovane, and Tristani (1998).

of shocks to total reserve demand and to borrowed reserves. In terms of the model parameters, this adjustment requires that $\phi^d = 1$ and $\phi^b = -1$. Bernanke and Mihov (1998), using both monthly and biweekly data, reported that these restrictions are not rejected for the period 1972:11 to 1979:09. Thus, innovations in the funds rate provide an appropriate measure of monetary policy during this period.

11.5.2   1979–1982

In October 1979, as part of a policy shift to lower inflation, the Fed moved to a non-borrowed reserves operating procedure. An operating procedure that focused on a reserve quantity was viewed as more consistent with reducing money growth rates to bring down inflation.

The Fed had, in fact, begun announcing target growth rates for several monetary aggregates in 1975. Under the Humphrey-Hawkins Act, the Fed was required to establish monetary targets and report these to Congress.[45] Because growth rate target ranges were set for several measures of the money supply (there were targets for $M1$, $M2$, $M3$, and debt), the extent to which these targets actually influenced policy was never clear. The move to a nonborrowed reserves operating procedure was thought by many economists to provide a closer link between the policy instrument (nonborrowed reserves) and the intermediate target of policy (the monetary growth targets). B. Friedman and Kuttner (1996) provided an evaluation of the actual effects of these targets on the conduct of policy.

Under a nonborrowed reserves procedure, an increase in expected inflation would no longer automatically lead to an accommodative increase in bank reserves. Instead, interest rates would be allowed to rise, reducing nominal asset demand and restraining money growth. Similarly, if money growth rose above the Fed's target growth rate, reserve demand would rise, pushing up the funds rate. The resulting rise in the funds rate would tend to reduce money demand automatically.

Whether the Fed actually followed a nonborrowed reserves procedure after October 1979 has often been questioned. The funds rate was clearly both higher and more volatile after the switch in policy procedures than before.[46] Many commentators felt that the policy shift in late 1979 was designed to allow the Fed to increase interest rates substantially while reducing the political pressures on the Fed to prevent rates from rising. Under the former funds rate procedure, changes in short-term

---

45. The targets for $M1$ for the period 1975–1986 and for $M2$ and $M3$ for the period 1975–1991 are reported in Bernanke and Mishkin (1993, table 1). Preliminary targets for the following calendar year were set each July and confirmed in January. Discussions of the targets can be found in the various issues of the Federal Reserve's "Monetary Report to Congress." The Fed stopped setting growth rate targets for $M1$ after 1986 because of the apparent breakdown in the relationship between $M1$ and nominal income.

46. See figure 1.5. Much of the increased volatility in early 1980 was caused by the imposition and then removal of credit controls.

interest rates were (correctly) perceived as reflecting Fed decisions. By adopting a nonborrowed reserves operating procedure and focusing more on achieving its targeted growth rates for the money supply, the Fed could argue that the high interest rates were due to market forces and not Fed policy. Cook (1989) estimated, however, that fully two-thirds of all funds rate changes during this period were the result of "judgmental" Fed actions; only one-third represented automatic responses to nonpolicy disturbances.

The 1979–1982 period was characterized by increased attention by the Fed to its monetary targets. In principle, nonborrowed reserves were adjusted to achieve a targeted growth rate for the money stock. If the money stock was growing faster than desired, the nonborrowed reserve target would be adjusted downward to place upward pressure on the funds rate. This in turn would reduce money demand and tend to bring the money stock back on target. As a result, market interest rates responded sharply to each week's new information on the money supply. If the money supply exceeded the market's expectation, market interest rates rose in anticipation of future policy tightening (see Roley and Walsh 1985 and the references listed there).

The actual practice under the nonborrowed reserves procedure was complicated by several factors. First, the Fed established and announced targets for several different definitions of the money stock.[47] This policy reduced the transparency of the procedure because often one monetary aggregate might be above its target while another would be below, making the appropriate adjustment to the nonborrowed reserves path unclear. Second, under the system of lagged reserve accounting then in effect, the level of reserves a bank was required to hold during week t was based on its average deposit liabilities during week $t - 2$. With reserve demand essentially predetermined each week, variations in the funds rate had little contemporaneous effect on reserve demand. Changes in reserve supply required large swings in the funds rate to equilibrate the reserve market. A rise in interest rates had no immediate effect on the banking sector's reserve demand, leading to a delay in the impact of a policy tightening on money growth. This system was criticized as reducing the ability of the Fed to control the growth rate of the monetary aggregates (see McCallum and Hoehn 1983).[48]

Referring to the earlier reserve market model, with $\phi^d = \phi^b = 0$ under a nonborrowed reserves operating procedure, (11.30) implies that

47. The Fed established target cones for each aggregate. For example, the target cone for $M1$ set in January 1980 was 4.0–6.5 percent from a base of the actual level of $M1$ in the fourth quarter of 1979. The use of actual levels as the base for new target cones resulted in base drift; past target misses were automatically incorporated into the new base. See Broaddus and Goodfriend (1984). For a discussion of the optimal degree of base drift, see Walsh (1986).

48. Lagged reserve accounting was replaced by contemporaneous reserve accounting in 1984. See Hamilton (1996) for a detailed discussion of the reserve accounting system.

$$i^f_{\text{NBR}} = \left(\frac{b}{a+b}\right) i^d - \left(\frac{1}{a+b}\right) [v^s + v^b - v^d], \tag{11.38}$$

so that, ignoring discount rate changes, the variance of funds rate innovations rises from $\sigma_g^2/(a+b)^2$ under a pure funds rate operating procedure to $[\sigma_s^2 + \sigma_d^2 + \sigma_b^2]/(a+b)^2$ under a pure nonborrowed reserves operating procedure, where σ_i^2 is the variance of v^i for $i = s, d, b$. The variance of funds rate innovations is decreasing in a, and with lagged reserve accounting, $a = 0$, further increasing the variance of the funds rate. Changes in reserve supply would require large swings in the funds rate to equilibrate the reserve market.

In practice, it was argued that the Fed actually set its nonborrowed reserves target to achieve the level of the funds rate it desired. That is, the Fed started with a desired path for the money stock; since equilibrium required that money demand equal money supply, it used an estimated money demand function to determine the level of the funds rate consistent with the targeted level of money demand. Then, based on total reserve demand (predetermined under lagged reserve accounting) and an estimated borrowed reserve function, it determined the level of nonborrowed reserves required to achieve the desired funds rate. A nonborrowed reserves operating procedure designed to achieve a desired funds rate is simply an inefficient funds rate procedure. However, by shifting the focus of policy away from a concern for stabilizing interest rates, the 1979 policy shift did reflect a substantive policy shift consistent with reducing the rate of inflation.

Using biweekly data for the period October 1979 to October 1982, Bernanke and Mihov (1998) reported estimates of ϕ^d and ϕ^b; neither estimate is statistically significantly different from zero. These estimates are consistent, then, with the actual use of a nonborrowed-reserves operating procedure during this period.

Key to a nonborrowed reserves operating procedure is the need to predict the relationship between changes in nonborrowed reserves and the resulting impact on broader monetary aggregates, inflation, and real economic activity. During the late 1970s and early 1980s, there seemed to be a fairly stable relationship between monetary aggregates such as $M1$ and nominal income. This relationship could be used to work backward from a desired path of nominal income growth to a growth path for $M1$ to a growth path for nonborrowed reserves. Unfortunately, this relationship appeared to break down in the early and mid-1980s (see, e.g., B. Friedman and Kuttner 1996). In the absence of a reliable link between reserve measures and nominal income, the Fed eventually moved away from a nonborrowed reserves operating procedure.

11.5.3   1982–1988

After 1982 the Fed generally followed a borrowed reserves operating procedure. As noted earlier, such a procedure is, in practice, similar to a funds rate operating procedure, at least in the face of reserve demand shocks (see table 11.2). The basic Poole analysis implied that an operating procedure oriented toward interest rates will tend to dominate one oriented toward monetary aggregates as the variance of money demand shocks rises relative to aggregate demand shocks. B. Friedman and Kuttner (1996) provided a plot of the ratio of the variance of money demand shocks to the variance of aggregate demand shocks based on an estimated VAR. The plot shows this ratio reaching a minimum during 1981 and then steadily increasing. The shift back to an interest rate operating procedure after 1982 is consistent with the recommendations of Poole's model.

From the earlier discussion, a borrowed reserves operating procedure implies values of 1 and a/b for ϕ^d and ϕ^b. Bernanke and Mihov (1998) obtained point estimates for ϕ^d and ϕ^b for February 1984 to October 1988 that are more consistent with a funds rate procedure ($\phi^d = 1; \phi^b = -1$) than with a borrowed reserves procedure. However, for biweekly data during the post-1988 period, Bernanke and Mihov found estimates consistent with a borrowed reserves procedure with $a = 0$. This last parameter restriction agrees with the characterization of policy provided by Strongin (1995).

Cosimano and Sheehan (1994) estimated a biweekly reserve-market model using data from 1984 to 1990. Their results are consistent with a borrowed reserves procedure over this period and not with a funds rate procedure, although they noted that actual policy under this procedure was similar to what would occur under a funds rate procedure. The evidence also suggests that after the October 1987 stock market crash, the Fed moved toward a more direct funds rate procedure.

11.5.4 After 1988

Since the late 1980s, the Fed has targeted the funds rate directly ($\phi^d = 1; \phi^b = -1$). Open market operations are conducted once each day, so the actual funds rate can fluctuate slightly around the target rate on a daily basis. Taylor (1993) was one of the earliest to model Fed interest rate–setting behavior in terms of a policy rule. He showed that a simple rule that made the funds rate a function of inflation and the output gap did a good job in tracking the actual behavior of the funds rate. Taylor rules have become a standard way of representing policy by the Fed and other central banks and have generated a huge literature estimating Taylor rules for different time periods and for different central banks (see, e.g., Clarida, Galí, and Gertler 1999; Orphanides 2001). Taylor rules, usually augmented to include past interest rates, are commonly used to represent policy in empirical DSGE models (Christiano, Eichenbaum, and Evans 2005; Smets and Wouter 2003). Interest rate rules in new Keynesian models are discussed in chapter 8, and more references to the literature are provided.

One of the biggest changes in operating procedures since 1990 is the increase in the transparency with which the Fed and other central banks conduct monetary policy.

Since 1994 the Federal Open Market Committee (FOMC) has announced its policy decisions at the time they are made. These announced changes in the target rate receive prominent coverage in the press, and the FOMC's press releases serve to convey its assessment of the economy to the public and to give some signal of possible future changes in policy. The Fed has begun providing more information on FOMC members' projections of future growth and inflation. The medium-term projections for inflation have been interpreted as giving the implicit inflation targets of the members of the FOMC.[49] While these statements contribute to policy transparency, the Fed, unlike many other central banks, has never formally translated its "long-run goals of price stability" into an explicit target for the rate of inflation. Nor has it published projections for its policy interest rate, as several central banks have done.

The financial market crisis that began during the second half of 2007 has led to major changes in the operating procedures of the Federal Reserve. During 2008, the Fed cut the funds rate target, and the effective funds rate was essentially at zero by the end of 2008. In such an environment, policy clearly can no longer be represented in terms of a simple rule for setting the policy interest rate. To deal with the financial crisis and the sharp decline in economic activity, the Fed developed new policy tools. For example, new auction facilities were introduced to expand the range of institutions able to borrow from the Fed, and the assets that qualified as collateral were greatly expanded. However, even as the funds rate fell to zero, rates on corporate debt rose, reflecting increases in risk premiums, and the Fed moved directly to reduce risk spreads. Cecchetti (2008) discussed some of these new policies, and Taylor and Williams (2008) provided some empirical evidence that initial attempts by the Fed to alter interest rates by changing the composition of its balance sheet were ineffective. It is too early to tell which of the new tools of the Fed will remain active components of monetary policy once the economy rebounds or what role asset prices and credit market variables may play in the future conduct of policy.

11.6 Other Countries

The preceding discussion focused on the United States. If measuring monetary policy requires an understanding of operating procedures, then the appropriate measure of policy in the United States will not necessarily be appropriate for other countries. Operating procedures generally depend on the specific institutional structure of a country's financial sector, and the means used to implement monetary policy have varied over time in most countries as financial markets have evolved as the result of

---

49. Eijffinger and Geraats (2006) and Dincer and Eichengreen (2007) constructed indexes of central bank transparency. Gerrats (2002) provided a survey of research on monetary policy transparency. Recent work on transparency is cited in Walsh (2007).

either deregulation or financial innovation. Borio (1997) provided a survey of policy implementation in the industrial economies. Detailed discussions of the operating procedures in France, Germany, Japan, the United Kingdom, and the United States can be found in Batten et al. (1990). Bernanke and Mishkin (1993) provided case studies of monetary policy strategies in the United States, the United Kingdom, Canada, Germany, Switzerland, and Japan. These countries, plus France, are discussed in Kasman (1993) and Morton and Wood (1993). The behavior of the Bundesbank is examined by Clarida and Gertler (1997). Cargill, Hutchison, and Ito (1997) provided a discussion of Japan. Goodhart and Viñals (1994) discussed policy behavior in a number of European and Antipodian countries. A recent survey of central bank operating procedures is provided in Bank for International Settlements (2007).

The experiences with monetary policy operating procedures in all these countries have been broadly similar over the past 20 years. Beginning in the mid-1970s, many countries publicly established monetary targets. Germany, Canada, and Switzerland began announcing money targets in 1975, the United Kingdom in 1976, and France in 1977. The weight placed on these targets, however, varied greatly over time. In general, the financial innovations that occurred in the 1980s, together with significant deregulation of financial markets that took place after 1985, reduced reliance on monetary targets. This finding is consistent with the implications of Poole's model, which suggested that increased financial market instability that makes money demand less predictable would lessen the advantages of an operating procedure oriented toward monetary aggregates.

Morton and Wood (1993) argued that a common theme among the six industrial countries they examined was a move to more flexible interest rate policies. Rather than rely on officially established interest rates, often combined with direct credit controls, central banks moved toward more market-oriented interest rate policies.[50] These involve control over a reserve aggregate (such as nonborrowed reserves in the United States) through which the central bank influences liquidity in the money market. This provides the central bank with control over a short-term money market rate that balances reserve supply and demand. Typically, central banks do not intervene in the market continuously; instead they estimate reserve demand and then add or subtract bank reserves to achieve the targeted interbank interest rate. Because these operations are based on reserve projections and because actual reserve demand may differ from projections, the actual value of the interest rate can differ from the central bank's target. However, by intervening daily, the central bank can normally keep target deviations quite small.

---

50. Similarly, Kasman (1993) noted that innovation and liberalization in financial markets have made the institutional setting in which policy is conducted increasingly similar among the industrial countries.

Finally, it is worth emphasizing that the choice of operating procedure is, in principle, distinct from the choice of ultimate goals and objectives of monetary policy. For example, a policy under which price stability is the sole objective of monetary policy could be implemented through either an interest rate procedure or a reserve aggregate procedure. A policy that incorporates output stabilization or exchange rate considerations can similarly be implemented through different procedures. The choice of operating procedure is significant, however, for interpreting the short-term response of financial markets to economic disturbances. And inefficient procedures can introduce unnecessary volatility into financial markets.

11.7 Problems

1. Suppose the basic Poole model, (11.1) and (11.2), is modified by allowing the disturbances to be serially correlated. Specifically, assume that the disturbance in (11.1) is given by $u_t = \rho_u u_{t-1} + \varphi_t$, and the disturbance in (11.2) is given by $v_t = \rho_v v_{t-1} + \psi_t$, where φ and ψ are white noise processes (assume that all shocks can be observed with a one-period lag). Assume the central bank's loss function is $E(y_t)^2$.

a. Under a money supply operating procedure, derive the value of m_t that minimizes $E(y_t)^2$.

b. Under an interest rate operating procedure, derive the value of i_t that minimizes $E(y_t)^2$.

c. Explain why your answers in (a) and (b) depend on ρ_u and ρ_v.

d. Does the choice between a money supply procedure and an interest rate procedure depend on ρ_u and ρ_v? Explain.

e. Suppose the central bank sets its instrument for two periods (for example, $m_t = m_{t+1} = m^*$) to minimize $E(y_t)^2 + \beta E(y_{t+1})^2$, where $0 < \beta < 1$. How is the instrument choice problem affected by ρ_u and ρ_v?

2. Suppose (11.1) is replaced by a forward-looking IS curve of the form

$$y_t = E_t y_{t+1} - \alpha i_t + u_t.$$

The LM curve is given by (11.2). Assume u_t and v_t are given by $u_t = \rho_u u_{t-1} + \varphi_t$ and $v_t = \rho_v v_{t-1} + \psi_t$, where φ and ψ are white noise processes (assume that all shocks can be observed with a one-period lag). Assume the central bank's loss function is $E(y_t)^2$.

a. Under a money supply operating procedure, derive the value of m_t that minimizes $E(y_t)^2$.

b. Under an interest rate operating procedure, derive the value of i_t that minimizes $E(y_t)^2$.

c. Explain why your answers in (a) and (b) depend on ρ_u and ρ_v.

d. Does the choice between a money supply procedure and an interest rate procedure depend on ρ_u and ρ_v? Explain.

3. Suppose the utility of the representative household depends on consumption, leisure, and real money balances, as in the MIU models of chapter 2. In the context of a new Keynesian model of the sort developed in chapter 8 (optimizing agents, sticky prices), discuss how consumption, leisure, and real money balances would respond to a positive money demand shock under the following policies:

a. The central bank stabilizes the nominal supply of money.

b. The central bank stabilizes the nominal rate of interest (subject to satisfying the Taylor principle for determinacy).

c. Given your results in parts (a) and (b), is there a clear ranking of the two policies in terms of their implications for welfare?

4. Suppose the utility of the representative household depends on consumption, leisure, and real money balances, as in the MIU models of chapter 2. In the context of a new Keynesian model of the sort developed in chapter 8 (optimizing agents, sticky prices), discuss how consumption, leisure, and real money balances would respond to a positive fiscal spending shock under the following policies:

a. The central bank stabilizes the nominal supply of money.

b. The central bank stabilizes the nominal rate of interest (subject to satisfying the Taylor principle for determinacy).

c. Given your results in parts (a) and (b), is there a clear ranking of the two policies in terms of their implications for welfare?

5. Solve for the δ_i coefficients appearing in (11.11), and show that the optimal rule for the monetary base is the same as that implied by the value of μ^* given in (11.10).

6. Suppose the money demand relationship is given by $m = -c_1 i + c_2 y + v$. Show how the choice of an interest rate versus a money supply operating procedure depends on c_2. Explain why the choice depends on c_2.

7. Prices and aggregate supply shocks can be added to Poole's analysis by using the following model:

$$y_t = y_n + a(\pi_t - E_{t-1}\pi_t) + e_t$$

$$y_t = y_n - \alpha(i_t - E_t\pi_{t+1}) + u_t$$

$$m_t - p_t = c_0 - ci_t + y_t + v_t.$$

Assume that the central bank's objective is to minimize $E[\lambda(y - y_n)^2 + \pi^2]$ and that disturbances are mean zero white noise processes. Both the private sector in setting

$E_{t-1}\pi_t$ and the monetary authority in setting its policy instrument must act prior to observing the current values of the disturbances.

a. Calculate the expected loss function if i_t is used as the policy instrument. (Hint: Given the objective function, the instrument will always be set to ensure that expected inflation is equal to zero.)

b. Calculate the expected loss function if m_t is used as the policy instrument.

c. How does the instrument choice comparison depend on

i. the relative variances of the aggregate supply, demand, and money demand disturbances?

ii. the weight on stabilizing output fluctuations λ?

8. Using the intermediate target model of section 11.3.3 and the loss function (11.15), rank the policies that set i_t equal to $\hat{\imath}_t$, i_t^T, and $\hat{\imath}_t + \mu^* x_t$.

9. Show that if the nominal interest rate is set according to (11.17), the expected value of the nominal money supply is equal to $\hat{m}$ given in (11.19).

10. Suppose the central bank is concerned with minimizing the expected value of a loss function of the form

$$L = \mathrm{E}(\mathrm{TR})^2 + \chi \mathrm{E}(i^f)^2,$$

which depends on the variances of innovations to total reserves and the funds rate (χ is a positive parameter). Using the reserve-market model of this chapter, find the values of ϕ^d and ϕ^b that minimize this loss function. Are there conditions under which a pure nonborrowed reserves or a pure borrowed reserves operating procedure would be optimal?

11. Assume $i^d = i^f + s$ in (11.27) where s is a penalty for discount window borrowing. How does this modification change (11.27)? How are (11.30)–(11.32) affected? How does the Fed's operating procedure affect the interpretation of movements in nonborrowed reserves, borrowed reserves, and the federal funds rate as measures of monetary policy shocks?

12. Suppose the central bank operates a channel system of the sort analyzed in section 11.4.3 with $s = 0.50$ (i.e., 50 basis points). Assume end-of-day bank settlement balances are $T + \varepsilon$, where ε is normally distributed with mean zero and variance σ^2. The supply of settlement balances is fixed at $\bar{T}$ and the target interest rate is i^*.

a. Explain how the equilibrium market interest rate is affected by an increase in σ^2.

b. Explain how the equilibrium market interest rate is affected by an increase in s.

c. Explain why i^* is not a complete description of monetary policy under a channel system unless s is also known.

References

Abel, A. B. 1985. "Dynamic Behavior of Capital Accumulation in a Cash-in-Advance Model." *Journal of Monetary Economics* 16(1): 55–71.

Abel, A. B., and B. Bernanke. 1995. *Macroeconomics*. 2d ed. Addison-Wesley.

Abel, A. B., N. G. Mankiw, L. H. Summers, and R. Zeckhauser. 1989. "Assessing Dynamic Efficiency: Theory and Evidence." *Review of Economic Studies* 56(1): 1–20.

Abreu, D. 1988. "On the Theory of Infinitely Repeated Games with Discounting." *Econometrica* 56: 383–396.

Adao, B., I. Correia, and P. Teles. 1999. "The Monetary Transmission Mechanism: Is It Relevant for Policy?" Banco de Portugal.

———. 2003. "Gaps and Triangles." *Review of Economic Studies* 70(4): 699–713.

Adolfson, M. 2007. "Monetary Policy with Incomplete Exchange Rate Pass-Through." *Journal of International Money and Finance* 26(3): 468–494.

Adolfson, M., S. Laseén, J. Lindé, and M. Villani. 2007a. "Bayesian Estimation of an Open Economy DSGE Model with Incomplete Pass-Through." *Journal of International Economics* 72(2): 481–511.

———. 2007b. "RAMSES—A New General Equilibrium Model for Monetary Policy Analysis." Sveriges Riksbank *Economic Review* 2: 5–39.

———. 2008. "Evaluating an Estimated New Keynesian Small Open Economy Model." *Journal of Economic Dynamics and Control* 32(8): 2690–2721.

Adolfson, M., S. Laseén, J. Lindé, and L.E.O. Svensson. 2008. "Monetary Policy Trade-Offs in an Estimated Open-Economy DSGE Model." NBER Working Paper 14510.

Aiyagari, S. R., and M. Gertler. 1985. "The Backing of Government Bonds and Monetarism." *Journal of Monetary Economics* 16(1): 19–44.

Aizenman, J., and J. A. Frankel. 1986. "Targeting Rules for Monetary Policy." *Economic Letters* 21: 183–187.

Akerlof, G. A. 1970. "The Market for 'Lemons': Quality Uncertainty and the Market Mechanism." *Quarterly Journal of Economics* 84(3): 488–500.

Akerlof, G. A., and J. L. Yellen. 1985. "Can Small Deviations from Rationality Make Significant Differences to Economic Equilibria?" *American Economic Review* 75(4): 708–721.

Albanesi, S., V. V. Chari, and L. J. Christiano. 2003. "Expectation Traps and Monetary Policy." *Review of Economic Studies* 70: 715–741.

Alchian, A. A. 1977. "Why Money?" *Journal of Money, Credit, and Banking* 9(1): 133–140.

Alesina, A. 1987. "Macroeconomic Policy in a Two-Party System as a Repeated Game." *Quarterly Journal of Economics* 102(3): 651–678.

———. 1989. "Macroeconomics and Politics." In *NBER Macroeconomics Annual 1988*, 11–55. Cambridge, Mass.: MIT Press.

Alesina, A., and R. Gatti. 1995. "Independent Central Banks: Low Inflation at No Cost?" *American Economic Review* 85(3): 196–200.

Alesina, A., and N. Roubini. 1992. "Political Cycles in OECD Countries." *Review of Economics and Statistics* 59(4): 663–688.

Alesina, A., N. Roubini, with G. D. Cohen. 1997. *Political Cycles and the Macroeconomy*. Cambridge, Mass.: MIT Press.

Alesina, A., and J. Sachs. 1988. "Political Parties and the Business Cycles in the United States: 1948–1984." *Journal of Money, Credit, and Banking* 20(1): 63–82.

Alesina, A., and L. Summers. 1993. "Central Bank Independence and Macroeconomic Performance." *Journal of Money, Credit, and Banking* 25(2): 157–162.

al-Nowaihi, A., and P. Levine. 1994. "Can Reputation Resolve the Monetary Policy Credibility Problem?" *Journal of Monetary Economics* 33(2): 355–380.

———. 1996. "Independent But Accountable: Walsh Contracts and the Credibility Problem." CEPR Discussion Paper 1387.

Altig, D., L. J. Christiano, M. Eichenbaum, and J. Linde. 2005. "Firm-Specific Capital, Nominal Rigidities, and the Business Cycle." NBER Working Paper 11034.

Altissimo, F., M. Ehrmann, and F. Smets. 2006. "Inflation Persistence and Price-Setting Behaviour in the Euro Area." European Central Bank Occasional Paper 46.

Alvarez, F., A. Atkeson, and P. J. Kehoe. 2002. "Money, Interest Rates, and Exchange Rates with Endogenously Segmented Markets." *Journal of Political Economy* 110(1): 73–112.

Alvarez, F., R. E. Lucas Jr., and W. Weber. 2001. "Interest Rates and Inflation." *American Economic Review* 91(2): 219–225.

Álvarez, L. J., E. Dhyne, M. M. Hoeberichts, C. Kwapil, H. L. Bihan, P. Lunnemann, F. Martins, R. Sabbatini, H. Stahl, P. Vermeulen, and J. Vilmunen. 2005. "Sticky Prices in the Euro Area: A Summary of New Micro Evidence." European Central Bank Working Paper 563.

Amano, R., D. Coletti, and T. Macklem. 1998. "Monetary Policy Rules When Economic Behavior Changes." Research Department, Bank of Canada.

Amato, J. D., and S. Gerlach. 2002. "Inflation Targeting in Emerging Market and Transition Economies." *European Economic Review* 46(4/5): 781–790.

Ammer, J., and R. T. Freeman. 1995. "Inflation Targeting in the 1990s: The Experiences of New Zealand, Canada, and the United Kingdom." *Journal of Economics and Business* 47(2): 165–192.

Andersen, L., and J. Jordon. 1968. "Monetary and Fiscal Actions: A Test of Their Relative Importance in Economic Stabilization." Federal Reserve Bank of St. Louis *Review* 50 (Nov.): 11–24.

Andersen, T. M. 1989. "Credibility of Policy Announcements: The Output and Inflation Costs of Disinflationary Policies." *European Economic Review* 33(1): 13–30.

Ang, A., and M. Piazzesi. 2003. "A No-Arbitrage Vector Autoregression of Term Structure Dynamics with Macroeconomic and Latent Variables." *Journal of Monetary Economics* 50: 745–787.

Angelini, P. 1994a. "More on the Behavior of the Interest Rates and the Founding of the Fed." *Journal of Monetary Economics* 34(3): 537–553.

———. 1994b. "Testing for Structural Breaks: Trade-off Between Power and Spurious Effects." *Journal of Monetary Economics* 34(3): 561–566.

Angeloni, I., L. Aucremanne, M. Ehrmann, J. Galí, A. Levin, F. Smets. 2006. "New Evidence on Inflation Persistence and Price Stickiness in the Euro Area: Implications for Macro Modelling." *Journal of the European Economic Association* 4(2/3): 562–574.

Asako, K. 1983. "The Utility Function and the Superneutrality of Money on the Transition Path." *Econometrica* 51(5): 1593–1596.

Ascari, G. 2000. "Optimizing Agents, Staggered Wages, and Persistence in the Real Effects of Money Shocks." *Economic Journal* 110: 664–686.

———. 2004. "Staggered Prices and Trend Inflation: Some Nuisances." *Review of Economic Dynamics* 7: 642–667.

Ascari, G., and T. Ropele. 2007. "Optimal Monetary Policy under Low Trend Inflation." *Journal of Monetary Economics* 54: 2568–2583.

Athey, S., V. V. Chari, and P. Kehoe. 2005. "The Optimal Degree of Discretion in Monetary Policy." *Econometrica* 73(5): 1431–1475.

Atkinson, A. B., and J. E. Stiglitz. 1972. "The Structure of Indirect Taxation and Economic Efficiency." *Journal of Public Economics* 1(1): 97–119.

Attfield, C.L.F., D. Demery, and N. W. Duck. 1991. *Rational Expectations in Macroeconomics.* 2d ed. Oxford: Blackwell.

Auernheimer, L. 1974. "The Honest Government's Guide to the Revenue from the Creation of Money." *Journal of Political Economy* 82(3): 598–606.

Backus, D. K., and J. Driffill. 1985. "Inflation and Reputation." *American Economic Review* 75(3): 530–538.

Backus, D. K., and P. J. Kehoe. 1992. "International Evidence on the Historical Properties of Business Cycles." *American Economic Review* 82(4): 864–888.

Bade, R., and M. Parkin. 1984. "Central Bank Laws and Monetary Policy." Department of Economics, University of Western Ontario, Canada.

Bailey, M. J. 1956. "The Welfare Costs of Inflationary Finance." *Journal of Political Economy* 64(2): 93–110.

Balduzzi, P., G. Bertola, S. Foresi, and L. Klapper. 1998. "Interest Rate Targeting and the Dynamics of Short-Term Rates." *Journal of Money, Credit, and Banking* 30(1): 26–50.

Ball, L. 1991. "The Genesis of Inflation and the Costs of Disinflation." *Journal of Money, Credit, and Banking* 23(3): 439–452.

———. 1993. "How Costly Is Disinflation? The Historical Evidence." Federal Reserve Bank of Philadelphia *Business Review* (Nov./Dec.): 17–28.

———. 1994a. "Credible Disinflation with Staggered Price-Setting." *American Economic Review* 84(1): 282–289.

———. 1994b. "What Determines the Sacrifice Ratio?" In *Monetary Policy,* ed. N. G. Mankiw, 155–182. Chicago: University of Chicago Press.

———. 1995. "Time Consistent Inflation Policy and Persistent Changes in Inflation." *Journal of Monetary Economics* 36(2): 329–350.

———. 1999. "Efficient Rules for Monetary Policy." *International Finance* 2(1): 63–83.

———. 2001. "Another Look at Long-Run Money Demand." *Journal of Monetary Economics* 47(1): 31–44.

Ball, L., and N. G. Mankiw. 1994. "A Sticky-Price Manifesto." *Carnegie-Rochester Conference Series on Public Policy* 41 (Dec.): 127–151.

Ball, L., N. G. Mankiw, and R. Reis. 2005. "Monetary Policy for Inattentive Economies." *Journal of Monetary Economics* 52: 703–725.

Ball, L., and D. Romer. 1991. "Sticky Prices as Coordination Failure." *American Economic Review* 81(3): 539–552.

Bank of Canada. 1993. *Economic Behavior and Policy Choice under Price Stability.*

Bank for International Settlements. 2007. *Monetary Policy Frameworks and Central Bank Market Operations.*

Barnett, W. A. 1980. "Economic Monetary Aggregates: An Application of Index Number and Aggregation Theory." *Journal of Econometrics* 14(1): 11–48.

Barr, D. G., and J. Y. Campbell. 1997. "Inflation, Real Interest Rates, and the Bond Market: A Study of UK Nominal and Index-Linked Government Bond Prices." *Journal of Monetary Economics* 39(3): 361–383.

Barro, R. J. 1974. "Are Government Bonds Net Wealth?" *Journal of Political Economy* 82(6): 1095–1118.

———. 1976. "Rational Expectations and the Role of Monetary Policy." *Journal of Monetary Economics* 2(1): 1–32.

———. 1977. "Unanticipated Money Growth and Unemployment in the United States." *American Economic Review* 67(1): 101–115.

———. 1978. "Unanticipated Money, Output, and the Price Level in the United States." *Journal of Political Economy* 86(4): 549–580.

———. 1979a. "On the Determination of the Public Debt." *Journal of Political Economy* 87(5): 940–971.

———. 1979b. "Unanticipated Money Growth and Unemployment in the United States: Reply." *American Economic Review* 69(5): 1004–1009.

———. 1981. *Money, Expectations, and Business Cycles.* New York: Academic Press.

———. 1986. "Reputation in a Model of Monetary Policy with Incomplete Information." *Journal of Monetary Economics* 17(1): 3–20.

———. 1989. "Interest-Rate Targeting." *Journal of Monetary Economics* 23(1): 3–30.

———. 1995. "Inflation and Economic Growth." Bank of England *Quarterly Bulletin* (May): 39–52.

———. 1996. "Inflation and Growth." Federal Reserve Bank of St. Louis *Review* 78(3): 153–169.

Barro, R. J., and D. B. Gordon. 1983a. "A Positive Theory of Monetary Policy in a Natural-Rate Model." *Journal of Political Economy* 91(4): 589–610.

———. 1983b. "Rules, Discretion, and Reputation in a Model of Monetary Policy." *Journal of Monetary Economics* 12(1): 101–121.

Barro, R. J., and R. G. King. 1984. "Time-Separable Preferences and Intertemporal-Substitution Models of Business Cycles." *Quarterly Journal of Economics* 99(4): 817–839.

Barro, R. J., and M. Rush. 1980. "Unanticipated Money and Economic Activity." In *Rational Expectations and Economic Policy*, ed. S. Fischer, 23–48. Chicago: University of Chicago Press.

Barth, M. J. III, and V. A. Ramey. 2002. "The Cost Channel of Monetary Transmission." In *NBER Macroeconomics Annual 2001*, 199–239. Cambridge, Mass.: MIT Press.

Bartolini, L., G. Bertola, and A. Prati. 2002. "Day-to-Day Monetary Policy and the Volatility of the Federal Funds Rate." *Journal of Money, Credit, and Banking* 34(1): 136–159.

Bassetto, M. 2002. "A Game-Theoretic View of the Fiscal Theory of the Price Level." *Econometrica* 70(6): 2167–2195.

Batini, N., and D. Baxton. 2007. "Under What Conditions Can Inflation Targeting Be Adopted?" In *Monetary Policy under Inflation Targeting*, ed. F. S. Mishkin and K. Schmidt-Hebbel, 467–506. Santiago: Banco Central de Chile.

Batini, N., and A. Haldane. 1999. "Forward-Looking Rules for Monetary Policy." In *Monetary Policy Rules*, ed. J. B. Taylor, 157–192. Chicago: University of Chicago Press.

Batini, N., and A. Yates. 2001. "Hybrid Inflation and Price Level Targeting." London: Bank of England.

Batten, D. S., M. P. Blackwell, I. Kim, S. E. Nocera, and Y. Ozeki. 1990. "The Conduct of Monetary Policy in the Major Industrial Countries: Instruments and Operating Procedures." International Monetary Fund Occasional Paper 70.

Baumol, W. 1952. "The Transactions Demand for Cash." *Quarterly Journal of Economics* 67(4): 545–556.

Bean, C. 1983. "Targeting Nominal Income: An Appraisal." *Economic Journal* 93: 806–819.

Beaudry, P., and M. B. Devereux. 1995. "Monopolistic Competition, Price Setting, and the Effects of Real and Monetary Shocks." University of British Columbia, Canada.

Beck, G. W., and V. Wieland. 2007. "Money in Monetary Policy Design: A Formal Characterization of ECB-Style Cross-Checking." *Journal of the European Economic Association* 5(2/3): 524–533.

Beetsma, R., and H. Jensen. 1998. "Inflation Targets and Contracts with Uncertain Central Banker Preferences." *Journal of Money, Credit, and Banking* 30(3): 384–403.

Bénassy, J.-P. 1995. "Money and Wage Contracts in an Optimizing Model of the Business Cycle." *Journal of Monetary Economics* 35(2): 303–315.

Benhabib, J., S. Schmitt-Grohé, and M. Uribe. 2001a. "The Perils of Taylor Rules." *Journal of Economic Theory* 96: 40–69.

———. 2001b. "Monetary Policy and Multiple Equilibria." *American Economic Review* 91(1): 167–186.

———. 2002. "Avoiding Liquidity Traps." *Journal of Political Economy* 110: 535–563.

Benigno, G., and P. Benigno. 2002. "Implementing Monetary Cooperation through Inflation Targeting." CEPR Discussion Paper 3226.

Benigno, P., and M. Woodford. 2005. "Inflation Stabilization and Welfare: The Case of a Distorted Steady State." *Journal of the European Economic Association* 3(4): 1185–1236.

Berentsen, A., G. Menzio, and R. Wright. 2008. "Inflation and Unemployment in the Long Run." NBER Working Paper 13924.

Berentsen, A., and C. Monnet. 2008. "Monetary Policy in a Channel System." *Journal of Monetary Economics* 55(6): 1067–1080.

Bernanke, B. S. 1983. "Nonmonetary Effects of the Financial Crisis in the Propagation of the Great Depression." *American Economic Review* 73(3): 257–276.

———. 1986. "Alternative Explanations of the Money-Income Correlation." *Carnegie-Rochester Conference Series on Public Policy* 25 (Autumn): 49–99.

———. 1993. "Credit in the Macroeconomy." Federal Reserve Bank of New York *Quarterly Review* 18(1): 50–70.

Bernanke, B. S., and A. S. Blinder. 1988. "Credit, Money, and Aggregate Demand." *American Economic Review* 78(2): 435–439.

———. 1992. "The Federal Funds Rate and the Channels of Monetary Transmission." *American Economic Review* 82(4): 901–921.

Bernanke, B. S., and M. Gertler. 1989. "Agency Costs, Net Worth, and Business Fluctuations." *American Economic Review* 79(1): 14–31.

———. 1995. "Inside the Black Box: The Credit Channel of Monetary Policy Transmission." *Journal of Economic Perspectives* 9(4): 27–48.

Bernanke, B. S., M. Gertler, and S. Gilchrist. 1996. "The Financial Accelerator and the Flight to Quality." *Review of Economics and Statistics* 78(1): 1–15.

———. 1999. "The Financial Accelerator in a Quantitative Business Cycle Framework." In *Handbook of Macroeconomics*, ed. J. B. Taylor and M. Woodford. Vol. 1C, 1341–1393. Amsterdam: North-Holland.

Bernanke, B. S., T. Laubach, F. S. Mishkin, and A. Posen. 1998. *Inflation Targeting: Lessons from the International Experience.* Princeton: Princeton University Press.

Bernanke, B. S., and C. Lown. 1992. "The Credit Crunch." *Brookings Papers on Economic Activity*, no. 2, 205–239.

Bernanke, B. S., and I. Mihov. 1998. "Measuring Monetary Policy." *Quarterly Journal of Economics* 113(3): 869–902.

Bernanke, B. S., and F. Mishkin. 1993. "Central Bank Behavior and the Strategy of Monetary Policy: Observations from Six Industrialized Countries." In *NBER Macroeconomics Annual 1992*, 183–228. Cambridge, Mass.: MIT Press.

———. 1997. "Inflation Targeting: A New Framework for Monetary Policy?" *Journal of Economic Perspectives* 11: 97–116.

Bernanke, B. S., and M. Woodford. 1997. "Inflation Forecasts and Monetary Policy." *Journal of Money, Credit, and Banking* 29(4): 653–684.

Betts, C., and M. Devereux. 2000. "Exchange Rate Dynamics in a Model with Pricing-to-Market." *Journal of International Economics* 50(1): 215–244.

Bewley, T. 1983. "A Difficulty with the Optimum Quantity of Money." *Econometrica* 51(5): 1485–1504.

Bils, M., and P. J. Klenow. 2004. "Some Evidence on the Importance of Sticky Prices." *Journal of Political Economy* 112(5): 947–985.

Black, R., V. Cassino, A. Drew, E. Hansen, B. Hunt, D. Rose, and A. Scott. 1997. "The Forecasting and Policy System: The Core Model." Reserve Bank of New Zealand Research Paper 43.

Blake, A. P. 2001. "A 'Timeless Perspective' on Optimality in Forward-Looking Rational Expectations Models." NIESR Discussion Paper 188.

Blanchard, O. J. 1989. "A Traditional Interpretation of Economic Fluctuations." *American Economic Review* 79(5): 1146–1164.

———. 1990. "Why Does Money Affect Output? A Survey." In *Handbook of Monetary Economics*, ed. B. M. Friedman and F. H. Hahn, 779–835. Amsterdam: North-Holland.

Blanchard, O. J., and S. Fischer. 1989. *Lectures on Macroeconomics*. Cambridge, Mass.: MIT Press.

Blanchard, O. J., and J. Galí. 2007. "Real Wage Rigidity and the New Keynesian Model." *Journal of Money, Credit, and Banking* 39 (1s): 35–66.

———. 2008. "A New Keynesian Model with Unemployment." CEPR Discussion Paper 6765.

Blanchard, O. J., and C. M. Kahn. 1980. "The Solution of Linear Difference Models under Rational Expectations." *Econometrica* 48(5): 1305–1311.

Blanchard, O. J., and N. Kiyotaki. 1987. "Monopolistic Competition and the Effects of Aggregate Demand." *American Economic Review* 77(4): 647–666.

Blanchard, O. J., and D. Quah. 1989. "The Dynamic Effects of Aggregate Demand and Supply Disturbances." *American Economic Review* 79(4): 655–673.

Blanchard, O. J., and M. W. Watson. 1986. "Are Business Cycles All Alike?" In *The American Business Cycle: Continuity and Change*, ed. R. J. Gordon, 123–165. Chicago: University of Chicago Press.

Blinder, A. 1995. "Central Banking in Theory and Practice. Lecture II: Credibility, Discretion, and Independence." Marshall Lecture, Cambridge University.

Blinder, A. S., and J. B. Rudd. 2008. "The Supply-Shock Explanation of the Great Stagflation Revisited." NBER Working Paper 14563.

Bohn, H. 1991a. "Budget Balance through Revenue or Spending Adjustments? Some Historical Evidence for the United States." *Journal of Monetary Economics* 27(3): 333–359.

———. 1991b. "On Cash-in-Advance Models of Money Demand and Asset Pricing." *Journal of Money, Credit, and Banking* 23(2): 224–242.

———. 1991c. "The Sustainability of Budget Deficits with Lump-Sum and with Income-Based Taxation." *Journal of Money, Credit, and Banking* 23(3): 580–604.

———. 1991d. "Time Inconsistency of Monetary Policy in the Open Economy." *Journal of International Economics* 30(3/4): 249–266.

———. 1992. "Budget Deficits and Government Accounting." *Carnegie-Rochester Conference Series on Public Policy* 37 (Dec.): 1–83.

———. 1995. "The Sustainability of Budget Deficits in a Stochastic Economy." *Journal of Money, Credit, and Banking* 27(1): 257–271.

———. 1998. "The Behavior of U.S. Public Debt and Deficits." *Quarterly Journal of Economics* 113(3): 949–964.

———. 1999. "Comment: A Frictionless View of U.S. Inflation." In *NBER Macroeconomics Annual 1998*, 384–389. Cambridge, Mass.: MIT Press.

———. 2007. "Are Stationarity and Cointegration Restrictions Really Necessary for the Intertemporal Budget Constraint?" *Journal of Monetary Economics* 54: 1837–1847.

Boianovsky, M. 2002. "Simonsen and the Early History of the Cash-In-Advance Approach." *European Journal of the History of Economic Thought* 9(1): 57–71.

Bonser-Neal, C., V. V. Roley, and G. H. Sellon Jr. 1998. "Monetary Policy Actions, Intervention, and Exchange Rates: A Re-examination of the Empirical Relationships Using Federal Funds Rate Target Data." *Journal of Business* 71(2): 147–177.

Borio, C.E.V. 1997. "The Implementation of Monetary Policy in Industrial Countries: A Survey." Bank for International Settlements Economic Paper 47.

Boschen, J. F., and L. O. Mills. 1991. "The Effects of Countercyclical Monetary Policy on Money and Interest Rates: An Evaluation of Evidence from FOMC Documents." Federal Reserve Bank of Philadelphia. WP-91-02.

———. 1995a. "The Relation Between Narrative and Money Market Indicators of Monetary Policy." *Economic Inquiry* 33(1): 24–44.

———. 1995b. "Tests of Long-Run Neutrality Using Permanent Monetary and Real Shocks." *Journal of Monetary Economics* 35(1): 25–44.

Brainard, W. 1967. "Uncertainty and the Effectiveness of Policy." *American Economic Review* 57(2): 411–425.

Braun, R. A. 1991. "Comment on Optimal Fiscal and Monetary Policy: Some Recent Results." *Journal of Money, Credit, and Banking* 23(3): 542–546.

Brayton, F., A. Levin, R. Tryon, and J. C. Williams. 1997. "The Evolution of Macro Models at the Federal Reserve Board." *Carnegie-Rochester Conference Series on Public Policy* 47 (Dec.): 43–81.

Brayton, F., and E. Mauskopf. 1985. "The Federal Reserve Board MPS Quarerly Econometric Model of the U.S. Economy." *Economic Modelling* 2(3): 170–292.

Brayton, F., E. Mauskopf, D. Reifschneider, P. Tinsley, and J. C. Williams. 1997. "The Role of Expectations in the FRB/US Macroeconomic Model." Federal Reserve *Bulletin* 83(4): 227–246.

Brayton, F., and P. Tinsley. 1996. "A Guide to the FRB/US: A Macroeconomic Model of the United States." Federal Reserve Board Finance and Economics Discussion Paper 1996-42.

Briault, C., A. Haldane, and M. King. 1996. "Independence and Accountability." Institute for Monetary and Economic Studies Discussion Paper 96-E-17. Bank of Japan.

Broaddus, A., and M. Goodfriend. 1984. "Base Drift and the Longer-Run Growth of M1: Evidence from a Decade of Monetary Targeting." Federal Reserve Bank of Richmond *Economic Review* 70(6): 3–14.

Brock, W. A. 1974. "Money and Growth: The Case of Long-Run Perfect Foresight." *International Economic Review* 15(3): 750–777.

———. 1975. "A Simple Perfect Foresight Monetary Model." *Journal of Monetary Economics* 1(2): 133–150.

———. 1990. "Overlapping Generations Models with Money and Transaction Costs." In *Handbook of Monetary Economics*, ed. B. Friedman and F. Hahn. Vol. 1, 263–295. Amsterdam: North-Holland.

Brunner, K., and A. H. Meltzer. 1972. "Money, Debt, and Economic Activity." *Journal of Political Economy* 80(5): 951–977.

———. 1988. "Money and Credit in the Monetary Transmission Process." *American Economic Review* 78(2): 446–451.

Brunner, K., A. H. Meltzer, and A. Cukierman. 1980. "Stagflation, Persistent Unemployment, and the Permanence of Economic Shocks." *Journal of Monetary Economics* 6: 467–492.

Bruno, M., and S. Fischer. 1990. "Seigniorage, Operating Rules, and the High Inflation Trap." *Quarterly Journal of Economics* 105(2): 353–374.

Bryant, R., P. Hooper, and C. Mann, eds. 1992. *Evauating Policy Regimes: New Research in Empirical Macroeconomics*. Washington, D.C.: Brookings Institution.

Buiter, W. 2002. "The Fiscal Theory of the Price Level: A Critique." *Economic Journal* 112(481): 459–480.

Buiter, W., and I. Jewitt. 1981. "Staggered Wage Setting with Real Wage Relativities: Variations on a Theme of Taylor." *Manchester School* (Sept.): 211–228.

Bullard, J. 1999. "Testing Long-Run Monetary Neutrality Propositions: Lessons from the Recent Research." Federal Reserve Bank of St. Louis *Review* 81(6): 57–77.

Bullard, J., and J. W. Keating. 1995. "The Long-Run Relationship between Inflation and Output in Postwar Economies." *Journal of Monetary Economics* 36(3): 477–496.

Bullard, J., and K. Mitra. 2002. "Learning about Monetary Policy Rules." *Journal of Monetary Economics* 49(6): 1105–1129.

Buttiglione, L., P. Del Giovane, and O. Tristani. 1998. "Monetary Policy Actions and the Term Structure of Interest Rates: A Cross-Country Analysis." In *Monetary Policy and Interest Rates*, ed. I. Angeloni and R. Rovelli. New York: St. Martins Press.

Caballero, R. J., and E. M. Engel. 2007. "Price Stickiness in Ss Models: New Interpretations of Old Results." *Journal of Monetary Economics* 54 (1s): 100–121.

Cagan, P. 1956. "The Monetary Dynamics of Hyperinflation." In *Studies in the Quantity Theory of Money*, ed. M. Friedman, 25–117. Chicago: University of Chicago Press.

Calvo, G. A. 1978. "On the Time Consistency of Optimal Policy in a Monetary Economy." *Econometrica* 46(6): 1411–1428.

———. 1983. "Staggered Prices in a Utility-Maximizing Framework." *Journal of Monetary Economics* 12(3): 983–998.

Calvo, G. A., and P. E. Guidotti. 1993. "On the Flexibility of Monetary Policy: The Case of the Optimal Inflation Tax." *Review of Economic Studies* 60(3): 667–687.

Calvo, G. A., and L. Leiderman. 1992. "Optimal Inflation Tax under Precommitment: Theory and Evidence." *American Economic Review* 82(1): 179–194.

Campbell, J. Y. 1994. "Inspecting the Mechanism: An Analytical Approach to the Stochastic Growth Model." *Journal of Monetary Economics* 33(3): 463–506.

Campbell, J. Y., and N. G. Mankiw. 1990. "Consumption, Income, and Interest Rates: Reinterpreting the Time Series Evidence." In *NBER Macroeconomics Annual 1989*, 185–216. Cambridge, Mass.: MIT Press.

———. 1991. "The Response of Consumption to Income: A Cross-Country Investigation." *European Economic Review* 35(4): 723–756.

Campbell, J. Y., and R. J. Shiller. 1991. "Yield Spreads and Interest Rate Movements: A Bird's Eye View." *Review of Economic Studies* 58(3): 495–514.

Campillo, M., and J. Miron. 1997. "Why Does Inflation Differ across Countries?" In *Reducing Inflation: Motivation and Strategy*, ed. C. D. Romer and D. H. Romer, 335–357. Chicago: University of Chicago Press.

Candel-Sánchez, F., and J. C. Campoy-Miñarroy. 2004. "Is the Walsh Contract Really Optimal?" *Public Choice* 120(1/2): 29–39.

Canzoneri, M. B. 1985. "Monetary Policy Games and the Role of Private Information." *American Economic Review* 75(4): 1056–1070.

Canzoneri, M. B., R. E. Cumby, and B. T. Diba. 2001. "Is the Price Level Determined by the Needs of Fiscal Solvency?" *American Economic Review* 91(5): 1221–1238.

———. 2007. "Euler Equations and Money Market Interest Rates: A Challenge for Monetary Policy Models." *Journal of Monetary Economics* 54(7): 1863–1881.

Canzoneri, M. B., and H. Dellas. 1998. "Real Interest Rates and Central Bank Operating Procedures." *Journal of Monetary Economics* 42(3): 471–494.

Canzoneri, M. B., and D. Henderson. 1989. *Noncooperative Monetary Policies in Interdependent Economies*. Cambridge, Mass.: MIT Press.

Canzoneri, M. B., D. Henderson, and K. Rogoff. 1983. "The Information Content of the Interest Rate and Optimal Monetary Policy." *Quarterly Journal of Economics* 98(4): 545–566.

Canzoneri, M. B., C. Nolan, and A. Yates. 1997. "Mechanisms for Achieving Monetary Stability: Inflation Targeting versus the ERM." *Journal of Money, Credit, and Banking* 29(1): 46–60.

Caplin, A., and J. Leahy. 1991. "State-Dependent Pricing and the Dynamics of Money and Output." *Quarterly Journal of Economics* 106(3): 683–708.

Caplin, A., and D. Spulber. 1987. "Menu Costs and the Neutrality of Money." *Quarterly Journal of Economics* 102: 703–726.

Carare, A., and M. R. Stone. 2002. "Inflation Targeting Regimes." International Monetary Fund.

Cargill, T. 1995a. "The Bank of Japan and the Federal Reserve: An Essay on Central Bank Independence." In *Monetarism and the Methodology of Economics*, ed. K. Hoover and S. Sheffrin, 198–214. Aldershot, UK: Edward Elgar Publishing.

———. 1995b. "The Statistical Association between Central Bank Independence and Inflation." *Banca Nazionale del Lavoro Quarterly Review* 48(193): 159–172.

Cargill, T. F., M. M. Hutchison, and T. Ito. 1997. *The Political Economy of Japanese Monetary Policy*. Cambridge, Mass.: MIT Press.

Carlson, K. M. 1978. "Does the St. Louis Equation Now Believe in Fiscal Policy?" Federal Reserve Bank of St. Louis *Review* 60(2): 13–19.

Carlstrom, C. T., and T. S. Fuerst. 1995. "Interest Rate Rules vs. Money Growth Rules: A Welfare Comparison in a Cash-in-Advance Economy." *Journal of Monetary Economics* 36(2): 247–267.

———. 1997. "Agency Costs, Net Worth, and Business Fluctuations: A Computable General Equilibrium Analysis." *American Economic Review* 87(5): 893–910.

———. 1999. "The Fiscal Theory of the Price Level." Federal Reserve Bank of Cleveland (Dec.).

———. 2001. "Timing and Real Indeterminacy in Monetary Models." *Journal of Monetary Economics* 47(2): 285–298.

Carvalho, C. V. de. 2006. "Heterogeneity in Price Stickiness and the Real Effects of Monetary Shocks." *Frontiers of Macroeconomics* 2(1).

Cecchetti, S. G. 1995. "Distinguishing Theories of the Monetary Transmission Mechanism." Federal Reserve Bank of St. Louis *Review* 77(3): 83–97.

———. 2008. "Crisis and Responses: The Federal Reserve and the Financial Crisis of 2007–2008." NBER Working Paper 14134.

Champ, B., and S. Freeman. 1994. *Modeling Monetary Economies*. New York: Wiley.

Chari, V. V., L. J. Christiano, and M. Eichenbaum. 1995. "Inside Money, Outside Money, and Short-Term Interest Rates." *Journal of Money, Credit, and Banking* 27(4): 1354–1386.

Chari, V. V., L. J. Christiano, and P. J. Kehoe. 1991. "Optimal Fiscal and Monetary Policy: Some Recent Results." *Journal of Money, Credit, and Banking* 23(3): 519–539.

———. 1996. "Optimality of the Friedman Rule in Economies with Distorting Taxes." *Journal of Monetary Economics* 37(2): 203–223.

Chari, V. V., and P. J. Kehoe. 1990. "Sustainable Plans." *Journal of Political Economy* 98(4): 783–802.

———. 1999. "Optimal Fiscal and Monetary Policy." In *Handbook of Macroeconomics*, ed. J. B. Taylor and M. Woodford, Vol. 1C, 1671–1745. Amsterdam: North-Holland.

Chari, V. V., P. J. Kehoe, and E. R. McGrattan. 2000. "Sticky Price Models of the Business Cycle: Can the Contract Multiplier Solve the Persistence Problem?" *Econometrica* 68(5): 1151–1179.

Chiang, A. C. 1992. *Elements of Dynamic Optimization*. New York: McGraw-Hill.

Chortareas, G. E., and S. M. Miller. 2003. "Monetary Policy Delegation, Contract Costs, and Contract Targets." *Bulletin of Economic Research* 55(1): 101–112.

———. 2007. "The Walsh Contracts for Central Bankers Prove Optimal After All!" *Public Choice* 131(1): 243–247.

Christiano, L. J. 1991. "Modelling the Liquidity Effect of a Money Shock." Federal Reserve Bank of Minneapolis *Quarterly Review* 15(1): 3–34.

Christiano, L. J., and M. Eichenbaum. 1992a. "Liquidity Effects and the Monetary Transmission Mechanism." *American Economic Review* 82(2): 346–353.

———. 1992b. "Current Real Business Cycle Theories and Aggregate Labor-Market Fluctuations." *American Economic Review* 82(3): 430–450.

———. 1995. "Liquidity Effects, Monetary Policy, and the Business Cycle." *Journal of Money, Credit, and Banking* 27(4): 1113–1136.

Christiano, L. J., M. Eichenbaum, and C. Evans. 1996a. "The Effects of Monetary Policy Shocks: Evidence from the Flow of Funds." *Review of Economics and Statistics* 78(1): 16–34.

———. 1996b. "Identification and the Effects of Monetary Policy Shocks." In *Financial Factors in Economic Stabilization and Growth*, ed. M. Blejer, Z. Eckstein, Z. Hercowitz, and L. Leiderman, 36–74. Cambridge: Cambridge University Press.

———. 1997. "Sticky Prices and Limited Participation Models: A Comparison." *European Economic Review* 41(6): 1201–1249.

———. 1999. "Monetary Policy Shocks: What Have We Learned and to What End?" In *Handbook of Macroeconomics*, ed. J. B. Taylor and M. Woodford. Vol. 1A, 65–148. Amsterdam: North-Holland.

———. 2005. "Nominal Rigidities and the Dynamic Effects of a Shock to Monetary Policy." *Journal of Political Economy* 113(1): 1–45.

Christiano, L. J., and T. J. Fitzgerald. 2000. "Understanding the Fiscal Theory of the Price Level." NBER Working Paper 7668.

Christiano, L., R. Motto, and M. Rostagno. 2007. "Financial Factors in Business Cycles." ⟨http://www.ecb.int/events/pdf/conferences/ecbcf_cbfm/MottoRostagno_paper.pdf?⟩.

Clarida, R., J. Galí, and M. Gertler. 1999. "The Science of Monetary Policy: A New Keynesian Perspective." *Journal of Economic Perspectives* 37(4): 1661–1707.

———. 2000. "Monetary Policy Rules and Macroeconomic Stability: Evidence and Some Theory." *Quarterly Journal of Economics* 115(1): 147–180.

———. 2001. "Optimal Monetary Policy in Open vs. Closed Economies." *American Economic Review* 91(2): 248–252.

———. 2002. "A Simple Framework for International Monetary Policy Analysis." *Journal of Monetary Economics* 49(5): 877–904.

Clarida, R., and M. Gertler. 1997. "How Does the Bundesbank Conduct Monetary Policy?" In *Reducing Inflation: Motivation and Strategy*, ed. C. D. Romer and D. H. Romer, 363–406. Chicago: University of Chicago Press.

Clower, R. W. 1967. "A Reconsideration of the Microfoundations of Monetary Theory." *Western Economic Journal* 6(1): 1–9.

Cochrane, J. H. 1998. "What Do the VARs Mean? Measuring the Output Effects of Monetary Policy." *Journal of Monetary Economics* 41(2): 277–300.

———. 1999. "A Frictionless View of U.S. Inflation." In *NBER Macroeconomics Annual 1998*, 323–384. Cambridge, Mass.: MIT Press.

———. 2007. "Identification with Taylor Rules: A Critical Review." NBER Working Paper 13410.

Cochrane, J., and M. Piazzesi. 2002. "The Fed and Interest Rates: A High-Frequency Identification." *American Economic Review* 92(1): 90–95.

Cogley, T., and J. M. Nason. 1995. "Output Dynamics in a Real Business Cycle Model." *American Economic Review* 85(3): 492–511.

Cogley, T., and A. M. Sbordone. 2006. "Trend Inflation and Inflation Persistence in the New Keynesian Phillips Curve." Federal Reserve Bank of New York. WP-270.

Coibion, O. 2008. "Testing the Sticky Information Phillips Curve." ⟨http://wmpeople.wm.edu/asset/index/ocoibion/testingthesipcrestatfinal⟩.

Coibion, O., and Y. Gorodnichenko. 2008. "Monetary Policy, Trend Inflation, and the Great Moderation: An Alternative Interpretation." NBER Working Paper 14621.

Cole, H. L., and L. E. Ohanian. 2002. "Shrinking Money: The Demand for Money and the Non-neutrality of Money." *Journal of Monetary Economics* 49(4): 653–686.

Coleman, W. J. III. 1996. "Money and Output: A Test of Reverse Causation." *American Economic Review* 86(1): 90–111.

Collard, F., and H. Dellas. 2005. "Poole in the New Keynesian Model." *European Economic Review* 49(4): 887–907.

Cook, T. 1989. "Determinants of the Federal Funds Rate: 1979–1982." Federal Reserve Bank of Richmond *Economic Review* 75(1): 3–19.

Cook, T., and T. Hahn. 1989. "The Effect of Interest Rate Changes in the Federal Funds Rate Target on Market Interest Rates in the 1970s." *Journal of Monetary Economics* 24(3): 331–351.

Cooley, T. F., ed. 1995. *Frontiers of Business Cycle Research*. Princeton, N.J.: Princeton University Press.

Cooley, T. F., and G. D. Hansen. 1989. "The Inflation Tax in a Real Business Cycle Model." *American Economic Review* 79(4): 733–748.

———. 1991. "The Welfare Costs of Moderate Inflations." *Journal of Money, Credit, and Banking* 23(3): 483–503.

———. 1995. "Money and the Business Cycle." In *Frontiers of Business Cycle Research*, ed. T. F. Cooley, 175–216. Princeton, N.J.: Princeton University Press.

Cooley, T. F., and E. Prescott. 1995. "Economic Growth and Business Cycles." In *Frontiers of Business Cycle Research*, ed. T. F. Cooley, 1–38. Princeton, N.J.: Princeton University Press.

Cooley, T. F., and V. Quadrini. 1999. "A Neoclassical Model of the Phillips Curve Relation." *Journal of Monetary Economics* 44(2): 165–193.

Correia, I., and P. Teles. 1996. "Is the Friedman Rule Optimal When Money Is an Intermediate Good?" *Journal of Monetary Economics* 38(2): 223–244.

———. 1999. "The Optimal Inflation Tax." *Review of Economic Dynamics* 2: 325–346.

Corsetti, G., and P. Presenti. 2001. "Welfare and Macroeconomic Interdependence." *Quarterly Journal of Economics* 116(2): 421–445.

———. 2002. "International Dimensions of Optimal Monetary Policy." University of Rome III and Federal Reserve Bank of New York.

Cosimano, T. F., and R. G. Sheehan. 1994. "The Federal Reserve Operating Procedure, 1984–1990: An Empirical Analysis." *Journal of Macroeconomics* 16(4): 573–588.

Costain, J., and A. Nakov. 2008. "Price Adjustment in a General Model of State-Dependent Pricing." Bank of Spain.

Cover, J. P. 1992. "Asymmetric Effects of Positive and Negative Money Supply Shocks." *Quarterly Journal of Economics* 107(4): 1261–1282.

Cox, J. C., J. E. Ingersol, and S. A. Ross. 1985. "A Theory of the Term Structure of Interest Rates." *Econometrica* 53(2): 385–407.

Croushore, D. 1993. "Money in the Utility Function: Functional Equivalence to a Shopping-Time Model." *Journal of Macroeconomics* 15(1): 175–182.

Cubitt, R. P. 1992. "Monetary Policy Games and Private Sector Precommitment." *Oxford Economic Papers* 44(3): 513–530.

Cukierman, A. 1992. *Central Bank Strategies, Credibility and Independence.* Cambridge, Mass.: MIT Press.

———. 2002. "Are Contemporary Central Banks Transparent about Economic Models and Objectives, and What Difference Does It Make?" Federal Reserve Bank of St. Louis *Review* 84(4): 15–35.

Cukierman, A., S. Edwards, and G. Tabellini. 1992. "Seigniorage and Political Instability." *American Economic Review* 82(3): 537–555.

Cukierman, A., and S. Gerlach. 2003. "The Inflation Bias Revisited: Theory and Some International Evidence." *Manchester School* 71(5): 541–565.

Cukierman, A., P. Kalaitzidakis, L. H. Summers, and S. B. Webb. 1993. "Central Bank Independence, Growth, Investment, and Real Rates." *Carnegie-Rochester Conference Series on Public Policy* 39 (Dec.): 95–140.

Cukierman, A., and F. Lippi. 2001. "Labour Markets and Monetary Union: A Strategic Analysis." *Economic Journal* 111(473): 541–565.

Cukierman, A., and N. Liviatan. 1991. "Optimal Accommodation by Strong Policymakers under Incomplete Information." *Journal of Monetary Economics* 27(1): 99–127.

Cukierman, A., and A. Meltzer. 1986. "A Theory of Ambiguity, Credibility, and Inflation under Discretion and Asymmetric Information." *Econometrica* 54(5): 1099–1128.

Cukierman, A., S. B. Webb, and B. Neyapti. 1992. "Measuring the Independence of Central Banks and Its Effects on Policy Outcomes." *World Bank Economic Review* 6(3): 353–398.

Cúrdia, V., and M. Woodford. 2008. "Credit Frictions and Optimal Monetary Policy." ⟨http://ideas.repec.org/p/nbb/reswpp/200810-21.html⟩.

Currie, D., and P. Levine. 1991. "The International Coordination of Monetary Policy: A Survey." In *Surveys in Monetary Economics*, ed. C. Green and D. Llewellyn. Vol. 1, 379–417. Cambridge, Mass.: Blackwell.

Dahlquist, M., and L.E.O. Svensson. 1996. "Estimating the Term Structure of Interest Rates for Monetary Policy Analysis." *Scandinavian Journal of Economics* 98(2): 163–183.

Dai, Q., and K. Singleton. 2000. "Specification Analysis of Affine Term Structure Models." *Journal of Finance* 55: 1943–1978.

Damjanovic, T., V. Damjanovic, and C. Nolan. 2008. "Unconditional Optimal Monetary Policy." *Journal of Monetary Economics* 55: 491–500.

Daniel, B. 2001. "The Fiscal Theory of the Price Level in an Open Economy." *Journal of Monetary Economics* 48(2): 293–308.

———. 2007. "The Fiscal Theory of the Price Level and Initial Government Debt." *Review of Economic Dynamics* 10(2): 193–206.

de Brouwer, G., and J. O'Regan. 1997. "Evaluating Simple Monetary-Policy Rules for Australia." In *Monetary Policy and Inflation Targeting*, ed. P. Lowe, 244–276. Reserve Bank of Australia.

De Fiore, F., and O. Tristani. 2009. "Optimal Monetary Policy in a Model of the Credit Channel." Paper presented at Macroeconomic Models for Monetary Policy conference, Federal Reserve Bank of San Francisco, March.

De Gregorio, J. 1993. "Inflation, Taxation, and Long-Run Growth." *Journal of Monetary Economics* 31(3): 271–298.

de Haan, J., and G. J. van't Hag. 1995. "Variation in Central Bank Independence across Countries: Some Provisional Empirical Evidence." *Public Choice* 85(3/4): 335–351.

De Prano, M., and T. Mayer. 1965. "Tests of the Relative Importance of Autonomous Expenditures and Money." *American Economic Review* 55(4): 729–752.

Debelle, G., and S. Fischer. 1994. "How Independent Should a Central Bank Be?" In *Goals, Guidelines, and Constraints Facing Monetary Policymakers*, ed. J. C. Fuhrer, 195–221. Federal Reserve Bank of Boston.

Demirel, U. D. 2007. "Optimal Monetary Policy in a Financially Fragile Economy."

Demopoulos, G. D., G. M. Katsimbris, and S. M. Miller. 1987. "Monetary Policy and Central-Bank Financing of Government Budget Deficits." *European Economic Review* 31(5): 1023–1050.

Den Haan, W. J. 2000. "The Co-movement between Output and Prices." *Journal of Monetary Economics* 46(1): 3–30.

Den Haan, W. J., S. W. Summer, and G. M. Yamashiro. 2007. "Bank Loan Portfolios and the Monetary Transmission Mechanism." *Journal of Monetary Economics* 54(4): 904–924.

Dennis, R. 2001a. "Pre-commitment, the Timeless Perspective, and Policymaking from behind a Veil of Uncertainty." Federal Reserve Bank of San Francisco. WP-01-19.

———. 2001b. "The Policy Preferences of the US Federal Reserve." Federal Reserve Bank of San Francisco.

———. 2008. "The Frequency of Price Adjustment and New Keynesian Business Cycle Dynamics." Federal Reserve Bank of San Francisco.

Dhyne, E., L. J. Álvarez, H. L. Bihan, G. Veronese, D. Dias, J. Hoffmann, N. Jonker, P. Lunnemann, F. Rumler, and J. Vilmunen. 2006. "Price Setting in the Euro Area and the United States: Some Facts from Individual Consumer Price Data." *Journal of Economic Perspectives* 20(2): 171–192.

Diamond, P. A. 1983. "Money in Search Equilibrium." *Econometrica* 52(1): 1–20.

Diamond, P. A., and J. A. Mirlees. 1971. "Optimal Taxation and Public Production. I: Production and Efficiency; II: Tax Rules." *American Economic Review* 61(3): 8–27; 261–278.

Diba, B. T., and H. I. Grossman. 1988a. "Explosive Rational Bubbles in Stock Prices." *American Economic Review* 78(3): 520–530.

———. 1988b. "Rational Inflationary Bubbles." *Journal of Monetary Economics* 21(1): 35–46.

Diebold, F. X., M. Piazzesi, and G. D. Rudebusch. 2005. "Modeling Bond Yields in Finance and Macroeconomics." *American Economic Review* 95(2): 415–420.

Dincer, N. N., and B. Eichengreen. 2007. "Central Bank Transparency: Where, Why, and with What Effects?" NBER Working Paper 13003.

Dittmar, R., W. T. Gavin, and F. Kydland. 1999. "The Inflation-Output Variability Trade-off and Price-Level Targeting." Federal Reserve Bank of St. Louis *Review* 81(1): 23–31.

———. 2002. "Inflation Persistence and Flexible Prices." Federal Reserve Bank of St. Louis Working Paper.

Dixit, A. K. 1990. *Optimization in Economic Theory*. 2d ed. Oxford: Oxford University Press.

———. 2000. "A Repeated Game Model of Monetary Union." *Economic Journal* 110(466): 759–780.

Dixit, A. K., and H. Jensen. 2001. "Equilibrium Contracts for the Central Bank of a Monetary Union." Princeton University and University of Copenhagen.

Dixit, A. K., and L. Lambertini. 2002. "Symbiosis of Monetary and Fiscal Policies in a Monetary Union." Princeton University.

Dixit, A. K., and J. E. Stiglitz. 1977. "Monopolistic Competition and Optimum Product Diversity." *American Economic Review* 67(3): 297–308.

Dornbusch, R. 1976. "Expectations and Exchange Rate Dynamics." *Journal of Political Economy* 84(6): 1161–1176.

Dotsey, M., and P. Ireland. 1995. "Liquidity Effects and Transaction Technologies." *Journal of Money, Credit, and Banking* 27(4): 1441–1457.

———. 1996. "The Welfare Cost of Inflation in General Equilibrium." *Journal of Monetary Economics* 37(1): 29–47.

Dotsey, M., and R. G. King. 2001. "Pricing, Production, and Persistence." NBER Working Paper 8407.

———. 2005. "Implications of State-Dependent Pricing for Dynamic Macroeconomic Models." *Journal of Monetary Economics* 52(1): 213–242.

Dotsey, M., R. G. King, and A. L. Wolman. 1999. "State-Contingent Pricing and the General Equilibrium Dynamics of Money and Output." *Quarterly Journal of Economics* 114(2): 655–690.

———. 2006. "Inflation and Real Activity with Firm-Level Productivity Shocks: A Quantitative Framework." Federal Reserve Bank of Richmond.

Drazen, A. 1979. "The Optimal Rate of Inflation Revisited." *Journal of Monetary Economics* 5(2): 231–248.

———. 2001. "The Political Business Cycle after 25 Years." In *NBER Macroeconomics Annual 2000*, 75–117. Cambridge, Mass.: MIT Press.

Drazen, A., and P. R. Masson. 1994. "Credibility of Policies versus Credibility of Policymakers." *Quarterly Journal of Economics* 109(3): 735–754.

Driffill, J. 1988. "Macroeconomic Policy Games with Incomplete Information: A Survey." *European Economic Review* 32(2/3): 513–541.

Driffill, J., G. E. Mizon, and A. Ulph. 1990. "Costs of Inflation." In *Handbook of Monetary Economics*, ed. B. Friedman and F. Hahn. Vol. 2, 1012–1066. Amsterdam: North-Holland.

Duguay, P. 1994. "Empirical Evidence on the Strength of the Monetary Transmission Mechanism in Canada." *Journal of Monetary Economics* 33(1): 39–61.

Eggertsson, G. B., and M. Woodford. 2003. "The Zero Bound on Interest Rates and Optimal Monetary Policy." *Brookings Papers on Economic Activity*, no. 1, 139–211.

Ehrmann, M., and F. Smets. 2001. "Uncertain Potential Output: Implications for Monetary Policy." European Central Bank Working Paper 59.

Eichenbaum, M. 1992. "Comments: 'Interpreting the Macroeconomic Time Series Facts: The Effects of Monetary Policy' by Christopher Sims." *European Economic Review* 36(5): 1001–1011.

Eichenbaum, M., and C. L. Evans. 1995. "Some Empirical Evidence on the Effects of Shocks to Monetary Policy on Exchange Rates." *Quarterly Journal of Economics* 110(4): 975–1009.

Eichenbaum, M., and J.D.M. Fisher. 2007. "Estimating the Frequency of Price Reoptimization in Calvo-Style Models." *Journal of Monetary Economics* 54(7): 2032–2047.

Eichenbaum, M., and K. J. Singleton. 1987. "Do Equilibrium Real Business Cycle Theories Explain Postwar U.S. Business Cycles?" In *NBER Macroeconomics Annual 1986*, 91–135. Cambridge, Mass.: MIT Press.

Eijffinger, S., and J. de Haan. 1996. "The Political Economy of Central-Bank Independence." Special Papers in International Economics 19. Princeton University.

Eijffinger, S., and P. Geraats. 2006. "How Transparent Are Central Banks?" *European Journal of Political Economy* 22: 1–22.

Eijffinger, S., M. Hoeberichts, and E. Schaling. 1995. "Optimal Conservativeness in the Rogoff (1985) Model: A Graphical and Closed-Form Solution." CentER Discussion Paper 95121.

Eijffinger, S., and E. Schaling. 1993. "Central Bank Independence in Twelve Industrialized Countries." Banca Nazionale del Lavoro *Quarterly Review*, no. 184, 49–89.

———. 1995. "Optimal Commitment in an Open Economy: Credibility vs. Flexibility." CentER Discussion Paper 9579.

Engel, C. 2002. "The Responsiveness of Consumer Prices to Exchange Rates and the Implications for Exchange-Rate Policy: A Survey of a Few Recent New Open-Economy Macro Models." NBER Working Paper 8725.

Engle, R., and C. Granger. 1987. "Cointegration and Error Correction: Representation, Estimation, and Testing." *Econometrica* 55(2): 251–276.

Erceg, C. J., D. Henderson, and A. T. Levin. 2000. "Optimal Monetary Policy with Staggered Wage and Price Contracts." *Journal of Monetary Economics* 46(2): 281–313.

Erceg, C. J., and A. T. Levin. 2003. "Imperfect Credibility and Inflation Persistence." *Journal of Monetary Economics* 50(4): 915–944.

Estrella, A., and J. C. Fuhrer. 2002. "Dynamic Inconsistencies: Counterfactual Implications of a Class of Rational Expectations Models." *American Economic Review* 92(4): 1013–1028.

Evans, G. W. 1991. "Pitfalls in Testing for Explosive Bubbles in Asset Prices." *American Economic Review* 81(4): 922–930.

Evans, G. W., and S. Honkapohja. 2001. *Learning and Expectations in Macroeconomics*. Princeton, N.J.: Princeton University Press.

———. 2009. "Expectations, Learning, and Monetary Policy: An Overview of Recent Research." In *Monetary Policy under Uncertainty and Learning*, ed. K. Schmidt-Hebbel and C. E. Walsh. Banco Central de Chile.

Faig, M. 1988. "Characterization of the Optimal Tax on Money When It Functions as a Medium of Exchange." *Journal of Monetary Economics* 22(1): 137–148.

Fair, R. C. 1984. *Specification, Estimation, and Analysis of Macroeconometric Models*. Cambridge, Mass.: Harvard University Press.

Farmer, R. 1993. *The Macroeconomics of Self-Fulfilling Prophecies*. Cambridge, Mass.: MIT Press.

Faust, J. 1996. "Whom Can You Trust? Theoretical Support for the Founders' Views." *Journal of Monetary Economics* 37(2): 267–283.

Faust, J., and J. Irons. 1996. "Money, Politics and the Post-War Business Cycles." Federal Reserve Board International Finance Discussion Paper 572.

Faust, J., and E. Leeper. 1997. "When Do Long-Run Identifying Restrictions Give Reliable Results?" *Journal of Business Economics and Statistics* 15(3): 345–354.

Federal Reserve Bank of New York. 1994. *Studies on Causes and Consequences of the 1989–92 Credit Slowdown*.

Federal Reserve System. 1981. *New Monetary Control Procedures*. Washington, D.C.

———. 2001. *88th Annual Report*. Washington, D.C.

Feenstra, R. C. 1986. "Functional Equivalence between Liquidity Costs and the Utility of Money." *Journal of Monetary Economics* 17(2): 271–291.

Feldstein, M. 1978. "The Welfare Costs of Capital Income Taxation." *Journal of Political Economy* 86(2): 529–551.

———. 1979. "The Welfare Costs of Permanent Inflation and Optimal Short-Run Economic Policy." *Journal of Political Economy* 87(4): 749–768.

———. 1998. "The Costs and Benefits of Going from Low Inflation to Price Stability." In *Monetary Policy and Inflation*, ed. C. Romer and D. Romer, 123–156. Chicago: University of Chicago Press.

Feldstein, M., J. Green, and E. Sheshinski. 1978. "Inflation and Taxes in a Growing Economy with Debt and Equity Finance." *Journal of Political Economy* 86(2): S53–S70.

Fischer, A. M. 1996. "Central Bank Independence and Sacrifice Ratios." *Open Economy Review* 7: 5–18.

Fischer, M. E., and J. J. Seater. 1993. "Long-Run Neutrality and Superneutrality in an ARIMA Framework." *American Economic Review* 83(3): 402–415.

Fischer, S. 1972. "Keynes-Wicksell and Neoclassical Models of Money and Growth." *American Economic Review* 62(5): 880–890.

———. 1974. "Money and the Production Function." *Economic Inquiry* 12(4): 517–533.

———. 1977. "Long-Term Contracts, Rational Expectations, and the Optimal Money Supply Rule." *Journal of Political Economy* 85(1): 191–206.

———. 1979a. "Anticipations and the Non-neutrality of Money." *Journal of Political Economy* 87(2): 225–252.

———. 1979b. "Capital Accumulation on the Transition Path in a Monetary Optimizing Model." *Econometrica* 47(6): 1433–1439.

———. 1994. "Modern Central Banking." In *The Future of Central Banking*, ed. F. Capie, C. Goodhart, S. Fischer, and N. Schnadt, 262–308. Cambridge: Cambridge University Press.

———. 1996. "The Unending Search for Monetary Salvation." In *NBER Macroeconomics Annual 1995*, 275–286. Cambridge, Mass.: MIT Press.

Fishe, R., and M. Wohar. 1990. "The Adjustment of Expectations to a Change in Regime: Comment." *American Economic Reivew* 80(4): 968–976.

Fisher, I. 1896. *Appreciation and Interest*. New York: Macmillan.

Flood, R., and P. Isard. 1988. "Monetary Policy Strategies." NBER Working Paper 2770.

Frankel, J., and M. Chinn. 1995. "The Stabilizing Properties of a Nominal GNP Rule." *Journal of Money, Credit, and Banking* 27(2): 318–334.

Fratianni, M., J. von Hagen, and C. Waller. 1997. "Central Banking as a Principal Agent Problem." *Economic Inquiry* 35(2): 378–393.

Friedman, B. M. 1975. "Targets, Instruments, and Indicators of Monetary Policy." *Journal of Monetary Economics* 1(4): 443–473.

———. 1977a. "Even the St. Louis Model Now Believes in Fiscal Policy." *Journal of Money, Credit, and Banking* 9(2): 365–367.

———. 1977b. "The Inefficiencies of Short-Run Monetary Targets for Monetary Policy." *Brookings Papers on Economic Activity*, no. 2, 293–335.

———. 1990. "Targets and Instruments of Monetary Policy." In *Handbook of Monetary Economics*, ed. B. Friedman and F. Hahn. Vol. 2, 1183–1230. Amsterdam: North-Holland.

Friedman, B. M., and K. N. Kuttner. 1992. "Money, Income, Prices, and Interest Rates." *American Economic Review* 82(3): 472–492.

———. 1996. "A Price Target for U.S. Monetary Policy? Lessons from the Experience with Money Growth Targets." *Brookings Papers on Economic Activity*, no. 1, 77–125.

Friedman, M. 1968. "The Role of Monetary Policy." *American Economic Review* 58(1): 1–17.

———. 1969. "The Optimum Quantity of Money." In *The Optimum Quantity of Money and Other Essays*. Chicago: Aldine.

———. 1977. "Nobel Lecture: Inflation and Unemployment." *Journal of Political Economy* 85(3): 451–472.

Friedman, M., and D. Meiselman. 1963. "The Relative Stability of Monetary Velocity and the Investment Multiplier in the United States: 1897–1958." In *Stabilization Policies*, 165–268. Englewood Cliffs, N.J.: Prentice Hall.

Friedman, M., and A. Schwartz. 1963a. *A Monetary History of the United States, 1867–1960*. Princeton, N.J.: Princeton University Press.

———. 1963b. "Money and Business Cycles." *Review of Economics and Statistics* 45(1): 32–64.

———. 1982. *Monetary Trends in the United States and the United Kingdom: Their Relation to Income, Prices, and Interest Rates, 1867–1975*. Chicago: University of Chicago Press.

Froot, K. A., and R. H. Thaler. 1990. "Anomalies: Foreign Exchange." *Journal of Economic Perspectives* 4(3): 179–192.

Froyen, R. T., and R. N. Waud. 1995. "Central Bank Independence and the Output-Inflation Trade-off." *Journal of Economics and Business* 47(2): 137–149.

Fudenberg, D., and E. Maskin. 1986. "Folk Theorems for Repeated Games with Discounting or with Incomplete Information." *Econometrica* 54(3): 533–554.

Fuerst, T. S. 1985. "Monetary and Financial Interactions in the Business Cycle." *Journal of Money, Credit, and Banking* 27(4): 1321–1338.

———. 1992. "Liquidity, Loanable Funds, and Real Activity." *Journal of Monetary Economics* 29(1): 3–24.

Fuhrer, J. C. 1994a. "A Semi-Classical Model of Price Level Adjustment: A Comment." *Carnegie-Rochester Conference Series on Public Policy* 41 (Dec.): 285–294.

———. 1994b. "Optimal Monetary Policy and the Sacrifice Ratio." In *Goals, Guidelines, and Constraints Facing Monetary Policymakers*, ed. J. C. Fuhrer, 43–69. Federal Reserve Bank of Boston.

———. 1996. "Monetary Policy Shifts and Long-Term Interest Rates." *Quarterly Journal of Economics* 111(4): 1183–1209.

———. 1997a. "Inflation/Output Variance Trade-offs and Optimal Monetary Policy." *Journal of Money, Credit, and Banking* 29(2): 214–234.

———. 1997b. "The (Un)importance of Forward-Looking Behavior in Price Specifications." *Journal of Money, Credit, and Banking* 29(3): 338–350.

———. 1997c. "Towards a Compact, Empirically Verified Rational Expectations Model for Monetary Policy Analysis." *Carnegie-Rochester Conference Series on Public Policy* 47 (Dec.): 197–230.

Fuhrer, J. C., and G. R. Moore. 1995a. "Inflation Persistence." *Quarterly Journal of Economics* 110(1): 127–159.

———. 1995b. "Monetary Policy Trade-offs and the Correlation between Nominal Interest Rates and Real Output." *American Economic Review* 85(1): 219–239.

Furfine, C. H. 2000. "Interbank Payments and the Daily Federal Funds Rate." *Journal of Monetary Economics* 46(2): 535–553.

Furfine, C. H., and J. Stehem. 1998. "Analyzing Alternative Intraday Credit Policies in Real-Time Gross Settlement Systems." *Journal of Money, Credit, and Banking* 30(4): 832–848.

Galí, J. 1992. "How Well Does the IS-LM Model Fit the Postwar U.S. Data?" *Quarterly Journal of Economics* 107(2): 709–738.

———. 2002. "New Perspectives on Monetary Policy, Inflation, and the Business Cycle." NBER Working Paper 8767.

———. 2008. *Monetary Policy, Inflation, and the Business Cycle: An Introduction to the New Keynesian Framework*. Princeton, N.J.: Princeton University Press.

Galí, J., and M. Gertler. 1999. "Inflation Dynamics: A Structural Econometric Analysis." *Journal of Monetary Economics* 44(2): 195–222.

———. 2007. "Macroeconomic Modeling for Monetary Policy Evaluation." *Journal of Economic Perspectives* 21(4): 25–46.

Galí, J., M. Gertler, and J. D. López-Salido. 2001. "European Inflation Dynamics." *European Economic Review* 45(7): 1237–1270.

———. 2002. "Markups, Gaps, and the Welfare Costs of Business Fluctuations." NBER Working Paper 8850.

Gallmeyer, M. F., B. Hollifield, and S. E. Zin. 2005. "Taylor Rules, McCallum Rules, and the Term Structure of Interest Rates." *Journal of Monetary Economics* 52: 921–950.

Garber, P. M., and L.E.O. Svensson. 1995. "The Operation and Collapse of Fixed Exchange Rate Systems." In *Handbook of International Economics*, ed. G. M. Grossman and K. Rogoff, 1865–1911. Amsterdam: North-Holland.

Garcìa de Paso, J. I. 1993. "Monetary Policy with Private Information: A Role for Monetary Targets." Instituto Complutense de Analisis Economico Working Paper 9315.

———. 1994. "A Model of Appointing Governors to the Central Bank." Instituto Complutense de Analisis Economico Working Paper 9416.

Garfinkel, M., and S. Oh. 1993. "Strategic Discipline in Monetary Policy with Private Information: Optimal Targeting Horizons." *American Economic Review* 83(1): 99–117.

Geraats, P. M. 2002. "Central Bank Transparency." *Economic Journal* 112: 532–565.

Gerali, A., and F. Lippi. 2003. "Optimal Control and Filtering in Linear Forward-Looking Economies: A Toolkit." CEPR Discussion Paper 3706.

Gertler, M. 1988. "Financial Structure and Aggregate Activity: An Overview." *Journal of Money, Credit, and Banking* 20(3): 559–588.

Gertler, M., and S. Gilchrist. 1993. "The Role of Credit Market Imperfections in the Monetary Transmission Mechanism: Arguments and Evidence." *Scandinavian Journal of Economics* 95(1): 43–64.

———. 1994. "Monetary Policy, Business Cycles and the Behavior of Small Manufacturing Firms." *Quarterly Journal of Economics* 109(2): 309–340.

Gertler, M., S. Gilchrist, and F. M. Natalucci. 2007. "External Constraints on Monetary Policy and the Financial Accelerator." *Journal of Money, Credit, and Banking* 39(2–3): 295–330.

Gertler, M., and J. Leahy. 2008. "A Phillips Curve with an Ss Foundation." *Journal of Political Economy* 116(3): 533–572.

Geweke, J. 1986. "The Superneutrality of Money in the United States: An Interpretation of the Evidence." *Econometrica* 54(1): 1–22.

Giavazzi, F., and M. Pagano. 1988. "The Advantage of Tying One's Hands: EMS Discipline and Central Bank Credibility." *European Economic Review* 32: 1055–1082.

Gillman, M. 1995. "Comparing Partial and General Equilibrium Estimates of the Welfare Costs of Inflation." *Contemporary Economic Policy* 13(4): 60–71.

Goldfeld, S. M. 1976. "The Case of the Missing Money." *Brookings Papers on Economic Activity*, no. 3, 683–730.

Goldfeld, S. M., and D. E. Sichel. 1990. "The Demand for Money." In *Handbook of Monetary Economics*, ed. B. Friedman and F. Hahn. Vol. 1, 299–356. Amsterdam: North-Holland.

Golosov, M., and R. E. Lucas Jr. 2007. "Menu Costs and the Phillips Curve." *Journal of Political Economy* 115(2): 171–199.

Gomme, P. 1993. "Money and Growth Revisited: Measuring the Costs of Inflation in an Endogenous Growth Model." *Journal of Monetary Economics* 32(1): 51–77.

Goodfriend, M. 1983. "Discount Window Borrowing, Monetary Policy, and the Post–October 6, 1979 Federal Reserve Operating Procedure." *Journal of Monetary Economics* 12(3): 343–356.

———. 1987. "Interest-Rate Smoothing and Price Level Trend-Stationarity." *Journal of Monetary Economics* 19(3): 335–348.

———. 1991. "Interest Rate Policy and the Conduct of Monetary Policy." *Carnegie-Rochester Conference Series on Public Policy* 34 (Spring): 7–30.

———. 1993. "Interest Rate Policy and the Inflation Scare Problem, 1979–1992." Federal Reserve Bank of Richmond *Economic Quarterly* 79(1): 1–24.

———. 2000. "Overcoming the Zero Bound on Interest Rate Policy." *Journal of Money, Credit, and Banking* 32(4): 1007–1035.

———. 2002. "Interest on Reserves and Monetary Policy." Federal Reserve Bank of New York *Economic Policy Review* 8(1).

Goodfriend, M., and R. G. King. 1998. "The New Neoclassical Synthesis and the Role of Monetary Policy." In *NBER Macroeconomics Annual 1997*, 231–283. Cambridge, Mass.: MIT Press.

———. 2001. "The Case for Price Stability." NBER Working Paper 8423.

Goodfriend, M., and D. Small, eds. 1993. *Operating Procedures and the Conduct of Monetary Policy: Conference Proceedings*. Federal Reserve System.

Goodhart, C.A.E., and J. Viñals. 1994. "Strategy and Tactics of Monetary Policy: Examples from Europe and the Antipodes." In *Goals, Guidelines, and Constraints Facing Monetary Policymakers*, ed. J. C. Fuhrer, 139–187. Federal Reserve Bank of Boston.

Gordon, D. B., and E. M. Leeper. 1994. "The Dynamic Impacts of Monetary Policy: An Exercise in Tentative Identification." *Journal of Political Economy* 102(6): 1228–1247.

Gordon, R. J. 1982. "Why Stopping Inflation May Be Costly: Evidence from Fourteen Historical Episodes." In *Inflation: Causes and Effects*, ed. R. E. Hall, 11–40. Chicago: University of Chicago Press.

Gordon, R. J., and S. King. 1982. "The Output Costs of Disinflation in Traditional and Vector Autoregressive Models." *Brookings Papers on Economic Activity*, no. 1, 205–242.

Gouvea, S., A. Minella, R. Santos, and N. Souza-Sobrinho. 2008. "Samba: Stochastic Analytical Model with a Bayesian Approach." Central Bank of Brazil.

Grandmont, J., and Y. Younes. 1972. "On the Role of Money and the Existence of a Monetary Equilibrium." *Review of Economic Studies* 39: 355–372.

Gray, J. A. 1978. "On Indexation and Contract Length." *Journal of Political Economy* 86(1): 1–18.

Grier, K. B., and H. E. Neiman. 1987. "Deficits, Politics and Money Growth." *Economic Inquiry* 25(2): 201–214.

Grilli, V., D. Masciandaro, and G. Tabellini. 1991. "Political and Monetary Institutions and Public Financial Policies in the Industrial Countries." *Economic Policy* 6(2): 341–392.

Grossman, S., and L. Weiss. 1983. "A Transactions-Based Model of the Monetary Transmission Mechanism." *American Economic Review* 73(5): 871–880.

Guerrieri, L. 2000. "Staggered Wage and Price Setting in General Equilibrium." Stanford University.

Guidotti, P. E., and C. A. Végh. 1993. "The Optimal Inflation Tax When Money Reduces Transactions Costs: A Reconsideration." *Journal of Monetary Economics* 31(2): 189–205.

Guthrie, G., and J. Wright. 2000. "Open Mouth Operations." *Journal of Monetary Economics* 46(2): 489–516.

Hahn, F. H. 1965. "On Some Problems of Proving the Existence of an Equilibrium in a Monetary Economy." In *The Theory of Interest Rates*, ed. F. H. Hahn and F.P.R. Brechling, 126–135. London: Macmillan.

Hakkio, C., and M. Rush. 1991. "Is the Budget Deficit Too Large?" *Economic Inquiry* 29(3): 429–445.

Haldane, A. G., ed. 1995. *Targeting Inflation: A Conference of Central Banks on the Use of Inflation Targets*. Bank of England.

Haldane, A. G. 1997. "Designing Inflation Targets." In *Monetary Policy and Inflation Targeting*, ed. P. Lowe, 76–112. Reserve Bank of Australia.

Hall, R. E., and N. G. Mankiw. 1994. "Nominal Income Targeting." In *Monetary Policy*, ed. N. G. Mankiw, 71–92. Chicago: University of Chicago Press.

Hall, R. E., and J. B. Taylor. 1997. *Macroeconomics*. 5th ed. New York: Norton.

Hamada, K. 1976. "A Strategic Analysis of Monetary Interdependence." *Journal of Political Economy* 84(4): 677–700.

Hamilton, J. 1994. *Time Series Analysis.* Princeton, N.J.: Princeton University Press.

———. 1996. "The Daily Market for Federal Funds." *Journal of Political Economy* 104(1): 26–56.

Hamilton, J., and M. Flavin. 1986. "On the Limitations of Government Borrowing: A Framework for Empirical Testing." *American Economic Review* 76(4): 808–819.

Hansen, G. D., and E. C. Prescott. 1994. "Recursive Methods for Computing Equilibria of Business Cycle Models." In *Frontiers of Business Cycle Research,* ed. T. F. Cooley, 39–64. Princeton, N.J.: Princeton University Press.

Hartley, P. 1988. "The Liquidity Services of Money." *International Economic Review* 29(1): 1–24.

Haubrich, J. G., and R. G. King. 1991. "Sticky Prices, Money, and Business Fluctuations." *Journal of Money, Credit, and Banking* 23(2): 243–259.

Havrilesky, T., and J. Gildea. 1991. "The Policy Preferences of FOMC Members as Revealed by Dissenting Votes." *Journal of Money, Credit, and Banking* 23(1): 130–138.

———. 1992. "Reliable and Unreliable Partisan Appointees to the Board of Governors." *Public Choice* 73 (June): 397–417.

———. 1995. "The Biases of Federal Reserve Bank Presidents." *Economic Inquiry* 33(2): 274–284.

Heller, D., and Y. Lengwiler. 2003. "Payment Obligations, Reserve Requirements, and the Demand for Central Bank Balances." *Journal of Monetary Economics* 50(2): 419–432.

Herrendorf, B. 1995. "Why Inflation Targets May Partly Substitute for Explicit Precommitment."

———. 1997. "Time-Consistent Collection of Optimal Seigniorage: A Unifying Framework." *Journal of Economic Surveys* 11(1): 1–46.

———. 1998. "Inflation Targeting as a Way of Precommitment." *Oxford Economic Papers* 50(3): 431–448.

———. 1999. "Transparency, Reputation, and Credibility under Floating and Pegged Exchange Rates." *Journal of International Economics* 49(1): 31–50.

Herrendorf, B., and B. Lockwood. 1997. "Rogoff's 'Conservative' Central Banker Restored." *Journal of Money, Credit, and Banking* 29(4): 476–495.

Herrendorf, B., and M.J.M. Neumann. 2003. "The Political Economy of Inflation, Labor Market Distortions, and Central Bank Independence." *Economic Journal* 113(484): 43–64.

Hobijn, B., F. Ravenna, and A. Tambalotti. 2006. "Menu Costs at Work: Restaurant Prices and the Introduction of the Euro." *Quarterly Journal of Economics* 121(3): 1103–1131.

Hoffman, D. L., and R. H. Rasche. 1991. "Long-Run Income and Interest Elasticities of Money Demand in the United States." *Review of Economics and Statistics* 73: 665–674.

Hoffman, D. L., R. H. Rasche, and M. A. Tieslau. 1995. "The Stability of Long-Run Money Demand in Five Industrial Countries." *Journal of Monetary Economics* 35(2): 317–339.

Holman, J. A. 1998. "GMM Estimation of a Money-in-the-Utility-Function Model: The Implications of Functional Forms." *Journal of Money, Credit, and Banking* 30(4): 679–698.

Hoover, K. D. 1995. "Resolving the Liquidity Effect: Commentary." Federal Reserve Bank of St. Louis *Review* 77(3): 26–32.

Hoover, K. D., J. Hartley, and K. Salyer, eds. 1998. *Real Business Cycles: A Reader.* New York: Routledge.

Hoover, K. D., and S. J. Perez. 1994. "Post Hoc Ergo Propter Once More: An Evaluation of 'Does Monetary Policy Matter?' in the Spirit of James Tobin." *Journal of Monetary Economics* 34(1): 89–99.

Hosios, A. J. 1990. "On the Efficiency of Matching and Related Models of Search and Unemployment." *Review of Economic Studies* 57(2): 279–298.

Huang, K.X.D., and Z. Liu. 2002. "Staggered Price-Setting, Staggered Wage-Setting, and Business Cycle Persistence." *Journal of Monetary Economics* 49(2): 405–433.

Hubbard, R. G. 1995. "Is There a Credit Channel for Monetary Policy?" *Federal Reserve Bank of St. Louis Review* 77(3): 63–77.

Hutchison, M. M., and C. E. Walsh. 1992. "Empirical Evidence on the Insulation Properties of Fixed and Flexible Exchange Rates: The Japanese Experience." *Journal of International Economics* 32(3/4): 241–263.

——. 1998. "The Output-Inflation Trade-off and Central Bank Reform: Evidence from New Zealand." *Economic Journal* 108: 703–725.

Imrohoroğlu, A. 1992. "The Welfare Costs of Inflation under Imperfect Insurance." *Journal of Economic Dynamics and Control* 16(1): 79–91.

Imrohoroğlu, A., and E. C. Prescott. 1991. "Seigniorage as a Tax: A Quantitative Evaluation." *Journal of Money, Credit, and Banking* 23(3): 462–475.

Ireland, P. N. 1996. "The Role of Countercyclical Monetary Policy." *Journal of Political Economy* 104(4): 704–723.

——. 1997a. "A Small, Structural, Quarterly Model for Monetary Policy Evaluation." *Carnegie-Rochester Conference Series on Public Policy* 47 (Dec.): 83–108.

——. 1997b. "Sustainable Monetary Policies." *Journal of Economic Dynamics and Control* 22(1): 87–108.

——. 1999. "Does the Time-Inconsistency Problem Explain the Behavior of Inflation in the United States?" *Journal of Monetary Economics* 44: 279–292.

——. 2001a. "Sticky-Price Models of the Business Cycle: Specification and Stability." *Journal of Monetary Economics* 47(1): 3–18.

——. 2001b. "The Real Balance Effect." NBER Working Paper 8316.

——. 2004. "Money's Role in the Monetary Business Cycle." *Journal of Money, Credit, and Banking* 36(6): 969–983.

——. 2009. "On the Welfare Cost of Inflation and the Recent Behavior of Money Demand." *American Economic Review* 99(3): 1040–1052.

Jaffee, D., and T. Russell. 1976. "Imperfect Information, Uncertainty, and Credit Rationing." *Quarterly Journal of Economics* 90(4): 651–666.

Jaffee, D., and J. E. Stiglitz. 1990. "Credit Rationing." In *Handbook of Monetary Economics*, ed. B. Friedman and F. Hahn. Vol. 2, 837–888. Amsterdam: North-Holland.

Jeanne, O. 1998. "Generating Real Persistent Effects of Monetary Shocks: How Much Nominal Rigidity Do We Really Need?" *European Economic Review* 42(6): 1009–1032.

Jensen, C., and B. T. McCallum. 2002. "The Nonoptimality of Proposed Monetary Policy Rules under Timeless-Perspective Commitment." NBER Working Paper 8882.

——. 2008. "Optimal Continuation versus the Timeless Perspective in Monetary Policy."

Jensen, H. 1997. "Credibility of Optimal Monetary Delegation." *American Economic Review* 87(5): 911–920.

——. 2000. "Optimal Degrees of Transparency in Monetary Policymaking." University of Copenhagen. ⟨http://papers.ssrn.com/sol3/papers.cfm?abstract_id=243028⟩.

——. 2002. "Targeting Nominal Income Growth or Inflation?" *American Economic Review* 92(4): 928–956.

Johnson, D. R., and P. L. Siklos. 1994. "Empirical Evidence on the Independence of Central Banks." Wilfrid Laurier University, Waterloo, Ontario, Canada.

Joines, D. H. 1985. "Deficits and Money Growth in the United States 1872–1983." *Journal of Monetary Economics* 16(3): 329–351.

Jones, R. A. 1976. "The Origin and Development of Media of Exchange." *Journal of Political Economy* 84(4): 757–775.

Jonsson, G. 1995. "Institutions and Incentives in Monetary and Fiscal Policy." Ph.D. diss., Institute for International Economic Studies, Stockholm University. Monograph Series No. 28.

————. 1997. "Monetary Politics and Unemployment Persistence." *Journal of Monetary Economics* 39: 303–325.

Jovanovic, B. 1982. "Inflation and Welfare in the Steady-State." *Journal of Political Economy* 90(3): 561–577.

Judd, J. P., and B. Motley. 1991. "Nominal Feedback Rules for Monetary Policy." Federal Reserve Bank of San Francisco *Economic Review* (Summer), 3–17.

————. 1992. "Controlling Inflation with an Interest Rate Instrument." Federal Reserve Bank of San Francisco *Economic Review* (Summer), 3–22.

Judd, J. P., and G. D. Rudebusch. 1997. "A Tale of Three Chairmen." Federal Reserve Bank of San Francisco.

Judd, J. P., and J. Scadding. 1982. "The Search for a Stable Money Demand Function." *Journal of Economic Literature* 20(3): 993–1023.

Judd, J. P., and B. Trehan. 1989. "Unemployment Rate Dynamics: Aggregate Demand and Supply Interactions." Federal Reserve Bank of San Francisco *Economic Review* (Fall), 20–37.

————. 1995. "The Cyclical Behavior of Prices: Interpreting the Evidence." *Journal of Money, Credit, and Banking* 27: 789–797.

Kahn, M., S. Kandel, and O. Sarig. 2002. "Real and Nominal Effects of Central Bank Monetary Policy." *Journal of Monetary Economics* 49(8): 1493–1519.

Kareken, J. H., T. Muench, and N. Wallace. 1973. "Optimal Open Market Strategies: The Use of Information Variables." *American Economic Review* 63(1): 156–172.

Kasa, K., and H. Popper. 1995. "Monetary Policy in Japan: A Structural VAR Analysis." Federal Reserve Bank of San Francisco. WP-PB95-12.

Kashyap, A. K., O. A. Lamont, and J. C. Stein. 1994. "Credit Conditions and the Cyclical Behavior of Inventories." *Quarterly Journal of Economics* 109(3): 565–592.

Kashyap, A. K., and J. C. Stein. 1994. "Monetary Policy and Bank Lending." In *Monetary Policy*, ed. N. G. Mankiw, 221–256. Chicago: University of Chicago Press.

Kashyap, A. K., J. C. Stein, and D. W. Wilcox. 1993. "Monetary Policy and Credit Conditions: Evidence from the Composition of External Finance." *American Economic Review* 83(1): 78–98.

Kasman, B. 1993. "A Comparison of Monetary Policy Operating Procedures in Six Industrial Countries." In *Operating Procedures and the Conduct of Monetary Policy: Conference Proceedings*, ed. M. Goodfriend and D. Small. Federal Reserve System.

Keeton, W. 1979. *Equilibrium Credit Rationing*. New York: Garland Press.

Kerr, W., and R. King. 1996. "Limits on Interest Rate Rules in the IS Model." Federal Reserve Bank of Richmond *Economic Quarterly* 82(2): 47–75.

Khan, A., R. G. King, and A. L. Wolman. 2000. "Optimal Monetary Policy." Federal Reserve Bank of Philadelphia.

Khan, H., and Z. Zu. 2006. "Estimates of the Sticky-Information Phillips Curve for the United States." *Journal of Money, Credit, and Banking* 38(1): 195–207.

Khoury, S. 1990. "The Federal Reserve Reaction Function." In *The Political Economy of American Monetary Policy*, ed. T. Mayer, 27–49. Cambridge: Cambridge University Press.

Kiley, M. T. 1996. "The Lead of Output over Inflation in Sticky Price Models." Federal Reserve Board, Finance and Economics Discussion Series 96-33.

————. 2000. "Endogenous Price Stickiness and Business Cycle Persistence." *Journal of Money, Credit, and Banking* 32(1): 28–53.

————. 2002. "Partial Adjustment and Staggered Price Setting." *Journal of Money, Credit, and Banking* 34(2): 283–298.

————. 2007a. "A Quantitative Comparison of Sticky-Price and Sticky-Information Models of Price Setting." *Journal of Money, Credit, and Banking* 39 (1s): 101–125.

———. 2007b. "Is Moderate-to-High Inflation Inherently Unstable?" *International Journal of Central Banking* 3(2): 173–201.

Kimbrough, K. P. 1986a. "Inflation, Employment, and Welfare in the Presence of Transaction Costs." *Journal of Money, Credit, and Banking* 28(2): 127–140.

———. 1986b. "The Optimum Quantity of Money Rule in the Theory of Public Finance." *Journal of Monetary Economics* 18(3): 277–284.

King, R. G., and M. Goodfriend. 2001. "The Case for Price Stability." Federal Reserve Bank of Richmond. WP-01-2.

King, R. G., and C. I. Plosser. 1984. "Money, Credit, and Prices in a Real Business Cycle." *American Economic Review* 74(3): 363–380.

———. 1985. "Money, Deficits, and Inflation." *Carnegie-Rochester Conference Series on Public Policy* 22 (Spring): 147–196.

King, R. G., C. I. Plosser, and S. Rebelo. 1988. "Production, Growth, and Business Cycles. I. The Basic Neoclassical Model." *Journal of Monetary Economics* 21(2/3): 195–232.

King, R. G., and M. W. Watson. 1996. "Money, Prices, Interest Rates, and the Business Cycle." *Review of Economics and Statistics* 78(1): 35–53.

———. 1997. "Testing Long-Run Neutrality." Federal Reserve Bank of Richmond *Economic Quarterly* 83(3): 69–101.

———. 1998. "The Solution of Singular Linear Difference Systems under Rational Expectations." *International Economic Review* 39(4): 1015–1026.

King, R. G., and A. L. Wolman. 1996. "Inflation Targeting in a St. Louis Model of the 21st Century." Federal Reserve of St. Louis *Review* 78(3): 83–107.

———. 1999. "State-Dependent Pricing and the General Equilibrium Dynamics of Money and Output." *Quarterly Journal of Economics* 114(2): 655–690.

King, S. R. 1986. "Monetary Transmission: Through Bank Loans or Bank Liabilities?" *Journal of Money, Credit, and Banking* 18(3): 290–303.

Kiyotaki, N., and J. Moore. 1997. "Credit Cycles." *Journal of Political Economy* 105(2): 211–248.

Kiyotaki, N., and R. Wright. 1989. "On Money as a Medium of Exchange." *Journal of Political Economy* 97(4): 927–954.

———. 1993. "A Search-Theoretic Approach to Monetary Economics." *American Economic Review* 83(1): 63–77.

Klein, M., and M.J.M. Neumann. 1990. "Seigniorage: What Is It and Who Gets It?" *Weltwirtschaftliches Archiv* 126(2): 205–221.

Klenow, P. J., and O. Kryvtsov. 2008. "State-Dependent or Time-Dependent Pricing: Does it Matter for Recent U.S. Inflation?" *Quarterly Journal of Economics* 123(3): 863–904.

Klenow, P., and J. Willis. 2007. "Sticky Information and Sticky Prices." *Journal of Monetary Economics* 54: 79–99.

Knell, M., and H. Stix. 2005. "The Income Elasticity of Money Demand: A Meta-Analysis of Empirical Results." *Journal of Economic Surveys* 19(3): 513–533.

Kocherlakota, N. R. 2000. "Creating Business Cycles through Credit Constraints." Federal Reserve Bank of Minneapolis *Quarterly Review*, 2–10.

Kocherlakota, N. R., and C. Phelan. 1999. "Explaining the Fiscal Theory of the Price Level." Federal Reserve Bank of Minneapolis *Quarterly Review* 23 (Fall): 14–23.

Kollman, R. 2001. "The Exchange Rate in a Dynamic-Optimizing Business Cycle Model with Nominal Rigidities." *Journal of International Economics* 55: 243–262.

Kormendi, R. C., and P. G. Meguire. 1984. "Cross-Regime Evidence of Macroeconomic Rationality." *Journal of Political Economy* 92(5): 875–908.

———. 1985. "Macroeconomic Determinants of Growth: Cross-Country Evidence." *Journal of Monetary Economics* 16(2): 141–163.

Krause, M. U., D. López-Salido, and T. A. Lubik. 2007. "Do Search Frictions Matter for Inflation Dynamics?" Kiel Working Paper 1353.

Kreps, D., and R. Wilson. 1982. "Reputation and Imperfect Information." *Journal of Economic Theory* 27(2): 253–279.

Krugman, P. R. 1979. "A Model of Balance of Payments Crises." *Journal of Money, Credit, and Banking* 11(3): 311–325.

———. 1991. "Target Zones and Exchange Rate Dynamics." *Quarterly Journal of Economics* 106(3): 669–682.

Kurozumi, T. 2008. "Optimal Sustainable Monetary Policy." *Journal of Monetary Economics* 55: 1277–1289.

Kurozumi, T., and W. Van Zandwedge. 2008. "Labor Market Search and Interest Rate Policy." Federal Reserve Bank of Kansas City. WP-08-03.

Kydland, F. E., and E. C. Prescott. 1977. "Rules Rather Than Discretion: The Inconsistency of Optimal Plans." *Journal of Political Economy* 85(3): 473–491.

———. 1982. "Time to Build and Aggregate Fluctuations." *Econometrica* 50(6): 1345–1370.

———. 1990. "Business Cycles: Real Facts and a Monetary Myth." Federal Reserve Bank of Minneapolis *Quarterly Review* 14 (Spring): 3–18.

Lacker, J. M. 1988. "Inside Money and Real Output." *Economic Letters* 28(1): 9–14.

Lagos, R., and G. Rocheteau. 2005. "Inflation, Output, and Welfare." *International Economic Review* 46(2): 495–522.

Lagos, R., and R. Wright. 2005. "A Unified Framework for Monetary Theory and Policy Analysis." *Journal of Political Economy* 113(3): 463–484.

Laidler, D.E.W. 1985. *The Demand for Money: Theories, Evidence, and Problems*. 3d ed. New York: Harper and Row.

Lancaster, K. J. 1966. "A New Approach to Consumer Theory." *Journal of Political Economy* 74(2): 132–157.

Lane, P. 2001. "The New Open Economy Macroeconomics: A Survey." *Journal of International Economics* 54(2): 235–266.

Lansing, K. J. 2002. "Real-Time Estimation of Trend Output and the Illusion of Interest Rate Smoothing." Federal Reserve Bank of San Francisco *Economic Review*, 17–34. ⟨http://ssrn.com/abstract =298870⟩.

Lansing, K. J., and B. Trehan. 2001. "Forward-Looking Behavior and the Optimality of the Taylor Rule." Federal Reserve Bank of San Francisco. WP-2001-03.

Laubach, T., and A. S. Posen. 1997. "Disciplined Discretion: The German and Swiss Monetary Targeting Frameworks in Operation." Federal Reserve Bank of New York Research Paper 9707.

Leeper, E. M. 1991. "Equilibria under 'Active' and 'Passive' Monetary and Fiscal Policies." *Journal of Monetary Economics* 27(1): 129–147.

———. 1993. "Has the Romers' Narrative Approach Identified Monetary Policy Shocks?" Federal Reserve Bank of Atlanta. WP-93-1.

———. 1997. "Narrative and VAR Approaches to Monetary Policy: Common Identification Problems." *Journal of Monetary Economics* 40(3): 641–657.

Leeper, E. M., and D. B. Gordon. 1992. "In Search of the Liquidity Effect." *Journal of Monetary Economics* 29(3): 341–369.

Leeper, E. M., C. A. Sims, and T. Zha. 1996. "What Does Monetary Policy Do?" *Brookings Papers on Economic Activity*, no. 2, 1–63.

Leiderman, L., and L.E.O. Svensson, eds. 1995. *Inflation Targets*. London: CEPR.

LeRoy, S. 1984a. "Nominal Prices and Interest Rates in General Equilibrium: Money Shocks." *Journal of Business* 57(2): 177–195.

———. 1984b. "Nominal Prices and Interest Rates in General Equilibrium: Endowment Shocks." *Journal of Business* 57(2): 197–213.

Levhari, D., and D. Patinkin. 1968. "The Role of Money in a Simple Growth Model." *American Economic Review* 58(4): 713–753.

Levin, A., A. Onatski, J. C. Williams, and N. Williams. 2006. "Monetary Policy under Uncertainty in Micro-Founded Macroeconometric Models." In *NBER Macroeconomics Annual 2005*, 229–287.

Levin, A., J. Rogers, and B. Tryon. 1997. "A Guide to FRB/Global." Federal Reserve Board.

Levin, A., V. Wieland, and J. C. Williams. 1999. "Robustness of Simple Monetary Policy Rules under Model Uncertainty." In *Monetary Policy Rules*, ed. J. B. Taylor, 263–299. Chicago: University of Chicago Press.

Lindé, J. 2005. "Estimating New-Keynesian Phillips Curves: A Full Information Maximum Likelihood Approach." *Journal of Monetary Economics* 52(6): 1135–1149.

Lippi, F. 1997. *Central Bank Independence and Credibility: Essays on the Delegation Arrangements for Monetary Policy*. Tinbergen Institute Research Series No. 146. Erasmus University, Rotterdam.

Litterman, R., and L. Weiss. 1985. "Money, Real Interest Rates, and Output: A Reinterpretation of the Postwar U.S. Data." *Econometrica* 53(1): 129–156.

Ljungquist, L., and T. Sargent. 2000. *Recursive Macroeconomics*. Cambridge, Mass.: MIT Press.

Llosa, G., and V. Tuesta. 2006. "E-stability of Monetary Policy When the Cost Channel Matters." Central Bank of Peru.

Lockwood, B. 1997. "State-Contingent Inflation Contracts and Unemployment Persistence." *Journal of Money, Credit, and Banking* 29(3): 286–299.

Lockwood, B., and A. Philippopoulos. 1994. "Insider Power, Employment Dynamics, and Multiple Inflation Equilibria." *Economica* 61(241): 59–77.

Lohmann, S. 1992. "Optimal Commitment in Monetary Policy: Credibility versus Flexibility." *American Economic Review* 82(1): 273–286.

Lowe, P., ed. 1997. *Monetary Policy and Inflation Targeting*. Reserve Bank of Australia.

Lubik, T., and F. Schorfheide. 2004. "Testing for Indeterminacy: An Application to U.S. Monetary Policy." *American Economic Review* 94(1): 190–217.

———. 2006. "A Bayesian Look at New Open Economy Macroeconomics." In *NBER Macroeconomics Annual 2005*, 313–366. Cambridge, Mass.: MIT Press.

———. 2007. "Do Central Banks Respond to Exchange Rates? A Structural Investigation." *Journal of Monetary Economics* 54(4): 1069–1087.

Lucas, R. E. Jr. 1972. "Expectations and the Neutrality of Money." *Journal of Economic Theory* 4(2): 103–124.

———. 1973. "Some International Evidence on Output-Inflation Tradeoffs." *American Economic Review* 63(3): 326–334.

———. 1976. "Econometric Policy Evaluation: A Critique." *Carnegie-Rochester Conference Series on Public Policy*, no. 1, 19–46.

———. 1980a. "Equilibrium in a Pure Currency Economy." In *Models of Monetary Economics*, ed. J. H. Karaken and N. Wallace, 131–145. Reserve Bank of Minneapolis.

———. 1980b. "Two Illustrations of the Quantity Theory of Money." *American Economic Review* 70(5): 1005–1014.

———. 1982. "Interest Rates and Currency Prices in a Two-Country World." *Journal of Monetary Economics* 10(3): 335–359.

———. 1988. "Money Demand in the United States: A Quantitative Review." *Carnegie-Rochester Conference Series on Public Policy* 29: 137–168.

———. 1990. "Liquidity and Interest Rates." *Journal of Economic Theory* 50(2): 237–264.

———. 1994. "The Welfare Costs of Inflation." CEPR Publication 394. Stanford University.

———. 1996. "Nobel Lecture: Monetary Neutrality." *Journal of Political Economy* 104(4): 661–682.

————. 2000. "Inflation and Welfare." *Econometrica* 68(2): 247–274.

Lucas, R. E. Jr., and N. Stokey. 1983. "Optimal Fiscal and Monetary Policy in an Economy without Capital." *Journal of Monetary Economics* 12(1): 55–93.

————. 1987. "Money and Interest in a Cash-in-Advance Economy." *Econometrica* 55(3): 491–514.

Lucas, R. E. Jr., N. Stokey, with E. C. Prescott. 1989. *Recursive Methods in Economic Dynamics*. Cambridge, Mass.: Harvard University Press.

Maddala, G. S. 1992. *Introduction to Econometrics*. 2d ed. New York: Macmillan.

Mankiw, N. G. 1985. "Small Menu Costs and Large Business Cycles: A Macroeconomic Model of Monopoly." *Quarterly Journal of Economics* 101(2): 529–537.

————. 1987. "The Optimal Collection of Seigniorage: Theory and Evidence." *Journal of Monetary Economics* 20(2): 327–341.

————. 1997. *Macroeconomics*. 3d ed. New York: Worth.

Mankiw, N. G., and J. A. Miron. 1986. "The Changing Behavior of the Term Structure of Interest Rates." *Quarterly Journal of Economics* 101(2): 211–228.

Mankiw, N. G., J. A. Miron, and D. N. Weil. 1987. "The Adjustment of Expectations to a Change in Regime: A Study of the Founding of the Federal Reserve." *American Economic Review* 77(3): 358–374.

————. 1994. "The Founding of the Fed and the Behavior of Interest Rates: What Can Be Learned from Small Samples?" *Journal of Monetary Economics* 34(3): 555–559.

Mankiw, N. G., and R. Reis. 2002. "Sticky Information versus Sticky Prices: A Proposal to Replace the New Keynesian Phillips Curve." *Quarterly Journal of Economics* 117(4): 1295–1328.

————. 2003. "Sticky Information: A Model of Monetary Non-neutrality and Structural Slumps." In *Knowledge, Information, and Expectations in Modern Macroeconomics*, ed. P. Aghion, R. Frydman, J. E. Stiglitz, and M. Woodford, 64–86. Princeton, N.J.: Princeton University Press.

————. 2006a. "Pervasive Stickiness." *American Economic Review* 96(2): 164–169.

————. 2006b. "Sticky Information in General Equilibrium." *Journal of the European Economic Association* 2(2/3): 603–613.

Mankiw, N. G., and L. H. Summers. 1986. "Money Demand and the Effects of Fiscal Policy." *Journal of Money, Credit, and Banking* 18(4): 415–429.

Marshall, D. A. 1993. "Comment on 'Search, Bargaining, Money, and Prices: Recent Results and Policy Implications.'" *Journal of Money, Credit, and Banking* 25(3): 577–581.

Maskin, E., and J. Tirole. 1988. "Models of Dynamic Oligopoly. I: Overview and Quality Competition with Large Fixed Costs." *Econometrica* 56(3): 549–569.

Mattey, J., and R. Meese. 1986. "Empirical Assessment of Present Value Relationships." *Econometric Review* 5(2): 171–233.

McCallum, B. T. 1983a. "On Nonuniqueness in Rational Expectations Models: An Attempt at Perspective." *Journal of Monetary Economics* 11(2): 139–168.

————. 1983b. "The Role of Overlapping Generations Models in Monetary Economics." *Carnegie-Rochester Conference Series on Public Policy* 18: 9–44.

————. 1984a. "A Linearized Version of Lucas's Neutrality Model." *Canadian Journal of Economics* 17(1): 138–145.

————. 1984b. "On Low-Frequency Estimates of Long-Run Relationships in Macroeconomics." *Journal of Monetary Economics* 14(1): 3–14.

————. 1986. "Some Issues Concerning Interest Rate Pegging, Price Level Determinacy, and the Real Bills Doctrine." *Journal of Monetary Economics* 17(1): 135–160.

————. 1988. "Robustness Properties of a Rule for Monetary Policy." *Carnegie-Rochester Conference Series on Public Policy* 29: 173–204.

————. 1989. *Monetary Economics: Theory and Policy*. New York: Macmillan.

————. 1990a. "Inflation: Theory and Evidence." In *Handbook of Monetary Economics*, ed. B. Friedman and F. Hahn. Vol. 2, 963–1012. Amsterdam: North-Holland.

———. 1990b. "Targets, Instruments, and Indicators of Monetary Policy." In *Monetary Policy for a Changing Financial Environment*, ed. W. S. Haraf and P. Cagan, 44–70. Washington, D.C.: AEI Press.

———. 1994a. "A Reconsideration of the Uncovered Interest Parity Relationship." *Journal of Monetary Economics* 33(1): 105–132.

———. 1994b. "Monetary Policy and the Term Structure of Interest Rates." NBER Working Paper 4938.

———. 1995. "Two Fallacies Concerning Central Bank Independence." *American Economic Review* 85(2): 207–211.

———. 1997a. "Critical Issues Concerning Central Bank Independence." *Journal of Monetary Economics* 39(1): 99–112.

———. 1997b. "Inflation Targeting in Canada, New Zealand, Sweden, the United Kingdom, and in General." In *Towards More Effective Monetary Policy*, ed. I. Kuroda, 211–241. London: Macmillan.

———. 1997c. "The Alleged Instability of Nominal Income Targeting." Reserve Bank of New Zealand Discussion Paper G97/6.

———. 1999a. "Analysis of the Monetary Transmission Mechanism: Methodological Issues." NBER Working Paper 7395.

———. 1999b. "Issues in the Design of Monetary Policy Rules." In *Handbook of Macroeconomics*, ed. J. B. Taylor and M. Woodford. Vol. 1C, 1483–1530. Amsterdam: North-Holland.

———. 1999c. "Recent Developments in the Analysis of Monetary Policy Rules." Federal Reserve Bank of St. Louis *Review* 81(6): 3–11.

———. 2000. "Theoretical Analysis Regarding a Zero Lower Bound on Nominal Interest Rates." *Journal of Money, Credit, and Banking* 32(4): 870–904.

———. 2001. "Indeterminacy, Bubbles, and the Fiscal Theory of Price Level Determination." *Journal of Monetary Economics* 47(1): 19–30.

McCallum, B. T., and M. S. Goodfriend. 1987. "Demand for Money: Theoretical Studies." In *The New Palgrave Dictionary of Economics*, ed. P. Newman, M. Milgate, and J. Eatwell, 775–781. Houndmills, U.K.: Palgrave Macmillan.

McCallum, B. T., and J. G. Hoehn. 1983. "Instrument Choice for Money Stock Control with Contemporaneous and Lagged Reserve Accounting: A Note." *Journal of Money, Credit, and Banking* 15(1): 96–101.

McCallum, B. T., and E. Nelson. 1999. "An Optimizing IS-LM Specification for Monetary Policy and Business Cycle Analysis." *Journal of Money, Credit, and Banking* 31(3): 296–316.

———. 2000a. "Monetary Policy for an Open Economy: An Alternative Framework with Optimizing Agents and Sticky Prices." *Oxford Review of Economic Policy* 16: 74–91.

———. 2000b. "Timeless Perspective vs. Discretionary Monetary Policy in Forward-Looking Models." NBER Working Paper 7915.

———. 2005. "Fiscal and Monetary Theories of the Price Level: The Irreconcilable Differences." *Oxford Review of Economic Policy* 21: 565–583.

McCandless, G. T. Jr., and W. E. Weber. 1995. "Some Monetary Facts." Federal Reserve Bank of Minneapolis *Quarterly Review* 19(3): 2–11.

McGough, B., G. D. Rudebusch, and J. C. Williams. 2005. "Using a Long-Term Interest Rate as the Monetary Policy Instrument." *Journal of Monetary Economics* 52(5): 855–879.

McKinnon, R., and K. Ohno. 1997. *Dollar and Yen: Resolving Economic Conflicts between the United States and Japan*. Cambridge, Mass.: MIT Press.

Meese, R. A., and K. Rogoff. 1983. "Empirical Exchange Rate Models of the Seventies: Do They Fit Out of Sample?" *Journal of International Economics* 14(1): 3–24.

Metzler, L. 1951. "Wealth, Saving, and the Rate of Interest." *Journal of Political Economy* 59(2): 93–116.

Meulendyke, A.-M. 1998. *U.S. Monetary Policy and Financial Markets*. Federal Reserve Bank of New York.

Minford, P. 1995. "Time-Inconsistency, Democracy, and Optimal Contingent Rules." *Oxford Economic Papers* 47(2): 195–210.

Mino, K., and S. Tsutsui. 1990. "Reputational Constraint and Signalling Effects in a Monetary Policy Game." *Oxford Economic Papers* 42(3): 603–619.

Mishkin, F. S. 1982. "Does Anticipated Policy Matter? An Econometric Investigation." *Journal of Political Economy* 90(1): 22–51.

———. 1992. "Is the Fisher Effect for Real? A Reexamination of the Relationship between Inflation and Interest Rates." *Journal of Monetary Economics* 30(2): 195–215.

Mishkin, F. S., and A. S. Posen. 1997. "Inflation Targeting: Lessons from Four Countries." Federal Reserve Bank of New York *Economic Policy Review* 3(3): 9–110.

Mishkin, F. S., and K. Schmidt-Hebbel. 2002. "One Decade of Inflation Targeting in the World: What Do We Know and What Do We Need to Know?" In *Inflation Targeting: Design, Performance, Challenges*, ed. N. Loayza and R. Soto, 171–219. Banco Central de Chile.

———. 2007. "Does Inflation Targeting Make a Difference?" In *Monetary Policy under Inflation Targeting*, ed. F. S. Mishkin and K. Schmidt-Hebbel, 291–372. Banco Central de Chile.

Mixon, F. G. Jr., and M. T. Gibson. 2002. "The Timing of Partisan and Nonpartisan Appointments to the Central Bank: Some New Evidence." *Journal of Money, Credit, and Banking* 34(2): 361–375.

Modigliani, F. 1963. "The Monetary Mechanism and Its Interaction with Real Phenomena." *Review of Economics and Statistics* 45(1): 79–107.

Modigliani, F., and A. Ando. 1976. "Impacts of Fiscal Actions on Aggregate Income and the Monetarist Controversy: Theory and Evidence." In *Monetarism*, ed. J. L. Stein, 17–42. Amsterdam: North-Holland.

Modigliani, F., R. Rasche, and J. P. Cooper. 1970. "Central Bank Policy, the Money Supply, and the Short-Term Rate of Interest." *Journal of Money, Credit, and Banking* 2(2): 166–218.

Monacelli, T. 2005. "Monetary Policy in a Low Pass-Through Environment." *Journal of Money, Credit, and Banking* 37(6): 1047–1066.

———. 2008. "Optimal Monetary Policy with Collateralized Household Debt and Borrowing Constraints." In *Asset Prices and Monetary Policy*, ed. J. Y. Campbell, 103–141. Chicago: University of Chicago Press.

Monnet, C., and W. Weber. 2001. "Money and Interest Rates." Federal Reserve Bank of Minneapolis *Quarterly Review* 25(4): 2–13.

Morton, J., and P. Wood. 1993. "Interest Rate Operating Procedures of Foreign Central Banks." In *Operating Procedures and the Conduct of Monetary Policy: Conference Proceedings*, ed. M. Goodfriend and D. Small. Federal Reserve System.

Motley, B. 1994. "Growth and Inflation: A Cross-Country Study." Paper prepared for the CEPR/SF Federal Reserve Conference on Monetary Policy in a Low-Inflation Environment.

Mulligan, C. B., and X. Sala-i-Martin. 1997. "The Optimum Quantity of Money: Theory and Evidence." *Journal of Money, Credit, and Banking* 24(4): 687–715.

———. 2000. "Extensive Margins and the Demand for Money at Low Interest Rates." *Journal of Political Economy* 108(5): 961–991.

Muscatelli, A. 1998. "Optimal Inflation Contracts and Inflation Targets with Uncertain Central Bank Preferences: Accountability through Independence." *Economic Journal* 108: 529–542.

———. 1999. "Delegation versus Optimal Inflation Contracts: Do We Really Need Conservative Central Bankers?" *Economica* 66: 241–254.

Nakamura, E., and J. Steinsson. 2008a. "Five Facts about Prices: An Evaluation of Menu Cost Models." *Quarterly Journal of Economics* 123(4): 1415–1464.

———. 2008b. "Monetary Non-neutrality in a Multi-Sector Menu Cost Model." NBER Working Paper 14001.

Neiss, K. S., and E. Nelson. 2001. "The Real Interest Rate Gap as an Inflation Indicator." Bank of England Working Paper 130.

———. 2002. "Inflation Dynamics, Marginal Costs, and the Output Gap: Evidence from Three Countries." Bank of England.

Nelson, E. 1998. "Sluggish Inflation and Optimizing Models of the Business Cycle." *Journal of Monetary Economics* 42(2): 303–322.

Nessén, M., and D. Vestin. 2000. "Average Inflation Targeting." Sveriges Riksbank Working Paper 119.

Niehans, J. 1978. *The Theory of Money*. Baltimore: Johns Hopkins University Press.

Niepelt, D. 2004. "The Fiscal Myth of the Price Level." *Quarterly Journal of Economics* 119(1): 277–300.

Nolan, C., and E. Schaling. 1996. "Monetary Policy Uncertainty and Central Bank Accountability." Bank Of England.

Obstfeld, M., and K. Rogoff. 1983. "Speculative Hyperinflations in Maximizing Models: Can We Rule Them Out?" *Journal of Political Economy* 91(4): 675–687.

———. 1986. "Ruling Out Divergent Speculative Bubbles." *Journal of Monetary Economics* 17(3): 349–362.

———. 1995. "Exchange Rate Dynamics Redux." *Journal of Political Economy* 103(3): 624–660.

———. 1996. *Foundations of International Macroeconomics*. Cambridge, Mass.: MIT Press.

———. 2000. "New Directions in Stochastic Open Economy Models." *Journal of International Economics* 48: 117–153.

O'Flaherty, B. 1990. "The Care and Handling of Monetary Authorities." *Economics and Politics* 2(1): 25–44.

Oh, S. 1989. "A Theory of a Generally Accepted Medium of Exchange and Barter." *Journal of Monetary Economics* 23(1): 101–119.

Ohanian, L., and A. Stockman. 1995. "Resolving the Liquidity Effect." Federal Reserve Bank of St. Louis *Review* 77(3): 3–25.

Oliner, S. D., and G. D. Rudebusch. 1995. "Is There a Bank Lending Channel for Monetary Policy?" Federal Reserve Bank of San Francisco *Economic Review*, Spring, 3–20.

———. 1996a. "Is There a Broad Credit Channel for Monetary Policy?" Federal Reserve Bank of San Francisco *Economic Review*, Winter, 3–13.

———. 1996b. "Monetary Policy and Credit Conditions: Evidence from the Composition of External Finance: Comment." *American Economic Review* 86(1): 300–309.

Olson, M. Jr. 1996. "Big Bills Left on the Sidewalk: Why Some Nations Are Rich and Others Poor." *Journal of Economic Perspectives* 10(2): 3–24.

Orphanides, A. 2000. "The Quest for Prosperity without Inflation." European Central Bank Working Paper 15.

———. 2001. "Monetary Policy Rules Based on Real-Time Data." *American Economic Review* 91(4): 964–985.

Orphanides, A., and R. Solow. 1990. "Money, Inflation and Growth." In *Handbook of Monetary Economics*, ed. B. Friedman and F. Hahn. Vol I, 223–261. Amsterdam: North-Holland.

Orphanides, A., and J. C. Williams. 2002. "Robust Monetary Policy Rules: The Case of Unknown Natural Rates of Interest and Unemployment." Federal Reserve Board.

Papell, D., T. Molodtsova, and A. Nikolsko-Rzhevskyy. 2008. "Taylor Rules with Real-Time Data: A Tale of Two Countries and One Exchange Rate." *Journal of Monetary Economics* 55: S63–S79.

Parsley, D. C., and S.-J. Wei. 1996. "Convergence to the Law of One Price with Trade Barriers or Currency Fluctuations." *Quarterly Journal of Economics* 111(4): 1211–1236.

Patinkin, D. 1965. *Money, Interest, and Prices: An Integration of Monetary and Value Theory*. 2d. ed. New York: Harper and Row.

Pearce, D. 1993. "Discount Window Borrowing and Federal Reserve Operating Regimes." *Economic Inquiry* 31(4): 564–579.

Peek, J., and E. Rosengren, eds. 1995. *Is Bank Lending Important for the Transmission of Monetary Policy?* Federal Reserve Bank of Boston Conference Series No. 39.

Perez, S. J. 2001. "Looking Back at Forward-Looking Monetary Policy." *Journal of Economics and Business* 53(5): 509–521.

Peristiani, S. 1991. "The Model Structure of Discount Window Borrowing." *Journal of Money, Credit, and Banking* 23(1): 13–34.

Persson, T., and G. Tabellini. 1993. "Designing Institutions for Monetary Stability." *Carnegie-Rochester Conference Series on Public Policy* 39 (Dec.): 53–84.

———. 1996. "Monetary Cohabitation in Europe." CEPR Discussion Paper 1380.

———. 1999. "Political Economics and Macroeconomic Policy." In *Handbook of Macroeconomics*, ed. J. Taylor and M. Woodford. Vol. 1C, 1397–1482. Amsterdam: North-Holland.

Persson, T., and G. Tabellini, eds. 1990. *Macroeconomic Policy, Credibility, and Politics*. Chur, Switzerland: Harwood Academic Publishers.

———. 1994a. *Monetary and Fiscal Policy*. Volume 1: *Credibility*. Cambridge, Mass.: MIT Press.

———. 1994b. *Monetary and Fiscal Policy*. Volume 2: *Politics*. Cambridge, Mass.: MIT Press.

Phelps, E. S. 1968. "Money-Wage Dynamics and Labor Market Equilibrium." *Journal of Political Economy* 76(4): 678–711.

———. 1973. "Inflation in the Theory of Public Finance." *Swedish Journal of Economics* 75(1): 67–82.

Phillips, A. W. 1957. "Stabilisation Policy and the Time-Forms of Lagged Responses." *Economic Journal* 67(2): 265–277.

Pollard, P. S. 1993. "Central Bank Independence and Economic Performance." Federal Reserve Bank of St. Louis *Review* 75(4): 21–36.

Poloz, S., D. Rose, and R. Tetlow. 1994. "The Bank of Canada's New Quarterly Projections Model (QPM): An Introduction." Bank of Canada *Review*, Autumn, 23–39.

Poole, W. 1968. "Commercial Bank Reserve Management in a Stochastic Model: Implications for Monetary Policy." *Journal of Finance* 23: 769–791.

———. 1970. "Optimal Choice of Monetary Policy Instrument in a Simple Stochastic Macro Model." *Quarterly Journal of Economics* 84(2): 197–216.

Posen, A. 1993. "Why Central Bank Independence Does Not Cause Low Inflation: There Is No Institutional Fix for Politics." In *Finance and the International Economy*, ed. R. O'Brien. Vol. 7, 40–65. Oxford: Oxford University Press.

———. 1996. "Declarations Are Not Enough: Financial Sector Sources of Central Bank Independence." In *NBER Macroeconomics Annual 1995*, 253–274. Cambridge, Mass.: MIT Press.

Poterba, J. M., and J. J. Rotemberg. 1990. "Inflation and Taxation with Optimizing Governments." *Journal of Money, Credit, and Banking* 22(1): 1–18.

Ramey, V. 1993. "How Important Is the Credit Channel in the Transmission of Monetary Policy?" *Carnegie-Rochester Conference Series on Public Policy* 39 (Dec.): 1–45.

Ramsey, F. P. 1928. "A Mathematical Theory of Saving." *Economic Journal* 38(152): 543–559.

Rasche, R. H. 1973. "A Comparative Static Analysis of Some Monetarist Propositions." Federal Reserve Bank of St. Louis *Review* 55: 15–23.

Ravenna, F. 2000. "The Impact of Inflation Targeting in Canada: A Structural Analysis." New York University.

Ravenna, F., and J. Seppälä. 2007a. "Monetary Policy and Rejections of the Expectations Hypothesis." University of California, Santa Cruz, Working Paper.

———. 2007b. "Monetary Policy, Expected Inflation, and Inflation Risk Premia." Bank of Finland Research Discussion Paper.

Ravenna, F., and C. E. Walsh. 2006. "Optimal Monetary Policy with the Cost Channel." *Journal of Monetary Economics* 53: 199–216.

———. 2008. "Vacancies, Unemployment, and the Phillips Curve." *European Economic Review* 52: 1494–1521.

Ravn, M. O., and H. Uhlig. 2001. "On Adjusting the HP-Filter for the Frequency of Observations." CESifo Working Paper 479.

Rebelo, S., and D. Xie. 1999. "On the Optimality of Interest Rate Smoothing." *Journal of Monetary Economics* 43(2): 263–282.

Reichenstein, W. 1987. "The Impact of Money on Short-Term Interest Rates." *Economic Inquiry* 25(1): 67–82.

Reifschneider, D. L., D. J. Stockton, and D. W. Wilcox. 1997. "Econometric Models and the Monetary Policy Process." *Carnegie-Rochester Conference Series on Public Policy* 47 (Dec.): 1–37.

Reis, R. 2006a. "Inattentive Consumers." *Journal of Monetary Economics* 53(8): 1731–1800.

———. 2006b. "Inattentive Producers." *Review of Economic Studies* 73(3): 793–821.

———. 2007. "The Analytics of Monetary Non-Neutrality in the Sidrauski Model." *Economics Letters* 94(1): 129–135.

Reynard, S. 2004. "Financial Market Participation and the Apparent Instability of Money Demand." *Journal of Monetary Economics* 51: 1297–1317.

Ritter, J. A. 1995. "The Transition from Barter to Fiat Money." *American Economic Review* 85(1): 134–149.

Roberts, J. M. 1995. "New Keynesian Economics and the Phillips Curve." *Journal of Money, Credit, and Banking* 27(4): 975–984.

———. 1997. "Is Inflation Sticky?" *Journal of Monetary Economics* 39(2): 173–196.

———. 2001. "How Well Does the New Keynesian Sticky-Price Model Fit the Data?" Federal Reserve Board.

Rocheteau, G., and R. Wright. 2005. "Money in Search Equilibrium, in Competitive Equilibrium, and in Competitive Search Equilibrium." *Econometrica* 73(1): 175–202.

Rogoff, K. 1985a. "Can International Policy Coordination Be Counterproductive?" *Journal of International Economics* 18(3/4): 199–217.

———. 1985b. "The Optimal Commitment to an Intermediate Monetary Target." *Quarterly Journal of Economics* 100(4): 1169–1189.

———. 1989. "Reputation, Coordination, and Monetary Policy." In *Modern Business Cycle Theory*, ed. R. Barro, 236–264. Cambridge, Mass.: Harvard University Press.

Roley, V. V., and G. H. Sellon. 1996. "The Response of the Term Structure of Interest Rates to Federal Funds Rate Target Changes." Federal Reserve Bank of Kansas City.

Roley, V. V., and C. E. Walsh. 1985. "Monetary Policy Regimes, Expected Inflation, and the Response of Interest Rates to Money Anouncements." *Quarterly Journal of Economics* 100(5): 1011–1039.

Rolnick, A. J., and W. E. Weber. 1994. "Inflation, Money, and Output under Alternative Monetary Standards." Research Department Staff Report 175. Federal Reserve Bank of Minneapolis.

Romer, C. D., and D. H. Romer. 1990a. "Does Monetary Policy Matter? A New Test in the Spirit of Friedman and Schwartz." In *NBER Macroeconomics Annual 1989*, 121–170. Cambridge, Mass.: MIT Press.

———. 1990b. "New Evidence on the Monetary Transmission Mechanism." *Brookings Papers on Economic Activity*, no. 1, 149–198.

———. 1997. "Institutions for Monetary Stability." In *Reducing Inflation: Motivation and Strategy*, ed. C. Romer and D. Romer, 307–329. Chicago: University of Chicago Press.

———. 2002. "The Evolution of Economic Understanding and Postwar Stabilization Policy." In *Rethinking Stabilization Policy*, 11–78. Federal Reserve Bank of Kansas City.

Romer, D. H. 1985. "Financial Intermediation, Reserve Requirements, and Inside Money: A General Equilibrium Analysis." *Journal of Monetary Economics* 16(2): 175–194.

———. 1986. "A Simple General Equilibrium Version of the Baumol-Tobin Model." *Quarterly Journal of Economics* 101(4): 663–685.

———. 1993. "Openness and Inflation: Theory and Evidence." *Quarterly Journal of Economics* 108(4): 869–903.

————. 1998. "A New Assessment of Openness and Inflation: Reply." *Quarterly Journal of Economics* 113(2): 649–652.

————. 2006. *Advanced Macroeconomics.* 3d. ed. New York: McGraw-Hill.

Rotemberg, J. J. 1982. "Sticky Prices in the United States." *Journal of Political Economy* 80: 1187–1211.

————. 1984. "A Monetary Equilibrium Model with Transaction Costs." *Journal of Political Economy* 92(1): 40–58.

————. 1988. "New Keynesian Microfoundations." In *NBER Macroeconomics Annual 1987*, 69–104. Cambridge, Mass.: MIT Press.

————. 2007. "The Persistence of Inflation Versus That of Real Marginal Cost in the New Keynesian Model." *Journal of Monetary Economics* 39(1): 237–239.

Rotemberg, J. J., and M. Woodford. 1995. "Dynamic General Equilibrium Models with Imperfectly Competitive Product Markets." In *Frontiers of Business Cycle Research*, ed. T. F. Cooley, 243–293. Princeton, N.J.: Princeton University Press.

————. 1998. "An Optimizing-Based Econometric Model for the Evaluation of Monetary Policy." In *NBER Macroeconomics Annual 1997*, 297–346. Cambridge, Mass.: MIT Press.

Rudd, J., and K. Whelan. 2005. "Does Labor's Share Drive Inflation?" *Journal of Money, Credit, and Banking* 37(2): 297–312.

Rudebusch, G. D. 1995. "Federal Reserve Interest Rate Targeting, Rational Expectations, and the Term Structure." *Journal of Monetary Economics* 35(2): 245–274.

————. 1998. "Do Measures of Monetary Policy in a VAR Make Sense?" *International Economic Review* 39(4): 907–931.

————. 2001. "Is the Fed Too Timid? Monetary Policy in an Uncertain World." *Review of Economics and Statistics* 83(2): 203–217.

————. 2002a. "Assessing Nominal Income Rules for Monetary Policy with Model and Data Uncertainty." *Economic Journal* 112(479): 402–432.

————. 2002b. "Term Structure Evidence on Interest Rate Smoothing and Monetary Policy Inertia." *Journal of Monetary Economics* 49(6): 1161–1187.

————. 2006. "Monetary Policy Inertia: A Fact or Fiction." *International Journal of Central Banking* 2: 865–935.

Rudebusch, G. D., and L.E.O. Svensson. 1999. "Policy Rules for Inflation Targeting." In *Monetary Policy Rules*, ed. J. Taylor, 203–246. Chicago: University of Chicago Press.

Rudebusch, G. D., and T. Wu. 2007. "Accounting for a Shift in Term Structure Behavior with No-Arbitrage and Macro-Finance Models." *Journal of Money, Credit, and Banking* 39(2/3): 395–422.

————. 2008. "A Macro-Finance Model of the Term Structure, Monetary Policy, and the Economy." *Economic Journal* 118: 906–926.

Ruge-Murcia, F. J. 2003a. "Does the Barro-Gordon Model Explain the Behavior of U.S. Inflation? A Reexamination of the Empirical Evidence." *Journal of Monetary Economics* 50(6): 1375–1390.

————. 2003b. "Inflation Targeting under Asymmetric Preferences." *Journal of Money, Credit, and Banking* 35(5): 763–785.

Rupert, P., M. Schindler, and R. Wright. 2001. "Generalized Search-Theoretic Models of Monetary Exchange." *Journal of Monetary Economics* 48(3): 605–622.

Sack, B. 2000. "Does the Fed Act Gradually? A VAR Analysis." *Journal of Monetary Economics* 46(1): 229–256.

Sala, L., U. Söderström, and A. Trigari. 2008. "Monetary Policy under Uncertainty in an Estimated Model with Labor Market Frictions." *Journal of Monetary Economics* 55: 983–1006.

Salyer, K. D. 1991. "The Timing of Markets and Monetary Transfers in Cash-in-Advance Economies." *Economic Inquiry* 29: 762–773.

Samuelson, P. A. 1958. "An Exact Consumption-Loan Model of Interest with or without the Social Contrivance of Money." *Journal of Political Economy* 66(6): 467–482.

Sargent, T. J. 1976. "The Observational Equivalence of Natural and Unnatural Rate Theories of Macroeconomics." *Journal of Political Economy* 84(3): 631–640.

———. 1982. "Beyond Supply and Demand Curves in Macroeconomics." *American Economic Review* 72(2): 382–389.

———. 1986. "The Ends of Four Big Inflations." In *Rational Expectations and Inflation*, 40–109. New York: Harper and Row.

———. 1987. *Dynamic Macroeconomic Theory*. Cambridge, Mass.: Harvard University Press.

———. 1999. *The Conquest of American Inflation*. Princeton, N.J.: Princeton University Press.

Sargent, T. J., and N. Wallace. 1975. "'Rational' Expectations, the Optimal Monetary Instrument, and the Optimal Money Supply Rule." *Journal of Political Economy* 83(2): 241–254.

———. 1981. "Some Unpleasant Monetarist Arithmetic." Federal Reserve Bank of Minneapolis *Quarterly Review* 5(3): 1–17.

Sbordone, A. M. 2001. "An Optimizing Model of U.S. Wage and Price Dynamics." Rutgers University.

———. 2002. "Prices and Unit Labor Costs: A New Test of Price Stickiness." *Journal of Monetary Economics* 49(2): 265–292.

———. 2007. "Inflation Persistence: Alternative Interpretations and Policy Implications." *Journal of Monetary Economics* 54: 1311–1339.

Schelde-Andersen, P. 1992. "OECD Country Experiences with Disinflation." In *Inflation, Disinflation and Monetary Policy*, ed. A. Blundell-Wignall, 104–173. Reserve Bank of Australia.

Schellekens, P. 2002. "Caution and Conservatism in the Making of Monetary Policy." *Journal of Money, Credit, and Banking* 34(1): 160–177.

Schlagenhauf, D. E., and J. M. Wrase. 1995. "Liquidity and Real Activity in a Simple Open Economy Model." *Journal of Monetary Economics* 35(3): 431–461.

Schmitt-Grohé, S., and M. Uribe. 2000a. "Liquidity Traps with Global Taylor Rules." Rutgers University.

———. 2000b. "Price Level Determinacy and Monetary Policy under a Balanced-Budget Requirement." *Journal of Monetary Economics* 45(1): 211–246.

Sheffrin, S. M. 1983. *Rational Expectations*. Cambridge: Cambridge University Press.

———. 1995. "Identifying Monetary and Credit Shocks." In *Monetarism and the Methodology of Economics*, ed. K. D. Hoover and S. M. Sheffrin, 151–163. Aldershot, UK: Edward Elgar.

Shi, S. 1995. "Money and Prices: A Model of Search and Bargaining." *Journal of Economic Theory* 67(2): 467–496.

———. 1997. "A Divisible Search Model of Fiat Money." *Econometrica* 65(1): 75–102.

———. 1999. "Search, Inflation, and Capital Accumulation." *Journal of Monetary Economics* 44(1): 81–103.

———. 2005. "Nominal Bonds and Interest Rates." *International Economic Review* 46(2): 579–612.

Shiller, R. J. 1981. "Do Stock Prices Move Too Much to Be Justified by Subsequent Changes in Dividends?" *American Economic Review* 71(3): 421–436.

———. 1990. "The Term Structure of Interest Rates." In *Handbook of Monetary Economics*, ed. B. Friedman and F. Hahn. Vol. 1, 626–722. Amsterdam: North-Holland.

Sidrauski, M. 1967. "Rational Choice and Patterns of Growth in a Monetary Economy." *American Economic Review* 57(2): 534–544.

Sims, C. A. 1972. "Money, Income and Causality." *American Economic Review* 62(4): 540–542.

———. 1980. "Comparison of Interwar and Postwar Business Cycles." *American Economic Review* 70(2): 250–257.

———. 1988. "Identifying Policy Effects." In *Empirical Macroeconomics for Interdependent Economies*, ed. R. C. Bryant, D. W. Henderson, G. Holtham, P. Hooper, and S. A. Symansky, 305–321. Washington, D.C.: Brookings Institution.

———. 1992. "Interpreting the Macroeconomic Time Series Facts: The Effects of Monetary Policy." *European Economic Review* 36(5): 975–1000.

———. 1994. "A Simple Model for Study of the Determination of the Price Level and the Interaction of Monetary and Fiscal Policy." *Economic Theory* 4: 381–399.

———. 1998a. "Comment on Glenn Rudebusch's 'Do Measures of Monetary Policy in a VAR Make Sense?'" *International Economic Review* 39(4): 933–941.

———. 1998b. "The Role of Interest Rate Policy in the Generation and Propagation of Business Cycles: What Has Changed Since the 30's?" In *Beyond Shocks: What Causes Business Cycles?* ed. J. Fuhrer and S. Schuh, 121–167. Federal Reserve Bank of Boston Conference Series No. 42.

———. 2003. "Implications of Rational Inattention." *Journal of Monetary Economics* 50(3): 665–690.

Small, D. H. 1979. "Unanticipated Money Growth and Unemployment in the United States: Comment." *American Economic Review* 69(5): 996–1003.

Smets, F., and R. Wouters. 2003. "An Estimated Dynamic Stochastic General Equilibrium Model of the Euro Area." *Journal of the European Economic Association* 1(5): 1123–1175.

———. 2007. "Shocks and Frictions in U.S. Business Cycles: A Bayesian Approach." *American Economic Review* 97(3): 586–606.

Smith, B. 1983. "Limited Information, Credit Rationing, and Optimal Government Lending Policy." *American Economic Review* 73(3): 305–318.

Söderlind, P. 1999. "Solution and Estimation of RE Macromodels with Optimal Policy." *European Economic Review* 43: 813–823.

Söderlind, P., and L.E.O. Svensson. 1997. "New Techniques to Extract Market Expectations from Financial Instruments." *Journal of Monetary Economics* 40(2): 383–429.

Söderström, U. 2001. "Targeting Inflation with a Prominent Role for Money." Sveriges Riksbank Working Paper 123.

———. 2002. "Monetary Policy with Uncertain Parameters." *Scandinavian Journal of Economics* 104(1): 125–145.

Soller, E. V., and C. J. Waller. 2000. "A Search Theoretic Model of Legal and Illegal Currency." *Journal of Monetary Economics* 45(1): 155–184.

Solow, R. 1956. "A Contribution to the Theory of Economic Growth." *Quarterly Journal of Economics* 70(1): 65–94.

Spindt, P. 1985. "Money Is What Money Does: Monetary Aggregation and the Equations of Exchange." *Journal of Political Economy* 93(1): 175–204.

Stein, J. 1969. "Neoclassical and Keynes-Wicksell Monetary Growth Models." *Journal of Money, Credit, and Banking* 1(2): 153–171.

Steinsson, J. 2003. "Optimal Monetary Policy in an Economy with Inflation Persistence." *Journal of Monetary Economics* 50(7): 1425–1456.

Stiglitz, J. E., and A. Weiss. 1981. "Credit Rationing in Markets with Imperfect Information." *American Economic Review* 71(3): 393–410.

Stock, J. H., and M. W. Watson. 1989. "Interpreting the Evidence on Money-Income Causality." *Journal of Econometrics* 40(1): 161–181.

———. 1993. "A Simple Estimator of Co-integrating Vectors in Higher-Order Integrated Systems." *Econometrica* 61: 783–820.

Stockman, A. 1981. "Anticipated Inflation and the Capital Stock in a Cash-in-Advance Economy." *Journal of Monetary Economics* 8(3): 387–393.

Stokey, N. 2003. "'Rules versus Discretion' after Twenty-Five Years." In *NBER Macroeconomics Annual 2002*, 9–45. Cambridge, Mass.: MIT Press.

Strongin, S. 1995. "The Identification of Monetary Policy Disturbances: Explaining the Liquidity Puzzle." *Journal of Monetary Economics* 35(3): 463–497.

Summers, L. H. 1981. "Optimal Inflation Policy." *Journal of Monetary Economics* 7(2): 175–194.

Svensson, L.E.O. 1985. "Money and Asset Prices in a Cash-in-Advance Economy." *Journal of Political Economy* 93(5): 919–944.

———. 1997a. "Inflation Forecast Targeting: Implementing and Monitoring Inflation Targets." *European Economic Review* 41(6): 1111–1146.

———. 1997b. "Optimal Inflation Contracts, 'Conservative' Central Banks, and Linear Inflation Contracts." *American Economic Review* 87(1): 98–114.

———. 1999a. "How Should Monetary Policy Be Conducted in an Era of Price Stability?" In *New Challenges for Monetary Policy*, 195–259. Federal Reserve Bank of Kansas City.

———. 1999b. "Inflation Targeting as a Monetary Policy Rule." *Journal of Monetary Economics* 43: 607–654.

———. 1999c. "Inflation Targeting: Some Extensions." *Scandinavian Journal of Economics* 101(3): 337–361.

———. 1999d. "Price Level Targeting vs. Inflation Targeting." *Journal of Money, Credit, and Banking* 31: 277–295.

———. 2000. "Open-Economy Inflation Targeting." *Journal of International Economics* 50(1): 155–183.

———. 2001. "The Zero Bound in an Open Economy: A Foolproof Way of Escaping from a Liquidity Trap." *Monetary and Economic Studies* 19(S-1): 277–312.

Svensson, L.E.O., and N. Williams. 2008. "Optimal Monetary Policy under Uncertainty: A Markov Jump-Linear-Quadratic Approach." Federal Reserve Bank of St. Louis *Review* 90(4): 275–293.

Svensson, L.E.O., and M. Woodford. 2003. "Indicator Variables for Optimal Policy." *Journal of Monetary Economics* 50: 691–720.

———. 2004. "Indicator Variables for Optimal Policy under Asymmetric Information." *Journal of Economic Dynamics and Control* 28(4): 661–690.

———. 2005. "Implementing Optimal Policy through Inflation-Forecast Targeting." In *The Inflation-Targeting Debate*, ed. B. S. Bernanke and M. Woodford, 19–83. Chicago: University of Chicago Press.

Tabellini, G. 1988. "Centralized Wage Setting and Monetary Policy in a Reputational Equilibrium." *Journal of Money, Credit, and Banking* 20(1): 102–118.

Taylor, J. B. 1975. "Monetary Policy during a Transition to Rational Expectations." *Journal of Political Economy* 83(5): 1009–1021.

———. 1979. "Staggered Wage Setting in a Macro Model." *American Economic Review* 69(2): 108–113.

———. 1980. "Aggregate Dynamics and Staggered Contracts." *Journal of Political Economy* 88(1): 1–24.

———. 1983. "Comments on 'Rules, Discretion and Reputation in a Model of Monetary Policy' by R. J. Barro and D. B. Gordon." *Journal of Monetary Economics* 12(1): 123–125.

———. 1985. "What Would Nominal GNP Targeting Do to the Business Cycle?" *Carnegie-Rochester Conference Series on Public Policy* 22: 61–84.

———. 1989. "Policy Analysis with a Multicountry Model." In *Macroeconomic Policies in an Interdependent World*, ed. R. Bryant, D. A. Currie, J. A. Frenkal, P. R. Masson, and R. Portes, 122–141. Washington, D.C.: Brookings Institution.

———. 1993a. "Discretion versus Policy Rules in Practice." *Carnegie-Rochester Conferences Series on Public Policy* 39 (Dec.): 195–214.

———. 1993b. *Macroeconomic Policy in a World Economy*. New York: W. W. Norton.

———. 1996. "How Should Monetary Policy Respond to Shocks While Maintaining Long-Run Price Stability? Conceptual Issues." In *Achieving Price Stability*, 181–195. Federal Reserve Bank of Kansas City.

———, ed. 1999. *Monetary Policy Rules*. Chicago: University of Chicago Press.

Taylor, J. B., and J. C. Williams. 2009. "A Black Swan in the Money Market." *American Economic Journal: Macroeconomics* 1(1): 58–83.

Tinbergen, J. 1956. *Economic Policy: Principles and Design*. Amsterdam: North-Holland.

Teles, P., and R. Zhou. 2005. "A Stable Money Demand: Looking for the Right Monetary Aggregate." Federal Reserve Bank of Chicago *Economic Perspectives* Q1: 50–63.

Temple, J. B. 2002. "Openness, Inflation, and the Phillips Curve: A Puzzle." *Journal of Money, Credit, and Banking* 34(2): 450–468.

Terra, C. T. 1998. "Openness and Inflation: A New Assessment." *Quarterly Journal of Economics* 113(2): 641–648.

Thomas, C. 2008. "Search and Matching Frictions and Optimal Monetary Policy." *Journal of Monetary Economics* 55: 936–956.

Tobin, J. 1956. "The Interest Elasticity of the Transactions Demand for Cash." *Review of Economics and Statistics* 38(3): 241–247.

———. 1965. "Money and Economic Growth." *Econometrica* 33(4): 671–684.

———. 1969. "A General Equilibrium Approach to Monetary Theory." *Journal of Money, Credit, and Banking* 1(1): 15–29.

———. 1970. "Money and Income: Post Hoc Ergo Proctor Hoc?" *Quarterly Journal of Economics* 84(2): 301–317.

Tobin, J., and W. Brainard. 1963. "Financial Intermediaries and the Effectiveness of Monetary Control." *American Economic Review* 53: 383–400.

Tootell, G. 1991. "Are District Presidents More Conservative Than Board Governors?" Federal Reserve Bank of Boston *New England Economic Review*, Sept./Oct., 3–12.

Townsend, R. 1979. "Optimal Contracts and Competitive Markets with Costly State Verification." *Journal of Economic Theory* 21(2): 265–293.

Trabandt, M. 2003. "Sticky Information vs. Sticky Prices: A Horse Race in a DSGE Framework." Kiel Working Paper 1369.

Trehan, B., and C. E. Walsh. 1988. "Common Trends, the Government's Budget Balance, and Revenue Smoothing." *Journal of Economic Dynamics and Control* 12(2/3): 425–444.

———. 1990. "Seigniorage and Tax Smoothing in the United States, 1914–1986." *Journal of Monetary Economics* 25(1): 97–112.

———. 1991. "Testing Intertemporal Budget Constraints: Theory and Applications to U.S. Federal Budget and Current Account Deficits." *Journal of Money, Credit, and Banking* 23(2): 206–223.

Trejos, A., and R. Wright. 1993. "Search, Bargaining, Money, and Prices: Recent Results and Policy Implications." *Journal of Money, Credit, and Banking* 25(3): 558–576.

———. 1995. "Search, Bargaining, Money, and Prices." *Journal of Political Economy* 103(1): 118–141.

Trigari, A. 2009. "Equilibrium Unemployment, Job Flows, and Inflation Dynamics." *Journal of Money, Credit, and Banking* 41(1): 1–33.

Turnovsky, S. 1995. *Methods of Macroeconomic Dynamics.* Cambridge, Mass.: MIT Press.

Uhlig, H. 1999. "A Toolkit for Analyzing Nonlinear Dynamic Stochastic Models Easily." In *Computational Methods for the Study of Dynamic Economies*, ed. R. Marimon and A. Scott, 30–61. Oxford: Oxford University Press.

Van Hoose, D. 1989. "Monetary Targeting and Price Level Non-Trend Stationarity." *Journal of Money, Credit, and Banking* 21(2): 232–239.

Vestin, D. 2006. "Price-Level Targeting versus Inflation Targeting." *Journal of Monetary Economics* 53(7): 1361–1376.

Vickers, J. 1986. "Signalling in a Model of Monetary Policy with Incomplete Information." *Oxford Economic Papers* 38(3): 443–455.

Wallace, N. 1981. "A Modigliani-Miller Theorem for Open-Market Operations." *American Economic Review* 71(3): 267–274.

Waller, C. J. 1989. "Monetary Policy Games and Central Bank Politics." *Journal of Money, Credit, and Banking* 21(4): 422–431.

———. 1990. "Administering the Window: A Game Theoretic Model of Discount Window Borrowing." *Journal of Monetary Economics* 25(2): 273–287.

——. 1992. "A Bargaining Model of Partisan Appointments to the Central Bank." *Journal of Monetary Economics* 29(3): 411–428.

——. 1995. "Performance Contracts for Central Bankers." Federal Reserve Bank of St. Louis *Review* 77(5): 3–14.

Waller, C. J., and C. E. Walsh. 1996. "Central Bank Independence, Economic Behavior and Optimal Term Lengths." *American Economic Review* 86(5): 1139–1153.

Walsh, C. E. 1982. "The Effects of Alternative Operating Procedures on Economic and Financial Relationships." In *Monetary Policy Issues in the 1980s*, 133–163. Federal Reserve Bank of Kansas City.

——. 1984. "Optimal Taxation by the Monetary Authority." NBER Working Paper 1375.

——. 1986. "In Defense of Base Drift." *American Economic Review* 76(4): 692–700.

——. 1987. "Monetary Targeting and Inflation, 1976–1984." Federal Reserve Bank of San Francisco *Economic Review*, Winter, 5–15.

——. 1990. "Issues in the Choice of Monetary Policy Operating Procedures." In *Monetary Policy for a Changing Financial Environment*, ed. W. S. Haraf and P. Cagan, 8–37. Washington, D.C.: AEI Press.

——. 1992. "The New View of Banking." In *The New Palgrave Dictionary of Money and Finance*, ed. J. Eatwell, M. Milgate, and P. Newman, 31–33. London: Macmillan.

——. 1993. "What Caused the 1990 Recession?" Federal Reserve Bank of San Francisco *Economic Review*, Spring, 33–48.

——. 1995a. "Central Bank Independence and the Short-Run Output-Inflation Trade-off in the EC." In *Monetary and Fiscal Policy in an Integrated*, ed. B. Eichengreen, J. Frieden, and J. von Hagan, 12–37. Berlin: Springer.

——. 1995b. "Is New Zealand's Reserve Bank Act of 1989 an Optimal Central Bank Contract?" *Journal of Money, Credit, and Banking* 27(4): 1179–1191.

——. 1995c. "Optimal Contracts for Central Bankers." *American Economic Review* 85(1): 150–167.

——. 1996. "Recent Central Bank Reforms and the Role of Price Stability as the Sole Objective of Monetary Policy." In *NBER Macroeconomics Annual 1995*, 237–252. Cambridge, Mass.: MIT Press.

——. 1999. "Announcements, Inflation Targeting, and Central Bank Incentives." *Economica* 66: 255–269.

——. 2000. "Market Discipline and Monetary Policy." *Oxford Economic Papers* 52: 249–271.

——. 2002. "When Should Central Bankers Be Fired?" *Economics of Governance* 3(1): 1–21.

——. 2003a. "Labor Market Search and Monetary Shocks." In *Elements of Dynamic Macroeconomic Analysis*, ed. S. Altuǧ, J. Chadha, and C. Nolan, 451–486. Cambridge: Cambridge University Press.

——. 2003b. "Speed Limit Policies: The Output Gap and Optimal Monetary Policy." *American Economic Review* 93(1): 265–278.

——. 2005a. "Endogenous Objectives and the Evaluation of Targeting Rules for Monetary Policy." *Journal of Monetary Economics* 52(5): 889–911.

——. 2005b. "Labor Market Search, Sticky Prices, and Interest Rate Policies." *Review of Economic Dynamics* 8(4): 829–849.

——. 2007. "Optimal Economic Transparency." *International Journal of Central Banking* 3(1): 5–36.

——. 2009. "Inflation Targeting: What Have We Learned?" *International Finance*, 12(2): 195–233.

Walsh, C. E., and J. A. Wilcox. 1995. "Bank Credit and Economic Activity." In *Is Bank Lending Important for the Transmission of Monetary Policy?* ed. J. Peek and E. Rosengren, 83–112. Federal Reserve Bank of Boston Conference Series No. 39.

Wang, P., and C. K. Yip. 1992. "Alternative Approaches to Money and Growth." *Journal of Money, Credit, and Banking* 24(4): 553–562.

West, K. D. 1986. "Targeting Nominal Income: A Note." *Economic Journal* 96: 1077–1083.

——. 1987. "A Specification Test for Speculative Bubbles." *Quarterly Journal of Economics* 102(3): 553–580.

———. 1988. "Dividend Innovation and Stock Price Volatility." *Econometrica* 56(1): 37–61.

Whitesell, W. 2006. "Interest Rate Corridors and Reserves." *Journal of Monetary Economics* 53(6): 1177–1195.

Wickens, M. 2008. *Macroeconomic Theory: A Dynamic General Equilibrium Approach*. Princeton, N.J.: Princeton University Press.

Wieland, V. 2000a. "Learning By Doing and the Value of Optimal Experimentation." *Journal of Economic Dynamics and Control* 24: 501–534.

———. 2000b. "Monetary Policy, Parameter Uncertainty, and Optimal Learning." *Journal of Monetary Economics* 46(1): 199–228.

Wilcox, D. W. 1989. "The Sustainability of Government Deficits: Implications of the Present-Value Borrowing Constraint." *Journal of Money, Credit, and Banking* 21(3): 291–306.

Williamson, S. D. 1986. "Costly Monitoring, Financial Intermediation, and Equilibrium Credit Rationing." *Journal of Monetary Economics* 18(2): 159–179.

———. 1987a. "Costly Monitoring, Loan Contracts, and Equilibrium Credit Rationing." *Quarterly Journal of Economics* 102(1): 135–145.

———. 1987b. "Financial Intermediation, Business Failures, and Real Business Cycles." *Journal of Political Economy* 95(6): 1196–1216.

———. 2004. "Limited Participation, Private Money, and Credit in a Spatial Model of Money." *Economic Theory* 24: 857–875.

———. 2005. "Limited Participation and the Neutrality of Money." Federal Reserve Bank of Richmond *Economic Quarterly* 91(2): 1–20.

Wolman, A. L. 1999. "Sticky Prices, Marginal Costs, and the Behavior of Inflation." Federal Reserve Bank of Richmond *Economic Quarterly* 85(4): 29–48.

Woodford, M. 1990. "The Optimum Quantity of Money." In *Handbook of Monetary Economics*, ed. B. Friedman and F. Hahn, 1067–1152. Amsterdam: North-Holland.

———. 1995. "Price Level Determinacy without Control of a Monetary Aggregate." *Carnegie-Rochester Conference Series on Public Policy* 43 (Dec.): 1–46.

———. 1998. "Doing without Money: Controlling Inflation in a Post-Monetary World." *Review of Economic Dynamics* 1: 173–219.

———. 1999a. "Comment: A Frictionless View of U.S. Inflation." In *NBER Macroeconomics Annual 1998*, 390–419. Cambridge, Mass.: MIT Press.

———. 1999b. "Price-Level Determination under Interest-Rate Rules." Princeton University.

———. 2000. "A Neo-Wicksellian Framework for the Analysis of Monetary Policy." Princeton University.

———. 2001a. "Fiscal Requirements for Price Stability?" *Journal of Money, Credit, and Banking* 33(3): 669–728.

———. 2001b. "Inflation Stabilization and Welfare." NBER Working Paper 8071.

———. 2001c. "Monetary Policy in the Information Economy." In *Economic Policy for the Information Economy*. Federal Reserve Bank of Kansas City.

———. 2003a. *Interest and Prices: Foundations of a Theory of Monetary Policy*. Princeton, N.J.: Princeton University Press.

———. 2003b. "Optimal Monetary Policy Inertia." *Review of Economic Studies* 70: 861–886.

———. 2005. "Comment on 'Using a Long-Term Interest Rate as the Monetary Policy Instrument.'"

Woolley, J. 1995. "Nixon, Burns, 1972, and Independence in Practice." University of California, Santa Barbara.

Yun, T. 1996. "Nominal Price Rigidity, Money Supply Endogeneity, and Business Cycles." *Journal of Monetary Economics* 37(2): 345–370.

Zha, T. 1997. "Identifying Monetary Policy: A Primer." Federal Reserve Bank of Atlanta *Economic Review* Q2: 26–43.

Name Index

Subject Index